Twelfth Edition

ELECTRONIC COMMERCE

Gary P. Schneider, Ph.D., CPA
California State University Monterey Bay

CENGAGE Learning

Australia • Brazil

d States

CENGAGE
Learning®

Electronic Commerce, Twelfth Edition
Gary P. Schneider

Vice President, General Manager, Social
Science & Qualitative Business: Erin Joyner

Product Director: Mike Schenk

Sr. Product Team Manager: Joe Sabatino

Content Developer: Ted Knight

Marketing Director: Michelle McTighe

Marketing Manager: Eric La Scola

Marketing Coordinator: Will Guiliani

Sr. Product Assistant: Adele Scholtz

Art and Cover Direction, Production
Management, and Composition:
Lumina Datamatics Inc.

Intellectual Property

Analyst: Brittani Morgan

Project Manager: Kathryn Kucharek

Manufacturing Planner: Ron Montgomery

Cover Image(s): alexmillos/shutterstock
Stokkete/Veer

For product information and technology assistance, contact us at
Cengage Learning Customer & Sales Support, 1-800-354-9706

For permission to use material from this text or product,
submit all requests online at **www.cengage.com/permissions**
Further permissions questions can be emailed to
permissionrequest@cengage.com

Library of Congress Control Number: 2015960926

ISBN: 978-1-305-86781-9

Cengage Learning
20 Channel Center Street
Boston, MA 02210
USA

Cengage Learning is a leading provider of customized learning solutions with
employees residing in nearly 40 different countries and sales in more than
125 countries around the world. Find your local representative at
www.cengage.com.

Cengage Learning products are represented in Canada by
Nelson Education, Ltd.

To learn more about Cengage Learning Solutions, visit **www.cengage.com**

Purchase any of our products at your local college store or at our preferred
online store **www.cengagebrain.com**

Printed in the United States of America
Print Number: 01   Print Year: 2016

Brief Contents

Part 4: Integration

iv

Chapter 12

Table of Contents

Part 2: Business Strategies for Electronic Commerce

Chapter 6 *Social Networking, Mobile Commerce, and Online Auctions*   *257*

Preface

Electronic Commerce, Twelfth Edition, provides complete coverage of the key business and technology elements of electronic commerce. The book does not assume that readers have any previous electronic commerce knowledge or experience.

In 1998, having spent several years doing electronic commerce research, consulting, and corporate training, I began developing undergraduate and graduate business school courses in electronic commerce. Although I had used a variety of books and other materials in my corporate training work, I was concerned that those materials would not work well in university courses because they were written at widely varying levels and did not have the organization and pedagogic features, such as review questions, that are so important to students.

After searching for a textbook that offered balanced coverage of both the business and technology elements of electronic commerce, I concluded that no such book existed. The first edition of *Electronic Commerce* was written to fill that void. Since that first edition, I have worked to improve the book and keep it current with the rapid changes in this dynamic field.

New to This Edition

This edition includes the usual updates to keep the content current with the rapidly occurring changes in electronic commerce. It also includes new material on the following topics:

- The emergence of mobile apps as a driver of retail sales in the United States (Chapter 1)
- Technology developments such as Google's Project Loon, new wireless technologies, and the first commercial applications of Semantic Web research (Chapter 2)
- Revenue model developments in online video (Chapter 3)
- New online advertising standards and developments in mobile advertising (Chapter 4)
- How supply chain management enhances organizations' abilities to implement lean production and just-in-time inventory management (Chapter 5)
- Chinese banks' use of online auctions to sell off nonperforming loans (Chapter 6)
- Legal issues facing lodging brokers such as Airbnb and ride brokers such as Lyft and Uber (Chapter 7)
- Cloud computing and content-delivery networks (Chapter 8)
- Advanced shopping cart management services, enterprise resource planning systems in the form of software-as-a-service, and detailed coverage of customer relationship management system architectures (Chapter 9)

- LastPass hack, new viruses including Regin and TeslaCrypt, and emerging initiatives for making digital certificates more widely available (Chapter 10)
- Mobile device payment systems and electronic bill presentment and payment systems (Chapter 11)
- Business accelerators (Chapter 12)

ORGANIZATION AND COVERAGE

Electronic Commerce, Twelfth Edition, introduces readers to both the theory and practice of conducting business over the Internet and World Wide Web. The book is organized into four sections: an introduction, business strategies, technologies, and integration.

Introduction

The book's first section includes two chapters. Chapter 1, "Introduction to Electronic Commerce," defines electronic commerce and describes how companies use it to create new products and services, reduce the cost of existing business processes, and improve the efficiency and effectiveness of their operations. The concept of electronic commerce waves is presented and developed in this chapter. Chapter 1 also outlines the history of the Internet and the Web, explains the international environment in which electronic commerce exists, provides an overview of the economic structures in which businesses operate, and describes how electronic commerce fits into those structures. Two themes are introduced in this chapter and recur throughout later chapters: that examining a firm's value chain can reveal opportunities for electronic commerce initiatives, and reductions in transaction costs are important elements of many electronic commerce initiatives.

Chapter 2, "Technology Infrastructure: The Internet and the World Wide Web," introduces the technologies used to conduct business online, including topics such as Internet infrastructure, protocols, packet-switched networks, and the Internet of Things. Chapter 2 also describes the markup languages used on the Web (HTML and XML) and discusses Internet connection options and tradeoffs, including wireless technologies.

Business Strategies for Electronic Commerce

The second section of the book includes five chapters that describe the business strategies that companies and other organizations are using to do business online. Chapter 3, "Selling on the Web," describes revenue models that companies are using online and explains how some companies have changed their revenue models as the Web has matured. The chapter also explains how firms that understand the nature of communication on the Web can identify and reach the largest possible number of qualified customers.

Chapter 4, "Marketing on the Web," provides an introduction to Internet marketing and online advertising. It includes coverage of market segmentation, technology-enabled customer relationship management, rational branding, contextual advertising, localized advertising, viral marketing, and permission marketing. The chapter also explains how online businesses can share and transfer brand benefits through affiliate marketing and cooperative efforts among brand owners. Effective use of mobile apps to advertise and promote products and services is also included here.

Chapter 5, "Business-to-Business Activities: Improving Efficiency and Reducing Costs," explores the variety of methods that companies are using to improve their purchasing and logistics primary activities with Internet and Web technologies. The chapter describes how companies are using EDI, and outsourcing or offshoring some of their business processes to less-developed countries, and using collaborative commerce in precision manufacturing supply chains. Chapter 5 describes how businesses are using technologies such as e-procurement, radio-frequency identification, and reverse auctions in the practice of supply chain management online.

Chapter 6, "Social Networking, Mobile Commerce, and Online Auctions," explains how companies now use the Web to do things that they have never done before, such as creating social networks, engaging in mobile commerce, and operating auction sites. The chapter describes how businesses are developing social networks and using existing social networking Web sites to increase sales and do market research. The development of mobile commerce, order and pay services, and location-aware online services is discussed. The chapter also explains how companies are using Web auctions to sell goods and generate advertising revenue.

Chapter 7, "The Environment of Electronic Commerce: Legal, Ethical, and Tax Issues," discusses the legal and ethical aspects of intellectual property usage, the privacy rights of customers, and the protection of children who use the Internet. Online crime, terrorism, and warfare are covered as well. The chapter also explains that the large number of government units that have jurisdiction and power to tax makes it essential that companies doing business on the Web understand the potential liabilities of doing business with customers in those jurisdictions.

Technologies for Electronic Commerce

The third section of the book includes four chapters that describe the technologies of electronic commerce and explains how they work. Chapter 8, "Web Server Hardware and Software," describes the computers, operating systems, e-mail systems, utility programs, and Web server software that organizations use in the operation of their electronic commerce Web sites, including cloud computing technologies. The chapter describes the problem of unsolicited commercial e-mail (UCE, or spam) and outlines both technical and legal solutions to the problem.

Chapter 9, "Electronic Commerce Software," describes the basic functions that all electronic commerce Web sites must accomplish and explains the various software options used to perform those functions. This chapter includes an overview of Web services, database management, shopping carts, content delivery networks, cloud computing, and other types of software used in electronic commerce. The chapter also includes a discussion of Web hosting options for online businesses of various sizes.

Chapter 10, "Electronic Commerce Security," discusses security threats and countermeasures that organizations can use to ensure the security of client computers (and smartphones and tablet devices), communications channels, and Web servers. The chapter emphasizes the importance of a written security policy and explains how encryption and digital certificates work. The chapter also includes an overview of significant computer viruses, worms, and other threats that have affected online business activities.

Chapter 11, "Payment Systems for Electronic Commerce," presents a discussion of electronic payment systems, including electronic bill presentment and payment, mobile banking, digital cash, digital wallets, and the technologies used to make stored-value cards, credit cards, debit cards, and charge cards work. The chapter describes how payment systems operate, including approval of transactions and disbursements to merchants, and describes how banks use Internet technologies to improve check clearing and payment-processing operations. The use of mobile devices as digital wallets to make payments and doing online banking is outlined. The chapter also includes a discussion of the threats that phishing attacks and identity theft crimes pose for individuals and online businesses.

Integration

The fourth and final section of the book includes one chapter that integrates the business and technology strategies used in electronic commerce. Chapter 12, "Managing Electronic Commerce Implementations," presents an overview of key elements that are typically included in business plans for electronic commerce implementations, such as the setting of objectives and estimating project costs and benefits. The chapter describes online business incubators and accelerators, outsourcing strategies, and the use of project management and project portfolio management as formal ways to plan and control tasks and resources used in electronic commerce implementations. This chapter includes a discussion of change management and outlines specific jobs available in organizations that conduct electronic commerce.

FEATURES

The twelfth edition of *Electronic Commerce* includes a number of features and offers additional resources designed to help readers understand electronic commerce. These features and resources include:

- **Business Case Approach** The introduction to each chapter includes a real business case that provides a unifying theme and backdrop for the material described in the chapter. Each case illustrates an important topic from the chapter and demonstrates its relevance to the current practice of electronic commerce.
- **Learning From Failures** Not all electronic commerce initiatives have been successful. Each chapter in the book includes a short summary of an electronic commerce failure related to the content of that chapter. We all learn from our mistakes—this feature is designed to help readers understand the missteps of electronic commerce pioneers who learned their lessons the hard way.
- **Summaries** Each chapter concludes with a Summary that concisely recaps the most important concepts in the chapter.
- **Web Links** The Web Links are a set of Web pages maintained by the publisher for readers of this book. The Web Links complement the book by linking to Web sites mentioned in the book and to other relevant online resources. The Web Links are continually monitored and updated for changes so they

continue to lead to useful Web resources for each chapter. You can find the Web Links for this book by visiting the companion site.

- **Web Links References in Text** Throughout each chapter, there are Web Links references that indicate the name of a link included in the Web Links. Text set in bold, green, sans-serif letters (**Metabot Pro**) indicates a like-named link in the Web Links. The links are organized under chapter and subchapter headings that correspond to those in the book. The Web Links also contains many supplemental links to help students explore beyond the book's content.

- **Review Questions and Exercises** Each chapter concludes with meaningful review materials including both conceptual discussion questions and hands-on exercises. The review questions are ideal for use as the basis for class discussions or as written homework assignments. The exercises give students hands-on experiences that yield computer output or a written report.

- **Cases** Each chapter concludes with two comprehensive cases. One case uses a fictitious setting to illustrate key learning objectives from that chapter. The other case gives students an opportunity to apply what they have learned from the chapter to an actual situation that a real company or organization has faced. The cases offer students a rich environment in which they can apply what they have learned and provide motivation for doing further research on the topics.

- **For Further Study and Research** Each chapter concludes with a comprehensive list of the resources that were consulted during the writing of the chapter. These references to publications in academic journals, books, and the IT industry and business press provide a sound starting point for readers who want to learn more about the topics contained in the chapter.

- **Key Terms and Glossary** Terms within each chapter that may be new to the student or have specific subject-related meaning are highlighted by boldface type. The end of each chapter includes a list of the chapter's key terms. All of the book's key terms are compiled, along with definitions, in a Glossary at the end of the book.

TEACHING TOOLS

When this book is used in an academic setting, instructors may obtain the following teaching tools:

- **Instructor's Manual** The Instructor's Manual has been carefully prepared and tested to ensure its accuracy and dependability. The Instructor's Manual is available on the instructor companion site.

- **Cengage Learning Testing Powered by Cognero** is a flexible, online system that allows you to:

  - author, edit, and manage test bank content from multiple Cengage Learning solutions

- create multiple test versions in an instant
- deliver tests from your LMS, your classroom, or wherever you want

- **PowerPoint Presentations** Microsoft PowerPoint slides are included for each chapter as a teaching aid for classroom presentations, to make available to students on a network for chapter review, or to be printed for classroom distribution. Instructors can add their own slides for additional topics they introduce to the class. The presentations are available on the instructor companion site.

ACKNOWLEDGMENTS

I owe a great debt of gratitude to my good friends at Cengage who made this book possible, including Jason Guyler, Product Manager; Ted Knight, Content Developer; and Divya Divakaran, Project Manager. I am also indebted to Amanda Brodkin, who served as Development Editor on the first 11 editions.

I want to thank the following reviewers for their insightful comments and suggestions on previous editions:

Paul Ambrose	University of Wisconsin, Milwaukee
Kirk Arnett	Mississippi State University
Tina Ashford	Macon State College
Rafael Azuaje	Sul Ross State University
Robert Chi	California State University-Long Beach
Chet Cunningham	Madisonville Community College
Roland Eichelberger	Baylor University
Mary Garrett	Michigan Virtual High School
Barbara Grabowski	Benedictine University
Milena Head	McMaster University
Perry M. Hidalgo	Gwinnett Technical Institute
Brent Hussin	University of Wisconsin, Green Bay
Cheri L. Kase	Legg Mason Corporate Technology
Joanne Kuzma	St. Petersburg College
Rick Lindgren	Graceland University
Victor Lipe	Trident Technical College
William Lisenby	Alamo Community College
Diane Lockwood	Seattle University
Jane Mackay	Texas Christian University
Michael P. Martel	University of Alabama
William E. McTammany	Florida State College at Jacksonville
Leslie Moore	Jackson State Community College
Martha Myers	Kennesaw State University
Pete Partin	Forethought Financial Services
Andy Pickering	University of Maryland University College
David Reavis	Texas A&M University

George Reynolds	Strayer University
Barbara Warner	University of South Florida
Gene Yelle	Megacom Services

Special thanks go to reviewer A. Lee Gilbert of Nanyang Technological University in Singapore, who provided extremely detailed comments and many useful suggestions for improving Chapter 12. My thanks also go to the many professors who have used the previous editions in their classes and who have sent me suggestions for improving the text. In particular, I want to acknowledge the detailed recommendations made by David Bell of Pacific Union College regarding the coverage of IP addresses in Chapter 2.

The University of San Diego provided research funding that allowed me to work on the first edition of this book and gave me fellow faculty members who were always happy to discuss and critically evaluate ideas for the book, including Tom Buckles (now at Azusa Pacific University), Rahul Singh (now at the University of North Carolina-Greensboro), Carl Rebman, and Jim Perry, who co-authored the first two editions of this book with me. The University of San Diego School of Business also provided the research assistance of many graduate students who helped me with work on the first seven editions of this book. Among those research assistants were Sebastian Ailioaie, a Fulbright Fellow who did substantial work on the Web Links, and Anthony Coury, who applied his considerable legal knowledge to reviewing Chapter 7 and suggesting many improvements. I also thank Quinnipiac University for providing a graduate student, Arienne Kvetkus, who made many helpful comments on the content of Chapter 6.

Many of my graduate students have provided helpful suggestions and ideas over the years. My special thanks go to two of those students, Dima Ghawi and Dan Gordon. Dima shared her significant background research on reverse auctions and helped me develop many of the ideas presented in Chapters 5 and 6. Dan gave me the benefit of his experiences as manager of global EDI operations for a major international firm and provided an in-depth review of Chapter 5. Other students who provided valuable suggestions include Maximiliano Altieri, Adrian Boyce, Karl Flaig, Kathy Glaser, Emilie Johnson Hersh, Robin Lloyd, Chad McManamy, Dan Mulligan, Firat Ozkan, Suzanne Phillips, Susan Soelaiman, Carolyn Sturz, Leila Worthy, and Zu-yo Wang.

Finally, I want to express my deep appreciation for the support and encouragement of my wife, Cathy Cosby. Without her support and patience, writing this book would not have been possible.

DEDICATION

To the memory of my father, Anthony J. Schneider.

ABOUT THE AUTHOR

Gary Schneider is currently a Professor at the California State University Monterey Bay College of Business. His previous appointments include the William S. Perlroth Professorship at Quinnipiac University and the Clarence L. Steber Professorship at the University of San Diego. He has also taught at the University of Cincinnati, Northern

Kentucky University, the University of Tennessee, and Xavier University. He has won a number of teaching and research awards at these universities and served as academic director of the University of San Diego's graduate programs in electronic commerce and information systems. Gary has published more than 50 books and 100 research papers on a variety of accounting, information systems, and management topics. His books have been translated into Chinese, French, Italian, Korean, and Spanish. Gary's research has been funded by the Irvine Foundation and the U.S. Office of Naval Research. His work has appeared in *Accounting Horizons*, the *Journal of Information Systems*, *Interfaces*, *Issues in Accounting Education*, and the *Information Systems Audit and Control Journal*. He has served as editor of the *Business Studies Journal* and the *Accounting Systems and Technology Reporter*, as accounting discipline editor of *Advances in Accounting, Finance and Economics*, as associate editor of the *Journal of Global Information Management*, and on the editorial boards of the *Journal of Information Systems*, the *Journal of Electronic Commerce in Organizations*, the *Journal of Database Management*, and the *Information Systems Audit & Control Journal*. Gary has lectured on electronic commerce topics at universities and businesses in the United States, Europe, South America, and Asia. He has provided consulting and training services to a number of major clients, including Gartner, Gateway, Honeywell, the National Science Foundation, Qualcomm, and the U.S. Department of Commerce. In 1999, he was named a Fellow of the Gartner Institute. In 2013, he was named a Distinguished Visiting Professor at the *Instituto Tecnológico y de Estudios Superiores de Monterrey* in Guadalajara, Mexico. Gary is a licensed CPA in Ohio, where he practiced public accounting for 14 years. He holds a Ph.D. in accounting information systems from the University of Tennessee, an M.B.A. in accounting from Xavier University, and a B.A. in economics from the University of Cincinnati.

PART 1

Introduction

Blend Images Photography/Veer

Introduction to Electronic Commerce

LEARNING OBJECTIVES

In this chapter, you will learn:

- What electronic commerce is and how it has evolved in three waves of development
- Why companies concentrate on revenue models and the analysis of business processes instead of business models when they undertake electronic commerce initiatives
- How to identify opportunities for and barriers to electronic commerce initiatives
- How economic forces have led to the development and continued growth of electronic commerce
- How businesses use value chains and SWOT analysis to identify electronic commerce opportunities
- How the international nature of electronic commerce affects its growth and development

INTRODUCTION

Electronic commerce began in the United States and for many years was conducted primarily through English-language Web sites. As you will learn in this chapter, that has changed dramatically in recent years. Since 2013, China has been the leader in online retail sales, with a growing proportion of those sales being made on smartphones rather than computers.

With a population of 1.4 billion, some 650 million of whom have an Internet connection of some kind, China is the world's largest potential online market. Recent studies have identified the Chinese as especially active Internet users, with more than 90 percent reporting that they go online two to four times a day. Combined with an overall upward trend in economic growth in the country, current and projected online retail sales are expected to continue their recent upward trends. Although Chinese buyers do use U.S.-based sites such as Amazon (*Note*: This typeface indicates a corresponding link to a related Web page in the book's Web Links. Google's URL is http://www.amazon.com) and eBay, they are also frequent users of domestic sites with well-developed brand awareness such as JD.com and Tmall.

The differences between Chinese and U.S. online shoppers do not stop at the different languages they use. Chinese online buyers are more highly influenced by and want to consult online reviews far more often than shoppers elsewhere. They also like to discuss potential purchases with others online to a greater degree. These cultural characteristics have led to the development of independent online review sites and in sellers such as Nike becoming active participants in Chinese chat and messaging sites such as Sina Weibo and WeChat.

Sellers in China also find that they must take into account regional differences within a diverse country. In the major cities, shoppers are buying branded luxury goods and big-ticket items such as cars; while in smaller towns, consumers are more price-conscious and looking to find deals on everyday goods. Distribution and delivery can be tricky in parts of China that do not have well-developed roads and standardized shipping practices. Some sellers are overcoming these issues by creating their own distribution systems. For example, JD.com has built more than 80 warehouses in 34 cities which it uses to make faster and more reliable deliveries than its competitors.

In this chapter, you will learn how online businesses have emerged and grown to accommodate the various cultures and infrastructure challenges around the world.

The Evolution of Electronic Commerce

The business phenomenon that we now call electronic commerce has had an interesting history. From humble beginnings in the mid-1990s, electronic commerce grew rapidly until 2000, when a major downturn occurred prompting endless news stories describing how the "dot-com boom" had turned into the "dot-com bust." Between 2000 and 2003, many industry observers were writing obituaries for electronic commerce. Just as the unreasonable expectations for immediate success had fueled unwarranted high expectations during the boom years, overly gloomy news reports colored perceptions during this time.

Beginning in 2003, electronic commerce began to show signs of a profound rebirth. Companies that had survived the downturn were not only seeing growth in sales again, but many of them were showing profits for the first time. As the economy grew, electronic commerce also grew, but at a faster pace than the overall economy. Thus, electronic commerce gradually became a larger part of the total economy.

In the general economic recession that started in 2008, electronic commerce suffered far less than most of the economy. Looking back from today's perspective, we can see that as the general economy has expanded and contracted, electronic commerce has consistently expanded more in the good times and contracted less in the bad times than other economic sectors. This section defines electronic commerce and describes its evolution from a novelty to its current place as an important component of global business activity.

Electronic Commerce and Electronic Business

To many people, the term "electronic commerce" means shopping on the part of the Internet called the World Wide Web (the Web). However, **electronic commerce (or e-commerce)** also includes many other activities, such as businesses trading with other businesses and internal processes that companies use to support their buying, selling, hiring, planning, and other activities. Some people use the term **electronic business (or e-business)** when they are talking about electronic commerce in this broader sense. For example, IBM defines electronic business as "the transformation of key business processes through the use of Internet technologies." Most people use the terms "electronic commerce" and "electronic business" interchangeably. In this book, the term electronic commerce (or e-commerce) is used in its broadest sense and includes all business activities that use Internet technologies. Internet technologies include the Internet, the World Wide Web, and other technologies such as wireless transmissions on mobile telephone networks. Companies that operate only online are sometimes called **dot-com** or **pure dot-com** businesses to distinguish them from companies that operate in physical locations (solely or together with online operations); however, online business activity has become so integrated with everyday life in much of the world that few people worry about these distinctions any longer.

Categories of Electronic Commerce

Categorizing electronic commerce by the types of entities participating in the transactions or business processes is a useful and commonly accepted way to define online business.

The five general electronic commerce categories are business-to-consumer, business-to-business, transactions and business processes, consumer-to-consumer, and business-to-government. The three categories that are most commonly used are:

- Consumer shopping on the Web, often called **business-to-consumer (or B2C)**
- Transactions conducted between businesses on the Web, often called **business-to-business (or B2B)**
- Business processes in which companies, governments, and other organizations use Internet technologies to support selling and purchasing activities

A single company might participate in activities that fall under multiple e-commerce categories. Consider a company that manufactures stereo speakers. The company might sell its finished product to consumers on the Web, which would be B2C electronic commerce. It might also purchase the materials it uses to make the speakers from other companies on the Web, which would be B2B electronic commerce. Businesses often have entire departments devoted to negotiating purchase transactions with their suppliers. These departments are usually named **supply management** or **procurement**. Thus, B2B electronic commerce is sometimes called **e-procurement**.

In addition to buying materials and selling speakers, the company must also undertake many other activities to convert the purchased materials into speakers. These activities might include hiring and managing the people who make the speakers, renting or buying the facilities in which the speakers are made and stored, shipping the speakers, maintaining accounting records, obtaining customer feedback, purchasing insurance, developing advertising campaigns, and designing new versions of the speakers. An increasing number of these transactions and business processes can be done on the Web. Manufacturing processes (such as the fabrication of the speakers) can be controlled using Internet technologies within the business. All of these communication, control, and transaction-related activities have become an important part of electronic commerce. Some people include these activities in the B2B category; others refer to them as underlying or supporting business processes.

Business Processes

For more than 80 years, business researchers have been studying the ways people behave in businesses. This research has helped managers better understand how workers do their jobs and what motivates them to work more effectively. The research results have helped managers, and more recently, the workers themselves, improve job performance and productivity. An important part of doing these job studies is to learn what activities each worker performs. In this setting, a **business activity** is a task performed by a worker in the course of doing his or her job.

For a much longer time—centuries, in fact—business owners have kept records of how well their businesses are performing. The formal practice of accounting, or recording transactions, dates back to the Middle Ages. A **transaction** is an exchange of value, such as a purchase, a sale, or the conversion of raw materials into a finished product. By recording transactions, accountants help business owners keep score and measure how well they are doing. All transactions involve at least one activity, and some transactions involve many activities. Not all activities result in measurable (and therefore recordable) transactions. Thus, a transaction always has one or more activities associated with it, but an activity might not be related to a transaction.

The group of logical, related, and sequential activities and transactions in which businesses engage are often collectively referred to as **business processes**. Transferring funds, placing orders, sending invoices, and shipping goods to customers are all types of activities or transactions. For example, the business process of shipping goods to customers might include a number of activities (or tasks, or transactions), such as inspecting the goods, packing the goods, negotiating with a freight company to deliver the goods, creating and printing the shipping documents, loading the goods onto the truck, and sending payment to the freight company.

One important way that the Web is helping people work more effectively is by enabling employees of many different kinds of companies to work at home or from other locations (such as while traveling). In this arrangement, called **telecommuting** or **telework**, the employee logs in to the company network through the Internet instead of traveling to an office.

Relative Size of Electronic Commerce Elements

Figure 1-1 shows the two main types of electronic commerce as subsets of the overall business processes in which a company might engage. The figure presents a rough approximation of the relative sizes of these three elements (B2C commerce, B2B commerce, and overall business processes). In terms of dollar volume and number of transactions, B2B electronic commerce is much greater than B2C electronic commerce. However, the number of business processes that are conducted using online technologies is far greater than the number of all B2C and B2B transactions combined.

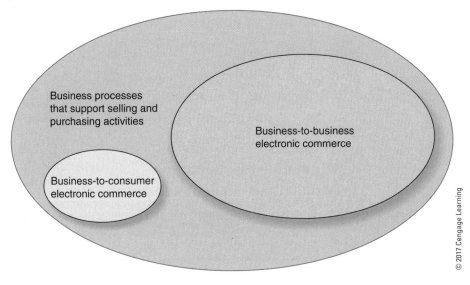

Business processes that support selling and purchasing activities

Business-to-business electronic commerce

Business-to-consumer electronic commerce

© 2017 Cengage Learning

FIGURE 1-1   Elements of electronic commerce

The large oval in Figure 1-1 that represents the business processes that support selling and purchasing activities is the largest element of electronic commerce.

Some researchers define a fourth category of electronic commerce, called **consumer-to-consumer (or C2C)**, which includes individuals who buy and sell items among themselves. For example, C2C electronic commerce occurs when a person sells an item through a Web auction site to another person. In this book, C2C sales are included in the B2C category because the person selling the item acts much as a business would for purposes of the transaction.

Finally, some researchers also define a category of electronic commerce called **business-to-government (or B2G)**; this category includes business transactions with government agencies, such as paying taxes and filing required reports. An increasing number of states have Web sites that help companies do business with state government agencies. In this book, B2G transactions are included in the discussions of B2B electronic commerce. Figure 1-2 summarizes these five categories of electronic commerce.

Category	Description	Example
Business-to-consumer (B2C)	Businesses sell products or services to individual consumers.	Walmart.com sells merchandise to consumers through its Web site.
Business-to-business (B2B)	Businesses sell products or services to other businesses.	Grainger.com sells industrial supplies to large and small businesses through its Web site.
Business processes that support buying and selling activities	Businesses and other organizations maintain and use information to identify and evaluate customers, suppliers, and employees. Increasingly, businesses share this information in carefully managed ways with their customers, suppliers, employees, and business partners.	Dell Computer uses secure Internet connections to share current sales and sales forecast information with suppliers. The suppliers can use this information to plan their own production and deliver component parts to Dell in the right quantities at the right time.
Consumer-to-consumer (C2C)	Participants in an online marketplace can buy and sell goods to each other. Because one party is selling, and thus acting as a business, this book treats C2C transactions as part of B2C electronic commerce.	Consumers and businesses trade with each other in the eBay.com online marketplace.
Business-to-government (B2G)	Businesses sell goods or services to governments and government agencies. This book treats B2G transactions as part of B2C electronic commerce.	CA.gov procurement site allows businesses to sell online to the state of California.

FIGURE 1-2   Electronic commerce categories

The Development and Growth of Electronic Commerce

Over the thousands of years that people have engaged in commerce with one another, they have adopted the tools and technologies that became available. For example, the advent of sailing ships in ancient times opened new avenues of trade to buyers and sellers. Later innovations, such as the printing press, steam engine, and telephone, have changed the way people conduct commerce activities. The Internet has changed the way people buy, sell, hire, and organize business activities in more ways and more rapidly than any other technology in the history of business.

Early Electronic Commerce

Although the Web has made online shopping possible for many businesses and individuals, in a broader sense, electronic commerce has existed for many years. Since the mid-1960s, banks have been using **electronic funds transfers (EFTs**, also called **wire transfers)**, which are electronic transmissions of account exchange information over private communications' networks. Initially used to transfer money between business checking accounts, the use of EFTs gradually expanded to include payroll deposits to employees' accounts, automatic payment of auto and mortgage loans, and deposit of government payments to individuals, such as U.S. Social Security System remittances.

Businesses have also used a form of electronic commerce, known as electronic data interchange, for many years. **Electronic data interchange (EDI)** occurs when one business transmits computer-readable data in a standard format to another business. In the 1960s, businesses realized that many of the documents they exchanged were related to the shipping of goods; for example, invoices, purchase orders, and bills of lading. These documents included the same set of information for almost every transaction. Businesses also realized that they were spending a good deal of time and money entering this data into their computers, printing paper forms, and then reentering the data on the other side of the transaction. Although the purchase order, invoice, and bill of lading for each transaction contained much of the same information—such as item numbers, descriptions, prices, and quantities—each paper form usually had its own unique format for presenting the information. By creating a set of standard formats for transmitting the information electronically, businesses were able to reduce errors, avoid printing and mailing costs, and eliminate the need to reenter the data.

Businesses that engage in EDI with each other are called **trading partners**. The standard formats used in EDI contain the same information that businesses have always included in their standard paper invoices, purchase orders, and shipping documents. Firms such as General Electric, Sears, and Walmart were pioneers in using EDI to improve their purchasing processes and their relationships with suppliers. The U.S. government, which is one of the largest EDI trading partners in the world, was also instrumental in bringing businesses into EDI.

One problem that EDI pioneers faced was the high cost of implementation. Until the late 1990s, doing EDI meant buying expensive computer hardware and software and then either establishing direct network connections (using leased telephone lines) to all trading partners or subscribing to a value-added network. A **value-added network (VAN)** is an independent firm that offers connection and transaction-forwarding services to buyers and sellers engaged in EDI. Before the Internet came into existence as we know it today, VANs provided the connections between most trading partners and were responsible for ensuring the security of the data transmitted. EDI continues to be a large portion of B2B electronic commerce and is growing steadily every year in number of transactions and dollar volume. You will learn more about EDI, VANs, and new B2B transaction technologies in Chapter 5.

The First Wave of Electronic Commerce, 1995–2003

Many researchers have concluded that the development of electronic commerce is a major change in the way business is conducted and compare it to other historic changes in economic organization, such as the Industrial Revolution. A growing number of business scholars have determined that major changes in economic structures do not occur as single events but occur as a series of developments, or waves, that occur over an extended period of time. For example, the Industrial Revolution is no longer studied as a single event but as a series of developments that took place over a 50- to 100-year period. Economists Chris Freeman and Francisco Louçã describe four distinct waves (or phases) that occurred in the Industrial Revolution in their book *As Time Goes By* (see the For Further Study and Research section at the end of this chapter). In each wave, they found that different business strategies were successful.

Electronic commerce and the information revolution brought about by the Internet will likely go through a series of waves, too. This section outlines the defining characteristics of the first wave of electronic commerce. Subsequent sections of this chapter discuss the evolution of electronic commerce through its second and third waves.

The first wave of electronic commerce was characterized by its rapid growth, often called a "boom," which was followed by a rapid contraction, often called a "bust." Between 1997 and 2000, more than 12,000 Internet-related businesses were started with more than $100 billion of investors' money. In an extended burst of optimism, and what many later described as irrational exuberance, investors feared that they might miss the moneymaking opportunity of a lifetime. As more investors competed for a fixed number of good ideas, the price of those ideas increased. Many good ideas suffered from poor implementation. Worse, a number of bad ideas were proposed and funded.

More than 5000 of these Internet start-up firms went out of business or were acquired in the downturn that began in 2000. The media coverage of the "dot-com bust" from 2000 to 2003 was extensive. However, during that time, more than $200 billion was spent bailing out troubled electronic commerce businesses and starting completely new online ventures. Although this injection of financial investment was not reported widely in either the general or business media, these investments set the stage for significant growth in online business activity in subsequent years. This rebirth provided another chance at success for many good online business ideas that had been poorly implemented in the early days of the Internet.

The Second Wave of Electronic Commerce, 2004–2009

The first wave of electronic commerce was predominantly a U.S. phenomenon. Web pages were primarily in English, particularly on commerce sites. The second wave was characterized by an expanding international scope, with sellers beginning to do business in other countries and languages. Language translation and currency conversion were two impediments to rapid global expansion of electronic commerce in its second wave. You will learn more about the issues that occur today in global electronic commerce later in this chapter, in Chapter 7, which concerns legal issues, and in Chapter 11, which concerns online payment systems.

In the first wave, easy access to start-up capital led to an overemphasis on creating entirely new enterprises to exploit electronic commerce opportunities. Investors were excited about electronic commerce and wanted to participate, no matter how much it cost or how weak the underlying ideas were. In the second wave, established companies began using their own internal funds to finance gradual expansion of electronic commerce opportunities. These measured and carefully considered investments are helping electronic commerce grow more steadily, though more slowly.

The Internet technologies used in the first wave, especially in B2C commerce, were slow and inexpensive. Although businesses typically had broadband connections, most consumers connected to the Internet using dial-up modems. The increase in broadband connections in homes is a key element in the B2C component of the second wave. In 2004, the number of U.S. homes with broadband connections began to increase rapidly. Most industry estimates showed that about 12 percent of U.S. homes had broadband connections in early 2004. By 2009, those estimates were ranging between 70 and 80 percent. Other countries, such as South Korea, began to subsidize their citizens' Internet access, which led to an even higher rate of broadband usage.

The increased use of home Internet connections to transfer large audio and video files is generally seen as the reason large numbers of people spent the extra money required to obtain a broadband connection during the second wave. The increased speed of broadband not only makes Internet use more efficient, but it also can alter the way people use the Web. For example, a broadband connection allows a user to watch movies and television programs online—something that is impossible to do with a dial-up connection. This opens up more opportunities for businesses to make online sales. It also changes the way that online retailers can present their products to Web site visitors. Although business customers, unlike retail customers, have had fast connections to the Internet for many years, the increasing availability of wireless Internet connections increased the volume and nature of B2B electronic commerce during the second wave. For example, salespeople using laptop computers could stay in touch with customers, prepare quotes, and check on orders being fulfilled from virtually anywhere. You will learn more about different types of connections in Chapter 2 and how connection speed can affect consumers' online shopping experiences in Chapters 3 and 4.

Electronic mail (or e-mail) was used in the first wave as a tool for relatively unstructured communication. In the second wave, both B2C and B2B sellers began using e-mail as an integral part of their marketing and customer contact strategies. You will learn about e-mail technologies in Chapter 2 and e-mail marketing in Chapter 4.

Online advertising was the main intended revenue source of many failed dot-com businesses in the first wave. After a pronounced dip in online advertising activity and revenues near the end of the first wave, companies began the second wave with a renewed interest in making the Internet work as an effective advertising medium. Some categories of online advertising, such as employment services (job-wanted ads) have grown rapidly and have replaced traditional advertising outlets. Companies such as Google have devised ways of delivering specific ads to Internet users who are most likely to be interested in the products or services offered by those ads. You will learn about these advertising strategies in Chapter 4.

The sale of digital products was fraught with difficulties during the first wave of electronic commerce. The music recording industry was unable (or, some would say, unwilling) to devise a way to distribute digital music on the Web. This created an environment in which digital piracy—the theft of musical artists' intellectual property— became rampant. The promise of electronic books was also unfulfilled. The second wave fulfilled the promise of available technology by supporting the legal distribution of music, video, and other digital products on the Web. Apple Computer's iTunes Web site is an example of a second-wave digital product distribution business that is meeting the needs of consumers and its industry. You will learn more about digital product distribution strategies in Chapter 3 and about the related legal issues in Chapter 7.

Another group of technologies emerged in the second wave that made new online businesses possible. The general term for these technologies is **Web 2.0**, and they include software that allows users of Web sites to participate in the creation, editing, and distribution of content on a Web site owned and operated by a third party. Sites such as Wikipedia, YouTube, and Facebook use Web 2.0 technologies. Customer relationships management software that runs from the Web, such as Salesforce.com, also uses Web 2.0 technologies. You will learn about Web 2.0 business opportunities throughout this book and you will learn about the technologies used to implement them in Chapter 9.

In the first wave of electronic commerce, many companies and investors believed that being the first Web site to offer a particular type of product or service would give them an opportunity to be successful. This strategy is called the **first-mover advantage**. As business researchers studied companies who had tried to gain a first-mover advantage, they learned that being first did not always lead to success (see the Suarez and Lanzolla article reference in the For Further Study and Research section at the end of this chapter). First movers must invest large amounts of money in new technologies and make guesses about what customers will want when those technologies are functioning. The combination of high uncertainty and the need for large investments makes being a first mover very risky. As many business strategists have noted, "It is the second mouse that gets the cheese." An approach in which a business observes first-mover failures and enters a business later, when large investments are no longer required and business processes have been tested, is called a **smart-follower strategy**.

First movers that were successful tended to be large companies that had an established reputation (or brand) and that also had marketing, distribution, and production expertise. First movers that were smaller or that lacked the expertise in these areas tended to be unsuccessful. Also, first movers that entered highly volatile markets or in those industries with high rates of technological change often did not do well. In the second wave, more businesses followed a smart-follower strategy when they took their businesses online.

The Third Wave of Electronic Commerce, 2010–Present

In 2010, a number of factors came together to start a third wave in the development of electronic commerce. Some of these factors include:

- A critical mass of mobile users with powerful devices (smartphones and tablets) that, for the first time, allowed them to interact online with businesses along with proliferation of high-speed mobile phone networks throughout the world that provide useful connections among users and companies
- An increase in electronic commerce activity, both domestic and across borders, in developing countries, especially those with large populations such as China, India, and Brazil
- Widespread participation in social networking platforms combined with businesses' increased willingness to use them for advertising, promotion, and sales
- Increased online participation by smaller businesses in sales, purchasing, and capital-raising activities
- Highly sophisticated analysis of the large amounts of data that companies collect about their online customers
- Increased integration of tracking technologies into B2B electronic commerce and the management of business processes within companies

EMERGENCE OF MOBILE COMMERCE

Since about 2001, industry analysts have been predicting the emergence of mobile telephone-based commerce (often called **mobile commerce or m-commerce**) every year. And year after year, they were surprised that the expected development of mobile commerce did not occur. The limited capabilities of mobile telephones were a major impediment.

In the third wave of electronic commerce, mobile commerce finally took off with the increasingly widespread use of mobile phones that allow Internet access and smartphones. **Smartphones** are mobile phones that include a Web browser, a full keyboard, and an identifiable operating system that allows users to run various software packages. These phones are available with usage plans that include very high or even unlimited data transfers at a fixed monthly rate.

Another technological development was the introduction of tablet computers. These handheld devices are larger than a smartphone but smaller than a laptop computer. Most tablet computers (and smartphones) can connect to the Internet through a wireless phone service carrier or a local wireless network. This flexibility is important, especially if the wireless data plan restricts the amount of data that can be downloaded. The availability of these devices and the low cost of Internet connectivity have made mobile commerce possible on a large scale for the first time. Leading online business research firms, including Forrester and Internet Retailer, estimate mobile commerce to be about $76 billion in 2015 and forecast continued rapid growth to over $130 billion by 2018.

Both tablet devices and smartphones allow users to access the Internet using Web browsers; however, an increasing number of mobile shoppers use **mobile software applications (mobile apps)** to make purchases on their mobile devices. Mobile apps are issued by the seller to make shopping at their store easier and more convenient. In 2014, *Internet Retailer* reported that 42 percent of all B2C mobile sales in the United States were made using these apps.

EMERGENCE OF GLOBAL ELECTRONIC COMMERCE

One force driving the growth in global online sales to consumers is the ever-increasing number of people who have access to the Internet. Today, billions of people around the world still do not have computers and, therefore, do not have computer access to the Internet. The increases in global online business, especially in less developed countries, are due in part to the growing numbers of people using inexpensive devices such as mobile phones and tablet devices to access the Internet. This growth is expected to be especially dramatic in highly populated countries that also have rapidly growing economies such as China, India, and Brazil. In fact, online retail sales in China have exceeded those in the United States since 2010.

The pervasiveness of interconnected handheld devices makes the Internet truly available everywhere. This constant availability can change buyer behavior in many ways (discussed in Chapters 3 and 4) and it can provide new opportunities for online businesses that could not exist without such broad-based connectivity, especially in the sale and delivery of digital products and content. In Chapter 5, you will learn how the pervasiveness of computers (laptops and tablets) and mobile phones that can access the Internet is changing B2B electronic commerce, and you will learn about the growing opportunities for B2C mobile commerce in Chapter 6.

WIDESPREAD SOCIAL NETWORKING

The Web 2.0 technologies that enabled part of the growth in electronic commerce that occurred in the second wave will play a major role in the third wave. For example, social networking sites such as Facebook and microblogging technologies such as Twitter can be used to engage in social commerce.

Social commerce is the use of interpersonal connections online to promote or sell goods and services. Because a handheld device connected to the Internet can put a user online virtually all the time, businesses can use online social interactions to advertise, promote, or suggest specific products or services. Although sales traceable directly to social commerce activities are estimated to be about $20 billion per year, most industry analysts believe that the effect of these activities on overall online business is much greater. You will learn more about social networking, microblogging, and social commerce in Chapter 6.

INCREASED PARTICIPATION BY SMALL BUSINESSES

Large businesses—both existing businesses and new businesses that had obtained large amounts of capital early on—dominated the first wave. The second wave saw a major increase in the participation of small businesses (those with fewer than 200 employees) in the online economy. Still, more than 30 percent of small businesses in the United States do not have Web sites. In other parts of the world, this percentage is much higher. The third wave of electronic commerce will include the participation of a significantly larger proportion of these smaller businesses.

One way that smaller businesses can obtain funding for operations is by using Web sites and social commerce activities for raising capital. Web sites used to gather multiple small investors together for specific business funding activities are called **crowdsourcing** sites. These allow businesses to post their ideas and solicit funding for them from the general public, replacing banks and private investors as the source of the money they need for expansion or creating new products and services. You will learn more about these funding opportunities in Chapter 12. Providing services that help smaller companies use electronic commerce will also be a substantial area of growth in the third wave.

SOPHISTICATED ANALYSIS OF LARGE DATASETS

Companies that do business online found that they could track the detailed behavior of customers as they navigate the company Web site. They also found that they could store large amounts of this information and use it to improve their operations and interactions with customers. The availability of so much data, which was available to physical companies only through expensive surveys and focus groups, was a major force in the development of sophisticated software tools for analyzing large amounts of data. The term **big data** is used in business to describe very large stores of information such as that collected by online sellers about their customers. The highly sophisticated tools for investigating patterns and knowledge contained in big data are called **data analytics**.

Companies that store large amounts of data about their customers' behavior on their Web sites can combine that information with their existing data about customers' past purchases to predict the kinds of products, services, or special offers in which each customer might be interested. You will learn more about how companies use big data to tailor their product offerings, advertising, and marketing strategies to groups of customers and even individual customers in Chapter 4.

The study of data analytics, which includes the development and use of statistical software to detect patterns in big data and the modeling of customer behavior, has become a popular subject area at many universities around the world. You will learn more about the use of data analytics in managing customer relationships in Chapter 4 and the software used to perform these activities in Chapter 9.

INTEGRATION OF TRACKING TECHNOLOGIES INTO B2B

In the first two waves, Internet technologies were integrated into B2B transactions and internal business processes by using bar codes and scanners to track parts, assemblies, inventories, and production status. These tracking technologies were not well integrated. Also, companies sent transaction information to each other using a patchwork of communication methods, including fax, e-mail, and EDI. In the third wave, Radio Frequency Identification (RFID) devices and smart cards are being combined with biometric technologies, such as fingerprint readers and retina scanners, to control more items and people in a wider variety of situations. These technologies are increasingly integrated with each other and with communication systems that allow companies to communicate with each other and share transaction, inventory level, and customer demand information effectively. You will learn more about how these technologies are integrated with B2B electronic commerce in Chapter 5.

Figure 1-3 shows a summary of these and other key characteristics of third-wave electronic commerce as compared to those discussed earlier regarding the first and second waves.

Not all of the future of electronic commerce is based on second- and third-wave developments. Some of the most successful first-wave companies, such as Amazon.com, eBay, and Yahoo!, continue to grow by offering increasingly innovative products and services. However, the third wave of electronic commerce will provide new opportunities for these businesses, too.

Electronic Commerce Characteristic	First Wave	Second Wave	Third Wave
International Character of Electronic Commerce	Dominated by U.S. companies	Global enterprises in many countries participating in electronic commerce	Emergence of China, India, Brazil, and other countries as major centers of electronic commerce activity
Languages	Most electronic commerce Web sites in English	Many electronic commerce Web sites available in multiple languages	English is no longer the dominant language on Web sites worldwide
Funding	Many new companies started with outside investor money	Established companies funding electronic commerce initiatives with their own capital	Wide variety of funding sources available, including crowdsourcing
Connection Technologies	Many electronic commerce participants used slow Internet connections	Rapidly increasing use of broadband technologies for Internet connections	High bandwidth mobile telephone networks become an additional important connection technology
Contact with Customers	Unstructured e-mail communication with customers	Customized e-mail strategies are integral to customer contact	Social networking tools are important additions to e-mail contact
Advertising and Electronic Commerce Integration	Reliance on simple forms of online advertising as main revenue source	Use of multiple sophisticated advertising approaches and better integration of electronic commerce with existing business processes and strategies	Increasingly, advertising and marketing strategies are driven by available online communication technologies
Distribution of Digital Products	Widespread piracy due to ineffective distribution of digital products	New approaches to the sale and distribution of digital products	Sale and distribution of digital products becomes commonplace
First-Mover Advantage	Rely on first-mover advantage to ensure success in all types of markets and industries	Realize that first-mover advantage leads to success only for some companies in certain specific markets and industries	First-mover advantage no longer seen as a key element in electronic commerce initiatives

© 2017 Cengage Learning

FIGURE 1-3   Key characteristics of the first three waves of electronic commerce

The "Boom and Bust" Myth

Despite the many news stories that appeared between 2000 and 2002 proclaiming the death of electronic commerce, the growth in online B2C sales actually had continued through that period, although at a slower pace than during the boom years of the late 1990s. Thus, viewed with an historical perspective, the "bust" that was so widely reported in the media actually turned out to be more of a minor slowdown than an all-out collapse. After four years of doubling or tripling every year, growth in online sales slowed to an annual rate of 20–30 percent starting in 2001, which is a very high rate of expansion. This growth rate continued through the recession of 2008–2009.

The 2008–2009 global recession devastated many traditional retailers, particularly in the United States and Europe. Large Asian economies, such as those in China and India, were affected less and continued to expand. Around the globe, online sales overall continued to grow during that period, although at a lower rate than the 20–30 percent annual rates achieved earlier in the decade. As many traditional businesses remained mired in the aftereffects of that recession, online business activity picked up and was at the leading edge of economic growth. Online business growth in Asia continued at relatively high rates throughout the recessionary period, which boosted global online sales totals.

In addition to the growth in the B2C sector, B2B sales online have been increasing steadily for almost two decades. The dollar total of B2B online sales has been greater than B2C sales because B2B incorporates EDI, a technology that accounted for more than $400 billion per year in transactions in 1995, when Internet-based electronic commerce was just beginning. This book defines B2B sales as including companies' transactions with other businesses, with their employees, and with governmental agencies (for example, when they pay their taxes) because these business processes are all candidates for the application of Internet technologies.

The total volume of all worldwide business activities on the Web is expected to exceed $14 trillion by 2018. Figure 1-4 summarizes the growth of actual and estimated global online sales for the B2C and B2B categories.

Business Models, Revenue Models, and Business Processes

A **business model** is a set of processes that combine to achieve a company's primary goal, which is typically to yield a profit. In the first wave of electronic commerce, many investors tried to find start-up companies that had new, Internet-driven business models. These investors expected that the right business model would lead to rapid sales growth and market dominance. If a company was successful using a new "dot-com" business model, investors would clamor to copy that model or find a start-up company that planned to use a similar business model. This strategy led the way to many business failures, some of them quite dramatic.

In the wake of the dot-com debacle that ended the first wave of electronic commerce, many business researchers analyzed the efficacy of this "copy a successful business model" approach and began to question the advisability of focusing great attention on a company's business model. One of the main critics, Harvard Business School professor Michael Porter, argued that business models not only did not matter, they also probably

Year	B2C Sales: Actual and Estimated $ Billions	B2B Sales (Including EDI): Actual and Estimated $ Billions
2015	1170	14,300
2014	1080	13,100
2013	963	11,900
2012	821	10,600
2011	681	9500
2010	573	8600
2009	487	7500
2008	453	6500
2007	426	5600
2006	361	4800
2005	255	4100
2004	179	2800
2003	103	1600
2002	91	900
2001	73	730
2000	52	600
1999	26	550
1998	11	520
1997	5	490
1996	Less than 1	460

Adapted from reports by ClickZ Network (http://www.clickz.com/stats/stats_toolbox/); eMarketer (http://www.emarketer.com/); Forrester Research (http://www.forrester.com); Gartner (http://www.gartner.com); Internet Retailer (http://www.internetretailer.com); the Statistical Abstract of the United States, 2008, Washington: U.S. Census Bureau); the Statistical Abstract of the United States, 2011, Washington: U.S. Census Bureau; and the Statistical Abstract of the United States, 2012, Washington: U.S. Census Bureau.

FIGURE 1-4   Actual and estimated global online sales in B2C and B2B categories

did not exist. (You can read more about Porter's criticisms of the business model approach in the articles cited in the For Further Study and Research section at the end of this chapter.)

Today, most companies realize that copying or adapting someone else's business model is neither an easy nor wise road map to success. Instead, companies should examine the elements of their business; that is, they should identify business processes that they can streamline, enhance, or replace with processes driven by Internet technologies.

Companies and investors do use the idea of a **revenue model**, which is a specific collection of business processes used to identify customers, market to those customers, and generate sales to those customers. The revenue model idea is helpful for classifying revenue-generating activities for communication and analysis purposes. The details of revenue models that are used on the Web are presented in Chapter 3.

Focus on Specific Business Processes

In addition to the revenue model grouping of business processes, companies think of the rest of their operations as specific business processes. Those processes include purchasing raw materials or goods for resale, converting materials and labor into finished goods, managing transportation and logistics, hiring and training employees, managing the finances of the business, and many other activities.

An important function of this book is to help you learn how to identify those business processes that firms can accomplish more effectively by using electronic commerce technologies. In some cases, business processes use traditional commerce activities very effectively, and technology cannot improve them. Products that buyers prefer to touch, smell, or examine closely can be difficult to sell using electronic commerce. For example, customers might be reluctant to buy items that have an important element of tactile feel or condition such as high-fashion clothing (you cannot touch it online, and subtle color variations that are hard to distinguish on a computer monitor can make a large difference) or antique jewelry (for which elements of condition that require close inspection can be critical to value) if they cannot closely examine the products before agreeing to purchase them.

This book will help you learn how to use Internet technologies to improve existing business processes and identify new business opportunities. An important aspect of electronic commerce is that firms can use it to help them adapt to change. The business world is changing more rapidly than ever before. Although much of this book is devoted to explaining technologies, the book's focus is on the business of electronic commerce; the technologies only enable the business processes.

Role of Merchandising

Retail merchants have years of traditional commerce experience in creating store environments that help convince customers to buy. This combination of store design, layout, and product display knowledge is called **merchandising**. In addition, many salespeople have developed skills that allow them to identify customer needs and find products or services that meet those needs.

The skills of merchandising and personal selling can be difficult to practice remotely. However, companies must be able to transfer their merchandising skills to the Web for their Web sites to be successful. Some products are easier to sell on the Internet than others because the merchandising skills related to those products are easier to transfer to the Web. You will learn more about how merchandising can be accomplished online in Chapters 3 and 4.

Product/Process Suitability to Electronic Commerce

Some products, such as books or CDs, are good candidates for electronic commerce because customers do not need to experience the physical characteristics of the particular item before they buy it. Because one copy of a new book is identical to other copies, and because the customer is not concerned about fit, freshness, or other such qualities, customers are usually willing to order a title without examining the specific copy they will receive. In later chapters, you will learn how to evaluate the advantages and disadvantages of using electronic commerce for specific business processes. Figure 1-5 lists examples of business processes categorized by suitability for electronic commerce and traditional commerce. As technologies develop, many processes that were strictly handled through traditional commerce have become more suitable for electronic commerce. This trend will likely continue. You will learn more about transitions of this type in Chapter 3.

One business process that is especially well suited to electronic commerce is the selling of commodity items. A **commodity item** is a product or service that is hard to distinguish from the same products or services provided by other sellers; its features have become standardized and well known. The only difference a buyer perceives when shopping for a commodity item is its price. Gasoline, office supplies, soap, computers, and airline transportation are all examples of commodity products or services, as are the books and DVDs sold by Amazon.com.

Not all commodity items are good candidates for electronic commerce. They must have an attractive shipping profile to be sold online. A product's **shipping profile** is the collection of attributes that affect how easily that product can be packaged and delivered. A high value-to-weight ratio can help by making the overall shipping cost a small fraction of the selling price. A DVD is an excellent example of an item that has a high value-to-weight ratio. Products that are consistent in size, shape, and weight can make warehousing and shipping much simpler and less costly. Commodity items that have an

Well Suited to Electronic Commerce	Suited to a Combination of Electronic and Traditional Commerce Strategies	Well Suited to Traditional Commerce
Sale/purchase of books and CDs	Sale/purchase of automobiles	Sale/purchase of impulse items for immediate use
Sale/purchase of goods that have strong brand reputations	Banking and financial services	Sale/purchase of used, unbranded goods
Online delivery of software and digital content, such as music and movies	Roommate-matching services	
Sale/purchase of travel services	Sale/purchase of residential real estate	
Online shipment tracking	Sale/purchase of high-value jewelry and antiques	
Sale/purchase of investment and insurance products		

FIGURE 1-5 Business process suitability to type of commerce

attractive shipping profile include books, clothing, shoes, kitchen accessories, and many other small household items.

A product that has a strong brand reputation—such as a Sony television—is easier to sell on the Web than an unbranded item, because the brand's reputation reduces the buyer's concerns about quality when buying that item sight unseen. Expensive jewelry has a high value-to-weight ratio, but many people are reluctant to buy it without examining it in person unless the jewelry is sold under a well-known brand name or with a generous return policy.

Other items that are well suited to electronic commerce are those that appeal to small, but geographically dispersed, groups of customers. Collectible comic books are an example of this kind of product.

Traditional commerce, rather than electronic commerce, can be a better way to sell items that rely on personal selling skills. For example, sales of commercial real estate involve large amounts of money and a high degree of interpersonal trust. Even if commercial real estate is listed online, it will usually require personal contact to negotiate the deal. Many businesses are using a combination of personal contact enhanced by an online presence to sell items such as high-fashion clothing, antiques, or specialized food items.

A combination of electronic and traditional commerce strategies works best when the business process includes both commodity and personal inspection elements. For example, most people find information on the Web about new and used automobiles and do considerable research on specific makes and models before they visit a dealership to buy. In the case of used cars, electronic commerce provides a good way for buyers to obtain information about available models, features, reliability, prices, and dealerships, and also helps buyers find specific vehicles that meet their exact requirements. The range of conditions of used cars makes the traditional commerce component of personal inspection a key part of the transaction negotiation.

Another approach to combining online and traditional selling strategies has been developed to great success by Home Depot. Many of the items sold by hardware stores and home improvement centers are large and heavy; that is, they have terrible shipping profiles. However, Home Depot has a large number of physical store locations. By offering online shoppers the option to pick up purchased items at a nearby store, Home Depot has combined the best of both worlds. Today, more than 40 percent of the company's online sales are picked up in a store, where many customers then make additional purchases.

Electronic Commerce: Opportunities, Cautions, and Concerns

Electronic commerce has changed the way business is conducted in many industries. However, not every business process is suitable for electronic commerce. As technologies advance, more and more types of business processes become candidates for electronic commerce. This section outlines some opportunities and points out some cautions that businesses should consider in evaluating opportunities to engage in online business activities.

Opportunities for Electronic Commerce

Electronic commerce is attractive to businesses because, quite simply, it can help increase profits. It can do this because electronic commerce can increase sales and decrease business costs. Advertising done well on the Web can get even a small firm's promotional message out to potential customers in every country in the world. A firm can use electronic commerce to reach small groups of customers that are geographically scattered. The Web is particularly useful in creating virtual communities that become ideal target markets for specific types of products or services. A **virtual community** is a gathering of people who share a common interest, but instead of this gathering occurring in the physical world, it takes place on the Internet. In recent years, virtual communities have taken advantage of Web 2.0 technologies to make their activities more accessible and interesting to community members. Thomas Petzinger has written extensively in his *Wall Street Journal* newspaper columns and his book, *The New Pioneers*, about new patterns of work and commerce that have evolved from these virtual communities. As you learned earlier in this chapter, businesses in the third wave of electronic commerce are starting to use virtual community structures and tools to conduct social commerce. You will learn about Web sites (called **social networking sites)** that individuals and businesses use to conduct social interactions online and the business opportunities they present in Chapter 6.

Just as electronic commerce increases sales opportunities for the seller, it also increases purchasing opportunities for the buyer. Businesses can use electronic commerce to identify new suppliers and business partners. Negotiating price and delivery terms is easier in electronic commerce because the Internet can help companies efficiently obtain competitive bid information. Electronic commerce increases the speed and accuracy with which businesses can exchange information, which reduces costs on both sides of transactions. Many companies are reducing their costs of handling sales inquiries, providing price quotes, and determining product availability by using electronic commerce in their sales support and order-taking processes.

Cisco Systems, a leading manufacturer of computer networking equipment, currently sells almost all its products online. Because no customer service representatives are involved in making these sales, Cisco operates very efficiently. In 1998, the first year in which its online sales initiative was operational, Cisco made 72 percent of its sales on the Web. Cisco avoided handling 500,000 calls per month and saved $500 million in that first year. Today, Cisco conducts more than 99 percent of its purchase and sales transactions online.

Electronic commerce provides buyers with a wider range of choices than traditional commerce because buyers can consider many different products and services from a wider variety of sellers. This wide variety is available for consumers to evaluate 24 hours a day, every day. Some buyers prefer a great deal of information in deciding on a purchase; others prefer less. Electronic commerce provides buyers with an easy way to customize the level of detail in the information they obtain about a prospective purchase. Instead of waiting days for the mail to bring a catalog or product specification sheet, buyers can have instant access to detailed information on the Web. Allowing customers to create their own ideal information environment saves money and provides an opportunity for increased sales.

Most digital products, such as software, music, video, or images, can be delivered through the Internet to reduce the time buyers must wait to begin using their purchases. The ability to deliver digital products online is not just a cost-reduction strategy; it can provide an opportunity for increased sales. Intuit sells its TurboTax income tax preparation software online and lets customers download the software immediately if they wish. Intuit sells a considerable amount of TurboTax software late in the evening on April 14 each year. (April 15 is the deadline for filing personal income tax returns in the United States.)

The benefits of electronic commerce extend to the general welfare of society. Electronic payments of tax refunds, public retirement, and welfare support cost less to issue and arrive securely and quickly when transmitted over the Internet. Furthermore, electronic payments can be easier to audit and monitor than payments made by check, providing protection against fraud and theft losses. To the extent that electronic commerce enables people to telecommute, everyone benefits from the reduction in commuter-caused traffic and pollution. Electronic commerce can also make products and services available in remote areas. For example, distance learning makes it possible for people to learn skills and earn degrees no matter where they live or which hours they have available for study.

Electronic Commerce: Current Barriers

Some business processes might never lend themselves to electronic commerce. For example, perishable foods and high-cost, unique items such as custom-designed jewelry can be very difficult to inspect adequately from a remote location, regardless of any technologies that might be devised in the future. Four issues currently act as barriers to electronic commerce. These issues might be addressed as online business knowledge and technology develop. They are as follows:

- The need for a critical mass of potential buyers to be equipped with the technology necessary to buy online and be comfortable using that technology,
- A level of predictability in costs and revenues related to the technologies used to undertake electronic commerce,
- Sufficient tools for both hardware and software technology integration, and
- The ability to overcome cultural and legal barriers that can prevent companies from doing business online efficiently.

THE NEED FOR A CRITICAL MASS

Some products and services require that a critical mass of potential buyers be equipped and willing to buy through the Internet. For example, online grocers such as Peapod initially offered their delivery services only in a few cities. As more of Peapod's potential customers became connected to the Internet and felt comfortable with purchasing online, the company was able to expand slowly and carefully into more geographic areas. After more than 10 years of operation, Peapod operates in fewer than 20 U.S. metropolitan areas. Most online grocers focus their sales efforts on packaged goods and branded items. Perishable grocery products, such as fruits and vegetables, are much harder to sell online because customers want to examine and select specific items for freshness and quality. Peapod is a good example of how challenging it can be to build a business in an industry that requires this kind of critical mass. Although it was one of the first online grocery stores, Peapod has had a difficult time staying in business, and was even offline for a short time in 2000. Peapod was subsequently acquired by Royal Ahold, a European firm that was willing to invest additional cash to keep it in operation. Two of Peapod's major competitors, WebVan and HomeGrocer, were unable to stay in business long enough to attract a sufficient customer base.

Established traditional grocery chains in the United States, such as Safeway, also offer online ordering and delivery services in a second wave of using Internet technologies in the grocery business. By using their existing infrastructure (including warehouses, purchasing systems, and physical stores in multiple locations), they are able to avoid having to make the large capital investment in facilities that led to the demise of first-wave dot-com grocers such as WebVan and HomeGrocer.

One online grocer that has successfully implemented an updated version of the WebVan and HomeGrocer operational approach is **FreshDirect**. By limiting its service area to the densely populated region in and around New York City, FreshDirect has found the right combination of operating scale and market. The company started in 2002 and achieved profitability in 2004 with sales of $90 million. This is a much smaller sales volume than either WebVan or HomeGrocer would have needed to be profitable.

Outside the United States, online grocers have done quite well. Three of the most successful online grocery efforts in the world are **Grocery Gateway** in Toronto, **Disco Virtual** in Buenos Aires, and **Tesco** in the United Kingdom. Grocery Gateway and Disco Virtual operate in densely populated urban environments that offer sufficiently large numbers of customers within relatively small geographic areas, which make their delivery routes profitable. Tesco started its operations in London, which offers a similar densely populated urban area. However, Tesco has also expanded its operations to selected rural areas that are near a Tesco supermarket.

PREDICTABILITY OF COSTS AND REVENUES

Businesses often calculate return-on-investment numbers before committing to any new technology. This has been difficult to do for investments in electronic commerce because the costs and benefits are often hard to quantify or predict with any degree of accuracy. Costs that are a function of technology can change dramatically even during a short-lived online business implementation project because the underlying technologies are changing so rapidly. As companies move into the third wave and increasingly use big data and related analytical tools, they are getting better at predicting some costs and revenues. But the difficulty of cost and revenue prediction remains an issue for most companies.

Many firms have had trouble recruiting and retaining employees with the technological, design, or business process skills needed to take their business online. Larger firms often try to use existing personnel who are steeped in traditional ways of doing business. These employees often have difficulty adapting what they have learned about the business to an online environment in which the risks and benefits are often very different. You will learn more about return-on-investment calculations and employee recruitment and retention issues in Chapter 12.

TECHNOLOGY INTEGRATION ISSUES

Another problem facing firms that want to do business on the Internet is the difficulty of integrating existing databases and transaction-processing software designed for traditional commerce into the software that enables electronic commerce. Although a number of companies offer software design and consulting services that promise to tie existing systems into new online business systems, these services can be expensive. The outcome of any systems integration effort can be highly uncertain as well.

In the third wave, more companies are introducing tracking technologies that can help them integrate operations more efficiently. You will learn more about how companies are using tracking technologies in Chapter 5 and how they are beginning to deal with software integration issues in Chapter 9.

CULTURAL AND LEGAL CONCERNS

In addition to technology and software issues, many businesses face cultural and legal obstacles to conducting all types of electronic commerce. B2C electronic commerce must deal with the fact that many consumers are still fearful of sending their credit card numbers over the Internet and having online merchants—merchants they have never met—know so much about them. Other consumers are simply resistant to change and are uncomfortable viewing merchandise on a computer screen rather than in person.

B2B electronic commerce is also affected by cultural and legal considerations. The details of business transactions are often not specified; businesses frequently rely on a long history of doing business a particular way. These established business practices can vary greatly from country to country, and making assumptions when engaging in international commerce can be disastrous. You will learn more about electronic commerce security, privacy issues, and payment systems later in this book.

The legal environment in which electronic commerce is conducted is full of unclear and conflicting laws. In many cases, government regulators have not kept up with technologies. As you will learn in Chapter 7, laws that govern commerce were written when signed documents were a reasonable expectation in any business transaction. However, as more businesses and individuals find the benefits of electronic commerce to be compelling, many of these technology- and culture-related disadvantages will be resolved or seem less problematic.

Economic Forces and Electronic Commerce

Economics is the study of how people allocate scarce resources. One important way that people allocate resources is through commerce (the other major way is through government actions, such as taxes or subsidies). Many economists are interested in how people organize their commerce activities. One way people do this is to participate in markets. Economists use a formal definition of **market** that includes two conditions: first, that the potential sellers of a good come into contact with potential buyers, and second, that a medium of exchange is available. This medium of exchange can be currency or barter. Most economists agree that markets are strong and effective mechanisms for allocating scarce resources. Thus, one would expect most business transactions to occur

LEARNING FROM FAILURES

Pets.com

In February 1999, Pets.com launched its Web site with the hopes of making substantial sales to the 60 percent of U.S. households that own pets and spend more than $20 billion each year feeding, entertaining, and caring for them. More than 10,000 stores sold pet supplies. These stores included small retail outlets, grocery stores, discount retailers (such as Walmart and Costco), and a new generation of pet superstores. Pets.com had acquired an excellent domain name and intended to exploit the opportunities presented by high levels of investor interest in funding electronic commerce companies. The plan for Pets.com was to spend heavily to develop a brand and a Web presence that would rapidly make the company the premier online source for pet-related products.

After launching the site, Pets.com raised $110 million from private investors in 1999, and another $80 million in a public sale of stock in early 2000. Pets.com spent more than $100 million of the money on advertising during its short life. It also spent significant sums to create a Web store that offered more than 12,000 different products. In November 2000—less than two years after launching its Web site—Pets.com went out of business.

Pets.com had created an electronic commerce initiative in an industry in which online business offered few advantages over traditional commerce. The products had a very low value-to-weight ratio. The shipping costs for pet food, one of the company's best-selling product categories, caused it to lose money on every sale. Pet products come in all shapes, sizes, and weights, and are, therefore, difficult to pack and ship efficiently. Pets.com was also spending money rapidly at a time when investors were beginning to question the long-run viability of all electronic commerce businesses. The lesson here is that Pets.com could not develop any sustainable advantage over traditional pet stores. Without such an advantage, the business was doomed.

In the years following the Pets.com failure, a number of companies such as PETCO and PetFoodDirect.com began selling pet food and related items online. These companies were more careful than Pets.com was about what they offered for sale. By selling only items that had an appropriate shipping profile, many of these companies have now become successful. For example, veterinarians who formulate foods that meet the needs of specific pet diets are finding they can charge enough for those products to make online sales profitable.

within markets. However, much business activity today occurs within large **hierarchical business organizations,** which economists generally refer to as **firms,** or **companies.**

Most hierarchical organizations are headed by a top-level president or chief operating officer. Reporting to the president are a number of executives who, in turn, have a larger number of middle managers who report to them, and so on. An organization can have a relatively flat hierarchy, in which there are only a few levels of management, or it can have many reporting levels. In either case, the bottom level includes the largest number of employees and is usually made up of production workers or service providers. Thus, the hierarchical organization always has a pyramid-shaped structure.

These large firms often conduct many different business activities entirely within the organizational structure of the firm and participate in markets only for purchasing raw materials and selling finished products. If markets are indeed highly effective mechanisms for allocating scarce resources, these large corporations should participate in markets at every stage of their production and value-generation processes. The late Nobel laureate Ronald Coase wrote an essay in 1937 in which he questioned why individuals who engaged in commerce often created firms to organize their activities. He was particularly interested in the hierarchical structure of these business organizations. Coase concluded that transaction costs were the main motivation for moving economic activity from markets to hierarchically structured firms.

Transaction Costs

Transaction costs are the total of all costs that a buyer and seller incur as they gather information and negotiate a purchase-and-sale transaction. Although brokerage fees and sales commissions can be a part of transaction costs, the cost of information search and acquisition is often far larger. Another significant component of transaction costs can be the investment a seller makes in equipment or in the hiring of skilled employees to supply the product or service to the buyer.

To understand better how transaction costs occur in markets, consider the following example: A sweater dealer could obtain sweaters by engaging in market transactions with a number of independent sweater knitters. Each knitter could sell sweaters to one or several dealers. Transaction costs incurred by the dealer would include the costs of identifying the independent knitters, visiting them to negotiate the purchase price, arranging for delivery of the sweaters, and inspecting the sweaters on arrival. The knitters would also incur costs, such as the purchase of knitting supplies. Because individual knitters could not know whether any sweater dealer would ever buy sweaters from them, the investments they make to enter the sweater-knitting business have an uncertain yield. This risk is a significant transaction cost for the knitters.

After purchasing the sweaters, sweater dealers take them to a different market in which sweater dealers meet and do business with the retail shops that sell sweaters to the consumer. The dealers can learn which colors, patterns, and styles are in demand from price and quantity negotiations with the retail shops in this market. The sweater dealers can then use that information to negotiate price and other terms in the knitters' market. A diagram of this set of markets appears in Figure 1-6.

Markets and Hierarchies

Coase reasoned that when transaction costs were high, businesspeople would form organizations to replace market-negotiated transactions. These organizations would be hierarchical and would include strong supervision and worker-monitoring elements. Instead of negotiating with individuals to purchase sweaters they had knit, a hierarchical organization would hire knitters, and then supervise and monitor their work activities.

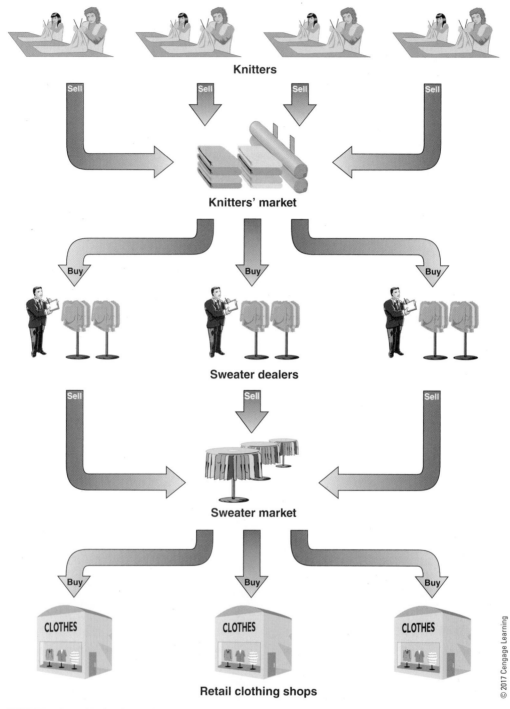

Knitters

Knitters' market

Sweater dealers

Sweater market

CLOTHES   **CLOTHES**   **CLOTHES**

Retail clothing shops

FIGURE 1-6   Market form of economic organization

This supervision and monitoring system would include flows of monitoring information from the lower levels to the higher levels of the organization. It would also have control of information flowing from the upper levels of the organization to the lower levels. Although the costs of creating and maintaining a supervision and monitoring system are high, they can be lower than transaction costs in many instances.

In the sweater example, the sweater dealer would hire knitters, supply them with yarn and knitting tools, and supervise their knitting activities. This supervision could be done mainly by first-line supervisors, who might be drawn from the ranks of the more skilled knitters. The practice of an existing firm replacing one or more of its supplier markets with its own hierarchical structure for creating the supplied product is called **vertical integration**. Figure 1-7 shows how the sweater example would look after the knitters and the individual sweater dealers were vertically integrated into the hierarchical structure of a single sweater dealer.

Oliver Williamson, an economist who extended Coase's analysis, noted that firms in industries with complex manufacturing and assembly operations tended to be hierarchically organized and vertically integrated. Many of the manufacturing and administrative innovations that occurred in businesses during the twentieth century increased the efficiency and effectiveness of hierarchical monitoring activities. Assembly lines and other mass-production technologies allowed work to be broken down into small, easily supervised procedures. The advent of computers brought tremendous increases in the ability of upper-level managers to monitor and control the detailed activities of their

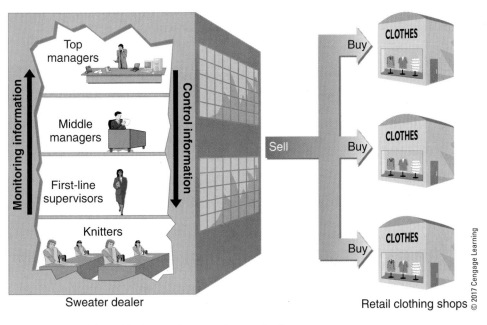

FIGURE 1-7   Hierarchical form of economic organization

subordinates. Some of these direct measurement techniques are even more effective than the first-line supervisors on the shop floor.

During the years from the Industrial Revolution through the present, improvements in monitoring became commonplace and the size and level of vertical integration of firms have increased. In some very large organizations, however, monitoring systems have not kept pace with the organization's increase in size. This has created problems because the economic viability of a firm depends on its ability to track operational activities effectively at the lowest levels of the firm. These firms have instituted decentralization programs that allow business units to function as separate organizations, negotiating transactions with other business units as if they were operating in a market rather than as part of the same firm. Economists argue that large companies decentralize because they have grown too large to be managed effectively as hierarchical structures, so their managers need the information provided by market mechanisms.

To expose their decentralized operations to market mechanisms, these companies allow their divisions to operate as independent business units. A **strategic business unit**, or simply **business unit**, is an autonomous part of a company that is large enough to manage itself but small enough to respond quickly to changes in its business environment. Strategic business units have their own mission and objectives; therefore, they have their own strategies for marketing, product development, purchasing, and long-term growth. General Electric, one of the largest companies in the world, has used strategic business units to organize its diverse business operations since the 1960s. For example, General Electric makes both jet engines and light bulbs. These two businesses have different products, distribution channels, and customer types; therefore, they require different objectives, product development strategies, marketing plans, and manufacturing operations. General Electric's Jet Engine division and Light Bulb division operate as separate strategic business units. Although a strategic business unit operates as a participant in a market (rather than as part of the hierarchical structure of the owning company), the strategic business unit itself is organized internally as a hierarchy.

Exceptions to the general trend toward hierarchies do exist. Many commodities, such as wheat, sugar, and crude oil, are still traded in markets. The commodity nature of the products traded in these markets significantly reduces transaction costs. There are a large number of potential buyers for an agricultural commodity such as wheat, and farmers do not make any special investment in customizing or modifying the product for particular customers. Thus, neither buyers nor sellers in commodity markets experience significant transaction costs.

Using Electronic Commerce to Reduce Transaction Costs

Businesses and individuals can use electronic commerce to reduce transaction costs by improving the flow of information and increasing the coordination of actions. By reducing the cost of searching for potential buyers and sellers and increasing the number of potential market participants, electronic commerce can change the attractiveness of vertical integration for many firms.

To see how electronic commerce can change the level and nature of transaction costs, consider an employment transaction. The agreement to employ a person has high transaction costs for the seller—the employee who sells his or her services.

These transaction costs include a commitment to forego other employment and career development opportunities. Individuals make a high investment in learning and adapting to the culture of their employers. If accepting the job involves a move, the employee can incur very high costs, including actual costs of the move and related costs, such as the loss of a spouse's job. Much of the employee's investment is specific to a particular job and location; the employee cannot transfer the investment to a new job.

If a sufficient number of employees throughout the world can telecommute, then many of these transaction costs could be reduced or eliminated. Instead of uprooting a spouse and family to move, a worker could accept a new job by simply logging on to a different company server.

Mobile technologies, which are becoming more prevalent in the third wave, can also reduce transaction costs. For example, a construction supervisor could review architectural drawings on her tablet device and place an immediate order for a building component using the tablet.

Network Economic Structures

Some researchers argue that many companies and strategic business units operate today in an economic structure that is neither a market nor a hierarchy. In this **network economic structure**, companies coordinate their strategies, resources, and skill sets by forming long-term stable relationships with other companies and individuals based on shared purposes. These relationships are often called **strategic alliances** or **strategic partnerships**, and when they occur between or among companies operating on the Internet, these relationships are also called **virtual companies**.

In some cases, these entities, called **strategic partners**, come together as a team for a specific project or activity. The team dissolves when the project is complete; however, the partners maintain contact with each other through the ensuing period of inactivity. When the need for a similar project or activity arises, the same organizations and individuals build teams from their combined resources. In other cases, the strategic partners form many intercompany teams to undertake a variety of ongoing activities. Later in this book, you will see many examples of strategic partners creating alliances of this sort on the Web. In a hierarchically structured business environment, these types of strategic alliances would not last very long because the larger strategic partners would buy out the smaller partners and form a larger single company.

Network organizations are particularly well suited to technology industries that are information intensive. In the sweater example, the knitters might organize into networks of smaller organizations that specialize in certain styles or designs. Some of the particularly skilled knitters might leave the sweater dealer to form their own company to produce custom-knit sweaters. Some of the sweater dealer's marketing employees might form an independent firm that conducts market research on what the retail shops plan to buy in the upcoming months. This firm could sell its research reports to both the sweater dealer and the custom-knitting firm. As market conditions change, these smaller and more nimble organizations could continually reinvent themselves and take advantage of new opportunities that arise in the sweater markets. An illustration of such a network organization appears in Figure 1-8.

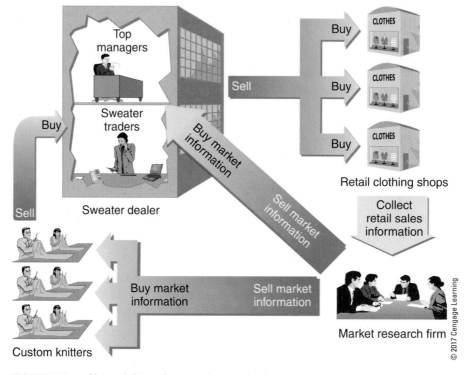

FIGURE 1-8 Network form of economic organization

Electronic commerce can make such networks, which rely extensively on information sharing, much easier to construct and maintain. Some researchers believe that these network forms of organizing commerce will become predominant in the near future. One of these researchers, Manuel Castells, even predicts that economic networks will become the prevalent organizing structure for all social interactions among people.

Network Effects

Economists have found that most activities yield less value as the amount of consumption increases. For example, a person who consumes one hamburger obtains a certain amount of value from that consumption. As the person consumes more hamburgers, the value provided by each hamburger decreases. Few people find the fifth hamburger as enjoyable as the first. This characteristic of economic activity is called the **law of diminishing returns**. In networks, an interesting exception to the law of diminishing returns occurs. As more people or organizations participate in a network, the value of the network to each participant increases. This increase in value is called a **network effect**.

To understand how network effects work, consider an early user of the telephone in the 1800s. When telephones were first introduced, few people had them. The value of each telephone increased as more people had them installed. As the network of telephones grew, the capability of each individual telephone increased because it could be used to communicate with more people. This increase in the value of each telephone as more and more telephones are able to connect to each other is the result of a network effect. Imagine how much less useful (and therefore, less valuable) your mobile phone today would be if you could only use it to talk with other people who had the same mobile phone carrier.

Your e-mail account, which gives you access to a network of other people with e-mail accounts, is another example of a network effect. If your e-mail account were part of a small network, it would be less valuable than it is. Most people today have e-mail accounts that are part of the Internet (a global network of computers, about which you will learn more in Chapter 2). In the early days of e-mail, most e-mail accounts only connected people in the same company or organization. Today's Internet e-mail accounts are far more valuable than single-organization e-mail accounts were because of the network effect.

Regardless of how businesses in a particular industry organize themselves—as markets, hierarchies, or networks—you need a way to identify business processes and evaluate whether electronic commerce is suitable for each process. The next section presents one useful structure for examining business processes.

Identifying Electronic Commerce Opportunities

Internet technologies can be used to improve such a wide range of business processes that it can be difficult for managers to decide where and how to use them. One way to focus on specific business processes as candidates for electronic commerce is to break the business down into a series of value-adding activities that combine to generate profits and meet other goals of the firm. In this section, you will learn how to analyze business activities as a sequence of activities that create value for the firm.

Business activities are conducted by firms of all sizes. Smaller firms might combine business activities to create one product, sell through one distribution channel, or sell to one type of customer. Larger firms combine business activities to sell many different products and services through a variety of distribution channels to several types of customers. In these larger firms, managers organize their business activities into strategic business units, which you learned about earlier in this chapter. Multiple business units owned by a common set of shareholders make up a firm, or company, and multiple firms that sell similar products to similar customers make up an **industry**.

Strategic Business Unit Value Chains

In his 1985 book, *Competitive Advantage*, Michael Porter introduced the idea of value chains. A **value chain** is a way of organizing the activities that each strategic business unit undertakes to design, produce, promote, market, deliver, and support the products or services it sells. In addition to these **primary activities**, Porter also includes **supporting activities**, such as human resource management and purchasing, in the value chain model. Figure 1-9 shows a value chain for a strategic business unit, including both primary and supporting activities. These value chain activities will occur in some form in any strategic business unit.

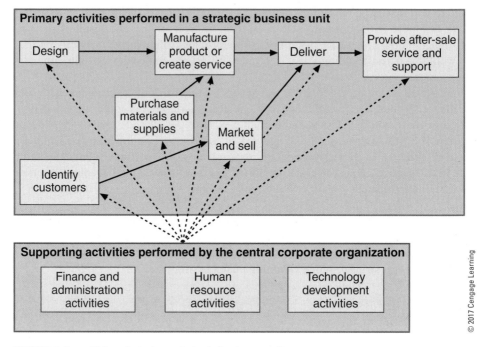

FIGURE 1-9   Value chain for a strategic business unit

The left-to-right flow in Figure 1-9 does not imply a strict time sequence for these processes. For example, a business unit might engage in marketing activities before purchasing materials and supplies. Each strategic business unit conducts the following primary activities:

- *Design*: activities that take a product from concept to manufacturing, including concept research, engineering, and test marketing
- *Identify customers*: activities that help the firm find new customers and new ways to serve existing customers, including market research and customer satisfaction surveys
- *Purchase materials and supplies*: procurement activities, including vendor selection, vendor qualification, negotiating long-term supply contracts, and monitoring quality and timeliness of delivery
- *Manufacture product or create service*: activities that transform materials and labor into finished products, including fabricating, assembling, finishing, testing, and packaging
- *Market and sell*: activities that give buyers a way to purchase and that provide inducements for them to do so, including advertising, promoting, managing salespeople, pricing, and identifying and monitoring sales and distribution channels
- *Deliver*: activities that store, distribute, and ship the final product or provide the service, including warehousing, handling materials,

consolidating freight, selecting shippers, and monitoring timeliness of delivery

- *Provide after-sales service and support*: activities that promote a continuing relationship with the customer, including installing, testing, maintaining, repairing, fulfilling warranties, and replacing parts

The importance of each primary activity depends on the product or service the business unit provides and to which customers it sells. Each business unit must also have support activities that provide the infrastructure for the unit's primary activities. The central corporate organization typically provides the support activities that appear in Figure 1-9. These activities include the following:

- *Finance and administration activities*: providing the firm's basic infrastructure, including accounting, paying bills, borrowing funds, reporting to government regulators, and ensuring compliance with relevant laws
- *Human resource activities*: coordinating the management of employees, including recruiting, hiring, training, compensation, and managing benefits
- *Technology development activities*: improving the product or service that the firm is selling and that helps improve the business processes in every primary activity, including basic research, applied research and development, process improvement studies, and field tests of maintenance procedures

Industry Value Chains

Porter's book also identifies the importance of examining where the strategic business unit fits within its industry. Porter uses the term **value system** to describe the larger stream of activities into which a particular business unit's value chain is embedded. However, many subsequent researchers and business consultants have used the term **industry value chain** when referring to value systems. When a business unit delivers a product to its customer, that customer might use the product as purchased materials in its value chain. By becoming aware of how other business units in the industry value chain conduct their activities, managers can identify new opportunities for cost reduction, product improvement, or channel reconfiguration.

Every product or service is sold within an industry value chain that can be identified and analyzed for these opportunities. To create an industry value chain, start with the inputs to your strategic business unit and work backward to identify your suppliers' suppliers, then the suppliers of those suppliers, and so on. Then start with your customers and work forward to identify your customers' customers, then the customers of those customers, and so on.

An example of an industry value chain appears in Figure 1-10. This value chain is for a wooden chair and traces the life of the product from its inception as trees in a forest to its grave in a landfill or at a sawdust recycler.

Each business unit (logger, sawmill, lumberyard, chair factory, retailer, consumer, and recycler) shown in Figure 1-10 has its own value chain. For example, the sawmill purchases logs from the tree harvester and combines them in its manufacturing process

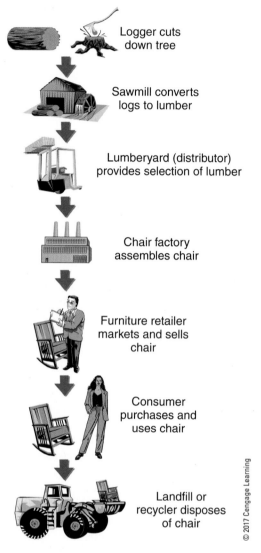

Logger cuts
down tree

Sawmill converts
logs to lumber

Lumberyard (distributor)
provides selection of lumber

Chair factory
assembles chair

Furniture retailer
markets and sells
chair

Consumer
purchases and
uses chair

Landfill or
recycler disposes
of chair

© 2017 Cengage Learning

FIGURE 1-10   Industry value chain for a wooden chair

with inputs, such as labor and saw blades, from other sources. Among the sawmill
customers are the chair factory, shown in Figure 1-10, and other users of cut lumber.
Examining this industry value chain could be useful for the sawmill that is considering
entering the tree-harvesting business or the furniture retailer who is thinking about
partnering with a trucking line. The industry value chain identifies opportunities up and
down the product's life cycle for increasing the efficiency or quality of the product.

Many managers have found ways to use electronic commerce technologies to reduce
costs, improve product quality, reach new customers or suppliers, or create new ways of
selling existing products. For example, software developers now almost universally use

the Internet to distribute updates. Doing so modified software developers' industry value chains and has provided additional opportunities for sales revenue (software developers now retain the profit that retailers and distributors once added to the price of updates), but this revenue opportunity was not a part of the software developers' business unit value chains. By examining elements of the value chain outside the individual business unit, managers can identify many business opportunities, including those that can be exploited using electronic commerce.

The value chain concept is a useful way to think about business strategy in general. When firms are considering electronic commerce, the value chain can be an excellent way to organize the examination of business processes within their business units and in other parts of the product's life cycle. Using the value chain reinforces the idea that electronic commerce should be a business solution, not a technology implemented for its own sake.

SWOT Analysis: Evaluating Business Unit Opportunities

Now that you have learned about industry value chains and SBUs, you can learn one popular technique for analyzing and evaluating business opportunities. Most electronic commerce initiatives add value by either reducing transaction costs, creating some type of network effect, or a combination of both. In **SWOT analysis** (the acronym is for strengths, weaknesses, opportunities, and threats), the analyst first looks into the business unit to identify its strengths and weaknesses. The analyst then reviews the environment in which the business unit operates and identifies opportunities presented by that environment and the threats posed by that environment. Figure 1-11 shows questions that an analyst would ask in conducting a SWOT analysis for any company or strategic business unit.

Strengths	**Weaknesses**
• What does the company do well? • Is the company strong in its market? • Does the company have a strong sense of purpose and the culture to support that purpose?	• What does the company do poorly? • What problems could be avoided? • Does the company have serious financial liabilities?

Opportunities	**Threats**
• Are industry trends moving upward? • Do new markets exist for the company's products/services? • Are there new technologies that the company can exploit?	• What are competitors doing well? • What obstacles does the company face? • Are there troubling changes in the company's business environment (technologies, laws, and regulations)?

© 2017 Cengage Learning

FIGURE 1-11   SWOT analysis questions

By considering all of the issues that it faces in a systematic way, a business unit can formulate strategies to take advantage of its opportunities by building on its strengths, avoiding any threats, and compensating for its weaknesses.

In the mid-1990s, **Dell Computer** used a SWOT analysis to create a business strategy that helped it become a strong competitor in its industry value chain. Dell identified its strengths in selling directly to customers and in designing its computers and other products to reduce manufacturing costs. It acknowledged the weakness of having no relationships with local computer dealers. Dell faced threats from competitors such as Compaq (now a part of Hewlett-Packard) and IBM, both of which had much stronger brand names and reputations for quality at that time. Dell identified an opportunity by noting that its customers were becoming more knowledgeable about computers and could specify exactly what they wanted without having Dell salespeople answer questions or develop configurations for them. It also saw the Internet as a potential marketing tool. Dell carefully considered and answered the SWOT analysis questions shown in Figure 1-11. The results of Dell's SWOT analysis appear in Figure 1-12.

The strategy that Dell followed after doing the analysis took all four of the SWOT elements into consideration. Dell decided to offer customized computers built to order and sold over the phone and, eventually, over the Internet. Dell's strategy capitalized on its strengths and avoided relying on a dealer network. The brand and quality threats posed by Compaq and IBM were lessened by Dell's ability to deliver higher perceived quality because each computer was custom-made for each buyer. Ten years later, Dell observed that the environment of personal computer sales had changed and did start selling computers through dealers.

Strengths	**Weaknesses**
• Sell directly to consumers • Keep costs below competitors' costs	• No strong relationships with computer retailers
Opportunities	**Threats**
• Consumer desire for one-stop shopping • Consumers know what they want to buy • Internet could be a powerful marketing tool	• Competitors have stronger brand names • Competitors have strong relationships with computer retailers

© 2017 Cengage Learning

FIGURE 1-12   Results of Dell's SWOT analysis

International Nature of Electronic Commerce

Because the Internet connects computers all over the world, any business that engages in electronic commerce instantly becomes an international business, with exposure to potential customers in other countries and cultures. When companies use the Web to improve a business process, they are automatically operating in a global environment. The first wave of electronic commerce was dominated by U.S. businesses. In the second wave, European and Asian businesses expanded online.

In the third wave, a rapidly increasing proportion of online business activity is based outside the United States. Countries with large populations, such as China, India, and Brazil, have seen enormous recent growth in both the number of people who have Internet access and the number of online businesses. The proliferation of smartphones and tablet devices has greatly increased the size of potential markets for companies operating in these countries. B2C sales in China have exceeded those in the United States since 2013. Figure 1-13 shows the proportions of online B2C sales that arise in the main geographic regions of the world.

Although much of the online sales activity in each of the world regions depicted in the figure occurs within its originating region, a substantial proportion of online business today occurs across international boundaries. The key issues that a company faces when it conducts international commerce include trust, culture, language, government, and infrastructure. These topics are covered in the following sections. The related issues of international law and currency conversion are covered in Chapter 7.

Trust Issues on the Web

It is important for all businesses to establish trusting relationships with their customers. Companies with established reputations in the physical world often create trust by ensuring that customers know who they are. These businesses can rely on their established brand names to create trust on the Web. New companies that want to do

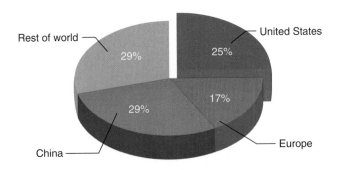

Source: *Internet Retailer* reports of Goldman Sachs, Forrester Research, U.S. Department of Commerce, United Nations Conference on Trade and Development, and China National Bureau of Statistics estimates

FIGURE 1-13   Proportion of online B2C sales by geographic region, 2015

business online face a more difficult challenge because a kind of anonymity exists for companies trying to establish a Web presence.

For example, a U.S. bank can establish a Web site that offers services throughout the world. No potential customer visiting the site can determine just how large or well established the bank is simply by browsing through the site's pages. Because Web site visitors will not become customers unless they trust the company behind the site, a plan for establishing credibility is essential. Sellers on the Web cannot assume that visitors will know that the site is operated by a trustworthy business.

Customers' inherent lack of trust in "strangers" on the Web is logical and to be expected; after all, people have been doing business with their neighbors—not strangers—for thousands of years. When a company grows to become a large corporation with multinational operations, its reputation grows commensurately. Before a company can do business in dozens of countries, it must prove its trustworthiness by satisfying customers for many years as it grows. Businesses on the Web must find ways to overcome this well-founded tradition of distrusting strangers, because today a company can incorporate one day and, through the Web, be doing business the next day with people all over the world. For businesses to succeed on the Web, they must find ways to quickly generate the trust that traditional businesses take years to develop.

Language Issues

Most companies realize that the only way to do business effectively in other cultures is to adapt to those cultures. The phrase "think globally, act locally" is often used to describe this approach. The first step that a Web business usually takes to reach potential customers in other countries, and thus in other cultures, is to provide local language versions of its Web site. This may mean translating the Web site into another language or regional dialect. Researchers have found that customers are far more likely to buy products and services from Web sites in their own language, even if they can read English well. Only about 400 million of the world's 7 billion people learned English as their native language. Electronic commerce began in the United States; however, it has become a global phenomenon and the proportion of Web sites available only in English has declined dramatically in recent years. Today, about 25 percent of Web sites are in English.

Some languages require multiple translations for separate dialects. For example, the Spanish spoken in Spain is different from that spoken in Mexico, which is different from that spoken elsewhere in Latin America. People in parts of Argentina and Uruguay use yet a fourth dialect of Spanish. Many of these dialect differences are spoken inflections, which are not important for Web site designers (unless their sites include audio or video elements); however, a significant number of differences occur in word meanings and spellings. You might be familiar with these types of differences, because they occur in the United States and British dialects of English. The U.S. spelling of *gray* becomes *grey* in Great Britain, and the meaning of *bonnet* changes from a type of hat in the United States to an automobile hood in Great Britain. Chinese has two main systems of writing: simplified Chinese, which is used in the Peoples Republic of China, and traditional Chinese, which is used in Hong Kong and Taiwan.

Most companies that translate their Web sites choose to translate all of their pages. A number of firms translate Web pages and maintain them for a fee that is usually between 15 and 50 cents per word for translations done by skilled human translators. Languages that are complex or that are spoken by relatively few people are generally more expensive to translate than other languages. Different approaches can be appropriate for translating the different types of text that appear on an electronic commerce site. For key marketing messages, the touch of a human translator can be essential to capture subtle meanings. For more routine transaction-processing functions, automated software translation may be an acceptable alternative. Software translation, also called **machine translation**, can reach speeds of 400,000 words per hour, so even if the translation is not perfect, businesses might find it preferable to a human who can translate only about 500 words per hour. Many of the companies in this field are working to develop software and databases of previously translated material that can help human translators work more efficiently and accurately.

The translation services and software manufacturers that work with electronic commerce sites do not generally use the term "translation" to describe what they do. They prefer the term **localization**, which means a translation that considers multiple elements of the local environment, such as business and cultural practices, in addition to local dialect variations in the language. The cultural element is very important because it can affect—and sometimes completely change—the user's interpretation of text.

Cultural Issues

An important element of business trust is anticipating how the other party to a transaction will act in specific circumstances. A company's brand conveys expectations about how the company will behave; therefore, companies with established brands can build online businesses more quickly and easily than a new company without a reputation. For example, a potential buyer might like to know how the seller would react to a claim by the buyer that the seller misrepresented the quality of the goods sold. Part of this knowledge derives from the buyer and seller sharing a common language and common customs. Buyers are more comfortable doing business with sellers they know are trustworthy.

The combination of language and customs is often called **culture**. Most researchers agree that culture varies across national boundaries and, in many cases, varies across regions within nations. For example, the concept of private property is an important cultural value and underlies laws in many European and North American countries. Asian cultures do not value private property in the same way, so laws and business practices in those countries can be quite different. All companies must be aware of the differences in language and customs that make up the culture of any region in which they intend to do business.

For example, managers at Virtual Vineyards (now a part of Wine.com), a company that sells wine and specialty food items on the Web, were perplexed by the unusually high number of complaints from customers in Japan about short shipments. Virtual Vineyards sold most of its wine in case (12 bottles) or half-case quantities. Thus, to save on operating costs, it stocked shipping materials only in case, half-case, and two-bottle sizes. After an investigation, the company determined that many of its Japanese customers ordered only one bottle of wine, which was shipped in a two-bottle container. To these Japanese customers, who consider packaging to be an important element of a high-quality product such as wine, it was inconceivable that anyone would ship one bottle of wine in a two-bottle container. They were e-mailing to ask where the other bottle was, notwithstanding the fact that they had ordered only one bottle.

Some errors stemming from subtle language and cultural standards have become classic examples that are regularly cited in international business courses and training sessions. For example, General Motors' choice of name for its Chevrolet Nova automobile amused people in Latin America—*no va* means "it will not go" in Spanish. Pepsi's "Come Alive" advertising campaign fizzled in China because its message came across as "Pepsi brings your ancestors back from their graves."

Another story that is widely used in international business training sessions is about a company that sold baby food in jars adorned with the picture of a very cute baby. The jars sold well everywhere they had been introduced except in parts of Africa. The mystery was solved when the manufacturer learned that food containers in those parts of Africa always carry a picture of their contents. This story is particularly interesting because it never happened. However, it illustrates a potential cultural issue so dramatically that it continues to appear in marketing textbooks and international business training materials.

Designers of Web sites for international commerce must be very careful when they choose icons to represent common actions. For example, in the United States, a shopping cart is a good symbol to use when building an electronic commerce site. However, many Europeans use shopping *baskets* when they go to a store and may never have seen a shopping *cart*. In Australia, people would recognize a shopping cart image but would be confused by the text "shopping cart" if it were used with the image. Australians call them shopping *trolleys*. In the United States, people often form a hand signal (the index finger touching the thumb to create a circle) that indicates "OK" or "everything is just fine." A Web designer might be tempted to use this hand signal as an icon to indicate that the transaction is completed or the credit card is approved, unaware that in some countries, including Brazil, this hand signal is an obscene gesture.

The cultural overtones of simple design decisions can be dramatic. In India, for example, it is inappropriate to use the image of a cow in a cartoon or other comical setting. Potential customers in Muslim countries can be offended by an image that shows human arms or legs uncovered. Even colors or Web page design elements can be troublesome. For example, white, which denotes purity in Europe and the Americas, is associated with death and mourning in China and many other Asian countries. A Web page that is divided into four segments can be offensive to a Japanese visitor because the number four is a symbol of death in that culture.

Initially, Japanese shoppers resisted the U.S. version of electronic commerce because they preferred to pay in cash or by cash transfer instead of by credit card, and they had a high level of apprehension about doing business online. Softbank, a major Japanese firm that invests in Internet companies, created a joint venture with 7-Eleven, Yahoo! Japan, and Tohan (a major Japanese book distributor) to sell books and CDs online. This venture, called eS-Books, allowed customers to order items on the Internet, and then pick them up and pay for them in cash at the local 7-Eleven convenience store. By adding an intermediary that satisfied the needs of the Japanese customer, Softbank was highly successful in bringing B2C electronic commerce to Japan.

Culture and Government

Some parts of the world have cultural environments that are extremely inhospitable to the type of online discussion that occurs on the Internet. These cultural conditions, in some cases, lead to government controls that can limit electronic commerce development. The Internet is a very open form of communication. This type of unfettered communication is not desired or even considered acceptable in some cultures. For example, Human Rights Watch regularly reports on countries that do not allow their citizens unrestricted access to the Internet; China, Russia, Saudi Arabia, Yemen, and the United Arab Emirates all filter the Web content that is available in their countries.

In some countries, officials have publicly denounced the Internet as a medium that helps distribute materials that are sexually explicit, antireligion, or that cast doubts on the traditional role of women in their societies. In many of these countries, uncontrolled use of Internet technologies is so at odds with existing traditions, cultures, and laws that electronic commerce is unlikely to exist locally at any significant level in the near future.

A number of governments in the world control Internet access as a way to prevent the formation and growth of internal independent political activist organizations. By limiting access or monitoring all Internet traffic, the planners of rebellions against the government can be thwarted. The censorship of Internet content and communications restricts electronic commerce because it prevents certain types of products and services from being sold or advertised. Further, it reduces the interest level of many potential participants in online activities. If large numbers of people in a country are not interested in being online, businesses that use the Internet as an information and product delivery channel will not develop in those countries.

Countries such as the People's Republic of China and Singapore are wrestling with the issues presented by the growth of the Internet as a vehicle for doing business. These countries have a tradition of controlling their citizens' access to information from outside the country, but they want their economies to reap the benefits of electronic commerce. China created a complex set of registration requirements and regulations that govern any business that engages in electronic commerce. These regulations are enforced by the Public Security Bureau, which is a branch of the state police, not an independent administrative agency. For example, companies in China that sell Internet services must register all of their customers with the Public Security Bureau and must retain copies of all e-mail messages and chat room conversations for 60 days.

The Chinese government regularly conducts reviews of ISPs and their records. Every year, the Chinese Public Security Bureau shuts down thousands of Internet cafes for failing to keep adequate records and requires many others to suspend operations while they implement required electronic record-keeping procedures. Operators of Web sites in China are required to monitor all content that appears on their sites. Hundreds of people have been jailed in China for posting "subversive" content on Web pages.

At times, the Chinese government has required the installation of censoring software on all computers used in schools and Internet cafes in the country. One example of such software, the Green Dam Youth Escort, blocked any Web sites on a government-banned list and tracked details of the use of the computer on which it was installed. A requirement that all computers sold in China have this software installed was withdrawn in 2009; however, other government efforts to limit access to the Internet are in place. China's Golden Shield Project is an $800 million effort to limit its citizens' access to information on the Internet that it deems to be forbidden. The Chinese government actively monitors developments in the world to determine what it will censor. For example, Chinese human rights activist Liu Xiaobo became a forbidden topic when he won the 2010 Nobel Peace Prize and discussion of the 2013 arrest of Xu Zhiyong, another human rights activist, also was forbidden.

Some countries, although they do not ban electronic commerce entirely, have strong cultural requirements that have found their way into the legal codes that govern business conduct. In France, an advertisement for a product or service must be in French. Thus, a business in the United States that advertises its products on the Web and is willing to ship goods to France must provide a French version of its pages if it intends to comply with French law. Many U.S. electronic commerce sites include in their Web pages a list of the countries from which they will accept orders through their Web sites to limit their exposure to laws such as this.

Infrastructure Issues

Businesses that successfully meet the challenges posed by trust, language, and culture issues still face the challenges posed by variations and inadequacies in the infrastructure that supports the Internet throughout the world. Internet infrastructure includes the computers and software connected to the Internet and the communications networks over which the message packets travel. In many countries other than the United States, the telecommunications industry is either government-owned or heavily regulated by the government. In many cases, regulations in these countries have inhibited the development of the telecommunications infrastructure or limited the expansion of that infrastructure to a size that cannot reliably support Internet traffic.

Local connection costs through the existing telephone networks in many developing countries are very high compared to U.S. costs for similar access. This can have a profound effect on the behavior of electronic commerce participants. For example, in countries where Internet connection costs are high, few businesspeople would spend time surfing the Web to shop for a product. They would use a Web browser only to navigate to a specific site that they know offers the product they want to buy. Thus, to be successful in selling to businesses in such countries, a company would need to advertise its Web presence in traditional media instead of relying on Web search engines to deliver customers to their Web sites. This problem continues in many countries even as they move to mobile devices for Internet access. In India and China, data plans for smartphones are very expensive. These costs limit Internet usage, especially B2C Web shopping, just as high telephone network costs have in the past.

More than half of all businesses on the Web turn away international orders because they do not have the processes in place to handle such orders. Some of these companies are losing millions of dollars' worth of international business each year. This problem is increasingly global; not only are U.S. businesses having difficulty reaching their international markets, but businesses in other countries are having even greater difficulties reaching the U.S. market.

The paperwork and often-convoluted processes that accompany international transactions are targets for technological solutions. Most firms that conduct business internationally rely on a complex array of freight-forwarding companies, customs brokers, international freight carriers, bonded warehouses, and importers to navigate the maze of paperwork that must be completed at every step of the transaction to satisfy government and insurance requirements. A **freight forwarder** is a company that arranges shipping and insurance for international transactions. A **customs broker** is a company that arranges the payment of tariffs and compliance with customs laws for international shipments. A number of companies combine these two functions and offer a full range of export management services. A **bonded warehouse** is a secure location where incoming international shipments can be held until customs requirements are satisfied or until payment arrangements are completed. The multiple flows of information and transfers of physical objects that occur in a typical international trade transaction are illustrated in Figure 1-14.

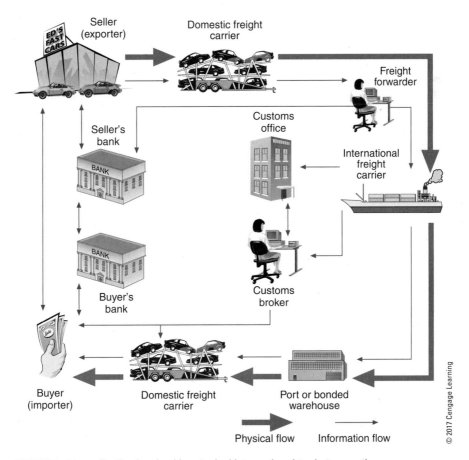

FIGURE 1-14   Parties involved in a typical international trade transaction

As you can see in Figure 1-14, the information flows can be complex. Domestic transactions usually include only the seller, the buyer, their respective banks, and one freight carrier. International transactions almost always require physical handling of goods by several freight carriers, storage in a freight forwarder's facility before international shipment, and storage in a port or bonded warehouse facility in the destination country. This handling and storage require monitoring by government customs offices in addition to the monitoring by seller and buyer that occurs in domestic transactions. International transactions usually require the coordinated efforts of customs brokers and freight-forwarding agencies because the regulations and procedures governing international transactions are so complex. You will learn more about how businesses transfer money in international transactions in Chapter 11.

Industry experts estimate that the annual cost of handling paperwork for international transactions is $700 billion. Companies sell software that can automate some of the paperwork; however, many countries have their own paper-based forms and procedures with which international shippers must comply. To further complicate matters, some countries that have automated some procedures use computer systems that are incompatible with those of other countries.

Some governments provide assistance to companies that want to do international business on the Web. The Argentine government operates the **Argentina Empresas** Web site to provide information to companies that want to do business in Argentina. The U.S. Department of Commerce's International Trade Administration operates the **Export.gov** site, a portal for U.S. companies that want to sell abroad.

Infrastructure issues will continue to prevent international business from reaching its full potential until technology is adapted to overcome barriers instead of being a part of those barriers.

Summary

In this chapter, you learned that electronic commerce is the application of new technologies, particularly Internet and Web technologies, to help individuals, businesses, and other organizations conduct business more effectively. Electronic commerce is being adopted in waves of change. The first wave of electronic commerce ran from about 1995 through 2003 and was characterized by a period of rapid growth and innovation, with many companies pursuing a first-mover advantage. This period included much experimentation with a wide range of revenue models and business strategies and developed primarily in the United States. The second wave, which ran from 2004 through 2009, saw global expansion of electronic commerce driven by improvements in the technologies of the Internet and the Web. Digital product distribution grew dramatically as content providers came to terms with piracy and developed strategies for succeeding in the online environment. An increasing number of companies used a smart-follower strategy rather than pursuing a first-mover advantage. A third wave of electronic commerce began in 2010 and is exploiting the critical mass of mobile users who have powerful smartphones and tablet devices and are eager to do business and participate in social networking online. Other characteristics of the third wave include increased participation by smaller businesses, rapid electronic commerce growth in developing countries with large populations, sophisticated analysis of the large amounts of data generated by electronic commerce activities, and increased integration of tracking technologies into business operations.

You also learned that, when viewed through an historical perspective, the "boom and bust" characterization of the development of electronic commerce often portrayed in the media is largely incorrect. Although online business activity has increased and decreased with changes in the overall economy, it has a long record of consistently outperforming traditional business activity throughout its history.

Using electronic commerce, some businesses have been able to create new products and services, and others have improved the promotion, marketing, and delivery of existing offerings. Firms have also found many ways to use electronic commerce to improve purchasing and supply activities; identify new customers; and operate their finance, administration, and human resource management activities more efficiently. You learned that electronic commerce can help businesses reduce transaction costs or create network economic effects that can lead to greater revenue opportunities.

You examined an overview of markets, hierarchies, and networks—the economic structures in which businesses operate—and learned how electronic commerce fits into those structures. Porter's ideas about value chains at the business unit and industry levels were presented, and you learned how to use value chains and SWOT analysis as ways to understand business processes and analyze their suitability for electronic commerce implementation.

The inherently global nature of electronic commerce leads to many opportunities and a number of challenges. You learned that companies engaged in international electronic commerce must understand the trust, cultural, language, infrastructure, and legal issues that arise when doing business across national borders.

Key Terms

big data	business activity
bonded warehouse	business model

business processes

business unit

business-to-business (B2B)

business-to-consumer (B2C)

business-to-government (B2G)

commodity item

consumer-to-consumer (C2C)

crowdsourcing

culture

customs broker

data analytics

dot-com

e-procurement

electronic business (e-business)

electronic commerce (e-commerce)

electronic data interchange (EDI)

electronic funds transfers (EFT)

firms, or companies

first-mover advantage

freight forwarder

hierarchical business organizations

industry

industry value chain

law of diminishing returns

localization

machine translation

market

merchandising

mobile commerce (m-commerce)

mobile software applications (mobile apps)

network economic structure

network effect

primary activities

procurement

pure dot-com

revenue model

shipping profile

smart-follower strategy

smartphones

social commerce

social networking site

strategic alliance

strategic business unit

strategic partners

strategic partnerships

supply management

supporting activities

SWOT analysis

telecommuting

telework

trading partners

transaction

transaction costs

value-added network (VAN)

value chain

value system

vertical integration

virtual community

virtual companies

Web 2.0

wire transfer

Review Questions

1. What are the two main categories of electronic commerce?
2. List several activities that might be considered business processes.
3. List several activities that might be considered a part of business-to-government electronic commerce.

4. Name the technology that businesses have used since the 1960s to exchange transaction information electronically.

5. What is a value-added network?

6. What drove the burst of enthusiasm that led to a rapid growth of investment in online business during the first wave of electronic commerce?

7. What are some of the drawbacks to a strategy that attempts to capitalize on the first-mover advantage?

8. What specific Internet technologies led to a growth in electronic commerce in developing countries during the third wave of electronic commerce?

9. In what specific ways can businesses use online social interactions?

10. What is crowdsourcing?

11. How can online businesses use data analytics to increase sales?

12. Briefly explain the difference between a business model and a revenue model.

13. What is a shipping profile?

14. Briefly explain why many industry observers believe that describing the history of electronic commerce as a series of "booms and busts" is incorrect.

15. Why is most business activity conducted today in hierarchical organizations rather than in markets?

16. What is a network economic structure?

17. List four primary activities that might be conducted in a particular business value chain.

18. Briefly explain why an online business can find it difficult to establish trust with its customers.

19. In what ways does localization differ from language translation?

20. Briefly describe the functions performed by a freight forwarder in international electronic commerce.

Exercises

1. In two or three paragraphs, distinguish between the terms "business activity," "business process," and "transaction."

2. Some writers have called the emergence of electronic commerce to be a "revolution." Others have described it as a series of waves. In about 100 words, briefly discuss the merits of each point of view.

3. In about 100 words, outline the changes in Internet technology that drove much of the expanded consumption of digital content during the second wave of electronic commerce.

4. The use of online advertising in the second wave of electronic commerce was significantly different than in the first wave. In a paragraph or two, briefly describe this change.

5. In the first wave of electronic commerce, many businesses tried to capitalize on a first-mover advantage. In the second wave, businesses were more likely to employ a smart-follower strategy. In about 100 words, compare the first-mover advantage to the smart-follower strategy.

6. Many customers who use mobile devices prefer to make purchases using a mobile app instead of their devices' Web browsers. It is less clear that these customers search for and

select specific products using only the merchant's dedicated mobile app. In about 200 words, outline the advantages and disadvantages of using a specific merchant's mobile app to select and purchase products.

7. Many companies are combining their online business activities with an existing physical presence. In about 100 words, explain which elements they are combining and what problems they are solving by doing so.

8. Briefly define the term "transaction cost" and, in about 100 words, outline several specific ways in which electronic commerce can reduce transaction costs.

9. In a paragraph or two, explain how the Internet creates or enhances the network effect.

10. Write a paragraph in which you distinguish between a business value chain and an industry value chain.

11. Political and cultural issues can limit the ability of companies to do business in other countries. In about 100 words, provide examples of how specific government rules and cultural norms can interfere with the conduct of electronic commerce across international borders.

Cases

C1. Silvercar

Renting a car at the airport has, for many, become an unpleasant experience. After a long day (or night) of navigating airports and flight delays, the weary traveler must trudge or take a bus to a rental counter, wait in a line, and finally be greeted with a selection of choices: which type of car, what insurance options, prepaid fuel or refill on the way back to the airport, which navigation aids, and so on. Frequent travelers can make this process less burdensome by selecting choices in advance, but the likelihood that a chosen car model will be unavailable is still high.

Although car-sharing services, such as Zipcar, and chauffeur services, such as Lyft and Uber, have used Internet technologies as a key element from their beginnings, most car rental companies have made limited use of those technologies as an add-on to their core airport-based operations. In 2012, the launch of Silvercar airport rental cars was intended to change that. From its original operation in Austin, Silvercar had grown to 10 airport locations by 2015 with plans to add a new location every few months. Billing itself as the "first hassle-free car rental company," Silvercar designed its workflow to minimize the time customers would spend dealing with the airport car rental experience.

Silvercar customers must download the company's mobile app to their phones or tablet devices to make a reservation. The reservation includes insurance options, but there is no need to select a car type or option since all Silvercar vehicles are identically equipped Audi A4 sedans that are painted silver, of course. Once they arrive at the airport, customers receive a text that directs them to either pick up their car at the curb, delivered by a Silvercar employee, or to a nearby lot. The app includes a scan code that unlocks the car. The app reminds the customer when it is time to return the vehicle and provides directions through the app and on the car's built-in GPS system. If the customer is unable to return the car with a full fuel tank, Silvercar will fill it at the prevailing local price plus a $5 refueling charge.

The company has established rental rates that are competitive in each location with other companies' rates for midsize sedans. The rentals include additional drivers and roadside assistance. The equipment included with each car includes GPS, Wi-Fi, satellite radio, and a toll-tracking system that charges the customer automatically for the exact amount of tolls incurred (most rental car companies charge a daily rental fee for a toll transponder in addition to the toll amounts).

REQUIRED:

1. Silvercar's business process design implicitly excludes being able to provide services to certain customers. In about 100 words, identify the characteristics of those customers and outline the costs and benefits to Silvercar of choosing not to serve them.

2. Assume you are the Customer Experience Manager at an established rental car company. Prepare a memo of about 200 words to your Board of Directors that summarizes the competitive threats presented to your business by Silvercar and outline specific actions you believe your company can take to reduce those threats.

3. Many rental car companies in the past have promoted their services by highlighting the helpfulness and friendliness of their employees. In about 100 words, assess the role and importance of employee characteristics such as helpfulness in Silvercar's business process design.

Note: Your instructor might assign you to a group to complete this case and might ask you to prepare a formal presentation of your results to your class.

C2. Hal's Woodworking

Hal Donovan started an ordinary hardware store, named Hal's Hardware in Sandusky, Ohio, in 1988. He had been working during his summer vacations from college for a long-established hardware store and decided he liked the business. Hal's Hardware developed an excellent reputation as a friendly neighborhood store. The store managers are all active in the community and the store regularly sponsors youth sports teams and supports local charities. When hired, salespeople go through a comprehensive training program that includes skill training in the areas of the store in which they will work (plumbing, electrical, power tools, flooring, garden, and so on), and they are trained in customer service skills. As a result of this focus on service, Hal's Hardware became a community gathering place.

Hal offers classes and workshops for the homeowner and hobbyist three evenings each month and regularly schedules seminars for professional customers on weekday mornings. Many of these workshops and seminars are underwritten and taught by manufacturers to promote their products, but an increasing number are being created by Hal's Hardware staff members.

In recent years, Hal has become concerned that the business is no longer growing. The store is facing increasing competition from hardware chains such as Home Depot and Lowe's. These national chains have opened many new stores, and they are larger, carry more items, and offer lower prices on some items. The competition is fierce; for example, Hal's Hardware closed its lumber department because of this competition. The national chains buy lumber in such large quantities that they can offer far lower prices. Hal matched his larger competitors' prices, but found he was unable to earn a profit on lumber sales and that department consumed a large amount of floor space in the store.

Hal was worried that this sort of problem could develop in other departments, so he began looking for ways to add value to the customer experience, especially in ways that the national chains were not willing or able to do. For example, Hal has found that many people want to try out a new power tool in person before they spend hundreds of dollars on a purchase. Thus, Hal's Hardware created a tool demonstration area staffed with salespeople who are experts in power tool operation. For each major type of power tool (drills, power saws, joiners, grinding tools, and so on), Hal created a small booklet of hints for using that type of tool. Hal's salespeople give these booklets to customers as free handouts. They also sell Hal's own low-cost instructional DVDs.

Hal's Hardware currently has a Web site that includes general information about the company, directions to the store, and hours of operation. Hal is thinking about expanding the Web site to include online shopping. He is hoping that customers might find the Web site to be a useful way to order items, see whether items are in stock at the store, and comparison shop among different brands of a particular item. Hal also hopes that the Web site might reach customers who are not located near the store, but he realizes that some of his products do not have ideal shipping profiles.

Hal has been talking with Sarah Johnson, his most senior store manager, about his idea for adding online sales to the Web site. Sarah has been with the company for 20 years and has organized a number of the classes held on Saturday afternoons in the tool demonstration area. After hearing Hal's ideas, she expressed some concerns. Sarah explained that going online with their entire product line might not make any sense because the competition for common tools is likely to be just as fierce online as it is in the store now. She has noticed that there seems to be a solid core of customers who are interested in serious woodworking and who show up for a lot of the classes. These customers buy some of the best, and most expensive, tools that the store sells. Many times, she finds that she has to specially order tools for these customers when they are working on a specific project.

Sarah suggests to Hal that they might want to take the business in a different direction online and sell only the high-end specialty tools to dedicated woodworkers and cabinetmakers. These items yield much higher margins than the regular tools and the salespeople who Hal has hired are eager to develop videos and instruction sheets that would appeal to this more skilled and specialized audience. Sarah suggests that they call the new online business Hal's Woodworking to distinguish it from the general hardware store business. She suggested that Hal take a look at Web sites such as Highland Woodworking and Woodworker's Supply to get a better idea of the online store she has in mind.

REQUIRED:

1. Conduct a SWOT analysis for the existing Hal's Hardware store. You can use the information in the case narrative, your personal knowledge of the retail hardware and tool industry, and information you obtain by following the Web Links or doing independent searches of the Web as you conduct your analysis. Create a diagram similar to Figure 1-12 to summarize your SWOT analysis results.

2. Conduct a SWOT analysis for Sarah's proposed Hal's Woodworking online business. You can use the information in the case narrative, your personal knowledge of the retail hardware and tool industry, and information you obtain by following the Web Links or doing independent searches of the Web as you conduct your analysis. Create a diagram similar to Figure 1-12 to summarize your SWOT analysis results.

3. Based on your SWOT analysis of the proposed online business, write a report of about 400 words that includes a summary of your assumptions and a list of specific recommendations for Hal's Woodworking. These recommendations should specify the types of content that should appear on the Web site, the features that Hal should make available on the site, and how the site might overcome any of the weaknesses or threats you identified in the SWOT analysis.

4. In about 100 words, outline any costs or benefits that the company might experience by operating both businesses at the same time.

Note: Your instructor might assign you to a group to complete this case and might ask you to prepare a formal presentation of your results to your class.

For Further Study and Research

Bannan, K. 2006. "Lost in Translation," *B to B*, 91(7), June, 21–23.

Berthon, P., L. Pitt, D. Cyr, and C. Campbell. 2008. "E-readiness and Trust: Macro and Micro Dualities for E-commerce in a Global Environment," *International Marketing Review*, 25(6), 700–714.

Boles, C. and S. Morrison. 2007. "Yahoo Settles Suit Over Jailed Chinese Dissidents," *The Wall Street Journal*, November 14, A2.

Brady, P. 2015. "This New Company May Change the Rental Car Game," *Condé Nast Traveler*, May 1. http://www.cntraveler.com/stories/2015-05-01/this-new-company-may-change-the-rental-car-game

Brohan, M. 2015. "E-commerce Sales Grow Six Times Faster for U.S. Top 500 Merchants than Total Retail Sales," *Internet Retailer*, April 13. https://www.internetretailer.com/2015/04/13/e-commerces-sales-outgrow-total-retail-sales-2014

Buckley, C. 2013. "Formal Arrest of Advocate Is Approved by China," *The New York Times*, August 24, A9.

Castells, M. 1996. *The Rise of the Network Society*. Cambridge, MA: Blackwell.

Chen, T. and V. Wang. 2010. "Web Filtering and Censoring," *Computer*, 43(3), March, 94–97.

Coase, R. 1937. "The Nature of the Firm," *Economica*, 4(4), November, 386–405.

Collett, S. 1999. "SWOT Analysis," *Computerworld*, 33(29), July 19, 58.

Columbus, L. 2013. "Getting a Head Start on Five Factors Reshaping E-commerce," *Forbes*, March 23. http://www.forbes.com/sites/louiscolumbus/2013/03/23/getting-a-head-start-on-five-factors-reshaping-e-commerce/

Computerworld. 2001. "Autopsy of a Dot Com," January 19. http://www.computerworld.com/article/2590458/e-commerce/autopsy-of-a-dot-com.html

Correia, J. and G. Alvarez. 2013. *Market Insight: Three Compelling Reasons to Update Your E-commerce Product Strategy*. Stamford, CT: Gartner.

Drickhamer, D. 2003. "EDI Is Dead! Long Live EDI!" *Industry Week*, 252(4), April, 31–35.

Enright, A. 2011. "Classy Examples: Luxury Brands Show How to Sell High-ticket Items Online," *Internet Retailer*, May 31, 74–80.

Enright, A. 2015. "Digital Disruptors," *Internet Retailer*, May 1. https://www.internetretailer.com/2015/05/01/editors-greeting-digital-disruptors

Foer, F. 2014. "Amazon Must Be Stopped," *The New Republic*, October 9. http://www.newrepublic.com/article/119769/amazons-monopoly-must-be-broken-radical-plan-tech-giant

Freeman, C. and F. Louçã. 2001. *As Time Goes By: From the Industrial Revolutions to the Information Revolution*. Oxford: Oxford University Press.

Goldstein, E. 1999. *The Internet in the Mideast and North Africa: Free Expression and Censorship*. Washington: Human Rights Watch.

Grau, J. 2011. *U.S. Retail Ecommerce Forecast: Growth Opportunities in a Maturing Channel*. New York: eMarketer.

Gudivada, V., R. Baeza-Yates, and V. Raghavan. 2015. "Big Data: Promises and Problems," *Computer*, March, 20–23.

Hajli, N. and J. Sims. 2015. "Social Commerce: The Transfer of Power from Sellers to Buyers," *Technological Forecasting and Social Change*, 94, May, 350–358.

Harsany, J. 2004. "Web Grocer Hits Refresh: Online Grocer FreshDirect Takes the Hassle Out of City Shopping," *PC Magazine*, May 18, 76.

Hill, C., G. Zhang, and G. Scudder. 2009. "An Empirical Investigation of EDI Usage and Performance Improvement in Food Supply Chains," *IEEE Transactions on Engineering Management*, 56(1), February, 61–75.

Holahan, C. 2007. "Yahoo! Agrees to Pay Prisoners' Families," *Business Week*, November 14. http://www.bloomberg.com/bw/stories/2007-11-14/yahoo-agrees-to-pay-prisoners-familiesbusinessweek-business-news-stock-market-and-financial-advice

Honan, M. 2014. "Don't Diss Cheap Smartphones. They Are About To Change Everything," *Wired*, May 16. http://www.wired.com/2014/05/cheap-smartphones/

Horrigan, J. and L. Rainie. 2002. *Getting Serious Online*. Washington, DC: Pew Internet & American Life Project.

Internet Retailer. 2014. "Hot Mobile Retailers Ride a Wild Mobile Wave," December, 14.

Kearney, A. T. 2015. *Global Retail E-commerce Keeps on Clicking*. Chicago: A. T. Kearney.

Kell, J. 2015. "Home Depot Finds Its Footing in Online Shopping," *Fortune*, May 19. http://fortune.com/2015/05/19/home-depot-web-strategy/

Knight, K. 2014. "Study: Consumers Find Driving Need to Be Always On," *BizReport*, November 19. http://www.bizreport.com/2014/11/study-consumers-find-driving-need-to-be-always-on.html

Kristof, N. 2005. "Death by a Thousand Blogs," *The New York Times*, May 24, A21.

LaValle, S., E. Lesser, R. Shockley, M. Hopkins, and N. Kruschwitz. 2011. "Big Data, Analytics, and the Path from Insights to Value," *MIT Sloan Management Review*, Winter, 52(2), 21–31.

Lightman, S. 2007. "Web Globalization," *B to B*, 92(13), October, 11.

MacKinnon, M. 2010. "Jailed Dissident's Nobel Peace Prize Infuriates China," *The Globe and Mail*, October 8. http://www.theglobeandmail.com/news/world/jailed-dissidents-nobel-peace-prize-infuriates-china/article1750923/

MacLaggan, C. 2004. "Global Grocer," *Latin Trade*, 12(4), April, 51–54.

Mayer-Schönberger, V. and K. Cukier. 2013. *Big Data: A Revolution That Will Transform How We Live, Work, and Think*. London: John Murray.

Moon, J., D. Chadee, and S. Tikoo. 2008. "Culture, Product Type, and Price Influences on Consumer Purchase Intention to Buy Personalized Products Online," *Journal of Business Research*, 61(1), January, 31–39.

Ozcan, P. and K. Eisenhardt. 2009. "Origin of Alliance Portfolios: Entrepreneurs, Network Strategies, and Firm Performance," *Academy of Management Journal*, 52(2), 246–279.

Panditrao, M. 2015. "How Can Small Retailers Gain from Social Commerce?" *ETRetail.com*, April 27. http://retail.economictimes.indiatimes.com/re-tales/How-can-small-retailers-gain-from-social-commerce/597

Petzinger, T. 1999. *The New Pioneers: The Men and Women Who Are Transforming the Workplace and Marketplace*. New York: Simon & Schuster.

Porter, M. 1985. *Competitive Advantage: Creating and Sustaining Superior Performance*. New York: Free Press.

Porter, M. 1998. "Clusters and the New Economics of Competition," *Harvard Business Review*, 76(6), November–December, 77–90.

Porter, M. 2001. "Strategy and the Internet," *Harvard Business Review*, 79(3), March, 63–78.

Powell, W. 1990. "Neither Market nor Hierarchy: Network Forms of Organization," *Research in Organizational Behavior*, 12(3), 295–336.

Ramdeen, C., J. Santos, and H. Chatfield. 2009. "EDI and the Internet in the E-Business Era," *International Journal of Hospitality & Tourism Administration*, 10(3), 270–282.

Rayport, J. and B. Jaworski. 2001. *E-Commerce*. New York: McGraw-Hill/Irwin.

Ring, P. and A. Van de Ven. 1992. "Structuring Cooperative Relationships Between Organizations," *Strategic Management Journal*, 13(4), 483–498.

Schneider, G. 2005. "Digital Products on the Web: Pricing Issues and Revenue Models," 154–174. In Kehal, H. and V. Singh, eds., *Digital Economy: Impacts, Influences, and Challenges*. Hershey, PA: Idea Group.

Shapiro, A. 1999. *The Control Revolution: How the Internet Is Putting Individuals in Charge and Changing the World We Know*. New York: The Century Foundation.

Shapiro, C. and H. Varian. 1999. *Information Rules: A Strategic Guide to the Network Economy*. Boston: Harvard Business School Press.

Siwicki, B. 2011. "Stores Link to the Online World," *Internet Retailer*, September, 22–29.

Suarez, F. and G. Lanzolla. 2005. "The Half-Truth of First-Mover Advantage," *Harvard Business Review*, 83(4), April, 121–127.

Tai, Z. 2010. "Casting the Ubiquitous Net of Control: Internet Surveillance in China from Golden Shield to Green Dam," *International Communication Association Annual Meeting*, Suntec City, Singapore.

Tapscott, D. 2001. "Rethinking Strategy in a Networked World: Or Why Michael Porter Is Wrong About the Internet," *Strategy + Business*, 21(3), 1–8.

Taylor, D. and A. Terhune. 2001. *Doing E-Business: Strategies for Thriving in an Electronic Marketplace*. New York: John Wiley & Sons.

Thompson, D. 2014. "What in the World Is Amazon?" *The Atlantic*, October 10. http://www.theatlantic.com/business/archive/2014/10/is-amazon-evil/381357/

Thynne, J. 2008. "The E-revolution," *Bookseller*, October, 20–21.

U.S. Census Bureau. 2011. *Statistical Abstract of the United States*. Washington, DC: U.S. Census Bureau.

U.S. Census Bureau. 2012. *Statistical Abstract of the United States*. Washington, DC: U.S. Census Bureau.

Vascellaro, J. 2009. "Google to Tie Ads to Surfers' Habits," *The Wall Street Journal*, March 12, B8.

Vora, S. 2015. "The Car Rental Company Silvercar Adds Locations," *The New York Times*, May 12. http://www.nytimes.com/2015/05/13/travel/the-car-rental-company-silvercar-adds-locations.html

W3Techs. 2013. *Usage of Content Languages for Websites*. September. Maria Enzerdorf, Austria: W3Techs. http://w3techs.com/technologies/overview/content_language/all

Williamson, O. 1975. *Markets and Hierarchies: Analysis and Antitrust Implications*. New York: Free Press.

Williamson, O. 1985. *The Economic Institutions of Capitalism*. New York: Free Press.

Yang, K. 2011. "The Aborted Green Dam-Youth Escort Censor-ware Project in China," *Telematics and Informatics*, 26(2), May, 101–111.

Blend Images Photography/Neer

Technology Infrastructure: The Internet and the World Wide Web

INTRODUCTION

As you learned in Chapter 1, a growing number of Internet users, especially those in developing countries, use a smartphone or a tablet device instead of a computer to go online. For many of these users, a mobile device is their main or only connection to the Internet, and many companies have developed Web sites that work well on the smaller screens and keyboards of these devices. As the number of Internet users connected through mobile telephone networks increases, however, the volume of traffic is taxing existing technologies and threatening to overload those networks.

Chapter 2

As you will learn in this chapter, wireless telephone networks are built on a cellular technology that uses antennas on towers to collect the mobile device signals and transfer them into a wired network through equipment at the base of those towers. As more users operate their devices within range of a particular cell tower, the speed of the service each user experiences slows down. As the number of users and the amount of data they transmit increases (playing videos, for example, requires a much larger amount of data than sending e-mail or talking on a phone), the speed can slow significantly or even drop a connection entirely. The only current technological solution within the wireless network is for the telecommunications companies to add more cell towers, which is expensive and requires additional tower locations that can be hard to acquire.

With mobile data traffic expected to double by 2017 and triple by 2018, the search for solutions to this problem is underway. Steve Perlman, the entrepreneur who developed WebTV and sold it to Microsoft in 1997 for $425 million, has been working on one such solution for the past eight years with his company, **Artemis Networks**. His approach, called pCell, has been shown in laboratory tests to operate at about 35 times the speed of current telephone wireless network technologies. Some critics have challenged the results of these tests, but in 2015, Perlman launched the technology for a two-year commercial application test with Dish Network in San Francisco.

Instead of building a network based on cell towers that serve all users within a range of 200–15,000 feet, pCell creates a network of "personal cells" based on each device. The system uses a series of small radio transmitters that work with mobile devices to create these personal cells, each with a range of less than one inch. Thus, instead of competing with hundreds or even thousands of mobile devices for a single cell tower's signal, each device gets access to the full speed of the network. In its current stage of development, pCell is designed to work with existing mobile devices.

In this chapter, you will learn about the technologies that created the Internet and enabled the World Wide Web to emerge as a powerful platform for conducting business globally in ways that were not possible before. The continuing development of those technologies will make new digital products and services available in the future.

The Internet and the World Wide Web

A **computer network** is any technology that allows people to connect computers to each other. An **internet** (small "i") is a group of computer networks that have been interconnected. In fact, "internet" is short for "interconnected network." One particular internet, which uses a specific set of rules and connects networks all over the world to each other, is called the **Internet** (capital "I"). Networks of computers and the Internet that connects them to each other form the basic technological structure that underlies virtually all electronic commerce.

This chapter introduces you to many of the hardware and software technologies that make electronic commerce possible. First, you will learn how the Internet and the World Wide Web work. Then, you will learn about other technologies that support the Internet, the Web, and electronic commerce. In this chapter, you will be introduced to several complex networking technologies. If you are interested in learning more about how computer networks operate, you can consult one of the computer networking books cited in the For Further Study and Research section at the end of this chapter, or you can take courses in data communications and networking.

The part of the Internet known as the **World Wide Web**, or, more simply, the **Web**, is a subset of the computers on the Internet that are connected to one another in a specific way that makes them and their contents easily accessible to each other. The most important thing about the Web is that it includes an easy-to-use standard interface. This interface makes it possible for people who are not computer experts to use the Web to access a variety of Internet resources.

Origins of the Internet

In the early 1960s, the U.S. Department of Defense became concerned about the possible effects of nuclear attack on its computing facilities. The Defense Department realized that the weapons of the future would require powerful computers for coordination and control. The powerful computers of that time were all large mainframe computers.

The Defense Department began examining ways to connect these computers to each other and also to connect them to weapons installations distributed all over the world. Employing many of the best communications technology researchers, the Defense Department funded research at leading universities and institutes. The goal of this research was to design a worldwide network that could remain operational, even if parts of the network were destroyed by enemy military action or sabotage. These researchers determined that the best path to accomplishing their goals was to create networks that did not require a central computer to control network operations.

The computer networks that existed at that time used leased telephone company lines for their connections. These telephone company systems established a single connection between sender and receiver for each telephone call, and then that connection carried all data along a single path. When a company wanted to connect computers it owned at two different locations, the company placed a telephone call to establish the connection, and then connected one computer to each end of that single connection.

The Defense Department was concerned about the inherent risk of this single-channel method for connecting computers, and its researchers developed a different method of sending information through multiple channels. In this method, files and messages are broken into packets that are labeled electronically with codes for their origins, sequences, and destinations. You will learn more about how packet networks operate later in this chapter.

In 1969, Defense Department researchers in the Advanced Research Projects Agency (ARPA) used this direct connection network model to connect four computers—one each at the University of California at Los Angeles, SRI International, the University of California at Santa Barbara, and the University of Utah—into a network called the ARPANET. The ARPANET was the earliest of the networks that eventually combined to become what we now call the Internet. Throughout the 1970s and 1980s, many researchers in the academic community connected to the ARPANET and contributed to the technological developments that increased its speed and efficiency. At the same time, researchers at other universities were creating their own networks using similar technologies.

New Uses for the Internet

Although the goals of the Defense Department network were to control weapons systems and transfer research files, other uses for this vast network began to appear in the early 1970s. E-mail was born in 1972 when Ray Tomlinson, a researcher who used the network, wrote a program that could send and receive messages over the network. This new method of communicating became widely used very quickly. The number of network users in the military and education research communities continued to grow. Many of these new participants used the networking technology to transfer files and access computers remotely.

The first e-mail mailing lists also appeared on these military and education research networks. A **mailing list** is an e-mail address that forwards any message it receives to any user who has subscribed to the list. In 1979, a group of students and programmers at Duke University and the University of North Carolina started **Usenet**, an abbreviation for **User's News Network**. Usenet allows anyone who connects to the network to read and post articles on a variety of subjects. Usenet survives on the Internet today, with more than 1000 different topic areas that are called **newsgroups**.

Although the people using these networks were developing many creative applications, use of the networks was limited to those members of the research and academic communities who could access them. Between 1979 and 1989, these network applications were improved and tested by an increasing number of users. The

Defense Department's networking software became more widely used in academic and research institutions as these organizations recognized the benefits of having a common communications network. As the number of people in different organizations using these networks increased, security concerns arose; these concerns continue to be problematic. You will learn more about these network security issues in Chapter 10. The explosion of personal computer use during the 1980s also helped more people become comfortable with computers. During the 1980s, other independent networks (such as Bitnet) were developed by academics worldwide and researchers in specific countries other than the United States (such as the United Kingdom's academic research network, Janet). In the late 1980s, these independent academic and research networks from all over the world merged into what we now call the Internet.

Commercial Use of the Internet

As personal computers became more powerful, affordable, and available during the 1980s, companies increasingly used them to construct their own internal networks. Although these networks included e-mail software that employees could use to send messages to each other, businesses wanted their employees to be able to communicate with people outside their corporate networks. The Defense Department network and most of the academic networks that had teamed up with it were receiving funding from the National Science Foundation (NSF). The NSF prohibited commercial network traffic on its networks, so businesses turned to commercial e-mail service providers to handle their e-mail needs. Larger firms built their own networks that used leased telephone lines to connect field offices to corporate headquarters.

In 1989, the NSF permitted two commercial e-mail services, MCI Mail and CompuServe, to establish limited connections to the Internet for the sole purpose of exchanging e-mail transmissions with users of the Internet. These connections allowed commercial enterprises to send e-mail directly to Internet addresses, and allowed members of the research and education communities on the Internet to send e-mail directly to MCI Mail and CompuServe addresses. The NSF justified this limited commercial use of the Internet as a service that would primarily benefit the Internet's noncommercial users. As the 1990s began, people from all walks of life—not just scientists or academic researchers—started thinking of these networks as the global resource that we now know as the Internet. Although this network of networks had grown from four Defense Department computers in 1969 to more than 300,000 computers on many interconnected networks by 1990, the greatest growth of the Internet was yet to come.

Growth of the Internet

In 1991, the NSF further eased its restrictions on commercial Internet activity and began implementing plans to privatize the Internet. The privatization of the Internet was substantially completed in 1995, when the NSF turned over the operation of the main Internet connections to a group of privately owned companies. The new structure of the Internet was based on four **network access points (NAPs)** located in San Francisco, New York, Chicago, and Washington, DC, each operated by a separate telecommunications

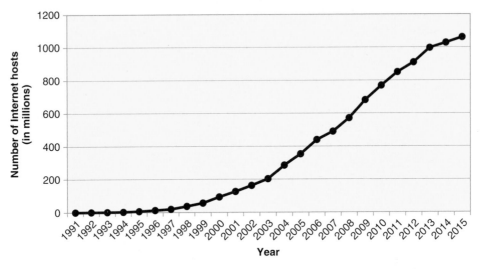

Source: Internet Software Consortium (http://www.isc.org/) and author's estimates

FIGURE 2-1   Growth of the Internet

company. As the Internet grew, more companies opened more NAPs in more locations. These companies, known as **network access providers**, sell Internet access rights directly to larger customers and indirectly to smaller firms and individuals through other companies, called **Internet service providers (ISPs)**.

The Internet was a phenomenon that had truly sneaked up on an unsuspecting world. The researchers who had been so involved in the creation and growth of the Internet just accepted it as part of their working environment. However, people outside the research community were largely unaware of the potential offered by a large interconnected set of computer networks. Figure 2-1 shows the consistent and dramatic growth in the number of **Internet hosts**, which are computers directly connected to the Internet, to more than 1 billion today.

The Internet of Things

The most common perception of the Internet is that it connects computers to one another and, by doing so, connects the users of those computers to each other. In recent years, devices other than computers have been connected to the Internet, such as mobile phones and tablet devices. Once again, the connection of these devices to the Internet serves to connect the users of those devices to each other. However, the connection of devices to the Internet that are not used by persons is increasing rapidly. These devices—such as switches; optical scanners; sensors that detect changes in temperature, light, moisture, or the existence of vibration or movement—can be connected to the Internet and used by computers to manage automatically environmental conditions (such as heating and cooling or lighting levels) or security procedures. These interconnected devices can be located in houses, offices, factories, autos, appliances, and so on.

Computers can also be connected to each other using the Internet to conduct business transactions without human intervention. For example, a computer that monitors inventory levels using sensors connected to it over the Internet can use its Internet connection to place inventory orders with a vendor's computer automatically. The subset of the Internet that includes these computers and sensors connected to each other for communication and automatic transaction processing is often called the **Internet of Things**. Industry analysts estimate that the number of devices, sensors, switches, and computers that are interconnected in the Internet of Things is 10 billion (more than the number of people on Earth) and will reach 40 billion by 2020. Examples of how the Internet of Things has been used to make business processes more efficient, safer, and less expensive include:

- Coca-Cola added Internet-connected voice recognition devices to its inventory control, shipping, and service support systems, saving more than $2 million and improving order accuracy from 90 percent to 99.8 percent.
- BC Hydro, an electric utility in British Columbia, Canada, uses Internet-connected smart electric meters and remote monitoring devices to manage the flow of electricity more precisely throughout its grid and reduce theft, saving more than $500 million.
- Argentine bank Banco de Cordoba used the Internet to connect 2600 video cameras, a new network, and digital signs located in 243 branch locations to its central control and security system and found significant cost savings in the distribution of training and marketing messages to employees along with an eight-fold increase in electronic transactions, which cost less to process.
- SK Solutions, a provider of construction safety services in Dubai, uses Internet-connected sensors that continually monitor the weight, position, movement, and inertia of machinery and equipment along with ambient wind speed and temperature to give its customers increased worker safety, faster project completions, and reduced downtime.
- The Rio Tinto coal mining operation in Western Australia uses Internet-connected control systems to operate a fleet of 54 autonomous trucks, an autonomous railway system, and drilling operations, removing safety hazards to the surrounding community and reducing risky work conditions for employees.

From its humble beginnings in 1969, the Internet has grown to become one of the most significant technological and social accomplishments of the last millennium. Nearly one-third of the world's population now uses this network of computers on which billions of dollars change hands each year in exchange for all kinds of products and services.

The Internet is a set of interconnected networks. To understand the technologies used to build the Internet, you must first learn about the structure of its component networks.

Packet-Switched Networks

A network of computers that are located close together—for example, in the same building—is called a **local area network (LAN)**. Networks of computers that are connected over greater distances are called **wide area networks (WANs)**.

The early models (dating back to the 1950s) for WANs were the circuits of the local and long-distance telephone companies of the time because the first early WANs used leased telephone company lines for their connections. A telephone call establishes a single connection path between the caller and receiver, then transmits data along that single path, which is called a **circuit**. Telephone company equipment selects specific telephone lines to connect to one another by closing switches that resemble the switches you use to turn lights on and off in your home, except that they open and close much faster, and are controlled by mechanical or electronic devices instead of human hands. This single path of connected circuits switched into each other is maintained for the entire length of the call. This type of centrally controlled, single-connection model is known as **circuit switching**.

Circuit-switched networks are not resistant to failure because a break in any one of the connected circuits causes the circuit to be interrupted and data to be lost. The Internet was designed to be failure-resistant and instead uses packet switching to move data between two points. In a **packet-switched** network, files and e-mail messages are broken down into small pieces, called **packets**, that are labeled electronically with their origins, sequences, and destination addresses. Packets travel from computer to computer along the interconnected networks until they reach their destinations. Each packet can take a different path through the interconnected networks, and the packets may arrive out of order. The destination computer collects the packets and reassembles the original file or e-mail message from the pieces in each packet. If any packets are missing, the destination computer can request that the transmission be resent so it can reconstruct the sent file or message.

Routing Packets

As an individual packet travels from one network to another, the computers through which the packet travels determine the most efficient route for getting the packet to its destination. The most efficient route changes from second to second, depending on how much traffic each computer on the Internet is handling at each moment. The computers that decide how best to forward each packet are called **routing computers**, **router computers**, **routers**, **gateway computers** (because they act as the gateway from a LAN or WAN to the Internet), **border routers**, or **edge routers** (because they are located at the border between the organization and the Internet or at the edge of the organization). The programs on router computers that determine the best path on which to send each packet contain rules called **routing algorithms**. The programs apply their routing algorithms to information they have stored in **routing tables** or **configuration tables**. This information includes lists of connections that lead to particular groups of other routers, rules that specify which connections to use first, and rules for handling instances of heavy packet traffic and network congestion.

Individual LANs and WANs can use a variety of different rules and standards for creating packets within their networks. The network devices that move packets from one part of a network to another are called hubs, switches, and bridges. Routers are used to connect networks to other networks. You can take a data communications and networking class to learn more about these network devices and how they work.

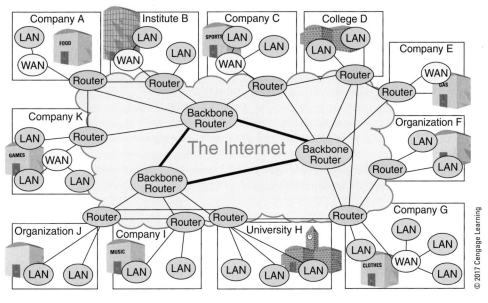

FIGURE 2-2   Router-based architecture of the Internet

When packets leave a network to travel on the Internet, they must be translated into a standard format. Routers usually perform this translation function. As you can see, routers are an important part of the infrastructure of the Internet. When a company or organization becomes part of the Internet, it must connect at least one router to the other routers (owned by other companies or organizations) that make up the Internet. Figure 2-2 is a diagram of a small portion of the Internet that shows its router-based architecture. The figure shows only the routers that connect each organization's WANs and LANs to the Internet, not the other routers that are inside the WANs and LANs or that connect them to each other within the organization.

The Internet also has routers that handle packet traffic along the Internet's main connecting points. These routers and the telecommunications lines connecting them are collectively referred to as the **Internet backbone**. These routers, sometimes called **backbone routers**, are very large computers that can each handle more than 5 billion packets per second. You can see in the figure that a router connected to the Internet always has more than one path to which it can direct a packet. By building in multiple packet paths, the designers of the Internet created a degree of redundancy in the system that allows it to keep moving packets, even if one or more of the routers or connecting lines fails.

Public and Private Networks

A **public network** is any computer network or telecommunications network that is available to the public. The Internet is one example of a public network. Public networks such as the Internet, as you will learn in later chapters, do not provide much security as part of their basic structures.

A **private network** is a leased-line connection between two companies that physically connects their computers and/or networks to one another. A **leased line** is a permanent, continually active, telephone line connection between two points. An advantage of a leased line is security. Only the two parties that lease the line to create the private network have access to the connection. Drawbacks to private networks include the cost of the leased lines, which can range from a few hundred to several thousand dollars each, and the need to have a dedicated line for every connection needed. For example, if a company wants to set up private network connections with seven other companies, the company must pay the cost of seven leased lines, one for each company.

Virtual Private Networks (VPNs)

A **virtual private network (VPN)** is a connection that uses public networks and their protocols to send data in a way that protects the data as well as a private network would, but at a lower cost. VPN software must be installed on the computers at both ends of the transmission. The technology that most VPN software uses is called IP tunneling or encapsulation.

IP tunneling creates a private passageway through the public Internet that provides secure transmission from one computer to another. The passageway is created by VPN software that encrypts the packet content and then places the encrypted packets inside another packet in a process called **encapsulation**. The outer packet is called an **IP wrapper**. The Web server sends the encapsulated packets to their destinations over the Internet, which is a public network. The computer that receives the packet unwraps it and decrypts the message using VPN software that is the same as, or is compatible with, the VPN software used to encrypt and encapsulate the packet at the sending end.

The word *virtual* is used as part of VPN because, although the connection appears to be a permanent connection, it is actually temporary. The VPN is created, carries out its work over the Internet, and is then terminated.

The VPN is like a separate, covered commuter lane on a highway (the Internet) in which the passengers cannot be seen by vehicles traveling in the other lanes. Company employees in remote locations can send sensitive information to company computers using the VPN private tunnels established on the Internet. You will learn more about VPNs, firewalls, and other network security devices in Chapter 10.

Intranets and Extranets

In the early days of the Internet, the distinction between private and public networks was clear. Organizations could have one or more private networks that they operated internally. They could also participate in public networks with other organizations. The Internet was one such public network. However, as networking (and inter-networking) technologies became less expensive and easier to deploy, organizations began building more and more internets (small "i"), or interconnected networks. An internet that does not extend beyond the boundaries of a single organization is often called an **intranet**. In the past, most intranets were constructed by interconnecting a number of private networks; however, organizations today can create secure intranets using VPN technologies.

An **extranet** was originally defined as an intranet that had been extended to include specific entities outside the boundaries of the organization, such as business partners, customers, or suppliers. Extranets were used to save money and increase efficiency by replacing traditional communication tools such as fax, telephone, and overnight express document carriers. To maintain security within extranets, almost all organizations that created them did so by interconnecting private networks. However, as the Internet became more widely used, many organizations began using it as part of their extranets (and, in some cases, intranets). The addition of VPN technologies allowed organizations to use the Internet (a public network), yet have the same level of security over their data that had been provided by their use of private networks in the past.

This evolution of technologies over time has led to some confusion today when people use the terms public network, private network, VPN, intranet, and extranet. Remember that "intranet" is used when the internet does not extend beyond the boundaries of a particular organization; "extranet" is used when the internet extends beyond the boundaries of an organization and includes networks of other organizations. The technologies used (public networks, private networks, or VPNs) are independent of organizational boundaries. For example, an intranet could use private networks, VPNs, or even public networks.

Internet Protocols

A **protocol** is a collection of rules for formatting, ordering, and error checking data sent across a network. For example, protocols determine how the sending device indicates that it has finished sending a message and how the receiving device indicates that it has received (or not received) the message. A protocol also includes rules about what is allowed in a transmission and how it is formatted. Computers that communicate with each other must use the same protocol for data transmission. As you learned earlier in this chapter, the first packet-switched network, the ARPANET, connected only a few universities and research centers. Following its inception in 1969, this experimental network grew during the next few years and began using the **Network Control Protocol (NCP)**. In the early days of computing, each computer manufacturer created its own protocol, so computers made by different manufacturers could not be connected to each other. This practice was called **proprietary architecture** or **closed architecture**. NCP was designed so it could be used by any computer manufacturer and was made available to any company that wanted it. This **open architecture** philosophy that was developed for the evolving ARPANET, which later became the core of the Internet, included the use of a common protocol for all computers connected to the Internet and four key rules for message handling:

- Independent networks should not require any internal changes to be connected to the network.
- Packets that do not arrive at their destinations must be retransmitted from their source network.
- Router computers act as receive-and-forward devices; they do not retain information about the packets that they handle.
- No global control exists over the network.

The open architecture approach has contributed to the success of the Internet because computers manufactured by different companies (Apple, Dell, Hewlett-Packard, and so on) can be interconnected. The ARPANET and its successor, the Internet, use routers to isolate each LAN or WAN from the other networks to which they are connected. Each LAN or WAN can use its own set of protocols for packet traffic within the LAN or WAN, but must use a router (or similar device) to move packets onto the Internet in its standard format (or protocol). Following these simple rules makes the connections between the interconnected networks operate effectively.

TCP/IP

The Internet uses two main protocols: the **Transmission Control Protocol (TCP)** and the **Internet Protocol (IP)**. Developed by Internet pioneers Vinton Cerf and Robert Kahn, these protocols are the rules that govern how data moves through the Internet and how network connections are established and terminated. The acronym **TCP/IP** is commonly used to refer to the two protocols. TCP/IP was technologically superior to other protocols available at the time (such as the NCP). Once its use became pervasive on the Internet, the network effects, which you learned about in Chapter 1, have prevented any other protocol from challenging TCP/IP.

The TCP controls the disassembly of a message or a file into packets before it is transmitted over the Internet, and it controls the reassembly of those packets into their original formats when they reach their destinations. The IP specifies the addressing details for each packet, labeling each with the packet's origination and destination addresses. Soon after the new TCP/IP protocol set was developed, it replaced the NCP that ARPANET originally used.

In addition to its Internet function, TCP/IP is used today in many LANs. The TCP/IP protocol is provided in most personal computer operating systems commonly used today, including Linux, Macintosh, Microsoft Windows, and UNIX.

IP Addressing

The version of IP that has been in use since 1981 on the Internet is **Internet Protocol version 4 (IPv4)**. It uses a 32-bit number to identify computers connected to the Internet. This address is called an **IP address**. Computers do all of their internal calculations using a **base 2** (or **binary**) number system in which each digit is either a 0 or a 1, corresponding to a condition of either off or on. IPv4 uses a 32-bit binary number that allows for more than 4 billion different addresses ($2^{32} = 4,294,967,296$).

When a router breaks a message into packets before sending it onto the Internet, the router marks each packet with both the source IP address and the destination IP address of the message. To make them easier to read, IP numbers (addresses) appear as four numbers separated by periods. This notation system is called **dotted decimal** notation. An IPv4 address is a 32-bit number, so each of the four numbers is an 8-bit number ($4 \times 8 = 32$) that can have binary values from 00000000 to 11111111; the decimal equivalents of which are 0 and 255, respectively.

Because each of the four parts of a dotted decimal number can range from 0 to 255, IP addresses range from 0.0.0.0 (written in binary as 32 zeros) to 255.255.255.255 (written in binary as 32 ones). Although some people find dotted decimal notation to be confusing at first, most do agree that writing, reading, and remembering a computer's address as 216.115.108.245 is easier than 11011000011100110110110011110101, or its full decimal equivalent, which is 3,631,433,189.

Today, IP addresses are assigned by three not-for-profit organizations: the American Registry for Internet Numbers (ARIN), the Réseaux IP Européens (RIPE), and the Asia-Pacific Network Information Center (APNIC). These registries assign and manage IP addresses for various parts of the world: ARIN for North America, South America, the Caribbean, and sub-Saharan Africa; RIPE for Europe, the Middle East, and the rest of Africa; and APNIC for countries in the Asia-Pacific area.

You can use the ARIN Whois page at the ARIN Web site to search the IP addresses owned by organizations in North America. Enter an organization name into the search box on the page, then click the Search WHOIS button, and the Whois server returns a list of the IP addresses owned by that organization. For example, performing a search on the word *Carnegie* displays the IP address blocks owned by Carnegie Bank, Carnegie Mellon University, and a number of other organizations whose names begin with Carnegie. You can also enter an IP address and find out who owns that IP address. If you enter "3.0.0.0" (without the quotation marks), you will find that General Electric owns the entire block of IP addresses from 3.0.0.0 to 3.255.255.255. General Electric can use these addresses, which number approximately 16.7 million, for its own computers, or it can lease them to other companies or individuals to whom it provides Internet access services.

In the early days of the Internet, the 4 billion addresses provided by the IPv4 rules certainly seemed to be more addresses than an experimental research network would ever need. However, the increase in mobile devices and the Internet of Things has dramatically increased the need for more IP addresses.

Network engineers have devised a number of techniques to stretch the supply of IP addresses. One of the most popular techniques is **subnetting**, which is the use of reserved private IP addresses within LANs and WANs to provide additional address space. **Private IP addresses** are a series of IP numbers that are not permitted on packets that travel on the Internet. In subnetting, a computer called a **Network Address Translation (NAT) device** converts those private IP addresses into normal IP addresses when it forwards packets from those computers to the Internet.

The Internet Engineering Task Force (IETF) worked on several new protocols that could solve the limited addressing capacity of IPv4, and in 1997, approved **Internet Protocol version 6 (IPv6)** as a replacement for IPv4. The process of switching the Internet completely over to IPv6 is taking many years; however, network engineers have devised ways to run both protocols in parallel on interconnected networks.

The worldwide growth in the number of mobile devices and the Internet of Things has consumed existing IPv4 addresses much faster than anyone had predicted and the last available IPv4 addresses were allocated in the summer of 2015. Companies that still need IPv4 addresses can buy them on secondary markets or can use subnetting and their NAT devices to adapt their traffic to IPv6. The major advantage of IPv6 is that it uses a 128-bit number for addresses instead of the 32-bit number used in IPv4. The number of available addresses in IPv6 (2^{128}) is 34 followed by 37 zeros—billions of times larger than the address space of IPv4. The new IP also changes the format of the packet itself.

Improvements in networking technologies over the past 20 years have made many of the fields in the IPv4 packet unnecessary. IPv6 eliminates those fields and adds fields for security and other optional information.

IPv6 has a shorthand notation system for expressing addresses, similar to the IPv4 dotted decimal notation system. However, because the IPv6 address space is much larger, its notation system is more complex. The IPv6 notation uses eight groups of 16 bits (8 × 16 = 128). Each group is expressed as four hexadecimal digits separated by colons. A **hexadecimal (base 16)** numbering system uses 16 characters (0, 1, 2, 3, 4, 5, 6, 7, 8, 9, a, b, c, d, e, and f). An example of an IPv6 address expressed in this notation is: CD18 :0000:0000:AF23:0000:FF9E:61B2:884D. To save space, the zeros can be omitted, which reduces this address to: CD18:::AF23::FF9E:61B2:884D.

Electronic Mail Protocols

Electronic mail, or **e-mail**, that is sent across the Internet must also be formatted according to a common set of rules. Most organizations use a client/server structure to handle e-mail. The organization has a computer called an **e-mail server** that is devoted to handling e-mail. Software that runs on the e-mail server stores and forwards e-mail messages. People in the organization might use a variety of programs, called **e-mail client software**, to read and send e-mail. These programs include Microsoft Outlook, Mozilla Thunderbird, and many others. The e-mail client software communicates with the e-mail server software on the e-mail server computer to send and receive e-mail messages.

Many people also use e-mail on their computers at home. In most cases, the e-mail servers that handle their messages are operated by the companies that provide their connections to the Internet. An increasing number of people use e-mail services that are offered by Web sites such as Yahoo! Mail, or Google's Gmail. In these cases, the e-mail servers and the e-mail clients are operated by the owners of the Web sites. The individual users only see the e-mail client software (and not the e-mail server software) in their Web browsers when they log on to the Web mail service.

With so many different e-mail client and server software choices, standardization and rules are very important. If e-mail messages did not follow standard rules, an e-mail message created by a person using one e-mail client program could not be read by a person using a different e-mail client program. As you have already learned in this chapter, rules for computer data transmission are called protocols.

SMTP and POP are two common protocols used for sending and retrieving e-mail. **Simple Mail Transfer Protocol (SMTP)** specifies the format of a mail message and describes how mail is to be administered on the e-mail server and transmitted on the Internet. An e-mail client program running on a user's computer can request mail from the organization's e-mail server using the **Post Office Protocol (POP)**. A POP message can tell the e-mail server to send mail to the user's computer and delete it from the e-mail server; send mail to the user's computer and not delete it; or simply ask whether new mail has arrived. POP provides support for **Multipurpose Internet Mail Extensions (MIME)**, a set of rules for handling binary files, such as word-processing documents, spreadsheets, photos, or sound clips that are attached to e-mail messages.

The **Interactive Mail Access Protocol (IMAP)** performs the same basic functions as POP, but includes additional features. For example, IMAP can instruct the e-mail server to send only selected e-mail messages to the client instead of all messages. IMAP also allows the user to view only the header and the e-mail sender's name before deciding to download the entire message, which avoids the POP requirement that users download e-mail messages to their computers before they can search, read, forward, delete, or reply to those messages. IMAP lets users create and manipulate e-mail folders and messages while the messages are still on the e-mail server; that is, the user does not need to download e-mail before working with it.

IMAP lets users manipulate and store their e-mail on the e-mail server and access it from any computer, which is important to people who access their e-mail from different computers at different times. The main drawback to IMAP is that e-mail messages are stored on the server and, over time, can exceed the user's space allowance on the server.

Web Page Request and Delivery Protocols

The Web is software that runs on computers that are connected to each other through the Internet. **Web client computers** run software called **Web client software** or **Web browser software**. Widely used Web browser software includes Google Chrome, Microsoft Internet Explorer, Apple Safari, and Mozilla Firefox. Web browser software sends requests for Web page files to other computers, which are called Web servers. A Web server computer runs software called **Web server software**. Web server software receives requests from many different Web clients and responds by sending files back to those Web client computers. Each Web client computer's Web client software renders those files into a Web page. Thus, the purpose of a Web server is to respond to requests for Web pages from Web clients. This combination of client computers running Web client software and server computers running Web server software is an example of a **client/server architecture**.

The set of rules for delivering Web page files over the Internet is in a protocol called the **Hypertext Transfer Protocol (HTTP)**, which was developed by Tim Berners-Lee in 1991. When a user types a domain name (for example, www.yahoo.com) into a Web browser's address bar, the browser sends an HTTP-formatted message to a Web server computer at Yahoo! that stores Web page files. The Web server computer at Yahoo! then responds by sending a set of files (one for the Web page and one for each graphic object, sound, or video clip included on the page) back to the client computer. These files are sent within a message that is HTTP formatted.

To initiate a Web page request using a Web browser, the user types the name of the protocol, followed by the characters "//:" before the domain name. Thus, a user would type http://www.yahoo.com to go to the Yahoo! Web site. Most Web browsers today automatically insert the http:// if the user does not include it. The combination of the protocol name and the domain name is called a **Uniform Resource Locator (URL)** because it lets the user locate a resource (the Web page) on another computer (the Web server).

Emergence of the World Wide Web

At a technological level, the Web is nothing more than software that runs on computers that are connected to the Internet. The network traffic generated by Web software is the largest single category of traffic on the Internet today, outpacing e-mail, file transfers, and other data-transmission traffic. But the ideas behind the Web developed from innovative ways of thinking about and organizing information storage and retrieval. These ideas go back many years. Two important ideas that became key technological elements of the Web are hypertext and graphical user interfaces.

The Development of Hypertext

In 1945, Vannevar Bush, who was director of the U.S. Office of Scientific Research and Development, wrote an article in *The Atlantic Monthly* about ways that scientists could apply the skills they developed during World War II to peacetime activities. The article included a number of visionary ideas about future uses of technology to organize and facilitate efficient access to information. Bush speculated that engineers would eventually build a machine that he called the Memex, a memory extension device that would store all of a person's books, records, letters, and research results on microfilm. Bush's Memex would include mechanical aids, such as microfilm readers and indexes, that would help users quickly and flexibly consult their collected knowledge.

In the 1960s, Ted Nelson described a similar system in which text on one page links to text on other pages. Nelson called his page-linking system **hypertext**. Douglas Engelbart, who also invented the computer mouse, created the first experimental hypertext system on one of the large computers of the 1960s. In 1987, Nelson published *Literary Machines*, a book in which he outlined project Xanadu, a global system for online hypertext publishing and commerce. Nelson used the term *hypertext* to describe a page-linking system that would interconnect related pages of information, regardless of where in the world they were stored.

In 1989, Tim Berners-Lee was trying to improve the laboratory research document-handling procedures for his employer, CERN: European Laboratory for Particle Physics. CERN had been connected to the Internet for two years, but its scientists wanted to find better ways to circulate their scientific papers and data among the high-energy physics research community throughout the world. Berners-Lee proposed a hypertext development project intended to provide this data-sharing functionality.

Over the next two years, Berners-Lee developed the code for a hypertext server program and made it available on the Internet. A **hypertext server** is a computer that stores files written in **Hypertext Markup Language (HTML)**, the language used for the creation of Web pages. The hypertext server is connected through the Internet to other computers that can connect to the hypertext server and read those HTML files. Hypertext servers used on the Web today are usually called **Web servers**. HTML, which Berners-Lee developed from his original hypertext server program, is a language that includes a set of codes (or tags) attached to text. These codes describe the relationships among text elements. For example, HTML includes tags that indicate which text is part of a header element, which text is part of a paragraph element, and which text is part of a numbered list element. One important type of tag is the hypertext link tag. A **hypertext link**, or **hyperlink**, points to another location in the same or another HTML document. The details of HTML and other markup languages are covered later in this chapter.

Graphical Interfaces for Hypertext

As you learned earlier in this chapter, a **Web browser** is software that lets users read (or browse) HTML documents and move from one HTML document to another through text formatted with hypertext link tags in each file. If the HTML documents are on computers connected to the Internet, you can use a Web browser to move from an HTML document on one computer to an HTML document on any other computer on the Internet.

An HTML document differs from a word-processing document in that it does not specify how a particular text element will appear. For example, you might use word-processing software to create a document heading by setting the heading text font to Arial, its font size to 14 points, and its position to centered. The document displays these exact settings whenever you open the document in that word processor. In contrast, an HTML document simply includes a heading tag with the heading text. Many different browser programs can read an HTML document. Each program recognizes the heading tag and displays the text in whatever manner each program normally displays headings. Different Web browser programs might each display the text differently, but all of them display the text with the characteristics of a heading.

A Web browser presents an HTML document in an easy-to-read format in the browser's graphical user interface. A **graphical user interface (GUI)** is a way of presenting program control functions and program output to users and accepting their input. It uses pictures, icons, and other graphical elements instead of displaying just text. Almost all personal computers today use a GUI such as Microsoft Windows or the Macintosh user interface.

The World Wide Web

Berners-Lee called his system of hyperlinked HTML documents the World Wide Web. The Web caught on quickly in the scientific research community, but few people outside that community had software that could read the HTML documents. In 1993, a team of students led by Marc Andreessen at the University of Illinois wrote Mosaic, the first GUI program that could read HTML and use HTML hyperlinks to navigate from page to page on computers anywhere on the Internet. Mosaic was the first Web browser that became widely available for personal computers, and some Web surfers still use it today.

Programmers quickly realized that a system of pages connected by hypertext links would provide many new Internet users with an easy way to access information on the Internet. Businesses recognized the profit-making potential offered by a worldwide network of easy-to-use computers. In 1994, Andreessen and other members of the Mosaic team joined with James Clark of Silicon Graphics to found Netscape Communications (the company was acquired by Time Warner in 1998 but was disbanded in 2003). Its first product, the Netscape Navigator Web browser program based on Mosaic, was an instant success. Netscape became one of the fastest-growing software companies ever. Microsoft created its Internet Explorer Web browser and entered the market soon after Netscape's

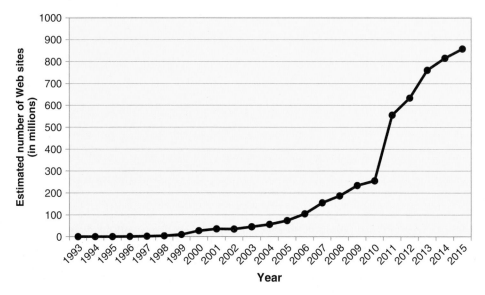

Adapted from Netcraft Web Server Surveys (http://www.netcraft.com) and author's estimates

FIGURE 2-3   Growth of the World Wide Web

success became apparent. Internet Explorer and Mozilla Firefox, a descendant of Netscape Navigator, are still widely used along with Web browsers such as Google's Chrome and Apple's Safari.

The number of Web sites has grown even more rapidly than the Internet itself. The number of Web sites is currently estimated at more than 800 million, and individual Web pages likely number more than a trillion (each Web site might include hundreds or even thousands of individual Web pages). Figure 2-3 shows the overall rapid growth rate of the Web. Noteworthy is the increase from 2010 to 2011, a year in which the number of Web sites doubled. This growth was driven in part by the large number of new Web sites opening in developing countries, primarily in Asia and Eastern Europe.

The Deep Web

In addition to Web pages that are specifically programmed to exist in a permanent form, the Web provides access to customized Web pages that are created in response to a particular user's query. Such Web pages pull their content from databases. For example, if you visit Amazon.com and search for a book about "online business," computers at Amazon.com query their databases of information about books and create a Web page that is a customized response to your search. The Web page that lists your search results never existed before your visit. This store of information that is available through the Web is called the **deep Web**.

Researchers estimate the number of possible pages in the deep Web to be in the tens of trillions. The deep Web can be difficult or impossible to search because its information is not stored on the Web, but in databases that provide results only when a user requests specific information through the Web site that maintains the database. In other words, available data that is never requested remains hidden.

Domain Names

The founders of the Internet were concerned that users might find the dotted decimal notation difficult to remember. To make the numbering system easier to use, they created an alternative addressing method that uses words. In this system, an address such as www. cengage.com is called a domain name. **Domain names** are sets of words that are assigned to specific IP addresses. Domain names can contain two or more word groups separated by periods. The rightmost part of a domain name is the most general. Each part of the domain name becomes more specific as you move to the left.

For example, the domain name www.sandiego.edu contains three parts separated by periods. Beginning at the right, the name "edu" indicates that the computer belongs to an educational institution. The institution, University of San Diego, is identified by the name "sandiego." The "www" indicates that the computer is running software that makes it a part of the World Wide Web. Most, but not all, Web addresses follow this "www" naming convention. For example, the group of computers that operate the Yahoo! Games service is named games.yahoo.com.

The rightmost part of a domain name is called a **top-level domain (TLD)**. For many years, these domains have included a group of generic domains—such as .edu, .com, and .org—and a set of country domains. Since 1998, the Internet Corporation for Assigned Names and Numbers (ICANN) has had the responsibility of managing domain names and coordinating them with the IP address registrars. ICANN is also responsible for setting standards for the router computers that make up the Internet. Since taking over these responsibilities, ICANN has added a number of new TLDs. Some of these TLDs are **generic top-level domains (gTLDs)**, which are available to specified categories of users. ICANN is itself responsible for the maintenance of gTLDs. Other new domains are **sponsored top-level domains (sTLDs)**, which are TLDs for which an organization other than ICANN is responsible.

The sponsor of a specific sTLD must be a recognized institution that has expertise regarding and is familiar with the community that uses the sTLD. For example, the .aero sTLD is sponsored by SITA, an air transport industry association that has expertise in and is familiar with airlines, airports, and the aerospace industry. Individual countries are permitted to maintain their own TLDs, which their residents can use alone or in combination with other TLDs. For example, the URL of the University of Queensland in Brisbane, Australia, is www.uq.edu.au, which combines .edu with .au to indicate that it is an educational institution in Australia. Figure 2-4 presents a list of some commonly used TLDs, including gTLDs and some of the more frequently used country TLDs.

Although ICANN has always chosen new gTLDs after much deliberation and careful consideration, many people have been highly critical of the selections (see, for example, the ICANNWatch Web site). In 2011, ICANN decided to stop managing the addition of new gTLDs so tightly. Since 2012, individuals and businesses have been able to petition for just about any TLD they would like to have. This has generated some controversy; you

TLD	Use
.com	U.S. commercial
.edu	Four-year educational institution
.gov	U.S. federal government
.mil	U.S. military
.net	U.S. general use
.org	U.S. not-for-profit organization
.us	U.S. general use
.asia	Companies, individuals, and organizations based in Asian–Pacific regions
.biz	Businesses
.info	General use
.name	Individual persons
.pro	Licensed professionals (such as accountants, lawyers, physicians)
.au	Australia
.ca	Canada
.de	Germany
.fi	Finland
.fr	France
.jp	Japan
.se	Sweden
.uk	United Kingdom

Source: Internet Assigned Numbers Authority Root Zone Database, http://www.iana.org/domains/root/db/

FIGURE 2-4   Commonly used domain names

can learn more about the related issues on the Web sites of the Internet Governance Project and the Center for Convergence and Emerging Networking Technologies, both at Syracuse University. Increases in the number of TLDs can make it more difficult for companies to protect their corporate and product brand names, as you will learn in Chapter 7.

Markup Languages and the Web

Web pages can include many elements, such as graphics, photographs, sound clips, and even small programs that run in the Web browser. Each of these elements is stored on the Web server as a separate file. The most important parts of a Web page, however, are the structure of the page and the text that makes up the main part of the page. The page structure and text are stored in a text file that is formatted, or marked up, using a text markup language. A **text markup language** specifies a set of tags that are inserted into the text. These **markup tags**, or **tags**, provide formatting instructions that Web client software can understand. The Web client software uses those instructions as it renders the text and page elements contained in the other files into the Web page that appears on the screen of the client computer.

The markup language most commonly used on the Web is HTML, which is a subset of a much older and more complex text markup language called **Standard Generalized Markup Language (SGML)**. SGML was developed in the 1960s to create documents that can be formatted once, stored electronically, and then printed many times in various layouts that each interpret the formatting differently. U.S. Department of Defense contractors used SGML to create manuals and parts lists for weapons systems. These documents contained many information elements that were often reprinted in different versions and formats. Using electronic document storage and programs that could interpret the formats to produce different layouts saved significant retyping time and cost.

The **World Wide Web Consortium (W3C)**, a not-for-profit group that maintains standards for the Web, presented its first draft form of XML in 1996; the W3C issued its first formal version recommendation in 1998. Thus, it is a much newer markup language than HTML. In 2000, the W3C released the first version of a recommendation for a new markup language called **Extensible Hypertext Markup Language (XHTML)**, which is a reformulation of HTML version 4.0 as an XML application. The Web Links include a link to the W3C XHTML Version 1.0 Specification.

Hypertext Markup Language

HTML includes tags that define the format and style of text elements in an electronic document. HTML also has tags that can create relationships among text elements within one document or among several documents. The text elements that are related to each other are called **hypertext elements**.

HTML is easier to learn and use than SGML. HTML is the prevalent markup language used to create documents on the Web today. The early versions of HTML let Web page designers create text-based electronic documents with headings, title bar titles, bullets, lines, and ordered lists. As the use of HTML and the Web itself grew, HTML creator Berners-Lee turned over the job of maintaining versions of HTML to the W3C. Later versions of HTML included tags for tables, frames, and other features that helped Web designers create more complex page layouts. The W3C maintains detailed information about HTML versions and related topics on its W3C HTML Working Group page.

The latest version of HTML is 5.0, which was finalized in 2014. You can learn more about this latest HTML version by visiting the W3C HTML 5 page.

Figure 2-5, on the next page, shows how HTML, XML, and XHTML have descended from the original SGML specification. SGML was used for many years by the publishing industry to create documents that needed to be printed in various formats and that were revised frequently. In addition to its role as a markup language, SGML is a **metalanguage**, which is a language that can be used to define other languages. Another markup language that was derived from SGML for use on the Web is **Extensible Markup Language (XML)**,

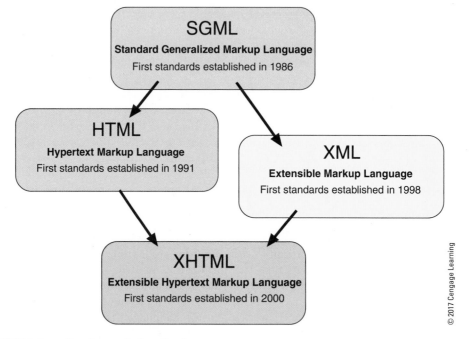

FIGURE 2-5   Development of markup languages

which is increasingly used to tag information that companies share with each other over the Internet. The X in XML comes from the word *extensible*; you might see the word *extensible* shown as eXtensible. XML is also a metalanguage because users can create their own markup elements that extend the usefulness of XML (which is why it is called an "extensible" language).

HTML TAGS

An HTML document contains document text and elements. The tags in an HTML document are interpreted by the Web browser and used by it to format the display of the text enclosed by the tags. In HTML, the tags are enclosed in angle brackets (<>). Most HTML tags have an **opening tag** and a **closing tag** that format the text between them. The closing tag is preceded by a slash within the angle brackets (</>). The general form of an HTML element is:

```
<tagname properties>Displayed information affected by tag</tagname>
```

Two good examples of HTML tag pairs are the strong character-formatting tags and the emphasis character-formatting tags. For example, a Web browser reading the following line of text:

```
<strong>A Review of the Book <em>HTML Is Fun!</em></strong>
```

would recognize the <strong> and </strong> tags as instructions to display the entire line of text in bold and the <em> and </em> tags as instructions to display the text enclosed by those tags in italics. The Web browser would display the text as:

A Review of the Book *HTML Is Fun!*

Some Web browsers allow the user to customize the interpretations of the tags so that different Web browsers might display the tagged text differently. For example, one Web browser might display text enclosed by strong tags in a blue color instead of displaying the text as bold. Tags are generally written in lowercase letters; however, older versions of HTML allowed the use of either case and you might still see Web pages that include uppercase (or mixed case) HTML tags. Although most tags are two-sided (they require both an opening and a closing tag), some require only an opening tag and are known as one-sided tags. The tag that creates a line break (</br>) is a common one-sided tag. Some tags, such as the paragraph tag (<p>...</p>), are two-sided tags for which the closing tag is optional. Designers sometimes omit the optional closing tags, but this practice is poor markup style.

Some opening tags contain one or more property modifiers that further refine how the tag operates. A tag's property might modify a text display, or it might designate where to find a graphic element. Figure 2-6 (on the next page) shows some sample text marked up with HTML tags and Figure 2-7 (on page 81) shows this text as it appears in a Web browser. The tags in these two figures are among the most common HTML tags in use today on the Web.

Other frequently used HTML tags (not shown in the figures) let Web designers include graphics on Web pages and format text in the form of tables. Online sources (such as the **W3C Getting Started with HTML** page) and textbooks are available to help you learn more about HTML.

HTML LINKS

The Web organizes interlinked pages of information residing on sites around the world. Hyperlinks on Web pages form a "web" of those pages. A user can traverse the interwoven pages by clicking hyperlinked text on one page to move to another page in the web of pages. Users can read Web pages in serial order or in whatever order they prefer by following hyperlinks. The way links lead customers through pages can affect the usefulness of the site. Two commonly used link structures are linear and hierarchical. A **linear hyperlink structure** resembles conventional paper documents in that the reader begins on the first page and clicks the Next button to move to the next page in a serial fashion. This structure works well when customers fill out forms prior to a purchase or other agreement. In this case, the customer reads and responds to page one, and then moves on to the next page. This process continues until the entire form is completed. The only Web page navigation choices the user typically has are Back and Next. Figure 2-8 illustrates the differences between reading a paper catalog in a linear way and reading a hypertext catalog in a nonlinear way.

Many Web sites use a **hierarchical hyperlink structure** in which the Web site opens to an introductory page called a **home page** or **start page**. This page contains one or more links to other pages, and those pages, in turn, link to other pages. This hierarchical arrangement resembles an inverted tree in which the root is at the top and the branches

```
<html>

    <head>

        <title>HTML Tag Examples</title>

    </head>

    <body>

    <h1>This text is set in Heading one tags</h1>
    <h2>This text is set in Heading two tags</h2>
    <h3>This text is set in Heading three tags</h3>

    <p>
    This text is set within Paragraph tags. It will appear as one paragraph: the
    text will wrap at the end of each line that is rendered in the Web browser no
    matter where the typed text ends. The text inside Paragraph tags is rendered
    without regard to extra spaces typed in the text, such as these:
    Character formatting can also be applied within Paragraph tags. For
    example, <strong>the Strong tags will cause this text to appear bolded in
    most Web browsers</strong> and <em>the emphasis tags will cause this to
    appear italicized in most Web browsers</em>.
    </p>

    <pre>
    HTML includes tags that instruct the Web browser to render the text
    Exactly      the       way      it      is       typed,
    as in this example.
    </pre>

    <p>
    HTML includes tags that instruct the Web browser to place text in bulleted or
    numbered lists:
    </p>

    <ul>
        <li>Bulleted list item one</li>
        <li>Bulleted list item two</li>
        <li>Bulleted list item three</li>
    </ul>

    <ol>
        <li>Numbered list item one</li>
        <li>Numbered list item two</li>
        <li>Numbered list item three</li>
    </ol>

    <p>
    The most important tag in HTML is the Anchor Hypertext Reference tag,
    which is the tag that provides a link to another Web page (or another location
    in the same Web page). For example, the underlined text
    <a href="http://www.w3c.org/">World Wide Web Consortium</a>
    is a link to the not-for-profit organization that develops Web technologies.
    </p>

    </body>

</html>
```

FIGURE 2-6   Text marked up with HTML tags

This text is set in Heading one tags

This text is set in Heading two tags

This text is set in Heading three tags

This text is set within Paragraph tags. It will appear as one paragraph: the text will wrap at the end of each line that is rendered in the Web browser no matter where the typed text ends. The text inside Paragraph tags is rendered without regard to extra spaces typed in the text, such as these: Character formatting can also be applied within Paragraph tags. For example, **the Strong tags will cause this text to appear bolded in most Web browsers** and *the emphasis tags will cause this to appear italicized in most Web browsers.*

```
HTML includes tags that instruct the Web browser to render the text
Exactly     the     way     it     is     typed,
as in this example.
```

HTML includes tags that instruct the Web browser to place text in bulleted or numbered lists:

- Bulleted list item one
- Bulleted list item two
- Bulleted list item three

1. Numbered list item one
2. Numbered list item two
3. Numbered list item three

The most important tag in HTML is the Anchor Hypertext Reference tag, which is the tag that provides a link to another Web page (or another location in the same Web page). For example, the underlined text <u>World Wide Web Consortium</u> is a link to the not-for-profit organization that develops Web technologies.

© 2017 Cengage Learning

FIGURE 2-7   Text marked up with HTML tags as it appears in a Web browser

are below it. Hierarchical structures can help lead customers from general topics to specific products or services. Hybrid designs that combine linear and hierarchical structures are also possible. Figure 2-9 illustrates these three common Web page organization structures.

In HTML, hyperlinks are created using the HTML **anchor tag**. Whether you are linking to text within the same document or to a document on a distant computer, the anchor tag has the same basic form:

```
<a href="address">Visible link text</a>
```

Anchor tags have opening and closing tags. The opening tag has a hypertext reference (HREF) property, which specifies the remote or local document's address. Clicking the text following the opening link transfers control to the HREF address, wherever that happens to be. A person creating an electronic résumé on the Web might want to make a university's name and address under the Education heading a hyperlink instead of plain text. Anyone viewing the résumé can click the link, which leads the reader to the

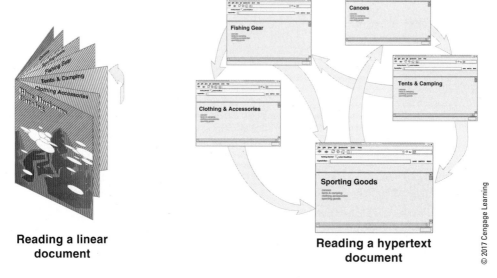

**Reading a linear
document**

**Reading a hypertext
document**

© 2017 Cengage Learning

FIGURE 2-8   Linear versus nonlinear paths through documents

university's home page. The following example shows the HTML code to create a hyperlink
to another Web server:

```
<a href="http://www.gsu.edu">Georgia State University </a>
```

Similarly, the résumé could include a local link to another part of the same document
with the following marked-up text:

```
<a href="#references">References are found here</a>
```

In both of these examples, the text between the anchors appears on the Web page
as a hyperlink. Most browsers display the link in blue and underline it. In most browser
software, the action of moving the mouse pointer over a hyperlink causes the mouse
pointer to change from an arrow to a pointing hand.

CASCADING STYLE SHEETS

A **style sheet** is a set of instructions that gives Web developers more control over the
format of displayed pages. Similar to document styles in word-processing programs, style
sheets let designers define formatting styles in one place that can be applied to multiple
Web pages. The style sheet is usually stored in a separate file and is referenced using the
HTML style tag; however, it can be included as part of a Web page's HTML file.

Most Web designers today use a specific type of style sheet called a **cascading style sheet
(CSS)**, so named because many CSSs can be applied to each Web page, one on top of the
other, and the styles from each style sheet flow (or cascade) into the next. For example, a
three-stage cascade might include one style sheet with formatting instructions for text within
heading 1 tags, a second style sheet with formatting instructions for text within heading 2 tags,
and a third style sheet with formatting instructions for text within paragraph tags. A designer

Linear structure

Hierarchical structure

Hybrid structure

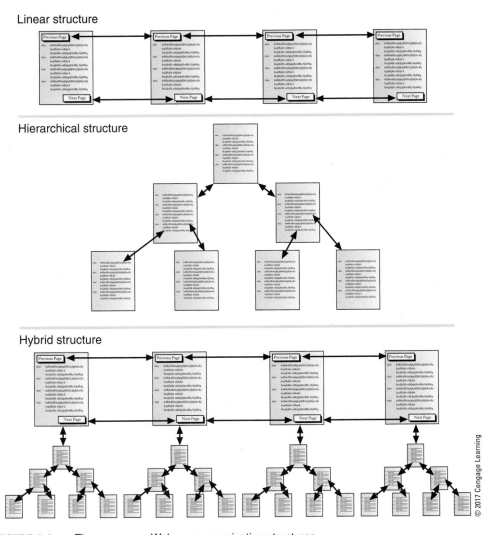

© 2017 Cengage Learning

FIGURE 2-9   Three common Web page organization structures

who later decides to change the formatting of heading 2 text can just replace the second style sheet with a different one. Those changes would cascade into the third style sheet.

Extensible Markup Language (XML)

As the Web grew, HTML continued to provide a useful tool for Web designers who wanted to create attractive layouts of text and graphics on their pages. However, as companies began to conduct business online, they needed to present large amounts of data such as lists of inventory items, sales invoices, and purchase orders. The tool that had helped Web designers create useful Web pages, HTML, was not such a good tool for presenting and maintaining large amounts of business data, so they turned to XML.

```
<html>

  <head>

    <title>Countries</title>

  </head>

  <body>

    <h1>Countries</h1>

    <h2>CountryName</h2>
    <h3>CapitalCity</h3>
    <h4>AreaInSquareKilometers</h4>
    <h5>OfficialLanguage</h5>
    <h6>VotingAge</h6>

    <h2>Argentina</h2>
    <h3>Buenos Aires</h3>
    <h4>2,766,890</h4>
    <h5>Spanish</h5>
    <h6>18</h6>

    <h2>Austria</h2>
    <h3>Vienna</h3>
    <h4>83,858</h4>
    <h5>German</h5>
    <h6>19</h6>

    <h2>Barbados</h2>
    <h3>Bridgetown</h3>
    <h4>430</h4>
    <h5>English</h5>
    <h6>18</h6>

    <h2>Belarus</h2>
    <h3>Minsk</h3>
    <h4>207,600</h4>
    <h5>Byelorussian</h5>
    <h6>18</h6>

  </body>

</html>
```

© 2017 Cengage Learning

FIGURE 2-10   Country list data marked up with HTML tags

XML uses paired start and stop tags to define the structure of a collection of data. For example, a company might maintain descriptions and photos of the products it sells in XML documents. The Web pages are created in HTML, but the product information elements themselves, such as prices, identification numbers, and quantities on hand, are contained in an XML document that can be embedded within the HTML document.

XML includes data-management capabilities that HTML cannot provide. To better understand the differences between XML and HTML, consider a list of countries that includes some basic facts about each country. HTML can show each fact formatted the same way for each country. Figure 2-10 shows the data and the HTML heading tags for four countries (this is only an example; the actual list would include more than 150 countries). Each type of fact is given a different heading style (h1, h2, and so on) that causes each fact to be formatted differently when displayed in a Web browser (as shown in Figure 2-11).

Countries

CountryName

CapitalCity

AreaInSquareKilometers

OfficialLanguage

Voting Age

Argentina

Buenos Aires

2,766,890

Spanish

18

Austria

Vienna

83,858

German

19

Barbados

Bridgetown

430

English

18

Belarus

Minsk

207,600

Byelorussian

18

© 2017 Cengage Learning

FIGURE 2-11   Country list data as it appears in a Web browser

```
declaration ──<?xml version="1.0"?>

root        ┌─<CountriesList>
element

              <Country Name = "Argentina">
                <CapitalCity>Buenos Aires</CapitalCity>
                <AreaInSquareKilometers>2,766,890</AreaInSquareKilometers>
                <OfficialLanguage>Spanish</OfficialLanguage>
                <VotingAge>18</VotingAge>
              </Country>

              <Country Name = "Austria">
                <CapitalCity>Vienna</CapitalCity>
                <AreaInSquareKilometers>83,858</AreaInSquareKilometers>
                <OfficialLanguage>German</OfficialLanguage>
                <VotingAge>19</VotingAge>
              </Country>

              <Country Name = "Barbados">
                <CapitalCity>Bridgetown</CapitalCity>
                <AreaInSquareKilometers>430</AreaInSquareKilometers>
                <OfficialLanguage>English</OfficialLanguage>
                <VotingAge>18</VotingAge>
              </Country>

              <Country Name = "Belarus">
                <CapitalCity>Minsk</CapitalCity>
                <AreaInSquareKilometers>207,600</AreaInSquareKilometers>
                <OfficialLanguage>Byelorussian</OfficialLanguage>
                <VotingAge>18</VotingAge>
              </Country>

            </CountriesList>
```

© 2017 Cengage Learning

FIGURE 2-12   Country list data marked up with XML tags

As you can see, HTML has some limits when used to represent the meaning of data elements. HTML has only six levels of heading tags, so if more elements than shown in this example were needed (such as population and continent), this approach would not be ideal. The Web designer could use various combinations of text attributes such as size, font, color, bold, or italics to distinguish among items, but none of these tags would convey the meaning of the individual data elements.

XML solves these problems. Since XML tags are not defined by default, the user can create their own tags and definitions to convey the meaning (the semantics) of the information included within them. Consider the list of countries example again, but with XML tags created for each fact that convey the meaning of the item. Figure 2-12 shows the countries data marked up with XML tags (such as CapitalCity and VotingAge). Figure 2-13 shows the country list XML file as it would appear in a browser window.

The first line in the XML file is the declaration, which indicates that the file uses version 1.0 of XML. XML markup tags are similar in appearance to SGML markup tags,

```
<?xml version="1.0" ?>
<CountriesList>
- <Country Name="Argentina">
    <CapitalCity>Buenos Aires</CapitalCity>
    <AreaInSquareKilometers>2,766,890</AreaInSquareKilometers>
    <OfficialLanguage>Spanish</OfficialLanguage>
    <VotingAge>18</VotingAge>
  </Country>
- <Country Name="Austria">
    <CapitalCity>Vienna</CapitalCity>
    <AreaInSquareKilometers>83,858</AreaInSquareKilometers>
    <OfficialLanguage>German</OfficialLanguage>
    <VotingAge>19</VotingAge>
  </Country>
- <Country Name="Barbados">
    <CapitalCity>Bridgetown</CapitalCity>
    <AreaInSquareKilometers>430</AreaInSquareKilometers>
    <OfficialLanguage>English</OfficialLanguage>
    <VotingAge>18</VotingAge>
  </Country>
- <Country Name="Belarus">
    <CapitalCity>Minsk</CapitalCity>
    <AreaInSquareKilometers>207,600</AreaInSquareKilometers>
    <OfficialLanguage>Byelorussian</OfficialLanguage>
    <VotingAge>18</VotingAge>
  </Country>
</CountriesList>
```

© 2017 Cengage Learning

FIGURE 2-13   Country list data marked up with XML tags displayed in a Web browser

thus the declaration can help avoid confusion in organizations that use both. The second line and the last line are the root element tags. The root element of an XML file contains all of the other elements in that file and is usually assigned a name that describes the purpose or meaning of the file.

The other elements are called child elements; for example, Country is a child element of CountriesList. Each of the other attributes is, in turn, a child element of the Country element. The names of these child elements were created specifically for use in this file. If programmers in another organization were to create a file with country information, they might use different names for these elements (for example, "Capital" instead of "CapitalCity"), which would make it difficult for the two organizations to share information. Thus, the greatest strength of XML, that it allows users to define their own tags, is also its greatest weakness.

To overcome that weakness, many companies have agreed to follow common standards for XML tags. These standards, in the form of **data-type definitions (DTDs)** or **XML schemas**, are available for a number of industries, including **LegalXML** for information in the legal profession, **MathML** for mathematical and scientific information, and **Extensible Business Reporting Language (XBRL)** for accounting and financial information standards. XBRL is probably one of the most widely used XML schemas in the world. The U.S. Securities and Exchange Commission and similar agencies in other countries have begun requiring publicly traded companies to submit their annual financial information electronically using XBRL instead of filing paper documents. Individual investors and professional financial analysts can import the XBRL data from these filings directly into their own spreadsheet software to easily review and study the companies' reported financial results.

A number of industry groups have formed to create standard XML tag definitions that can be used by all companies in that industry. RosettaNet is an example of such an industry group. In 2001, the W3C released a set of rules for XML document interoperability that many researchers believe will help resolve incompatibilities between different sets of XML tag definitions. A set of XML tag definitions is sometimes called an **XML vocabulary**. Hundreds of publicly defined XML vocabularies have been developed or are currently circulating. You can find links to many of them on the Oasis Cover Pages: XML Applications and Initiatives Web page. You can learn more about XML by reading the W3C XML Pages.

Although it is possible to display XML files in some Web browsers, they are usually intended to be translated using another file that contains formatting instructions or to be read by a program. Formatting instructions are often written in the **Extensible Stylesheet Language (XSL)**, which are read by programs, sometimes called **XML parsers**, that can display an XML file on the screen of a computer, a tablet device, a smartphone, an Internet-capable mobile phone, or some other device. A diagram showing one way that a Web server might process HTTP requests for Web pages generated from XML documents in different formats for different Web browsing devices appears in Figure 2-14.

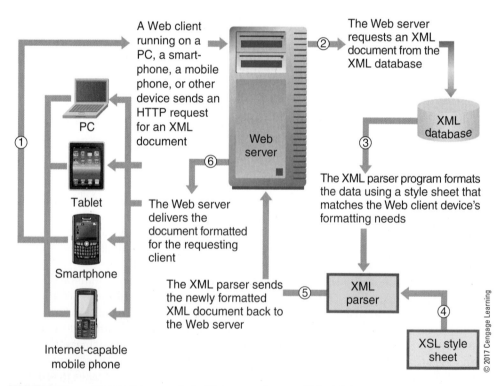

FIGURE 2-14   Processing requests for Web pages from an XML database

Internet Connection Options

The Internet is a set of interconnected networks. Most organizations have their computers connected to each other using a network. Many families have their home computers connected to each other in a network. Mobile phones are connected to the wireless phone service provider's network. These networks can be connected to the Internet in a number of ways, as described in this section. Companies that provide Internet access to individuals, businesses, and other organizations, called **Internet access providers (IAPs)** or ISPs, usually offer several connection options. This section briefly describes current connection choices and presents their advantages and disadvantages.

Connectivity Overview

ISPs offer several ways to connect to the Internet. The most common connection options are voice-grade telephone lines, various types of broadband connections, leased lines, and wireless. One of the major distinguishing factors between various ISPs and their connection options is the bandwidth they offer. **Bandwidth** is the amount of data that can travel through a communication medium per unit of time. The higher the bandwidth, the more data can be transmitted in each second and the faster Web pages appear on your screen. Each connection option offers different bandwidths, and each ISP offers varying bandwidths for each connection option. Traffic on the Internet and at your local service provider greatly affects **net bandwidth**, which is the actual amount of data that is transmitted per second. When few people are competing for service from an ISP, net bandwidth approaches the carrier's upper limit. On the other hand, users experience slowdowns during high-traffic periods.

Bandwidth can differ for data traveling to or from the ISP depending on the user's connection type. Connection types include:

- **Symmetric connections** that provide the same bandwidth in both directions.
- **Asymmetric connections** that provide different bandwidths for each direction.

The two bandwidth types in an asymmetric connection are as follows:

- **Upstream bandwidth**, also called **upload bandwidth**, is a measure of the amount of information that can travel from the user to the Internet in a given amount of time.
- **Downstream bandwidth**, also called **download bandwidth** or **downlink bandwidth**, is a measure of the amount of information that can travel from the Internet to a user in a given amount of time (for example, when a user receives a Web page from a Web server).

Voice-Grade Telephone Connections

In the early days of the Web, most individuals connected to their ISPs through a modem connected to their local telephone service providers. **Plain old telephone service (POTS)** uses existing telephone lines and an analog modem to provide a bandwidth of between 28 and 56 Kbps. Today, most people use higher bandwidth connection options. Connections that operate at speeds of greater than about 200 Kbps are called **broadband** services.

Broadband Services

One broadband option is a higher grade of telephone service called the **Digital Subscriber Line (DSL)** protocol. DSL connection methods do not use a modem. They use a piece of equipment that is a form of network switch, but many people call this piece of equipment (incorrectly) a "DSL modem." One of the oldest broadband services to use the DSL protocol is **asymmetric digital subscriber line** (**ADSL**, usually abbreviated **DSL**). It provides transmission bandwidths from 100 to 640 Kbps upstream and from 1 to 15 Mbps (million bits per second) downstream. DSL is a private line with no competing traffic.

Cable modems—connected to the same broadband coaxial cable that serves a television—typically provide bandwidths between 500 Kbps and 15 Mbps from the client to the server. The downstream bandwidth can be as high as 10 Mbps. In recent years, DSL monthly fees have been slightly lower than those of cable companies in markets where they compete. Unlike DSL, cable modem connection bandwidths vary with the number of other subscribers competing for the shared resource. Connection bandwidth can decrease dramatically in heavily subscribed neighborhoods at prime times—in neighborhoods where many people are using cable modems simultaneously.

Leased-Line Connections

Large firms with large amounts of Internet traffic can connect to an ISP using higher bandwidth connections that they can lease from telecommunications carriers. These connections use a variety of technologies and are usually classified by the equivalent number of telephone lines they include. (The connection technologies they use were originally developed to carry large numbers of telephone calls.)

A telephone line designed to carry one digital signal is called DS0 (digital signal zero, the name of the signaling format used on those lines) and has a bandwidth of 56 Kbps. A T1 line (also called a DS1) carries 24 DS0 lines and operates at 1.544 Mbps. T3 service (also called DS3) offers 44.736 Mbps (the equivalent of 30 T1 lines or 760 DS0 lines). All of these leased telephone line connections are much more expensive than POTS, ISDN, or DSL connections.

Large businesses and government organizations that need to connect hundreds or thousands of individual users to the Internet require very high bandwidth. These organizations use T1 and T3 lines. NAPs and the computers that perform routing functions on the Internet backbone also use technologies such as **frame relay** and **asynchronous transfer mode (ATM)** connections and **optical fiber** (instead of copper wire) connections with bandwidths determined by the class of fiber-optic cable used. An OC3 (optical carrier 3) connection provides 156 Mbps, an OC12 provides 622 Mbps, an OC48 provides 2.5 Gbps (gigabits, or 1 billion bits per second), an OC192 provides 10 Gbps, and an OC768 provides 40 Gbps.

Wireless Connections

Although the Internet was built on telephone company wires and infrastructure when it was created in the 1960s, many Internet users today use some form of wireless connection. In this section, you will learn about wireless options for connecting to the Internet.

LEARNING FROM FAILURES

NorthPoint Communications

In 1997, Michael Malaga was a successful telecommunications executive with an idea. He wanted to sell broadband Internet access to small businesses in urban areas. DSL technology was just gaining acceptance, and leased telephone lines were available from telephone companies. He wanted to avoid residential customers because they would soon have inexpensive cable modem access to meet their broadband needs. He also wanted to avoid suburban and rural businesses to keep the telephone line leasing costs low (lease charges are higher for longer distances). He and five friends started NorthPoint Communications with $500,000 of their combined savings and raised another $11 million within a few months. After six months, the company had raised more money from investors and had acquired 1500 customers, but it was posting a net loss of $30 million. On the strength of its number of customers, the company began the task of raising the $100 million that Malaga estimated it would need to create the network infrastructure.

Independent DSL providers such as NorthPoint were pressed by customers to install service rapidly, but had to rely on local telephone companies to ensure that their lines would support DSL. In many cases, the telephone companies had to install switches and other equipment to make DSL work on a particular line. The telephone companies often were in no rush to do this because they also sold DSL service, and speedy service would be helping a competitor. The delays led to unpredictable installation holdups and many unhappy NorthPoint customers. Customers with problems after the service was installed were often bounced from the telephone company to NorthPoint, without obtaining satisfactory or timely resolutions of their problems.

Although NorthPoint was unable to make its relationship with each customer profitable, Malaga and his team were rapidly raising money in the hot capital markets of the time. The company raised $162 million before its first stock offering in 1999, which brought in an additional $387 million. At that time, the company had 13,000 customers, which means that NorthPoint had raised more than $42,000 from outside investors for each customer. Considering that each customer would generate revenue of about $1000 per year, the economics of the business did not look good. By the end of 1999, NorthPoint had spent $300 million of the cash it had raised to build its network infrastructure and reported an operating loss of $184 million. At this point, NorthPoint was operating in 28 cities.

During the next year, the company continued to raise additional funds, gain more customers, and lose money on each customer. In August 2000, the telephone company Verizon agreed to purchase 55 percent of the company for $800 million paid in installments. The total funding that NorthPoint had obtained by the end of 2000, including the partial payments received from Verizon, added up to $1.2 billion. By the end of the year, NorthPoint was in 109 cities and needed to spend $66 million in cash per month just to stay in business. Verizon withdrew from the purchase agreement, the stock plunged, and the layoffs began.

NorthPoint filed for bankruptcy in January 2001 and sold its networking hardware to AT&T in March for $135 million. AT&T was not interested in continuing the DSL

(Continued)

business (it just wanted the hardware), so NorthPoint's 87,000 small business customers lost their Internet service overnight. In many of the cities that NorthPoint had served, there were no competitors to pick up the service.

Because the capital markets of the late 1990s were so eager to invest in anything that appeared to be connected with the Internet, NorthPoint was able to raise incredible amounts of money. However, NorthPoint sold Internet access to customers for less than it cost to provide the service. No amount of investor money could overcome that basic business mistake.

WIRELESS ETHERNET (WI-FI)

The most common wireless connection technology in use today is called **Wi-Fi, wireless Ethernet**. The technology is also known by its network specification number, 802.11, the latest version of which is 802.11ac, which is replacing 802.11n in many networks because it has greater bandwidth. The 802.11ac specification bandwidth ranges up to 2.5 Gbps in typical installations as compared with 802.11n's typical bandwidth of 450Mbps. Both versions have a range of about 500 feet.

In actual installations, the achieved bandwidth and range can be dramatically affected by the construction material of the objects (such as walls, floors, doors, and windows) through which the signals must pass. For example, reinforced concrete walls and certain types of tinted glass windows greatly reduce the effective range of Wi-Fi. Despite these limitations, organizations can make Wi-Fi a key element of their LAN structures by installing a number of WAPs throughout their premises. A computer equipped with a Wi-Fi network card can communicate through a wireless access point connected to a LAN to become a part of that LAN. A **wireless access point (WAP)** is a device that transmits network packets between Wi-Fi-equipped computers and other devices that are within its range.

Wi-Fi devices are capable of **roaming**; that is, shifting from one WAP to another, without requiring intervention by the user. Some organizations, including airports, convention centers, and hotels, operate WAPs that are open to the public. These access points are called **hot spots**. Some organizations allow free access to their hot spots; others charge an access fee. A number of restaurants and fast-food retailers, such as McDonald's, Panera, and Starbucks, offer hot spots. Hotels and office buildings have found that installing a WAP can be cheaper and easier than running network cable, especially in older buildings. Some hotels offer wireless access free; others charge a small fee. Users of fee-based networks authorize a connection charge when they log in.

PERSONAL AREA NETWORKS

One of the first wireless protocols, designed for personal use over short distances, is called **Bluetooth**. (The protocol was developed in Norway and is named for Harald Bluetooth, a tenth-century Scandinavian king.) Bluetooth operates reliably over distances of up to 35 feet and can be a part of up to 10 networks of eight devices each. It is a low-bandwidth technology, with speeds of up to 722 Kbps. Bluetooth is useful for tasks such as wireless synchronization of laptop computers with desktop computers and wireless printing from laptops or mobile phones. These small Bluetooth networks are called **personal area networks (PANs)** or **piconets**.

One major advantage of Bluetooth technology is that it consumes very little power, which is an important consideration for mobile devices. Another advantage is that Bluetooth devices can discover one another and exchange information automatically. For example, a person using a laptop computer in a temporary office can print to a local Bluetooth-enabled printer without logging in to the network or installing software on either device. The printer and the laptop computer electronically recognize each other as Bluetooth devices and can immediately begin exchanging information.

Another wireless communication technology, **Ultra Wideband (UWB)**, provides wide bandwidth (up to about 480 Mbps in current versions) connections over short distances (30 to 100 feet). UWB was developed for short-range secure communications in military applications during the 1960s. Many observers believe that UWB technologies will be used in future personal area networking applications such as home media centers (for example, a PC could beam stored video files to a nearby television) and in linking mobile phones to the Internet. UWB is faster and more reliable than the wireless Ethernet technologies now used for these purposes.

A short-range wireless technology that was developed to be low cost and run on very little power is **ZigBee** (the name is a reference to the waggle dance a honeybee performs when returning to its hive). With intentionally low bandwidth (20–250 Kbps) to limit power consumption, ZigBee has a range of 30 to 300 feet. An increasing number of applications have been developed to run on ZigBee that control home energy management systems (including lighting, heating, cooling), commercial building automation, security systems, and remote controls for consumer electronic products. You can learn more about this technology by visiting the ZigBee Alliance Web site.

FIXED-POINT WIRELESS

In a growing number of rural areas that do not have cable TV service or telephone lines with the high-grade wires necessary to provide Internet bandwidths, some small companies have begun to offer fixed-point wireless service as an inexpensive alternative to satellite service. One version of **fixed-point wireless** uses a system of repeaters to forward a radio signal from the ISP to customers. The **repeaters** are transmitter–receiver devices (also called **transceivers**) that receive the signal and then retransmit it toward users' roof-mounted antennas and to the next repeater, which receives the signal and passes it on to the next repeater, which can be up to 20 miles away. The users' antennas are connected to a device that converts the radio signals into Wi-Fi packets that are sent to the users' computers or wireless LANs. Another version of fixed-point wireless directly transmits Wi-Fi packets through hundreds, or even thousands, of short-range transceivers that are located close to each other. This approach is called **mesh routing**. As Wi-Fi technologies improve, the number and variety of options for wireless connections to the Internet should continue to increase.

One of the most interesting current applications that use mesh routing is Google's Project Loon, which uses a network of balloons that float in the stratosphere to connect the Internet to each other and to ground stations. Started as a research project in 2013, the initiative is still experimental but could become commercially viable in 2016. The balloons drift in the prevailing low-speed winds that exist between 10 and 30 miles above the Earth's surface and must be replaced periodically (currently, about every 100 days). The electronics on board the balloons are powered by solar panels. The ground stations can be operated by telecommunications companies or other ISPs. During the testing phase of the project, the balloon-based mesh network has been used to connect directly to smartphones and tablet devices. When fully operational, Google expects this network to help reach the 60 percent of the world's population that currently does not have an Internet connection.

SATELLITE MICROWAVE

For many people in rural areas, satellite microwave transmissions made connections to the Internet possible for the first time. These connections use a microwave transmitter that provides upload bandwidths in the range of 120 Kbps to 5 Mbps and downloads in the 1–16 Mbps range. Initially, installation charges for satellite were much higher than for other residential Internet connection services because a professional installer was needed to carefully aim the transmitter's dish antenna at the satellite. As the accuracy of the antennas improved, more of these companies offered a self-installation option that drastically reduced the initial cost. For installations in North America, the antennas must have a clear line of sight into the southwestern sky. This requirement can make these services unusable for many people living in large cities or on the wrong side of an apartment building. Many airlines now provide Internet access to passengers in flight through a combination of satellite and ground-based wireless connections.

Although satellite connections were once the only wireless Internet access media for many years, many types of wireless networks are available now. People today use Internet-capable mobile phones, smartphones, game consoles, and notebook computers equipped with wireless network cards to connect to a variety of wireless networks that, in turn, are connected to the Internet.

MOBILE TELEPHONE NETWORKS

In 2014, the number of mobile phones in the world, nearly 8 billion, was greater than the planet's population for the first time in history (although many people in the world do not have a mobile phone, many more own multiple mobile phones and devices). These phones are sometimes called cellular (or cell) phones because they broadcast signals to (and receive signals from) antennas that are placed about 3 miles apart in a grid, and the hexagonal area that each antenna covers within this grid is called a cell.

Many mobile phones have a small screen and can be used to send and receive short text messages using a protocol called **short message service (SMS)**. Internet-enabled mobile phones and smartphones are very popular in highly developed countries as convenient ways to stay connected while on the go. But more important, mobile phones are giving large numbers of people in developing countries their first access to the online world.

Although mobile phones were originally designed to handle voice communications, they have always been able to transmit data. However, their data transmission speeds were very low, ranging from 10 to 384 Kbps. Most mobile telephone networks today use

Service	Upstream Bandwidth (Kbps)	Downstream Bandwidth (Kbps)	Capacity (Number of Simultaneous Users)	One-Time Start-Up Costs	Continuing Monthly Costs
Residential-Small Business Services					
POTS	28–56	28–56	1	$0–$20	$9–$20
Wireless 3G network	10–800	10–2000	1	$0–$120	$30–150
DSL	100–640	1000–15,000	4–20	$50–$100	$20–$300
Cable	300–1500	500–15,000	4–10	$0–$100	$35–$200
Satellite	120–5000	1000–16,000	1–3	$0–$800	$40–$100
Fixed-point wireless	250–1500	500–3000	1–4	$0–$350	$50–$150
Wireless 4G network	500–5000	1000–12,000	1	$0–$200	$80–$200
Business Services					
Leased digital line (DS0)	64	64	1–50	$50–$200	$40–$150
Fixed-point wireless	500–10,000	500–10,000	5–1000	$0–$500	$150–$4000
T1 leased line	1544	1544	100–1000	$100–$2000	$200–$300
T3 leased line	44,736	44,736	1000–10,000	$500–$5000	$2500–$3000
Large Organizations					
OC3 leased line	156,000	156,000	1000–50,000	$3000–$12,000	$5000–$20,000
OC12 leased line	622,000	622,000	Backbone	Negotiated	$25,000–$100,000
Network Access Providers					
OC48 leased line	2,500,000	2,500,000	Backbone	Negotiated	Negotiated
OC192 leased line	10,000,000	10,000,000	Backbone	Negotiated	Negotiated
OC768 leased line	40,000,000	40,000,000	Backbone	Negotiated	Negotiated

© 2017 Cengage Learning

FIGURE 2-15   Internet connection options

one of a series of technologies called **third-generation (3G) wireless technology** that offer download speeds up to 2 Mbps and upload speeds up to 800 Kbps. However, the major U.S. wireless carriers are rapidly introducing newer technologies, including **Long Term Evolution (LTE)** and **Worldwide Interoperability for Microwave Access (WiMAX)**, that are generally referred to as **fourth-generation (4G) wireless technology**. These 4G technologies offer download speeds up to 14 Mbps and upload speeds up to 8 Mbps.

Most tablet devices, mobile phones, and smartphones have the ability to use either a mobile telephone network or a locally available wireless network and most can switch automatically to a wireless network when one is available. Using a local wireless network can be less expensive than using a mobile telephone network.

Although mobile phone networks are under pressure from the increased amount of data transmitted through them by Internet users, a number of research efforts directed at increasing the bandwidth of those networks are underway, including the pCell technology you learned about in the introduction to this chapter.

Figure 2-15 summarizes speed and cost information for the most commonly available wired and wireless options for connecting a home or business to the Internet.

Internet2 and the Semantic Web

When the National Science Foundation turned over the Internet backbone to commercial interests in 1995, many scientists felt that they had lost a large, living laboratory. A group of network research scientists from nearly 200 universities and a number of major corporations joined together in 1996 to recapture the original enthusiasm of the ARPANET and created an advanced research network called **Internet2**. An experimental test bed for new networking technologies that is separate from the original Internet, Internet2 has achieved bandwidths of 10 Gbps and more on parts of its network.

Internet2 is also used by universities to conduct large collaborative research projects that require several supercomputers connected at very fast speeds, or that use multiple video feeds—things that would be impossible on the Internet given its bandwidth limits. For example, doctors at medical schools that are members of Internet2 regularly use its technology to do live videoconference consultations during complex surgeries, and particle physicists use it to collect and analyze large amounts of information while doing experiments using the Large Hadron Collider (a large particle physics laboratory near Geneva, Switzerland), which can generate 10 Gb of data per second. Internet2 serves as a proving ground for new technologies and applications of those technologies that will eventually find their way to the Internet. Many of the technologies that are now part of the Internet of Things (about which you learned earlier in this chapter) were first developed as Internet2 initiatives. You can learn more about current activities conducted on this network by following the Web Link to **Internet2**.

The Internet2 project is focused mainly on technology development. In contrast, Tim Berners-Lee began a project in 2001 that has a goal of blending technologies and information into a next-generation Web. This **Semantic Web** project envisions words on Web pages being tagged (using XML) with their meanings. The Web would become a huge machine-readable database of meanings rather than words. People could use intelligent programs called **software agents** to read the XML tags to determine the meaning of the words in their contexts rather than identifying the words themselves or relying on keyword descriptors included by the Web site creator. For example, a software agent given the instruction to find an airline ticket with certain terms (date, cities, cost limit) would launch a search on the Web and return with an electronic ticket that meets the criteria. Instead of a user having to visit several Web sites to gather information, compare prices and itineraries, and make a decision, the software agent would automatically do the searching, comparing, and purchasing.

For software agents to perform these functions, Web standards must include XML, a resource description framework, and an ontology. You have already seen how XML tags can describe the semantics of data elements. A **resource description framework (RDF)** is a set of standards for XML syntax. It would function as a dictionary for all XML tags used on the Web. An **ontology** is a set of standards that defines, in detail, the relationships among RDF standards and specific XML tags within a particular knowledge domain. For example, the ontology for cooking would include concepts such as ingredients, utensils, and ovens; however, it would also include rules and behavioral expectations, such as that ingredients can be mixed using utensils, that the resulting product can be eaten by people, and that ovens generate heat within a confined area. Ontologies and the RDF would provide the intelligence about the knowledge domain so that software agents could make decisions as humans would.

The development of the Semantic Web is expected to take many years. The first step in this project is to develop ontologies for specific subjects. Thus far, several areas of scientific inquiry have begun developing ontologies that will become the building blocks of the Semantic Web in their areas. Biology, genomics, and medicine have all made progress toward specific ontologies. These fields can benefit greatly from a tool like the Semantic

Web, which can increase the speed with which research results, experimental data, and new procedures can be made available to all researchers in the field. Thus, these fields have a high incentive to collaborate on the hard work involved in creating ontologies.

Other sciences, such as climatology, hydrology, and oceanography, have similar incentives (as many researchers around the world work on common problems such as global warming) and scientists are developing ontologies for their disciplines. The government of the United Kingdom is also developing an ontology for data it collects with the hope that it will be useful to a wide range of researchers.

One ongoing Semantic Web project that is of general interest is DBpedia, which is building a knowledge base that describes the content of the Wikipedia online encyclopedia. The DBpedia dataset currently includes more than five million things, including persons, places, creative works, organizations, species, and diseases.

Although many researchers involved in the Semantic Web project have expressed frustration at its slow progress, a number of users of the Semantic Web have developed important ontologies that will allow the project to continue moving forward. You can learn more about the current status of this project by following the Web Links to the W3C Semantic Web pages.

Current commercial applications of the research conducted by the Semantic Web community include the natural language interfaces of mobile phone search utilities such as Siri on the Apple iPhone and Google Now on Android phones. Facebook also provides its advertisers with Graph Search, a semantic search technology that helps them better target their messages.

Summary

In this chapter, you learned about the history and growth of the Internet and the Web, including intranets and extranets and how they can be implemented using public network, private network, or VPN technologies. You also learned about the wide variety of devices that can be connected to the Internet today, including the Internet of Things.

You also learned about packet-switching networks and the protocols, programs, languages, and architectures that support the Internet and the World Wide Web. You learned how IP addressing and domain names work; how HTTP provides rules for transferring Web pages and requests for those Web pages on the Internet; and that POP, SMTP, and IMAP are protocols that help manage e-mail. You learned the history of markup languages and how specific versions, including HTML, XHTML, and XML, are used to display Web pages and manage the data content behind them.

You learned that Internet service providers offer many different types of wired connections to the Internet and that wireless connection options available through mobile phones and tablet devices are important pathways to the Internet, especially in developing countries. You also learned that Internet2 is an experimental network built by a consortium of research universities and businesses to provide test bed for creating and perfecting the high-speed networking technologies of tomorrow and that the Semantic Web project is providing some commercial benefits while slowly moving toward its goal of making research data widely available and helping intelligent software agents become a productive part of electronic commerce.

Key Terms

ADSL	closed architecture
anchor tag	closing tag
asymmetric connections	computer network
asymmetric digital subscriber line (ADSL)	configuration tables
asynchronous transfer mode (ATM)	data-type definitions (DTDs)
backbone routers	deep Web
bandwidth	Digital Subscriber Line (DSL)
base 2	domain names
binary	dotted decimal
Bluetooth	downlink bandwidth
border routers	download bandwidth
broadband	downstream bandwidth
cascading style sheet (CSS)	DSL
circuit	edge router
circuit switching	electronic mail
client/server architecture	e-mail

e-mail client software

e-mail server

encapsulation

Extensible Business Reporting Language (XBRL)

Extensible Hypertext Markup Language (XHTML)

Extensible Markup Language (XML)

Extensible Stylesheet Language (XSL)

extranet

fixed-point wireless

fourth-generation (4G) wireless technology

frame relay

gateway computers

generic top-level domains (gTLDs)

graphical user interface (GUI)

hexadecimal (base 16)

hierarchical hyperlink structure

home page

hot spots

hyperlink

hypertext

hypertext elements

hypertext link

Hypertext Markup Language (HTML)

hypertext server

Hypertext Transfer Protocol (HTTP)

Interactive Mail Access Protocol (IMAP)

internet

Internet

Internet access providers (IAPs)

Internet backbone

Internet hosts

Internet of Things

Internet Protocol (IP)

Internet Protocol version 4 (IPv4)

Internet Protocol version 6 (IPv6)

Internet service providers (ISPs)

Internet2

intranet

IP address

IP tunneling

IP wrapper

leased line

LegalXML

linear hyperlink structure

local area network (LAN)

Long Term Evolution (LTE)

mailing list

markup tags

MathML

mesh routing

metalanguage

Multipurpose Internet Mail Extensions (MIME)

net bandwidth

network access points (NAPs)

network access providers

Network Address Translation (NAT) device

Network Control Protocol (NCP)

newsgroups

ontology

open architecture

opening tag

optical fiber

packet-switched (network)

packets

pCell

personal area networks (PANs)

piconets

plain old telephone service (POTS)

Post Office Protocol (POP)

Private IP addresses

private network

proprietary architecture

protocol

public network

repeaters

resource description framework (RDF)

roaming

router computers

routers

routing algorithms

routing computers

routing tables

Semantic Web

short message service (SMS)

Simple Mail Transfer Protocol (SMTP)

software agents

sponsored top-level domains (sTLDs)

Standard Generalized Markup Language (SGML)

start page

style sheet

subnetting

symmetric connections

tags

TCP/IP

text markup language

third-generation (3G) wireless technology

top-level domain (TLD)

transceivers

Transmission Control Protocol (TCP)

Ultra Wideband (UWB)

Uniform Resource Locator (URL)

upload bandwidth

upstream bandwidth

Usenet

User's News Network

virtual private network (VPN)

Web

Web browser

Web browser software

Web client computers

Web client software

Web server software

Web servers

wide area networks (WANs)

Wi-Fi

wireless access point (WAP)

wireless Ethernet

World Wide Web

World Wide Web Consortium (W3C)

Worldwide Interoperability for Microwave Access (WiMAX)

XML parsers

XML schemas

XML vocabulary

ZigBee

Review Questions

1. What is an internet (small "i")?

2. Why did the U.S. Department of Defense undertake the research project that would become the Internet?

3. What were Bitnet and Janet?

4. On the Internet, what is the function of a network access point?

5. Briefly describe one example of how the Internet of Things might be used to reduce costs or increase efficiency in a business.

6. What is a border router?

7. What are the key elements of a private network?

8. What is a protocol?

9. Briefly describe what the TCP/IP protocol does for the Internet.

10. Why was it necessary for the Internet to adopt IPv6?

11. Briefly describe the function of Web browser software.

12. What is a Uniform Resource Locator?

13. In what ways does an HTML document differ from a word-processing document?

14. Briefly explain how the deep Web contains hidden information.

15. Describe, in general, the function of HTML tags.

16. Describe, in general, the function of XML tags.

17. What is bandwidth and why do people often think of it as a measure of connection speed?

18. List the Internet connection options that might be suitable for a small business in an urban location with five employees.

19. What is the main function of a wireless access point?

20. What is roaming?

21. What is mesh routing?

22. Briefly describe the goals of the Internet2 project.

23. List some commercial applications that have emerged from the Semantic Web research project.

Exercises

1. In a paragraph or two, evaluate the NSF's 1989 decision to introduce limited commercial activity on the Defense Department network that would eventually become the Internet.

2. In about 100 words, outline the advantages and disadvantages of using circuit-switched and packet-switched networks to transmit data.

3. In about 100 words, briefly describe the function of each type of router that might exist in an interconnected network.

4. In a paragraph or two, describe how a VPN maintains security over data transmitted through it.

5. In a paragraph, briefly explain the differences between closed and open architectures; then, in an additional two or three paragraphs, outline the reasons an open architecture was chosen for the Internet.

6. In about 100 words, explain why the IMAP e-mail protocol is better than the POP e-mail protocol.

7. In a paragraph or two, explain why the Web is often described as having a client/server architecture.

8. In a paragraph or two, explain how Vannevar Bush's idea of a Memex machine presaged the Web.

9. In about 100 words, explain how top-level Web domain names are proposed and approved.

10. In two or three paragraphs, explain the hyperlinked structure of the Web and why it is important.

11. HTML and XML are both markup languages, but they have very different objectives. In about 100 words, describe the objectives of each and provide at least one example of when using XML would be preferable to using HTML.

12. In about 100 words, describe two or three situations (business or personal) in which you might find a personal area network to be useful.

Cases

C1. Internet Access in Hyderabad

Hyderabad is the fourth-largest city in India, with a population of 9 million in the city itself and more than 15 million in the metropolitan area. It is the capital of the State of Andhra Pradesh, which has 86 million people and a $100 billion-per-year economy. Hyderabad itself accounts for about half of that annual activity, much of it in information technology (the city houses the Indian headquarters of Amazon.com, Google, and Microsoft, for example) and pharmaceuticals. With more than a dozen universities, the city is a leader in education and research.

Like the rest of the country, however, citizens in the Hyderabad metropolitan area are less connected to the Internet than the city's strong presence in the information technology industry would suggest. Overall, only about 1.7 million residents (about 19 percent of the population) have regular online access. About half of those with regular access use an Internet-capable phone as their primary access device. Approximately 85 percent of Hyderabad citizens own mobile phones, but most of them are not Internet-capable.

Although the level of Internet access in Hyderabad is greater than the average for India, it lags far behind the United States, where more than 90 percent of the population has regular online access. It also lags behind online access in China, where about 46 percent of the population has regular online access (about 80 percent of that through mobile devices).

REQUIRED:

1. What are the implications of the low Internet access rates for the citizens of Hyderabad as they become active participants in the world economy over the next five years? Summarize your thoughts in about 100 words.

2. Using your library or your favorite search engine, identify current trends in the growth of Internet-capable phones and other online access devices in India. In a report of about 200 words, evaluate the prospects for significant changes in online access rates over the next few years.

3. Use what you learned about online access technologies in this chapter to outline several alternatives that the government of Hyderabad should consider developing (perhaps in partnership with local information technology companies) that might increase online access rates for its citizens. Prepare a report of about 200 words in which you discuss at least two of these alternatives.

Note: Your instructor might assign you to a group to complete this case and might ask you to prepare a formal presentation of your results to your class.

C2. Quick Fix Repair Systems

You are the assistant to Yin Chan, the service manager of Quick Fix Repair Systems. Quick Fix offers repair and maintenance services to homeowners throughout the tri-state area. Quick Fix service technicians are licensed and qualified to do minor plumbing, electrical, and carpentry work in addition to repairs on most major appliances.

Yin wants to equip each service technician with the technology they need to report their time and materials usage on each job. Today, the service technicians carry a notebook computer for recording this information at job sites. They also each carry a smartphone to stay in touch with the office, order parts that they do not have with them, and keep track of their schedule. These smartphones are currently connected through a corporate wireless phone plan that provides free data transfers of up to 5 Gb per phone per month.

Yin would like to ensure that service technicians have access to the Quick Fix main computers while they are on the job site so they can check supplies inventory and access Quick Fix service guides that help them make repairs in the most effective ways possible.

REQUIRED:

1. Investigate various options for giving Yin's service technicians wireless remote access to the Quick Fix main computers. You should consider options that use the technicians' notebook computers, their smartphones, or new tablet devices. In your report of about 200 words, outline the advantages and disadvantages of having the technicians use each type of device for access to the Quick Fix main computers. Be sure to consider whether the technicians' needs could be met by having them carry only one device.

2. You should consider at least three options for connecting the device or devices you chose, writing no more than two paragraphs for each option. Then select the best option and write a one-page evaluation of your choice's strengths and weaknesses.

3. Yin has been reading about the Internet of Things and is concerned that his technicians might begin encountering devices such as thermostats and lighting controls that are connected to the Internet or that include computerized components (such as an automobile's onboard diagnostics system). Using your favorite search engine or your school's library, identify at least one such device that is currently sold or likely to be sold soon and write two or three paragraphs about what technology Quick Fix technicians will need to deal with it.

Note: Your instructor might assign you to a group to complete this case and might ask you to prepare a formal presentation of your results to your class.

For Further Study and Research

Bergman, M. 2001. *The Deep Web: Surfacing Hidden Value*. Sioux Falls, SD: BrightPlanet.com. http://brightplanet.com/technology/deepweb.asp

Bonson, E., V. Cortijo, and T. Escobar. 2009. "Toward the Global Adoption of XBRL Using International Financial Reporting Standards (IFRS)," *International Journal of Accounting Information Systems*, 10(1), March, 46–60.

Buckler, C. 2011. "HTML5 Completion Date Announced," *Sitepoint*, February 16. http://www .sitepoint.com/html5-completion-date-announced-by-w3c/

Campbell, T. 1998. "The First E-Mail," *PreText Magazine*, March.

Chester, J. 2006. "The End of the Internet?" *The Nation*, February 1. http://www.thenation.com/ doc/20060213/chester

Chmielewski, D. 2015. "WebTV Founder's Super-Fast Wireless Network to Launch in San Francisco," *re/code*, February 23. http://recode.net/2015/02/23/ webtv-founders-super-fast-wireless-network-to-launch-in-sf/

China Internet Network Information Center (CINIC). 2015. *Statistical Report on Internet Development in China*. Beijing: CINIC.

Davidson, N. 2015. "Global Internet: Google's Project Loon," *Popular Science*, April, 42–43.

Dominque, J., D. Fensel, and J. Hendler. 2011. *Handbook of Semantic Web Technologies*. London: Springer.

Dooley, M. and T. Rooney. 2013. *IPv6 Deployment and Management*. Hoboken, NJ: Wiley.

Dyck, T. 2002. "Going Native: XML Databases," *PC Magazine*, 21(12), June 30, 136–139.

The Economist, 2008. "India: 3G at Last," *The Economist Intelligence Unit Country Monitor*, 16(28), July 28, 1.

EContent. 2009. "XML for the Masses," 32(3), April, 45.

Goldfarb, C. 1981. "A Generalized Approach to Document Markup," *ACM Sigplan Notices*, (16)6, June, 68–73.

Gompa, N. 2013. "IPv6 Makes Mobile Networks Faster," *PC Magazine*, March 20, 6.

Hardy, Q. 2015. "Tim O'Reilly Explains the Internet of Things," *The New York Times*, February 4. http://bits.blogs.nytimes.com/2015/02/04/tim-oreilly-explains-the-internet-of-things/

Hawn, C. 2001. "Management By Stock Market: NorthPoint Rode the Web Wave," *Forbes*, 167(10), April 30, 52–53.

Internet Society. 2011. "World IPv6 Day." http://www.worldipv6day.org/

Jeffrey, R. and A. Doron. 2013. *The Great Indian Phone Book: How Cheap Mobile Phones Change Business*. Cambridge, MA: Harvard University Press.

Kerravala, Z. 2014. "Ten Enterprise Internet of Things Deployments With Actual Results," *Network World*, November 17. http://www.networkworld.com/article/2848714/cisco-subnet/10-enterprise-internet-of-things-deployments-with-actual-results.html

Kumaravel, K. 2011. "Comparative Study of 3G and 4G in Mobile Technology," *International Journal of Computer Science Issues*, 8(5), September, 256–263.

Lawson, L. 2013. "Why CIOs Need to Prepare for Big Data from Internet of Things," *IT Business Edge*, August 22. http://www.itbusinessedge.com/blogs/integration/why-cios-need-to-prepare-for-big-data-from-internet-of-things.html

Lawton, C. 2009. "Making the Connection," *The Wall Street Journal*, April 20, R4.

Lawton, G. 2011. "4G: Engineering Versus Marketing," *IEEE Computer*, 44(3), March, 14–16.

Lendino, J. 2015. "What is 802.11ac WiFi, and How Much Faster Than 801.11n Is It? *ExtemeTech*, April 20. http://www.extremetech.com/computing/160837-what-is-802-11ac-and-how-much-faster-than-802-11n-is-it

Liebman, L. 2001. "XML's Tower Of Babel," *InternetWeek*, April 30, 25–26.

Luckerson, V. 2015. "Google's Nuttiest Project Is Making Big Progress," *Time*, May 29. http://time.com/3902045/googles-project-loon/

Markelevich, A. and T. Riley. 2013. "Embracing and Integrating XBRL," *The CPA Journal*, 83(6), 70–72.

McMillan, R. 2013. "How the Large Hadron Collider Will Bring the Internet to Everything," *Wired*, June 21. http://www.wired.com/wiredenterprise/2013/06/open-garden/

Metz, C. 2015. "This Guy Is Creating an All-New Cell Network Built by You," *Wired*, March 6. http://www.wired.com/2015/03/perlman/

Nelson, T. 1987. *Literary Machines*. Swarthmore, PA: Nelson.

Newman, D. 2014. "The Future of Marketing Is Semantic: Search Predicts The Future," *Forbes*, August 12. http://www.forbes.com/sites/danielnewman/2014/08/12/the-future-of-marketing-is-semantic-search-predicts-the-future-part-3/

Nielsen, J. 2009. "Mobile Usability," *Alertbox*, July 20. http://www.useit.com/alertbox/mobile-usability.html

Panko, R. and J. Panko. 2015. *Business Data Networks and Telecommunications*. Tenth Edition. Upper Saddle River, NJ: Prentice Hall.

Perlman, S. and A. Forenza. 2015. *pCell: Wireless Reinvented*. San Francisco: Artemis Networks.

Recker, K. 2014. "Search Today and Beyond: Optimizing for the Semantic Web," *Wired*, February. http://www.wired.com/2014/02/search-today-beyond-optimizing-semantic-web/

Rodenbaugh, M. 2009. "Abusive Domain Registrations: ICANN Policy Developments (or Lack Thereof?)," *Computer & Internet Lawyer*, 26(5), May, 17–22.

Shadbolt, N., T. Berners-Lee, and W. Hall. 2006. "The Semantic Web Revisited," *IEEE Intelligent Systems*, 21(3), 96–101.

Singh, S. 2013. "With Growing Internet Penetration and Data Usage, India Is Facebook's New Lab," *The Economic Times*, July 30, 3.

Stansbury, M. 2015. "How Three Prominent Universities Are Becoming Video Trailblazers," *eCampus News*, May 1. http://www.ecampusnews.com/technologies/university-video-internet2-281/

Steele, B. 2015. "Google's Project Loon Improves Launch and Range to Expand Its Reach," *Engadget*, May 29. http://www.engadget.com/2015/05/29/google-project-loon-launcher-range-boost/

Strategic Finance. 2009. "XBRL Reporting Is Now Mandatory," 90(7), January, 61.

Telecommunications Reports. 2011. "ICANN Approves Expansion of gTLDs," 77(13), July 1, 22.

Thurm, S. 2002. "Cisco Profit Exceeds Expectations," *The Wall Street Journal*, May 8, A3.

Tech Media Network. 2013. *Top Ten Reviews: Satellite Internet*. New York: Tech Media Network. http://satellite-internet-review.toptenreviews.com/

Tribunella, T. and H. Tribunella. 2010. "Using XBRL to Analyze Financial Statements," *The CPA Journal*, 80(3), 69–72.

Violino, B. 2013. "The 'Internet of Things' Will Mean Really, Really Big Data," *InfoWorld*, July 29. http://www.infoworld.com/d/big-data/the-internet-of-things-will-mean-really-really-big-data-223314

Weinberger, D. 2009. "The Dream of the Semantic Web," *KM World*, 18(3), March, 1–3.

White, C. 2011. *Data Communications and Computer Networks: A Business User's Approach*. 6th Edition. Cincinnati: South-Western.

Wood, G. 2011. "IPv6: Making Room for the World on the Future Internet," *IEEE Internet Computing*, 15(4), July–August, 88–89.

Yoo, S., Y. Kim, and S. Park. 2013. "An Educational Tool for Browsing the Semantic Web," *Informatics in Education*, 12(1), 143–151.

Zhang, Z., G. Dong, Z. Peng, and Z. Yan. 2011. "A Framework for Incremental Deep Web Crawler Based on URL Classification," *Lecture Notes in Computer Science*, 6988, 302–310.

Zhu, H. and H. Wu. 2011. "Interoperability of XBRL Financial Statements in the U.S," *International Journal of E-Business Research*, 7(2), April–June, 19–33.

PART 2

Business Strategies for Electronic Commerce

Blend Images Photography/Veer

Chapter 3

Selling on the Web

LEARNING OBJECTIVES

In this chapter, you will learn:

- What a revenue model is and how companies use various revenue models online
- Which characteristics identify specific revenue models
- How some companies experiment with alternative revenue models to achieve success
- About revenue strategy choices that companies face when selling online
- How to create an effective business presence on the Web
- What factors enhance Web site usability
- How companies use the Web to connect with customers

INTRODUCTION

People have always liked to take pictures. With cameras now built into almost every mobile phone sold in the world, it is easy for almost everyone to take a great number of photos and videos. They not only capture important family events such as birthdays and weddings but also take pictures of mundane things. Many people find that their smartphones become packed with photos and videos that they would hate to lose if something happened to their phone. Some people even find that they run out of storage space on their phone.

Given this demand, the business of offering storage services for these photos and videos has become an ideal online business, especially with the continually decreasing cost of storage space and high-bandwidth Internet connections. Indeed, a number of businesses do offer free or low-cost versions of these services, including Amazon (as part of its Prime subscription), Dropbox, OneDrive, and Yahoo!'s Flickr (which is supported by selling advertising, a revenue strategy about which you will learn in this chapter). However, all of the firms in this business face similar costs; that is, digital storage and high-bandwidth Internet connections are commodities, so it is difficult for any one of them to compete as the lowest-cost provider. Success in online photo storage will thus likely go to the company that can provide the most effective, easy-to-use, and intuitive interface along with tools to manage customers' ever-larger photo collections. That is, the competition will be on features, not cost.

In 2015, Google launched a photo storage service called **Google Photos** that it designed to provide the features most users want in this type of service. Although every one of its competitors has tried to do the same thing, Google's developers combined the company's technical capabilities with research on how customers interact with technology (an approach you will learn about in this chapter). They also knew that most people who take photos do not have time to organize them in any way.

Google's technology includes a collection of software tools that can analyze image data and detect meaning in the elements of images (you learned about the general nature of this semantics research in Chapter 1). By using these software tools to analyze collections of meanings about each photo, Google computers can place photos into categories. This semantic detection process is not perfect, but it does a good job of identifying objects in photos and sorting them into groups that include common or related objects. Many photos are tagged with geographic location coordinates when they are taken, and this information can also be used in category identification.

By itself, the technology could do a good job of categorizing photos, especially using faces it identified as similar. But the development team also interviewed a large number of potential customers and asked them to describe the last 10 photos they had taken. They found that most people describe their photos using four categories: what people are in the photo, where the photo was taken, what objects are in the photo, and what are its characteristics (photo or video, portrait or landscape orientation, and so on).

By combining their technology with the information they gathered from potential customers, the development team could enable the service to organize photos into categories automatically.

In this chapter you will learn how companies choose revenue models and use their knowledge of customer needs to build useful experiences into their online business designs that will attract and keep those customers.

Revenue Models for Online Business

As you learned in Chapter 1, a useful way to think about electronic commerce implementations is to consider the various strategies that can be used to generate revenue, which are called revenue models. Not all electronic commerce initiatives have the goal of providing revenue; some are undertaken to reduce costs or improve customer service. You will learn about those types of initiatives in Chapter 5. In this chapter, you will learn about various models that online businesses currently use to generate revenue, including Web catalog, digital content, advertising-supported, advertising-subscription mixed, and fee-based models.

These approaches can work for both business-to-consumer (B2C) and business-to-business (B2B) electronic commerce. Many companies create one Web site to handle both B2C and B2B sales. Even when companies create separate sites (or separate pages within one site), they often use the same revenue model for both types of sales.

Web Catalog Revenue Models

Many companies sell goods and services on the Web using an adaptation of a revenue model that is more than 100 years old. In 1872, a traveling salesman named Aaron Montgomery Ward started selling dry goods to farmers through a one-page list. Richard Sears and Alvah Roebuck began mailing catalogs to farmers and small-town residents in 1895. Both Montgomery Ward and Sears, Roebuck & Company grew to become dominant retailers in the United States by the 1950s, with retail stores serving urban markets and the catalog business well established in serving rural and small-town markets. The general acceptance of the mail order catalog business built a solid base for the Web-based version that would evolve from it in the 1990s.

In the traditional catalog-based retail revenue model, the seller establishes a brand image, and then uses the strength of that image to sell through printed information mailed to prospective buyers, who place orders by mail or telephone. For more than a century, this revenue model, called the **mail-order** or **catalog model**, has been successful for a wide variety of consumer items, including apparel, computers, electronics, housewares, and gifts. Other companies that succeeded as mail-order businesses in the twentieth century include J.C. Penney, L.L. Bean, and Hickory Farms.

Many companies have adapted this revenue model to the online world by replacing or supplementing their print catalogs with information on their Web sites. This revenue model is called the **Web catalog revenue model**. Most customers today place orders through the Web site, but in the early years of electronic commerce, many shoppers used the Web to obtain information about products and compare prices and features, and then made their purchases by telephone. Types of retail businesses that use the Web catalog revenue model include sellers of computers, consumer electronics, books, music, videos, jewelry, clothing, flowers, and gifts. Many general merchandisers also use the Web catalog revenue model. B2B sellers have also been avid adopters of the Web catalog model. Items such as tools, electrical and plumbing parts, and every imaginable industrial supply item from sandpaper to valve gaskets are now offered for sale online.

Many of the most successful online businesses using the Web catalog revenue model are firms that were already operating in the mail-order business and simply extended their operations to the Web. Other companies that use the Web catalog revenue model adopted it after realizing that the products they sold in their physical stores could also be sold on the Web. This additional sales outlet did not require them to build additional stores, yet provided access to new customers throughout the world.

DISCOUNT RETAILERS: GETTING A GREAT DEAL ONLINE

In the first wave of electronic commerce, a number of new discounters, such as Buy.com (now **Rakuten**), began their first retail operations online using the Web catalog revenue model. Borrowing the low-cost strategy used by traditional discount retailers (such as Costco, Kmart, and Walmart), these online businesses sell merchandise at extremely low prices. Most traditional discount retailers were reluctant to implement online sales at that time because they had huge investments in their physical stores, were making large amounts of sales in those stores, and did not really understand the world of online retailing. During the second wave of electronic commerce, however, these traditional discounters also adopted the Web catalog revenue model for their online sales efforts. They did encounter some false starts and learning challenges, but all eventually found online sales to be an important contributor to their overall revenues and profits.

USING MULTIPLE MARKETING CHANNELS

Having more than one way to reach customers is often a good idea for companies, as Montgomery Ward and Sears found out many years ago. They used one channel (retail

LEARNING FROM FAILURES

Walmart.com

Walmart is the world's largest retailer, with thousands of stores and annual sales exceeding $470 billion. Founded in 1962 by retailing legend Sam Walton, the company has won numerous awards for business innovation. However, Walmart's moves into online retailing have been troubled.

Walmart launched its first Web site in July 1996. Like most company sites of that time, it contained some information about the company, but did not offer any products for sale. Walmart did little to develop the Web site over the next three years, but it did add a Web store—just in time to participate in the disastrous 1999 holiday shopping season. Walmart was not the only Web retailer to have trouble in 1999. Many companies found that they were ill prepared for the large number of customers who decided to try electronic commerce in that year's holiday season. Lost orders, unfilled orders, and shipments that failed to arrive until January 2000 were common for many Web retailers that year. Walmart was noted as an industry leader in shipping and logistics management; however, the announcement on its Web site that it could not promise Christmas delivery for items ordered after December 14 was particularly embarrassing. To make matters worse, Walmart was in the middle of developing a new Web site that it had hoped to launch before the holiday season. The project, which industry analysts estimate cost more than $100 million, ran months late and did not operate until January 2000.

After eight months of operating the new Web site, Walmart found itself with low levels of customer traffic (well below those of its major rivals) and high levels of criticism from Web site design experts who found the site slow, difficult to use, and lacking customer service features. In October 2000, Walmart closed the site completely for four weeks.

Earlier in the year, it had created Walmart.com, a joint venture with Accel Partners to develop a new Web site, but the new site was not ready to launch until November. Industry analysts widely criticized Walmart's decision to completely shut down its Web operations for such a long time period at the beginning of the holiday shopping season.

The new Web site was a vast improvement with better organization and improved search functions. Although the new site offered about the same number of items as the previous site (about 500,000 items, a physical Walmart store at the time carried about 100,000 items), the newer site had more consumer electronics, toys, and sporting goods and far fewer consumable products. Walmart also created a separate distribution center for online sales fulfillment rather than continuing to make the distribution network designed to supply the physical stores do double duty.

A decade later, Walmart's online operations were once again in the news. In 2011, industry analysts estimated that Walmart.com was the sixth-largest online retailer in North America and noted that this was not a particularly impressive showing for the world's largest retailer. Later that year, the company announced that it was ending sales of music downloads after failing to compete successfully against Apple's iTunes store and that two of its top online executives were leaving the company. In the wake of these developments, Walmart announced a major reorganization of its online operations in North America, the United Kingdom, and Japan to

(Continued)

(Continued)

better integrate online and physical store operations. Online business managers would now report to retail operations directors in each country rather than to a global e-commerce director.

Walmart's experience is a testament to how difficult it can be to get Web retailing right. Success eluded the largest retailer in the world for years. Walmart is estimated to have spent hundreds of millions of dollars over 16 years on various Web implementations and product distribution strategies since it began selling online and many industry observers believe the company has not yet reached its full potential.

stores) to reach urban customers and another channel (mail order catalog) to reach rural customers. Each different pathway to customers is called a **marketing channel**.

Companies find that having several marketing channels lets them reach more customers at less cost. For example, it is expensive to stock a large number of different items in a physical store, so a company such as Best Buy will stock the most popular items in its stores but will sell a wider variety of items (including those that are not in high demand at every one of its retail locations) on its Web site. Customers who want to have physical contact with a product (putting fingers on a laptop computer's keyboard, for example) before buying can visit the retail location. A customer who wants a high-end and expensive home theater system can find it on the Web site. By having two marketing channels (retail store and Web site), Best Buy reaches more customers and offers more products than it could by using either channel alone. Like many other retailers, Home Depot encourages online sales by offering an option to have online orders shipped free to a nearby physical store location for the customer to pick up. This is an especially attractive option for large or heavy items.

Some retailers, such as Talbots, combine the benefits of these two marketing channels by offering in-store online ordering. This allows customers to examine a product in the store, and then find their exact size or the color they like by placing an order on the retailer's Web site from the store.

Similarly, a retailer that mails print catalogs might include a product's general description and photo in the catalog, but refer customers to the retailer's Web site for detailed specifications or more information about the product. Mailed catalogs (or newspaper advertising inserts) continue to be an effective marketing tool because they inform customers of products they might not otherwise know about. The catalog arrives in the mail (or the newspaper insert arrives with the newspaper) to inform them. In contrast, a Web site only delivers the marketing message if the customer visits the Web site.

Using multiple marketing channels to reach the same set of customers can be an effective strategy for retailers. Figure 3-1 shows two examples (there are many other possibilities) of how retailers might combine two marketing channels.

ADDING THE PERSONAL TOUCH

A number of apparel sellers have adapted their catalog sales model to the Web. These Web stores display photos of casual and business clothing categorized by style and described

Retailer with physical stores and Web site

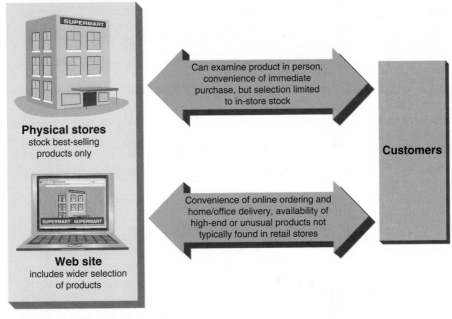

Physical stores
stock best-selling products only

Can examine product in person, convenience of immediate purchase, but selection limited to in-store stock

Customers

Web site
includes wider selection of products

Convenience of online ordering and home/office delivery, availability of high-end or unusual products not typically found in retail stores

Retailer with mailed catalogs and Web site

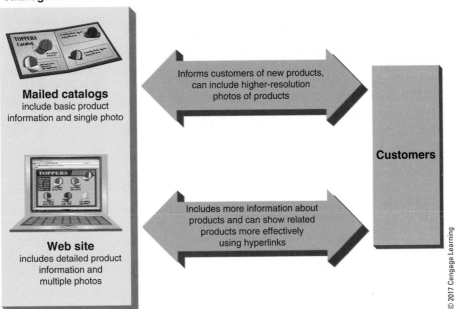

Mailed catalogs
include basic product information and single photo

Informs customers of new products, can include higher-resolution photos of products

Customers

Web site
includes detailed product information and multiple photos

Includes more information about products and can show related products more effectively using hyperlinks

FIGURE 3-1   Combining marketing channels: two retailer examples

with prices, sizes, colors, and tailoring details. Their intent is to have customers examine the clothing and place orders through the Web site. Lands' End pioneered the idea of online Web shopping assistance with its Lands' End Live feature in 1999. Today, many Web sites offer a chat feature that is activated by the Web site visitor clicking a button on the Web page. Many sites activate a chat window when a visitor remains on a particular Web page longer than a certain time interval. These chat windows simulate the experience of having a helpful salesperson approach the customer in a physical retail store. In addition to text chat, some online retailers use video to communicate with customers who have Webcams attached to or built into their computers. Some online stores include a feature that lets two shoppers browse the Web site together from different computers.

Many online clothing retailers offer personal shopper and virtual model features. The **personal shopper** is an intelligent agent program that learns the customer's preferences and makes suggestions. The **virtual model** is a graphic image built from customer measurements and descriptions on which customers can try clothes. Some retailers report that the dollar amount of orders placed by customers who use the virtual model is significantly higher than other orders. The Canadian company that developed this Web site feature, My Virtual Model, has sold the technology to a number of other clothing retailers. The increase in sales and the decrease in returns on Web sites that use these services, generally called **virtual fitting rooms**, is so dramatic that a number of other companies now offer similar services that include, in some cases, body scans performed at a physical location.

One problem that the Web presents for clothing retailers of all types is that the color settings on computer monitors vary widely. It is difficult for customers to get an accurate idea of what the product's color will look like when it arrives. Most online clothing stores will send a fabric swatch on request. The swatch also gives the customer a sense of the fabric's texture—an added benefit not provided by catalogs. Many Web catalog retailers also have generous return policies that allow customers to return unused merchandise for any reason. One company that used its return policy as a competitive advantage is online shoe retailer Zappos (now owned by Amazon). Recognizing that shoe styles and fit can be difficult to evaluate online, Zappos distinguished itself from its competitors by offering fast delivery and free returns.

Fee-for-Content Revenue Models

Firms that own written information (words or numbers) or rights to that information have embraced the Web as a highly efficient distribution mechanism. Many of these companies use a **digital content revenue model**; that is, they sell rights to access the information they own. Many companies sell subscriptions that give customers the right to access all or a specified part of the information; others sell the right to access individual items. A number of companies combine these two approaches and sell both subscriptions and individual access rights.

LEGAL, ACADEMIC, BUSINESS, AND TECHNICAL CONTENT

Many digital content providers specialize in legal, academic research, business, or technical material; however, all types of content are now available online. Whether you are an engineer who needs to find out if an idea you have has already been patented by someone else or a physician checking on a potential prescription interaction, you can find an appropriate digital content provider online. For example, LexisNexis offers a variety of information services for lawyers and law enforcement officials that include laws, regulations, court case decisions, public records, and legal treatises. In the past, law firms had to subscribe to and install expensive dedicated computer systems to obtain access to this information, but the Web has given LexisNexis customers much more flexibility in how they access their subscriptions.

Many academic and professional organizations, such as the American Psychological Association and the Association for Computing Machinery, sell subscriptions to their journals online. Academic publishing has always been a difficult business in which to make a profit because the base of potential subscribers is so small. Even highly regarded academic journals might have fewer than 2000 subscribers, most of which are university libraries. To cover their costs, academic journals must often charge each subscriber hundreds or even thousands of dollars per year. Publishing online eliminates the high costs of paper, printing, and delivery, and makes dissemination of research results less expensive and more timely. Some academic publishers are experimenting with new revenue models, including letting authors pay a fee to make their research available free online to readers. Academic information aggregation services, such as ProQuest Dialog and EBSCO Information Services, purchase the rights to academic journals, newspapers, and other publications and resell those rights in various subscription packages to schools, libraries, companies, and not-for-profit institutions.

Not all technical content is business related, and the Web provides a way for technical content developers to reach retail customers. For example, persons who do scrapbooking, knitting, sewing, and other craft activities can purchase and download digital files for patterns, fonts, stock photos, and electronic files that can control hobbyist machines (die-cutting, sewing, knitting, or quilting).

ELECTRONIC BOOKS

Another type of digital content sold online is the electronic book. Companies such as Audible and Books-on-Tape (now both owned by Amazon) sold audio editions of books for many years, first as cassette tapes, then as CDs. Today, electronic books (that can be read or listened to) are available for dedicated devices such as Amazon's Kindle products. Electronic books are also sold as digital content by online stores such as Apple's iTunes and Google Play alongside digital music and video offerings. Electronic books sold for the physical readers can also be displayed on smartphone and tablet device apps as well as on computers using the appropriate book reader software.

Sales of electronic books grew rapidly in the first few years in which physical readers were available; for example, Amazon announced in 2011 it was selling more electronic books than paper books. However, there are some signs that electronic book sales growth has slowed. Estimates for 2015 suggest that U.S. electronic books make up about 23 percent of total book sales and that proportion might plateau in a few years and stabilize at about 25 percent. Outside the United States, however, inexpensive electronic books might become widely distributed through apps on mobile phones in the future, something that is now popular in India. Many industry experts note that electronic books serve some purposes well (frequent recreational reading) but not others (reference books) and thus, physical books and electronic books will likely coexist for many years to come.

An interesting example of how electronic books can be more flexible than print editions is the Amazon Kindle Singles product line, which publishes original works of between 5000 and 30,000 words that generally sell for one to three dollars. In the past, short stories were a staple of various print magazines, but many of those magazines have reduced length of stories they publish or have gone out of business. This reduced the number of outlets for budding fiction writers, many of whom develop their skills by writing short stories before moving on to full-length novels. Amazon Singles Kindle Editions provide an entire new online distribution channel for this type of work.

ONLINE MUSIC

The recording industry was slow to embrace online distribution of music because audio files are digital products that can be easily copied once purchased. Following a period of years during which audio files were illegally shared among thousands of users, much of the recording industry finally stopped resisting digital sales of audio files. Starting around 2006, the major recording companies began to identify ways they could capture some of the market for music files by selling their audio tracks online.

The largest online music stores today include Amazon MP3, Apple's iTunes, and Google Play. These sites sell single songs (tracks) for about a dollar each and sell albums at various prices (most are between $5 and $12). Other companies, such as Pandora, Spotify, and Rhapsody offer subscription services that stream music to devices for a monthly fee rather than charging for specific songs or albums. To introduce potential customers to their services, some of these companies offer free, advertising-supported, limited versions of their subscriptions.

The early development of the online music market was complicated because no single store offered all of the music that is available in digital format and because many of the stores tried to promote their own music file formats. Artists and recording companies sometimes only offered their music through one store and some refused to offer their music online at all. By promoting their own file formats, sellers tried to encourage music consumers to use one store exclusively. Some online music sellers required buyers to download and install software, called **Digital Rights Management (DRM)** software, that limited the number of copies that could be made of each audio file.

In 2007, the Amazon MP3 store was the first major online retailer to offer music tracks from several major recording companies in DRM-free MP3 format. Since then, most other online music companies have come to offer their music in DRM-free, compatible file formats as well. After years of suffering declines due to illegal copying, the music industry in 2013 reported that sales of recorded music had increased for the first time in 14 years. In 2014, global sales of recorded music totaled $15 billion, still substantially below the 1999 peak of $38 billion. The proportion of these sales that were digital and physical (CDs, vinyl records) were about the same, with royalties paid for performances and by online subscription services contributing a much smaller share, as shown in Figure 3-2.

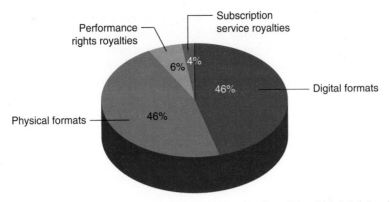

Source: International Federation of the Phonographic Industry, http://www.ifpi.org/global-statistics.php

FIGURE 3-2   Global recorded music sales, 2014

ONLINE VIDEO

Digital video can be sold or rented online as either a file download or as a streaming video. DRM software provides control over the number of copies that can be made of the downloaded video, the devices on which the video can be installed, and restrictions on how long the video remains available for watching. Videos offered for sale online include previously released movies, television shows, and programming that is developed specifically for the online market. In the past, video sales were limited by three main issues: the large size of video files (which can make download times long and streaming feeds uneven), concern that such sales would limit other sales of the video, and technological barriers that prevented downloaded videos from being played on a variety of devices. Online businesses have been working to overcome these issues and have had success in addressing all three issues.

First, videos are still the largest types of files that are regularly transmitted on the Internet, but companies are continually experimenting with technologies that improve the delivery of large files and video streams. You will learn more about these content delivery enhancement technologies, pioneered by companies such as Akamai, Amazon, and Google, in Chapter 8.

Second, the companies that produce media are learning more about how online distribution fits into their overall revenue strategy. Movies were released traditionally by the major Hollywood studios (20th Century Fox, Paramount, Sony, Walt Disney, Warner Brothers, and Universal) into different markets in a well-defined pattern. Movies were first distributed to theaters, which paid a high price for the right to show the movie first. After its initial theater run, the movie might then have been sold to airlines for in-flight showings and to premium cable channels such as HBO or Starz. Next, the movie was released on DVD and became available for purchase or rental through retail video stores. Eventually, the movie was sold to broadcast television stations and basic cable channels. This serial release pattern was designed to provide the movie's creators with the highest revenue obtainable at each point in the life of the product. The major studios released movies in this pattern for years, out of fear that any online distribution might steal sales away from one of their traditional outlets. These media producers now are experimenting with alternative distribution strategies. Some are now releasing movies online and on DVD simultaneously. As the number of online content distributors that charge either a subscription or a per-view fee for movies increases, media producers will be more amenable to releasing their product online because they know they will get paid for it.

Finally, video delivery technologies are becoming more transparent. For example, HTML 5 allows the delivery of movies through a standard Web browser without requiring plug-ins or external software. The availability of Web browsers on devices other than computers (for example, smartphones, tablet devices, and television sets) has reduced concerns about technology barriers to video delivery on multiple devices.

Amazon sells the right to view movies and television shows on its Web site. Netflix offers online subscription access to television shows, movies, and original content either separately or as part of its DVD rental plan. Crackle, an online video provider launched by Sony in 2007, offers television shows, movies, and original content supported by advertising, just as the traditional television networks have for decades. Apple's iTunes service includes video offerings for rent or purchase in addition to many free video downloads. Three of the major U.S. broadcast networks (ABC, Fox, and NBC) formed a joint venture to operate Hulu, which offers video clips of popular television programs and movies. Hulu offers much of its content free (using an advertising-supported revenue model) but also offers a monthly subscription, which makes premium content available. The other major U.S. broadcast network, CBS, operates TV.com, which offers free selected CBS-owned content, using an advertising-supported revenue model.

Premium cable channel providers such as HBO and Showtime offer online access to their content for customers who have subscriptions to their services through their local cable company. In 2015, HBO added a separate online service available by subscription to customers who do not subscribe through their local cable provider.

Google's YouTube has become a leading source of free videos on the Web. These videos are often used to show trailers and other promotional clips for movies, television shows, and live performances that are sold elsewhere online, through network or cable television outlets, or in theaters. Some entertainers, such as comedian Louis CK, are selling performance videos to fans online in addition to using online video as a promotional device.

Advertising as a Revenue Model Element

Instead of charging a fee or subscription for content, many online businesses display advertising on their Web sites. The fees they charge advertisers are used to support the operation of the Web site and pay for the development or purchase of its content. Some sites rely entirely on advertising for their revenue; others use it only to provide part of their revenue. In this section, you will learn how advertising revenue is incorporated into the revenue models of various content-providing online businesses.

ADVERTISING-SUPPORTED REVENUE MODELS

The **advertising-supported revenue model** is the one used by broadcast network television in the United States. Broadcasters provide free programming to an audience along with advertising messages. The advertising revenue is sufficient to support the operations of the network and the creation or purchase of the programs. On the Web, advertising revenue has increased steadily since the mid-1990s. As you will learn in Chapter 4, online advertising is now well established as an important component of the advertising mix used by businesses of all types. This growth has enabled more and more Web sites to use it as a revenue source, either alone or in combination with other revenue sources.

The use of online advertising as the sole revenue source for a Web site has faced two major challenges. First, there has been little consensus on how to measure and charge for site visitor views, even after almost 20 years of experience with the medium. Because Web sites can take multiple measurements, such as number of visitors, number of unique visitors, number of click-throughs, and can measure other attributes of visitor behavior, Web advertisers have struggled to develop standards for advertising charges. In addition to the number of visitors or page views, stickiness is a critical element in creating a presence that attracts advertisers. The **stickiness** of a Web site is its ability to keep visitors at the site and attract repeat visitors. People spend more time at a **sticky** Web site and are thus exposed to more advertising.

The second issue is that very few Web sites have sufficiently large numbers of visitors to compete with mass media outlets such as radio or television. Although a few Web sites have succeeded in attracting the large general audience that major advertisers have traditionally wanted to reach, most successful advertising on the Web is targeted at specific groups. The set of characteristics that marketers use to group visitors is called **demographic information** and includes things such as address, age, gender, income level, type of job held, hobbies, and religion. It can be difficult to determine whether a given Web site is attracting a specific market segment unless that site collects demographic information from its visitors—information that visitors often are reluctant to provide because of privacy concerns.

One solution to this second problem has been found by an increasing number of specialized information Web sites. These sites are successful in using an advertising-supported revenue model because they draw a specialized audience that certain advertisers want to reach. These sites do not need to gather demographic information from their visitors because anyone drawn to the site will have the specific set of interests that makes them a prized target for certain advertisers. In most cases, advertisers will pay high enough rates to support the operation of the site and in some cases, the advertising revenue is large enough to make these sites quite profitable.

Two examples of successful advertising-supported sites that appeal to audiences with specific interests are The Huffington Post and the Drudge Report. Each of these Web sites appeals to people who are interested in politics (liberal and conservative, respectively). Advertisers that want to target an audience with a specific political interest are willing to pay rates that are high enough to make these sites profitable enterprises. Online news sites that focus their coverage on a particular town or metropolitan area can use the advertising-supported revenue model successfully. Companies that want to reach potential customers in that area would find such sites to be useful for targeted marketing, since the Web sites would draw visitors with a specific interest in the geographic area.

Similarly, **HowStuffWorks** is a Web site that explains, as the name suggests, how things work. Each set of Web pages in the site attracts visitors with a highly focused interest. For example, a visitor looking for an explanation of how heating stoves work would be a good prospect for advertisers that sell heating stoves. HowStuffWorks does not need to obtain any specific information from its visitors; the fact that visitors are viewing the heating stoves information page is enough justification for charging heating stove companies a higher rate for ads on those pages. HowStuffWorks has a collection of pages that appeal to an array of visitors with highly focused interests. Thus, it is an attractive online advertising option for a wide variety of companies because the site has a collection of pages on a broad range of very specific products and processes that would be attractive to a variety of consumers, each of whom has a highly focused interest in one or more of them.

These three strategies—general interest, specific interest, and collection of specific interests—for implementing an advertising-supported revenue model are summarized in Figure 3-3.

Some companies have been successful using the general interest strategy shown in Figure 3-3 by operating a Web portal. A **portal** or **Web portal** is a site that people use as a launching point to enter the Web (the word "portal" means "doorway"). A portal almost always includes a Web directory or search engine, but it can also include other features that help visitors find what they are looking for on the Web such as shopping directories,

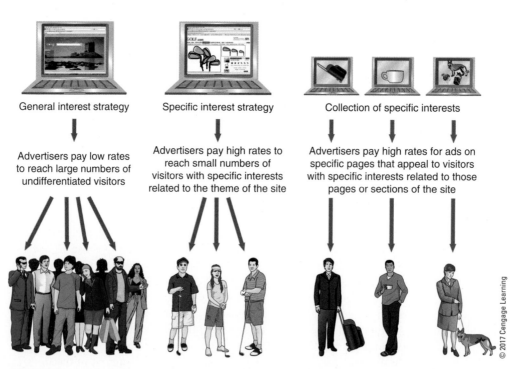

FIGURE 3-3   Three strategies for an advertising-supported revenue model

© 2017 Cengage Learning

free e-mail, chat rooms, file and photo storage services, games, messaging tools, and calendar tools.

One of the leading Web portal sites is **Yahoo!**, which was one of the first Web directories. A **Web directory** is a listing of hyperlinks to Web pages. Because the Yahoo! portal's search engine presents visitors' search results on separate pages, it can include advertising on each results page that is triggered by the terms in the search. For example, when the Yahoo! search engine detects that a visitor has searched on the term *new car deals*, it can place a Ford ad at the top of the search results page. Ford is willing to pay more for this ad because it is directed only at visitors who have expressed interest in new cars. Besides Yahoo!, portal sites that use the general interest strategy today include **Google** and **Bing**. Smaller general interest sites, such as the Web directory **refdesk.com**, have had more difficulty attracting advertisers than the larger sites.

Not all portals use a general interest strategy. Instead, they focus on helping site visitors find information within a specific knowledge domain. For example, technology portal **C-NET** is devoted to technology products and includes reviews of specific technologies and related products. Advertisers pay more to have their ad appear near a discussion of a technology related to their product or on a page that reviews the product.

Travel portals such as **Kayak** have also been successful as advertising-supported online businesses. The Kayak site allows visitors to specify travel dates and destinations, and then searches multiple sites to find the best airfares, car rentals, and hotel rooms. It searches provider sites such as those of the airlines, hotels, and car rental companies, but it also searches sites that consolidate travel products and sell them at reduced prices. Kayak benefits its visitors by saving them the trouble of visiting multiple sites to find the best travel deals. And it sells targeted advertising space to companies that want to reach travelers with near-term travel plans.

ADVERTISING-SUPPORTED NEWSPAPERS

Many newspapers and magazines publish all or part of their print content on the Web. They sell advertising to cover the costs of converting their print content to an online format and operating the Web site. Some publications, such as local shopping news and alternative press newspapers, have always been fully supported by advertising revenues and are distributed at retail locations and newsstands without charge. Many of these publications have made an easy transition to an advertising-supported revenue model. A number of small-town weekly newspapers have always used a pure advertising-supported revenue model, and many that have not are now moving in that direction. Most newspapers and magazines, however, have relied on subscription and newsstand revenue to supplement their advertising revenue. These publications have had a more difficult time in making their online editions generate sufficient advertising revenue to support their full operations.

Although a Web site can provide greater exposure for a newspaper's name and a larger audience for advertising that it carries, an online edition also can divert sales from the print edition. Like retailers or distributors whose online sales lead to the loss of their brick-and-mortar sales, publishers also experience sales losses as a result of online distribution. Newspapers and other publishers worry about these sales losses because they are very difficult to measure.

Many publishers continue to experiment with various other ways of generating revenue from their Web sites. There is no consensus among media industry analysts regarding whether a pure advertising-supported revenue strategy can work for newspapers or magazines in the long run.

One mixed revenue model for newspapers provides some content at no cost but charges a fee for other content. Newspapers (and other Web sites that offer valuable content) can allow visitors to access a limited number of items for free each month and then charge a fee for continued access. This approach, where free content is available up to a point at which fees begin, is called a **paywall** (that is, a visitor can access free content until hitting a wall, and then must pay to pass over that wall). You will learn more about the technologies that are used to create paywalls in Chapter 11. An increasing number of newspaper and other content-providing Web sites are experimenting with various combinations of mixed advertising, subscription, and fee-for-content revenue models, and this experimentation will likely continue into the foreseeable future.

ADVERTISING-SUPPORTED ONLINE CLASSIFIED AD SITES

In the past, newspapers generated a significant percentage of their revenue from their classified advertising pages. You have already learned that targeted advertising can command higher rates than general advertising and newspaper classified advertising was an early form of targeted advertising. Each ad is placed in a specific classification and only readers interested in that type of ad will read that classification. For example, a person looking for an apartment to rent would look in the Rentals classification. The rapid growth of online classified advertising has taken a large amount of revenue from newspapers, replacing them in their historical role as the primary carriers of classified advertising. Sites such as craigslist now carry free classified ads that would once have produced substantial classified advertising revenue for local newspapers. Craigslist and similar sites run most ads for free, only charging for a small proportion of the ads they carry (craigslist charges for job ads, brokered rental ads in New York City, and a few other categories).

The most successful targeted classified advertising category has been Web employment sites. Companies such as CareerBuilder.com offer international distribution of employment ads. These sites offer advertisers access to targeted markets. When a visitor specifies an interest in, for example, engineering jobs in Dallas, the results page can include a targeted ad for which an advertiser will pay more because it is directed at a specific market segment. Other employment ad sites charge both job seekers and employers for ads and access to those ads. Employment ad sites such as Monster.com also target specific categories of job seekers by including short articles on topics of interest. These articles increase the site's stickiness and attract people who are not necessarily looking for a job. This is a good tactic because people who are not looking for a job are often the candidates most highly sought by employers.

Another type of online classified advertising business is the used vehicle site. Trader Publishing has printed advertising newspapers for many years and now operates the AutoTrader.com site. Similar sites accept paid advertising from individuals and companies that want to sell cars, motorcycles, and boats.

ADVERTISING-SUBSCRIPTION MIXED REVENUE MODELS

In an **advertising-subscription mixed revenue model**, which has been used for many years by traditional print newspapers and magazines, subscribers pay a fee, but also accept some level of advertising. On Web sites that use the advertising-subscription mixed revenue model, subscribers are typically subjected to much less advertising than they are on sites supported completely by advertising. Firms have had varying levels of success in applying this mixed revenue model and a number of companies have moved to or from this model as they try to find the best way to generate revenue online.

Two of the world's most widely circulated newspapers, **The New York Times** and **The Wall Street Journal**, have each used an advertising-subscription mixed model since they first took their publications online. *The Wall Street Journal's* mixed model is weighted toward subscription revenue. The site allows nonsubscribing visitors to view the classified ads and certain stories from the newspaper, but most of the content is reserved for subscribers who pay an annual fee for access to the site. Visitors who already subscribe to the print edition are offered a reduced rate on subscriptions to the online edition. As you will learn later in this chapter, *The New York Times* has gone through a number of changes to its revenue model, but for most of its online life it has made considerable portions of its content available at no cost and relied more heavily on advertising than *The Wall Street Journal*.

Most newspapers and magazines that use the advertising-subscription mixed revenue model for their online publications make most of their content available online, but a number of them do restrict the amount of free content as *The Wall Street Journal* does. Figure 3-4 shows the revenue models used by a number of newspapers and magazines, including those that use the advertising-supported model, the advertising-subscription mixed model with substantial content freely available, and the advertising-subscription mixed model with most content available only to subscribers.

Advertising-Supported	Advertising-Subscription Mixed Supported	
Most or All Content Free to All Visitors	**Substantial Content Free to All Visitors**	**Most Content Available Only to Subscribers**
The Boston Globe	BusinessWeek	The Economist
Cleveland Plain Dealer	Chronicle of Higher Education	Foreign Affairs
Financial Times	Forbes	Harvard Business Review
Newsweek	Inc. Magazine	National Geographic
InStyle	The Los Angeles Times	Nature
PC Magazine	The New York Times	Scientific American
San Francisco Chronicle	The Washington Post	Sports Illustrated
Smithsonian		Technology Review
Time		The Times
		The Wall Street Journal

© 2017 Cengage Learning

FIGURE 3-4   Revenue models used by online editions of newspapers and magazines

Sports fans visit the ESPN site for all types of sports-related information. Leveraging its brand name from its cable television businesses, ESPN is one of the most-visited sports sites on the Web. It sells advertising and offers a vast amount of free information, but die-hard fans can subscribe to its Insider service to obtain access to even more sports information. Thus, ESPN uses a mixed model that includes advertising and subscription revenue, but it only collects the subscription revenue from Insider subscribers, who make up a small portion of site visitors.

Consumers Union, the publisher of product evaluations and ratings monthly magazine *Consumer Reports*, operates a Web site, ConsumerReports.org, that relies exclusively on subscriptions (that is, it is a purely subscription-supported site). Consumers Union is a not-for-profit organization that does not accept advertising as a matter of policy because it might appear to influence its research results. Thus, the site is supported by a combination of subscriptions and a small amount of charitable donations. The Web site does offer some free information as a way to attract subscribers and fulfill its organizational mission of encouraging improvements in product safety.

Fee-for-Transaction Revenue Models

In the **fee-for-transaction revenue model**, businesses offer services for which they charge a fee that is based on the number or size of transactions they process. Some of these services, including stock trading and online banking, lend themselves well to operating on the Web. To the extent that companies can offer Web site visitors the information they need about the transaction, companies can offer much of the personal service formerly provided by human agents. If customers are willing to enter transaction information into Web site forms, these sites can provide options and execute transactions much less expensively than traditional transaction service providers. The removal of these traditional service providers is an example of **disintermediation**, which occurs when an intermediary, such as a human agent, is cut from a value chain. The introduction of a new intermediary, such as a fee-for-transaction Web site, into a value chain is called **reintermediation**.

STOCK BROKERAGE FIRMS: TWO ROUNDS OF DISINTERMEDIATION

Online stock brokerage firms use a fee-for-transaction model. They charge their customers a commission for each trade executed. In the past, stockbrokers offered investment advice and made specific buy and sell recommendations to customers in addition to their transaction execution services. They did not charge for this advice, but they did charge substantial commissions on the trades they executed. In the United States, these commission rates were set by a government agency and were the same for each stockbroker. Thus, because they could not compete on price, the best way for brokerage firms to compete was to offer more and better investment advice.

After the U.S. government deregulated the securities trading business in the early 1970s, a number of discount brokers opened. These discount brokers distinguished themselves by not offering any investment advice and charging very low commissions. They did not employ account executives (as the traditional brokerage firms did) because they did not need to offer the same level of personalized service; the attraction to customers was their low commission rates. Traditional brokers had provided free research to all of their customers, but many of those customers neither wanted nor valued the research. Those customers were very happy to move their business to the discount brokers who provided fast, inexpensive trade execution only. As this shift occurred, individual stockbrokers were disintermediated from the industry value chain.

A second round of disintermediation occurred in the 1990s as new online brokerage firms took business away from the discount brokers who had earlier taken business away from traditional brokers. The Web made it possible for firms such as E*Trade Financial to compete with both traditional and discount brokers by offering investment advice posted on their Web pages or sent in e-mailed newsletters. This advice was similar to that offered by a traditional broker, but could be provided without many of the costs of distributing the advice that traditional brokers had incurred (such as stockbroker salaries, overhead, and the costs of printing and mailing paper newsletters). These Web-based brokerage firms could also offer fast execution of trades by having customers enter data into Web page forms, thus competing with the discount brokers.

Of course, the full-line brokers found that they were simultaneously losing business to both the discount brokers and the online brokers. In response, both discount brokers and the few surviving traditional brokers opened stock trading and research information Web sites in attempts to take back some of their business from the online brokers. After two rounds of disintermediation and the financial crisis of 2008, the brokerage firms that remain today do most of their business online.

INSURANCE BROKERS

Other sales agency and brokerage businesses have moved substantial portions of their operations online. Although insurance companies themselves were slow to offer policies and investments for sale online, a number of intermediaries that sell insurance policies from a variety of companies have been online since the early days of the Web. Quotesmith, which began business in 1984 as a policy-quoting service for independent insurance brokers, decided in 1996 to sell its policy price quotes directly to the public over the Internet. By quoting policies and accepting applications directly, Quotesmith disintermediated the independent insurance agents with whom it formerly worked. Although Quotesmith is no longer in business, similar sites continue to provide quotes from multiple insurance carriers online directly to consumers.

The General (General Automobile Insurance Services) uses its Web site to reach auto insurance buyers who might have had trouble getting insurance from other companies. By offering a comfortable environment to potential customers who have been rejected by other companies because of credit problems or traffic tickets, The General has been successful in this specific niche of the insurance market. Today, most major insurance companies offer information and policies for sale on their Web sites.

EVENT TICKETS

Before the Web made online sales possible, obtaining tickets for concerts, shows, and sporting events could be a challenge. Some venues only offered tickets for sale at their own box offices, and others sold tickets through ticket agencies that were difficult for patrons to find or impossible to reach by telephone. The Web gave event promoters the ability to sell tickets from one virtual location to customers practically anywhere in the world. Established ticket agencies such as Ticketmaster were early participants in online ticket sales and earn a fee on every ticket they sell.

In addition to the original sale of tickets, the Web created opportunities for those who deal in secondary market tickets (tickets that have already been sold by the event's producer and that are being offered for resale to other persons). Companies such as StubHub operate as brokers to connect owners of tickets with buyers in this market. These ticket resellers earn fees on tickets they resell for others, but they can also profit by buying blocks of tickets and reselling them at a higher price. Both ticket brokers and ticket resellers reduce transaction costs for both buyers and sellers of tickets by creating a central marketplace that is easy to find and that facilitates buyer–seller negotiation.

Individual entertainers, as you learned earlier in this chapter, operate their own Web sites to promote themselves and, in some cases, sell music or performance videos online. A few of these performers are experimenting with selling tickets to their live performances directly to consumers online. This allows them to disintermediate ticket brokers from the value chain and either reduce ticket prices or keep more ticket revenue for themselves.

ONLINE BANKING AND FINANCIAL SERVICES

Because financial services do not involve a physical product, they are easy to offer on the Web. Online banking was slow to take off on the Web, because many customers were concerned about the safety of their banking transaction data as it traveled the Internet. Today, however, the general level of trust in online services has increased and about 84 percent of all U.S. households use online banking services. That number is expected to reach 89 percent (a point that many financial services experts believe to be near saturation) by 2018. In Chapter 11, you will learn more about how online payments and other financial transactions are processed.

Most banks that entered the online banking business did so by offering some of their services on the Web. They generally began with sites that offered account balances and statements, then added bill pay, account transfers, loan applications, and other services. Some firms started completely new online banks that were not affiliated with any existing bank. Banks benefit from serving their customers online because it costs the bank less to provide services online than to provide those same services through personal interactions with bank employees in a branch office.

Although online banks let customers pay their bills electronically, many customers still receive their bills in the mail. Those who do receive their bills online must often visit a different Web site to view each online bill. A **bill presentment** service provides an electronic version of an invoice or billing statement (such as a credit card bill or a mobile phone services statement) with all of the details that would appear in the printed document. As online banks add bill presentment services that allow their customers to view all of their bills on the bank's Web site (and pay each of them with a single click), they are finding that more of their customers are willing to do their banking on the Web.

Another important feature that an increasing number of online banks now offer is **account aggregation**, which is the ability to obtain bank, investment, loan, and other financial account information from multiple Web sites and display it all in one location at the bank's Web site. Many of a bank's best customers have credit card, loan, investment, and brokerage accounts with several different financial institutions. Having all of this information collected in one place is very helpful to these customers.

TRAVEL

In the past, travel agents earned substantial commissions on each airplane ticket, hotel reservation, auto rental, or vacation that they booked. These commissions were paid to the travel agent by the transportation or lodging provider. Thus, the traditional revenue model in the travel agency business was a fee-for-transaction, similar to the model of stock brokerage firms.

When the Internet became available to commercial users, a number of online travel agencies began doing business on the Web. Existing travel agencies did not, in general, rush to the new medium. They believed that the key value they added, personal customer service, could not be replaced with a Web site.

In recent years, most airlines and auto rental companies have reduced the amount of the commissions they pay travel agents. In some cases, they have stopped paying commissions at all. Most cruise lines and hotels continue to pay commissions. And many hotels sell blocks of rooms to travel agents who can then resell them as part of vacation packages. Some airlines also sell blocks of seats to travel agents. Online travel sites have much larger volume than traditional travel agencies and are thus able to buy larger blocks of hotel rooms and airline seats.

Online travel sites have evolved to make money in various ways. They all collect any commissions that are paid. And they buy and sell rooms and airline seats, but most of them, including Travelocity, which was based on the Sabre computer system that traditional travel agencies used to book flights and hotel rooms (Travelocity is owned by Sabre), and Microsoft's Expedia subsidiary, run advertising on their Web sites in a combined advertising-fee revenue model. In 2001, a consortium of five major U.S. airlines launched Orbitz, which became one of the most visited travel sites on the Web. The online travel sites were able to disintermediate many traditional travel agencies. By expanding rapidly online, they were able to negotiate better deals on hotel rooms and airline seats that they purchased for resale. With their scale of operations and low cost per transaction, they were able to continue operating profitably on the reduced airline ticket commissions. These factors combined to hasten the end of the traditional travel agency.

Some smaller travel agencies have survived; these agencies most often specialize in cruise vacations. Cruise lines still view travel agents as an important part of their selling strategy and continue to pay commissions to travel agents on the sales that they make. Web sites that make discounted cruise packages easy to search, such as VacationsToGo .com, or that provide detailed information about cruises, have been successful in this travel industry niche.

Other small travel agencies have been successful by following a reintermediation strategy with a focus on specific groups of travelers. These travel agents identify a group of travelers with specific needs and sell travel packages designed for that group. For example, surf vacations have become increasingly popular. The stereotypical surfer of years gone by (a young unemployed male) has been replaced by a much broader demographic. Today's surfers often have significant financial resources and enjoy surfing in exotic locations. Web sites such as WaveHunters.com have followed a reintermediation strategy and cater to this specialized market. Travel agencies that specialize in unusual or exotic destinations, such as Antarctica, have also been successful as intermediaries if they have particular expertise, knowledge, or local contacts that help them create custom itineraries. These sites also include advertising as part of their online presences and revenue models.

AUTOMOBILE SALES

Traditional auto dealers buy cars from the manufacturer and sell them to consumers. They provide showrooms and salespeople to help customers learn about product features, arrange financing, and make a purchase decision. Dealers make their profits by charging a markup on each vehicle sale in addition to charging fees for service, warranty extensions, and other add-ons. In the United States, most states have laws that prevent auto manufacturers from selling directly to consumers, which provides some protection from disintermediation for auto dealers. Almost all auto dealers negotiate the prices at which they sell their cars; thus, the salesperson's job includes extracting the highest possible price from the consumer. Many people do not like negotiating car prices, especially if they have taken the time to learn about car features, arrange financing, and are ready to purchase a car without further assistance from a salesperson.

Some firms, such as Edmunds.com, provide an information service to car buyers. They offer an independent source of information, reviews, and recommendations regarding auto makes and models. Some of these firms offer customers the ability to select a specific car (model, color, options) at a price the firm determines. The firm then finds a local dealer that has such a car and is willing to sell it for the determined price. An alternative approach is for the firm to locate dealers in the buyer's area that are willing to sell the car specified by the buyer (including make, model, options, and color) for a small premium over the dealer's nominal cost. After the firm introduces the buyer to the dealer, that buyer can purchase the car without negotiating with a salesperson. The firm charges participating dealers a fee for this service. In effect, these firms are disintermediating the individual salesperson. To the extent that the salesperson provides little value to the consumer, these firms are reducing the transaction costs in the process. The car salesperson is disintermediated and the Web site becomes the new intermediary in the transaction, which is an example of reintermediation. Some auto sales sites also sell advertising on their sites, which makes them, like the online travel agencies, examples of mixed fee-for-transaction and advertising-supported revenue models.

REAL ESTATE AND MORTGAGE LOANS

Other fee-for-transaction businesses use Web sites to solicit business, including real estate brokers and mortgage loan brokers. Most real estate brokerage firms have a strong online presence, including information about properties they have for sale or rent, along with contact information for individual brokers affiliated with their offices. Many individual real estate brokers operate their own Web sites as well. The industry's trade association, the National Association of Realtors, sponsors a Web site, Realtor.com, that carries detailed descriptions and photos of houses listed for sale by its member firms. Although very few (if any) real estate transactions are completed online, these Web sites play an important role in bringing buyers and sellers together. Although the financial crisis of 2008 dramatically reduced the number of mortgage brokers in business, a number of them continue to do business online.

The complexity and size of real estate transactions have made it difficult for online activities to displace completely the work done by individual real estate and mortgage brokers. Thus, this is one line of business that has been highly resistant to disinter-mediation caused by online technologies. The changes caused by online elements in the real estate and mortgage businesses have been minor.

Fee-for-Service Revenue Models

Companies are offering an increasing variety of services on the Web for which they charge a fee. These are neither broker services nor services for which the charge is based on the number or size of transactions processed. The fee is based on the value of the service provided. These **fee-for-service revenue models** range from games and entertainment to financial advice and the professional services of accountants, lawyers, and physicians.

ONLINE GAMES

Computer and video games are a $66 billion worldwide industry. Although many sites that offer games relied on advertising revenue in the past, a growing number include premium games in their offerings. Site visitors must pay to play these premium games, either by buying and downloading software to install on their computers, or by paying a subscription fee to enter the premium games area on the site. Almost all game sites include some elements of advertising in their revenue models, but an increasing number of them rely on a "hook and pay" strategy. In this approach, a new game player is drawn in (hooked) by free play on a game that has a limited number of levels. The game then offers access to higher levels of game play, hints, or tools for playing the game better for a small fee. One of the fastest growing segments of the online games business is in the development and sale of games designed to be played as apps on mobile devices such as smartphones and tablets.

PROFESSIONAL SERVICES

State laws have been one of the main forces preventing U.S. professionals (such as physicians, lawyers, accountants, and engineers) from extending their practices to the Web. Since most professionals are licensed by individual states, state laws can prevent them from practicing their professions on the Web because online patients or clients would likely be located in other states. If they were to offer their services online to persons in other states, professionals could be charged with unlicensed practice in those other states. State laws concerning the imputed location of service delivery are vague; it can be difficult to determine exactly where a service provided online actually occurs. This uncertainty arises because most state professional practice laws were written long before the Internet existed.

Many medical, legal, and other professional practices allow patients to make appointments online, and an increasing number of professionals do online consultations.

Most professionals are still reluctant to conduct elements of their practices on the Web because they are concerned about protecting the privacy of their patients or clients online.

The Law on the Web site offers legal consultations on a variety of matters for residents of the United Kingdom. Accounting professionals in the United States can be located through the CPA Directory, and legal referral sites, often operated by local bar associations, can direct site visitors to attorneys. The online version of the well-known Martindale-Hubbell lawyer directory is also available online at Martindale.com.

Although a large number of Web sites offer general health information, physicians and other health care professionals have been reluctant to sell specific advice to specific patients online. The difficulty of diagnosing medical problems without a physical examination of the patient is a significant barrier to providing most types of health care services online, but a growing number of physicians now offer online consultations to patients with whom they have an ongoing, established relationship.

Some Web sites offer online mental health services to patients. Most sites connect potential patients with therapists licensed in the patient's jurisdiction, so the therapist providing the online consultation complies with state professional practice laws. Online consultations are done by text or video chat. The operators of these Web sites note that some conditions, such as depression or anxiety, might even be easier to treat online since the patient does not need to leave home to see a therapist.

Free for Many, Fee for a Few

Chris Anderson, the editor of *Wired Magazine*, argued in 2004 that the economics of producing and selling digital products is substantially different from the economics of producing and selling physical products. In his books (see references to his work in the For Further Study and Research section at the end of this chapter), he explains that physical products benefit from the production of standardized versions that generate economies of scale. Because each unit of production requires materials and labor, using the same materials allows large producers to buy those materials at lower costs by ordering in bulk. Labor costs can be reduced by training workers to do specific production tasks efficiently. Since most of the cost of a physical product is in the manufacture of each unit (as opposed to the design of the prototype), the key to making a profit is to reduce the costs of manufacturing.

The basic economics of selling digital products are different. Digital products have large up-front costs. Once those costs are incurred, additional units can be made at very low additional cost. For example, a software program can cost thousands (or even millions) of dollars to create because it requires many hours of expensive programmer time to design, code, and test. But once the software is in production, creating additional units costs very little (especially if those units are distributed in digital form, online). Making minor changes in the program so that it works better for different types of customers can be relatively inexpensive, too. Thus, the profitability of digital products depends on factors that are quite different from those that determine the profitability of physical products.

The result of Anderson's logic is that businesses can find it profitable to offer a digital product to a large number of customers for free, and then charge a small number of customers for an enhanced, specialized, or otherwise differentiated version of the product. If a company can charge the small number of customers enough to cover the cost of developing the digital product and yield a profit, it can give away many copies of the product, especially if those free copies lead to connecting with more customers willing to pay for the enhanced product.

For example, Yahoo! offers free e-mail accounts to site visitors. This draws visitors to the Yahoo! site and allows the company to sell some advertising on the pages that display the e-mail service. But some e-mail users will want an enhanced version of the service. Perhaps they want pages with no advertising, the ability to send large attachments with their e-mails, or more storage space for their e-mails. Yahoo! charges for a premium version of its service that offers these features. It costs the company very little to offer this service, but selling it generates considerable revenue.

You learned about another example of this revenue model earlier in this chapter. The subscription music services (such as Pandora, Internet Radio, Spotify, and Rhapsody) offer free, but limited and ad-bearing versions of their subscription services to introduce potential customers to their services.

In the physical world, this free sample logic works in reverse. Companies selling physical products have often used a mixture of free and for-sale products. For example, a bakery might have a plate of cookies available for customers to taste. The bakery hopes that enough customers will be impressed with the taste of the free cookies that they will buy cookies or other baked goods. They give away a small number of physical products to boost overall sales of that identical product. This is the opposite strategy used by sellers of a digital product; that is, to give away a large number of digital products to entice other customers to buy a small number of relatively expensive versions of the product.

Changing Strategies: Revenue Models in Transition

Many companies have gone through transitions in their revenue models as they learn how to do business successfully on the Web. As more people and businesses use the Web to buy goods and services, and as the behavior of those Web users changes, companies often find that they must change their revenue models to meet the needs of those new and changing Web users. Some companies created electronic commerce Web sites that needed many years to grow large enough to become profitable. This is not unusual; both CNN and ESPN took more than 10 years to become profitable and they had both created new businesses in television, which was an existing and well-established medium. Many Web companies found that their unprofitable growth phases were lasting longer than they had anticipated and were forced either to change their revenue models or go out of business.

This section describes the revenue model transitions undertaken by five different companies as they gained experience in the online world and faced the changes that occurred in that world. In the second wave of electronic commerce, these and other companies might well face the need to make further adjustments to their revenue models.

Subscription to Advertising-Supported Model

Microsoft founded its Slate magazine Web site as an upscale news and current events publication. Because *Slate* included experienced writers and editors on its staff, many people expected the online magazine to be a success. Microsoft believed that the magazine had a high value, too. At a time when most online magazines were using an advertising-supported revenue model, *Slate* began charging an annual subscription fee after a limited free introductory period.

Although *Slate* drew a wide readership and received acclaim for its incisive reporting and excellent writing, it was unable to draw a sufficient number of paid subscribers. At its peak, *Slate* had about 27,000 subscribers generating annual revenue of $500,000, which was far less than the cost of creating the content and maintaining the Web site. *Slate* is now operated as an advertising-supported site. Because it is a part of Microsoft, *Slate* does not report its own profit numbers. Microsoft maintains the *Slate* site as part of its Bing portal, so it is likely that the value of the publication to Microsoft is to increase the portal's stickiness.

Advertising-Supported to Advertising-Subscription Mixed Model

Another online magazine, Salon.com, which has also received acclaim for its innovative content, has moved its revenue model in the direction opposite of *Slate*'s transition. After operating for several years as an advertising-supported site, *Salon.com* began offering an optional subscription version of its site called *Salon Premium*, which was free of advertising and could be downloaded for later offline reading on the subscriber's computer.

The subscription version offering was motivated by the company's inability to raise the additional money from investors that it needed to continue operations. The subscription version has gone through a number of changes over the years and now includes access to additional content such as downloadable music, e-books, and audio books.

The premium version of the site, now called Salon Core, also includes subscriptions to various print magazines, access to sports content, music, and a preferential access to the site's writers and editors.

Advertising-Supported to Subscription Model

Northern Light was founded in August 1997 as a search engine, but a search engine that did more than search the Web. It also searched its own database of journal articles and other publications to which it had acquired reproduction rights. When a user ran a search, Northern Light returned a results page that included links to Web sites and abstracts of the items in its own database. Users could then follow the links to Web sites, which were free, or purchase access to the database items.

Thus, Northern Light's revenue model was a combination of the advertising-supported model used by most other Web search engines plus a fee-based information access service. The difference in the Northern Light model was that users could pay for just one or two articles (the cost was typically $1–$5 per article) instead of paying a large amount of money for unlimited access to its database on an annual subscription basis. Northern

Light also offered subscription access to most of its database to companies, schools, and libraries.

In January 2002, Northern Light decided that the advertising revenue it was earning from the ads it sold on search results pages was insufficient to justify continuing to offer that service. It stopped offering public access to its search engine and converted to a new revenue model that was primarily subscription supported. Northern Light's new model generates revenue from annual subscriptions to large corporate clients. Its main products today include Business News, Discovery—which searches life sciences conference proceedings—SinglePoint—a search engine that runs on corporate databases—and MI Analyst Text Analytics, a meaning extraction tool used in business research applications.

Multiple Changes to Revenue Models

Encyclopædia Britannica has developed one of the most respected brand names in research and education. Beginning in 1768 as a sort of precomputer-age frequently asked questions (FAQ) list, a group of academics developed the encyclopedia out of collected notes they had made while conducting research and decided to publish them as a series of articles.

The company has been through a number of revenue model transitions as it developed its current online business strategy. When Encyclopædia Britannica first moved online in 1994, it began with two Web-based offerings. The Britannica Internet Guide was a free Web navigation aid that classified and rated information-laden Web sites. It featured reviews written by Britannica editors who also selected and indexed the sites. The company's other Web site, Encyclopædia Britannica Online, contained the full text and pictures from the print encyclopedia. It was available for a subscription fee or as part of the Encyclopædia Britannica CD package. Britannica's intention was to use the free site to attract users to the paid subscription site.

In 1999, disappointed by low subscription sales of Encyclopædia Britannica Online, Britannica converted to a free, advertising-supported site. In terms of Web site traffic, the new revenue model was a huge success. The first day the new free site, Britannica.com, became available it had more than 15 million visitors, forcing Britannica to shut down for two weeks to upgrade its servers. The site offered full content of the encyclopedia's print edition in searchable form, plus access to the *Merriam-Webster's Collegiate Dictionary* and the *Britannica Book of the Year*. One of the most successful aspects of the site was the way it integrated the Britannica Internet Guide Web-rating service with its print content. The Britannica Store sold the CD version of the encyclopedia along with other educational and scientific products to help generate revenue.

Unfortunately, advertising sales were not what the company had hoped. After two years of trying to generate a profit using this advertising-supported model, Britannica returned to the mixed model it continues to use today. In this mixed model, the company offers free online access to summaries of encyclopedia articles and the *Merriam-Webster's Collegiate Dictionary*, but the full text of the encyclopedia is only available to visitors who pay an annual fee of about $70 for the Britannica Premium service, which is currently estimated to have about 500,000 subscribers. In 2012, the company printed its last print volumes, ending 244 years of continuous publication.

Britannica went from being a print publisher to a seller of information on the Web to an advertising-supported Web site to a mixed advertising subscription model—three major revenue model transitions—in just a few short years. The main value that Britannica has to sell is its reputation and the expertise of its editors, contributors, and advisors. After exploring these different revenue models, the company has decided that the best way to capitalize on its reputation and expertise is through a mixed revenue model of subscriptions and advertising support, with the bulk of its revenue coming from subscriptions to its premium service. Britannica also generates revenue by selling books, CDs, DVDs, and software with an educational theme through its online products store.

The New York Times Web site has gone through several revenue model transitions since opening in the mid-1990s. Originally, the site was purely advertising supported and included most of the content in the print edition of the newspaper. It has always charged a subscription fee for its premium crossword puzzles and chess columns. The first revenue model also included a fee for access to older articles stored in the newspaper's archives.

In 2005, *The New York Times* decided to limit access to much of its most desirable content to subscribers and began charging a fee for access to its Op Ed and news columns. The fee also allowed access to the crossword puzzles and the older articles in the archives. All of the limited-access content was also available to print edition subscribers. This program brought in about 227,000 subscribers, which at $44.95 per year generated about $10 million in revenue.

By 2007, the newspaper had become convinced that it could earn more advertising revenue by providing free access to those pages than it was earning in subscription fees, so it went back to relying on an advertising-supported revenue stream. The newspaper charged only for access to the crossword puzzles and for older articles in the archives. With this change, the traffic to *The New York Times* Web site nearly doubled, reaching an average of 30 million unique visitors per month. However, the recession of 2008 caused advertising revenue to drop and the company began considering other alternatives.

In 2011, disappointed with the level of advertising revenue, the company adopted a rather complex program that gave the newspaper some flexibility in what it would put online (in case there was a major story it wanted to cover broadly) yet that would generate more revenue than the advertising-based revenue model it had been using for the previous four years. In the new plan, *The New York Times* Web site visitors could read 20 articles a month at no charge. When a visitor attempted to view the 21st article, the site would invoke a paywall and offer several subscription plans (priced between $15 and $35 per month) that included unlimited access to the Web site and various levels of access through mobile phones. Subscribers to the print edition were given unlimited access to the site.

In 2012, a year after first introducing the paywall, the newspaper announced that it had gained more than 450,000 subscribers and, in an apparent confirmation of the success of its strategy, reduced the number of free articles allowed to nonsubscribers to 10 per month. The publishers of the newspaper hope that this mixed revenue model will provide an acceptable balance between the editors' desire to have as many people as possible read the paper and the need to generate sufficient revenue to keep the newspaper operating. Their experience with this revenue model has been, and will likely continue to be, watched closely by the entire industry.

Revenue Strategy Issues for Online Businesses

In the first part of this chapter, you learned about the revenue models that companies are using on the Web today. In this section, you will learn about some issues that arise when companies implement those models. You will also learn how companies deal with those issues.

Channel Conflict and Cannibalization

Companies that have existing sales outlets and distribution networks often worry that their Web sites will take away sales from those outlets and networks. For example, Levi Strauss & Company sells its Levi's jeans and other clothing products through department stores and other retail outlets. The company began selling jeans to consumers on its Web site in mid-1998. Many of the department stores and retail outlets that had been selling Levi's products for many years complained to the company that the Web site was now competing with them. In January 2000, Levi Strauss announced it would stop selling its clothing products on its own Web site. Such a **channel conflict** can occur whenever sales activities on a company's Web site interfere with its existing sales outlets. The problem is also called **cannibalization** because the Web site's sales consume sales that would be made in the company's other sales channels. In recent years, the Levi's Web site resumed selling products directly to consumers, but it includes a Store Locator link that helps customers find a nearby store if they want to buy in person. Both Levi Strauss and the retail stores it sells through have agreed that the sales through the Web site are insignificant. Over time, many Levi's retailers have opened online stores themselves, so they see the Levi's site as less of a threat than they did in 2000.

Maytag, the manufacturer of home appliances, found itself in the same position as Levi Strauss. It created a Web site that allowed customers to order directly from Maytag. After fewer than two years of making direct online sales and receiving many complaints from its authorized distributors and resellers, Maytag decided to incorporate online partners into its Web site store design. Now, after searching and gathering information about specific products from the Maytag Web site, a customer can click a Where to Buy link and be directed to a nearby Maytag retailer.

Both Levi's and Maytag faced channel conflict and cannibalization issues with their retail distribution partners. Their established retailers sold many times the dollar volume than either company could ever hope to sell on their own Web sites. Thus, to avoid angering their retailers, who could always sell competing products, both Levi's and Maytag decided that it would be best to work with their retail partners. Similar issues can also arise within a company if that company has established sales channels that would compete with direct sales on the company's own Web site.

Eddie Bauer, a retailer of clothing and outdoor gear, was selling through a catalog and retail stores located primarily in major shopping malls when it started selling products on its Web site. The company believed that it could make online sales more attractive by allowing customers to return unwanted products that they had purchased online at the retail store locations. The managers of these stores were concerned about the time it would take for their sales associates to process these returns and about having to add the items to their stores' inventories. In a retail store operation, managing labor costs and inventory are very important in achieving store profitability. The managers at the company's catalog division were also worried. They feared that sales through the Web site would cannibalize sales through the catalog.

By making adjustments in the managers' compensation and bonus plans, Eddie Bauer was able to convince all of the managers to support the Web site. The retail store managers were credited with an inventory and labor cost allowance for each Web site return they handled. The catalog division managers were given a credit for existing catalog customers who purchased goods from the Web site. By giving their customers access to the company's products through a coordinated presence in all three distribution channels, Eddie Bauer was able to increase overall sales to those customers. This type of solution is called **channel cooperation**.

Strategic Alliances

As you learned in Chapter 1, when two or more companies join forces to undertake an activity over a long period of time, they are said to create a strategic alliance. When companies form a strategic alliance, they are operating in the network form of organization that you learned about in Chapter 1. Companies form strategic alliances for many purposes. An increasing number of businesses are forming strategic alliances to sell on the Web. For example, the relationships that Levi's created with its retail partners by giving them space on the Levi's Web site to sell Levi's products is an example of a strategic alliance.

Amazon has forged a number of strategic alliances with existing firms over the years to sell clothing (with Target), music CDs (with CDnow), and other products. Amazon has also formed strategic alliances with many smaller companies to offer their products for sale on the Amazon Web site.

Luxury Goods Strategies

Some types of products can be difficult to sell online. This is particularly true for expensive luxury goods and high-fashion clothing items that customers generally want to see in person or touch. Many luxury brands hesitated to offer their products online for fear of alienating the upscale physical stores that sold their products. For example, clothier Lilly Pulitzer launched its Web site in 2000, but did not sell on the site until 2008, fearing that it would lose some of the luxury cachet it derived from limiting its sales outlets.

Some upscale brands overcome this obstacle by limiting the range of their online offerings. For example, luxury brand Chanel, which launched its retail site in 2010, and Calvin Klein do not offer all of their products online. Chanel sells fragrance and skincare products online but not its clothing lines. Calvin Klein does not sell its couture line online, but it does sell its ready-to-wear lines on its Web site.

In large part, luxury retailers limit their sales online out of concern that some or all of their products' features must be experienced in person and cannot be adequately represented online. One industry that has overcome this obstacle, however, is the retail jewelry business. After years of slow online sales, jewelry sales have grown rapidly in recent years. Retailers such as Blue Nile and Ice.com operate highly successful online jewelry stores. Even general retailers such as Costco offer $50,000 diamond rings online.

Helping these stores overcome resistance is the general availability of independent appraisal certificates for diamonds and other high-priced jewelry items. Another important factor is the stores' well-advertised "no questions asked" return policies.

Overstock Sales Strategies

In the fast-changing clothing business, retailers have always had to deal with the problem of overstocks—products that did not sell as well as hoped. Many retailers use outlet stores to sell their overstocks. Lands' End found that selling overstock items as clearance specials on its Web site worked so well that it was able to close some of its physical outlet stores. Many other retailer Web sites include a link to separate sections for overstocks or clearance sales of end-of-season merchandise.

An online overstocks store works well because it reaches more people than a physical store and it can be updated more frequently than a printed overstocks catalog. Overstocks and clearance sale pages have become a standard element of clothing retailers' Web sites and some, such as Overstock.com, are devoted entirely to the sale of overstocked items purchased from other retailers.

Creating an Effective Business Presence Online

Businesses have always created a presence in the physical world by building stores, factories, warehouses, and office buildings. An organization's **presence** is the public image it conveys to its stakeholders. The **stakeholders** of a firm include its customers, suppliers, employees, stockholders, neighbors, and the general public. Most companies tend not to worry much about the image they project until they grow to a significant size—until then, they are too focused on just surviving to spare the effort. On the Web, presence can be much more important. Many customers and other stakeholders of a Web business know the company only through its Web presence. Creating an effective Web presence can be critical even for the smallest and newest firms operating on the Web.

Identifying Web Presence Goals

When a business creates a physical space in which to conduct its activities, its managers focus on very specific objectives. Few of these objectives are image driven. The new company must find a location that will be convenient for its customers, with sufficient floor space and features to allow the selling activity to occur. A new business must balance its needs for inventory storage space and employee work space with the costs of obtaining that space. The presence of a physical business location results from satisfying these many other objectives and is rarely a main goal of designing the space.

A firm's physical location must satisfy so many other business needs that it often runs out of the resources it would need to convey a good presence. On the Web, businesses and other organizations have the luxury of building their Web sites with the main goal of creating a distinctive presence. A good Web site design can provide many image-creation and image-enhancing features very effectively—it can serve as a sales brochure, a product showroom, a financial report, an employment ad, and a customer contact point. Each entity that establishes a Web presence should decide which features the Web site can

Objectives	Strategies
Attracting visitors to the Web site	Include links to the Web site (or specific pages) in marketing e-mails
Making the site interesting enough that visitors stay and explore	Product reviews, comparison features, advice on how to use a product or service
Convincing visitors to follow the site's links to obtain information	Clearly labeled links that include a hint of the information to be obtained by following them
Creating an impression consistent with the organization's desired image	Using established branding elements such as logos, characters used in other advertising media, slogans, or catchphrases
Building a trusting relationship with visitors	Ensuring the validity and objectivity of information presented on the site
Reinforcing positive images that the visitor might already have about the organization	Presenting testimonials, information about awards, links to external reviews or articles about the organization or its products and services
Encouraging visitors to return to the site	Featuring current information about the organization or its products and services that is regularly updated

© 2017 Cengage Learning

FIGURE 3-5   Web presence objectives and strategies

provide and which of those features are the most important to include. An effective site is one that creates an attractive presence that meets the objectives of the business or organization. A list of these objectives, along with some examples of Web site design strategies that can help accomplish them, appears in Figure 3-5.

MAKING WEB PRESENCE CONSISTENT WITH BRAND IMAGE

Different firms, even those in the same industry, might establish different Web presence goals. For example, Coca Cola and Pepsi are two companies that have established powerful brand images in the same business, but they have developed significantly different Web presences. These two companies frequently change their Web pages, but the Coca Cola page always includes a trusted corporate image such as the Coke bottle. Alternatively, the Pepsi page is generally filled with links to a variety of activities and product-related promotions.

These Web presences convey the images each company wants to project. Each presence is consistent with other elements of the marketing efforts of these companies— Coca Cola's traditional position as a trusted classic, and Pepsi's position as the upstart product favored by a younger generation.

Most auto manufacturers' Web sites convey a consistent brand image. They usually include links to detailed information about each model, a dealer locator page, information about the company, and a set of shopping tools such as configuration pages for each model.

NOT-FOR-PROFIT ORGANIZATIONS

Auto makers enhance their images by providing useful information to customers on their Web sites. The main function of their Web sites, however, is to promote their products and get customers in touch with a dealer who can sell them a car. For other organizations, the image-enhancement capability is a key goal of their Web presence efforts. Not-for-profit organizations are an excellent example of this. They can use their Web sites as a central resource for communications with their varied and often geographically dispersed constituencies.

A key goal for the Web sites of many not-for-profit organizations is information dissemination. The Web allows these groups to integrate information dissemination with fund-raising in one location. Visitors who become engaged in the issues presented are usually just one or two clicks away from a page offering memberships or other opportunities to donate using a credit card. Web pages also provide a two-way contact channel for people who are engaged in the organization's efforts but who do not work directly for the organization—for example, many not-for-profits rely on volunteers and coordination with other organizations to accomplish their goals.

This combination of information dissemination and a two-way contact channel is a key element on any successful electronic commerce Web site. For example, the **American Civil Liberties Union (ACLU)**, which is devoted to the advocacy of individual rights in the United States, includes many communication opportunities on its Web site. The ACLU home page gives visitors an opportunity to learn about the organization and contribute money or join if their interests are piqued by what they see. The ACLU home page includes links to information about each major issue on which the ACLU has taken a position. The ACLU's Web site is especially valuable to it because the organization serves many different constituencies, not all of whom agree with the ACLU or with each other on all issues. If the ACLU were to create a print newsletter that contained interesting information for some of its supporters, that same information might offend other supporters. The Web site allows visitors to select the issues in which they are interested—and only those issues.

Not-for-profit organizations can use the Web to stay in touch with existing stakeholders and identify new opportunities for serving them. Political parties want to offer information about party positions on issues, recruit members, keep existing members informed, and provide communication links to visitors who have questions about the party. All the major U.S. political parties have Web sites, and each year candidates running for public office set up their own Web sites. In addition, political organizations that are not affiliated with a specific party, such as the nonpartisan Center for Responsive Politics, also accomplish similar goals with their Web presences.

Web Site Usability

Research indicates that few businesses accomplish all of their goals for their Web sites in their current Web presences. Even sites that succeed in achieving most of these goals often fail to provide sufficient interactive contact opportunities for site visitors.

In this section, you will learn how the Web is different from other ways in which companies have communicated with their customers, suppliers, and employees in the past. You will learn how companies can improve their Web presences by making their sites accessible to more people and easier to use, and by making sure that their sites encourage visitors to trust and even develop feelings of loyalty toward the organization behind the Web site.

How the Web Is Different

Through years of trial, error, and research, firms have come to realize that doing business online differs greatly from doing business in the physical world. When firms first started creating Web sites in the mid-1990s, they often built simple sites that conveyed basic information about their businesses. Few firms conducted any market research to see what kinds of things potential visitors might want to obtain from these Web sites, and even fewer considered what business infrastructure adjustments would be needed to service the site. For example, few firms had e-mail address links on their sites. Those firms that did include an e-mail link often understaffed the department responsible for answering visitors' e-mail messages. Thus, many site visitors sent e-mail messages that were never answered.

This failure to understand how the Web is different from other presence-building media continues to be an important reason that so many businesses do not achieve their Web objectives. To learn more about this issue, see Jakob Nielsen's classic **Failure of Corporate Websites** page in the Web Links; the article was written in 1998, but still accurately describes far too many Web sites. In revisiting the issue in 2009 (see **Top 10 Information Architecture Mistakes**), Nielsen found that a surprising number of Web sites still contained the same kinds of architectural and navigational flaws that impair site visitors' ability to find information.

Most Web sites that are designed to create an organization's presence in the Web medium include links to a fairly standard information set. The site should give the visitor easy access to the organization's history, a statement of objectives or mission statement, information about products or services, financial information, and a way to communicate with the organization. Sites achieve varying levels of success based largely on how they offer this information. Presentation is important, but so is realizing that the Web is an interactive medium. The Web gives even large companies the ability to engage in two-way, meaningful communication with their customers. Companies that do not make effective use of this ability will lose customers to competitors that do.

Meeting the Needs of Web Site Visitors

Businesses that are successful on the Web realize that every visitor to their Web site is a potential customer or partner. Thus, an important concern for businesses crafting Web presences is the variation in visitor characteristics. People who visit a Web site seldom arrive by accident; they are there for a reason.

VARIED MOTIVATIONS OF WEB SITE VISITORS

Web designers face some challenges when trying to create a site that is useful for everyone because visitors arrive for many different reasons, including the following:

- Learning about products or services that the company offers
- Buying products or services that the company offers

- Obtaining information about warranty, service, or repair policies for products they purchased
- Obtaining general information about the company or organization
- Obtaining financial information for making an investment or credit-granting decision
- Identifying the people who manage the company or organization
- Obtaining contact information for a person or department in the organization
- Following a link into the site while searching for information about a related product, service, or topic

Not only do Web site visitors arrive with different needs, they also arrive with different experience and expectation levels. In addition to the problems posed by the diversity of visitor characteristics, technology issues can also arise. These Web site visitors are connected to the Internet through a variety of communication channels that provide different bandwidths and data transmission speeds. They will also be using different Web browsers running on different devices (including computers, tablets, phones, television sets, and even video game consoles). Those using the same browser might be running different versions or have it configured in various ways with browser add-in and plug-in software. Addressing the implications of these many variations in visitor characteristics when building a Web site can help convert these visitors into customers.

MAKING WEB SITES ACCESSIBLE

One of the best ways to accommodate a broad range of visitor needs, including the needs of visitors with disabilities, is to build flexibility into the Web site's interface. For example, some sites offer a text-only version. As researchers at the University of Wisconsin's Trace Center note, this can be an especially important feature for visually impaired visitors who use special browser software to access Web site content. Approximately 15 percent of all Web users have some kind of disability. The W3C Web Accessibility Initiative site includes a number of useful links to information regarding these issues.

A site can give the visitor the option to select smaller versions of graphic images so that the page loads on a low-bandwidth connection in a reasonable amount of time. If the site includes streaming audio or video clips, it can give the visitor the option to specify a connection type so that the streaming media adjusts itself to the bandwidth for that connection.

A good site design lets visitors choose among information attributes, such as level of detail, forms of aggregation, viewing format, and downloading format. Many online stores let visitors select their preferred level of detail by presenting product information by product line. The site presents one page for each line of products. A product line page contains pictures of each item in that product line accompanied by a brief description. By using hyperlinked graphics for the product pictures, the site offers visitors the option of clicking the product picture, which opens a page of detailed specifications for that product.

The use of Adobe Flash to create animated graphic elements on Web pages has been controversial for years (see, for example, Jakob Nielsen's commentary on Ephemeral

Web-Based Applications). Although some Web site designers love Flash as a creative design tool, many electronic commerce sites are reluctant to use it because of the nonstandard interface it can present to customers. Web pages built with Flash (or large portions of those pages) are not rendered in HTML and do not provide the same navigation tools or visual hints that Web pages created in HTML offer. Flash files can be large and thus take a long time to download; another issue is that Flash does not work on Apple's iPhone and iPad products. This has increased concern about its use in Web sites designed to be viewed on smartphones and tablet devices.

As HTML 5 (which you learned in Chapter 2 includes the ability to include multimedia links directly in the markup language itself) becomes more widely used, most experts predict that the use of Flash will decline significantly. In the meantime, some sites provide an option on their home pages that allows users to select Flash or non-Flash versions of the site.

Some specific tasks that customers want to perform do lend themselves to animated Web pages. For example, the Lee® Jeans **FitFinder** is a series of Flash animation pages that can help customers find the right size and style of jeans. One of the Lee® Jeans FitFinder animation pages is shown in Figure 3-6.

Web sites can also offer visitors multiple information formats by including links to files in those formats. For example, a page offering financial information could include links to an HTML file, an Adobe PDF file, and an Excel spreadsheet file. Each of these files would contain the same financial information in different formats; visitors can then choose the format that best suits their immediate needs. Visitors looking for a specific financial fact might choose the HTML file so that the information appears in their Web browsers. Other visitors who want a copy of the entire annual report as it was printed would select the PDF file and either view it in their browsers or download and print the file. Visitors who want to conduct analyses on the financial data would download the spreadsheet file and perform calculations using the data in their own spreadsheet software.

To be successful in conveying an integrated image and offering information to potential customers, businesses should try to meet the accessibility goals shown in Figure 3-7 when constructing their Web sites.

Trust and Loyalty

When companies first started selling on the Web, many of them believed that their customers would use the abundance of information to find the best prices and disregard other aspects of the buying experience. For some products, this may be true; however, most products include an element of service. When customers buy a product, they are also buying that service element. A seller can create value in a relationship with a customer by nurturing the customer's trust and developing it into loyalty. Business researchers have found that a 5 percent increase in customer loyalty (measured as the proportion of returning customers) can yield profit increases of 25 to 80 percent.

Even when products are commodity items, the service element can be a powerful differentiating factor for which customers will pay extra. These services include such things as delivery, order handling, help with selecting a product, and after-sale support.

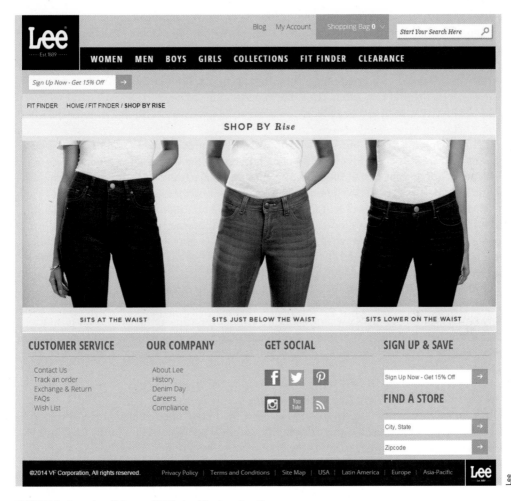

FIGURE 3-6   Lee® Jeans FitFinder Flash animation

Business Web sites need to:

- Offer easily accessible facts about the organization

- Allow visitors to experience the site in different ways and at different levels

- Provide visitors with a meaningful, two-way (interactive) communication link with the organization

- Sustain visitor attention and encourage return visits

- Offer easily accessible information about products and services and how to use them

FIGURE 3-7   Accessibility goals for business Web sites

Because many of these services are things that a potential customer cannot evaluate before purchasing a product, the customer must trust the seller to provide an acceptable level of service.

When a customer has a positive service experience with a seller, that customer begins to trust the seller. When a customer has multiple good experiences with a seller, that customer feels loyal to the seller. Thus, the repetition of satisfactory service can build customer loyalty, which can prevent a customer from seeking alternative sellers who offer lower prices.

Many companies doing business on the Web spend large amounts of money to obtain customers. If they do not provide levels of customer service that lead customers to develop trust in and loyalty to the firm, the companies are unlikely to recover the money they spend to attract the customers in the first place, much less earn a profit.

Customer service is a problem for many electronic commerce sites. Recent research indicates that customers rate most retail electronic commerce sites to be average or low in customer service. A common weak spot for many sites is the lack of integration between the companies' call centers and their Web sites. As a result, when a customer calls with a complaint or problem with a Web purchase, the customer service representative does not have information about Web transactions and is unable to resolve the caller's problem.

Even today, e-mail responsiveness of electronic commerce sites is disappointing. Many major companies are slow to respond to e-mail inquiries about product information, order status, or after-sale problems. A significant number of companies in these studies never acknowledged or responded to the e-mail queries.

Usability Testing

An increasing number of companies are realizing the importance of usability testing, however, most companies do not perform any usability testing on their Web sites. As its name suggests, **usability testing** is the testing and evaluation of a site by its owner to ensure ease of use for site visitors. As the practice of usability testing becomes more common, more Web sites will meet the goals outlined previously in this chapter.

Many electronic commerce Web sites frustrate their potential customers so much that they leave without buying anything. Even the best sites lose many customers because the sites are confusing or difficult to use. Simple changes in site usability can increase customer satisfaction and sales. For example, some Web sites do not include telephone contact information in the belief that not staffing a call center will save the business money. However, if your customers cannot reach you, they will not continue to do business with you. Most customers will give up when they cannot communicate with you when they need to using the medium they prefer.

Companies that have done usability tests, such as Eastman Kodak, T. Rowe Price, and Maytag, have found that they can learn a great deal about meeting visitor needs by conducting focus groups and watching how different customers navigate a series of Web site test designs. Industry analysts agree that the cost of usability testing is so low compared to the total cost of a Web site design or overhaul that it should almost always be included in such projects. Two pioneers of usability testing are Ben Shneiderman and Jakob Nielsen. Dr. Shneiderman founded the Computer Interaction Lab at the University of Maryland and has published a number of books on interface design. Dr. Nielsen and his colleagues post articles on the Nielsen Norman Group Web site that include information on how to conduct usability testing and use the results to improve Web site design and operation.

Because usability testing is fairly inexpensive to perform, many companies run usability tests periodically on their Web sites. Although user behavior is quite stable over time, Web sites evolve and are changed almost constantly. Many times these changes can affect Web site structure and navigation in unexpected and unintended ways. A regular program of usability testing can help organizations identify these issues and resolve them before they cause user frustration and lost sales.

Customer-Centric Web Site Design

An important part of a successful electronic business operation is a Web site that meets the needs of potential customers. In the list of goals for constructing Web sites that you learned about earlier in the chapter, the focus was on meeting the needs of all site visitors (which might include customers, potential customers, investors, potential contributors for charitable organizations, business partners, suppliers, potential employees, and the general public). Putting the customer at the center of all site designs is called a **customer-centric** approach to Web site design. A customer-centric approach leads to some guidelines that Web designers can follow when creating a Web site that is intended to meet the specific needs of *customers*, as opposed to all Web site visitors. These guidelines include the following:

- Design the site around how customers will navigate the links, not around the company's organizational structure.
- Help customers access information quickly.
- Use concise descriptive language rather than inflated marketing statements in product or service descriptions.
- Avoid using industry jargon and specialized terms that visitors might not understand.
- Build the site to work for visitors who are using older and slower devices connected through the lowest bandwidth connection, even if this means creating multiple versions of Web pages.
- Be consistent in use of design features and colors throughout the site.
- Avoid Web page design elements that look like banner ads (customers have learned to ignore anything that looks like an ad).
- Make sure that navigation controls are clearly labeled or otherwise distinguishable from other Web page design elements.
- Test text visibility on a range of monitor sizes; text can become too small to read on a small monitor (or mobile device) and so large it shows jagged edges on a large monitor.
- Check to make sure that color combinations do not impair viewing clarity for color-blind visitors.

Web sites that are designed for mobile device users should follow a few additional guidelines. These rules help accommodate the use of devices with very small screens (compared to laptop or desktop computer users) and the tendency of mobile device users to be even less patient than other Web users. These additional guidelines include the following:

- Text should be extremely concise; there is no space for excess verbiage on a mobile device screen.
- Navigation must be clear, intuitive, and easy to see.
- The set of available functions should be limited to those likely to be used by site visitors in a mobile setting (the page can include links to the more complete, nonmobile version of the site).
- Creating a dedicated Web site for mobile users is almost always essential because the needs of mobile users are so different from those of other users.
- Conduct usability tests by having potential site users navigate several mobile device versions of the site.
- Provide an option for mobile device users to switch easily to the full Web site.

Web marketing consultant Kristin Zhivago of Zhivago Management Partners has a number of recommendations for Web sites that are designed specifically to meet the needs of online customers. She encourages Web designers to create sites focused on the customer's buying process rather than the company's perspective and organization. For example, she suggests that companies examine how much information their Web sites provide and how useful that information is for customers. If the site does not provide substantial "content for your click" to visitors, they will not become customers.

Using these guidelines when you create your site can help make visitors' Web experiences more efficient, effective, and memorable. Usability is an important element of creating an effective Web presence.

Using the Web to Connect with Customers

An important element of a corporate Web presence is communicating with site visitors who are customers or potential customers. In this section, you will learn how Web sites can help firms identify and reach out to customers.

The Nature of Communication on the Web

Most businesses are familiar with two general ways of identifying and reaching customers: personal contact and mass media. These two approaches are often called **communication modes** because they each involve a characteristic way (or mode) of conveying information from one person to another (or communicating). In the **personal contact** model, the firm's employees individually search for, qualify, and contact potential customers. This personal contact approach to identifying and reaching customers is sometimes called **prospecting**. In the **mass media** approach, firms prepare advertising and promotional materials about the firm and its products or services. They then deliver these messages to potential customers by broadcasting them on television or radio, printing them in newspapers or magazines, posting them on highway billboards, or mailing them.

Some experts distinguish between broadcast media and addressable media. **Addressable media** are advertising efforts directed to a known addressee and include direct mail, telephone calls, and e-mail. Since few users of addressable media actually use address information in their advertising strategies, in this book, we consider addressable media to be mass media. Many businesses use a combination of mass media and personal contact to identify and reach customers. For example, Prudential uses mass media to create and maintain the public's general awareness of its insurance products and reputation, whereas its salespeople use prospecting techniques to identify potential customers. Once an individual becomes a customer, Prudential maintains contact through a combination of personal contact and mailings.

The Internet is a medium with unique qualities. It occupies a central space in the continuum of media choices. It is not a mass medium, even though a large number of people now use it and many companies seem to view their Web sites as billboards or broadcasts. Nor is the Internet a personal contact tool, although it can provide individuals the convenience of making personal contacts through e-mail and newsgroups. Jeff Bezos, founder of Amazon, described the Web as the ideal tool for reaching what he calls "the hard middle"—markets that are too small to justify a mass media campaign, yet too large to cover using personal contact. Figure 3-8 illustrates the position of the Web as a customer contact medium, located between the large markets addressed by mass media and the highly focused markets addressed by personal contact selling and promotion techniques.

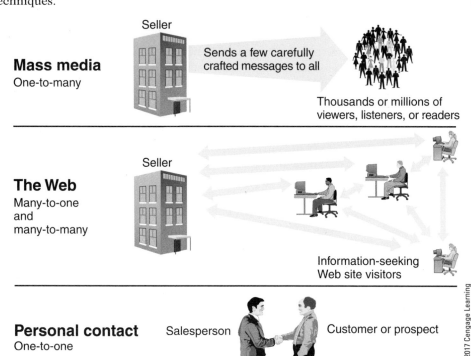

FIGURE 3-8   Business communication modes

To help you better understand the differences shown in Figure 3-8, read the following scenario. The scenario assumes that you have heard about a new book, but would like to learn more about it before buying it. Consider how your information acquisition process would vary, depending on the medium you used to gather the information.

- *Mass media*: You might have been exposed to general promotional messages from book publishers that have created impressions about quality associated with particular book brands. If your existing knowledge includes a brand identity for the book's publisher, these messages might influence your perceptions of the book. You might have been exposed to an ad for the title on television, radio, or in print. You might have heard the book's author interviewed on a radio program or read a review of the book in a publication such as *The New York Times Book Review* or *Booklist* magazine. Notice that most of these process elements involve you as a passive recipient of information. This communication channel is labeled "Mass media" and appears at the top of Figure 3-8. Communication in this model flows from one advertiser to many potential buyers and thus is called a **one-to-many communication model**. The defining characteristic of the mass media promotion process is that the seller is active and the buyer is passive.

- *Personal contact*: Small-value items are not frequently sold through this medium because the costs of devoting a salesperson's efforts to a small sale are prohibitive. However, in the case of books, local bookshop owners and employees often devote considerable time and resources to developing close relationships with their customers. Although each individual book sale is a small-value transaction, people who frequent local bookshops tend to buy large numbers of books over time. Thus, the bookseller's investment in developing personal contacts is often rewarded. In this scenario, you may visit your local bookshop and strike up a conversation with a knowledgeable bookseller. In the personal contact model, this would most likely be a bookseller with whom you have already established a relationship. The bookseller would offer an opinion on the book based on having read that book, books by the same author, or reviews of the book. This opinion would be expressed as part of a two-way conversational interchange. This interchange usually includes a number of conversational elements (small talk, such as discussions about the weather, local sports, or politics) that are not directly related to the transaction you are considering. These other interchanges are part of the trust-building and trust-maintaining activities that businesses undertake to develop the relationship element of the personal contact model. The underlying **one-to-one communication model** appears at the bottom of Figure 3-8 and is labeled "Personal contact." The defining characteristic of information gathering in the personal contact model is the wide-ranging interchange that occurs within the framework of an existing trust relationship. Both the buyer and the seller (or the seller's representative) actively participate in this exchange of information.

- *The Web*: To obtain information about a book on the Web, you could search for Web site references to the book, the author, or the subject of the book. You would likely identify a number of Web sites that offer such information. These sites might include those of the book's publisher, firms that sell books on the Web, independent book reviews, or discussion groups focused on the book's author or genre. *The New York Review of Books* and *Booklist* magazine, both staples of mass media book promotion, are available online. Book review sites that did not originate in a print edition, such as *BookBrowse*, also appear on the Web. Most online booksellers maintain searchable space on their sites for readers to post reviews and comments about specific titles. If the author of the book is famous, there might even be independent Web fan sites devoted to him or her. If the book is about a notable person, incident, or time period, you might find Web sites devoted to those notable topics that include reviews of books related to the topic. You could examine any number of these resources to any extent you desired. You might encounter some advertising material created by the publisher while searching the Web. However, if you choose not to view the publisher's ads, you will find it as easy to click the Back button on your Web browser as it is to surf television channels with your remote control. The Web affords you many communication channels. Figure 3-8 shows only one of the communication models that can occur when using the Web to search for product information. The model labeled "The Web" in Figure 3-8 is the **many-to-one communication model**. The Web gives you the flexibility to use a one-to-one model (as in the personal contact model) in which you communicate over the Web with an individual working for the seller, or engage in **many-to-many communications** with other potential buyers. The defining characteristic of a product information search on the Web is that the buyer actively participates in the search and controls the length, depth, and scope of the search.

Summary

In this chapter, you learned that businesses are using six main approaches to generate revenue on the Web, including: the Web catalog, digital content sales, advertising-supported, advertising-subscription mixed, fee-for-transaction, and fee-for-service models. You learned how these models work and what kinds of businesses use which models (or combinations of these models). You also learned that some companies have changed revenue models as they learned more about their customers and the business environment in which their Web sites operate. Changes in technology have also driven shifts in some companies' choice of revenue models.

You learned that companies can use multiple marketing channels, but must be careful to coordinate them to avoid cannibalization either within their own organizations or with the companies that have traditionally provided sales distribution to consumers for them. In accordance with the network model of organization that you learned about in Chapter 1, companies doing business online sometimes form strategic alliances with other companies to obtain their skills in Web site operation.

By understanding how the Web differs from other media and by designing Web sites that capitalize on those differences, companies can create effective Web presences that deliver value to visitors. Every organization must anticipate that visitors to its Web site arrive with a variety of expectations, prior knowledge, and skill levels, and are connected to the Internet through a variety of different technologies. Knowing how these factors can affect the visitor's ability to navigate the site and extract information from the site can help organizations design better, more usable Web sites. Enlisting the help of users when building test versions of the Web site is also a good way to create a Web site that represents the organization well.

Firms must understand the nature of communication on the Web so they can use it to identify and reach the largest possible number of customers and qualified prospects. Using a many-to-one communication model enables Web sites to effectively reach potential customers.

Key Terms

account aggregation	digital content revenue model
addressable media	Digital Rights Management (DRM)
advertising-subscription mixed revenue model	disintermediation
advertising-supported revenue model	fee-for-service revenue models
bill presentment	fee-for-transaction revenue model
cannibalization	mail-order
catalog model	many-to-many communications
channel conflict	many-to-one communication model
channel cooperation	marketing channel
communication modes	mass media
customer-centric	one-to-many communication model
demographic information	one-to-one communication model

paywall	stickiness
personal contact	sticky
personal shopper	usability testing
portal	virtual fitting rooms
presence	virtual model
prospecting	Web catalog revenue model
reintermediation	Web directory
stakeholders	Web portal

Review Questions

1. In the introduction to this chapter you learned about the development of the Google Photos service. Briefly describe two things the development team did that influenced the design of the service.

2. Why were many large discount retailers slow to sell online in the early days of electronic commerce?

3. What is a marketing channel?

4. Name two Web site features that an online clothing retailer might use to help customers find products in the right styles, colors, or sizes for them.

5. What is an academic information aggregation service?

6. How can an online music service provide free music to some customers?

7. What is the function of Digital Rights Management software?

8. Name one technology that has enabled the broad online distribution of video content.

9. What is meant by the "stickiness" of a Web site?

10. Why is demographic information about a Web site's visitors a factor in the pricing of advertising sold on that site?

11. What is a Web portal?

12. What is a Web directory?

13. What is a paywall?

14. Name two types of Web sites that might offer online classified ads.

15. What is a bill presentment service?

16. What is an account aggregation service?

17. Briefly describe the role an online information service could play in a used car purchase transaction.

18. What is a "hook and pay" strategy and how is it used by some online game play sites?

19. What is a strategic alliance?

20. Name one important element that a company should include in its Web presence.

21. Name two factors that can affect a Web site's usability.

22. What is addressable media?

Exercises

1. In about 100 words, outline the reasons a retailer might want to use more than one marketing channel.

2. In a paragraph or two, explain why an online retailer might mail printed catalogs to customers or potential customers.

3. Write a paragraph in which you explain how an online retailer might use its return policy to gain a competitive advantage.

4. In about 100 words, explain how online distribution might benefit the publisher of an academic journal.

5. In about 100 words, summarize the arguments for and against buying a novel as an electronic book instead of a printed paperback book.

6. In about 200 words, outline the changes that online distribution has prompted in the businesses of television program production and distribution.

7. Briefly explain what targeted advertising is and write a paragraph or two in which you describe what types of Web sites are likely able to sell it.

8. In about 100 words, outline the factors a local newspaper might need to consider when deciding whether to offer an online version.

9. In one or two paragraphs, define and distinguish between disintermediation and reintermediation.

10. In one or two paragraphs, outline the concerns a person might have when considering whether to do business with an online bank (that is, a bank with no physical offices).

11. In about 100 words, outline strategies that might allow a small, specialized travel agency to be successful doing business online.

12. In about 100 words, describe the issues that arise when a professional, such as a lawyer or physician, offer their services online.

13. Many businesses offer free samples of their products or services to potential customers to induce them to become customers. Write two or three paragraphs in which you describe how this strategy can be implemented online. Be sure to note how the amount of sampling that is likely to be beneficial differs in the online environment and the physical world.

14. In about 100 words, define "channel conflict" and describe how a consumer electronics company that sells its products both in retail stores and online might deal with this issue.

15. In general, custom-made luxury products sell better in physical stores than online because the unique nature of each individual product is easier to evaluate in person. In about 100 words, explain why expensive jewelry, especially diamond jewelry, sells well online in an apparent contradiction of this general tendency.

16. Visit the Web sites of two art museums that sell memberships online, then examine each site to find information about the memberships offered. Write a report of 200 words in which you describe the process on each site that a visitor would follow to shop for a membership. Evaluate how well each site describes its membership options and encourages a visitor to purchase one. Consider ease of shopping, how clearly the site describes membership options, and whether the site makes a convincing case for buying a membership. Provide at least one recommendation for improving each of the two sites you selected.

17. In about 100 words, describe the elements in a customer-centric approach to Web design.

Cases

C1. Progressive Insurance

In the 1980s, Progressive was a small auto insurance company that sold most of its policies to people who had poor driving records and could not qualify for the standard rate policies sold by other insurers. Progressive charged higher premiums for these policies, which the insurance industry calls substandard policies. Often, other insurers who could not write standard polices for customers would refer those customers to Progressive. The combination of high premiums and the lower cost of its smaller sales force enabled Progressive to earn good profits on this business. Eventually, other insurers noticed Progressive's success and began to offer their own substandard policies.

To respond to the increased competition, Progressive improved its claim service and became one of the first insurance companies to offer 24/7 service every day of the year. During the 1990s, Progressive gradually developed a full line of auto insurance products for all types of drivers and focused on offering the lowest prices in both standard and substandard markets. Although Progressive's advertising mentions the quality of its service, it always emphasizes its low prices.

Progressive was the first auto insurance company to launch a Web site (in 1995) and was the first to sell policies online (in 1997). Knowing that most potential insurance buyers shop multiple Web sites to find the best rate, the company began showing its competitors' rates on its Web site in 2002, allowing potential customers to compare prices without leaving Progressive's site. The site displays these rates even when Progressive's rate is higher than a competitor's rate on a particular policy.

Progressive's management has expressed a belief that people prefer to buy insurance from honest companies who offer the best prices. In 2008, Progressive introduced a female character, "Flo," who embodies openness, honesty, and a devotion to low prices. Flo appears in the company's television and radio ads, and is featured prominently on its Web site. In fact, the character often appears in television ad vignettes that tout the price comparison feature of the Web site.

REQUIRED:

1. Many managers would be reluctant even to mention competitors, much less provide their competitor's prices to potential customers. In about 200 words, outline Progressive's reasons for showing competitors' prices and analyze the costs and benefits of doing so.

2. In the chapter, you learned that it is important for a company to present an image consistent with its philosophy, principles, and identity on its Web site. In about 100 words, explain how Progressive does or does not accomplish this objective.

3. Visit the Progressive Web site and assume you are a potential customer who needs insurance for a used car you plan to buy. Evaluate the usability of the site and write a report of about 100 words in which you describe your experience. Be sure to mention specific site features that were or were not helpful and conclude with an overall impression of the site's effectiveness.

Note: Your instructor might assign you to a group to complete this case and might ask you to prepare a formal presentation of your results to your class.

C2. Association for the Study of International Business

The Association for the Study of International Business (ASIB) is an organization of researchers, professors, and business executives interested in the study, analysis, and promotion of business activities beyond domestic borders. Mario DiPonetti, ASIB's executive director, has hired you as a consultant to help him map out a future Web revenue strategy for the association.

The ASIB has about 3000 members located in countries throughout the world; however, about half of its members are in the United States. Each member pays an annual membership fee of $100, so ASIB's dues revenue totals about $300,000 per year. ASIB sponsors two conferences each year; it also publishes a monthly newsletter and two journals. The conferences generate about $50,000 per year; that is, conference and exhibitor fees exceed the costs of running the conferences by that amount. This $50,000 is used to cover general ASIB operating costs.

One of the journals, *Annals of International Business*, has an academic focus and is read by researchers interested in international business topics. All ASIB members receive a copy of this journal and ASIB sells about 300 subscriptions to the journal at $500 (a total of $150,000 per year). Most of the subscribers are university libraries. This journal is published four times each year.

The second journal, *International Business Today*, is written for business executives. It includes articles and features that report on current trends in international business and is published monthly. All ASIB members receive a copy of this journal and ASIB sells about 1000 subscriptions to the journal at $50 (a total of $50,000 per year).

The total subscription revenue from the two journals is $200,000 per year. *International Business Today* sells advertising that yields about $60,000 per year. ASIB uses that total revenue of $260,000 to cover the costs of producing and mailing both journals. The cost of producing one issue of either journal, which includes proofreading, editing, and typesetting costs, is about $2000. The printing and mailing costs, which have been increasing rapidly over the past several years, average about $3 per journal (the mailing costs to some members are much higher than others because they are located in distant countries). Each year, ASIB produces 16 issues (four of the academic journal and 12 of the business journal) and mails 61,200 journals (13,200 of the academic journal and 48,000 of the business journal) to members and subscribers at a total cost of $215,600 (16 × $2000 plus 61,200 × $3). Thus, ASIB's current journal operations yield a net profit of $44,400 ($260,000 − $215,600) that can help support other ASIB activities.

ASIB has a Web site that it constructed at a cost of $30,000 three years ago. One of ASIB's staff members spends approximately half of her time managing the site. One-half of this staff member's salary and benefits, along with other recurring expenses, such as software licenses and computer upgrades for the Web site, totals about $40,000 per year. Mario explains to you that one of the ASIB's greatest cost reduction successes was last year's decision to offer the monthly newsletter by e-mail. About half of the members chose to receive the newsletter by e-mail. The paper newsletters cost 50 cents each to print and mail, but creating and sending the e-mails took less than $50 worth of staff members' time. Thus, ASIB realized an immediate savings of about $700 (50% × 3000 × $.50 of mailing costs saved, less the $50 cost to send e-mails) each month, or $8400 per year. The newsletters are also placed on the Web site so that members can check there if they happen to miss the e-mailed newsletter. This success prompted Mario to think about ways to reduce the cost of distributing the journals. He wants to make sure, however, that ASIB continues to receive as much of the journal revenue as possible under any new revenue model.

One of the companies you learned about in the chapter, EBSCO, approached Mario with an offer to handle electronic distribution of the academic journal. EBSCO will take a copy of the journal when it is published, convert each article into Adobe Portable Document Format (PDF) and into HTML format, index the articles, and place them into several of EBSCO's databases. Many university and research libraries subscribe to EBSCO databases. The EBSCO representative explained to Mario that most of the libraries would continue their print subscriptions to the journal, but that about 30 percent of the libraries would stop subscribing and rely on their electronic access to the journal through the EBSCO database. Mario called some of his friends who are executive directors of other associations and confirmed that this percentage was correct in their experience. EBSCO would pay ASIB a flat annual fee of $10,000 for access to the journal plus $50 per year for every library that subscribed to an EBSCO database that included the journal. The EBSCO sales representative estimated that the number of subscribing libraries would be about 1000.

Mario outlined an alternative to the EBSCO contract. In this alternative, ASIB would itself scan the journals into PDF files and make them available on the ASIB Web site for a subscription fee. Mario estimated that it would cost about $1000 to create the PDF files for one issue and place them on the Web site. He also estimated that managing the accounts and passwords would consume about $500 per month of staff time and related costs. Mario believes that arranging for distribution of article abstracts through Google Scholar would increase the visibility of the organization and could possibly lead to additional subscription revenue. Note that Mario intends to make the abstract for each article available, not the entire text of each article.

EBSCO was not interested in purchasing access to the business journal, but Mario is evaluating ways to make some or all of the content from that journal available on the ASIB Web site. He is considering offering reduced-rate "Web access only" subscriptions to business executives. He is also thinking about offering some of the best stories from the print edition on the Web and including ads offering full subscriptions on each page. He is even considering placing the first part of the best stories on the Web site and offering readers a chance to subscribe so they can read the rest of the story.

Several companies that sell products and services to international businesses currently run ads in the business journal. These companies expressed an interest in placing ads on ASIB Web pages that contain content (such as stories from the business journal). Mario estimates that ASIB could earn between $3000 and $9000 per month from these ads, but he is concerned that having the best content from the business journal on the Web site might convince some business executives to drop their subscriptions to the print edition.

REQUIRED:

1. Review the requirements for listing the Association's journals on Google Scholar. Prepare a memo of about 100 words to Mario in which you outline what steps will be necessary to secure distribution of the journals' article abstracts through Google Scholar.

2. Mario and the ASIB face cannibalization issues in their decision to make the journals available online; however, the issues are somewhat different for the two journals because each is being sold to a different audience. In about 100 words, discuss these issues for the two journals. Be sure to note differences in these issues for the two journals.

3. Prepare a comprehensive report for Mario in which you outline and analyze the possible revenue models that ASIB might use for its Web site. You should address the two journals as separate issues. Be sure to include the role that a paywall could play in one or more of the possible revenue models. Your report should provide the basis for a presentation to the ASIB executive board and should include specific recommendations where possible.

Note: Your instructor might assign you to a group to complete this case and might ask you to prepare a formal presentation of your results to your class.

For Further Study and Research

Abrams, D. 2014. "Print Continues to Outsell Digital," *Publishing Perspectives*, October 15. http://publishingperspectives.com/2014/10/print-continues-outsell-digital-first-half-2014/

Anderson, C. 2008. *The Long Tail Revised and Updated Edition: Why the Future of Business is Selling Less of More*. New York: Hyperion.

Anderson, C. 2009. *Free: The Future of a Radical Price*. New York: Hyperion.

Bagchi, S. 2015. "E-books Help Personalize the Experience of Reading," *The Times of India*, May 3. http://timesofindia.indiatimes.com/tech/tech-news/E-books-help-personalize-the-experience-of-reading/articleshow/47136052.cms

Bedford, A. 2015. "Don't Prioritize Efficiency Over Expectations," *Nielsen Norman Group*, May 10. http://www.nngroup.com/articles/efficiency-vs-expectations/

Bustillo, M. 2011. "Wal-Mart Shakes Up its Online Business," *The Wall Street Journal*, August 13, B1.

Carlson, E. 2015. "Move Over Netflix, Amazon: Sony's Crackle Is Ramping Up," *Fortune*, April 29. http://fortune.com/2015/04/29/crackle-streaming-stars/

Carrns, A. 2014. "A Start-Up Offers Online Therapy for Anxiety and More," *The New York Times,* October 25, B5.

Christensen, C. and M. Overdorf. 2000. "Meeting the Challenge of Disruptive Change," *Harvard Business Review*, 78(2), March–April, 66–75.

Conditt, J. 2015. "Google Photos Offers Unlimited Storage for Mobile and Web," *Engadget*, May 28. http://www.engadget.com/2015/05/28/google-photos/

Crawford, W. 2004. "Keeping the Faith: Playing Fair with Your Visitors," *EContent*, 27(4), September, 42–43.

Davis, D. 2015. "Walmart Invests Heavily in E-commerce," *Internet Retailer*, May 19. https://www.internetretailer.com/2015/05/19/wal-mart-invests-e-commerce-q1-web-sales-grow-17

Demery, P. 2011. "Training, Technology, and Teamwork Help E-retailers Derive More Sales and Profits from Live Chat," *Internet Retailer*, November, 14–16.

The Economist. 2010. "Charging for Content: Media's Two Tribes," 396(8689), July 3–9, 63.

Enright, A. 2011. "Classy Examples: Luxury Brands Show How to Sell High-ticket Items Online and Build Trust," *Internet Retailer*, May 31. http://www.internetretailer.com/2011/05/31/classy-examples

Greenstein, S. and M. Devereux. 2006. *The Crisis at Encyclopaedia Britannica. Kellogg School of Management Case 5–306-504*. Evanston, IL: Northwestern University.

Gupta, S. and C. Mela. 2009. "What Is a Free Customer Worth?" *Harvard Business Review*, 86(11), 102–109.

Johnston, S. 2012. "Newspaper Paywalls Accelerating," *EByline*, July 30. http://ebyline.biz/2012/07/newspaper-paywalls-accelerating/

Jones, P. 2015. "Long Live the eBook: It's a Champion of the Printed Word," *The Guardian*, January 7. http://www.theguardian.com/commentisfree/2015/jan/07/ebook-printed-word-reader-e-reader

Kemp, T. 2000. "Wal-Mart No Web Mart," *Internet Week*, October 9, 1–2.

Kessler, S. 2012. "New York Times Paywall Gets Bigger, Halves Number of Free Online Articles," *Mashable*, March 20. http://mashable.com/2012/03/20/new-york-times-paywall-free-articles/

Kosner, A. 2013. "Blogger Andrew Sullivan and Filmmaker Larry Clark Monetize Themselves with Tinypass," *Forbes*, January 3. http://www.forbes.com/sites/anthonykosner/2013/01/03/blogger-andrew-sullivan-and-filmmaker-larry-clark-monetize-themselves-with-tinypass/

Leski, M. 2011. "Reading: From Paper to Pixels," *IEEE Security & Privacy*, 9(4), July–August, 76–79.

Lynch, J. 2015. "Why Crackle Wants You (and the Industry) to See It as a Mainstream TV Network," *Adweek*, April 9. http://www.adweek.com/news/television/why-streaming-service-crackle-ditched-newfronts-upfronts-163951

McIntyre, D. 2015. "Amazon Tops Walmart in Brand Survey," *24/7 Wall Street*, May 31. http://247wallst.com/retail/2015/05/31/amazon-tops-walmart-in-brand-survey/

Medical Economics. 2009. "Website to Offer Online Visits Nationwide," August 7, 18.

Miller, C. and J. Bosman. 2011. "E-books Outsell Print Books at Amazon," *The New York Times*, May 19. http://www.nytimes.com/2011/05/20/technology/20amazon.html

Morphy, E. 2012. "Pandora's Popularity—Too Much of a Good Thing?" *E-Commerce Times*, March 8. http://www.ecommercetimes.com/story/Pandoras-Popularity---Too-Much-of-a-Good-Thing-74595.html

Moynihan, T. 2015. "Google Photos Is Your New Essential Picture App," *Wired*, May 29. http://www.wired.com/2015/05/google-photos-new-essential-picture-app/

Newton, C. 2015. "How Google Solved Our Photo Backup Nightmare," *The Verge*, May 29. http://www.theverge.com/a/sundars-google/google-photos-google-io-2015

Nielsen, J. 1999. *Designing Websites with Authority: Secrets of an Information Architect*. Indianapolis, IN: New Riders.

Nielsen, J. 2001. "Usability Metrics," *Nielsen Norman Group*, January 21. http://www.nngroup.com/articles/usability-metrics/

Nielsen, J. 2011. "E-commerce Usability," *Nielsen Norman Group*, October 24. http://www.nngroup.com/articles/e-commerce-usability/

Nielsen Norman Group. 2011. *Non-profit and Charity Website Usability: 116 Design Guidelines*. Fremont, CA: Nielsen Norman Group.

Nyak, M. 2013. "FACTBOX: A Look at the $66 Billion Video Games Industry," *Reuters*, June 10. http://in.reuters.com/article/2013/06/10/gameshow-e-idINDEE9590DW20130610

Ojala, M. 2013. "The Big Three: Still Relevant? *Online Searcher*, 37(4), July/August, 67–69.

Osterwalder, A., Y. Pigneur, and C. Tucci. 2005. "Clarifying Business Models: Origins, Present, and Future of the Concept," *Communications of the Association for Information Systems*, 16, 1–25.

Oswald, E. 2012. "Wikipedia Kills Off Encyclopaedia Britannica, at Least in Print," *ExtremeTech*, March 14. http://www.extremetech.com/internet/122505-wikipedia-kills-of-encyclopaedia-britannica-at-least-in-print

Owen, L. 2012. "Newspaper Association of America Shows New Trends in Paywalls," *Paid Content*, August 1. http://paidcontent.org/2012/08/01/newspaper-association-of-america-shows-new-trends-in-paywalls/

Pérez-Peña, R. 2007. "Times to End Charges on Web Site," *The New York Times*, September 18. http://www.nytimes.com/2007/09/18/business/media/18times.html

Peters, J. 2011. "Times' Online Pay Model Was Years in the Making," *The New York Times*, March 20. http://www.nytimes.com/2011/03/21/business/media/21times.html

Pfanner, E. 2013. "Music Industry Sales Rise, and Digital Revenue Gets the Credit," *The New York Times*, February 27, B3.

Rawsthorn, A. 2013. "What Constitutes Good and Bad Web Design?" *The New York Times*, January 6. http://www.nytimes.com/2013/01/07/arts/design/what-constitutes-good-and-bad-web-design.html

Rayport, J. and J. Sviokla. 1995. "Exploiting the Virtual Value Chain," *Harvard Business Review*, 73(6), November–December, 75–85.

Rosenberger, R. 2013. "Why Don't People Want to Read E-books on Tablets?" *Slate*, August 15. http://www.slate.com/blogs/future_tense/2013/08/15/ebook_sales_decline_do_people_not_want_to_read_books_on_tablets.html

Rueter, T. 2011. "Home Depot Enables Online Shoppers to Pick Up Purchases Inside Stores," *Internet Retailer*, September 2. http://www.internetretailer.com/2011/09/02/home-depot-enables-online-shoppers-pick-items-stores

Sanderfoot, A. and C. Jenkins. 2001. "Content Sites Pursue Fee-Based Model," *Folio: The Magazine for Magazine Management*, 30(6), 15–16.

Schade, A. 2014. "Ecommerce User Experience Trends: Three Design Trends to Follow and Three to Avoid," *Nielsen Norman Group*, January 26. http://www.nngroup.com/articles/e-commerce-usability/

Schwartz, E. 1997. *Webonomics*. New York: Broadway Books.

Schwartz, E. 1999. *Digital Darwinism*. New York: Broadway Books.

Sharma, R. 2015. "Technology Will Help Target Boost Sales, But It Won't Solve Walmart's Problems," *TheStreet*, May 22. http://www.thestreet.com/story/13160495/1/technology-will-help-target-boost-sales-but-it-wont-solve-walmarts-problems.html

Shneiderman, B. 1997. *Designing the User Interface: Strategies for Effective Human-Computer Interaction*. Reading, MA: Addison-Wesley.

Sisario, B. 2015. "Global Online Music Sales Slightly Surpass CDs and LPs," *The New York Times*, April 15, B4.

Sklar, J. 2012. *Principles of Web Design*, Fifth Edition. Boston, MA: Course Technology.

Stambor, Z. 2011. "Customer Service: Video and Chat Help E-retailers Get Personal With Customers," *Internet Retailer*, June 30. http://www.internetretailer.com/2011/06/30/customer-service

Steel, E. 2007. "Job-Search Sites Face a Nimble Threat; Online Boards Become Specialized, Challenging Web-Print Partnerships," *The Wall Street Journal*, October 9, B10.

Stross, R. 2011. "The Therapist Will See You Now, Via the Web," *The New York Times*, July 9. http://www.nytimes.com/2011/07/10/technology/bringing-therapists-to-patients-via-the-web.html

Their, D. 2012. "Comedian Louis CK Is the King of Direct-to-Consumer Sales," *Forbes*, June 28. http://www.forbes.com/sites/davidthier/2012/06/28/comedian-louis-ck-is-the-king-of-direct-to-consumer-sales/

Tian, X. and B. Martin. 2011. "Impacting Forces on eBook Business Models Development," *Publishing Research Quarterly*, 27(3), 230–246.

Tognazzi, B. 2009. "How to Achieve Painless Registration," *AskTOG*, November–December. http://www.asktog.com/columns/081Registration.html

Tuttle, B. 2015. "Walmart Testing a Free Shipping Option to Compete with Amazon Prime," *Money*, May 14. http://time.com/money/3858616/walmart-free-shipping-amazon/

Weiss, T. 2000. "Walmart.com Back Online After Four-Week Overhaul," *Computerworld*, 34(45), November 6, 24.

Williams, T. 2005. "NYTimes.com to Offer Subscription Service," *The New York Times*, May 17, C5.

Zimmerman, A. 2000. "Wal-Mart Launches Web Site for a Third Time, This Time Emphasizing Speed and Ease," *The Wall Street Journal*, October 31, B12.

Blend Images Photography/Veer

Marketing on
the Web

LEARNING OBJECTIVES

In this chapter, you will learn:

- How firms use product-based and customer-based marketing strategies
- Strategies for communicating with different market segments
- To identify customers' characteristics as they move through the customer relationship life cycle
- How online advertising has developed and grown
- About e-mail marketing strategies
- About technology-enabled customer relationship management
- How to create and maintain brands online
- How businesses use social media in viral marketing campaigns
- About search engine positioning tactics and domain name selection strategies

INTRODUCTION

In the past, the humorous stereotype of a father who bumbles his way through housekeeping or child care duties was a staple of marketing messages for household products. In the story line of these ads, the poor fellow struggles to do laundry, make dinner, and care for the children and must scramble to get everything done or the evidence (everything from dirty dishes to soiled diapers) hidden before Mom returns.

When household product purchasing decisions were made primarily by women, this type of advertising might have made sense. But in recent years, men have been taking a larger role in these decisions. Thus, companies have begun to identify a new audience for their marketing messages and are beginning to turn away from advertising story lines that make a joke out of men's experiences.

In 2012, Kimberly-Clark ran a television ad for its Huggies brand diapers that became infamous for its portrayal of men as incompetent caregivers to their young children. In response to a firestorm of online criticism, the company replaced the ad immediately and initiated a complete review of its online brand message talking points. Today, it regularly engages with a number of "dad-focused" social media outlets and participates, along with many other consumer product companies, in the annual Dad 2.0 Summit. This conference, sponsored by Unilever's Dove Men+Care brand soap and shampoo products, is operated by XY Media, a consulting firm that advises companies on how to appeal to fathers.

In this chapter, you will learn how companies use advertising and marketing to develop long-term relationships with customers that their employees might never meet in person. The importance of telling an authentic, accurate, meaningful, and consistent story through online and physical channels underlies the principles of branding, marketing, relationship management, and communication that you will learn about in this chapter.

Web Marketing Strategies

In this chapter, you will learn how companies are using the Web in their marketing strategies to advertise their products and services and promote their reputations. Increasingly, companies are classifying customers into groups and creating targeted messages for each group. The sizes of these targeted groups can be smaller when companies are using the Web—in some cases, just one customer at a time can be targeted. New research into the behavior of Web site visitors has even suggested ways in which Web sites can respond to visitors who arrive at a site with different needs at different times. This chapter will also introduce you to some of the ways companies are making money by selling advertising on their Web sites.

Most companies use the term **marketing mix** to describe the combination of elements that they use to achieve their goals for selling and promoting their products and services. When a company decides which elements it will use, it calls that particular marketing mix its **marketing strategy**. As you learned in Chapter 3, companies—even those in the same industry—try to create unique brand presences in their markets. A company's marketing strategy is an important tool for conveying its branding and advertising messages to current and prospective customers. A company's Web presence is an element of that marketing strategy.

The Four Ps of Marketing

Most marketing classes organize the essential issues of marketing into the **four Ps of marketing**: product, price, promotion, and place. **Product** is the physical item or service that a company is selling. Elements such as quality, design, features, characteristics, and even the packaging make up the product. These intrinsic characteristics of the product are important, but customers' perceptions of the product, called the product's **brand**, can be as important as the actual characteristics of the product.

The **price** element of the marketing mix is the amount the customer pays for the product. In recent years, marketing experts have argued that companies should think of price in a broader sense—that is, the total of all financial costs that the customer pays (including transaction costs) to obtain the product. This total cost is subtracted from the benefits that a customer derives from the product to yield an estimate of the **customer value** obtained in the transaction. Later in this book, you will learn how the Web can create new opportunities for creative pricing and price negotiations through online auctions, reverse auctions, and group buying strategies. These Web-based opportunities are helping companies find new ways to create increased customer value.

Promotion includes any means of spreading the word about the product. It requires decisions about advertising, public relations, personal selling, and overall promotion of the product. On the Internet, possibilities abound for communicating with existing and potential customers. In this chapter, you will learn how organizations use their Web sites, e-mail strategies, and social media as communication tools for promoting their products and services.

For years, marketing managers dreamed of a world in which instant deliveries would give all customers exactly what they wanted when they wanted it. The issue of **place** (also called **distribution**) is the need to have products or services available in many different locations. The problem of getting the right products to the right places at the best time to sell them has plagued companies since commerce began. Although the Internet does not solve all of these logistics and distribution problems, it can certainly help. For example, digital products (such as information, news, software, music, video, and e-books) can be delivered almost instantly through the Internet. Companies that sell products that must be shipped have found that the Internet gives them much better shipment tracking and inventory control tools than they have ever had before. Figure 4-1 depicts the components of the four Ps of marketing and shows their contributions to overall marketing strategy.

Product-Based Marketing Strategies

Managers at many companies think of their businesses in terms of the products and services they sell. This **product-based marketing strategy** is a logical way to think of a business because companies spend a great deal of effort, time, and money to design and

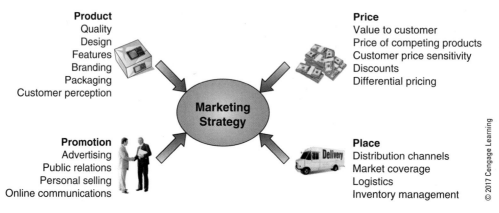

Product
Quality
Design
Features
Branding
Packaging
Customer perception

Price
Value to customer
Price of competing products
Customer price sensitivity
Discounts
Differential pricing

Marketing Strategy

Promotion
Advertising
Public relations
Personal selling
Online communications

Place
Distribution channels
Market coverage
Logistics
Inventory management

Delivery

© 2017 Cengage Learning

FIGURE 4-1   The four Ps of marketing contribute to marketing strategy

create those products and services. If you ask managers to describe what their companies are selling, they usually provide you with a detailed list of the physical objects they sell or use to create a service. When customers are likely to buy items from particular product categories, or are likely to think of their needs in terms of product categories, this type of product-based organization works well. Most office supplies stores on the Web believe their customers think of their needs using a product category structure. For example, both Office Depot and Staples use product categories (paper, ink and toner, printers) as the primary organizing theme in the design of their Web sites. Sears, a company that sold its products through catalogs and later in physical stores for many years before adding online sales, also organizes its Web site using a product-based structure. Many companies that used print catalogs in the past organized them by product category, and this design theme has been carried over into their Web sites.

Many retailers that began as catalog-based businesses organize their Web sites from an internal viewpoint; that is, according to the way that they arranged their products on store shelves or printed catalog pages. If customers arrive at these Web sites looking for a specific type of product, this approach can work well. However, customers who are shopping to fulfill a specific need, such as redecorating a room or choosing a graduation gift rather than to find a specific product, might not find these Web sites to be efficient to use.

Marketing consultants often advise retailers to design their Web sites using an external viewpoint by imagining themselves as customers and creating enabling experiences that meet their needs. Sometimes this requires a Web site design that offers alternative shopping paths. The next section describes how companies can implement this external viewpoint, or customer-based, approach to Web site design.

Customer-Based Marketing Strategies

In Chapter 3, you learned that the Web creates an environment that allows buyers and sellers to communicate with each other in multiple ways. The communication structures on the Web can become much more complex than in the one-way interactions that characterize traditional mass media outlets such as broadcast and print advertising.

For example, when a company takes its business online, it can create a Web site that is flexible enough to meet the needs of many different users. Instead of thinking of their Web sites as collections of products, companies can build their sites to meet the differing needs of various types of customers. For example, an online florist's Web site could allow customers to specify an arrangement that includes specific flowers or colors (satisfying customers with a desire for a specific product), yet provide a separate shopping path for customers who want to buy an arrangement for a specific occasion (birthday, anniversary, Mother's Day, and so on). Similarly, toy sites provide users with filtering options so they can select price range, type of toy, recipient age range, cost, and so on. The approach to Web site design that accommodates the differing needs of various types of customers is called a **customer-based marketing strategy**.

The first step in building a customer-based marketing strategy is to identify groups of customers who share common characteristics (such a group is often called a **demographic**). Creating a Web site that acknowledges the differences among those groups and treats each accordingly can make the site more accessible and useful to each group. Organizations find this difficult to accomplish because most managers, quite naturally, think about their Web sites as models of their activities, and they view those activities from their own internal perspective. For example, early university Web sites were often organized around the internal elements of the school (such as departments, colleges, and programs) in an implementation of their own internal perspective. Today, most university home pages include links to separate sections of the Web site designed for specific stakeholders, such as current students, prospective students, parents of students, potential donors, and faculty. This construction reflects the external perspective of each different user group that might use the Web site.

Communicating with Different Market Segments

Identifying groups of potential customers is just the first step in selling to those customers. An equally important component of any marketing strategy is the selection of communication media to carry the marketing message.

Media selection, or choosing where to market and advertise a company, can be critical for an online-only firm because it does not have a physical presence. The only contact a potential customer might have with an online firm could be the image it projects through the media and through its Web site. The challenge for online businesses, especially new online businesses, is to convince customers to trust them even though they do not have a physical presence.

Trust, Complexity, and Media Choice

As you learned in Chapter 3, the Web provides a communication mode that is an intermediate step between mass media and personal contact, but it is a very broad step. Using the Web to communicate with potential customers combines many of the advantages of personal contact selling with some of the cost savings of mass media. Figure 4-2 shows how these three information dissemination modes compare on the important dimensions of trust and product (or service) complexity.

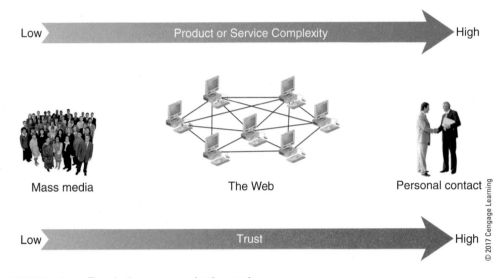

FIGURE 4-2   Trust in three communication modes

Although mass media offers the lowest level of trust, many companies continue to use it successfully. The cost of mass media advertising can be spread over the many people in its large audiences. For example, the cost of creating and running a television ad can be millions of dollars, but that ad will be viewed by millions of people. Thus, the cost of advertising per viewer is very low. Its low cost per viewer makes mass media advertising attractive to many companies.

After years of being barraged by television and radio commercials, many people have developed a resistance to the messages conveyed in mass media. The impact on an audience of the shouted expression "New and improved!" is very low. The overuse of superlatives has caused many people to distrust or ignore much mass media. Television remote controls have mute buttons and make channel surfing easy for a reason. Attempts to re-create mass media advertising on the Web are likely to fail for the same reasons—many people ignore or resist messages that lack content of any specific personal interest to them.

Mass media advertising campaigns that are successful often rely on the passive nature of the media consumption experience. People watching television or listening to radio are usually in a passive and receptive state of mind. Thus, advertisers can include messages in mass media advertising that recipients might not consider valid or convincing if they were actively evaluating those statements. The messages are accepted by recipients because they are in a nonquestioning and passive state of mind. In contrast, Web users are actively engaged in the medium, with hands on the keyboard or touchscreen, as they view Web pages. This active state of mind makes Web users far more likely to evaluate critically the advertising messages they see and less likely to accept the content of those messages in the same passive way that television viewers accept the content of television commercials. One exception to this general rule is when video entertainment is distributed online. Web sites that offer television shows or video clips as entertainment can incorporate mass media advertising into the video successfully because the visitor viewing the video is in the same nonquestioning and passive state of mind as a television viewer.

The level of complexity inherent in the product or service is also an important factor in media choice. Products that have few characteristics or that are easy to understand can be promoted well using mass media. Because mass media is expensive to produce, most companies use it to deliver short messages (although there are exceptions, such as infomercials). Highly complex products and services are best promoted through personal contact, which allows the potential customer to ask clarifying questions during the promotional presentation.

The Web occupies a wide middle ground and can be used for delivering short but focused messages that promote, but it can also be used to deliver longer and more complex messages. The Web can even be used to engage the potential customer in a back-and-forth dialog similar to that used in personal contact selling. Most important, a properly designed Web site can give potential customers the ability to choose their level of interaction. A company can present a mass media type of message that a site visitor can click to access a more detailed message. If the visitor still wants more information, the site can offer the opportunity for interactive communication (such as an online chat) with a customer service representative. Thus, the Web can offer elements of mass media messaging, personal contact interaction, and anything in between.

Companies can use the Web to capture some of the benefits of personal contact, yet avoid some of the costs inherent in that approach. One way to do this is to use some of the new communication tools that the Internet provides. For example, people can post their thoughts on a Web site and invite others to add commentary. Individuals have used this type of Web site, known as a **Web log** or **blog**, as an outlet for expressing their political, religious, and other strongly felt beliefs. Today, many companies use blogs as a communication device. For example, retailers use blogs to give their online stores a personality and provide customers with a reason to visit their Web sites even if they are not shopping.

In Chapter 1, you learned about social commerce, and in the introduction to this chapter, you saw how companies are starting to use storytelling techniques to tie their branding themes into a consistent set of messages across all media channels they use to communicate with customers and prospects. Social media can help companies create consistently themed discussions about new products, promotions, and even advertising campaigns. **Social media** is a general term for Web sites such as Facebook or Instagram and online communication technologies such as Twitter that allow participants to exchange ideas and report news and information updates to each other. You will learn more about social media and the mobile device applications that many people use with social media in Chapter 6.

Blogs and social media provide ways for companies to engage in two-way online communications that more closely resemble the high-trust personal contact mode of communication than the low-trust mass media mode. They also allow companies to achieve these benefits without incurring the high cost of traditional personal contact techniques.

Market Segmentation

Companies' responses to the decrease in advertising effectiveness were to identify specific portions of their markets and target them with specific advertising messages. This practice, called **market segmentation**, divides the pool of potential customers into groups, or **segments**. Segments are usually defined in terms of customer characteristics such as age, gender, marital status, income level, and geographic location. Thus, for example, unmarried men between the ages of 19 and 25 might be one market segment.

In the early 1990s, firms began identifying smaller and smaller market segments for specific advertising and promotion efforts. This practice of targeting very small market segments is called **micromarketing**. However, the low cost per viewer of traditional mass media advertising campaigns becomes much higher when mass media methods are used to target very small market segments. This cost increase hampered the success of micromarketing strategies. Even though micromarketing was an improvement over mass media advertising, it still used the same basic approach and suffered from the weaknesses of that approach.

Marketers have traditionally used three categories of variables to identify market segments. One variable is location. Firms divide their customers into groups by where they live or work. In this type of segmentation, called **geographic segmentation**, companies create different combinations of marketing efforts for each geographical group of customers. The grouping can be by nation, state (or province), city, or even by neighborhood. Alternatively, companies can develop one marketing strategy for urban customers, another for suburban customers, and yet a third for rural customers.

The second category uses information about age, gender, family size, income, education, religion, or ethnicity to group customers. This type of segmentation is called **demographic segmentation**. Demographic variables are frequently used by traditional marketers because research has shown that customers' need for and usage of products are strongly related to these types of variables. Demographic segmentation also exists on the Web. For example, a number of sites are devoted to women's issues or directed at specific age groups (such as teenagers) whose members tend to download music and purchase trendy clothing or video games. Often, demographic and geographic segmenting strategies are combined. For example, an airline might target middle-income families living in Wisconsin and Michigan with midwinter advertising for vacation trips to Florida.

In **psychographic segmentation**, marketers try to group customers by variables such as social class, personality, or their approach to life. For example, an auto company might direct advertising for a sports car to customers who are gregarious and have a high need for achievement. The use of psychographic segmentation has increased dramatically in recent years as marketers attempt to identify characteristic lifestyles and then design advertising to reach people who see themselves as having a particular lifestyle.

Companies that advertise on television often create messages designed to reach the likely audiences of various types of programs. These audiences represent one or more market segments. The market segments can be geographic, demographic, psychographic, or a combination of these. Figure 4-3 presents some examples from the television medium that show how companies do this.

Children's television shows are likely to feature advertising for products that appeal to children. Ads on daytime dramas are directed at people who are home during the day

Type of Television Program	Type of Advertising
Children's cartoons	Children's toys and games
Daytime dramas	Household and laundry goods, pet foods
Late-night talk shows	Snack foods and nonprescription sleep aids
Golf tournaments	Golf equipment, investment services, and life insurance
Baseball and football games	Snack foods, beer, autos
Documentary films	Books, CDs, educational DVDs

© 2017 Cengage Learning

FIGURE 4-3   Television advertising messages tailored to program audience

and who thus might be interested in household and laundry care products. These people are more likely than others to own pets, so they also will see ads for pet foods. Advertisers on late-night talk shows often direct their ads at people who might have trouble falling asleep. Advertisers also believe that this late-night audience is receptive to promotions for snack foods to eat while watching these programs or for nonprescription medications for ailments that might be keeping them up so late.

Advertisers use sports programming as a vehicle for two different market segments. Some sports shows, such as golf tournaments or tennis matches, appeal to higher-income viewers. Other sports shows, such as baseball or football game broadcasts, appeal to viewers with more moderate incomes. As a result, programs that cover golf or tennis are more likely to include ads for investment and insurance products and luxury automobiles than are baseball or football programs. Also, because viewers of golf tournaments and tennis matches are likely to play the sport, these programs often include ads for game equipment. Baseball or football games rarely include ads for game equipment because few viewers of these games participate in the sport themselves.

Programs that feature documentaries (such as those on the History Channel or the Discovery Channel) often carry ads for books, book clubs, and educational DVDs. Advertisers have found that these types of products appeal to the intellectual, arts-loving audiences of these programs.

Companies do much more than just match advertising messages to market segments. They also build a sales environment for their product or service that corresponds to the market segment they are trying to reach. In the physical world, store design and layout are often directed at specific market segments. If you walk through a shopping mall, you can observe that colors, displays, lighting, background music, and even the clothes worn by sales clerks vary with the targeted segment. For example, a clothing store for teenagers presents a completely different experience to its customers than a clothing store that sells expensive, conservative attire targeted toward more mature women with larger incomes.

Market Segmentation on the Web

The Web gives companies an opportunity to present different store environments online. For example, if you visit the home pages of Juicy Couture and Talbots, you will find that both pages are well designed and functional. However, they are each directed to very different market segments. The Juicy Couture site is targeted at young, fashion-conscious buyers. The site uses a wide variety of typefaces, bold graphics, and photos of brightly colored products to convey its tone. The emphasis is to make a bold fashion statement and, presumably, become the envy of your friends. In contrast, the Talbots site is rendered in a more subtle, conservative style. The messages emphasized are stability and timeless elegance. The site is designed to appeal to an older customer looking for classics instead of the latest trends.

In the physical world, retail stores have limited floor and display space. These limitations often force physical stores to decide on one particular message to convey. Exceptions do exist, such as a large department store that uses lighting and display space differently in each department; however, smaller retail stores usually choose the one image that appeals to most of their customers. On the Web, retailers can provide separate virtual spaces for different market segments. For example, the Verizon home page offers links for residential, business, and wireless customers. The Business page breaks down the options further, offering links to separate pages for small business, medium and enterprise business, and government agency customers. Some Web retailers provide the ultimate in targeted marketing—they allow their customers to create their own stores, as you will learn in the next section.

Offering Customers a Choice on the Web

Dell Premier accounts give users a high level of customer-based market segmentation. In these accounts, Dell offers each customer its own Dell Web site. Dell can customize a company's Premier account pages to show product selections for which price and terms have already been negotiated. Dell even allows individual employees of its customers to create their own personalized pages within their companies' Premier pages. This highly customized approach to offering products and services that match the needs of a particular customer is called **one-to-one marketing**. The Internet gives marketers the best opportunity for highly customized interactions with customers that they have had since the heyday of the door-to-door salesperson in the 1950s.

Beyond Market Segmentation: Customer Behavior and Relationship Intensity

In the previous sections, you learned how companies can target as market segments groups of customers that share common characteristics. You also learned how one-to-one marketing gives companies a chance to create Web experiences that are unique to each individual customer. The next step—beyond market segmentation, even beyond one-to-one marketing—is when companies use the Web to target specific customers in different ways at different times.

Segmentation Using Customer Behavior

In the physical world, businesses can sometimes create different experiences for customers in response to their needs. For example, a company might decide that its mission is to sell prepared meals to hungry customers. A given potential customer responds to hunger in different ways at different times. If a person is hungry in the morning, but late for work, that person might drive through a fast-food restaurant or grab a quick cup of coffee at the train station.

The point is that the same person requires different combinations of products and services depending on the occasion. In general, the creation of separate experiences for customers based on their behavior is called **behavioral segmentation**. When based on things that happen at a specific time or occasion, behavioral segmentation is sometimes called **occasion segmentation**.

Usually, businesses that operate in the physical world can meet only one or a few of a customer's differing behavioral needs. For example, the Chinese restaurant mentioned earlier might offer dining room service and take-out service, but it probably would not offer a drive-through window or a morning coffee kiosk. Very few, if any, restaurants offer everything from fast food through a five-course dinner. In the online world, it is much easier to design a single Web site that meets the needs of visitors who arrive in different behavioral modes. Thus, a Web site design can include elements that appeal to different behavioral segments.

Marketing researchers study how and why people prefer different combinations of products, services, and Web site features and how these preferences are affected by their modes of interaction with the site. Market researchers know that people want Web sites that offer a range of interaction possibilities. Remember that a particular person might visit a particular Web site at different times with different needs and will want an interaction that meets those needs on each visit. Customizing visitor experiences to match the site usage behavior patterns of each visitor or type of visitor is called **usage-based market segmentation**. Researchers have identified common patterns of online behavior and grouped patterns into categories. One set of categories that marketers use today includes browsers, buyers, and shoppers.

BROWSERS

Some visitors to a company's Web site are just surfing or browsing. Web sites intended to appeal to potential customers in this mode must offer them something that piques their interest. The site should include words that are likely to jog the memories of visitors and remind them of something they want to buy on the site.

These keywords are often called **trigger words** because they prompt a visitor to stay and investigate the products or services offered on the site. Links to explanations about the site or instructions for using the site can be particularly helpful to this type of customer. A site should include extra content related to the product or service the site sells. For example, a Web site that sells camping gear might offer reviews of popular camping destinations with photos and online maps. Such content can keep a visitor who is in browser mode interested long enough to stay at the site and develop a favorable impression of the company. Once visitors have developed this favorable impression, they are more likely to buy on this visit or bookmark the site for a return visit.

BUYERS

Visitors who arrive in buyer mode are ready to make a purchase right away. The best thing a site can offer a buyer is a direct route into the purchase transaction. For visitors who first choose a product from a printed catalog, many Web sites include a text box on their home pages that allows visitors to enter the catalog item number. This places that item in the site's shopping cart and takes the buyer directly to the shopping cart page. A **shopping cart** is the part of a Web site that keeps track of selected items for purchase and automates the purchasing process.

The shopping cart page should offer a link that takes the visitor back into the shopping area of the site, but the primary goal is to get the buyer to the shopping cart as quickly as possible, even if the buyer is at the site for the first time. The shopping cart should allow the buyer to create an account and log in after placing the item into the cart. To avoid placing barriers in the way of customers who want to buy, the site should not require visitors to log in until they near the end of the shopping cart procedure. You will learn more about shopping carts in Chapter 9.

SHOPPERS

Some customers arrive at a Web site knowing that it offers items they are interested in buying. These visitors are motivated to buy, but they are looking for more information before they make a purchase decision. For the visitor who is in shopper mode, a site should offer comparison tools, product reviews, and lists of features. Sites such as Crutchfield and Best Buy allow customers to specify the level of detail presented for each product, sort products by brand, or price, and compare products with each other side by side.

Remember that a person might visit a Web site one day as a browser and then return later as a shopper or a buyer. People do not retain behavioral categories from one visit to the next—even for the same Web site.

ALTERNATIVE MODELS

Although many companies work with these three visitor categories, other researchers are exploring alternative models. Much of Web site visitor behavior is not yet well understood. One study conducted jointly by the consulting firms McKinsey & Company and MediaMetrix examined the online behavior of 50,000 active Internet users and identified the six behavior-based categories of Web site visitors shown in Figure 4-4.

Other research studies have identified similar sets of characteristics and categories. Companies in different industries or lines of business identify somewhat different sets of characteristics and group their Web site visitors using different names. The challenge for Web businesses is to identify which groups are visiting their sites and formulate ways of generating revenue from each segment. For example, some of these groups (such as simplifiers and bargainers) are ready to buy and would be interested in seeing specific product or service offerings. Other groups (such as surfers, routiners, and sportsters) would be good targets for specific types of advertising messages. As the study of Web site visitor behavior becomes more sophisticated, companies are getting better at recognizing the various modes in which visitors arrive and channeling them into the appropriate sections of the site. For example, a beauty products Web site might track lipstick purchases and, knowing how long a lipstick should last, time e-mail promotions to reach a customer when she might be looking for a replacement. Similarly, online vitamin shops

Category	Online Objective	Web Site Characteristics That Attract These Visitors
Simplifiers	Convenience	Tools or facilities that make doing business easier, faster, or more efficient
Surfers	Find information, new ideas	Content that is entertaining, attractive, well displayed, and constantly updated
Bargainers	Find a good deal	Auctions, discounts, coupons, and sales
Connectors	Stay in touch with others	Chat rooms, discussion boards, social networking features, online greeting cards, e-mail services
Routiners	Information in one place	News, financial information, a familiar and stable user interface
Sportsters	Information in one place	Sports, entertainment, a familiar and stable user interface

Source: Forsyth, J., T. McGuire, J. Lavoie. 2000. *All Visitors Are Not Created Equal*. Boston: McKinsey & Co. and MediaMetrix.

FIGURE 4-4   Web site visitor categories based on a behavioral segmentation study

know how long each bottle of pills should last each customer and can design sales and promotion efforts to appeal to customers at just the right time to prompt a reorder.

Customer Relationship Intensity and Life-Cycle Segmentation

One goal of marketing is to create strong relationships between a company and its customers. The reason that one-to-one marketing and usage-based segmentation are so valuable is that they help to strengthen companies' relationships with their customers. Good customer experiences can help create an intense feeling of loyalty toward the company and its products or services.

Researchers have identified several stages of loyalty as customer relationships develop over time: the stages include awareness, exploration, familiarity, and commitment. The commitment stage can last a long time; indeed, it is every marketer's hope that it goes on forever. However, many customers lose their connections to a particular seller and enter a final stage called separation. A five-stage model of customer loyalty that is typical of these models appears in Figure 4-5.

This model shows the increase in intensity of the relationship as the customer moves through the first four stages. Not all customers go through the full five stages; some stop at a stage and continue the relationship at that level of intensity or terminate the relationship at that point. Some customers in a particular stage might have contact with the company online, while other customers in the same stage encounter the company offline. Companies should strive for a consistent customer experience at a particular life-cycle stage—that is, customers should experience the same level and quality of service whether they encounter the company online or offline. Online and offline customer

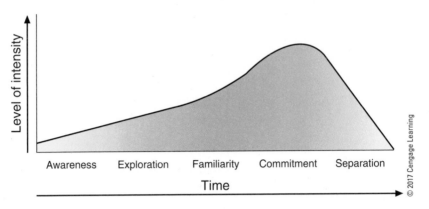

FIGURE 4-5   Five stages of customer loyalty

contact points are often called **touchpoints**, and the goal of providing similar levels and quality of service at all touchpoints is called **touchpoint consistency**.

As the figure shows, changes in the nature of the relationship do not occur suddenly as a customer moves from one stage to the next. Within each stage, the level of intensity changes gradually as the customer moves through that stage. The characteristics of the five stages are outlined in the next sections.

- *Awareness.* Customers who recognize the name of the company or one of its products are in the awareness stage of customer loyalty. They know that the company or product exists but have not had any interaction with the company. Advertising a brand or a company name is a common way for companies to achieve this level of relationship with potential customers.

- *Exploration.* In the exploration stage, potential customers learn more about the company or its products. The potential customer might visit the company's Web site to learn more, and the two parties will often communicate by telephone or e-mail. A large amount of information interchange can occur between the parties at this stage.

- *Familiarity.* Customers who have completed several transactions and are aware of the company's policies regarding returns, credits, and pricing flexibility are in the familiarity stage of their relationship with the company. In this stage, they are as likely to shop and buy from competitors as they are from the company.

- *Commitment.* After experiencing a considerable number of highly satisfactory encounters with a company, some customers develop a fierce loyalty or strong preference for the products or brands of that company. These customers have reached the commitment stage and are often willing to tell others about how happy they are with their interactions. To lure customers from the familiarity stage to the commitment stage, companies sometimes make concessions on prices or terms. Usually, the value of the strong relationship is worth more to the company than the costs of these concessions.

- *Separation*. Over time, the conditions that made the relationship valuable might change. The customer might be disappointed by changes in the level of service (either as provided by the company or as perceived by the customer) or product quality. The company can also evaluate the relationship and conclude that a particular loyal and committed customer is simply costing too much to maintain. As the intensity of the relationship fades, the parties enter a separation stage.

An important goal of any marketing strategy should be to move customers into the commitment stage as rapidly as possible and keep them there as long as possible. Companies want to see customers move into the separation stage only if they are costing more to serve than they are worth.

LIFE-CYCLE SEGMENTATION

Analyzing how customers' behavior changes as they move through the five stages can yield information about how they interact with the company and its products in each stage. The five stages are sometimes called the **customer life cycle**, and using these stages to create groups of customers that are in each stage is called **life-cycle segmentation**. Two companies that undertake continuing research into market segmentation and how companies can use segment information to develop better relationships with their customers are Claritas and Donnelley Marketing.

Claritas created one of the first segment marketing databases, named PRIZM, in the early 1970s. Claritas built PRIZM to take advantage of people's tendency to live near other people with similar tastes and preferences. Thus, PRIZM identifies the demographic characteristics of people by neighborhood. Claritas developed a number of other products that offer marketers databases with specific demographic, financial, and psychographic characteristics. Donnelley Marketing offers similar products, such as its Buyer Behavior Indicator and Affluence Models databases. Both Donnelley and Claritas extended their research from traditional direct marketing to help firms sell online. You can learn more about these companies and their products by following their links in the Web Links for this chapter.

Customer Acquisition: The Funnel Model

To increase sales and build market share, managers must have a good sense of how their companies acquire and retain customers. They often must evaluate competing marketing strategies to determine which of the strategies is the most effective at attracting and retaining customers. The **funnel model of customer acquisition** is used as a conceptual tool to understand the overall nature of a marketing strategy, but it also provides a clear structure for evaluating specific strategy elements.

The funnel model is very similar to the customer life-cycle model you learned about earlier in this chapter; however, the funnel model is less abstract and does a better job of showing the effectiveness of two or more specific strategies. The funnel is a good analogy for the operation of a marketing strategy because almost every marketing strategy starts with a large number of prospects and converts fewer and fewer of those prospects into serious prospects, customers, and finally, loyal customers. One example of a funnel model appears in Figure 4-6.

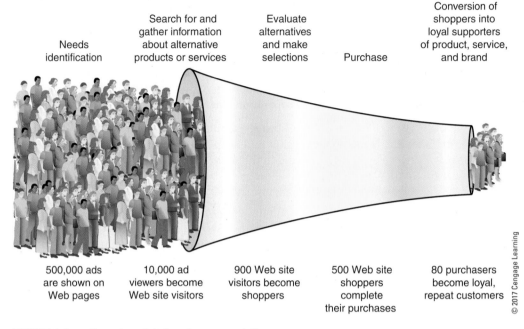

Needs identification • Search for and gather information about alternative products or services • Evaluate alternatives and make selections • Purchase • Conversion of shoppers into loyal supporters of product, service, and brand

500,000 ads are shown on Web pages • 10,000 ad viewers become Web site visitors • 900 Web site visitors become shoppers • 500 Web site shoppers complete their purchases • 80 purchasers become loyal, repeat customers

© 2017 Cengage Learning

FIGURE 4-6   Funnel model of customer acquisition

In this funnel model, repeat customers are on the right side of the figure. The top of the figure explains the increasing level of commitment that occurs in each step. Using market research and past history as a guide, the marketing manager develops the numbers that show the effectiveness of the planned strategy. The wider the right end of the funnel, the better the strategy—that is, the more prospects are converted into loyal customers. The funnel model can be used in planning marketing strategies by comparing the projected results shown in the diagram with the results for alternative strategies shown in separate diagrams. The funnel model can also be used to show results that can then be compared with the costs of running the marketing campaign. Either way, the model gives marketing managers a tool for conceptualizing and evaluating alternative strategies.

COSTS OF CUSTOMER ACQUISITION, CONVERSION, AND RETENTION

The benefits of acquiring new visitors are different for Web businesses with different revenue models. For example, an advertising-supported site is interested in attracting as many visitors as possible to the site and then keeping those visitors at the site as long as possible. That way, the site can display more advertising messages to more visitors, which is how the site earns a profit. For sites that operate a Web catalog, charge a fee for services, or are supported by subscriptions, attracting visitors to the site is only the first step in the process of turning those visitors into customers. The total amount of money that a site spends, on average, to draw one visitor to the site is called the **acquisition cost**.

The second step that a Web business wants to take is to convert the first-time visitor into a customer. This is called a **conversion**. For advertising-supported sites, the conversion is usually considered to happen when the visitor registers at the site, or, in some cases, when a registered visitor returns to a site several times. For sites with other revenue models, the conversion occurs when the site visitor buys a good or service or subscribes to the site's content. The total amount of money that a site spends, on average, to induce one visitor to make a purchase, sign up for a subscription, or (on an advertising-supported site) register is called the **conversion cost**. Most managers use a cumulative definition for conversion cost—that is, conversion cost includes acquisition cost.

For many Web businesses, the conversion cost is greater than the profit earned on the average sale (or the average first sale). In such cases, the Web business must induce the customer to return to the site and buy again (or renew the subscription, or view more advertising). Customers who return to the site one or more times after making their first purchases are called **retained customers**. Different businesses use different measures for determining when a customer is a retained customer. Some companies consider a customer retained if he or she returns just once and purchases again. Others use some number of subsequent purchases or some number of subsequent purchases within a specific time frame. The costs of inducing customers to return to a Web site and buy again are called **retention costs**.

Companies have found that measuring acquisition, conversion, and retention costs is important because it gives them an idea of which advertising and promotion strategies are successful. These measurements are more precise than classifying customers into the five stages of loyalty in the customer life-cycle model. It is much easier to determine, for example, whether a customer has been converted or retained than it is to determine whether that customer is in the familiarity stage or the commitment stage. A company that is evaluating its promotion campaign can measure the conversion costs and compare them to the profit generated by the average first-time sale. Most companies are very interested in retaining customers because the cost of acquiring a new customer is between 3 and 15 times (depending on the type of business) the cost of retaining an existing customer.

In the rest of this chapter, you will learn some specific techniques that can be elements of successful Web marketing strategies. Remember that each of these techniques makes sense only when used in concert with another. Not all techniques work well in all situations. For example, a retailer might find that a print catalog can be an integral part of promoting its online sales if it provides customers with recognizable value and augments the rest of the company's marketing strategy.

Advertising on the Web

Advertising is all about communication. The communication might be between a company and its current customers, potential customers, or even former customers that the company would like to regain. To be effective, firms should send different messages to each of these audiences; however, each message should tie into or be an element of a common theme, or story.

The five-stage customer loyalty model described in the previous section can be helpful in creating the messages to convey to each of these audiences. In the awareness stage, the advertising message should inform. The message could describe a new product, suggest new uses for existing products, or describe specific improvements to a product. Audiences in the exploration stage should receive messages that explain how a product or service works and encourage switching to that brand. In the familiarity stage, the advertising message should be persuasive—convincing customers to purchase specific products or request that a salesperson call. Customers in the commitment stage should be sent reminder messages. These ads should reinforce customers' good feelings about the brand and remind them to buy products or services. Companies generally do not target ads at customers who are in the separation stage.

Most companies that launch electronic commerce initiatives already have advertising programs in place. Online advertising should always be coordinated with existing advertising efforts. For example, print ads should include the company's URL. Display ads were the first advertising format to be used widely on the Web, but today's online ad formats also include pop-up, interstitial, rich media, and video ads.

Display Ads

The first widely used method of advertising on the Web was the placement of display ads on Web pages. A **display ad**, also called a **banner ad**, is a rectangular object on a Web page that displays a stationary or moving graphic and includes a link to the advertiser's Web site. Display ads are versatile advertising vehicles—their graphic images can help increase awareness, and users can click them to open the advertiser's Web site and learn more about the product. Thus, display ads can serve both informative and persuasive functions.

Early display ads used a simple graphic that loaded with the Web page and remained on the page until the user moved to another page or closed the browser. Today, a variety of technologies, including Shockwave, Java, or Flash, are used to make attention-grabbing ads that include audio and video elements. These ads are often rotated so that each time the Web page is loaded into a browser, the ad changes.

Although Web sites can create display ads in any dimensions, advertisers decided early on that it would be a good idea to standardize the sizes. The standard display ad sizes that most Web sites have voluntarily agreed to use are called **interactive marketing unit (IMU) ad formats**. The Interactive Advertising Bureau (IAB) is a not-for-profit organization that promotes the use of Internet advertising and encourages effective Internet advertising. The IAB has established voluntary standards for IMUs.

As the Web grew, so did the creativity of Web advertisers. They were using an increasing number of IMU ad formats, including pop-up ads, buttons, and ads that filled entire page borders. At one point, advertisers were using more than 15 different IMU ad formats and the IAB decided to encourage its members to agree to use only four standard formats, called the **universal ad package (UAP)**. They include the **leaderboard ad**, which is a display ad designed to span the top or bottom of a Web page; the **skyscraper ad**, which is a display ad that is designed to be placed on the side of a Web page and remain visible as the user scrolls down through the page; and two sizes of **rectangle ad**. These four ad formats and their specifications are shown in Figure 4-7.

Many advertisers use these four standard formats because they know that almost every Web site will be able to display their ads in those formats properly. You can learn

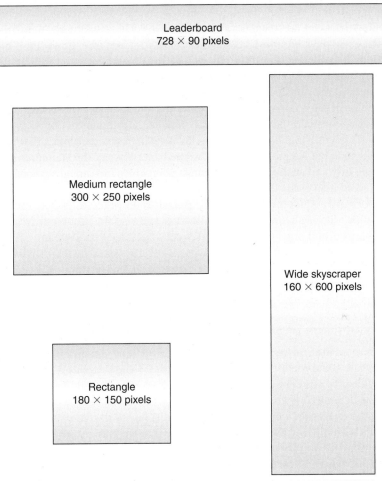

Source: Interactive Advertising Bureau, http://www.iab.net/guidelines/508676/508767/UAP.

FIGURE 4-7 Interactive Advertising Bureau Universal Ad Package format standards

more about display ads, including examples of the latest IAB-approved sizes, by following the Web Links to the IAB Web site.

Most advertising agencies that work with online clients can create display ads as part of their services. Web site design firms can also create display ads. Charges for creating display ads range from about $50 to more than $8000, depending on the complexity of the ad.

DISPLAY AD PLACEMENT

Companies have three different ways to arrange for other Web sites to host their display ads. The first is to use an **ad exchange network**, which coordinates ad sharing so that other sites run one company's ad while that company's site runs other exchange members' ads. Usually, the exchange requires each member site to accept two ads on its site for every one of its ads that appears on another member's site. The exchange then makes its profit by selling the extra ad space to other businesses. These exchange networks were popular in the early days of online business because they are free; however, it is often difficult to find an exchange that does not include direct competitors. This limitation prevents many businesses today from using banner exchange networks.

The second way that businesses can place their display advertising is to find Web sites that appeal to one of the company's market segments and then pay those sites to carry the ads. This can take considerable time and effort. Smaller sites might not have an established pricing policy for advertising. Larger sites usually have high standard rates that they discount for larger customers, but a smaller customer would generally pay the standard rates. To place online ads efficiently and at the lowest cost, most companies hire an advertising agency to negotiate rates and help with ad placement. A full-service advertising agency can help design the ads, create them, and identify appropriate Web sites on which to display them. Agencies can often negotiate lower advertising rates with sites because the agencies can consolidate their clients' budgets and buy large blocks of advertising space at one time.

A third way to place online advertising is to use a display advertising network. A **display advertising network** acts as a broker between advertisers and Web sites that carry ads. The larger networks, such as DoubleClick (owned by Google), offer many of the same services as comprehensive ad agencies.

NEW STRATEGIES FOR DISPLAY ADS

Click-through rates now range from .3 percent to .5 percent, depending on the site's content. Although some recent research suggests that Web site visitors see and are influenced by display ads that they do not click, advertisers are reluctant to pay for ads that do not produce directly measurable results.

To battle the decrease in click-through rates, display ad designers first introduced **animated GIFs** with moving elements in the hopes that they might be more attractive to the user's eye than stationary graphics. When animated GIFs failed to halt the decline, designers created ads that included rich media effects, such as video clips. They also added interactive effects by writing Java programs that could respond to a user's click with some action (other than simply loading the advertiser's page into the browser).

Some designers created display ads that appear to be dialog boxes in the hope that confused users would click them. Several examples of this type of display ad are shown in Figure 4-8. These ads are designed to induce users to click a button in the ad to fix

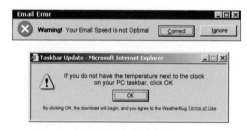

FIGURE 4-8   Disguised display ads

the "error," but the link actually leads to a Web site or begins installing a program on the user's computer.

Intrusive Ad Formats

The steady decline in the effectiveness of display ads has prompted advertisers to explore other formats for Web ads. One of these formats is the pop-up ad. A **pop-up ad** is an ad that appears in its own window when the user opens or closes a Web page. The window in which the ad appears does not include the usual browser controls. The only way to dismiss the ad is to find and click a small, often hard-to-identify, close button or link that might appear anywhere in the window. Many users find pop-up ads extremely annoying. A particularly irritating variation on the pop-up ad technique occurs at Web sites that open more than one pop-up ad when a user leaves the site or closes the browser. If the user does not act quickly enough, the browser spawns multiple windows and can even crash the computer. Some pop-up ads are delivered in a way that includes a quick follow-on command that returns the focus to the original browser window. The result is an ad that is parked behind the user's browser, waiting to appear when the browser is closed.

Despite user objections to pop-up ads (in all their variations), an increasing number of Web sites are using them as a way of delivering a larger advertising image in a more forceful way. Some users have responded by using **ad-blocking software** that prevents display ads and pop-up ads from loading. Most Web browsers can be configured not to display many of these ads; however, any site that uses methods for navigation that are similar to those used to deliver ads (such as pop-up information windows) cannot operate as intended in the reconfigured browser. Some researchers have found that beyond annoying users, pop-up ads actually create lasting bad will among users toward the company whose products are depicted in the ads. Despite these findings, many advertisers find pop-up ads to be effective tools for drawing customers to their sites and continue to use them.

Another intrusive ad format is the **interstitial ad**. When a user clicks a link to load a page, the interstitial ad opens in its own browser window, instead of the page that the user intended to load (the general meaning of the word "interstitial" is something that comes between two other things). Many interstitial ads close automatically, allowing the intended page to open in the existing browser window. Other interstitials require the user to click a button before they close. Because they open in a full-size browser window, interstitial ads offer the advertiser even more space than the pop-up ad format. These ads also completely cover the Web page that the user was trying to see. Many users find interstitials even more annoying than pop-up ads because they are larger and a more forceful interruption of the Web-browsing experience.

Rich Media and Video Ad Formats

Rich media ads generate graphical activity that "floats" over the Web page itself instead of opening in a separate window. These ads always contain moving graphics and usually include audio and video elements. One of the first rich media ads featured the figure of a little man who walked into the displayed Web page, unrolled a movie poster, and then pasted the poster onto the Web page (covering up part of the Web page content—content that a user might have been reading!). After about 10 seconds, the figure walked off the

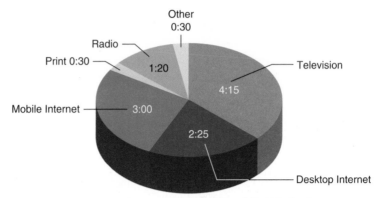

Source: Adapted from reports by eMarketer and ZenithOptimedia.

FIGURE 4-9   Average time spent (hours per day) with various media, 2016 U.S. population estimates

page and the poster disappeared. While it was open on the page, the poster was an active link to the movie's Web site.

A form of rich media ads is used on Web sites that deliver video. These **video ads** can be either free standing or integrated into videos that the site visitor selects to watch. For example, a Web site that provides television shows or news updates will often include a video ad at the beginning of the clip (in which case, it is called a **pre-roll video ad**). A visitor opens the video and must view all or part of the ad before the content begins to play. To be effective, the video ad should be long enough to deliver the advertiser's message, but not so long that the visitor loses interest. Most video ads today are between 10 and 30 seconds long.

As you learned in Chapter 3, an increasing number of people are watching television shows and other video entertainment online, so advertising in this channel has become more important. Today, the amount of time people spend online using either computers or mobile devices exceeds the amount of time people spend watching television. The amount of time the U.S. populations spend with various media is shown in Figure 4-9.

Text Ads

A **text ad** is a short promotional message that does not use any graphic elements and is often placed along the top or right side of a Web page. Google was the first company to use text ads successfully on the Web. Google places text ads on its search results pages. When you visit Google and use it to search for information, the page that provides the links relevant to your search query includes short text ads for products or services related to your search query. Google found that these ads were less obtrusive than display ads and that they were very effective because they reached people who were interested in learning more about something (as reflected in the search query they had entered) related to the advertisers' products or services.

Text ads were so unobtrusive that Google was criticized when it first included them on its pages. Observers noted that site visitors might not be able to distinguish the paid ads from the search results. In response to this criticism, Google and most other search sites that use text ads now clearly label the ads with language such as "sponsored links" to prevent users from being confused. The use of text ads was one of the innovations that helped Google become one of the leading search sites on the Web. It gave Google an effective way to earn money while providing users with a useful search experience.

A number of sites that provide information use text ads in another way by turning some of the text in the stories they display into hyperlinks that lead to advertisers' sites. This type of advertising is called an **inline text ad**. Newspaper, magazine, and other sites that users commonly visit to learn more about a topic often use this technique. For example, a newspaper site might have a story about local banks. Banks that are mentioned in the story could have their names presented in the story as links to ads for the banks' services. The newspaper would charge the advertising banks a fee for placing the link in the story.

Another way information sites use text ads is to include them in the middle of the running text of a story as a separate, blocked-off paragraph. These paragraphs are sometimes labeled as advertisements so that readers understand that they are looking at a link to an ad. This use of inline text ads is particularly common in online magazines devoted to specific industries. On such sites, these inline text ads are seen less as a nuisance than as a handy resource that leads an interested reader to more information from companies that sell products and services mentioned in or related to the topic of the article.

Mobile Device Advertising

In recent years, the use of mobile devices that are connected to the Internet, such as smartphones and tablets, has grown tremendously. The programs that run on these devices, called **mobile apps** (which is a short form of the term "mobile software applications"), perform a variety of functions such as calendar, contact management, Web browsing, e-mail, and entertainment. A number of mobile apps provide connectivity to specific Web sites or groups of Web sites. You will learn more about the business of selling mobile apps in Chapter 6.

Some of the sellers of mobile apps include an advertising element in their revenue models. These apps include **mobile ads** that display messages from advertisers (other than the seller of the app). For example, the mobile app of *The New York Times* has a small bar at the bottom of the screen that displays ads. Some productivity and game software also includes advertising that appears on a part of the screen or as a separate screen that must be clicked through to get to the productivity tool or game. The advertising space on mobile apps is sold in the same way that display advertising on Web sites is sold.

Mobile advertising is one of the fastest-growing types of online promotion. The rapid growth in the use of mobile devices and apps is driving this shift, which experts expect to continue as more people around the world use mobile devices to access the Internet.

Site Sponsorships

Some Web sites offer advertisers the opportunity to sponsor all or parts of their sites. These **site sponsorships** give advertisers a chance to promote their products, services, or brands in a more subtle way than by placing display or pop-up ads on the sites (although some sponsorship packages include a certain number of display and pop-up ads).

Companies that buy Web site sponsorships have goals that are similar to those of sporting event sponsors or television program sponsors—that is, they want to tie the company or product name to an event or a set of information. The idea is that the quality of the event or information set will carry over to the company's products, services, or brands. In general, sponsorships are used to build brand images and develop reputations rather than to generate immediate sales. A site sponsorship can be exclusive, which prevents any other companies from sponsoring the site, or it can be shared, which means that other companies can be co-sponsors of the site. In general, an exclusive site sponsorship will cost more than a shared site sponsorship.

In some cases, the sponsor is given the right to create content for the site or to weave its advertising message into the site's content. This practice can raise ethical concerns if not done carefully. Sites that offer content spots to sponsors should always identify the content as an advertisement or as provided by the sponsor. Unfortunately, many sites do not use clear labels for sponsored content. This can confuse site visitors who are unable to distinguish between editorial content and advertising. Sites that offer medical information, for example, should be especially careful to distinguish between information that is generated by the site's reporters or editorial staff and information that is provided by pharmaceutical companies or medical device manufacturers.

Online Advertising Cost and Effectiveness

As more companies rely on their Web sites to make a favorable impression on potential customers, the issue of measuring Web site effectiveness has become important. Mass media efforts are measured by estimates of audience size, circulation, or number of addressees. When a company purchases mass media advertising, it pays a dollar amount for every thousand people in the estimated audience. This pricing metric is called **cost per thousand** (CPM; the "M" is an abbreviation of "mille," which is Latin for "thousand").

Measuring Web audiences is more complicated because of the Web's interactivity and because the value of a visitor to an advertiser depends on how much information the site gathers from the visitor (for example, name, address, e-mail address, telephone number, and other demographic data). Because each visitor voluntarily chooses whether to provide these bits of information, all visitors are not of equal value. Internet advertisers have developed some Web-specific metrics for site activity, but these are not generally accepted and are currently the subject of considerable debate. One alternative to CPM for online advertising is called **cost per click** (CPC), in which the site monitors the number of visitors who click an ad and charges for each click rather than for each time the ad is shown on a Web page. However, CPC measures are difficult to compare with the CPM measures used in all other (not online) modes of advertising. This limits general use of CPC measures by advertisers who buy all types of advertising.

A **visit** occurs when a visitor requests a page from the Web site. Further page loads from the same site are counted as part of the visit for a specified period of time. This period of time is chosen by the administrators of the site and depends on the type of site. A site that features stock quotes might use a short time period because visitors may load the page to check the price of one stock and reload the page 15 minutes later to check another stock's price. A museum site would expect a visitor to load multiple pages over a longer time period during a visit and would use a longer visit time window. The first time

Medium	Description	Audience Size	Cost per Thousand (CPM)
Network television	30-second commercial	10 million–50 million	$10–$50
Local television station	30-second commercial	50,000–2 million	$3–$25
Cable television	30-second commercial	100,000–500,000	$8–$25
Radio	60-second commercial	50,000–2 million	$2–$8
Major metro newspaper	Full-page ad	100,000–600,000	$5–$40
Regional edition of a national magazine	Full-page ad	50,000–900,000	$40–$100
Local magazine	Full-page ad	3000–80,000	$100–$140
Direct mail coupon pack	Mailed in letter-sized envelope	10,000–200,000	$15–$20
Billboard	Highway billboard	100,000–3 million	$1–$8
Online	Display ad	10,000–50 million	$1–$15
Online	Video/Rich media	10,000–50 million	$2–$50
Online	Text ad	10,000–50 million	$1–$500
Targeted e-mail	Single mailing	10,000–10 million	$5–$15
Mobile ads	App-embedded	10,000–5 million	$1–$5

© 2017 Cengage Learning

FIGURE 4-10　　CPM rates for advertising in various media

that a particular visitor loads a Web site page is called a **trial visit**; subsequent page loads are called **repeat visits**. Each page loaded by a visitor counts as a **page view**. If the page contains an ad, the page load is called an **ad view**.

Some Web pages have display ads that continue to load and reload as long as the page is open in the visitor's Web browser. Each time the display ad loads is an **impression**. If the visitor clicks the display ad to open the advertiser's page, that action is called a **click** or **click-through**. Display ads are often sold on a CPM basis where the "thousand" is 1000 impressions. Rates vary greatly and depend on how much demographic information the Web site obtains about its visitors and what kinds of visitors the site attracts. Figure 4-10 shows a comparison of CPM rates for display ads and other Web advertising media to CPM rates for advertising placed in traditional media outlets.

One of the most difficult things for companies to do as they move onto the Web is gauge the costs and benefits of advertising on the Web. Many companies have developed new metrics to evaluate the number of desired outcomes their advertising yields. For example, instead of metrics based on the number of ads displayed (CPM) or click-throughs (CPC), they measure the number of new visitors to their site who buy for the first time after arriving at the site by way of a click-through. They can then calculate the advertising cost of acquiring one customer on the Web and compare that to how much it costs them to acquire one customer through traditional channels.

Most marketing analysts do agree that online advertising is much more effective if it is properly targeted. Online ads that reach site visitors who are looking for something specific that is related to the ad's message are much more successful than ads viewed by a general population. Thus, market segmentation is an important element in online advertising success. One useful marketing tool that uses market segmentation effectively is e-mail marketing, the subject of the next section.

E-Mail Marketing

Sociologists and cultural anthropologists have proclaimed e-mail to be one of the greatest tools for human communication to be developed in the twentieth century. Because advertising is a process of communication, it is easy to see that e-mail can be a very powerful element in any company's advertising strategy. Many businesses would like to send e-mail messages to their customers and potential customers to announce new products, new product features, or sales on existing products. However, industry analysts have severely criticized some companies for sending e-mail messages to customers or potential customers. Some companies have even faced legal action after sending out mass e-mailings.

Unsolicited Commercial E-Mail (UCE, Spam)

Spam, also known as **unsolicited commercial e-mail (UCE)** or **bulk mail**, is electronic junk mail and can include solicitations, advertisements, or e-mail chain letters. The origin of the term *spam* is generally believed to have come from a song performed by the British comedy troupe, Monty Python, about Hormel's canned meat product, SPAM. In the song, an increasing number of people join in repeating the song's chorus: "Spam spam spam spam, spam spam spam spam, lovely spam, wonderful spam…" Just as in the song, e-mail spam is a tiresome repetition of meaningless text that eventually drowns out any other attempt at communication.

Spam wastes time and storage space on servers and individuals' computers and it consumes bandwidth on the Internet. A considerable number of spam messages include content that can be offensive to recipients. Some employers worry that their employees might sue them, arguing that the offensive spam they receive while working contributes to a hostile work environment, which can be grounds for harassment allegations. Industry analysts estimate that spam costs businesses more than $20 billion per year in the direct costs of dealing with it and in lost productivity of employees who are subjected to it. You will learn about the legal issues surrounding spam in Chapter 7, and you will learn about the technical issues related to spam and some strategies for battling it in Chapter 8.

Sending e-mail messages to Web site visitors who expressly request the e-mail messages is a completely different story. A key element in any e-mail marketing strategy is to obtain customers' approvals before sending them any e-mail that includes a marketing or promotional message. By obtaining these approvals, as you will learn in the next section, companies can avoid being accused of engaging in spam.

Permission Marketing

Many businesses are finding that they can maintain an effective dialog with their customers by using automated e-mail communications. Sending one e-mail message to a customer can cost less than 1 cent if the company already has the customer's e-mail address. Purchasing the e-mail addresses of people who ask to receive specific kinds of e-mail messages adds between a few cents and a dollar to the cost of each message sent. Another factor to consider is the conversion rate. The **conversion rate** of an advertising method is the percentage of recipients who respond to an ad or promotion. Conversion rates on requested e-mail messages range from 10 percent to more than 30 percent. These are much higher than the click-through rates on display ads, which are currently under one-half of one percent and decreasing.

The practice of sending e-mail messages to people who request information on a particular topic or about a specific product is called **opt-in e-mail** and is part of a marketing strategy called **permission marketing**. Most marketing efforts that traditional businesses use to promote their products or services depend on potential customers having enough time to listen to sales pitches and pay attention to the best ones. As time becomes more precious to everyone, people no longer wish to hear and evaluate advertising and promotional appeals for products and services in which they have no interest. ConstantContact and Yesmail are two companies that offer permission-based e-mail and related services.

Thus, a marketing strategy that sends specific information only to people who have indicated an interest in receiving information about the product or service being promoted should be more successful than a marketing strategy that sends general promotional messages through the mass media. Companies such as Return Path offer opt-in e-mail services. These services provide the e-mail addresses to advertisers at rates that vary depending on the type and price of the product being promoted, but range from a minimum of about $1 to a maximum of 25–30 percent of the selling price of the product.

Combining Content and Advertising

One strategy for getting e-mail accepted by customers and prospects that many companies have found successful is to combine useful content with an advertising e-mail message. Articles and news stories that would interest specific market segments are good ways to increase acceptance of e-mail.

E-mail messages that include large articles or large attachments (such as graphics, audio, or video files) can fill up recipients' inboxes very quickly, so many advertisers send content by inserting hyperlinks into e-mail messages. The hyperlinks should take customers to the content, which is stored on the company's Web site. Once customers are viewing pages on the Web site, it is easier to induce them to stay on the site and consider making purchases. Using hyperlinks that lead to a Web page instead of embedding content in e-mail messages is especially important if the content requires a browser plug-in to play (as many audio and video files do). The Web page can provide a link to the needed plug-in software.

An important element in any marketing strategy is coordination across media outlets. If a company is using e-mail to promote its products or services, it should make sure that any other marketing efforts it is undertaking at the same time, such as press releases, print media ads, or broadcast media ads, are delivering a message that is consistent with the e-mail campaign's message.

Outsourcing E-Mail Processing

Many companies find that the number of customers who opt-in to information-laden e-mails can grow rapidly. The job of handling e-mail lists and mass mailing software can quickly outgrow the capacity of the company's information technology staff. A number of companies offer e-mail management services, and most small to midsized companies outsource their e-mail processing operations to an e-mail processing service provider.

The Additional Information section of the Web Links for this chapter includes links to several companies that offer e-mail processing and management services. These companies will manage an e-mail campaign for a cost of between 1 and 5 cents per valid e-mail address. Many of these companies will also help their clients purchase lists of e-mail addresses from companies that compile such lists.

Technology-Enabled Customer Relationship Management

The nature of the Web, with its two-way communication features and traceable connection technology, allows firms to gather much more information about customer behavior and preferences than they can gather using micromarketing approaches. Now, companies can measure a large number of things that are happening as customers and potential customers gather information and make purchasing decisions. The information that a Web site can gather about its visitors (which pages were viewed, how long each page was viewed, the sequence, and similar data) is called a **clickstream**.

Technology-enabled relationship management is important when promoting and selling on the Web. **Technology-enabled relationship management** occurs when a firm obtains detailed information about a customer's behavior, preferences, needs, and buying patterns, *and* uses that information to set prices, negotiate terms, tailor promotions, add product features, and otherwise customize its entire relationship with that customer.

Although companies can use technology-enabled relationship management concepts to help manage relationships with vendors, employees, and other stakeholders, most companies currently use these concepts to manage customer relationships. Thus, technology-enabled relationship management is often called **customer relationship management (CRM)**, **technology-enabled customer relationship management**, or **electronic customer relationship management (eCRM)**. Figure 4-11 lists seven dimensions of the customer interaction experience and shows how technology-enabled customer relationship management differs from traditional seller-customer interactions in each of those dimensions.

CRM as a Source of Value

Harvard Business School researchers Jeffrey Rayport and John Sviokla observed that firms today do business in both a physical world and a virtual, information world. Rayport and Sviokla distinguish between commerce in the physical world, or marketplace, and

Dimensions	Technology-Enabled Customer Relationship Management	Traditional Relationships with Customers
Advertising	Provide information in response to specific customer inquiries	"Push and sell" a uniform message to all customers
Targeting	Identify and respond to specific customer behaviors and preferences	Market segmentation
Promotions and discounts offered	Individually tailor to customer	Same for all customers
Distribution channels	Direct or through intermediaries; customer's choice	Through intermediaries chosen by the seller
Pricing of products or services	Negotiated with each customer	Set by the seller for all customers
New product features	Created in response to customer demands	Determined by the seller based on research and development
Measurements used to manage the customer relationship	Customer retention; total value of the individual customer relationship	Market share; profit

© 2017 Cengage Learning

FIGURE 4-11 Technology-enabled relationship management and traditional customer relationships

commerce in the information world, which they term the **marketspace**. In the information world's marketspace, digital products and services can be delivered through electronic communication channels, such as the Internet.

In Chapter 1, you learned that the value chain model described the primary and support activities that firms use to create value. This value chain model is valid for activities in the physical world and in the marketspace. However, value creation requires different processes in the marketspace. By understanding that value creation in the marketspace is different, firms can identify value opportunities effectively in both the physical and information worlds.

For years, businesses have viewed information as a part of the value chain's supporting activities, but they have not considered how information itself might be a source of value. In the marketspace, firms can use information to create new value for customers. Many electronic commerce Web sites today offer customers the convenience of an online order history, make recommendations based on previous purchases, and show current information about products in which the customer might be interested.

Successful Web-marketing approaches all involve enabling the potential customer to find information easily and customizing the depth and nature of that information; such approaches should encourage the customer to buy. Firms should track and examine the behaviors of their Web site visitors, and then use that information to provide customized, value-added digital products and services in the marketspace. Companies that use these technology-enabled relationship management tools to improve their contact with customers are more successful on the Web than firms that adapt advertising and promotion strategies that were successful in the physical world but are less effective in the virtual world.

In the early days of the Web, many companies attempted to create comprehensive CRM systems that captured every bit of information about every customer. Many of these systems failed because they were overly complex and required company staff to spend too much time entering data. In recent years, companies have had more success with CRM systems that are less ambitious in scope. By limiting data collection to key facts that matter to salespeople and customers, these systems provide valuable information, yet they do not overly burden sales and administrative staff with data entry work. More companies are getting better at automating the collection of data, which also increases the likelihood that a CRM implementation will be successful.

Today's CRM systems use information gathered from customer interactions on the company's Web site and combine them with information gathered from other customer interactions, such as calls to customer service departments. As you learned earlier in this chapter, the occurrence of contact between the customer and any part of the company is called a customer touchpoint. A good CRM system will gather information from every customer touchpoint and combine it with information from other sources about industry trends, general economic conditions, and market research about changes in general preference levels that might affect demand for the company's products or services.

In a CRM system, the multiple sources of information about customers, their preferences, and their behavior is entered into a large database called a **data warehouse**. On a regular basis, analysts query the data warehouse using sophisticated software tools to perform data mining and statistical modeling. **Data mining** (also called **analytical processing**) is a technique that examines stored information and looks for patterns in the data that are not yet known or suspected. In CRM, analysts might apply data mining techniques to the data warehouse and find that customers often buy two specific products at the same time. By offering both products together at a reduced price whenever a customer views either product page, the company could increase sales of both products. **Statistical modeling** is a technique that tests theories that CRM analysts have about relationships among elements of customer and sales data. For example, a statistical model could be used to test whether free shipping increases sales enough to cover the cost of offering the free shipping. Figure 4-12 shows the elements in a typical CRM system. In Chapter 9, you will learn more about software tools and other technologies that companies are using to implement CRM.

Creating and Maintaining Brands on the Web

A known and respected brand name can present to potential customers a powerful statement of quality, value, and other desirable characteristics in one recognizable element. Branded products are easier to advertise and promote because each product carries the

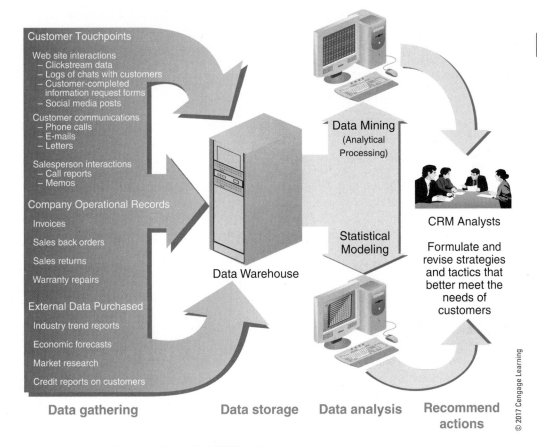

Data gathering   **Data storage** **Data analysis** **Recommend actions**

© 2017 Cengage Learning

FIGURE 4-12 Elements of a typical CRM system

reputation of the brand name. Companies have developed and nurtured their branding programs in the physical marketplace for many years. Consumer brands such as Ivory soap, Walt Disney entertainment, Maytag appliances, and Ford automobiles have been developed over many years with the expenditure of tremendous amounts of money. However, the value of these and other trusted major brands far exceeds the cost of creating them.

Elements of Branding

The key elements of a brand, according to researchers at the advertising agency Young & Rubicam, are differentiation, relevance, and perceived value. Product differentiation is the first condition that must be met to create a product or service brand. The company must clearly distinguish its product from all others in the market. This makes branding difficult for commodity products such as salt, nails, or plywood—difficult, but not impossible.

A classic example of branding a near-commodity product is Procter & Gamble's creation of the Ivory brand more than 100 years ago. The company was experimenting with manufacturing processes and had accidentally created a bar soap that contained a

Element	Meaning to Customer
Differentiation	In what significant ways is this product or service unlike its competitors?
Relevance	How does this product or service fit into my life?
Perceived value	Is this product or service good?

© 2017 Cengage Learning

FIGURE 4-13   Elements of a brand

high percentage of air. When one of the workers noted that the soap floated in water, the company decided to sell the soap using this differentiating characteristic in packaging and advertising by claiming "it floats." Thus was the Ivory soap brand born. Procter & Gamble maintains this brand differentiation on its Web site even today by maintaining a separate Facebook page for the brand.

The second element of branding—relevance—is the degree to which the product offers utility to a potential customer. The brand only has meaning to customers if they can visualize its place in their lives. Many people understand that Tiffany & Co. creates a highly differentiated line of jewelry and gift products, but very few people can see themselves purchasing and using such goods.

The third branding component—perceived value—is a key element in creating a brand that has value. Even if your product is different from others on the market and potential customers can see themselves using this product, they will not buy it unless they perceive value. Some large fast-food outlets have well-established brands that actually work against them. People recognize these brands and avoid eating at these restaurants because of negative associations—such as low overall quality and high-fat-content menu items. Figure 4-13 summarizes the elements of a brand.

If a brand has established that it is different from competing brands and that it is relevant and inspires a perception of value to potential purchasers, those purchasers will buy the product and become familiar with how it provides value. Brands become established only when they reach this level of purchaser understanding and acceptance.

Unfortunately, brands can lose their value if the environment in which they have become successful changes. A dramatic example is Digital Equipment Corporation (DEC). For years, DEC was a leading manufacturer of midrange computers. When the market for computing shifted to personal computers, DEC found that its branding did not transfer to the personal computers that it produced. The consumers in that market did not see the same perceived value or differentiation in DEC's personal computers that the buyers of midrange systems had seen for years. This is an important element of branding for Web-based firms to remember because the Web is still evolving and changing at a rapid pace.

Emotional Branding vs. Rational Branding

Companies have traditionally used emotional appeals in their advertising and promotion efforts to establish and maintain brands. Branding experts Ted Leonhardt and Bill Faust have described "brand" as "an emotional shortcut between a company and its customer." These emotional appeals work well on television, radio, billboards, and in print media

The business of selling search engine inclusions and placements is complex because many search engines do not sell inclusion and placement rights on their pages directly to advertisers. They use **search engine placement brokers**, which are companies that aggregate inclusion and placement rights on multiple search engines and then sell those combination packages to advertisers. Another reason for the complexity in this business is that recent years have brought a flurry of mergers and acquisitions. For example, in 2003, Yahoo! purchased Overture, a search engine placement broker. The most popular search engine, Google, does not use a placement broker to sell search term inclusion and placement for its site. Google sells these services directly through its Google AdWords program.

Two excellent resources for keeping up with the rapid changes in this business are Danny Sullivan's two related Web sites, Search Engine Land and Marketing Land. These sites include many free resources and explanations that are useful for learning about search engines, placement brokers, online marketing, and search engine optimization in general.

Web sites that offer content can also participate in paid placement. Google offers its AdSense program to sites that want to carry ads that match the content offered on the site. Other companies offer similar ad brokerage services, but Google is the leader in this market. The content site receives a placement fee from the broker in exchange for the ad placement and the broker sells the placement slots to interested advertisers. These techniques in which ads are placed in proximity to related content are sometimes called **contextual advertising**.

Of course, this approach is not without its flaws. In 2003, the *New York Post* ran a sensational story that described a gruesome murder. The murder victim's body had been cut into pieces, which the murderer hid in a suitcase. When the newspaper's Web site ran the story, it appeared with a paid placement ad for luggage. The ad broker's software had noted the word "suitcase" in the story and decided that it would be the perfect place for a luggage ad. Today, ad brokers use more sophisticated software and human reviewers to prevent this type of error; however, some industry analysts believe that contextual advertising on content sites will never be as successful as paid placement on search engine pages. They argue that search engine pages are provided to site visitors looking for something specific, often as part of a purchasing process. Content sites are used to explore and learn about more general things. Thus, an ad on a search engine results page will always be more effective than an ad on a content site page.

Another variation of paid placement ads uses search engine results pages that are generated in response to a search for products or services in a specific geographical area. This technique, called **localized advertising**, places ads related to the location on the search results page. Localized advertising came about as a result of local search services. In 2004, Google launched a local search service that lets users search by ZIP code or local address. All of the other major search engine and Web directory sites followed Google's lead and now offer some form of localized search, either as part of their main search page or as a separate service. The local advertising market is estimated to be more than $30 billion and is growing worldwide, especially as mobile devices become the primary target for such advertising. You will learn more about localization and mobile commerce in Chapter 6.

Web Site Naming Issues

Companies that have a well-established brand name or reputation in a particular line of business usually want the URLs for their Web sites to reflect that name or reputation. Obtaining identifiable names to use on the Web can be an important part of establishing a Web presence that is consistent with the company's existing image in the physical world.

Two airlines that started their online businesses with troublesome domain names have both purchased more suitable domain names. Southwest Airlines' domain name was www.iflyswa.com until it purchased www.southwest.com. Delta Air Lines' original domain name was www.delta-air.com. After several years of complaints from confused customers who could never remember to include the hyphen, the company purchased the domain name www.delta.com.

Companies often buy more than one domain name. Some companies buy additional domain names to ensure that potential site visitors who misspell the URL will still be redirected (through the misspelled URL) to the intended site. For example, Yahoo! owns the name Yahow.com. Other companies own many URLs because they have many different names or forms of names associated with them. For example, General Motors' main URL is GM.com, but the company also owns GeneralMotors.com, Chevrolet.com, Chevy.com, GMC.com, and many others.

BUYING, SELLING, AND LEASING DOMAIN NAMES

In 1998, a poster art and framing company named Artuframe opened for business on the Web. With quality products and an appealing site design, the company was doing well, but it was concerned about its domain name, which was www.artuframe.com. After searching for a more appropriate domain name, the company's president found the Web site of Advanced Rotocraft Technology, an aerospace firm, at the URL www.art.com. After finding out that Advanced Rotocraft Technology's site was drawing 150,000 visitors each month who were looking for something art related, Artuframe offered to buy the URL. The aerospace firm agreed to sell the URL to Artuframe for $450,000. Artuframe immediately relaunched as Art.com and experienced a 30 percent increase in site traffic the day after implementing the name change.

The newly named site did not rely on the name change alone, however. It entered a joint marketing agreement with Yahoo! that placed ads for Art.com on art-related search results pages. Art.com also created an affiliate program with businesses that sell art-related products and not-for-profit art organizations. Although Art.com was ultimately unsuccessful in building a profitable business on the Web and liquidated in mid-2001, the domain name was snapped up immediately by already profitable Allwall.com for an undisclosed amount. The new Allwall.com site, relaunched with the Art.com domain name, experienced a 100 percent increase in site visitors within the first month.

The market for domain names continues to be active, with names that include general topic terms (especially those that are sensational) often bringing high prices. Many domain name sales details are kept private, but some of the highest prices paid that have been reported in the media appear in Figure 4-17.

Although most domains that have high value are in the .com TLD, the name engineering.org sold at auction to the American Society of Mechanical Engineers, a not-for-profit organization, for just under $200,000.

Domain Name	Price
Insurance.com	$35.6 million
VacationRentals.com	$35.0 million
PrivateJet.com	$30.0 million
Internet.com	$18.0 million
360.com	$17.0 million
Insure.com	$16.0 million
Sex.com	$14.0 million
Hotels.com	$11.0 million
Fund.com	$10.0 million
Porn.com	$9.5 million
Porno.com	$8.9 million
FB.com	$8.5 million
Business.com	$7.5 million
Diamond.com	$7.5 million
Beer.com	$7.0 million
iCloud.com	$6.0 million
Israel.com	$5.9 million
Casino.com	$5.5 million
Slots.com	$5.5 million
AsSeenOnTV.com	$5.1 million
Toys.com	$5.1 million

© 2017 Cengage Learning

FIGURE 4-17   Domain names that sold for more than $5 million

Some companies and individuals invested their money in the purchase of highly desirable domain names. Instead of selling these names to the highest bidder, some of these domain name owners decided to retain ownership of the domain names and lease the rights to the names to companies for a fixed time period. Usually, these domain name lessors rent their domain names through URL brokers.

URL BROKERS AND REGISTRARS

Several legitimate online companies, known as **URL brokers**, are in the business of selling, leasing, or auctioning domain names that they believe others will find valuable. Companies selling "good" (short and easily remembered) domain names include BuyDomains.com and Sedo.

Companies can also obtain domain names that have never been issued, or that are currently unused, from a domain name registrar. The Internet Corporation for Assigned Names and Numbers (ICANN; about which you learned in Chapter 2) maintains a list of accredited registrars. Many of these registrars offer domain name search tools on their Web sites. A company can use these tools to search for available domain names that might meet their needs. Another service offered by domain name registrars is domain name parking. **Domain name parking**, also called **domain name hosting**, is a service that permits the purchaser of a domain name to maintain a simple Web site (usually one page) so that the domain name remains in use. The fees charged for this service are usually much lower than those for hosting an active Web site.

LEARNING FROM FAILURES

Nuts Online

In 1929, Sol Braverman began selling nuts and dried fruit at a stall on Mulberry Street in Newark, New Jersey. The family business grew to become the Newark Nut Company and, in 2003, Sol's grandson Jeffrey joined the business with ideas about doing business online. He purchased the domain name NutsOnline.com and found that selling nuts online was indeed a good business. Although the business was successful, Braverman felt that a better domain name might help the business become even more successful.

In 2009, he tracked down the owner of the domain name Nuts.com, which was a name that he thought would be an improvement. More important, he did not want that domain to fall into the hands of a competitor. After two years of negotiations with the owner, he finally paid several hundred thousand dollars for the name. This was a substantial price for a company with annual revenues in the $20 million range; however, Braverman was optimistic that the new name would increase traffic to the company's Web site and pay for itself within a few years.

Working with a Web consultant, the company set up redirects on each NutsOnline page that would take site visitors to the exact same page on the new site and followed Google's published guidelines for Webmasters. When the new site was launched on January 6, 2012, the company was in for a big surprise. Instead of increasing, the site's Web traffic plummeted 70 percent during the first two weeks after the change. Three months later, traffic was still down 50 percent, costing the company more than 100 orders per day.

When the company consulted other experts, it found that Web sites usually experience a small drop off in traffic when they change to a new domain name, but this drop is usually no more than 5 percent. After doing further research, the company learned that Google had failed to credit Nuts.com with the seller reviews that had accumulated for NutsOnline.com over many years. It took several months for this transition to occur.

One expert noted that Nuts.com had been a content-free site for the past 10 years, which made the name switch similar to moving into what had been an abandoned building. The company could have minimized the drop in traffic by putting some content, perhaps a small version of the full Web site, on Nuts.com a few months before making the transition. Also, a considerable amount of Web traffic going to Nuts.com was the result of searches originating in England (a British magazine has a similar name), and the company was able to change its geographic targeting to associate the site with U.S.-based searches. This made Google more likely to show Nuts.com in U.S. searches for "nuts" and similar words (for example, "almonds" or "walnuts"). Within a month after making these changes, the Web site's traffic levels returned to normal and the company was on its way to making the new domain name earn its keep.

Summary

In this chapter, you learned how companies can use the principles of marketing strategy and the four Ps of marketing to develop a mix of advertising and promotion that achieves their goals for selling their products and services online. In addition to traditional promotional strategies, companies now use multiple online contact points, including social media outlets such as Facebook and Twitter, to get their message out. Some companies use a product-based marketing strategy and some use a customer-based strategy. The Web enables companies to mix these strategies and give customers a choice about which approach they prefer. An increasing number of sellers use knowledge about their customers' specific buying habits to customize the Web site experience they encounter when shopping online.

Market segmentation using geographic, demographic, and psychographic information can work as well on the Web as it does in the physical world. The Web gives companies the powerful added ability to segment markets by customer behavior and life-cycle stage, even when the same customer exhibits different behavior during different visits to the company's site. These additional segmentation capabilities can lead to one-to-one online marketing efforts that result in greater relationship intensity than most non-online approaches.

You learned how companies are creating and delivering various types of online ads, including displays, pop-ups, inline text, interstitials, rich media, and video, to sell products and services online. Permission marketing and opt-in e-mail offer alternatives that can be used with or instead of Web page ads. Context-sensitive text ads are a rapidly growing form of online advertising that users find less intrusive than other online advertising media. Mobile ads served on the Web and through specific apps are one of the fastest-growing segments of online advertising today.

Many companies are using the Web to manage their relationships with customers. By understanding the nature of communication on the Web, companies can use it to identify and reach the largest possible number of qualified customers. Technology-enabled customer relationship management can provide better returns for businesses on the Web than the traditional unaided approaches of market segmentation and micromarketing.

Firms on the Web can use rational branding instead of the emotional branding techniques that work well in mass media advertising. Some businesses on the Web are sharing and transferring brand benefits through affiliate marketing and cooperative efforts among brand owners. Others are using viral marketing strategies in online social media to increase awareness of their brands and the size of their customer bases.

Successful search engine positioning and domain name selection can be critical for many businesses in their quests for new online customers. The most important theme in this chapter is that companies must integrate the Web marketing tools they use into a cohesive and customer-sensitive overall marketing strategy.

Key Terms

acquisition cost	ad exchange network
ad view	affiliate marketing
ad-blocking software	affiliate program broker

analytical processing

animated GIFs

behavioral segmentation

blog

bot

brand

bulk mail

cause marketing

click

clickstream

click-through

contextual advertising

conversion

conversion cost

conversion rate

cost per click (CPC)

cost per thousand (CPM)

crawler

customer-based marketing strategy

customer life cycle

customer relationship management (CRM)

customer value

data mining

data warehouse

database

demographic

demographic segmentation

display ad (banner ad)

display advertising network

distribution

domain name hosting

domain name parking

electronic customer relationship management (eCRM)

fan base

fans

four Ps of marketing

funnel model of customer acquisition

geographic segmentation

impression

index

inline text ad

interactive marketing unit (IMU) ad formats

interstitial ad

leaderboard ad

life-cycle segmentation

localized advertising

market segmentation

marketing mix

marketing strategy

marketspace

micromarketing

mobile ads

mobile apps

occasion segmentation

one-to-one marketing

opt-in e-mail

page view

paid placement

pay-per-click model

pay-per-conversion model

permission marketing

place

pop-up ad

pre-roll video ad

price

product

product-based marketing strategy

promotion

psychographic segmentation

rational branding

rectangle ad

repeat visits

retained customers

retention costs

rich media ads

robot

search engine

search engine optimization

search engine placement

search engine placement brokers

search engine positioning

search engine ranking

search term sponsorship

search utility

segments

shopping cart

site sponsorships

skyscraper ad

social media

spam

spider

sponsorship

statistical modeling

technology-enabled customer relationship management

technology-enabled relationship management

text ad

touchpoint consistency

touchpoints

trial visit

trigger words

universal ad package (UAP)

unsolicited commercial e-mail (UCE)

URL brokers

usage-based market segmentation

video ad

viral marketing

visit

Web log

Review Questions

1. Briefly explain why two different firms in the same industry might decide to use different marketing strategies.

2. Name four elements that a company might choose to include in its marketing mix.

3. What are the four Ps of marketing?

4. How do transaction costs play a role in determining customer value?

5. What are three elements of promotion that can be conducted online?

6. What is a product-based marketing strategy?

7. How can an external viewpoint help a company develop a customer-based online selling strategy?

8. What makes mass media advertising attractive to many companies?

9. What makes mass media advertising ineffective in many online settings?

10. What type of promotional media works best for highly complex products or services?

11. Many online retailers include blogs on their Web sites. Name and briefly describe one purpose for which an online retailer might use a blog?

12. Briefly define psychographic market segmentation and explain how it differs from demographic market segmentation.

13. Name and briefly describe one category of usage-based market segmentation.

14. Name and briefly describe one category of behavioral segmentation.

15. Why is touchpoint consistency an important feature of a company's relationship with its customers?

16. Outline the main characteristics of a Web site visitor who is in the exploration state of a relationship with the business owning the Web site.

17. Briefly define conversion cost and explain why companies should calculate it.

18. Why is acquisition cost for most online retailers higher than retention cost?

19. Why do most online advertisers comply with the Interactive Advertising Bureau's display ad format standards?

20. What is an ad exchange network and how does it differ from a display advertising network?

21. What is an interstitial ad?

22. What is a pre-roll video ad and in what specific situations can it be used effectively?

23. Explain what online text ads are and briefly describe their advantages over online display ads.

24. Briefly explain why mobile advertising is growing so rapidly.

25. What is a Web site sponsorship?

26. As the terms are used in online advertising, what is the difference between an "impression" and a "click-through"?

27. What are the basic ideas that underlie permission marketing?

28. Briefly define and distinguish between emotional and rational branding.

29. Briefly define the term "viral marketing."

30. Briefly define search engine positioning and explain why companies use it.

31. What is domain name parking?

Exercises

1. Many organizations find it difficult to incorporate a customer-based marketing strategy into their Web site designs. In about 100 words, explain why this is a challenge and outline things an organization can do to overcome these difficulties.

2. One of the four Ps of marketing is price. In about 100 words, explain what elements are involved in price besides the amount of money a customer pays for a product. In your answer, be sure to consider the concept of customer value.

3. In about 100 words, outline the ways in which a company can use the Internet to improve the logistics of a product's distribution.

4. In about 200 words, compare the use of a product-based marketing strategy to a customer-based product strategy. Include a discussion of the benefits and drawbacks of each and include at least one example of an online business that uses each strategy.

5. Assume you are the marketing director for PerfectSeasons, a new line of cookware designed by a famous celebrity chef. In about 200 words, describe how you would use the chef's reputation to accomplish the differentiation elements of this new product line's brand.

6. One approach to customer-based marketing relies on identification of customer demographic groups. Find an online retailer that has incorporated customer-based marketing in its Web site design. In about 100 words, describe the Web site and outline how it offers various navigation paths for customers belonging to different demographic groups.

7. **Visit Harry and David Gourmet Gifts** to examine how that company implements occasion segmentation with its individual products and its monthly club services. Write a report in which you describe two clear examples of occasion segmentation on the site. Also identify two examples of product segmentation on the site and explain how the company uses its Web site design to channel customers into the segmentation path that is most appropriate for them. Your report should be about 200 words.

8. In two or three paragraphs, explain why mass media advertising is likely to be less successful online (either with computer or mobile device users) than with television viewers.

9. In about 100 words, explain how the level of complexity of a product can affect a company's choice of communication modes it might use to disseminate information about that product.

10. In about 200 words, explain how the achieved trust level of a company's communications using social media compare with similar communication efforts conducted using mass media and personal contact.

11. In about 100 words, briefly describe micromarketing and explain what weakness it shares with mass media advertising.

12. Assume you are a consultant to TopSpin, a tennis equipment manufacturer that sells its products directly to customers on the Web. TopSpin is considering the use of YouTube videos to promote its products. Some of the salespeople have suggested that the videos include detailed reviews of the company's products and endorsements by top tennis players. Other marketing staff have suggested including instructional tips and videos of the equipment being used at famous resorts. Write a 200-word report in which you evaluate these two alternatives proposed by the salespeople and the marketing staff.

13. Manufacturers of golf equipment often advertise on television broadcasts of golf tournaments; however, manufacturers of football equipment rarely advertise on television broadcasts of football games. In one or two paragraphs, explain why the advertising strategies of these two businesses differ.

14. In about 100 words, summarize the difficulties companies encounter when they attempt to measure the effectiveness of their online advertising campaigns.

15. In about 100 words, explain what online businesses can learn from data mining (or analytical processing) activities.

16. You have been employed by **ESPN** to sell space on its Web site to advertisers. Create a memo of approximately 200 words in which you describe the advantages of advertising on the site in a form that the company's sales team can use as a resource when they are making presentations to potential advertisers for space on the main page. The company has a permission-based e-mail marketing system that you can include as part of an advertising package you sell to advertisers. Be sure to include the benefits to advertisers provided by this e-mail marketing system in your memo.

Note: Your instructor might assign you to a group to complete this exercise and might ask you to prepare a formal sales presentation based on your memo to your class.

17. Marti Baron operates The Cannonball, an online store that sells parts, repair kits, books, and accessories to hobbyists who restore antique model trains. Many model train hobbyists and collectors have created Web sites on which they share photos and other information about model trains. Marti is interested in creating an affiliate marketing program that would allow those hobbyists to place links on their sites to The Cannonball and be rewarded with commissions on sales that result from visitors following those links. In a 200-word memo to Marti, outline the steps she should take as she evaluates affiliate program brokers and other

options for creating her affiliate network. Be sure to consider the characteristics of Marti's business in your analysis.

18. You are the new marketing manager for the *Midland Daily Courier*, a weekly newspaper that publishes local news, high school sports results, and feature stories about local businesses and political issues. The paper also publishes several regular columns written by local experts on gardening, home repair, and crafts. Like many small weeklies, the *Courier* has seen its subscriber base shrink gradually over the past 10 years. The newspaper has a Web site on which it posts all of the display ads that run in the print edition, its free classified ads, and all of the news content from the print edition. Your job is to work with the publisher and the editorial staff to revive interest in the paper and devise marketing plans that will either increase subscriptions directly or generate increased interest and awareness of the newspaper's value to potential subscribers. In about 400 words, provide a viral marketing plan that uses blogs and social media tools to generate interest in the *Courier*. Be specific about how you would promote each element of the newspaper's offerings, including which tool you would use for which element.

Cases

C1. Mothshop Corporate

Growing up in Georgia, George Dawes Green, a poet and novelist, spent many warm summer evenings with friends on a screened-in porch telling each other stories late into the night. A hole in the screen allowed moths to join them, so the group began calling themselves the Moths. After moving to New York City in 1997, Green missed those evenings of friendship and entertainment and decided to bring his storytelling tradition to the cafes and clubs of his new home. Thus The Moth, a not-for-profit storytelling organization, was born.

The Moth is best known for The Moth Radio Hour, a weekly live program that airs on National Public Radio stations, through which it has generated a broad interest in the art and craft of storytelling. Although most of The Moth's activities are directed at storytelling as entertainment, in 2010, Moth Senior Producer Kate Tellers began working with Publicis Groupe, a global advertising and marketing firm based in France, to help corporate clients who wanted to learn how to connect better with their customers.

Tellers first developed and delivered workshops to Publicis Groupe clients who were looking for an effective way to tell their stories to customers, but later expanded the workshop offerings under the name Mothshop Corporate Training and made them available to a wide variety of companies. Although these workshops include technical storytelling tools such as developing a story arc and reinforcing a theme, they also provide corporate marketers with an appreciation for the importance of authenticity and being specific with a message. According to The Moth, a key element in any story's success is its ability to convey an underlying, deep lesson to the listener.

Mothshop Corporate has worked with a wide range of major companies, including Kraft, Google, L.L. Bean, McDonalds, and Organic, Inc. Its corporate training programs include elements such as "Advancing New Concepts," working on "Perfecting the Pitch," developing a "Brand Story," and building a "Company/Project Identity" that turn the Moth storytelling principles (which include ideas such as "develop the arc" and "set up the stakes") into techniques for improving a company's marketing and communication efforts.

In the world of online marketing, a company has a limited window through which to communicate. Customers and prospects must see common themes in the blog posts, tweets,

YouTube videos, and other social media tools. These themes must be coordinated and consistent with its Web presence, e-mail strategies, and branding approaches across all available communication channels and physical locations (if the company has them). The Moth's training programs help companies create stories that can be told in various forms in each of those channels.

REQUIRED:

1. Many forms of online communication, such as e-mails, tweets, and the content of Web pages, requires short-form, concise writing. In two or three paragraphs, discuss how storytelling might motivate short-form writing that can convey elements of a company's or a product's brand image online.

2. Choose a product with which you are familiar and, in about 200 words, outline the elements (such as branding, product characteristics, product use benefits, comparison to competing products) you would include in a story about the product and recommend online communication media (Web page, e-mail, social networking, and so on) that you could use to expose potential customers to the story.

3. Storytelling is an important part of many online gaming environments. In about 100 words, compare the role storytelling plays in online games to the role it could play in product marketing and promotion.

Note: Your instructor might assign you to a group to complete this case and might ask you to prepare a formal presentation of your results to your class.

C2. Montana Mountain Biking

Jerry Singleton founded Montana Mountain Biking (MMB) 18 years ago. MMB offers one-week guided mountain biking expeditions based in four Montana locations. Most of MMB's new customers hear about the company and its tours from existing customers. Many of MMB's customers come back every year for a mountain biking expedition; about 80 percent of the riders on any given expedition are repeat customers.

Jerry is happy with this high repeat percentage, but he is worried that MMB is missing a large potential market. He has been reluctant to spend a lot of money on advertising. About 10 years ago, he spent $80,000 on a print advertising campaign that included ads in several outdoor interest and sports magazines, but the ads did not generate enough additional customers to cover the cost of the advertising. Five years ago, a marketing consultant advised Jerry that the ads had not been placed well. The magazines did not reach the serious mountain bike enthusiast, which is MMB's true target market. After all, a casual mountain bike rider would probably not be drawn to a week-long expedition.

Another concern of Jerry's is that more than 90 percent of MMB's customers come from neighboring states. Jerry has always thought that MMB was not reaching the sizable market of serious mountain bike enthusiasts in California. He talked to the marketing consultant about buying an address list and sending out a promotional mailing, but producing and mailing the letters seemed too expensive. The cost of renting the list was $0.10 per name, but the printing and mailing were $4 per letter. There were 60,000 addresses on the list, and the consultant told him to expect a conversion rate of between 1 and 3 percent. At best, the mailing would yield 1800 new customers and MMB's profit on the one-week expedition was only about $100 per customer. It looked like the conversion cost would be about $246,000 (60,000 × $4.10) to obtain a profit of $180,000 (1800 × $100). The consultant explained that it was an investment; because

MMB had such a high customer retention rate, the profit from the new customers in the second or third years would exceed the one-time cost of the mailing in the first year. Jerry was not convinced.

Nine years ago, MMB launched its first Web site. It included information about the company and its tours, but Jerry did not see any need to include an expedition-booking function on the site. He did think about selling caps and jackets with the MMB logo, but that idea never was implemented. The MMB logo is well known in the mountain biking community in the upper Midwest.

The MMB Web site includes an e-mail address so that visitors to the site can send an e-mail requesting more information about the expeditions. Robin Davis, one of MMB's expedition leaders, is an amateur photographer who has taken many photos while on the trails over the years. Last year, she had those photos digitized and put them on the MMB Web site. The number of e-mail inquiries increased dramatically within a month. Many of the inquiries were about MMB's expeditions, but a surprising number asked for permission to use the photos, or asked if MMB had more photos like those for sale. Jerry is not quite sure what to make of the popularity of those photos. He is, after all, in the mountain bike expedition business.

REQUIRED:

1. Review the five stages of customer loyalty shown in Figure 4-5 and prepare a report of about 200 words in which you classify MMB's customers. Estimate the percentage of MMB customers who fall into each of the five categories. Support your classification with logic and evidence from the case narrative.

2. In a report of about 200 words, recommend an e-mail marketing strategy for MMB. In your recommendation, consider the results of MMB's earlier print mail advertising campaign, your answer to the first requirement, and the potential offered by permission marketing.

3. In about 300 words, explain how MMB could use social media-based viral marketing tactics to gain new customers and cement its relationships with existing customers. In your answer, be sure to discuss features that MMB should include on its Web site and its Facebook page to support the viral marketing strategy.

4. Prepare a report of about 500 words in which you outline an affiliate marketing strategy for MMB. Include a description of the types of Web sites that MMB should attempt to recruit as affiliates, and present at least five examples of specific sites that would be good referral sources.

Note: Your instructor might assign you to a group to complete this case and might ask you to prepare a formal presentation of your results to your class.

For Further Study and Research

Alford, E. 2015. "StubHub Saves Its Rankings While Opening Up Personalization Possibilities," *Search Engine Watch*, July 8. http://searchenginewatch.com/sew/news/2416725/stubhub-saves-its-rankings-while-opening-up-personalization-possibilities

Bayer, J. and E. Servan-Schreiber. 2011. "Gaining Competitive Advantage Through the Analysis of Customers' Social Networks," *Direct, Data and Digital Marketing Practice*, 13(2), October, 106–118.

Beatty, S. and W. Hill. 2013. "A Segmentation of Adolescent Online Users and Shoppers," *Journal of Services Marketing*, 27(5), 347–360.

Beck, K. 2011. "Pizza Chain Goes Extreme on Facebook," *CRM Magazine*, 15(6), June, 38–39.

Bruton, C. and G. Schneider. 2003. "Multiple Channels for Online Branding," *Academy of Marketing Studies Journal*, 7(1) 109–114.

Buchanan, L. 2013. "Both Simple and True: The Secrets of Effective Storytelling," *Inc*. October. http://www.inc.com/magazine/201310/leigh-buchanan/the-moth-storytelling-secrets.html

Canhoto, A., M. Clark, and P. Fennemore. 2013. "Emerging Segmentation Practices in the Age of the Social Customer," *Journal of Strategic Marketing*, 21(5), 413–428.

Chan, Y. 2009. "Effects Beyond Click-through: Incidental Exposure to Web Advertising." *Journal of Marketing Communications*, 15(4), September, 227–246.

Chaney, P. 2015. "Multi-channel Marketing: An Introductory Guide," *Web Marketing Today*, July 13. http://webmarketingtoday.com/articles/Multi-channel-Marketing-An-Introductory-Guide/

Chen, Y., S. Fay, and Q. Wang. 2011. "The Role of Marketing in Social Media: How Online Consumer Reviews Evolve," *Journal of Interactive Marketing*, 25(2), 85–94.

De Vivo, M. 2015. "Five Ways to Reduce Touchpoints on the Social Media Conversion Funnel," *Search Engine Watch*, June 11. http://searchenginewatch.com/sew/how-to/2412370/5-ways-to-reduce-touchpoints-on-the-social-media-conversion-funnel

Dean, S. 2015. "It's 2015: You'd Think We'd Have Figured Out How to Measure Web Traffic by Now," *FiveThirtyEight*, July 7. http://fivethirtyeight.com/features/why-we-still-cant-agree-on-web-metrics/

Dillon, K. 2013. "Selling Narrative: A Storytelling Radio Show Teaches Corporate America," *Fortune*, September 16, 18.

Dover, D. 2011. *Search Engine Optimization Secrets*. Indianapolis, IN: Wiley.

eMarketer. 2014. "Advertisers Will Spend Nearly $600 Billion Worldwide in 2015," December 10. http://www.emarketer.com/Article/Advertisers-Will-Spend-Nearly-600-Billion-Worldwide-2015/1011691

eMarketer. 2015. "U.S. Adults Spend 5.5 Hours With Video Content Each Day," April 16. http://www.emarketer.com/Article/US-Adults-Spend-55-Hours-with-Video-Content-Each-Day/1012362

Gardner, E. 1999. "Art.com," *Internet World*, March 15, 13. http://www.iw.com/print/1999/03/15/

Godin, S. 2005. *All Marketers Are Liars: The Power of Telling Authentic Stories in a Low-Trust World*. New York: Portfolio.

Godin, S. and D. Peppers. 1999. *Permission Marketing: Turning Strangers into Friends, and Friends into Customers*. New York: Simon & Schuster.

Hanlon, P. and J. Hawkins. 2008. "Expand Your Brand Community Online," *Advertising Age*, January 7, 14–15.

Hansen, C. 2013. "Let's Use Data Not Just to Target Ads, but to Make Ads Better," *Ad Age Digital*, October 2. http://adage.com/article/digitalnext/data-target-ads-make-ads/244484/

Harvard Business Review. 2003. "How to Measure the Profitability of Your Customers," 81(6), June, 74.

Hayes, D. 2013. "Big Data vs. Better Data: Marketing Beyond Hunting and Gathering," *ClickZ*, October 9. http://www.clickz.com/clickz/column/2299386/big-data-vs-better-data-marketing-beyond-hunting-gathering

Heffernan, V. 2011. "Google's War on Nonsense," *The New York Times*, June 26. http://opinionator.blogs.nytimes.com/2011/06/26/googles-war-on-nonsense/

Hinz, O., B. Skiera, C. Barrot, and J. Becker. 2011. "Seeding Strategies for Viral Marketing: An Empirical Comparison," *Journal of Marketing*, 75 (6), November, 55–71.

Hjort, K., B. Lantz, D. Ericsson, and J. Gattorna. 2013. "Customer Segmentation Based on Buying and Returning Behavior," *International Journal of Physical Distribution & Logistics Management*, 43(10), 852–865.

Jenkins, S. 2015. "Recognizing Millennial Men's Adaptability for Brands," *eMarketer*, July 10. http://www.emarketer.com/Article/Recognizing-Millennial-Mens-Adaptability-Key-Brands/1012705

Jones, K. 2008. *Search Engine Optimization: Your Visual Blueprint for Effective Internet Marketing*. Indianapolis, IN: Wiley.

Jothi, P., M. Neelamalar, and R. Prasad. 2011. "Analysis of Social Networking Sites: A Study on Effective Communication Strategy in Developing Brand Communication," *Journal of Media and Communication Studies*, 3(7), July, 234–242.

Kaplan, A. and M. Haenlein. 2011. "The Early Bird Catches the News: Nine Things You Should Know About Micro-blogging," *Business Horizons*, 54(2), March–April, 105–113.

Kaye, K. 2013. "Is Online Advertising Getting Too Complex?" *Ad Age Dataworks*, November 1. http://adage.com/article/datadriven-marketing/online-advertising-complex/245070/

Kennedy, A. and K. Hauksson. 2012. *Global Search Engine Marketing*. Indianapolis, IN: Que.

Kiley, D. and B. Helm. 2009. "The Great Trust Offensive," *BusinessWeek*, September 28, 38–42.

Klapdor, S. 2013. *Effectiveness of Online Marketing Campaigns: An Investigation into Online Multichannel and Search Engine Advertising*. Dordrecht: Springer Gabler.

Kunz, M., B. Hackworth, P. Osborne, and J. High. 2011. "Fans, Friends, and Followers: Social Media in the Retailers' Marketing Mix," *Journal of Applied Business and Economics*, 12(3), 61–68.

Lambert, J. 2013. *Digital Storytelling: Capturing Lives, Creating Community*. London: Routledge.

Lee, K. and C. Seda. 2009. *Search Engine Advertising: Buying Your Way to the Top to Increase Sales*. Indianapolis, IN: New Riders.

Leonhardt, T. and B. Faust. 2001. "Brand Power: Using Design and Strategy to Create the Future," *Design Management Journal*, 12(1), Winter, 10–13.

Lunden, I. 2014. "Internet Ad Spend to Reach $121 Billion in 2014." *TechCrunch*, April 7. http://techcrunch.com/2014/04/07/internet-ad-spend-to-reach-121b-in-2014-23-of-537b-total-ad-spend-ad-tech-gives-display-a-boost-over-search/

Lunden, I. 2015. "2015 Ad Spend Rises to $187 Billion, Digital Inches Closer to One-Third of It," *TechCrunch*, January 20. http://techcrunch.com/2015/01/20/2015-ad-spend-rises-to-187b-digital-inches-closer-to-one-third-of-it/

Mandese, J. 2015. "Supply of Time Spent With Media Expands, Continues to Fragment: Digital Boosts Share," *Media Daily News*, June 1. http://www.mediapost.com/publications/article/250969/supply-of-time-spent-with-media-expands-continues.html

Marckini, F. 2001. *Search Engine Positioning*. San Antonio, TX: Republic of Texas Press.

Mark, T., K. Lemon, M. Vandenbosch, J. Bulla, and A. Maruotti. 2013. "Capturing the Evolution of Customer-firm Relationships: How Customers Become More (or Less) Valuable Over Time." *Journal of Retailing*, 89(3), 231–245.

McKay, L. 2009. "Microsites to Serve Microsegments," *CRM Magazine*, 13(8), August, 21–22.

Mount, I. 2012. "A Web Retailer Buys the Perfect Domain Name, Then Comes a Letdown," *The New York Times*, April 26, B6.

Neff, J. 2012. "After Dad-fueled Poop Storm, Huggies Alters Campaign," *Advertising Age*, March 8. http://adage.com/article/adages/dad-fueled-poop-storm-huggies-alters-campaign/233203/

Payne, A. and P. Frow. 2005. "A Strategic Framework for Customer Relationship Management," *Journal of Marketing*, 69(4), October, 167–176.

Ralphs, M. 2011. "Built In or Bolt On: Why Social Currency Is Essential to Social Media Marketing," *Direct, Data and Digital Marketing Practice*, 12(3), January, 211–215.

Rayport, J. and J. Sviokla. 1994. "Managing in the Marketspace," *Harvard Business Review*, 72(6), November–December, 141–150.

Rayport, J. and J. Sviokla. 1995. "Exploiting the Virtual Value Chain," *Harvard Business Review*, 73(6), November–December, 75–85.

Schneider, G. and C. Bruton. 2003. "Communication Modalities for Commercial Speech on the Internet," *Journal of Organizational Culture, Communication, & Conflict*, 7(2), 89–94.

Schwarz, E. 2010. "Snapshots From the Digital Media Marketsphere," *Technology Review: Business Impact*, October, 20–22.

Simonite, T. 2010. "Why Can't Internet Ads Be Sold Like TV Commercials?" *Technology Review: Business Impact*, October, 26–27.

Steinmetz, K. 2015. "The Dad 2.0 Summit: Making the Case for a New Kind of Manhood," *Time*, February 21. http://time.com/3717511/dad-summit-manhood/

Tedeschi, B. 2005. "Blogging While Browsing, But Not Buying," *The New York Times*, July 4. http://www.nytimes.com/2005/07/04/technology/04ecom.html

Tribby, M. 2013. "These Shoes Ain't Just Made for Walkin': The Cause Marketing Biz Model," *The Huffington Post*, October 3. http://www.huffingtonpost.com/maryellen-tribby/these-shoes-aint-just-mad_b_4030377.html

Willkey, M. 2015. "Big Loyalty, Small Price," *Internet Retailer*, May 1. https://www.internetretailer.com/2015/05/01/big-loyalty-small-price

Wong, V. 2012. "Want to Raise Online Display CPMs? Pull in Small Advertisers," *Ad Age Digital*, May 23. http://adage.com/article/digitalnext/raise-online-ad-inventory-prices-small-advertisers/234878/

Yu, J. 2015. "They Psychology of Search: Five Ways to Optimize for User Demand," *Search Engine Watch*, July 14. http://searchenginewatch.com/sew/opinion/2417534/the-psychology-of-search-5-ways-to-optimize-for-user-demand

Zaroban, S. 2015. "Email 'Batch and Blast' Is a Thing of the Past," *Internet Retailer*, July, 42.

Blend Images Photography/Neer

Business-to-Business Activities: Improving Efficiency and Reducing Costs

LEARNING OBJECTIVES

In this chapter, you will learn:

- How businesses use the Internet to improve purchasing, logistics, and other business process activities
- How the Internet facilitates implementation of outsourcing and offshoring business strategies
- How electronic data interchange works and how it has evolved using Internet technologies
- What supply chain management is and how it uses Internet technologies to improve efficiency and cooperation in supply chains
- How the various types of online business marketplaces operate to make B2B transactions easier and more efficient

INTRODUCTION

Since the first large companies evolved during the Industrial Revolution, they have tried to find ways to cut costs and operate more efficiently. Their first major efforts were directed at finding ways to manufacture products faster and cheaper. Later, purchasing, logistics, and analyzing the data gathered about all of these business operations became increasingly important. As more countries around the world developed increasingly reliable transportation and governmental infrastructures, companies felt more comfortable contracting with foreign providers for manufacturing and business services, despite technological and cultural differences between countries.

One potential source of business service workers exists in some of the poorest countries of the world. In the past, a lack of infrastructure (water, electricity, and roads) in less-developed countries often limited the kinds of business activities that could be accomplished in these countries. But the Internet has started to remove some of those limitations.

When California high school student Leila Janah won a scholarship, she decided to use it to fund a year of service in Ghana where she taught English and creative writing. She was impressed with the eagerness and talent of her students. When she returned to the United States, she completed a degree at Harvard and went to work in international development. In 2008, she started **Samasource**, a not-for-profit organization that facilitates connections between these potential workers and work that large high-tech companies need to have done.

Samasource contracts with large companies that have specific business processes they need accomplished, such as data entry, transcriptions, creating captions for images, error-checking information in databases, translating text, and so on. Samasource then breaks down these projects into small tasks that workers can perform anywhere in the world, as long as they have an Internet connection.

Samasource has lifted more than 6500 African, Asian, and Haitian workers and their families above the poverty line by providing them with computers and connectivity, then arranging work for them with companies such as Google, Microsoft, and Walmart. Although these workers are not highly skilled, they can accomplish useful work activities if the tasks are broken down and organized for them. Many of these workers were earning less than two dollars per day. With Samasource, they can earn two dollars an hour in many cases. In 2013, Samasource started job-training programs for low-income workers in the United States, building on its international model. Many of these workers had neither a smartphone nor Internet access through a computer at home.

Samasource and similar organizations, such as CrowdFlower and DDD, help businesses everywhere get tasks accomplished more cost effectively. At the same time, they help build worker knowledge and skills in less-developed countries that can help industries grow there. They can also give low-income workers in developed countries similar opportunities. Businesses welcome the development of better-trained workforces everywhere. Thus, the Internet helps bring together work and workers in a way that does a great deal of good for people in need around the world.

Purchasing, Logistics, and Business Support Processes

In this chapter, you will learn how companies use electronic commerce to improve their business processes, including purchasing and logistics primary activities and all of the processes relating to their support activities (which include finance and administration, human resources, and technology development). You can refer to Figure 1-9 in Chapter 1 for a review of primary activities and support activities. Although the work might not seem as creative as designing a Web site or developing an advertising campaign, the potential earnings impact of cost reductions and business process improvements in purchasing, logistics, and support activities is tremendous.

Outsourcing and Offshoring

An important characteristic of purchasing, logistics, and support activities is flexibility. A purchasing or logistics strategy that works this year may not work next year. Fortunately, economic organizations are evolving from the hierarchical structures used since the Industrial Revolution to new, more flexible network structures. These network structures are, in many cases, made possible by the transaction cost reductions that companies realize when they use Internet and Web technologies to carry out business processes. For example, the use of other organizations to perform specific activities is called **outsourcing**. U.S.-based companies such as Paychex and TriNet handle payroll, human resources, health insurance, and other employee benefit plans for thousands of companies that have decided to outsource those business processes.

When the outsourcing is done by organizations in other countries, it is often called **offshoring**. Outsourcing and offshoring have existed for decades, but the activities outsourced were typically manufacturing activities. For example, Apple or Motorola would offshore the manufacture of their U.S.-designed mobile phones by having them manufactured and assembled in less-developed Asian countries. The Internet has enabled companies to do the same thing with many of their nonmanufacturing activities as well.

Today, many companies perform functions such as purchasing, research and development, recordkeeping, and information management at lower-cost locations around the world. This type of offshoring is often called **business process offshoring**. Offshoring that is done by or through not-for-profit organizations who use the business activity to support training or charitable activities in less-developed parts of the world (such as the organizations described in the opening case for this chapter) is sometimes called **impact sourcing** or **smart sourcing**. It can be done in countries that do not yet have the infrastructure to support manufacturing activities.

Purchasing Activities

Purchasing activities include identifying and evaluating vendors, selecting specific products, placing orders, and resolving any issues that arise after receiving the ordered goods or services. These issues might include late deliveries, incorrect quantities, incorrect items, and defective items. By monitoring all relevant elements of purchase transactions, purchasing managers can play an important role in maintaining and improving product quality and reducing costs. In Chapter 1, you learned how companies can organize their strategic business unit activities using an industry value chain. The part of an industry value chain that precedes a particular strategic business unit is called that business unit's **supply chain**. A company's supply chain for a particular product or service includes all the activities undertaken by every predecessor in the value chain to design, produce, promote, market, deliver, and support each individual component of that product or service. For example, the supply chain of an automobile manufacturer includes every activity undertaken by each individual component supplier, including engine manufacturers, steel fabricators, glass manufacturers, wiring harness assemblers, and thousands of others.

The Purchasing Department within most companies traditionally has been charged with buying all of these components at the lowest price possible. Usually, Purchasing staff did this by identifying qualified vendors and asking them to prepare bids that described what they would supply and how much they would charge. The Purchasing staff would then select the lowest bid that still met the quality standards for the component. This bidding process led to a very competitive environment with a large number of suppliers; this process focused excessively on the cost of individual components and ignored the total supply chain costs, including the cost to the manufacturing organization of dealing with such a large number of suppliers. As you learned in Chapter 1, many managers call this function "procurement" instead of "purchasing" to distinguish the broader range of responsibilities. Procurement generally includes all purchasing activities, plus the monitoring of all elements of purchase transactions. It also includes managing and developing relationships with key suppliers.

Another term that is used to describe procurement activities is supply management. In many companies, procurement staff must have high levels of product knowledge to identify and evaluate appropriate suppliers. The part of procurement activity devoted to identifying suppliers and determining the qualifications of those suppliers is called **sourcing**. In Chapter 1, you learned that the use of Internet technologies in procurement activities is called e-procurement. Similarly, the use of Internet technologies in sourcing activities is called **e-sourcing**. Specialized Web-purchasing sites can be particularly useful to procurement professionals responsible for sourcing. The business purchasing process is usually much more complex than most consumer purchasing processes. Figure 5-1 shows the steps in a typical business purchasing process.

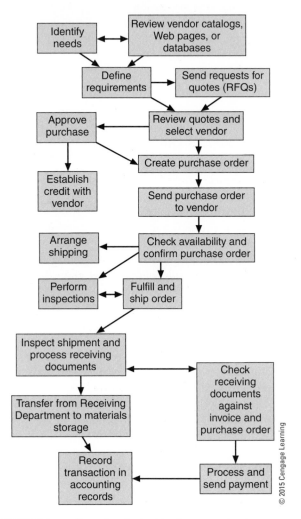

FIGURE 5-1   Steps in a typical business purchasing process

As you can see, the business purchasing process includes many steps. The business purchasing process also requires a number of people to coordinate their individual activities as part of the process. In large companies, the Procurement Department that supervises the purchasing process might include hundreds of employees who supervise the purchasing of materials, inventory for resale, supplies, and all of the other items that the company needs to buy. The total dollar amount of the goods and services that a company buys during a year is called its **spend**. In large companies, the spend can be many billions of dollars. Managing the spend in those companies is an important function and can be a key element in a company's overall profitability. Large manufacturing companies have annual spends that exceed $50 billion and process millions of purchase orders each year. By using Internet technologies in their purchasing, logistics, and support business processes, such companies can save billions of dollars each year.

The Institute for Supply Management (ISM) is the main organization for procurement professionals. ISM runs conferences, publishes a monthly journal (see the Web Link to Inside Supply Management), and offers helpful information on its Web site. Many of the articles in the journal discuss implementations of Internet technologies in purchasing and logistics. Full-time students who want to learn more about supply management can join ISM at no cost.

DIRECT VS. INDIRECT MATERIALS PURCHASING

Businesses make a distinction between direct and indirect materials. **Direct materials** are those materials that become part of the finished product in a manufacturing process. Steel manufacturers, for example, consider the iron ore that they buy to be a direct material. The procurement process for direct materials is an important part of any manufacturing business because the cost of direct materials is usually a very large part of the cost of the finished product. Large manufacturing companies, such as auto manufacturers, engage in two types of direct materials purchasing. In the first type, called **replenishment purchasing** (or **contract purchasing**), the company negotiates long-term contracts for most of the materials that it will need. For example, an auto manufacturer estimates how many cars it will make during a year and contracts with two or three steel mills to supply most of the steel it will need to build those cars. By negotiating the contracts in advance and guaranteeing the purchase, the auto manufacturer obtains low prices and good delivery terms. Of course, actual demand never matches expected demand perfectly. If demand is higher than the auto company's estimate, it must buy additional steel during the year. These purchases are made in a loosely organized market that includes steel mills, warehouses, speculators (who buy and sell contracts for future delivery of steel), and companies that have excess steel that they purchased on contract (demand for their products was lower than they had anticipated). This market is called a **spot market**, and buying in this market, the second type of direct materials purchasing, is called **spot purchasing**. **Indirect materials** are all other materials that the company purchases, including factory supplies such as sandpaper, hand tools, and replacement parts for manufacturing machinery.

Large companies usually assign responsibility for purchasing direct and indirect materials to separate departments. Most companies include the purchase of nonmanufacturing goods and services—such as office supplies, computer hardware and software, and travel expenses—in the responsibilities of the indirect materials Procurement Department. Many vendors that manufacture general industrial merchandise and standard machine tools for a variety of industries have created Web sites through which their customers can purchase materials. A number of customers buy these indirect material products on a recurring basis, and many of them are commodities—that is, standard items that buyers usually select using price as their main criterion. These indirect materials items are often called **maintenance**, **repair**, and **operating (MRO)** supplies. Procurement professionals generally use the terms "indirect materials" and "MRO supplies" interchangeably. Most companies have a difficult time controlling MRO spending from a centralized procurement office because many MRO purchases are numerous and small in dollar value. One way that Procurement Departments control MRO spending is by issuing **purchasing cards** (usually called **p-cards**). These cards, which resemble credit cards, give individual managers the ability to make multiple small purchases at their discretion while providing cost-tracking information to the procurement office.

By using a Web site to process orders, the vendors in this market can save the costs of printing and shipping catalogs and handling telephone orders. They can also keep price and quantity information continually updated, which would be impossible to do in a printed catalog. Some industry analysts estimate that the cost to process an MRO order through a Web site can be less than one-tenth of the cost of handling the same order by telephone.

Two of the largest MRO suppliers in the world are McMaster-Carr and W.W. Grainger. The Grainger Web site offers more than 900,000 different products for sale.

Office equipment and supplies are items that are used by a wide variety of organizations. Market leaders Office Depot and Staples each have well-designed Web sites devoted to helping their business customers buy these routine items easily. Digi-Key and Newark element 14 are leading online sellers of electronic parts.

Logistics Activities

The classic objective of logistics is to provide the right goods in the right quantities in the right place at the right time. Logistics management is an important support activity for both the sales and the purchasing activities in a company. Businesses need to ensure that the products they sell to customers are delivered on time and that the raw materials they buy from vendors and use to create their products arrive when needed. The management of materials as they go from the raw materials storage area through production processes to become finished goods is also an important part of logistics.

Logistics activities include managing the inbound movements of materials and supplies and the outbound movements of finished goods and services. Thus, receiving, warehousing, controlling inventory, scheduling and controlling vehicles, and distributing finished goods are all logistics activities. The Web and the Internet are providing an increasing number of opportunities to manage these activities better as they lower transaction costs and provide constant connectivity between firms engaged in logistics management. Web-enabled automated warehousing operations are saving companies millions of dollars each year. Major transportation companies such as Schneider National, Ryder Supply Chain, and J.B. Hunt now want to be seen by their customers as information management firms as well as freight carriers.

For example, the Schneider Track and Trace system delivers real-time shipment information to Web browsers on its customers' computers. This system shows the customer which freight carrier is transporting a shipment, where the shipment is, and when it should arrive at its destination. J.B. Hunt, with hundreds of thousands of trucks, trailers, containers, and other mobile operating assets, implemented a Web site that lets its customers track their shipments themselves. With customers doing their own tracking, J.B. Hunt needs far fewer customer service representatives. Also, J.B. Hunt found that its customers could monitor their own shipments more effectively than the company, saving J. B. Hunt more than $12,000 per week in labor and lost shipment costs. When transportation and freight companies engage in the business of operating all or a large portion of a customer's materials movement activities, the company is called a **third-party logistics (3PL) provider**. For example, Ryder has a multiyear contract to design, manage, and operate all of Whirlpool's inbound freight activities and is considered a 3PL provider to Whirlpool.

Both FedEx and UPS have freight-tracking Web pages available to their customers. Firms that run their own trucking operations have implemented tracking systems that use global positioning satellite (GPS) technology to monitor vehicle movements. With sensors in the vehicles that track speed, throttle positions, adjustable air suspension system settings, and fuel consumption, it is now possible to manage each vehicle in real time when those sensors are connected through mobile Internet access to a central operations location. Many of these freight-handling companies also provide 3PL services to other businesses as a way to generate additional revenue from their investments in tracking technologies.

Truckers themselves have benefitted from advances in Internet technologies, in particular the increase in mobile device connectivity. In the not-so-distant past, a long-haul truck driver relied on maps and updates heard on the radio to avoid traffic jams, weather-related slowdowns, and highway construction activity. Today, a variety of smartphone and tablet apps can warn a trucker of all these risks and more. Apps for truckers include information about permanent threats (low overpasses, tight turns, and roads that prohibit commercial vehicle traffic) and current threats (heavy traffic, construction, speed traps) as they develop. Truckers with mobile devices have continual access to the latest information about not only these risks, but also opportunities such as good prices on fuel or meals.

Logistics management is an area that illustrates well how electronic commerce has proceeded in waves of technological development. The marriage of GPS and portable computers with the Internet was one example of second-wave electronic commerce. The addition of mobile device technologies to the mix is an example of third-wave electronic commerce.

Business Process Support Activities

Activities that support all of a business's processes include finance and administration tasks, the operation of human resources, and technology development activities. Finance and administration business processes include activities such as making payments, processing payments received from customers, planning capital expenditures, and budgeting and planning to ensure that sufficient funds will be available to meet the organization's obligations as they come due. The operation of the computing infrastructure and database management functions of the organization is also an administration activity. Human resource processes include activities such as hiring, training, and evaluating employees; administering benefits; and complying with government record-keeping regulations. Technology development includes networking research scientists into virtual collaborative workgroups, sharing research results, publishing research papers online, and providing connections to outside sources of research and development services. Figure 5-2 summarizes these categories of support activities.

Finance and Administration	Human Resources	Technology Development
Making payments to suppliers	Hiring employees	Creating and maintaining virtual collaborative research workgroups
Processing payments from customers	Training employees	
Planning capital expenditures	Evaluating employees	Posting research results
Budgeting	Administering benefit programs	Publishing research reports online
Planning operations	Compliance with government record-keeping regulations	
Operating computing infrastructure		Connecting researchers to outside sources of research and development services

FIGURE 5-2   Categories of support activities

Human resources, payroll, and retirement plan services are all areas in which small and midsized companies often look for outside help. These business processes are subject to many detailed rules and regulations that often require an expert to decipher. A wide range of companies offer human resource management services online. Firms such as **CheckPointHR** offer a full range of services online; others, such as **Advantage Payroll**, specialize in payroll processing services, which are also available online. These business process outsourcing providers duplicate their clients' human resources and/or payroll functions on a password-protected Web site that is accessible to clients' employees. The employees can then access their employers' benefits information, find the answers to frequently asked questions, and even perform benefit option calculations. Larger firms build these types of functions into their own internal systems.

One common support activity that underlies multiple primary activities is training. In many companies, the Human Resources Department handles training. Other companies may decentralize this function and have individual departments administer it. For example, insurance firms expend large amounts of resources on sales training. In most insurance companies, the Sales and Marketing Department administers this training. By putting training materials on the company intranet, insurance companies can distribute the training materials to many different sales offices, yet coordinate the use of those materials in the corporate headquarters sales office.

The Swedish telecommunications giant Ericsson runs an extranet for current and former employees, families of those employees, and employees of approved business partners. Ericsson has more than 110,000 employees scattered across the globe. One part of this extranet includes a Web site that enables current employees, retirees, and other recipients of payments from the company's medical and retirement plans to efficiently track their benefits. Another part of the extranet includes a Web site designed to facilitate knowledge management. **Knowledge management** is the intentional collection, classification, and dissemination of information about a company, its products, and its processes. This type of knowledge is developed over time by individuals working for or with a company and is often difficult to gather and distill. You will learn more about knowledge management and the software tools used to facilitate it in Chapter 9.

Ericsson managers hope that their knowledge network will generate new ideas, help solve problems, and improve business processes throughout the international organization. Designers of the system have identified their biggest challenge: to direct the information they collect in the extranet to projects and product development activities that will benefit from that information. You can learn more about knowledge management in general at the KMWorld Web site. In Chapter 9, you will learn about software that companies can use to build knowledge management systems.

E-Government

Governments perform many important functions for the individual citizens, businesses, and other organizations that they serve. Many of these functions can be enhanced by the use of online technologies. Governments also perform businesslike activities; for example, they employ people, buy supplies from vendors, and distribute benefit payments of many kinds. Citizens can download blank tax forms, passport applications, and other documents from government Web sites. Governmental entities also collect a variety of taxes and fees from their constituents and can use the Internet to make that process more efficient, if not more pleasant (you will learn more about how governments use the Web in administering their tax laws in Chapter 7). The use of Internet technologies by governments and government agencies to perform these functions is often called **e-government**.

The U.S. government's Financial Management Service (FMS) is responsible for collecting trillions of dollars of tax, license, and other fee revenue. It also pays out trillions of dollars in Social Security benefits, veterans' benefits, tax refunds, and other disbursements. The FMS uses its Pay.gov Web site to handle much of this financial activity. The U.S. government's Bureau of Public Debt operates the TreasuryDirect site, which allows individuals to buy savings bonds and financial institutions to buy treasury bills, bonds, and notes.

Other countries' national governments use e-government to reduce administrative costs and provide better service to stakeholders as well. In the United Kingdom, the Department for Work and Pensions Web site provides information on unemployment, pension, and social security benefits. Smaller countries also have portal Web sites, such as Singapore Government Online, that provide information and enable citizens to interact with their governments online.

U.S. state governments also have Web sites for conducting business and interacting with their citizenry. The State of California's e-government activities are available at its one-stop portal site, CA.GOV, a recent version of which appears in Figure 5-3.

This site gives visitors access to every California government agency and state operation. Site visitors can transact a wide array of business with the state—from renewing a driver's license to reserving a campsite. The site gives Californians one site through which they can conduct virtually all of their business with their state. For businesses, the site offers the full text of all California business laws and regulations. It also provides information about how to sell to and buy from the state and its agencies.

link to business laws, regulations, and information about doing business with California

FIGURE 5-3   State of California portal site

Most other U.S. state governments (and, in other countries, provincial or regional governments) have similar Web sites. States can reduce the cost of providing services while providing those services more efficiently by using Web technologies to serve their stakeholders. The most common services offered by states and similar regional governments are the following: access to the text of state laws and regulations, renewal of licenses, promotion of the state to businesses considering new locations, job listings, promotion of tourism in the state, tax forms and filing information, and information for companies that want to do business with the state.

Most local U.S. governments now have Web sites that offer residents a variety of information. The Web sites of larger cities (such as Minneapolis or New Orleans) include transcripts of city council meetings, local laws and regulations, business license and tax administration functions, and promotional information about the city for new residents or businesses seeking new locations. Smaller cities, towns, and villages are also using the Web to communicate with residents (see the Cheviot, Ohio, Web site for one example). These local government Web sites have proven to be useful general communication tools in the aftermath of natural disasters.

Network Model of Economic Organization in Purchasing: Supply Webs

In Chapter 1, you learned about the three different forms of economic organization: markets, hierarchies, and networks. A significant trend in purchasing, logistics, and support activities is the shift away from hierarchical structures toward network structures. The traditional purchasing model had one hierarchically structured firm negotiating purchase terms with several similarly structured supplier firms, playing each supplier against the others. As is typical in a network organization, more businesses are now giving their Procurement Departments new tools to negotiate with suppliers, including the possibility of forming strategic alliances. For example, a buying firm might enter into an alliance with a supplier to develop new technology that will reduce overall product costs. The technology development might be done by a third firm using research conducted by a fourth firm.

While reading the previous sections in this chapter, you might have noticed that companies sometimes have other firms perform various support activities for them. These outsourcing arrangements are also examples of firms moving toward a network model of economic organization. Consider a business that uses one supplier to manage its payroll, another to administer its employee benefits plans, and a third to handle its document storage needs. The document storage service supplier might store the documents of the payroll service supplier and the benefits administration firm. The payroll service supplier might handle the payroll for the benefits administration firm. A fourth firm might provide online backup storage for the files of the other three companies. Of course, the payroll firm and the employee benefits firm might form a marketing partnership to sell both of their services to particular market segments.

Some researchers who study the interaction of firms within an industry value chain use the term **supply web** instead of "supply chain" because many industry value chains no longer consist of a single sequence of companies linked in a single line, but include many parallel lines that are interconnected in a web or network configuration made up of strategic alliances or complex configurations of outsourcing contracts.

Highly specialized firms can now exist and trade services efficiently on the Web. The Web is enabling this shift from hierarchical to network forms of economic organization. These emerging networks of firms are more flexible and can respond to changes in the economic environment much more quickly than hierarchically structured businesses. The roots of Web technology for business-to-business transactions, however, lie in a hierarchically structured approach to inter-firm information transfer: electronic data interchange.

Electronic Data Interchange

In Chapter 1, you learned that electronic data interchange (EDI) is a computer-to-computer transfer of business information between two businesses that uses a standard format of some kind. The two businesses that are exchanging information are trading partners. Firms that exchange data in specific standard formats are said to be **EDI compatible**. The business information exchanged is often transaction data; however, it can also include other information related to transactions, such as price quotes and order status inquiries. Transaction data in business-to-business (B2B) transactions includes the information traditionally included on paper documents. The data from invoices, purchase orders, requests for quotations, bills of lading, and receiving reports accounts for more than 75 percent of all information exchanged by U.S. trading partners. EDI was the first form of electronic commerce to be widely used in business—beginning some 20 years before anyone used the term *electronic commerce*—and it continues to be an important part of B2B, handling an estimated $4 trillion in transactions worldwide every year.

Understanding EDI is important because most B2B electronic commerce is based on EDI or adapted from EDI. It is also important because EDI is still the single most commonly used technology in online B2B transactions. The dollar amount of EDI transactions today is about equal to that of all other B2B transaction technologies combined. This section provides a brief history of EDI and explains how it works. It also explains why EDI is better than processing mountains of paper transactions.

Early Business Information Interchange Efforts

The emergence of large business organizations in the late 1800s and early 1900s brought with it the need to create formal records of business transactions. By the 1950s, companies were using computers to keep records of internal transactions, but information flows between businesses required paper documents (purchase orders, invoices, bills of lading, checks, remittance advices, and so on) because one company's computers could not communicate with other companies' computers. Generating these paper forms (by hand or as printed computer output), mailing them, and then having recipients enter the data from them into their computer systems was slow, inefficient, expensive, redundant, and unreliable. By the 1960s, businesses with large transaction volumes had begun exchanging information with each other by shipping punched cards or reels of magnetic tape. During the 1960s and 1970s, data communications technologies improved, allowing businesses to transfer much of this intercompany information over telephone lines instead.

Although these information transfer agreements between trading partners increased efficiency and reduced errors, they were not an ideal solution. Because the data translation programs that one business wrote would frequently not work on other businesses' computers, each company participating in these information exchanges had to spend considerable money to write their own programs. Only large companies could afford this investment. Smaller or lower-volume businesses could not afford to participate.

In 1968, a number of freight and shipping companies joined together to attack their collective paperwork burden. They created a standardized information set that included all the data elements that shippers commonly included on bills of lading, freight invoices, shipping manifests, and other paper forms. Instead of printing a paper form, shippers could convert information about shipments into a computer file that they could send to any freight company that had adopted the standard. The freight company could then transfer the standardized data into its own information systems. The costs saved by not printing or handling forms, not re-entering data, and avoiding errors were significant, even for smaller shippers and freight carriers.

Although these industry-specific data interchange standards were helpful, their benefits were limited to members of the standard-setting groups in those specific industries. Most businesses that are in one industry buy goods and services from businesses that are in other industries. For example, a machinery manufacturer might buy materials from steel mills, paint distributors, electrical assembly contractors, and container manufacturers. Almost every business needs to buy office supplies and the services of freight and transportation companies. Thus, full realization of economies and efficiencies required standards that could be used by companies in all industries.

Emergence of Broader Standards: The Birth of EDI

The **American National Standards Institute (ANSI)**, the coordinating body for standards in the United States since 1918, does not set standards, but maintains procedures for the development of national standards and accredits committees that follow those procedures. In 1979, ANSI chartered a new committee to develop uniform EDI standards. This committee is called the **Accredited Standards Committee X12 (ASC X12)**. The ASC X12 committee and its subcommittees include information systems professionals from hundreds of businesses. The administrative body that coordinates ASC X12 activities is the **Data Interchange Standards Association (DISA)**. The ASC X12 standard currently includes specifications for several hundred **transaction sets**, which are the names of the formats for specific business data interchanges.

The X12 standards were quickly adopted by major firms in the United States, but businesses in other countries continued to use their own national standards. In the mid-1980s, the United Nations Economic Commission for Europe invited North American and European EDI experts to work together on designing a common set of EDI standards based on the successful experiences of U.S. firms in using the ASC X12 standards. In 1987, the United Nations published its first standards under the title **EDI for Administration, Commerce, and Transport (EDIFACT, or UN/EDIFACT)**. The DISA and the UN/EDIFACT group have attempted to develop a single common set of international standards several times since 2000; however, these attempts have never succeeded. Today, both standards continue to exist. Companies that do business worldwide must either make their EDI software work with both standards or use a software product that does conversions between the standards. Figure 5-4 lists some of the more commonly used transaction sets, showing the paper document from which the transaction set was devised along with the identifiers of the ASC X12 and the UN/EDIFACT versions of the transaction set.

How EDI Works

Although the basic idea behind EDI is straightforward, its implementation can be complicated, even in fairly simple business situations. For example, consider a company

Transaction Description	Transaction Set Identifiers	
	ASC X12	UN/EDIFACT
Ordering Transactions		
Purchase Order	850	ORDERS
Purchase Order Acknowledgment	855	ORDRSP
Purchase Order Change	860	ORDCHG
Request for Quotation	840	REQOTE
Response to Request for Quotation	843	QUOTES
Shipping Transactions		
Ship Notice/Manifest (Advance Shipping Notice)	856	DESADV
Bill of Lading (Shipment Information)	858	IFTMCS
Receiving Advice	861	RECADV
Sales and Payment Transactions		
Invoice	810	INVOIC
Freight Invoice	859	IFTFCC
Payment Order/Remittance Advice	820	REMADV

FIGURE 5-4   Commonly used EDI transaction sets

that needs a replacement for one of its metal-cutting machines. This section describes the steps involved in making this purchase using a paper-based system and then explains how the process would change using EDI. In both of these examples, we assume that the vendor uses its own vehicles instead of a common carrier to deliver the purchased machine.

PAPER-BASED PURCHASING PROCESS

The buyer and the vendor in this example are not using any integrated software for business processes internally; thus, each information-processing step results in the production of a paper document that must be delivered to the department handling the next step. Information transfer between the buyer and vendor is also paper based and can be delivered by mail, courier, or fax. The information flows that occur in the paper-based version of the purchasing process example are shown in Figure 5-5.

Once the production manager in the operating unit decides that the metal-cutting machine needs to be replaced, the following process begins:

1. The production manager completes a purchase requisition form and sends it to Purchasing. This requisition describes the machine that is needed to perform the metal-cutting operation.

2. Purchasing contacts vendors to negotiate price and terms of delivery. When Purchasing has selected a vendor, it prepares a purchase order and forwards it to the mail room.

3. Purchasing also sends one copy of the purchase order to the Receiving Department so that Receiving can plan to accept delivery when scheduled; Purchasing sends another copy to Accounting to advise it of the financial implications of the order.

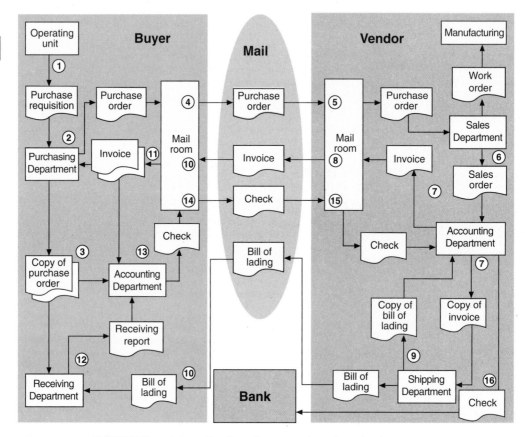

FIGURE 5-5 Information flows in a paper-based purchasing process

4. The mail room sends the purchase order it received from Purchasing to the selected vendor by mail or courier.

5. The vendor's mail room receives the purchase order and forwards it to its Sales Department.

6. The vendor's Sales Department prepares a sales order that it sends to its Accounting Department and a work order that it sends to Manufacturing. The work order describes the machine's specifications and authorizes Manufacturing to begin work on it. When the machine is completed, Manufacturing notifies Accounting and sends the machine to shipping.

7. The Accounting Department sends the original invoice to the mail room and a copy of the invoice to the Shipping Department.

8. The mail room mails the invoice to the buyer.

9. The vendor's Shipping Department uses its copy of the invoice to create a bill of lading and sends it with the machine to the buyer.

10. The buyer's mail room receives the invoice at about the same time as its Receiving Department receives the machine with its bill of lading.

11. The buyer's mail room sends one copy of the invoice to Purchasing so the Purchasing Department knows that the machine was received, and sends the original invoice to Accounting.

12. The buyer's Receiving Department checks the machine against the bill of lading and its copy of the purchase order. If the machine is in good condition and matches the specifications on the bill of lading and the purchase order, Receiving completes a receiving report, sends it to Accounting, and then delivers the machine to the operating unit.

13. Accounting makes sure that all details on its copy of the purchase order, the receiving report, and the original invoice match. If they do, Accounting issues a check and forwards it to the mail room.

14. The buyer's mail room sends the check by mail or courier to the vendor.

15. The vendor's mail room receives the check and sends it to Accounting.

16. Accounting compares the check to its copies of the invoice, bill of lading, and sales order. If all details match, Accounting deposits the check in the vendor's bank and records the payment received.

EDI PURCHASING PROCESS

The information flows that occur in the EDI version of this sample purchasing process are shown in Figure 5-6. The mail service has been replaced with the data communications of an EDI network, and the flows of paper within the buyer's and vendor's organizations have been replaced with computers running EDI translation software.

In the EDI purchasing process, when the operating unit manager decides that the metal-cutting machine needs to be replaced, the following process begins:

1. The operating unit manager sends an electronic message to its Purchasing Department. This message describes the machine that is needed to perform the metal-cutting operation.

2. Purchasing contacts vendors by telephone, e-mail, or through their Web sites to negotiate price and terms of delivery. After selecting a vendor, Purchasing sends a message that the buyer's EDI translator computer converts to a standard format purchase order transaction set that goes through an EDI network to the vendor where the message is routed through its EDI translator and sent to the Sales Department. At that point, the message is automatically entered into the vendor's Manufacturing Department production management system (where the machine's specifications are provided so Manufacturing can begin work on building it) and the vendor's accounting system (in their Accounting Department).

3. Purchasing also sends electronic messages to the buyer's Receiving Department (so it can plan to accept delivery when it is expected) and to the buyer's Accounting Department with details such as the agreed purchase price.

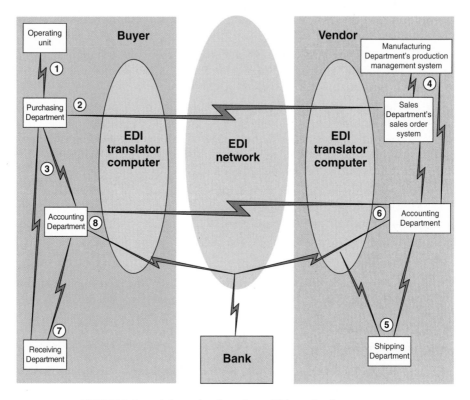

FIGURE 5-6   Information flows in an EDI purchasing process

4. When the machine is completed, Manufacturing notifies Accounting and sends the machine to the vendor's Shipping Department.

5. The vendor's Shipping Department sends an electronic message to its Accounting Department indicating that the machine is ready to ship. It also sends an electronic message to its EDI translator computer that indicates the machine is ready to ship. The EDI translator computer converts the message into a standard 856 transaction set (Advance Ship Notification) and forwards it through the EDI network to the buyer.

6. The vendor's Accounting Department sends a message to its EDI translator computer, which converts the message to the standard invoice transaction set and forwards it through the EDI network to the buyer's EDI translator computer before the buyer's Receiving Department receives the machine. The computer then converts the invoice data to a format that the buyer's information systems can use. The invoice data becomes immediately available to the buyer's Accounting Department.

7. When the machine arrives, the buyer's Receiving Department checks it against the purchase order data on its computer system. If the machine is in good condition and matches the specifications shown in the purchase order data,

Receiving sends a message to Accounting confirming that the machine has been received in good order. It then delivers the machine to the operating unit.

8. The buyer's Accounting Department system compares all details in the purchase order data, receiving data, and decoded invoice transaction set from the vendor. If all the details match, the accounting system notifies its bank to reduce the buyer's account and increase the vendor's account by the amount of the invoice. The EDI network may provide services that perform this task.

As you can see by comparing the paper-based purchasing process in Figure 5-5 to the EDI purchasing process in Figure 5-6, the same information is being provided to each department in each company, but EDI reduces paper flow and streamlines the information interchanges. The paper-based system has 16 individual steps compared to the eight steps required to complete this transaction using EDI. The three key elements (shown in Figure 5-6) that alter the process so dramatically are the EDI network (instead of the mail service) that connects the two companies and the two EDI translator computers that handle the conversion of data from the formats used internally by the buyer and the vendor to standard EDI transaction sets.

Value-Added Networks

Trading partners can implement the EDI network and EDI translation processes in several ways. Each of these ways uses one of two basic approaches: direct connection or indirect connection. The first approach, called **direct connection EDI**, requires each business in the network to operate its own on-site EDI translator computer (as shown in Figure 5-6). These EDI translator computers are then connected directly to each other using leased telecommunication lines. Because dedicated leased-lines are expensive, only a few very large companies still use direct connection EDI, which is illustrated in Figure 5-7.

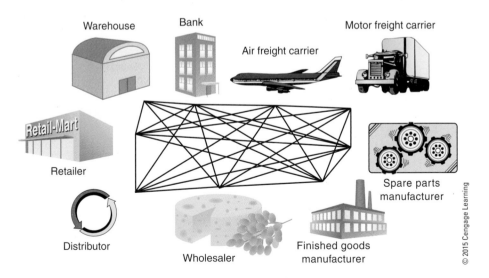

FIGURE 5-7   Direct connection EDI

Instead of connecting directly to each of its trading partners, a company might decide to use the services of a value-added network. As you learned in Chapter 1, a value-added network (VAN) is a company that provides communications equipment, software, and skills needed to receive, store, and forward electronic messages that contain EDI transaction sets. To use the services of a VAN, a company must install EDI translator software that is compatible with the VAN. Often, the VAN supplies this software as part of its operating agreement.

To send an EDI transaction set to a trading partner, the VAN customer connects to the VAN using a dedicated telecommunications line and then forwards the EDI-formatted message to the VAN. The VAN logs the message and delivers it to the trading partner's mailbox on the VAN computer. The trading partner then dials in to the VAN and retrieves its EDI-formatted messages from that mailbox. This approach is called **indirect connection EDI** because the trading partners pass messages through the VAN instead of connecting their computers directly to each other. Figure 5-8 illustrates indirect connection EDI using a VAN.

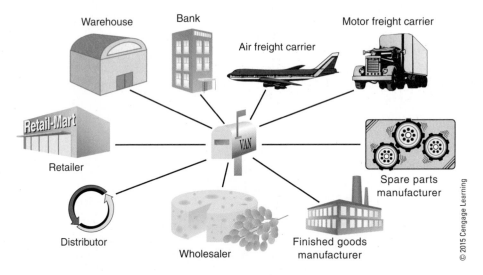

FIGURE 5-8   Indirect connection EDI through a VAN

Companies that provide VAN services include CovalentWorks, Kleinschmidt, and Promethean Software Services. Advantages of using a VAN are as follows:

1. Users need to support only the VAN's one communications protocol instead of many possible protocols used by trading partners.

2. The VAN can provide translation between different transaction sets used by trading partners (for example, the VAN can translate an ASC X12 set into a UN/EDIFACT set).

3. The VAN can perform automatic compliance checking to ensure that the transaction set is in the specified EDI format.

4. The VAN records message activity in an audit log. This VAN audit log becomes an independent record of transactions; this record can be helpful in resolving disputes between trading partners.

Because EDI transactions are business contracts and often involve large amounts of money, the existence of an independent audit log helps establish nonrepudiation. **Nonrepudiation** is the ability to establish that a particular transaction actually occurred. It prevents either party from repudiating, or denying, the transaction's validity or existence.

In the past, VANs had one serious disadvantage: cost. Most VANs required an enrollment fee, a monthly maintenance fee, and a transaction fee ranging from a few cents to a dollar that was levied on each transaction. The up-front cost of implementing indirect connection EDI, including software, VAN enrollment fee, and hardware, could easily exceed $20,000.

Today, VAN costs are much lower because VANs use the Internet instead of leased telecommunication lines to connect to their customers. Costs to begin EDI can be less than $5000, with monthly fees under $100 that include a generous transaction allowance. Even small companies find that they can engage indirect connection EDI and sell to large industrial and retail companies that require their vendors to use EDI.

Many companies that provide VAN services today all use the Internet as their main data communication technology. EDI on the Internet is called **Internet EDI** or **Web EDI**. It is also called **open EDI** because the Internet is an open architecture network, as you learned in Chapter 2. The **EDIINT (Electronic Data Interchange-Internet Integration**, also abbreviated **EDI-INT)** set of protocols is the most common set used for the exchange of EDI transaction sets over the Internet.

Most EDIINT exchanges today are encoded using the **AS2 (Applicability Statement 2)** specification, which is based on the HTTP rules for Web page transfers, although some companies are using a more secure specification, **AS3 (Applicability Statement 3)**. Both AS2 and AS3 transmissions return secure electronic receipts to the senders for every transaction, which helps establish nonrepudiation.

In the past, many companies tried to find the best single EDI solution (direct connection or VAN) to use for all of their purchases and/or sales. Today, a number of larger companies require all of their suppliers to use a specific method (usually direct connection). In general, a direct connection EDI approach is better if the company:

- Processes more than 500 EDI documents every month,
- Does business with relatively few large trading partners that have specific requirements, especially for data transmission protocols (AS2, AS3, and so on), and
- Has in-house information technology staff (or the ability to contract for such staff) that can maintain the various direct connection systems needed for each customer.

Conversely, companies will find a VAN EDI solution to be preferable if they:

- Process fewer than 500 EDI documents every month,
- Do business with a large number of smaller trading partners, and
- Do not have in-house information technology staff (or the ability to contract for such staff) that are familiar with EDI technologies.

The abilities of a company's accounting system to integrate with specific EDI technologies can also be an important factor to consider. Some systems have built-in mechanisms for direct connection EDI, whereas others are designed specifically for VAN EDI operations.

EDI Payments

Some EDI transaction sets provide instructions to a trading partner's bank. These transaction sets are negotiable instruments; that is, they are the electronic equivalent of checks. All banks have the ability to perform electronic funds transfers (EFTs), which are the movement of money from one bank account to another. The bank accounts involved in EFTs may be customer accounts or the accounts that banks keep on their own behalf with each other. When EFTs involve two banks, they are executed using an **automated clearing house (ACH)** system, which is a service that banks use to manage their accounts with each other. In the United States, banks can use the ACH operated by the U.S. Federal Reserve Banks or one of the private ACHs operated by a group of banks or a separate company. You will learn more about how banks process ACH payments in Chapter 11.

Supply Chain Management Using Internet Technologies

You learned earlier in this chapter that the part of an industry value chain that precedes a particular strategic business unit is called a supply chain. Many companies use strategic alliances, partnerships, and long-term contracts to create relationships with other companies in the supply chains for the products that they manufacture or sell. These relationships can be quite complex, with suppliers helping their customers develop new products, specify product features, refine product specifications, and identify needed product improvements. In many cases, companies are able to reduce costs by developing close relationships with a few suppliers rather than negotiating with a large number of suppliers each time they need to buy materials or supplies. When companies integrate their supply management and logistics activities across multiple participants in a particular product's supply chain, the job of managing that integration is called **supply chain management**. The ultimate goal of supply chain management is to achieve a higher-quality or lower-cost product at the end of the chain.

Value Creation in the Supply Chain

In recent years, businesses have realized that they can save money and increase product quality by taking a more active role in negotiations with suppliers. By engaging suppliers in cooperative, long-term relationships, companies have found that they can work together with these suppliers to identify new ways to provide their own customers with faster, cheaper, and better service. By coordinating the efforts of supply chain participants, firms that engage in supply chain management are reaching beyond the limits of their own organization's hierarchical structure and creating a new network form of organization among the members of the supply chain.

The use of technologies to improve the efficiency of a company's operations is sometimes called **supply chain competition**, and it can help companies implement management techniques such as just-in-time and lean production. Companies use **just-in-time inventory management** to reduce inventory stocks of component parts purchased by arranging for delivery of those parts to occur very close to the time at which they are used in the manufacturing process. This lowers the cost of storing, tracking, insuring, and managing inventory by reducing it as close to zero as possible. **Lean production** methods focus on eliminating waste and unnecessary processes throughout the manufacturing process. Both of these management techniques require readily available and continuously updated information about demand, production schedules, and inventory availability from suppliers—information that can be provided very effectively by a technology-enabled supply chain management system.

Supply chain management was originally developed as a way to reduce costs. It focused on very specific elements in the supply chain and tried to identify opportunities for process efficiency. Today, supply chain management is used to add value in the form of benefits to the ultimate consumer at the end of the supply chain.

Businesses that engage in supply chain management work to establish long-term relationships with a small number of very capable suppliers. These suppliers, called **tier-one suppliers**, in turn develop long-term relationships with a larger number of suppliers that provide components and raw materials to them. These **tier-two suppliers** manage relationships with the next level of suppliers, called **tier-three suppliers**, that provide them with components and raw materials. A key element of these relationships is trust between the parties. The long-term relationships created among participants in the supply chain are called **supply alliances**. The level of information sharing that must take place among the supply chain participants can be a major barrier to entering into these alliances. Firms are not accustomed to disclosing detailed operating information and often perceive that information disclosure might hurt the firm by placing it at a competitive disadvantage.

For example, Dell Computer has been able to reduce supply chain costs by sharing information with its suppliers. The moment Dell receives an order from a customer, it makes that information available to its tier-one suppliers, who can then better plan their production based on Dell's exact demand trends. For example, a supplier of disk drives can change its production plans immediately when it sees a shift in Dell's customer orders from computers with one size disk drive to another, usually larger, size disk drive. This prevents the supplier from overproducing the smaller drive, which reduces the supplier's costs (for unsold drives) and costs in the supply chain overall (the supplier does not need to charge more for the disk drives it does sell to Dell to recover the cost of the unsold drives).

In exchange for the stability of the closer, long-term relationships, buyers expect annual price reductions and quality improvements from suppliers at each stage of the supply chain. However, all supply chain participants share information and work together to create value. Ideally, the supply chain coordination creates enough value that each level of supplier can share the benefits of reduced cost and more efficient operations. Supply chain management has been gaining momentum during the past decade and is supported by major purchasing groups such as the **APICS Supply Chain Council** (APICS was originally known as the American Production and Inventory Control Society). By working together, supply chain members can reduce costs and increase the value of the product or service to the ultimate consumer.

A key element in the coordination of supply chain activities is the establishment of a consistent production strategy that is adopted by all supply chain participants. **Production strategy** is the way a company achieves competitive advantage in its product creation activities; the two most common strategies are efficient processing (in which the company tries to make products as quickly or as inexpensively as possible) or market-responsive flexibility (in which the company tries to produce the specific products demanded by the market as it changes). In other words, some companies structure themselves to be efficient producers, whereas others structure themselves to be flexible producers. Unfortunately, the kinds of things that allow a firm to be an efficient, low-cost producer are exactly the things that prevent a firm from being flexible enough to respond to market changes. For example, the efficient producer invests in expensive machines that can stamp out large numbers of low-cost items. This investment drives down the cost of production, but makes it difficult for the producer to be flexible. A large investment in specialized machinery prevents that producer from reconfiguring the plant layout. If even one member of the supply chain for a product that requires flexible production operates as an efficient producer (instead of as a flexible producer), every other firm in the supply chain suffers. The efficient producer creates bottlenecks that hamper the best efforts of all other supply chain members. Clear communication up and down the supply chain can keep each participant informed of what the ultimate consumer demands. The participants can then plot a strategy to meet those demands.

Clear communications, and quick responses to those communications, are key elements of successful supply chain management. Technologies, and especially the technologies of the Internet and the Web, can be very effective communications enhancers. For the first time, firms can effectively manage the details of their own internal processes and the processes of other members of their supply chains. Software that uses the Internet can help all members of the supply chain review past performance, monitor current performance, and predict when and how much of certain products need to be produced. When a company uses technology to respond quickly to changes in market demand and supplier conditions, it is said to have an **adaptive supply chain**, which can lead to higher efficiency, lower costs, and greater profits. Figure 5-9 lists the advantages of using Internet technologies in supply chain management. As you can see, the only major disadvantage of using Internet technologies in supply chain management is the cost of

Trading partners within a supply chain can:
- Share information about changes in customer demand
- Receive rapid notification of product design changes and adjustments
- Provide specifications and drawings more efficiently
- Increase the speed of processing transactions
- Reduce the cost of handling transactions
- Reduce errors in entering transaction data
- Share information about defect rates and types
- Better coordinate shipments with logistics partners and each other

FIGURE 5-9   Advantages of using Internet technologies in supply chain management

those technologies. For most companies, however, the advantages provide much greater value than the costs of implementing and maintaining the technologies.

Increasing Supply Chain Efficiency and Cooperation

Many companies are using Internet and Web technologies to manage supply chains in ways that yield increases in efficiency and cooperation throughout the chain. These companies have found ways to increase process speed, reduce costs, coordinate design efforts, and increase manufacturing flexibility so that they can respond to changes in the quantity and nature of ultimate consumer demand.

For example, Boeing, the largest producer of commercial aircraft in the world, faces a huge task in keeping its production on schedule. Each airplane requires more than 1 million individual parts and assemblies, and each airplane is custom configured to meet the purchasing airline's exact specifications. These parts and assemblies must be completed and delivered on schedule or the production process comes to a halt.

Using EDI and Internet links, Boeing works with suppliers so that they can provide exactly the right part or assembly at exactly the right time. Even before an airplane enters into production, Boeing makes the engineering specifications and drawings available to its suppliers through secure Internet connections. As work on the airplane progresses, Boeing keeps every member of the supply chain continually informed of completion milestones achieved and necessary schedule changes. Instead of waiting 36 months for delivery, customers can now have their new airplanes in 10 months or less. Using Internet technologies as Boeing and an increasing number of other precision manufacturing firms do—that is, to integrate the design, development, construction, testing, and refinement of products—is called **collaborative commerce**.

Although Dell Computer is famous for its use of the Web to sell custom-configured computers to individuals and businesses, it has also used technology-enabled supply chain management to give customers exactly what they want. Dell's tier-one suppliers have access to a secure Web site that shows them Dell's latest sales forecasts, along with other information about planned product changes, defect rates, and warranty claims. In addition, the Web site tells suppliers who Dell's customers are and what they are buying. All of this information helps these tier-one suppliers plan their production much better than they could otherwise. The information sharing goes in both directions in Dell's supply chain: tier-one suppliers are required to provide Dell with current information on their defect rates and production problems. As a result, all members of the supply chain work together to reduce inventories, increase quality, and provide high value to the ultimate consumer. The improved coordination between Dell and its tier-one suppliers has reduced the amount of inventory Dell must keep on hand from three weeks' sales to two hours' sales. Ultimately, Dell wants to see inventory levels measured in minutes. By increasing the amount of information it has about its customers, Dell has been able to dramatically reduce the amount of inventory it must hold. Dell has also shared this information with members of its supply chain. This kind of cooperative work requires a high level of trust. To enhance this trust and develop a sense of community, Dell maintains discussion boards as an open forum in which its supply chain members can share their experiences in dealing with Dell and with each other.

For Boeing, Dell, and other firms, the use of Internet and Web technologies in managing supply chains has yielded significantly increased process speed, reduced costs, and increased flexibility. All of these attributes combine to allow a coordinated supply chain to produce products and services that better meet the needs of the ultimate consumer.

Materials-Tracking Technologies

Tracking materials as they move from one company to another and as they move within the company has always been challenging. Companies have been using optical scanners and bar codes for many years to help track the movement of materials. In many industries, the integration of bar coding and EDI has become prevalent. Figure 5-10 shows a typical bar-coded shipping label that is used in the auto industry. Each bar-coded element is a representation of an element of the ASC X12 transaction set number 856, Advance Shipping Notice. Five of the 856 transaction set's elements are bar coded (including Part Number, Quantity Shipped, Purchase Order Number, Serial Number, and Packing List Number).

FIGURE 5-10   Shipping label with bar-coded elements from EDI transaction set 856, Advance Shipping Notice

These bar codes allow companies to scan materials as they are received and to track them as they move from the materials warehouse into production. Companies can use this bar-coded information along with information from their EDI systems to manage inventory flows and forecast materials needs across their supply chains.

Large online retailers such as Amazon.com, Target, and Kohl's maintain fulfillment centers from which they ship products that customers have ordered online. Tracking systems, called **real-time location systems (RTLS)**, in these fulfillment centers use bar codes to monitor inventory movements and ensure that goods are shipped as quickly as possible.

In the second wave of electronic commerce, companies are integrating new types of tracking into their Internet-based materials-tracking systems. The most promising technology now being used is **radio frequency identification devices (RFIDs)**, which are small chips that use radio transmissions to track inventory. RFID technology has existed for many years, but until recently, it required each RFID to have its own power supply (usually a battery). RFIDs that have their own power supply are called **active RFIDs**. RFIDs can be read much more quickly and with a higher degree of accuracy than bar codes. Bar codes must be visible to be scanned. RFIDs can be placed anywhere on or in most items and are readable even when covered with packing materials, dirt, or plastic bands. A bar-code scanner must be placed within a few inches of the bar code. Most RFID readers have a range of about six feet.

An important development in RFID technology is the passive RFID, which can be made cheaply and in very small sizes. A **passive RFID** does not need a power source. It receives a radio signal from a nearby transmitter and extracts a tiny amount of power from that signal. It uses the power it extracts to send a signal back to the transmitter. That signal includes information about the inventory item to which the RFID has been affixed. Passive RFIDs are small enough to be installed on the face of credit cards or sewn into clothing items. Figure 5-11 shows a typical passive RFID tag.

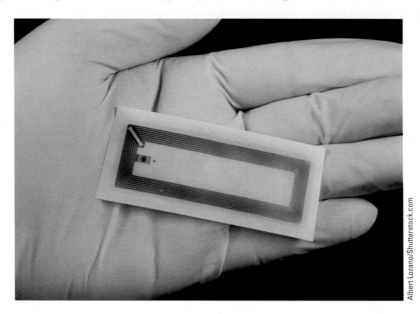

Albert Lozano/Shutterstock.com

FIGURE 5-11   Passive RFID tag

In 2003, Walmart began testing the use of RFIDs on its merchandise for inventory tracking and control. Walmart initiated a plan to have all of its suppliers install RFIDs in the goods they shipped to the retailer. Walmart wanted suppliers to do this within three years. Having all incoming inventory tagged with RFIDs would allow Walmart to manage its inventory better and reduce the incidence of stockouts. A **stockout** occurs when a retailer loses sales because it does not have specific goods on its shelves that customers want to buy. Many of Walmart's suppliers found the RFIDs, RFID readers, and the computer systems needed to manage RFID-tagged inventory to be quite expensive. These suppliers pushed Walmart to slow down the implementation of its plan. Walmart responded by encouraging suppliers to use RFIDs, but focused its energies on developing pilot projects within Walmart to test RFID-based inventory management systems. Some retailers, such as Target, devoted their resources to case-lot RFID tagging (where an RFID chip is placed in the packaging for a case of products rather than on each individual product).

Many industry observers have concluded that general acceptance of product-level RFID tagging will become widespread in retailing starting in 2017, with Macy's, American Apparel, Kohl's, Dillard's, and Target all projecting full RFID reading capabilities in all of their locations by then. Although the cost of a passive RFID tag is now between seven and fifteen cents (depending on quantity ordered), even that small cost can be prohibitive for companies that ship large volumes of low-priced goods. The cost of RFID tags is expected to continue dropping, and as it does, more and more companies will find them to be useful in an increasingly wide range of situations. The cost of RFID readers has also been dropping at the same time that the capabilities of those readers have been increasing. Some stationary RFID readers can scan everything within a 50-foot diameter simultaneously (potentially allowing thousands of RFID-tagged items to be read instantaneously), and small handheld RFID readers can be used to scan around metal shelving and liquids in containers (metal and liquid can interfere with RFID signals). You can learn more about current developments in this technology by visiting the RFID Journal online. Figure 5-12 summarizes the key features of bar codes, passive RFID, and active RFID technologies.

Feature	Bar Code	Passive RFID	Active RFID
Technology	Optical (laser)	Radio frequency signal	Radio frequency signal
Power source required	None	None	Battery
Must be visible to read?	Yes	No	No
Sources of interference	Dirt, oil/grease, torn tag	Some metals, liquids	Some metals, liquids
Tag reading rate	One at a time	Hundreds simultaneously	Hundreds simultaneously
Maximum read range	2–24 inches	20–40 feet	100–300 feet
Life of a tag	2–5 years	10 years	3–8 years
Cost of one tag	Fraction of a cent	7–15 cents	$15–$100
Cost of one reader	$80–$300	$500–$8000	$1000–$1500

Sources: http://www.inlogic.com/rfid/rfid_vs_barcode.aspx, http://www.amitracks.com/2013/10/simple-cost-analysis-for-rfid-options/, http://www.engineersgarage.com/contribution/rfid-vs-barcodes#

FIGURE 5-12   Key features of bar code, passive RFID, and active RFID technologies

Creating an Ultimate Consumer Orientation in the Supply Chain

One of the main goals of supply chain management is to help each company in the chain focus on meeting the needs of the consumer at the end of the supply chain. Companies in industries with long supply chains have, in the past, often found it difficult to maintain this customer focus, which is sometimes called an **ultimate consumer orientation**. Instead, companies have directed their efforts toward meeting the needs of the next member in the supply chain. This short-sighted approach can cause companies to miss opportunities to add value in subsequent steps of the chain.

One company that pioneered the use of Internet technology to go beyond the next step in its value chain is Michelin North America. Michelin has a highly respected brand name and reputation in the tire business. However, most consumers rely on local tire dealers to make specific recommendations when they need replacement tires for their vehicles. Michelin spends a great deal of money on direct advertising to its ultimate consumers. This advertising is directed at maintaining Michelin's well-known brand and convincing the consumer of the value of Michelin tires. The advertising and brand building effort can be wasted, however, if the consumer goes to a local tire dealer who recommends another brand.

Michelin launched an online business initiative in 1995 called BIB NET (after the company's famous Michelin Man mascot, whose name is Bibendum). The goal of this initiative was to sell more Michelin tires to consumers, but the initiative was directed at Michelin's tire dealers, not the ultimate consumers. BIB NET was an extranet that allowed tire dealers to access tire specifications, inventory status, and promotional information about Michelin products through a simple-to-use Web browser interface. Before BIB NET, dealers calling Michelin for product information were sometimes placed on hold. A dealer who is talking to a customer cannot afford to wait on hold. By giving dealers the power to access Michelin product information directly and immediately, Michelin saved money (maintaining a Web page is much less expensive than answering thousands of phone calls) and gave dealers better service. Michelin has found that tire retailers that use BIB NET are much less likely to recommend a competitor's tires to their customers.

Building and Maintaining Trust in the Supply Chain

The major issue that most companies must deal with in forming supply chain alliances is developing trust. Continual communication and information sharing are key elements in building trust. Because the Internet and the Web provide excellent ways to communicate and share information, they offer new avenues for building trust. Most procurement professionals have built trust on years of doing business with the same vendors. In many industries, vendors send sales representatives to call on buyers regularly. Vendors also participate actively in trade shows and conferences. By giving buyers frequent opportunities to interact with vendor representatives, vendors help build trust.

Vendors are finding that the Web gives them an opportunity to stay in contact with their customers more easily and less expensively. Although most buyers still see vendor sales representatives regularly, e-mail and the Web give them nearly instant access to their sales representative and other vendor personnel. By providing comprehensive information at a moment's notice, vendors can build buyers' trust in the vendor's ability to deliver products and provide the personalized service that buyers need.

Many supply chain management researchers are working on new ways to accumulate information about supplier performance and report that information to supply chain partners. This type of monitoring and reporting is being incorporated into the online marketplaces and business networks described in the next section.

Online Business Marketplaces and Networks

In the late 1990s, a number of industry-focused hubs opened and began offering marketplaces and auctions in which companies in the industry could contact each other and transact business. The idea was that these hubs would offer a doorway (or portal) to the Internet for industry members. Because these hubs were vertically integrated (that is, each hub would offer services to just one industry), they were called **vertical portals**. In this section, you will learn how these B2B marketplaces were conceived, developed, and operated as this sector of electronic commerce matured from 1997 through the present.

Independent Industry Marketplaces

The first vertical portals were trading exchanges focused on a particular industry. These vertical portals became known by various names that highlighted different elements of their collective nature, including **industry marketplaces** (focused on a single industry), **independent exchanges** (not controlled by a company that was an established buyer or seller in the industry), or **public marketplaces** (open to new buyers and sellers just entering the industry). These portals are also known collectively as **independent industry marketplaces**.

Ventro opened its first industry marketplace, Chemdex, in early 1997 to trade in bulk chemicals. To leverage the high investment it had made in trading exchange technology, Ventro followed Chemdex with Web marketplaces in a range of industries, including specialty medical supply, food service, and general business products. Many other companies followed Ventro's lead. By mid-2000, there were more than 2200 independent exchanges in a wide variety of industries but most of them were not earning profits and today fewer than 100 industry marketplaces are in operation. Some of the industry pioneers who closed their industry marketplace operations (including Ventro) were able to build successful businesses selling the software and technology that they had developed to run their marketplaces. Today, leading software vendors such as IBM, Microsoft, Oracle, and SAP also offer products that can be used to build B2B marketplaces. By 2010, various forms of B2B marketplaces gradually replaced independent marketplaces.

Alibaba.com, the China-based business marketplace, has been the biggest success in the general industrial marketplace category, providing suppliers in China and other developing economies easy access to buyers around the world. And Ariba, which was originally a set of software tools for building MRO catalogs, evolved into a company that provides software solutions (and is now owned by software company SAP) and the Ariba Network for Suppliers, which automates ordering, invoicing, payments, and catalog services for thousands of the world's largest buyers and suppliers. In 2012, Amazon. com launched AmazonSupply, a marketplace for industrial goods that is now a part of its Amazon Business Marketplace service offerings. Google followed a year later with Google Shopping for Suppliers, a similar service that was later folded into its Google Shopping site.

You will learn about four B2B marketplace models—private stores, customer portals, private company marketplaces, and industry consortia-sponsored marketplaces—in the remainder of this section.

LEARNING FROM FAILURES

MetalSite

Although a number of small steel manufacturing plants (called minimills) have opened in the past 20 years, most of the world's steel is still produced in very large steel mills. In these steel mills, it is economical to produce steel only in large batches. Because of the high cost of reconfiguring machinery, a steel mill set up to create one type of steel (for example, rolled sheets) requires significant time and money to change over to produce another type of steel (for example, bar steel). To minimize these changeover costs, steel mills produce steel products in large batches to meet estimated demand rather than actual orders. Because production quantities are designed to meet estimated demand instead of actual demand, steel mills often have overproduction of some items.

Companies such as Bethlehem Steel, one of the largest steel mills in the world, solved this problem in the past by sending faxes to potential buyers of their excess production. Buyers would respond with a bid on the product in which they were interested, and Bethlehem would negotiate with them to determine price and delivery terms.

In 1998, MetalSite was one of the first metal trading exchanges to begin doing business on the Web. These exchanges offered manufacturers such as Bethlehem an efficient way to reach a larger market for their excess production. By mid-2000, there were more than 200 metal exchanges operating on the Web. These exchanges were following a reintermediation strategy; that is, they were entering the supply chain of the steel industry to provide some added value that had not existed in the supply chain before. However, most industry analysts agreed that there was no need for

more than one or two exchanges in the steel industry. In 2001, metal trading exchange sites began to fail.

MetalSite had grown rapidly. With more than $35 million of investors' money, MetalSite was able to sign up 24,000 registered users and by mid-2001, was trading about $30 million worth of steel each month. However, its commissions of between 1 percent and 2 percent on each trade did not yield enough money to cover operating costs. The steel business was in a downturn along with the rest of the U.S. economy, and the downward pressure on commissions from competing exchanges was increasing rapidly. The major steel companies were discussing ways to form alliances to operate their own exchanges. After three years of operation and a desperate last-minute search for new investors, MetalSite closed in August 2001.

MetalSite had entered a business that could not support more than a few companies, and it was unable to become one of the survivors. The lesson from MetalSite's experience is that a reintermediation strategy must add significant value to the supply chain, and the company pursuing that strategy must be able to construct significant barriers that competitors must overcome to enter the business. MetalSite was unable to do either and thus failed. Many other B2B exchange sites that found themselves in similar competitive situations have also failed.

Private Stores and Customer Portals

As established companies in various industries watched new businesses open marketplaces, they became concerned that these independent operators would take control of transactions from them in supply chains—control that the established companies had spent years developing. Large companies that sell to many relatively small customers can exert great power in negotiating price, quality, and delivery terms with those customers. These sellers feared that industry marketplaces would dilute that power.

Many of these large sellers had already invested heavily in Web sites that they believed would meet the needs of their customers better than any industry marketplace. For example, Cisco and Dell offer private stores for each of their major customers within their selling Web sites. A **private store** has a password-protected entrance and offers negotiated price reductions on a limited selection of products—usually those that the customer has agreed to purchase in certain minimum quantities. Other companies, such as Grainger, provide additional services for customers on their selling Web sites. These **customer portal** sites offer private stores along with services such as part number cross referencing, product usage guidelines, safety information, and other services that would be needlessly duplicated if the sellers were to participate in an industry marketplace.

Private Company Marketplaces

Similarly, large companies that purchase from relatively small vendors can exert comparable power over those vendors in purchasing negotiations. The Procurement Departments of these companies can install procurement software (you will learn more about all types of electronic commerce software in Chapter 9), generally referred to as **e-procurement software**, that allows a company to manage its purchasing function through a Web interface. It automates many of the authorizations and other steps (see Figure 5-1) that are part of business procurement operations.

Although e-procurement software was originally designed to help manage the MRO procurement process, today it includes other marketplace functions, such as requests for quote posting areas, auctions, and integrated support for purchasing direct materials. E-procurement software for large companies can cost millions of dollars for licensing fees, installation, and customization; however, a growing number of companies are offering e-procurement software for smaller businesses.

Companies that implement e-procurement software usually require their suppliers to bid on their business. For example, an office supplies provider would create a schedule of prices at which it would sell to the company. The company would then compare that pricing to bids from other suppliers. The selected supplier would provide product price and description information to the company, which would insert that information into its e-procurement software. This permits authorized employees to order office supplies at the negotiated prices through a Web interface.

When industry marketplaces opened for business, these larger companies were reluctant to abandon their investments in e-procurement software or to make the software work with industry marketplaces' software—especially in the early years of industry marketplaces when there were many of them in each industry. These companies use their power in the supply chain to force suppliers to deal with them on their own terms rather than negotiate with suppliers in an industry marketplace.

As marketplace software became more reliable, many of these companies purchased software and technology consulting services from companies, such as Ventro and e-Steel, that had abandoned their industry marketplace businesses and were offering the software they had developed to companies that wanted to develop private marketplaces. A **private company marketplace** is a marketplace that provides auctions, request for quote postings, and other features (many of which are similar to those of e-procurement software) to companies that want to operate their own marketplaces. Today, many private company marketplaces have expanded to include functions to allow supply chain participants to manage multiple functions including manufacturing, tier-one and tier-two suppliers, distribution centers, transportation, orders, invoicing, and payments. These expanded arrangements are called **private industrial networks** or **private trading exchanges**.

Industry Consortia-Sponsored Marketplaces

Some companies had relatively strong negotiating positions in their industry supply chains, but did not have enough power to force suppliers to deal with them through a private company marketplace. These companies began to form consortia to sponsor marketplaces. An **industry consortia-sponsored marketplace** is a marketplace formed by several large buyers in a particular industry.

Figure 5-13 summarizes the characteristics of five general forms of marketplaces that exist in B2B electronic commerce today. The information in the figure comes from several sources, but the structure of the figure is adapted from one presented by Warren Raisch, a Web marketplace consultant, in his book *The eMarketplace*.

Although the figure shows five distinct B2B marketplace categories, the lines between them are not always clear. For example, Dell has from time to time sold other companies' products on its private store site, which would make it more like a customer portal than a private store. As the B2B marketplace industry matures, it is unlikely that one type of marketplace will become dominant. Most B2B experts believe that a variety of marketplaces with the characteristics of these five general categories will continue to exist for some time.

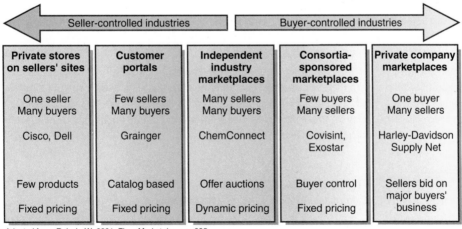

Adapted from: Raisch, W. 2001. *The eMarketplace, p. 225.*

FIGURE 5-13   Characteristics of B2B marketplaces

Summary

In this chapter, you learned how companies are using Internet technologies to improve their business processes for purchasing, logistics, and support activities and to implement strategies such as outsourcing and offshoring. Companies, government agencies, and other organizations are using Internet technologies to extend the reach of their enterprise planning and control activities beyond their organizations' legal definitions to include parts of other organizations. This emerging network model of organization was introduced in Chapter 1 and is used in this chapter to describe the growth in interorganizational communications and coordination.

Businesses of all sizes today use Internet technologies to purchase materials, services, and maintenance, repair, and operating supplies. Similarly, a growing number of companies use these technologies to manage their logistics and transportation operations, both internally and with outside providers of these services, including third-party logistics suppliers. Business services, such as benefits and payroll management, along with government services, are also provided increasingly online.

EDI, the earliest example of B2B electronic commerce, was initially developed by freight companies to reduce the paperwork burden of processing repetitive transactions. The spread of EDI to virtually all large companies has led smaller businesses to seek an affordable way to participate in EDI. The Internet is now providing the inexpensive communications channel that EDI lacked for so many years and is allowing smaller companies to participate in Internet EDI.

The increase in communications capabilities offered by the Internet and the Web have become an important force driving the adoption of supply chain management techniques, including supply chain competition, just-in-time inventory management, and lean production. Supply chain management can be implemented and enhanced through the use of online technologies, which can help to establish a consistent production strategy or make a specific supply chain more adaptive.

More and more companies are using the Internet to connect with their supply chain alliance partners to achieve comprehensive collaborative commerce objectives and provide more value to the ultimate consumer of their value chains' products and services. Increased integration of inventory tracking technologies, such as RFID, with Internet technologies has been driven by lower costs of implementation and operation, and their use is expected to continue to spread.

Early industry electronic marketplaces led to the development of several different models of online networks and marketplaces for B2B electronic commerce, including private stores, customer portals, private marketplaces, and industry consortia-sponsored marketplaces. Expanded versions of private marketplaces have emerged in the form of private industrial networks and private trading exchanges.

Key Terms

Accredited Standards Committee X12 (ASC X12)

active RFID (radio frequency identification device)

adaptive supply chain

American National Standards Institute (ANSI)

AS2 (Applicability Statement 2)

AS3 (Applicability Statement 3)

automated clearing house (ACH)

business process offshoring

collaborative commerce

contract purchasing

customer portal

Data Interchange Standards Association (DISA)

direct connection EDI

direct materials

EDI compatible

EDI for Administration, Commerce, and Transport (EDIFACT, or UN/EDIFACT)

EDIINT (Electronic Data Interchange-Internet Integration, EDI-INT)

e-government

e-procurement software

e-sourcing

impact sourcing

independent exchange

independent industry marketplace

indirect connection EDI

indirect materials

industry consortia-sponsored marketplace

industry marketplace

Internet EDI

just-in-time inventory management

knowledge management

lean production

maintenance, repair, and operating (MRO)

nonrepudiation

offshoring

open EDI

outsourcing

passive RFID

private company marketplace

private industrial network

private store

private trading exchange

production strategy

public marketplace

purchasing card (p-card)

Radio Frequency Identification Devices (RFIDs)

real-time location systems (RTLS)

replenishment purchasing

smart sourcing

sourcing

spend

spot market

spot purchasing

stockout

supply alliances

supply chain

supply chain competition

supply chain management

supply web

third-party logistics (3PL) provider

tier-one suppliers

tier-three suppliers

tier-two suppliers

transaction sets

ultimate consumer orientation

vertical portal

Web EDI

Review Questions

1. What is the difference between outsourcing and offshoring?
2. What is business process offshoring?
3. What is impact sourcing?
4. What activities are included in the procurement function called "sourcing"?

5. Briefly outline the differences between direct materials and indirect materials.

6. Briefly define the term *spend* as it is used in business purchasing.

7. What is spot purchasing?

8. What are MRO supplies?

9. What is a p-card?

10. What is a third-party logistics supplier?

11. Provide three specific examples of business support activities.

12. What is knowledge management?

13. Provide one specific example of how a government unit or agency could use the Web to operate more efficiently or service its constituents better.

14. What is a supply web?

15. Briefly describe the major problem faced by companies that want to use EDI for both U.S. and international transactions.

16. Briefly explain the differences between direct connection EDI and indirect connection EDI.

17. What is open EDI?

18. What is a supply alliance?

19. What is a production strategy?

20. Briefly explain how a company could benefit from being part of an adaptive supply chain.

21. What is the difference between collaborative commerce and EDI?

22. Briefly explain the differences between passive RFID and active RFID.

23. What is a private industrial network (also called a private trading exchange)?

Exercises

1. Impact sourcing, also called smart sourcing, was developed to provide opportunities for workers in less-developed countries. In two or three paragraphs, explain how and for what specific purposes impact sourcing can be used in developed countries.

2. The purchasing process in a business can be much more complex than most consumer purchasing processes. In about 100 words, outline the differences between a typical consumer purchase and a business purchase and explain why the business purchase decision is more complex in most cases.

3. Some business and political leaders argue that offshoring is dangerous because it can move jobs from developed countries to less-developed countries. Others argue that although offshoring might displace workers in the short run, in the longer term, everyone benefits by having developing economies create new industries, products, and markets for products and services that create high-level service and managerial jobs in the developed world. In recent years, some economists have argued that offshoring today is having a negative impact on service and professional employment in highly developed countries. Using resources in your library or online, write about 100 words in which you present two arguments for and two arguments against a U.S. company offshoring the management of its customer relationships to technical and managerial personnel in a less-developed country.

4. In a paragraph or two, explain how the Internet has reduced the spend of many U.S. manufacturing companies.

5. Would the use of purchasing cards be more helpful in controlling direct materials costs or indirect materials costs? In a paragraph or two, explain why.

6. Using your library or your favorite search engine, identify the main reason a large transportation company might want to use p-cards for its MRO spending. Summarize your findings in two or three paragraphs.

7. In about 100 words, explain why smaller companies might outsource elements of their human resources, payroll, or retirement plan management operations.

8. You have just started work as an intern in the purchasing department of Westridge Laboratories, an independent materials testing lab. You do not know much about the business, but your supervisor has given you the task of learning more about gas chromatographs, an instrument that the labs use for several regular tests they conduct. Use the ThomasNet Web site to locate at least three of these lab instruments and write a report that describes them, including their prices, specifications, and the vendors who sell them.

9. In about 200 words, explain how using EDI can lead to supply chain efficiencies. Include in your discussion the merits of using either direct connection or VAN-based EDI and how a company would choose between these approaches.

10. Internet access from smartphones and tablet devices has greatly improved the work environment of long-distance truck drivers. Using your favorite search engine, identify at least three apps that a trucker might use to do two or more of the following: obtain routing information, manage fuel consumption, find truck stops or truck-friendly rest areas, record what they have hauled and where they have hauled it, track required permits, locate Department of Transportation weigh stations, maintain electronic log books, or find potential loads and place bids to carry them. For each app you identify, write a paragraph that explains what the app does, how much it costs, and on what type of devices it runs.

11. In about 100 words, outline the advantages of using RFID technology instead of bar code scanning technology in managing the inventory and direct materials in a manufacturing company.

12. In about 100 words, explain how the Web can help build and maintain trust among participants in a specific supply chain.

13. Companies in a particular supply chain can work together to eliminate costs from the supply chain. In many cases, these cost savings are not shared evenly among the companies in the supply chain. Using research resources on the Web or in your library, identify an industry in which savings are not shared equally. In about 100 words, explain why some supply chain participants in your chosen industry can obtain more benefit than others from cost reductions in the supply chain.

14. In a paragraph or two, explain what a customer portal (also called a private store) is and describe the key features you would expect to find in one.

Cases

C1. Shrinkage at Walmart

In 2015, the world's largest retailer, Walmart, announced a quarterly increase in sales that was accompanied by an increase in expenses that reduced its hoped-for profit. In discussing the higher expenses, the company mentioned "shrinkage" three times in its written press release and 13 times in its conference call with financial analysts.

The company attributed a significant part of its increased shrinkage to shoplifting and outright theft, including one instance in which a team of thieves pushed a shopping cart full of electronics out a back door and loaded them into a waiting car. To combat these problems, which are unfortunately common in retailing, the company announced it was restarting a training program for employees that helps them learn how to spot shoplifters and fellow employees who are pilfering, along with adding staff to areas of the store that contain high-value or easy-to-steal items. They also plan to start checking customers' receipts at store exits.

In addition to these measures, however, the company also reported that a sizable portion of the shrinkage results from difficulties encountered in managing inventory flow throughout the company's distribution network and its stores. When warehouses and store backrooms become overstocked with inventory, it can be difficult to determine which items should be discounted and moved to the store's shelves. In recent years, Walmart has increased its sales of grocery and food items, which can be damaged more easily than its other inventory and for which failure to monitor expiration dates can be costly. To deal with these backroom inventory management issues, the company has added employees to staff those areas.

Walmart's U.S. supply chain includes more than 100 distribution centers from which the company makes deliveries to its more than 5000 stores and Sam's Club locations using its fleet of more than 6000 trucks. Managing the flow of inventory from the company's suppliers through its distribution centers and into its retail outlets is a mammoth task and, as discussed in this chapter, the company has made attempts to use technology in new and creative ways to address these challenges in the past.

REQUIRED

1. Become familiar with RFID technology and its potential uses in Walmart's supply chain using the information presented in this chapter and information you obtain through the Web Links, your favorite search engine, and your library. In about 200 words, outline the advantages Walmart might gain by using RFID in its retail stores. As you draft your answer, be sure to consider the nature of the stores' backroom environments, which include metal shelving. Also consider Walmart's possible use of RFID and other technologies as an alternative or addition to the increased staffing levels the company has announced for its backroom inventory storage areas.

2. In about 100 words, discuss the technologies that Walmart's trucking fleet might use to better manage their operations. Include a discussion of tracking technologies, GPS devices, and/or apps for use by truck drivers on their smartphones or tablet devices.

3. In about 100 words, discuss the advantages Walmart might gain if it were to use RFID tracking technologies in all of its retail stores to manage every single item as opposed to using either case-level RFID or tracking only part of each store's inventory at the item level.

Note: Your instructor might assign you to a group to complete this case and might ask you to prepare a formal presentation of your results to your class.

C2. Standard Metal Shaping Systems

Standard Metal Shaping Systems (SMSS) provides repair and maintenance services to companies that use large metal-shaping machinery to fold, bend, crease or otherwise shape aluminum, copper, steel, titanium, and other metals as part of a precision manufacturing process. These machines must be adjusted regularly, and they have hundreds of parts that can wear out gradually or fail suddenly. SMSS sells service contracts to cover most major metal-shaping machines. A typical service contract provides for an SMSS technician to make regular visits to the customer site to perform preventive maintenance and includes a certain number of emergency repair visits per year. SMSS also will send out technicians to perform repairs for companies that do not have service contracts, charging a fee based on materials and labor hours used to make the repair.

SMSS technicians are paid by the hour, with additional pay for overtime hours and time they work outside of standard working hours, such as weekends and holidays. SMSS technicians are members of the United Machinists International (IMU), a labor union that negotiates pay rates and working conditions for the technicians. SMSS subtracts union dues from each technician's weekly paycheck and submits the total dues collected each week to the IMU regional office. The union contract currently provides that SMSS technicians are covered by a medical and dental insurance plan underwritten by United MedCare. Although SMSS pays most of the insurance premium, technicians do pay a part of the premium cost. This contribution to the premium is withheld from their paychecks each week.

You are the director of online technology implementations for SMSS and you report to Carrie Liu, SMSS's Chief Information Officer (CIO). Carrie asks for your help in developing specifications for a new automated system she wants to install, which would use EDI and EFTs to handle SMSS's technician payroll and related transactions. She has provided the following narrative that describes how the system will work:

1. Technicians will record their time worked by entering the start and stop times for each job into a program that runs on their tablet devices (the technicians already use these tablet devices to look up wiring and mechanical diagrams for the machinery on which they work and to receive their job assignments). The time-worked information will be transmitted from the tablet device to SMSS's Payroll Department.

2. The Payroll Department will summarize the time-worked information and send it to supervisors' desktop computers. Each supervisor will indicate an authorization for each technician's time-worked, overtime, and holiday/weekend hours. That authorization will be returned by the system each day to the Payroll Department.

3. The Payroll Department will summarize the time-worked information each week and calculate gross pay, deductions, and net pay for each employee. The deductions include the federal and state taxes that must be withheld by law, the contribution to the medical insurance premium, and the union dues that are withheld under the IMU union contract.

4. The Payroll Department will send an electronic summary of the payroll information, including deductions, to the Accounting Department, which will prepare payroll tax returns and make the necessary entries in the SMSS accounting system to record payroll and the related tax expenses.

5. The Payroll Department will send electronic authorizations to SMSS's bank to make the necessary EFTs to deposit: the amount of each technician's net pay to that technician's bank account; the amount of each tax withheld to the account of the appropriate government agency; the amount of the total contributions to the medical insurance premium to the

insurance company's account; and the amount of the union dues withheld to the IMU's account. Most of these accounts are at other banks.

6. The Payroll Department will send electronic notifications to United MedCare and the IMU regional office, notifying them of the transferred amounts each week.

7. The Payroll Department will send an electronic summary of the hours worked by each technician and the amount of gross pay, including overtime and holiday/weekend pay, to the SMSS union steward's desktop computer. The union steward is an SMSS technician who is elected by the technicians to monitor the terms of the union contract and handle any grievances that arise between the technicians and SMSS management.

REQUIRED

1. Draw a diagram of the proposed payroll EDI and EFT system (you can use Figure 5-6 as a guide).

2. The technicians' tablet devices, like most tablet devices available today, include built-in cameras. In about 100 words, explain how the technicians might use the cameras to work better or more efficiently. Be specific, and remember that the cameras can record and transmit video as well as still images.

3. List and briefly describe any problems or issues that you think might arise in the design or implementation of the new system.

4. Provide a rationale and recommendation as to which elements of this system—if any—you think SMSS should hire an outside company to implement.

Note: Your instructor might assign you to a group to complete this case and might ask you to prepare a formal presentation of your results to your class.

For Further Study and Research

Adesnik, C. 2013. "Internet-Powered Jobs Transform Impoverished Youth into Lifelong Workers," *The Huffington Post*, July 30. http://www.huffingtonpost.com/charu-adesnik/cisco-internet-powered-jobs-tra_b_3676395.html

Benton, E. 2010. "Leila Janah, Founder of Samasource," *Fast Company*, March 23. http://www.fastcompany.com/article/leila-janah-samasource

Bornstein, D. 2011. "Workers of the World, Employed," *The New York Times*, November 3. http://opinionator.blogs.nytimes.com/2011/11/03/workers-of-the-world-employed/

Bovel, D. and M. Joseph. 2000. "From Supply Chain to Value Net," *Journal of Business Strategy*, 21(4), July–August, 24–28.

Bunyaratavej, K., J. Doh, E. Hahn, A. Lewing, and S. Massini. 2011. "Conceptual Issues in Services Offshoring Research: A Multidisciplinary Review," *Group & Organization Management*, 36(1), February, 70–102.

Chakravarty, V. 2013. "Managing a Supply Chain's Web of Risk," *Strategy & Leadership*, 41(2), 39–45.

Chang, H., Y.-C. Tsai, and C.-H. Hsu. 2013. " E-procurement and Supply Chain Performance," *Supply Chain Management: An International Journal*, 18(1), 34–51.

Clark, P. 2001. "MetalSite Kills Exchange, Seeks Funding," *B to B*, 86(13), June 25, 3.

Cleary, M. 2001. "Metal Meltdown Doesn't Deter New Ventures," *Interactive Week*, 8(27), July 9, 29.

Dobbs, J. 1999. *Competition's New Battleground: The Integrated Value Chain*. Cambridge, MA: Cambridge Technology Partners.

Drickhamer, D. 2003. "EDI Is Dead! Long Live EDI!" *Industry Week/IW*, 252(4), April, 31–35.

Duvall, M. 2007. " Wal-Mart Changes Its Faltering RFID Strategy to Lure More Suppliers, But Insists It's Not Turning Back," *Baseline*, October, 43–55.

Fisher, M. 1997. "What Is the Right Supply Chain for Your Product?" *Harvard Business Review*, 75(2), March–April, 105–116.

Friedman, T. 2006. *The World Is Flat: A Brief History of the Twenty-first Century*. New York: Farrar, Straus and Giroux.

Fries, J., A. Turri, D. Bello, and R. Smith. 2010. "Factors That Influence the Implementation of Collaborative RFID Programs," *Journal of Business & Industrial Marketing*, 25(8), 590–595.

Hempel, J. 2015. "The Woman Finding Tech Jobs for the World's Poorest People," *Wired*, July 28. http://www.wired.com/2015/07/leila-janah-samagroup/

Howland, D. 2015. "Wal-Mart Working on Reducing 'Shrink' as Theft Hits Earnings," *Retail Dive*, August 19. http://www.retaildive.com/news/wal-mart-working-on-reducing-shrink-as-theft-hits-earnings/404229/

Karpinski, R. 2002. " Wal-Mart Mandates Secure, Internet-Based EDI for Suppliers," *InternetWeek*, September 12.

Kenney, M., S. Massini, and T. Murtha. 2009. "Offshoring Administrative and Technical Work: New Fields for Understanding the Global Enterprise," *Journal of International Business Studies*, 40, 887–900.

Lewin, A. and H. Volberda. 2011. "Co-evolution of Global Sourcing: The Need to Understand the Underlying Mechanisms of Firm Decisions to Offshore," *International Business Review*, 20(3), June, 241–251.

Lynch, B. 2015. "Direct or VAN Based EDI, Which Is Best for Your Company?" *MSDynamicsWorld*, August 13. http://msdynamicsworld.com/story/how-do-you-communicate-direct-or-van-based-edi-which-best-your-company

Malone, M. 2012. "Did Walmart Love RFID to Death?" *Smartplanet.com,* February 14. http://www.smartplanet.com/blog/pure-genius/did-wal-mart-love-rfid-to-death/7459

Massini, S., N. Perm-Ajchariyawong, and A. Lewin. 2010. "The Role of Corporate-wide Offshoring Strategy in Directing Organizational Attention to Offshoring Drivers, Risks, and Performance," *Industry and Innovation*, 17(4), 337–371.

Napolitano, M. 2013. "RFID Settles In," *Logistics Management*, 52(4), 39–43.

Noormohammadi, M. 2011. "Samasource Provides Jobs for Poor Via the Internet," *Voice of America*, December 10. http://www.voanews.com/english/news/Samasource-Provides-Jobs-for-Poor-Via-the-Internet-135376738.html

Nowicki, A. 2014. "Google Shopping for Suppliers Shuts Down," *Modern Distribution Management*, July 8. http://www.mdm.com/blogs/20-distribution-operations/post/32192-google-shopping-for-suppliers-shuts-down

O'Connor, C. 2015. "Amazon Launches Amazon Business Marketplace, Will Close Amazon Supply," *Forbes*, April 28. http://www.forbes.com/sites/clareoconnor/2015/04/28/amazon-launches-amazon-business-marketplace-will-close-amazonsupply/

Preston, B. 2013. "Move Over, CB Radio: Trucker Apps Are Helping to Haul the Load," *The New York Times*, August 16. http://www.nytimes.com/2013/08/18/automobiles/move-over-cb-radio-trucker-apps-are-helping-to-haul-the-load.html

Purchasing. 2001. "MetalSite Shuts Operations While Seeking New Owner," July 5, 32.

Purchasing. 2004. "Easing into E-procurement with Indirect Spend," February 19, 35–36.

Raisch, W. 2001. *The eMarketplace: Strategies for Success in B2B Ecommerce*. New York: McGraw-Hill.

Robson, A. 2015. "Exposing the Top Five Myths of RFID Technology in Retail," *RetailWeek*, August 19. http://www.retail-week.com/technology/technology-blog/rfid-blog-exposing-the-top-five-myths-of-rfid-technology-in-retail/5078222.article

Rosenblum, P. 2014. "How Walmart Could Solve Its Inventory Problem and Improve Earnings," *Forbes*, May 22. http://www.forbes.com/sites/paularosenblum/2014/05/22/walmart-could-solve-its-inventory-problem-and-improve-earnings/

Rueter, T. 2011. "Faster Fulfillment," *Internet Retailer*, May 17. http://www.internetretailer.com/2011/05/17/faster-fulfillment

Stock, K. and S. Pettypiece. 2015. "Wal-Mart Is Getting Hit Hard by Thieves," *BloombergBusiness*, August 18. http://www.bloomberg.com/news/articles/2015-08-18/wal-mart-is-getting-hit-hard-by-thieves

Stockdale, R. and C. Standing. 2002. "A Framework for the Selection of Electronic Marketplaces: A Content Analysis Approach," *Internet Research: Electronic Networking Applications and Policy*, 12(3), 221–234.

Swedberg, C. 2015. "Target Announces Nationwide RFID Rollout," *RFID Journal*, May 20. http://www.rfidjournal.com/articles/view?13060

Taylor, D. and A. Terhune. 2001. *Doing E-Business: Strategies for Thriving in an Electronic Marketplace*. New York: John Wiley & Sons.

Ufelder, S. 2004. "B2B Survivors: Why Did Some Online Exchanges Survive While Many Others Failed?" *Computerworld*, February 2, 27–29.

Ustundag, A. 2013. *The Value of RFID: Benefits vs. Costs*. London: Springer.

Vandermey, A. 2013. "Forty under 40: Leila Janah," *Fortune*, September 19. http://money.cnn.com/gallery/magazines/fortune/2013/09/19/40-under-40-ones-to-watch.fortune/7.html

Wadhwa, V. 2015. "You Can Leave the Office, But There's No Getting Away from Work," *The Washington Post*, August 10. http://www.washingtonpost.com/news/innovations/wp/2015/08/10/you-can-leave-the-office-but-theres-no-getting-away-from-work/

Waugh, R. and S. Elliff. 1998. "Using the Internet to Achieve Purchasing Improvements at General Electric," *Hospital Material Management Quarterly*, 20(2), November, 81–83.

Yang, M.-H., H.-Y. Chao, S.-C. Liu, and H.-L. Chen. 2014. "Exploring the Determinants and Effects of Relationships in Collaborative Commerce," *Asia Pacific Management Review*, 19(3), 215–238.

Yao, Y., M. Dresner, and J. Palmer. 2009. "Private Network EDI vs. Internet Electronic Markets: A Direct Comparison of Fulfillment Performance," *Management Science*, 55(5), May, 843–852.

Zang, Y. and L Wu. 2010. "Application of RFID and RTLS Technology in Supply Chain Enterprise," *Proceedings of the 2010 Sixth International Wireless Communications Networking and Mobile Computing Conference*, September 23–25, 1–4.

Social Networking, Mobile Commerce, and Online Auctions

Blend Images Photography/Veer

INTRODUCTION

Many companies are now using technologies such as social media and mobile commerce to interact with customers, potential customers, and other stakeholders in new ways. Starbucks, the global coffee retailer, has been especially skillful in its use of these new technologies and is widely regarded to have been successful in leveraging them into its post-2008 recession financial success.

Participating actively in social media sites such as Facebook and Twitter along with buying large amounts of advertising on those services has been the approach taken by most companies in attaining social media success. However, Starbucks has found its success using a different strategy. Rather than flooding social media with its message, Starbucks monitors its customers' interactions with each other and then uses the information it gathers to improve its products and services and develop strategies for keeping those customers and attracting new ones.

Starbucks sees social media as an extension of the barista–customer relationships that develop in its stores and the relationships that arise among its customers as they enjoy Starbucks products in those stores. Instead of communications from Starbucks directed at customers, the company uses social media to provide a platform for customers to talk with each other about their favorite Starbucks products.

Starbucks also integrates mobile technology with the customer experience by accepting payments from mobile devices and by providing a Starbucks mobile device app that lets customers manage their loyalty program benefits.

Although most companies see social media and mobile technologies as just another advertising channel, Starbucks has taken a different approach: expanding its connection to individual users. Cementing these connections with insights gained by being a social media observer rather than an active participant has helped the company outperform most other consumer brands in the world of online consumer engagement.

From Virtual Communities to Social Networks

In Chapters 3 and 4, you learned how businesses use the Web to create online identities, reach customers, and sell products and services to those customers. In Chapter 5, you learned how businesses are using the Web to purchase goods and work with their suppliers more effectively. In all three of these chapters, the focus was on how companies are using the Web to improve the things that they have been doing for years, primarily buying and selling. In this chapter, you will learn how companies are using the Web to do things that were either very difficult or impossible to do before online connectivity became commonplace. The Web enables people to form online communities that are not limited by geography. Individuals and companies with common interests can connect online and discuss issues, share information, generate ideas, and develop valuable relationships.

As you learned in earlier chapters, the Internet reduces transaction costs in value chains and offers an efficient means of communication to anyone with an Internet connection. Combining the Internet's transaction cost-reduction potential with its role as a facilitator of communication among people has led companies to develop new ways of making money on the Web by serving as relationship facilitators.

This section begins with a brief history of online communities and then outlines how companies today engage in social networking activities that promote relationships among site visitors and businesses.

Virtual Communities

A **virtual community** is a gathering place for people and businesses that does not have a physical existence. Howard Rheingold described the characteristics of these communities in his 1993 book, *The Virtual Community*, which is widely recognized as the definitive book on the subject. Virtual communities began online even before the Internet was in general use. **Bulletin board systems (BBSs)** were computers that allowed users to connect using dial-up connections through telephone lines to read and post messages in a common discussion forum that resembled an electronic version of a physical bulletin board. BBSs often hosted discussions on specific topics or issues related to specific geographic regions. Most BBSs were free, but some charged a monthly membership fee. Eventually, commercial enterprises such as CompuServe, Prodigy, and GEnie created discussion board services that generated revenue by charging a monthly fee and selling advertising. In the education and research communities, Usenet newsgroups were a similar form of virtual community. Started at Duke University in 1979, **Usenet newsgroups** were message posting areas on a set of interconnected computers devoted to storing information on specific topics.

The social interaction in virtual communities was substantial and many sociologists believe that the communication and relationship-forming activities that occur online are similar to those that occur in physical communities. The rest of this section describes the evolution of these early virtual communities into the Web sites that people use today to form and maintain relationships online.

Early Web Communities

One of the first Web communities was the WELL. The WELL, which is an acronym for "whole earth 'lectronic link," predates the Web. It began in 1985 as a series of BBS dialogs among the authors and readers of the *Whole Earth Review*. The WELL was home to many of the researchers who created the Internet and the Web along with a number of noted writers and artists. In 1999, Salon.com bought the WELL and continues to operate it as a monthly subscription service.

By the mid-1990s, virtual communities formed in Web chat rooms and sites devoted to specific topics or the general exchange of information. As the bandwidths available to Internet users increased, photos and video clips became commonplace additions to the discussions in these communities. In 1995, Beverly Hills Internet opened a virtual community site that featured two Webcams aimed down Hollywood streets along with links to entertainment Web sites and free space for member-created Web pages. The

Webcams did not attract members, but the offer of free Web space did. As the site grew, it changed its name to GeoCities and earned revenue by selling advertising that appeared on members' Web pages and pop-up pages that opened whenever a visitor accessed a member's site. GeoCities grew rapidly and was purchased in 1999 by Yahoo! for $5 billion. Yahoo! also ran advertising on the individual GeoCities members' Web sites, but failed to engage the members in a functional virtual community and eventually closed GeoCities in 2009. During the 1995–2001 time period, other companies such as Tripod and Theglobe. com operated similar advertising-supported virtual communities that included free Web pages, chat rooms, and discussion areas. These virtual communities evolved into the social networking sites that emerged in the late 1990s as part of the second wave of electronic commerce, as you will learn in the next section.

Social Networking Emerges

Virtual communities provided an important service to the small number of people who regularly used the Internet in its early days. As the Internet and Web grew, many of these communities found that their original purpose as a place for sharing the new experiences of online communication began to fade. In the second wave of electronic commerce, a new phenomenon in online communication began. People who were using the Internet no longer found a single common bond in the very fact that they were using the Internet. Instead, they were finding that a variety of common interests—for example, gardening, specific medical issues, or parenting—created the basis for online interaction.

For these later Internet communities, the Internet was simply a tool that enabled communication among virtual community members. This intracommunity interaction among members is now called **social networking**. Web sites that facilitate those interactions are called social networking sites. Most **social networking sites** allow individuals who are members of the social network (or virtual community) to create and publish a profile, create a list of other users with whom they share a connection (or connections), control that list, and monitor similar lists made by other users. In this section, you will learn about the evolution of social networking sites.

One of the first sites, Six Degrees, started in 1997. Six Degrees was based on the idea that no more than six persons separated anyone in the world from any other person. The site was unable to generate sufficient revenue to continue operations and closed in 2000. More successful social networking sites followed several years later. Friendster was founded by Jonathan Abrams in 2002. Friendster was the first Web site to include most of the features found today in all social networking sites. The company's rapid growth outstripped its technological abilities and the company's management team was unable to agree on strategy for dealing with new competitors such as MySpace and Tribe.net. As Friendster faded, MySpace became the leading U.S. social networking site.

In 2006, Mark Zuckerberg expanded a virtual community site that he had developed with a few friends at Harvard by purchasing the domain name Facebook.com for $200,000 and signing a number of major advertising deals, including a three-year agreement with Microsoft. By 2008, Facebook had overtaken MySpace as the leading social networking site in the world and by 2014 was reporting more than a billion regular users and annual revenue of more than $6 billion.

The company's initial public offering in 2012 placed the market value of Facebook at $104 billion. Today, Facebook is the dominant general interest social networking site in North America, Europe, Australia, and parts of Africa. It is a significant presence in many other parts of the world as well. In 2011, Google introduced Google+ to compete with Facebook and, although Google+ has gained a substantial number of regular users, it remains well behind Facebook in every region of the world. In 2013, Google+ launched Hangouts and Photos as services for its members. During the 2014–2015 time period, both were split out of Google+ as separate offerings, a move that some industry observers interpreted as driven by Google+'s inability as a unified social networking service to surpass competitors such as Facebook.

In Asia, local language social networking sites such as GREE and mixi in Japan and Renren in China were launched within a year or two of Friendster and eroded that site's early successes in those countries. Also in China, the company Tencent Holdings created QQ in 1999 to compete with Six Degrees and, in 2009, relaunched the site along with two additional sites (WeChat and Weibo) that were expressly directed at the domestic Chinese language market. Today, social networking sites that started in each country's local language hold top positions in China, Russia, and Japan. In Iran, a Persian language social network named Cloob is the top site, aided by the Iranian government's continuing efforts to block U.S.-based sites such as Facebook and Twitter.

Orkut (named for the Google employee who developed the site in 2004) never really caught on in the United States but became the top social networking site in both Brazil and India between 2008 and 2010. Since then, Facebook has overtaken the top spot in those countries.

LinkedIn, a site devoted to facilitating business contacts, was founded in 2003 and allows users to create a list of trusted business contacts. Users then invite others to participate in several forms of relationships on the site, each of which is designed to help them find jobs, find employees, or develop connections to business opportunities. LinkedIn has become the dominant business-focused social networking site in North America, Europe, and South Africa.

Other social networking sites have met with varying degrees of success. Some sites have developed a following by offering specific features; for example, YouTube (owned by Google) popularized the inclusion of videos in social networking sites. Twitter offers users a way to send short messages to other users who sign up to follow their messages (called **tweets**). Figure 6-1 shows the launch year for some of the more successful social networking sites.

The general idea behind many of these sites is that people are invited to join by existing members who think they would be valuable additions to the community. Many of these sites provide a directory that lists members' locations, interests, and qualities; however, the directory does not disclose the name or contact information of members. A member can offer to communicate with any other member, but the communication does not occur until the intended recipient approves the contact (usually after reviewing the sender's directory information). In addition to searching the directory of the community, members can make connections with new contacts through friends they have established in the community (perhaps starting with the person who invited them to join). By

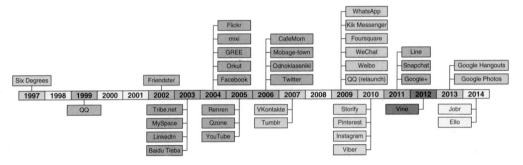

FIGURE 6-1   Social networking Web sites

gradually building up a set of connections, members can develop contacts within the community that might prove valuable later.

Some social networks are focused around specific interests or capabilities. For example, **Flickr**, **Instagram**, and **Pinterest** use photos and pictures as an organizing theme, whereas **Vine** features six-second video clips. **CafeMom** attracts participants who have young children. **Snapchat** allows its users to send text- and drawing-annotated photos and videos that expire after a short amount of time. **Jobr** is a mobile-based application to help users discover jobs. **Tumbler**, **Twitter**, and **WhatsApp** offer tools for short messaging (which you learn about later in this chapter). **Ello** was launched in 2014 as an ad-free alternative to Facebook.

The expansion of social networking sites into all corners of the world continues as we move into the third wave of electronic commerce. In addition to the Chinese and Japanese sites mentioned earlier, successful social networking sites in local languages have emerged in Germany (**Xing**), Israel (**Viber**), the Netherlands (**Hyves**), Russia (**VKontakte** and **Odnoklassniki**), Spain (**Tuenti**), and Taiwan (**Plurk**). Figure 6-2 shows the leading social networking sites in several areas of the world.

WEB LOGS (BLOGS), MICROBLOGS, AND PARTICIPATORY JOURNALISM

As you learned in Chapter 4, Web logs, or blogs, are Web sites that contain commentary on current events or specific issues written by individuals. Many blogs invite visitors to add comments, which the blog owner may or may not edit. The result is a continuing discussion of the topic with the possibility that many interested persons will contribute to that discussion. Because blog sites encourage interaction among people interested in a particular topic, they are a form of a social networking site. Sites such as Twitter are considered to be **microblogs** because they function as a very informal blog site with entries (messages, or tweets) that are limited to 140 characters in length.

Early blogs focused on technology topics or on topics about which people have strong beliefs (for example, political or religious issues). The 2004 U.S. presidential elections saw the first major use of blogs as a political networking tool in addition to the Web sites and e-mail messaging to supporters and potential donors that had been used before. Individuals working alone or with established political organizations set up Web sites that provided a place for people interested in a candidate or an issue to communicate with each other. These social networking sites allowed people to discuss issues, plan strategies,

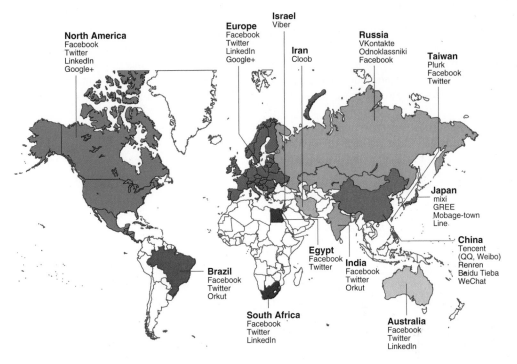

North America
Facebook
Twitter
LinkedIn
Google+

Europe
Facebook
Twitter
LinkedIn
Google+

Israel
Viber

Iran
Cloob

Russia
VKontakte
Odnoklassniki
Facebook

Taiwan
Plurk
Facebook
Twitter

Japan
mixi
GREE
Mobage-town
Line

China
Tencent
(QQ, Weibo)
Renren
Baidu Tieba
WeChat

Brazil
Facebook
Twitter
Orkut

Egypt
Facebook
Twitter

India
Facebook
Twitter
Orkut

South Africa
Facebook
Twitter
LinkedIn

Australia
Facebook
Twitter
LinkedIn

FIGURE 6-2   Leading social networking sites around the world

and arrange in-person meetings called **meetups** (facilitated, of course, by a social networking site named Meetup). Today, social media is used to organize a wide range of political and charitable fund-raising and communication activities.

After seeing the success of social media in political networking, many retailers embraced these tools as a way to engage Web site visitors who might not be ready to buy from the site but were interested in the products or services offered. Marketing and supply chain managers also saw the benefits of these social networking activities in enhancing their B2B relationships. Many companies that sell to other businesses include blogs and microblogs as part of their online presence to give customers a forum for discussing uses and technical specifications of the company's products or services.

CNN was a pioneer in including information from blogs and microblogs in its television newscasts. Other broadcasters and newspapers now incorporate social media in their Web sites, broadcasts, and print publications. Small-town newspapers often depend on readers to contribute information about community issues and events. Newspapers of all sizes would rather run a blog with reader contributions tied into microblogs and social media than pay reporters to write stories about events or issues that would interest only a small segment of their readership. By inviting information and opinion contributions, newspapers are finding they can reach younger readers who did not grow up reading print newspapers. This trend toward having readers help write their own news is called **participatory journalism**.

In addition to running a blog that is part of an existing activity (such as a political campaign, charitable organization, university, retail business, or newspaper), blogs can become a business in themselves if they can generate financial support through fees or advertising. Jake Dobkins writes about New York City on the blog site Gothamist. Instead of drawing a salary from a newspaper as a food and entertainment reporter, he blogs about the latest in New York nightlife. Advertising revenue has been sufficient to support Dobkins and the site's cofounder, Jen Chung. Now with a staff of bloggers, editors, and ad salespeople, these entrepreneurs have expanded to nine cities in four countries. Michael Arrington began blogging in 2005 about new online business startups. Again, instead of writing a column for a business magazine, he decided to put his research and reporting talents into his own business, which today is operating as TechCrunch, a successful advertising-supported Web site.

LOCATION-AWARE MOBILE SOCIAL NETWORKS

Later in this chapter, you will learn about the worldwide growth in the use of mobile devices for connecting to the Internet. Having a traveling Internet connection opens up many possibilities for social media that integrates with a user's specific location, especially as that location changes over time. Many mobile devices can transmit (with the user's permission) their locations to Web sites, which can use that location information to provide customized advertising or other services. These services are called **location-aware services**.

In 2015, about 35 percent of social media users tagged their posts with location information and 82 percent of mobile device owners obtained directions or other location-based information using those devices. Although Foursquare is the leading location-based social networking site and is designed to make interaction with location-specific resources easy for mobile devices, many people use their Facebook or Google+ accounts to access these services.

Business Uses of Social Networking

Business use of social media is still evolving and there are many opinions on what companies should and should not try to do with social networking tools. Many companies have been criticized for turning their social media interactions into thinly disguised advertising programs. Although social media allows companies to do many of the same kinds of things they can do with traditional advertising and promotion (building brand awareness, establishing trust and credibility, announcing new products or services, and so on), most experts agree that social media should be managed differently from advertising efforts. Managed effectively, social media engagement can provide much more information about customers and potential customers.

As you learned in the chapter introduction, Starbucks does not use social media to broadcast information about its products or build its brand. Instead, Starbucks uses social media to learn from their customers and find new ways to engage them with the company's brand, products, and services. By intentionally avoiding active participation in its own social media outreach, Starbucks's social media efforts are focused on listening to its customers' discussions with each other and learning from those discussions.

Brooks Running, a manufacturer of athletic shoes, expressly avoids using social media to sell products directly. Since its primary customers are in the community of active runners and are interested in health and fitness, Brooks participates in social media that focuses on these interests. By showing how their interests align with those of their customers, Brooks is able to enhance its brand image indirectly. By contributing to discussions in the health and fitness social media, the company contributes to the online communities that their customers inhabit and becomes known as a good neighbor, which enhances perceptions of trust.

Campbell's Soup has also been highly successful in developing a valuable social networking presence. After a beginning in which it focused on its products and recipes using its products, it found that the discussion areas devoted to what soup can do for families generated the most participation and interest in the company.

By using social media to participate in the environment of an industry or product, companies can interact with their customers (or suppliers) in ways that are different from and more expansive than the roles traditionally taken in buyer–seller relationships.

Figure 6-3 outlines some of the ways in which companies can benefit from participation in four types of social media. For each type of social media, the figure shows how companies can convey information to customers (similar to traditional advertising and promotion strategies), but can also receive information from customers and learn by listening to customers communicate with each other.

SOCIAL SHOPPING SITES

The practice of bringing buyers and sellers together in a social network to facilitate retail sales is called **social shopping**. One of the first of these was craigslist, an information resource for San Francisco area residents that was created in 1995 by WELL member Craig Newmark. That community has grown to include information for most major cities in the United States and in several other countries. The site is operated by a not-for-profit foundation, and all postings other than help-wanted ads are free.

The Etsy Web site provides a marketplace for people who want to sell handmade items. The social network here includes buyers and sellers interested in crafts of all types. The sense of community is so strong that a separate site, We Love Etsy, exists to provide a place where Etsy buyers and sellers share information. The existence of this separate site is an excellent example that shows how interactions among a company's customers can be as important (or more important) than the interactions between the company and its customers.

Other sites that combine social media elements such as microblogging and photo posting with shopping activities include Wanelo and Polyvore. Poshmark is a social shopping site devoted to women's clothing and fashion accessories. Members post photos of items they own but want to sell and other members make offers to buy them. Negotiating over price is done in private communications between the members but conducted through the site's social network. Poshmark has optimized all actions on its site for mobile phone users, so the social network is designed to work best when members are using their smartphones or tablet devices.

	Convey Information to Customers	Receive Information from Customers	Facilitate and Monitor Communications among Customers
Social networking sites	Purchase advertising, post offers and promotions, post information about products/services	Collect information from and summarize customer posts for analysis	Collect a body of shared knowledge from customer posts and use it to build customer loyalty
Blogs	Publish updates on forthcoming products, provide service information on existing products	Encourage customers to submit new ideas, purchase intentions, and reservations about existing products/services	Monitor and summarize customer discussions about products/services and the overall brand for analysis
Microblogs	Answer questions about products/services, respond to customer messages with specific answers	Actively solicit customer input on current products/ services and ideas for improvements and new products/services	Monitor carefully customer messages and summarize for analysis to identify new trends in their perceptions and thinking
Location-aware mobile social networks	Post information about new retail locations, specific promotions at particular locations	Encourage customers to contribute tips and comments regarding specific locations	Connect geographically disparate customers to each other and collect information about differences in customer experiences and perceptions at different locations

Source: Adapted from Table 1 in Chua and Banerjee (2013, p. 240), "Customer Knowledge Management Via Social Media: The Case of Starbucks," *Journal of Knowledge Management*, 17(2), 237–249.

FIGURE 6-3 Social media strategies for business

IDEA-BASED SOCIAL NETWORKING

Social networking sites form communities based on connections among people. Other Web sites create communities based on the connections between ideas. These more abstract communities are called **idea-based social media** and the people who participate in them are said to be engaging in **idea-based social networking**. The Delicious site calls itself a "social bookmarks manager." Individuals place Web page bookmarks with one-word tags that describe the Web page in a community-accessible location on the site. The bookmark-tag combinations are focused on ideas and the contributions of all community members build a shared base of knowledge about those ideas. Among the most active tag names on the site are words such as design, reference, tools, music, news, how to, and photography.

VIRTUAL LEARNING NETWORKS

One form of social network you might have used is the **virtual learning network**. Many colleges and universities now offer courses that use distance learning platforms such as Blackboard for student–instructor interaction. These distance learning platforms include tools such as bulletin boards, chat rooms, and drawing boards that allow students to interact with their instructors and each other in ways that are similar to the interactions that might occur in a physical classroom setting.

Although the concept dates back to 2008, **massive open online courses (MOOCs)** became widely known in 2012 with the formation of Coursera and Udacity by Stanford

University personnel who had developed MOOCs there. MOOCs are often offered at no cost and each one can attract hundreds of thousands of students. In 2013, Georgia Institute of Technology, partnering with Udacity, announced plans to offer the first entirely MOOC-based master's degree, at a fraction of its usual tuition.

Although many schools are launching MOOCs or using them in some way as part of their curricula, some academics question the value of this form of education. Most MOOCs have extremely low completion rates (in many cases, fewer than 2 percent of enrollees actually finish the course). MOOC defenders point out that they can extend the reach of educational experiences to nearly anyone in the world at a very low per-student cost. As more research is conducted on MOOC outcomes, we will have a better idea of when, how, and if MOOCs can contribute to education in a meaningful way in the future.

OPEN-SOURCE SOFTWARE

Some open-source software projects are devoted to the development of virtual learning communities, including Moodle and uPortal (maintained by the not-for-profit open-source software development organization, Jasig). **Open-source software** is developed by a community of programmers who make the software available for download at no cost. Other programmers then use the software, work with it, and improve it. Those programmers can submit their improved versions of the software back to the community.

Open-source software is an early and successful example of a virtual community that we would now call a social network. Each social network is devoted to the creation, improvement, and maintenance of a particular software application. You will learn more about open-source software in Chapters 8 and 9 because much open-source software is used to run the Internet itself, Web sites, and the electronic commerce activities at many of those sites.

Revenue Models for Social Networking Sites

By the late 1990s, virtual communities were selling advertising to generate revenue. Search engine sites and Web directories were also selling advertising to generate revenue. Beginning in 1998, a wave of purchases and mergers occurred among these sites. The new sites that emerged continued to use an advertising-only revenue-generation model and included many of the features offered by virtual community sites, search engine sites, Web directories, and other information-providing and entertainment sites in the early days of the Web. These Web portals, which you learned about in Chapter 3, are so named because their goal is to be every Web user's doorway to the Web. As you also learned in Chapter 3, sites that have higher numbers of visitors can charge more for advertising on the site. Figure 6-4 lists the most popular Web sites in the world based on the number of users who accessed the sites during the month of August 2015.

ADVERTISING-SUPPORTED SOCIAL NETWORKING SITES

Visitors spend a greater amount of time at portal sites than they do at most other types of Web sites, which is attractive to advertisers. Other types of social networking sites can also draw large numbers of visitors who spend considerable time on the sites. This section describes how these characteristics make social networking sites appealing to advertisers.

Web Site
Google
Facebook
YouTube
Baidu
Yahoo!
Amazon.com
Wikipedia
Tencent QQ
Twitter
Google India

Source: http://www.alexa.com/topsites

FIGURE 6-4   Popularity of leading Web sites

Smaller social networking sites that have a more specialized appeal can draw enough visitors to generate significant amounts of advertising revenue, especially compared to the costs of running such a site. For example, software developer Eric Nakagawa posted a picture of a grinning fat cat on his Web site in 2007 with the caption "I can has cheezburger?" as a joke. He followed that with several more cat photos and funny captions over the next few weeks and added a blog so that people could post comments about the pictures. Within a few months, the site was getting more than 100,000 visitors a day. Nakagawa found that a site with that kind of traffic could charge between $100 and $600 per day for a single ad. After generating a respectable income from the site, Nakagawa decided to sell I Can Has Cheezburger to Ben Huh for $2 million. Huh now operates the site as a part of network of more than 50 similar sites that together get 8 million visitors each month and generate annual revenue of more than $1 million, which supports a staff of about 40 employees.

Leading Web sites have much higher visitor traffic and often log more than 200 million unique visitors per month. The amounts that advertisers are willing to pay to place their messages before those visitors' eyes are substantial. Figure 6-5 shows recent and projected worldwide social network spending on advertising for recent and projected years.

MIXED-REVENUE AND FEE-FOR-SERVICE SOCIAL NETWORKING SITES

Although most social networking sites use advertising to support their operations, some do charge a fee for some services. For example, the Yahoo! Web portal offers most of its services free (supported by advertising), but it does sell some of its social networking features, such as its Games All-Star Central package. Yahoo! also sells other features, such as more space to store messages and attached files, as part of its premium e-mail service.

Feature	2013	2014	2015	2016	2017
North America	4940	7710	10,100	12,670	15,150
Asia-Pacific	3250	5180	7400	9660	11,910
Western Europe	2340	3680	4740	5820	6850
Latin America	350	540	680	850	1000
Central and Eastern Europe	410	520	610	700	790
Middle East and Africa	70	110	160	220	280
Worldwide totals	11,360	17,740	23,680	29,920	35,980

Source: eMarketer, April, 2015.

FIGURE 6-5   Worldwide social network spending, recent years and projections (in millions of U.S. dollars)

Some advertising-supported social networking sites have followed the lead of Yahoo! in a strategy called monetizing eyeballs or monetizing visitors. **Monetizing** refers to the conversion of existing regular site visitors seeking free information or services into fee-paying subscribers or purchasers of services. Sites that monetize visitors by charging them always worry about visitor backlash. They can never be sure how many existing visitors will pay for services that have been offered in some form at no cost. Most sites do not monetize their visitors by charging fees. For example, leading social networking sites Facebook and Twitter sell advertising only and do not charge any user fees. Social networking sites can sell information they gather about their members to advertisers and market researchers looking to identify connections between online behavior and purchases of products or services.

Other social networking sites that use a mixed-revenue model are the financial information sites The Motley Fool and TheStreet.com. These sites offer investment advice, stock quotes, and financial planning help. Some of the information is provided at no cost, additional information is available to subscribers who pay no fee but who are required to provide personal information, and even more information is available to subscribers who agree to pay a fee.

FEE-BASED SOCIAL NETWORKING

An early attempt to monetize social networking by charging visitors a fee for a specific service was the Google Answers site. Google Answers gave people a place to ask questions that were then answered by an expert (called a Google Answers Researcher). If the poster of the question was satisfied with the answer, they would pay the expert a small fee (usually $10–$50). Google administered a test to determine which members of the community were qualified to become Google Answers Researchers. Google operated this service from 2002 to 2006 (questions and answers posted during that time period are still available on the Web site). Similar services operated by Yahoo! (Yahoo! Answers) and Amazon.com (Askville) allow volunteers to answer questions, but as free services, they provide no opportunity for researchers to earn fees. These services do generate advertising revenue for the sites, however, and Askville includes many questions and answers about Amazon.com products and services, so it serves as an additional customer help resource for the company.

After Google closed its service, a number of the people who had been Google Researchers joined together and started a similar service on the site **Uclue**. Researchers earn 75 percent of the total fee paid to Uclue. Advocates of using paid researchers argue that the quality of the answers is higher than on free sites and that the questions tend to be more serious and better formulated. Both approaches are examples of how Web sites can generate revenue by providing a place in which virtual communities can interact.

MICROLENDING SITES

One of the most interesting uses of social networking on the Web has been the emergence of sites that function as clearinghouses for microlending activity. **Microlending** is the practice of lending very small amounts of money to people who are starting or operating small businesses, especially in developing countries. Microlending became famous in 2006 when Muhammad Yunus and the Grameen Bank won the Nobel Peace Prize for their work in developing microlending initiatives in Bangladesh.

A key element of microlending is working within a social network of borrowers. The borrowers provide support for each other and an element of pressure to ensure the loans are repaid by each member of the group. **Kiva** and **MicroPlace** are examples of social networking sites that bring together many small investors who lend money to groups and individuals all over the world who need loans to start or continue their small business ventures.

Kiva partners with microfinance institutions that are knowledgeable about business conditions in their parts of the world. These institutions select local individuals they believe are good credit risks and help them post a loan request on the Kiva site. Lenders can review the loan requests and agree to fund part (or all) of the loan amount using the Kiva Web site. The loans, which typically range from a few hundred to a few thousand dollars, are scheduled to be repaid within short time periods ranging from a few months to a year.

Most of the early interest in microlending was focused on lenders in highly developed countries and borrowers in less-developed countries because an amount of money that seemed small to a rich person can be a great deal of money to someone starting a business in a struggling economy. Although this mode of microlending continues to be substantial around the globe, business startups in prosperous economies are now using the technique. For example, a microlending program devoted to small Michigan businesses began in 2014. This program, a partnership among the Michigan Economic Development Corporation (MEDC), local community groups in the state, and Huntington Bank, is designed to help new businesses start and existing home-based businesses expand. Huntington Bank committed $25 million and the MEDC made available up to $225 million to fund loans between $500 and $50,000 for businesses with up to five employees.

CROWDFUNDING SITES

In addition to finding a lender who can provide funds for a business idea, entrepreneurs can sell partial ownership in their ventures to investors. Social networking sites that provide exactly this opportunity, called **crowdfunding**, include Kickstarter and IndieGoGo. These sites allow businesses and individuals to sell equity interests in their activities to participants around the world. Most new business owners fund their new ventures with savings and credit card debt at first. As the business grows, they might raise capital from friends and family members. However, few people are able to afford the risk of making large investments in new businesses.Crowdfunding addresses this issue; instead of a few people who each invest a lot of money, it relies on a large number of people who each have a small amount of money. Crowdfunding thus reduces the investors' individual risk but still can provide substantial total equity funding for new ventures.

The most common type of crowdfunding today is called **reward-based crowdfunding**, in which the investors pay in advance for products (or services) to be delivered when the company makes them using the invested funds. In this version of crowdfunding, the investors are basically customers who prepay for products, usually at a highly discounted price.

Crowdfunding is also used by artists and charitable organizations that have a specific project in mind. Funders learn about the project on a social media or crowdfunding site and make contributions to help the individual or organization complete the project. These appeals are generally for a small amount, often under $25, and the funders are rewarded by knowing that they have contributed to a worthy project and sometimes receive an acknowledgment.

INTERNAL SOCIAL NETWORKING

A growing number of organizations have built internal Web sites that provide opportunities for online social networking among their employees. These sites also include important information for employees. These sites run on the intranets you learned about in Chapter 2. Organizations have saved significant amounts of money by replacing the printing and distribution of paper memos, newsletters, and other correspondence with a Web site. Internal social networking pages also provide easy access to employee handbooks, newsletters, and employee benefits information.

An internal social networking Web site can become a good way of fostering working relationships among employees who are dispersed over a wide geographic area. Many service companies offer a discussion area on their internal social networks that allow service technicians to post questions that are then answered by more experienced technicians who might work anywhere in the company. Some companies create private pages on sites such as Facebook and use those as internal social networking tools. This saves the company the cost of creating the social networking site internally.

Many companies are extending the reach of their internal social networks by enabling employees who are traveling, meeting with customers or suppliers, or telecommuting to connect using their mobile devices. In the next section, you will learn more about how companies can combine mobile technologies with social networking to create new online business opportunities.

Mobile Commerce

Mobile phones today are used for much more than making voice calls. They are used to send and receive text messages, communicate over the Internet, and access satellite geographic positioning services.

Virtually all mobile phones sold today include **short messaging service (SMS)**, which allows mobile phone users to send short text messages to each other. Using SMS, usually called **texting**, became a common way to communicate in many countries (often, sending a text message was less expensive than a voice call), but it was much slower to catch on in the United States.

Internet-capable mobile phones first appeared in 1999, but the tiny screens made use of Web browsers difficult. Today's larger phones, with their high-resolution screens, are ideal devices for online purchasing and have helped usher in the third wave of electronic commerce. Two developments coincided in the United States in 2008 that made mobile phones truly viable Web browsing devices. First, high-speed mobile telephone networks grew dramatically in availability, and second, manufacturers began offering a wide variety of smartphones that included a Web browser and a screen large enough to make it usable, an operating system, and the ability to run applications on that operating system. In this section, you will learn how this confluence of technologies made doing business online using mobile devices, called **mobile commerce (m-commerce)**, an everyday occurrence throughout the world.

Mobile Phones

Internet-capable phones first caught on in Japan and parts of Southeast Asia because telecommunications companies there offered high-capacity mobile phone networks long before U.S. network providers did. NTT DoCoMo, which is still the largest phone company in Japan, launched mobile commerce there in 2000 with its i-mode service. Starting with the sale of games and other programs that run on the phones, NTT DoCoMo was a leader in global mobile commerce, including online shopping and payments.

In the United States, smartphones and the high-capacity networks that make them functional began appearing in 2008. These smartphones, such as the Apple iPhone and phones that use the Android operating system, opened the door for serious U.S. mobile commerce for the first time.

Tablet Devices

In 2010, Apple introduced the iPad, a tablet device that is smaller (with fewer capabilities) than a laptop computer, yet larger than a smartphone. **Tablet devices** can be connected to the Internet through a wireless phone carrier's service or through a local wireless network. Most tablet devices can use both access modes and can switch between them automatically. Within a year, many other manufacturers had introduced tablet devices to compete with the iPad. By 2012, some of these manufacturers were producing tablet-smartphone hybrids. Very large smartphones with high-resolution screens are called **phablets** (a combination of "phone" and "tablet").

These tablet devices became widely used throughout the world very rapidly. In 2015, the number of tablet devices sold was greater than the number of personal computers (both notebook and desktops) sold for the first time in history. Figure 6-6 shows this dramatic recent and projected growth in tablet device sales worldwide.

Apple's iPad tablet devices run the company's proprietary iOS operating system. Most other manufacturers' tablet devices (Samsung and Motorola are the two leading companies) run the Android operating system. Some of Amazon.com's electronic book products, such as the Kindle Fire, have the ability to be used as online tablet devices.

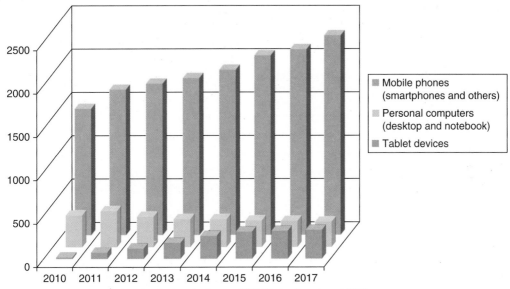

Sources: Research reports and projections by Gartner, NPD Display Search, and BGR.

FIGURE 6-6   Actual and projected worldwide sales of personal computers, tablet devices, and mobile phones (in millions of units)

The Android operating system was developed as an open-source software project funded by Google, which saw the software as a long-term effort that would increase mobile Web traffic (most of Google's revenue comes from advertising—more Web traffic leads to higher online advertising rates and more advertisers). Figure 6-7 shows several examples of smartphones, tablet devices, and phablets used today.

Some smartphones and internet-capable phones display Web pages using the **Wireless Application Protocol (WAP)**. WAP allows Web pages formatted in HTML to be displayed on devices with small screens, such as mobile phones. As mobile phones became larger and tablet (and phablet) devices were introduced, the use of WAP became optional. Normal Web pages can be displayed effectively on the larger, higher-resolution screens of these devices.

The Apple iPhone was one of the first devices to include touch screen controls that make viewing and navigating a normal Web page easy to do on a small handheld device. Almost all current-model smartphones use touch screen controls, although a few still include physical keyboards.

Mobile Device Operating Systems

Apple and BlackBerry use their own proprietary operating systems. In the past, other phone makers (including HTC, Motorola, and Samsung) created their own operating systems and apps for common functions such as calendar, contacts, and e-mail; these manufacturers now use a standard operating system provided by a third party. The most common of these third-party operating systems today are Android and Windows Phone. The fastest growing and most widely used third-party operating system in the world

FIGURE 6-7   Mobile devices, including smartphones, tablets, and phablets

today is Android, which was developed by Google. Android is open source, which allows smartphone manufacturers to use it at no cost. Most smartphone manufacturers that use Android add some customized features to the software's interface.

One of the first operating systems for Internet-capable phones was made by Palm for their phones and other portable devices; however, Palm's phones became less popular and, after an attempt to sell its software to other phone manufacturers, the company went out of business. Symbian, which started as Nokia's proprietary system, became open source in 2008. Few other phone manufacturers adopted the system and, in 2011, Nokia itself began using the Windows Phone operating system for its smartphones. Windows Phone is a proprietary operating system sold by Microsoft.

Figure 6-8 shows the change in worldwide market shares for leading smartphone operating systems over recent and projected near future years.

Once a manufacturer chooses an operating system for its phones, the user cannot switch easily to a different operating system. Unlike computers, the operating system is integrated into the software the carrier uses to make the phone operate on its network. Most carriers will void the warranty on a phone if they find a user has modified the operating system in any way, although some users with technical skills do so. Modifying an Apple iPhone's operating system is called **jailbreaking** the phone. Modifying an Android operating system is called **rooting** the phone.

Mobile Apps

In the past, each phone manufacturer wrote its own operating system software. Today, most mobile phones use a common operating system (such as Android and iOS). This

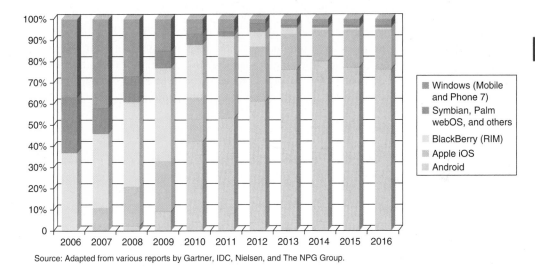

Source: Adapted from various reports by Gartner, IDC, Nielsen, and The NPG Group.

FIGURE 6-8   Actual and estimated worldwide smartphone operating system market percentages

change occurred because the way software applications are developed and sold has changed. In the past, U.S. mobile phone companies generated revenue by controlling the application software (usually called **apps**) that could run on their phones. Companies would license the apps from software developers and then charge subscribers a monthly usage fee for each app. Apple turned this revenue strategy on its head when AT&T agreed to be Apple's sole carrier for the iPhone (that is, iPhones would only operate on the AT&T network, an arrangement that lasted from the iPhone's introduction to 2011) and agreed to allow Apple to sell apps for the phone directly.

The Apple App Store was launched at the same time as the iPhone itself and became an instant success, making a wide variety of software available for the phone and later, for Apple's iPad tablet devices. Users of Android phones, phablets, and tablets can buy apps in a similar online store, Google Play, which offers software for that platform. Both Apple and Google allow independent software developers to create apps and sell them (on a revenue-sharing basis) through their respective stores. These developers found they could make thousands, even millions of dollars for their creations. Zynga, a company that creates game apps for mobile phones, generates more than $1 billion in revenues each year selling its game apps for phones. Other firms, such as Mutual Mobile, provide software design and development services for companies that want apps to use in their own organizations.

A number of apps do nothing more than provide a quick gateway to a company's Web site. Many online shopping destinations offer free apps that are optimized to provide users the best possible shopping experience on the small screen of a smartphone. Other apps are sold for a fee. Games, puzzles, productivity tools (such as contact managers, calendars, and task organizers), and reference works generally fall into this category. Most apps sell for $1 to $5, although prices can vary considerably. Newspaper, magazine, and media sites sometimes offer free access to their online content through apps (especially to their print subscribers); others sell subscriptions that can be accessed through their apps.

Some mobile app sellers include an advertising element in their revenue models. These apps include mobile ads that display messages from advertisers (other than the seller of the app). One common way to include ads is to display them in a small bar at the bottom of the app screen. Some apps include advertising that appears on a part of the screen or as a separate screen that must be clicked through to get to the app. The advertising space on mobile apps is sold in the same way that banner advertising on Web sites is sold (which you learned about in Chapter 4).

The use of mobile devices for banking and financial services (such as stockbrokers) is growing. The convenience of banking or executing stock trades from anywhere is very appealing to many consumers. In fact, basic apps are so easy to create that trade associations can provide apps to convention-goers that include maps of the convention floor and program agendas.

A growing number of hospitals and clinics are providing apps that give doctors access to detailed information needed for treating patients. For example, cardiologists can read electrocardiograms (EKGs) on their mobile devices at home, saving them time and often a trip to the hospital for an emergency consult. Other hospitals are creating equally creative apps. For example, diabetic patients can track food intake, insulin injections, blood sugar readings, and their level of physical activities on their phones. Doctors treating these patients can access the data using their own mobile devices and can better help patients manage their diabetes.

Virtually all mobile devices have global positioning satellite (GPS) service capabilities, which means that apps can combine the phone user's location with the availability of retail stores and services to create mobile business opportunities much like the location-based social networks you learned about earlier in this chapter. For example, some apps can direct the user to specific business locations (such as restaurants, movie theaters, or auto repair facilities) based on the user's current location.

Mobile Payment Apps

Since 2004, NTT DoCoMo has been selling mobile phones, called **mobile wallets** (*osaifu-ketai*, in Japanese), that function as credit cards. Although the individual applications on DoCoMo phones are not overwhelming (for example, one application lets you use a mobile phone to pay for a vending machine purchase in Japan), their combined capabilities generate a significant amount of business. Other countries that have a tradition of using cash for retail transactions have seen significant adoptions of mobile phone apps that allow them to be used to make payments. Very few people have credit cards in these countries and the convenience of using a mobile phone for payments has been very attractive.

In the United States, where the use of credit cards is widespread, the use of mobile device payment apps has not become popular. However, in 2011, a number of companies began to offer retail store technologies that allow the use of smartphones as payment devices. American Express, Visa, and MasterCard have all made phone readers available to retailers. Google Wallet for Android phones became more widely used in 2013 when it added the ability to send cash to any U.S. adult who has an e-mail address. In 2015, Starbucks attributed much of its recent sales growth to customers using its order and pay mobile app, which not only allows wireless payments, but lets customers order ahead and avoid the lines that form during their stores' busiest times (Starbucks also tracks its reward points in the app). You will learn more about the fast-changing area of mobile payment systems in Chapter 11.

In the next section, you will learn how online business pioneers adapted auctions, a very old business practice, to a new online business opportunity.

Online Auctions

In many ways, online auctions provide a business opportunity that is perfect for the Web. An auction site can charge both buyers and sellers to participate, and it can sell advertising on its pages. People interested in trading specific items can form a market segment that advertisers will pay extra to reach. Thus, the same kind of targeted advertising opportunities that search engine sites generate with their results pages are available to advertisers on auction sites. This combination of revenue-generating characteristics makes it relatively easy to develop online auctions that yield profits early in the life of the project.

One of the Internet's strengths is that it can bring together people who share narrow interests but are geographically dispersed. Online auctions can capitalize on that ability by either catering to a narrow interest or providing a general auction site that has sections devoted to specific interests.

Online auctions also create a natural social network. Since buyers and sellers interested in the same products (or product categories) congregate virtually on the auction site, a critical mass of highly interested participants occurs automatically. Thus, almost everything you learned about social networks earlier in this chapter applies to the business of online auctions. Before you learn more about online auctions, the next section introduces some basic auction terminology and principles.

Auction Basics

The earliest written records of auctions are from Babylon and date from 500 BC. Roman soldiers used auctions to liquidate the property they took from their vanquished foes. Auctions became common activities in seventeenth-century England, where taverns held regular auctions of art and furniture. The British settlers of the colonies that would become the United States brought auctions along and used them to sell farm equipment, animals, tobacco, and, sad to say, human beings.

In an auction, a seller offers an item or items for sale, but does not establish a price. Potential buyers are given information about the item or some opportunity to examine it; they then offer **bids**, which are the prices they are willing to pay for the item. The potential buyers, or **bidders**, each have developed **private valuations**, or amounts they are willing to pay for the item. The whole auction process is managed by an **auctioneer**. In some auctions, people employed by the seller or the auctioneer can make bids on behalf of the seller. These people are called **shill bidders**. Shill bidders can artificially inflate the price of an item and may be prohibited from bidding by the rules of a particular auction.

ENGLISH AUCTIONS

Many different kinds of auctions exist. Most people who have attended or seen an auction on television have experienced only one type of auction, the **English auction**, in which bidders publicly announce their successive higher bids until no higher bid is forthcoming. At that point, the auctioneer pronounces the item sold to the highest bidder at that bidder's price. This type of auction is also called an **ascending-price auction**. An English auction is sometimes called an **open auction** (or **open-outcry auction**) because the bids are publicly announced; however, there are other types of auctions that use publicly announced bids that are also called open auctions.

In some cases, an English auction has a minimum bid, or reserve price. A **minimum bid** is the price at which an auction begins. If no bidders are willing to pay that price, the item is removed from the auction and not sold. In some auctions, a minimum bid is not announced, but sellers can establish a minimum acceptable price, called a **reserve price**, or simply **reserve**. If the reserve price is not exceeded, the item is withdrawn from the auction and not sold.

English auctions that offer multiple units of an item for sale and allow bidders to specify the quantity they want to buy are called **Yankee auctions**. When the bidding concludes in a Yankee auction, the highest bidder is allotted the quantity he or she bid. If items remain after satisfying the highest bidder, those remaining items are allocated to successive lower (next highest) bidders until all items are distributed. Although all successful bidders (except possibly the lowest successful bidder) receive the quantity of items on which they bid, they only pay the price bid by the *lowest* successful bidder.

To understand Yankee auctions better, consider this example. A seller places nine items up for bid. When the bidders stop increasing their bids, the successful bidders include the following: the highest bidder, who bid $85, quantity five; the second-highest bidder, who bid $83, quantity three; and the third-highest bidder, who bid $81, quantity four. All three of the successful bidders pay $81 per item, but the highest bidder receives five items, the second-highest bidder receives three items, and the third-highest bidder receives the one remaining item, despite having bid for a quantity of four, because only one is left after satisfying the quantity bids of the higher bidders.

English auctions have drawbacks for both sellers and bidders. Because the winning bidder is only required to bid a small amount more than the next-highest bidder, winning bidders tend not to bid their full private valuations, which prevents sellers from obtaining the maximum possible price. Bidders risk becoming caught up in the excitement of competitive bidding and then bidding more than their private valuations. This psychological phenomenon, called the **winner's curse**, has been extensively documented by William Thaler (see the Thaler reference in the "For Further Study and Research" section at the end of this chapter) and other behavioral economists.

DUTCH AUCTIONS

The **Dutch auction** is a form of open auction in which bidding starts at a high price and drops until a bidder accepts the price. Because the price drops until a bidder claims the item, Dutch auctions are also called **descending-price auctions**. Farmers' cooperatives in the Netherlands use this type of auction to sell perishable goods such as produce and flowers, which is how it came to be known as a "Dutch" auction. In most Dutch auctions, the seller offers a number of similar items for sale. One common implementation of a Dutch auction uses a clock that drops the price with each tick. The first bidder to call out "stop," which stops the clock, becomes the winning bidder. The winning bidder can take all or any part of the auctioned items at that price. If any items remain, the clock is restarted and continues to run until all the items are taken by successive lower bidders. A Dutch auction is often better for the seller because the bidder with the highest private valuation will not let the bid drop much below that valuation for fear of losing the item to another bidder. Dutch auctions are particularly good for moving large numbers of commodity items quickly.

FIRST-PRICE SEALED-BID AUCTIONS

In **sealed-bid auctions**, bidders submit their bids independently and are usually prohibited from sharing information with each other. In a **first-price sealed-bid auction**, the highest bidder wins. If multiple items are auctioned, successive lower (next highest) bidders are awarded the remaining items at the prices they bid.

SECOND-PRICE SEALED-BID AUCTIONS

The **second-price sealed-bid auction** is the same as the first-price sealed-bid auction except that the highest bidder is awarded the item at the price bid by the *second*-highest bidder. At first glance, one might wonder why a seller would even consider such an auction because it gives the item to the winning bidder at a lower price; however, it yields higher returns for the seller, encourages all bidders to bid the amounts of their private valuations, and reduces the tendency for bidders to collude. Because the winning bidder is protected from an erroneously high bid, all bidders tend to bid higher than they would in a first-price sealed-bid auction. Second-price sealed-bid auctions are commonly called **Vickrey auctions**, named for William Vickrey, who won the Nobel Prize in Economics for his research on this auction type.

OPEN-OUTCRY DOUBLE AUCTIONS

The Chicago Board Options Exchange conducts **open-outcry double auctions** of commodity futures and stock options. The buy and sell offers are shouted by traders standing in a small area on the exchange floor called a trading pit. Each commodity or stock option is traded in its own pit. The action in a trading pit can become quite frenzied as 20 or 30 traders shout offers aloud. Double auctions, either sealed bid or open outcry, work well only for items of known quality, such as securities or graded agricultural products, that are regularly traded in large quantities because such items can be auctioned without bidders inspecting the items before placing their bids.

DOUBLE AUCTIONS

In a **double auction**, buyers and sellers each submit combined price-quantity bids to an auctioneer. The auctioneer matches the sellers' offers (starting with the lowest price and then going up) to the buyers' offers (starting with the highest price and then going down) until all the quantities offered for sale are sold to buyers. Double auctions can be operated in either sealed-bid or open-outcry formats. The New York Stock Exchange conducts sealed-bid double auctions of stocks and bonds in which the auctioneer, called a specialist, manages the market for a particular stock or bond issue. The specialist company must use its own funds, when necessary, to maintain a stable market in the specific security it manages. Although the specialist system has been in use for more than a century, critics have charged that specialists can and do use their knowledge to enrich themselves at the expense of investors. In 2007, the New York Stock Exchange added an electronic trading system that automatically matches buyer and seller offers and bypasses specialists. This system now handles most of the trading volume on the exchange.

REVERSE (SELLER-BID) AUCTIONS

In a **reverse auction** (also called a **seller-bid auction**), multiple sellers submit price bids to an auctioneer who represents a single buyer. The bids are for a given amount of a specific item that the buyer wants to purchase. The prices go down as the bidding continues until no seller is willing to bid lower. Most reverse auctions involve businesses as buyers and sellers. In many business reverse auctions, the buyer acts as auctioneer and screens sellers before they can participate. You will learn more about specific implementations of reverse auctions later in this chapter.

The seven auction types described in this section are the most commonly used in business today. Figure 6-9 summarizes the key characteristics of each of these seven major auction types.

Online Auctions and Related Businesses

Millions of people buy and sell all types of goods on consumer auction sites each year. Although the online auction business is changing rapidly as it grows, three broad categories of auction Web sites have emerged: general consumer auctions, specialty consumer auctions, and business-to-business auctions. Some industry analysts consider the two types of consumer auctions to be business-to-consumer electronic commerce, but others call it consumer-to-consumer or even **consumer-to-business** (because the bidders at a general consumer auction might be businesses). This argument is based on the idea that many sellers in general consumer auctions are ordinary people (not businesses) who use these auctions to sell personal items. Whether you prefer to think of online auctions as business-to-consumer, consumer-to-consumer, or consumer-to-business, the largest number of auction transactions occurs on general consumer auction sites.

GENERAL CONSUMER AUCTIONS

The most successful consumer auction Web site today is eBay. Sellers and buyers must register with eBay and agree to the site's basic terms of doing business. Sellers pay eBay a listing fee and a sliding percentage of the final selling price. Buyers pay nothing to eBay. In addition to paying the basic fees, sellers can choose from a variety of enhanced and extra-cost services, including having their auctions listed in boldface type and featured in lists of preferred auctions.

In an attempt to address buyer concerns about seller reliability, eBay instituted a rating system. Buyers can submit ratings of sellers after doing business with them. These ratings are converted into graphics that appear with the seller's nickname in each auction in which the seller participates. Although this system is not perfect, many eBay bidders feel that it affords them some protection from unscrupulous sellers. eBay also uses buyer ratings of sellers to place restrictions on sellers (such as withholding funds for three

Auction Type	Key Characteristics
English auction	Starting from a low price, bidding increases until no bidder is willing to bid higher.
Dutch auction	Starting from a high price, bidding automatically decreases until the bidder accepts the price.
First-price sealed-bid auction	Secret bidding process; the highest bidder pays the amount of the highest bid.
Second-price sealed-bid auction (Vickrey auction)	Secret bidding process; the highest bidder pays the amount of the *second*-highest bid.
Double auction (open-outcry)	Buyers and sellers declare combined price–quantity bids. The auctioneer matches seller offers (lowest to highest) with buyer offers (highest to lowest). Buyers and sellers can modify bids based on knowledge gained from other bids.
Double auction (sealed-bid)	Buyers and sellers declare combined price–quantity bids. The auctioneer (specialist) matches seller offers (lowest to highest) with buyer offers (highest to lowest). Buyers and sellers cannot modify their bids.
Reverse auction (seller-bid)	Multiple sellers submit price bids to an auctioneer that represents a single buyer. The bids are for a given amount of a specific item that the buyer wants to purchase. Prices go down as the bidding continues until no seller is willing to bid lower.

FIGURE 6-9   Key characteristics of seven major auction types

weeks) or, if the ratings are low enough, prohibit them from selling on eBay at all. The converse is true also; sellers rate buyers, which provides sellers some protection from unscrupulous buyers.

Although eBay does not release any statistics about buyer and seller frauds, most industry observers agree that sellers face larger potential losses than buyers. Sellers' greatest risks are from buyers who use stolen credit card numbers or who place the winning bid but never contact the seller to conclude the transaction. Buyers' risks include sellers who never deliver or who misrepresent their merchandise. You will learn about ways that sellers and buyers can protect themselves later in this chapter.

The most common format used on eBay is a computerized version of the English auction. The eBay English auction allows the seller to set a reserve price. In eBay English auctions, the bidders are listed, but the bid amounts are not disclosed until after the auction is over. This is a slight variation on the in-person English auction, but because eBay always shows a continually updated high bid amount, a bidder who monitors the auction can see the bidding pattern as it occurs. The main difference between eBay and a live English auction is that bidders do not see the details of the bidding history (which bidders placed which bids when) until the auction is over. The eBay English auction also allows sellers to specify that an auction be made private. In an eBay private auction, the site never discloses bidders' identities and the prices they bid. At the conclusion of the auction, eBay notifies only the seller and the highest bidder. Another auction type offered by eBay is an increasing-price format for multiple-item auctions that eBay calls a Dutch auction. However, these auctions are actually the Yankee auction variant of an English auction.

In either type of eBay auction, bidders must monitor closely the bidding activity if they intend to win the auction. All eBay auctions have a **minimum bid increment**, the amount by which one bid must exceed the previous bid, which is about 3 percent of the bid amount. Bidders can enter a **proxy bid**, which automatically increases to the next highest increment needed to exceed any bid, up to a bidder-specified maximum bid. As new bidders enter the auction, the eBay site software continually enters higher bids for all bidders who placed proxy bids. Although this feature is designed to make bidding require less bidder attention, if a number of bidders enter proxy bids on one item, the bidding rises rapidly to the highest proxy bid offered. This rapid rise in the current bid often occurs in the closing minutes of the auction, when multiple bidders each raise their maximum proxy bid levels.

To attract sellers who frequently offer items or who continually offer large numbers of items, eBay offers a platform called eBay stores within its auction site. Sellers can show items for sale as well as items being auctioned in their eBay stores, which can help sellers generate additional profits from sales of products related to their auction items.

GENERAL CONSUMER AUCTIONS: THE LOCK-IN EFFECT

By being the first major consumer auction site and by investing in substantial general media advertising, eBay was able to establish itself early. Its success has inspired competition from a number of powerful and well-financed companies over the years, including Yahoo! and Amazon.com, both of whom spent large amounts of money in their efforts to unseat eBay before giving up in 2006 and 2007, respectively. The economic structure of online markets is biased against new entrants. Because markets become more efficient (yielding fairer prices to both buyers and sellers) as the number of buyers and sellers increases, new auction participants are inclined to patronize established marketplaces. Thus, existing auction sites, such as eBay, are inherently more valuable to customers than new auction sites. This basic economic fact, which economists call a **lock-in effect**, has made the creation of alternative successful general consumer Web auction sites very difficult.

A somewhat ironic example of the lock-in effect occurred in the Japanese general consumer auction market. In this market, unlike in the United States, Yahoo! was the first major company to offer online auctions. At the time (early 1999), Yahoo! did not charge fees to sellers. When eBay entered the Japanese market five months later, it charged fees and found few people interested in its services. Even later, when Yahoo! began charging fees for its auctions, the lock-in effect preserved its strong lead in Japan. Today, Yahoo!

LEARNING FROM FAILURES

Auction Universe

One of the most promising early entrants into the general consumer auction business was Auction Universe. Times Mirror, the parent company of the *Los Angeles Times* newspaper, started Auction Universe in 1997 and then sold it in 1998 to a partnership of eight major newspaper companies (including Times Mirror itself) called Classified Ventures. These companies were concerned that classified advertising on the Web posed a threat to their newspapers' classified advertising, which is one of the most profitable elements in the newspaper business. Through their Classified Ventures partnership, these newspaper companies started their own Web sites for classified ads such as Apartments.com, Cars.com, and NewHomeNetwork.com. These sites earn revenue by charging for running ads, selling advertising on their pages, or both. Classified Ventures believed that the Auction Universe site could become an important and profitable part of its Web presence.

Auction Universe closed in August 2000, and Classified Ventures itself was dissolved in 2014 when Gannett, one of the original partners, bought out the other partners for $1.8 billion. Gannett continues to operate most of the Web sites. The Auction Universe site was modeled on eBay and offered similar types of auctions and services for buyers and sellers. Some critics believed that the Auction Universe interface was more intuitive than eBay's and included a better search engine; however, the site failed to mount a sustained challenge to eBay's dominance. Even with major corporate sponsorship and a $10 million advertising campaign behind it, Auction Universe was unable to displace the advantage eBay obtained from the lock-in effect it had on a large number of auction bidders and sellers.

Auctions holds more than 90 percent of the Japanese online auction market, whereas eBay's market share is less than 5 percent.

SPECIALTY CONSUMER AUCTIONS

Rather than struggle to compete with a well-established rival such as eBay in the general consumer auction market, a number of firms have decided to identify special-interest market targets and create specialized Web auction sites that meet the needs of those market segments.

JustBeads.com is one example of an auction site that caters to buyers and sellers who are geographically dispersed but share highly focused interests. Other specialty consumer auction sites include Cigarbid.com and Winebid. These sites gain an advantage by identifying a strong market segment with readily identifiable products that are desired by people with relatively high levels of disposable income. Cigars and wine meet those requirements. These specialized consumer auctions occupy profitable niches, which allows them to coexist successfully with large general consumer sites, such as eBay.

CONSUMER REVERSE AUCTIONS

In the past, a number of companies have created sites that allow site visitors to describe items or services they want to buy. The site then routes the visitor's request to a group of participating merchants who reply to the visitor by e-mail with offers to supply the item at a particular price. This type of offer is often called a **reverse bid**. The buyer can then accept the lowest offer or the offer that best matches the buyer's criteria. None of these sites were successful in developing a large enough following to interest merchants, so they have all closed.

Many people think of Priceline.com as a seller-bid auction site. Priceline.com allows site visitors to state a price they are willing to pay for airline tickets, car rentals, hotel rooms, and a few other services. If the price is sufficiently high, the transaction is completed. However, Priceline.com completes many of its transactions from an inventory that it has purchased from airlines, car rental agencies, and hotels.

GROUP SHOPPING AND COUPON SITES

Another type of business made possible by the Internet is the **group purchasing site**, or **group shopping site**. On these sites, the seller posts an item with a tentative price. As individual buyers enter bids on the item (these bids are agreements to buy one unit of that item, but no price is specified), the site operators negotiate with the seller to obtain a lower price. The posted price will decrease as the number of bids increases, but only if the number of bids increases. Thus, a group shopping site builds up the number of buyers sufficiently to encourage the seller to offer a quantity discount. The effect is similar to the outcome achieved by a reverse auction.

The types of products that work well for group shopping sites are branded products with well-established reputations, characteristics that help buyers to feel confident that they are getting a good bargain and are not just getting a lower price for a low-quality product. Ideal products also have a high value-to-size ratio and are not perishable.

Two companies, Mercata and LetsBuyIt.com, operated major group shopping sites for several years; however, both closed their doors after failing to find consistent sources of products that sold well on their sites. They found that few sellers of products that are well suited to group shopping efforts—such as computers, consumer electronics, and small appliances—were willing to work with them. These sellers did not see any compelling advantage in offering reduced prices on their merchandise to Web sites that were probably cannibalizing sales in their existing marketing channels. They also worried about offending the regular distributors of their products by selling through group shopping sites.

In 2008, Andrew Mason and Eric Lefkofsky decided to give the group shopping business another try. Starting in Chicago, they launched a site called **Groupon** (a shortening of "group coupon"). The site offered one coupon offer (called a "groupon") per day in the city. A groupon requires a certain number of people to sign up for it or it does not become available to anyone. For example, a $50 dinner coupon redeemable at a specific restaurant might be sold for $30. The consumer gets a $50 dinner for $30. Groupon would keep approximately half the money paid by the consumer ($15) and the remainder would go to the restaurant. Thus, the restaurant gets $15 for its $50 dinner, but it has a chance to impress a new customer and gain that customer's return business.

Further, the restaurant makes no up-front cash outlay, as it would if it were purchasing advertising.

Groupon promotes its business using social networking sites such as Facebook and Twitter to make contacts with consumers and to spread the word about the groupon deal for the day. Groupon's current customer base is primarily female, so the bulk of its business is in the health, beauty, and fitness markets. Similar services are offered by LivingSocial and Gilt. Industry analysts expect that the continued success of these group buying sites will bring competition from larger companies such as eBay and Google.

BUSINESS-TO-BUSINESS AUCTIONS

Unlike consumer online auctions, business-to-business online auctions evolved to meet a specific existing need. Many manufacturing companies periodically need to dispose of unusable or excess inventory. Despite the best efforts of procurement and production management, businesses occasionally buy more raw materials than they need. Many times, unforeseen changes in customer demand for a product can saddle manufacturers with excess finished goods or spare parts.

Depending on its size, a firm typically uses one of two methods to distribute excess inventory. Large companies sometimes have liquidation specialists who find buyers for these unusable inventory items. Smaller businesses often sell their unusable and excess inventory to **liquidation brokers**, which are firms that find buyers for these items. Online auctions are the logical extension of these inventory liquidation activities to a new and more efficient channel, the Internet.

Two of the three emerging business-to-business Web auction models are direct descendants of these two traditional methods for handling excess inventory. In the large-company model, the business creates its own auction site that sells excess inventory. In the small-company model, a third-party Web auction site takes the place of the liquidation broker and auctions excess inventory listed on the site by a number of smaller sellers. The third business-to-business Web auction model resembles consumer online auctions. In this model, a new business entity enters a market that lacked efficiency and creates a site at which buyers and sellers who have not historically done business with each other can participate in auctions. An alternative implementation of this model occurs when a Web auction replaces an existing sales channel.

In the second business-to-business auction model, smaller firms sell their obsolete inventory through an independent third-party auction site. In some cases, these online auctions are conducted by the same liquidation brokers that have always handled the disposition of obsolete inventory. These brokers adapted to the changed environment and implemented electronic commerce to stay in business. One example is the GoIndustry Dove Bid site, established by traditional liquidation broker the Ross-Dove Company and now operated by Liquidity Services. In 2015, a group of banks set up by the Chinese government to manage nonperforming loans began selling off the loans and/or the assets that secured the loans through online auctions. Since 2012, Taobao (the auction portal of Alibaba) has been using online auctions similarly to dispose of assets seized by the Chinese court system.

A number of hospitals and other organizations use a third type of business-to-business online auction to fill temporary employment openings. Health care workers, such as nurses, perform similar duties in specific health care settings in most hospitals. For example, the duties performed by an intensive care unit nurse at one hospital are almost identical to the duties performed by intensive care unit nurses at any other hospital. State licensing regulations require that all nurses have similar levels of knowledge, skills, and abilities. Having similar job functions in workplaces and having similarly qualified persons working in those jobs allows both nurses and employers to treat the nursing function as a commodity. Therefore, nurses can easily work for a variety of employers and do not require long periods of training or learning procedures specific to a particular hospital. In the past, nurse agencies would coordinate placement, matching nurses who wanted to work particular days or shifts with hospitals and other health care organizations who had shifts to fill. The agency would earn a commission on each placement. Today, employers operate their own shift auctions. Nurses bid on the shifts they would prefer to work and the software manages the auctions. In an efficient matching of supply and demand, employers meet their staffing needs efficiently, nurses get to work when they want, and the agency fee is avoided.

BUSINESS-TO-BUSINESS REVERSE AUCTIONS

In Chapter 5, you learned how businesses are creating various types of electronic marketplaces to conduct business-to-business (B2B) transactions. Many of these marketplaces include auctions and reverse auctions. Glass and building materials producer Owens Corning uses reverse auctions for items ranging from chemicals (direct materials) to conveyors (fixed assets) to pipe fittings (MRO). Owens Corning even held a reverse auction to buy bottled water. The company found that asking its suppliers to bid has reduced the cost of items purchased in reverse auctions by an average of 10 percent. Because Owens Corning buys billions of dollars' worth of materials, fixed assets, and MRO items each year, the potential for cost savings is significant. Both the U.S. Navy and the federal government's General Services Administration use reverse auctions to acquire some of the billions of dollars' worth of materials and supplies they purchase each year. Other companies that use reverse auctions include Agilent, Bechtel, Boeing, Raytheon, and Sony.

Not all companies are enthusiastic about reverse auctions, however. Some purchasing executives argue that reverse auctions cause suppliers to compete on price alone, which can lead suppliers to cut corners on quality or miss scheduled delivery dates. Others argue that reverse auctions can be useful for nonstrategic commodity items with established quality standards. Companies that have considered reverse auctions and decided not to use them include Cisco, Cubic, IBM, and Solar Turbines.

With compelling arguments on both sides, the advisability of using reverse auctions can depend on specific conditions that exist in a given company. For example, in some industry supply chains, the need for trust and long-term strategic relationships with suppliers makes reverse auctions less attractive. In fact, most purchasing managers today work to build trust-based relationships that can endure for many years. Using reverse auctions replaces trusting relationships with a bidding activity that pits suppliers against each other and is seen by many purchasing managers as a step backward.

In some industries, suppliers are larger and more powerful than the buyers. In those industries, suppliers simply will not agree to participate in reverse auctions. If enough important suppliers refuse to participate, it is impossible to conduct reverse auctions. In industries where a high degree of competition exists among suppliers, however, reverse auctions can be an efficient way to conduct and manage the price bidding that would naturally occur in that market. Figure 6-10 lists the supply chain characteristics that support or discourage reverse auctions identified in research conducted by Dima Ghawi and the author of this book.

Auction-Related Services

The growth of eBay and other auction sites has encouraged entrepreneurs to create businesses that provide auction-related services of various kinds. These include escrow services, auction directory and information services, auction software (for both sellers and buyers), and **auction consignment services**, which are described in this section.

AUCTION ESCROW SERVICES

A common concern among people bidding in online auctions is the reliability of the sellers. Surveys indicate that as many as 11 percent of all Web auction buyers either do not receive the items they purchased, or find the items to be different from the seller's representation in some significant way. About half of those buyers are unable to resolve their disputes to their satisfaction. When purchasing high-value items, buyers can use an escrow service to protect their interests.

An **escrow service** is an independent party that holds a buyer's payment until the buyer receives the purchased item and is satisfied that the item is what the seller represented it to be. Some escrow services take delivery of the item from the seller and perform the inspection for the buyer. In such situations, buyers give the escrow service authority to examine. Usually, escrow agents that perform this service are art appraisers, antique appraisers, and the like who are qualified to judge quality, usually with better judgment than the buyer. Escrow services do, however, charge fees ranging from 1 to 10 percent of the item's cost, subject to a minimum fee, typically between $5 and $50. The minimum fee provision can make escrow services too expensive for small purchases. Escrow.com is one of the leading Web auction escrow services. Some escrow firms also sell auction buyer's insurance, which can protect buyers from nondelivery and some quality risks. There have been cases of escrow fraud, especially in auctions of high-value items. The Better Business Bureau recommends that consumers determine whether an escrow service is licensed and bonded before using it. Consumers can do this by contacting the appropriate licensing agency in the state in which the escrow service is located. The Better Business Bureau recommends avoiding offshore escrow companies entirely.

Wary bidders in low-price auctions (for which the minimum escrow charges would be excessive) do have some other ways to protect themselves. One way is to check the seller's record on the auction site to see how the seller is rated. Also, some Web sites offer lists of auction sellers who have failed to deliver merchandise or who have otherwise cheated bidders in the past. These sites are operated as free services (often by bidders who have been cheated), so they sometimes contain unreliable information and they open and close periodically, but you can use your favorite search engine to locate sites that currently carry such lists.

Supply Chain Characteristics That Support Reverse Auctions:

- Suppliers are highly competitive.
- Product features can be clearly specified.
- Suppliers are willing to reduce the margin they earn on this product.
- Suppliers are willing to participate in reverse auctions.

Supply Chain Characteristics That Discourage Reverse Auctions:

- Product is highly complex or requires regular changes in design.
- Product has customized features.
- Long-term strategic relationships are important to buyers and suppliers.
- Switching costs are high.

FIGURE 6-10   Supply chain characteristics and reverse auctions

AUCTION DIRECTORY AND INFORMATION SERVICES

Another service offered by some firms on the Web is a directory of auctions. eCommerceBytes is an auction information site that publishes articles about developments in the online auction industry. It provides guidance for new auction participants and helpful hints and tips for more experienced buyers and sellers along with directories of online auction sites.

Price Watch is a site that lists current selling prices for computer hardware, software, and consumer electronics items. Although this monitoring is a retail pricing service designed to help shoppers find the best price on new items sold through the site, Web auction participants can use the site to help them formulate bidding strategies on auction sites.

AUCTION SOFTWARE

Both auction buyers and sellers can purchase software to help them manage their online auctions. Sellers often run many auctions at the same time. Companies such as AuctionHawk and Vendio sell auction management software and services for both buyers and sellers. For sellers, these companies offer software and services that can help with or automate tasks such as image hosting, advertising, page design, bulk repeatable listings, feedback tracking and management, report tracking, and e-mail management. Using these tools, sellers can create attractive layouts for their pages and manage hundreds of auctions.

For buyers, a number of companies sell auction sniping software. **Sniping software** observes auction progress until the last second or two of the auction clock. Just as the auction is about to expire, the sniping software places a bid high enough to win the auction (unless that bid exceeds a limit set by the sniping software's owner). The act of placing a winning bid at the last second is called a **snipe**. Because sniping software synchronizes its internal clock to the auction site clock and executes its bid with a computer's precision, the software almost always wins out over a human bidder. The first sniping software, named Cricket Jr., was written by David Eccles in 1997. He sells the software on his CricketSniper site. A number of other sniping software sellers have entered the market—each claiming that its software will outbid other sniping software. Some sites offer sniping services; that is, the sniping software runs on their Web site and customers enter their sniping instructions on that site. Some of these companies offer subscriptions; others use a mixed-revenue model in which they offer some free snipes supported by advertising, but require payment for additional snipes.

Summary

In this chapter, you learned how companies use Internet and mobile technologies to create social networks, make sales and increase operational efficiency, and operate online auctions.

The Web's ability to bring together people and organizations that share highly specific interests but that are scattered throughout the world gave birth to virtual communities and social networks. Businesses are creating their own online communities using social networking tools and are participating in social media sites to communicate to their customers, learn from their customers, and observe their customers' interactions with others. Knowledge gained from these interactions, as participants in the environment of their customers' activities, can be used to improve product and service offerings, design new products, or identify unmet customer needs. Social networks themselves have begun to generate sufficient revenue to cover their costs and generate a profit from advertising, sale of members' demographic and online behavior data, and, in some cases, charging fees.

A growing number of companies are exploiting the online business opportunities made possible by the growth in usage of Internet-connected mobile devices. As we continue in the third wave of electronic commerce, individuals and companies are using social networking media for personal and business-related interactions. Companies are using internal social networking sites and mobile apps to communicate with employees and coordinate work across various organizational units.

You learned about the key characteristics of the seven major auction types, and learned how firms are using online auctions to sell goods to their customers and buy from their suppliers. Although some specialty sites do conduct significant auction activities, the consumer online auction business is dominated by eBay, at least in the United States. B2B auctions give companies a new and efficient way to dispose of excess inventory, and B2B reverse auctions provide an effective procurement tool under some conditions. A number of businesses offer ancillary services to Web users who participate in online auctions. These businesses include escrow services, auction directories and information sites, auction management software for both sellers and bidders, and auction consignment sites.

Key Terms

apps	descending-price auctions
ascending-price auction	double auction
auction consignment services	Dutch auction
auctioneer	English auction
bidders	escrow service
bids	first-price sealed-bid auction
bulletin board systems (BBSs)	group purchasing site
consumer-to-business	group shopping site
crowdfunding	idea-based social media

idea-based social networking

jailbreaking

liquidation brokers

location-aware services

lock-in effect

massive open online course (MOOC)

meetups

microblogs

microlending

minimum bid

minimum bid increment

mobile commerce (m-commerce)

mobile wallets

monetizing

open auction

open-outcry auction

open-outcry double auctions

open-source software

participatory journalism

phablet

private valuations

proxy bid

reserve

reserve price

reverse auction

reverse bid

reward-based crowdfunding

rooting

sealed-bid auctions

second-price sealed-bid auction

seller-bid auction

shill bidders

short messaging service (SMS)

snipe

sniping software

social networking

social networking site

social shopping

tablet devices

texting

tweets

Usenet newsgroups

Vickrey auctions

virtual community

virtual learning network

winner's curse

Wireless Application Protocol (WAP)

Yankee auctions

Review Questions

1. What is a virtual community?

2. How did bulletin board systems and Usenet newsgroups provide early social networking opportunities for Internet users in the 1970s and 1980s?

3. Why did the social networking site Six Degrees fail?

4. Name three Web sites that created virtual communities or facilitated social networking before Facebook was founded in 2006.

5. What is a meetup?

6. What is the term for the practice of online newspapers and magazines to have their readers help write their own news?

7. What is social shopping?

8. What is a MOOC?

9. What does it mean to monetize Web site visitors?

10. What does a microlending Web site do?

11. What is crowdfunding?

12. How can companies use social networks internally; that is, by limiting access to employees of the company?

13. What is a phablet?

14. What does it mean to jailbreak or root a smartphone?

15. What is a shill bidder in an online auction?

16. What is a Yankee auction?

17. What is a Dutch auction?

18. What objective is a Vickrey auction designed to accomplish?

19. What is a reverse auction and when is it most likely to be used in a business-to-business setting?

20. What is a proxy bid?

21. What function is served by an online liquidation broker?

22. What is the main purpose of an auction escrow service?

Exercises

1. Drawing on the knowledge of cultural differences you learned about in Chapter 1, write one or two paragraphs in which you explain why people who live in one country might prefer to start their own social networking sites rather than use those created by companies in other countries.

2. Write about 100 words in which you describe specific changes that occurred in virtual community Web sites when the bandwidths available to Internet users increased. In your answer, be sure to explain why these changes occurred.

3. Some companies use a social networking strategy in which they avoid making direct advertising or brand statements. In about 100 words, outline the advantages and disadvantages of such a strategy.

4. In this and earlier chapters, you have learned that the development of open-source software has been facilitated by Internet technologies. In about 100 words, explain how a group of open-source software developers might be described as a virtual community using social networking tools to accomplish tasks related to both software creation and distribution.

5. In a paragraph, explain how blog sites such as Gothamist or TechCrunch generate revenue.

6. A number of Web sites offer a service that allows volunteers to answer questions posted by other site visitors. Uclue provides a similar service, but allows researchers to charge fees for their answers (and takes a percentage of that fee). In about 100 words, explain why a person might use a paid site such as Uclue rather than using a free site.

7. In about 100 words, describe the differences between a blog and a microblog. Be sure to discuss when a company might prefer to use a microblog in its social networking efforts rather than a blog.

8. In a paragraph or two, outline why most mobile phones are sold today with a common operating system rather than one developed by the phone manufacturer.

9. In about 100 words, outline at least three ways in which a mobile phone's GPS capabilities can be used to provide benefits to users of a social network.

10. In about 100 words, describe two or three social networking apps that could use a smartphone's GPS capability. Be sure to make clear the benefit of using the GPS in the app in each case.

11. In about 100 words, explain how the lock-in effect might operate in a general consumer auction.

12. In about 100 words, define the term *reserve price* and explain how the use of a reserve price can affect the progress and outcome of an auction.

13. In about 200 words, explain how sniping software works and why some auction participants feel its use is unfair to other bidders.

14. Assume you work in the procurement department of a packaging machinery systems manufacturer. The parts your company buys must meet precise specifications and the parts are not generally interchangeable; that is, your company's design engineers must work closely with your suppliers to design specific parts for particular systems. Your director of purchasing is interested in using online reverse auctions to buy these parts. In approximately 200 words, outline arguments for and against using online reverse auctions in this situation and conclude with a specific recommendation.

Cases

C1. Lego Mindstorms

Since 1947, Lego plastic blocks have been one of the world's favorite toys. Lego block kits let children build creations of their own design, or kids can follow instructions to build models of airplanes, cars, trucks, characters from movies and television shows, and robots. Lego uses its social networking efforts to stay connected to its customers in many ways. In 1998, Lego introduced its Mindstorms product, a programmable computerized brick that includes sensors and motors. Mindstorms was designed to be the basic building block of a programmable robot.

Although it is a toy, the Mindstorms product is also a powerful and functional robotics tool that allows people (young and old) to build robots without having advanced degrees in engineering and computer programming. In its current version, Mindstorms includes the programmable brick, several servo motors, a color sensor, a touch sensor, an infrared beacon, and several hundred building blocks to create more than a dozen different robots. The Mindstorms product comes with printed instructions and programming to build these basic robots, but the brick can be programmed and/or controlled by a personal computer or a mobile device (tablet, phablet, or smartphone) to create more robots. By adding additional Lego components, highly complex and large robots can be constructed and programmed.

Lego's Mindstorms social networking contains very little direct product advertising or promotion content, yet the company invests substantial resources in maintaining and developing its network of users. For example, Lego organizes in-person events and competitions where members can demonstrate their skills and learn from each other. An elite, invitation-only group called Mindstorms Community Partners tests new ideas, software, and hardware elements for the robotics system.

REQUIRED

1. As a toy manufacturer, Lego must always be sensitive to the needs of its customers, both children and their parents, which requires the company to pay close attention to changing preferences and trends. Visit the Lego Mindstorms Web site and identify specific social networking features. Based on what you learned in this chapter, write about 200 words in which you describe current developments in social networking that Lego will need to understand as it decides whether to continue, remove, or modify the social networking features you identified. In your discussion, identify at least two specific social networking features.

2. Lego provides a complete set of instructions with this product for building the basic robots. In about 200 words, explain how a new owner of this product might learn how to build and program complex robots using social networking elements provided by Lego.

3. In this chapter, you learned how newspapers, magazines, and broadcasters are using participatory journalism to have their readers to create news items and stories. In 200 words, outline at least five specific ways in which Mindstorms community members create value for Lego.

Note: Your instructor might assign you to a group to complete this case and might ask you to prepare a formal presentation of your results to your class.

C2. Betty's Treasures

Betty Shriver is the owner of Betty's Treasures, a small shop that sells collectible porcelain figurines and collectible pottery. Betty's shop carries many items that she purchased from estate sales and regional auctions, but the shop also sells handcrafted items made by local artisans, including greeting cards, stuffed toy animals, small pottery items, and knitted sweaters. The shop is located in Metamora, Indiana, which is a popular tourist destination for weekend travelers in the Midwest. The town of Old Metamora is a small historic area in a rural setting that is less than a day's drive from seven major metropolitan areas: Chicago, Cincinnati, Columbus, Detroit, Indianapolis, Louisville, and St. Louis.

The shop is very busy on weekends and during the spring and summer months when tourists flock to Old Metamora. In the early fall, the tourist traffic slows considerably, and in the winter months, the town becomes almost deserted. Several years ago, Betty began to pick up extra business during the off season by auctioning items on eBay. The auctions helped keep inventory moving during the slow months and Betty found that she could afford to carry a wider selection of items in the store. In the past, she would avoid buying unusual items at estate sales and auctions because they might not sell quickly in the shop. Now Betty knows that any item that does not sell in the shop can be auctioned online quite easily. Another unexpected benefit of participating in online auctions is that Betty developed relationships with regular buyers of figurines and with people who run collectibles stores in other parts of the country through their transactions on eBay.

Betty's online auction experiences prompted her to consider expanding the online portion of her business. She has heard from other shop owners that eBay allows people to create online stores within the eBay site and that Amazon.com offers a similar service that lists seller's items on Amazon.com's regular product pages. She is also interested in creating a Web site that contains photos and descriptions of popular figurines with additional information about how they are made. Betty is thinking that including a list of figurines that are no longer manufactured (which makes them more valuable) and a guide to buying collectible figurines that could help her customers and bidders on her auctions make more informed decisions as they add to their collections. She believes that such a site could attract a large number of people interested in figurines. She wants to find ways to direct these site visitors to her auctions and her proposed Web store. Betty has hired you as a consultant to build on her ideas and to help her develop an expansion strategy for her online business activities.

REQUIRED

1. Use your favorite Web search engine or your library to search for information about selling on Amazon Marketplace and eBay Stores. Based on your research, compare these two options for Betty's online sales of figurines. Include relevant facts, including specific costs of operating each type of store and specific benefits provided by each option. Summarize your recommendation and supporting facts in a report to Betty of about 200 words.

2. Using what you have learned in this chapter, outline a general social networking strategy that Betty could use to increase online sales of figurines that would work for either of the Amazon Marketplace or eBay Stores options. Be sure to consider including a Web site in your strategy that would be separate from the Betty's Treasures Amazon Marketplace or eBay Store presence. Summarize your strategy recommendations for Betty in about 200 words.

3. Visit the Etsy Web site and search online or in your library for information about selling on that site. Based on your research, evaluate Betty's potential use of that site to make online sales of the handcrafted items she sells that are made by local artisans. Summarize your findings in a report to Betty of about 200 words.

4. Both Etsy and the We Love Etsy Web sites include social networking features that could help Betty's Treasures become better known online. Identify specific ways in which Betty could use those features on both sites to increase the store's sales and develop a plan that includes them. Summarize your plan for Betty in about 200 words.

Note: Your instructor might assign you to a group to complete this case and might ask you to prepare a formal presentation of your results to your class.

For Further Study and Research

Albanesius, C. 2015. "Good Luck, Microsoft: Android, iOS on 96.8 Percent of Smartphones," *PC Magazine*, August 20. http://www.pcmag.com/article2/0,2817,2489815,00.asp

Barnes, N., A. Lescault, and S. Wright. 2013. *2013 Fortune 500 Are Bullish on Social Media*. Dartmouth, MA: University of Massachusetts-Dartmouth Center for Marketing Research. http://www.umassd.edu/cmr/socialmediaresearch/2013fortune500/

Belson, K., R. Hof, and B. Elgin. 2001. "How Yahoo! Japan Beat eBay at Its Own Game," *Business Week*, June 4, 58.

Bersin, J. 2013. "The MOOC Marketplace Takes Off," *Forbes*, November 30. http://www.forbes.com/sites/joshbersin/2013/11/30/the-mooc-marketplace-takes-off/

Boyd, D. and N. Ellison. (2007). "Social Network Sites: Definition, History, and Scholarship," *Journal of Computer-Mediated Communication*, 13(1). http://jcmc.indiana.edu/vol13/issue1/boyd.ellison.html

Breckenridge, M. 2008. "Old Meets New at Etsy," *Akron Beacon Journal*, March 6, D1.

Brown, J., L. Davison, and J. Hagel. 2010. *The Power of Pull*. New York: Basic Books.

Cassady, R. 1967. *Auctions and Auctioneering*. Berkeley, CA: University of California Press.

Chafkin, M. 2007. "How to Kill a Great Idea!" *Inc. Magazine*, June 1. http://www.inc.com/magazine/20070601/features-how-to-kill-a-great-idea.html

Chang, A. 2003. "Hospitals Auction Nursing Shifts Online," *The Boston Globe*, December 28, A28.

Chen, K. and K. Qiu Haixu. 2004. "Chinese E-Commerce Sites Allow Small Firms to Reach Wider Base," *The Wall Street Journal*, February 25, A12.

Chua, A. and S. Banerjee. 2013. "Customer Knowledge Management Via Social Media: The Case of Starbucks," *Journal of Knowledge Management*, 17(2), 237–249.

Cohen, A. 2001. "The Sniper King," *On Magazine*, May.

Colvin, J. 2013. "Questions for Starbucks' Chief Bean Counter," *Fortune*, December 9, 78–82.

Credit Union Management. 2007. "Focus on Microlending: Kiva Is People Helping People," May 12.

Denning, S. 2015. "Five Reasons Why Google+ Died," *Forbes*, April 17. http://www.forbes.com/sites/stevedenning/2015/04/17/five-reasons-why-google-died/

The Economist. 2015. "Alpine Android: Cyanogen Plots to Unseat Google's Platform," August 8, 54.

The Economist. 2015. "The Everything Creditor: Bad Loans for Sale in Online Auctions," June 6, 36.

Elliott, S. 2013. "Campbell Bets on the Wisdom of a Child," *The New York Times*, September 10, B5.

eMarketer. 2015. "Social Network Ad Spending to Hit $23.68 Billion Worldwide in 2015," April 15. http://www.emarketer.com/Article/Social-Network-Ad-Spending-Hit-2368-Billion-Worldwide-2015/1012357

Enge, E. 2015. "Hard Numbers for Public Posting Activity on Google Plus," *Stone Temple Consulting*, April 14. https://www.stonetemple.com/real-numbers-for-the-activity-on-google-plus/

Euchner, J. 2012. "The Evolution of Innovation," *Research-Technology Management*, September–October, 18–23.

Ferraro, N. 2008. "Lending & Philanthropy 2.0," *InformationWeek*, February 4, 40.

Flandez, R. 2008. "Building an Online Community of Loyal and Vocal Users," *The Wall Street Journal*, March 6, B5.

Ghawi, D. and G. Schneider. 2004. "New Approaches to Online Procurement," *Proceedings of the Academy of Information and Management Sciences*, 8(2), October, 25–28.

Gilbert, J. and A. Kerwin. 1999. "Newspapers Carve Slice of Auction Pie," *Advertising Age*, 70(26), June 21, 32–34.

Hagel, J. and J. Brown. 2012. "Why Most Online Communities Are Failures," *CNNMoney*, January 18. http://management.fortune.cnn.com/2012/01/18/why-most-online-communities-are-failures/

Hagel, J. and J. Brown, 2013. "What Every Company Can Learn from Lego," *CNNMoney*, August 6, 2013. http://management.fortune.cnn.com/2013/08/06/lego/

Hanlon, P. and J. Hawkins. 2008. "Expand Your Brand Community Online," *Advertising Age*, January 7, 14–15.

Harger, J. 2015. "Micro-loans for Small Businesses Get $5M Pledge from Huntington Bank," *MLive*, July 28. http://www.mlive.com/business/west-michigan/index.ssf/2015/07/micro-loans_for_small_business.html

Hayes, M. 2012. "The Pros and Cons of Selling on Amazon and eBay," *Shopify*, August 10. http://www.shopify.com/blog/6399562-the-pros-and-cons-of-selling-on-amazon-and-ebay

Heffernan, V. 2011. "The Old Internet Neighborhoods," *The New York Times*, July 10. http://opinionator.blogs.nytimes.com/2011/07/10/remembrance-of-message-boards-past/

Herrman, J. 2013. "Campbell's Go Soup Drives Advocacy Through Social Millennial Influencers," *Social Media Link*, November 1. http://www.socialmedialink.com/success/4

Holmes, R. 2013. "Big Global Social Networks Are Closing in on Facebook," *HootSource*, May 22. http://blog.hootsuite.com/global-networks-on-facebook/

IDC. 2015. "Android and iOS Squeeze the Competition," February 24. http://www.idc.com/getdoc .jsp?containerId=prUS25450615

Kennedy, J. 1998. "Radio Daze," *Technology Review*, 101(6), November–December, 68–71.

Lashinsky, A. 2013. "Jogging in Stride with Warren Buffet: Brooks Running CEO Jim Weber," *Fortune*, December 9, 50.

Lawler, R. 2014. "Tinder-For-Jobs App Jobr Raises $2 Million In Seed Funding," *TechCrunch*, July 17. http://techcrunch.com/2014/07/17/jobr-2m/

Lewin, T. 2013. "Universities Abroad Join Partnerships on the Web," *The New York Times*, February 21, A18.

MacMillan, D., P. Burrows, and S. Ante. 2009. "The App Economy," *Business Week*, November 2, 44–49.

Miller, C. 2011. "Another Try By Google to Take on Facebook," *The New York Times*, June 28. http:// www.nytimes.com/2011/06/29/technology/29google.html

Miller, K. 2007. "An eBay for the Arts and Crafts Set," *Business Week*, July 23, 70.

Morris, L. 2013. "MOOCs: Emerging Technologies and Quality," *Innovative Higher Education*, 38(4), 251–252.

Moth, D. 2013. "How Starbucks Uses Pinterest, Facebook, Twitter, and Google+," *Econsultancy*, March 6. http://econsultancy.com/us/blog/62281-how-starbucks-uses-pinterest-facebook-twitter-and-google

Murph, D. 2013. "Updated Google Wallet App for Android Delivers Easier Mobile Payments," *Engadget*, September 17. http://www.engadget.com/2013/09/17/updated-google-wallet-app-android-easier-mobile-payments/

Newton, C. 2015. "How Google Solved Our Photo Backup Nightmare," *The Verge*, May 29. http:// www.theverge.com/a/sundars-google/google-photos-google-io-2015

Olenick, D. 2015. "Apple iOS and Google Android Smartphone Market Share Flattening," *Forbes*, May 27. http://www.forbes.com/sites/dougolenick/2015/05/27/ apple-ios-and-google-android-smartphone-market-share-flattening-idc/

Olenski, S. 2013. "Social Media Usage Up 800% for U.S. Online Adults in Just Eight Years," *Forbes*, September 6. http://www.forbes.com/sites/steveolenski/2013/09/06/ social-media-usage-up-800-for-us-online-adults-in-just-8-years/

Okazaki, S. and M. Yague. 2012. "Responses to an Adver-gaming Campaign on a Mobile Social Networking Site: An Initial Research Report," *Computers in Human Behavior*, 28(1), January, 78–86.

Pappano, L. 2012. "The Year of the MOOC," *The New York Times*, November 4, ED26.

Pearson, B. 2015. "Mobile Order & Pay: The Ultimate Brand Experience (Just Ask Starbucks)," *Business2Community*, August 25. http://www.business2community.com/branding/ mobile-order-pay-ultimate-brand-experience-just-ask-starbucks-01310285

Petrecca, L. and B. Snyder. 1998. "Auction Universe Puts in $10 Mil Bid for Customers," *Advertising Age*, 43(8), October 26, 8.

Pierce, D. 2015. "Google+ as We Knew It Is Dead, But Google Is Still a Social Network," *Wired*, March 2. http://www.wired.com/2015/03/google-knew-dead-google-still-social-network/

Prochnow, D. 2010. "Creating Mobile Apps With a Point and a Click," *Popular Science*, January 22. http://www.popsci.com/diy/article/2010-01/point-and-click-apps

Purchasing. 2001. "What Top Supply Execs Say About Auctions," 130(12), June 21, S2–S3.

Quan, J. 1999. "Risky Business," *Rolling Stone*, March 4, 91–92.

Rheingold, H. 1993. *The Virtual Community: Homesteading on the Electronic Frontier*. New York: HarperCollins.

Rheingold, H. 2002. *Smart Mobs*. Cambridge, MA: Basic.

Robins, W. 2000. "Auctions.com Now a Dot-Goner," *Editor & Publisher*, August 28, 6.

Seligson, H. 2015. "Making Room (on the Internet) for Daddy," *The New York Times*, May 3, ST10.

Siegal, J. 2013. "Tablet Shipments Speed Ahead, Threaten to Lap the PC," *BGR*, October 21. http://bgr.com/2013/10/21/tablet-growth-2013-pc-shipments-decline/

Stambor, Z. 2015. "Retailers Can't Ignore Social Media's 70% of Active Daily Users," *Internet Retailer*, August 20. https://www.internetretailer.com/2015/08/20/why-retailers-cant-ignore-social-media

Tabuchi, H. 2011. "Facebook Wins Relatively Few Friends in Japan," *The New York Times*, January 10, B1.

Takahashi, T. 2010. "MySpace or Mixi? Japanese Engagement with Social Networking Sites in the Global Age," *New Media & Society*, 12(3), 453–475.

Taub, E. 2013. "The Path to Happy Employment, Contact by Contact on LinkedIn," *The New York Times*, December 5, B10.

Team, T. 2015. "Digital Payments and Ultra-Premium Coffee Drive Revenue Growth For Starbucks," *Forbes*, July 29. http://www.forbes.com/sites/greatspeculations/2015/07/29/digital-payments-ultra-premium-coffee-drive-revenue-growth-for-starbucks-in-q3/

Thaler, W. 1994. *The Winner's Curse: Paradoxes and Anomalies of Economic Life*. Princeton, NJ: Princeton University Press.

Tugend, A. 2009. "Losing Out After Winning an Online Auction," *The New York Times*, October 24. http://www.nytimes.com/2009/10/24/technology/24shortcuts.html

Vickrey, W. 1961. "Counterspeculation, Auctions, and Competitive Sealed Tenders," *Journal of Finance*, 16(1), March, 8–37.

Waldrop, M. 2013. "Massive Open Online Courses, aka MOOCs, Transform Higher Education and Science," *Scientific American*, March 13. http://www.scientificamerican.com/article.cfm?id=massive-open-online-courses-transform-higher-education-and-science

Wagner, M. 2009. "Smartphone App: What the Doctor Ordered." *InformationWeek*, Manhasset, NY.

Wireless Federation. 2009. "NTT DoCoMo's Credit Payment Subscriptions Reach 10 Million Mark," August 26. http://wirelessfederation.com/news/17894-ntt-docomos-credit-payment-subscriptions-reach-10mn-mark/

Young, J. 2013. *Beyond the MOOC Hype: A Guide to Higher Education's High-Tech Disruption*. Washington, DC: Chronicle of Higher Education Press.

Zhivago, K. 2012. "Are Your Customers Using Social Media to Warn Others to Stay Away?" *Revenue Journal*, June 17. http://www.revenuejournal.com/blog/are-your-customers-using-social-media-warn-others-stay-away

Zickuhr, K. 2013. *Location-Based Services*. Washington, DC: Pew Research Center's Internet & American Life Project.

Zimmerman, E. 2007. "Investing in the Women of Ghana," *FSB: Fortune Small Business*, 17(4), May, 101–102.

Zwilling, M. 2013. "The Old Ways of Social Media Marketing Are Broken," *Forbes*, November 29. http://www.forbes.com/sites/martinzwilling/2013/11/29/the-old-ways-of-social-media-marketing-are-broken/

The Environment of Electronic Commerce: Legal, Ethical, and Tax Issues

Blend Images Photography/Veer

LEARNING OBJECTIVES

In this chapter, you will learn:

*   How the legal environment affects electronic commerce activities
*   What elements combine to form a business contract online
*   When copyright, patent, and trademark laws govern the use of intellectual property online
*   How the Internet has opened doors for online crime, terrorism, and warfare
*   What ethics issues arise for companies conducting electronic commerce
*   Ways to resolve conflicts between companies' desire to collect and use their customers' data and the privacy rights of those customers
*   How taxes are levied on electronic commerce activities

INTRODUCTION

Apple's App Store gives iPhone and iPad users an easy and convenient way to purchase apps for their Apple smartphone and tablet device products, generating more than $10 billion each year in revenue for Apple. Many of these apps include the option to make further purchases while in the app itself. For example, a free app that has a premium version with more features can allow the user to upgrade the app from within the app itself. Another example is when a game app allows users to purchase hints or additional features from within the app. A number of games are provided free in the App Store and rely on such in-app purchases to generate revenue for the game creator.

To make these in-app purchases even more convenient, Apple decided to allow these transactions within the first 15 minutes after a user purchased an app without requiring the user to enter a password. Unfortunately, this convenience allowed children whose parents had purchased an app for them to buy an unlimited amount of additional content. In one case, a little girl spent $2600 to buy add-on content for her new app, Tap Pet Hotel, within that 15-minute window.

After receiving numerous complaints, Apple agreed in 2013 to refund these and similar charges, but a U.S. Federal Trade Commission (FTC) investigation had begun. In 2014, Apple agreed to settle with its customers, who had filed more than 37,000 claims, for $32.5 million. As part of the settlement, Apple agreed to make the 15-minute purchase authorization terms more clear to customers and to give those customers an explicit choice to accept or reject the purchase period.

In 2015, the FTC began another investigation of Apple, this time for the potential anticompetitive nature of Apple's practice of adding 30 percent to any commercial transaction processed through an app purchased in the company's App Store. For online music providers, such as Spotify and Rdio, this additional charge could make them less competitive with Apple's own iTunes music service. For example, Spotify sells it service for a monthly fee of $10 on its own Web site, but charges $13 per month to users who sign up through the Spotify app downloaded from Apple's App Store. The FTC probe is ongoing and could eventually prompt the U.S. Justice Department to launch its own investigation.

Companies that do business on the Web expose themselves, often unwittingly, to liabilities that arise from today's business environment. That environment includes laws and ethical considerations that may be different from those with which the business is familiar. As you will learn in this chapter, Apple is by no means the only Web business that has run afoul of laws and regulations. As companies do business online, they can find themselves subject to unfamiliar laws and different ethical frameworks much more rapidly than when they operated in familiar physical domains.

The Legal Environment of Electronic Commerce

Businesses that operate on the Web must comply with the same laws and regulations that govern the operations of all businesses. If they do not, they face the same penalties—including fines, reparation payments, court-imposed dissolution, and even jail time for officers and owners—that any business faces.

Businesses operating on the Web face two additional complicating factors as they try to comply with the law. First, the Web extends a company's reach beyond traditional boundaries. As you learned in Chapter 1, a business that uses the Web gains international reach instantly, which could subject it to many more laws more quickly than a traditional brick-and-mortar business based in a specific physical location. Second, the Web increases the speed and efficiency of business communications. As you learned in Chapters 3 and 4, customers often have much more interactive and complex relationships with online merchants than they do with traditional merchants. Further, the Web creates a network of customers who often have significant levels of interaction with each other. In Chapter 5, you learned how companies use online communications to facilitate complex strategic alliances and supply web relationships. These communication- and information-sharing channels also expose an organization's operations to other entities. In Chapter 6, you learned how online businesses use social networks to create and maintain relationships with their customers. Web businesses that violate the law or breach ethical standards can face rapid and intense reactions from large numbers of customers, vendors, and other stakeholders who become aware of the businesses' activities almost instantly.

Using Internet technologies can also change the structure of businesses in ways that create new legal questions. For example, taxi companies have done business for decades by buying cars, hiring drivers, and then providing those cars and drivers to customers. The law has evolved to regulate that business by requiring taxi companies to buy licenses to operate in specific geographic areas and by passing laws that require the companies to keep records and establish standards for driver qualifications and vehicle specifications. Today, companies such as Lyft and Uber are in a similar business, brokering rides between drivers/vehicle owners and riders, but face an unclear legal environment. Whether the brokers or the drivers/owners are subject to various vehicle-for-hire laws and regulations is a question that remains unresolved in many places around the world.

In this section, you will learn about the issues of borders, jurisdiction, and Web site content and how these factors affect a company's ability to conduct electronic commerce. You will also learn about legal and ethical issues that arise when the Web is used in the commission of crimes, terrorist acts, and even the conduct of war.

Borders and Jurisdiction

Territorial borders in the physical world serve a useful purpose in traditional commerce: They mark the range of culture and reach of applicable laws very clearly. Legal rules, languages, currency, and cultural customs differ from one country to another. In the physical world, geographic boundaries almost always coincide with legal and cultural boundaries. The limits of what constitutes acceptable behavior and the laws that are adopted in a geographic area are both influenced by that area's dominant culture. The relationships among a society's culture, laws, and ethical standards appear in Figure 7-1, which shows that culture affects laws directly and indirectly through its effect on ethical standards. The figure also shows that laws and ethical standards affect each other.

The geographic boundaries on culture are logical; for most of our history, slow methods of transportation and conflicts among various nations have prevented people from traveling great distances to learn about other cultures. Both restrictions have changed in recent years, however, and now people can travel easily from one country to another within many geographic regions. One example is the European Union (EU), which allows free movement within the EU for citizens of member countries. Most of the EU countries (Great Britain being a notable exception) now use a common currency (the euro) instead of their former individual currencies. Legal scholars define the relationship between geographic boundaries and legal boundaries in terms of four elements: power, effects, legitimacy, and notice.

POWER

Power is a form of control over physical space and the people and objects that reside in that space, and is a defining characteristic of statehood. For laws to be effective, a government must be able to enforce them. Effective enforcement requires the power both to exercise physical control over residents, if necessary, and to impose sanctions on those who violate the law. The ability of a government to exert control over a person or corporation is called **jurisdiction**.

Laws in the physical world do not apply to people who are not located in or do not own assets in the geographic area that created those particular laws. For example, the United States cannot enforce its copyright laws on a citizen of Japan who is doing business in Japan and owns no assets in the United States. Japanese citizens who bring goods into the United States to sell, however, are subject to applicable U.S. laws. A Japanese Web site that offers delivery of goods into the United States is, similarly, subject to applicable U.S. laws.

The level of power asserted by a government is limited to that which is accepted by the culture that exists within its geographic boundaries. Ideally, geographic boundaries, cultural groupings, and legal structures all coincide. When they do not, internal strife and civil wars can erupt.

EFFECTS

Laws in the physical world are grounded in the relationship between physical proximity and the effects, or impact, of a person's behavior. Personal or corporate actions have stronger effects on people and things that are nearby than on those that are far away. Government-provided trademark protection is a good example of this. For instance, the Italian government can provide and enforce trademark protection for a business named Casa di Baffi located in Rome. The effects of another restaurant using the same name

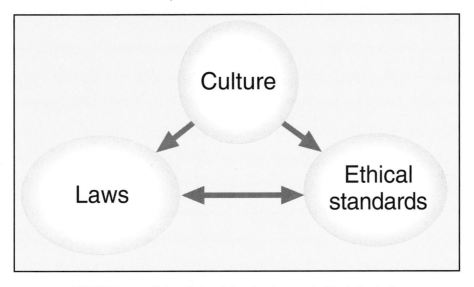

FIGURE 7-1   Culture helps determine laws and ethical standards

are strongest in Rome, somewhat less in geographic areas close to Rome, and even less in other parts of Italy. That is, the effects diminish as geographic distance increases. If someone were to open a restaurant in Kansas City and call it Casa di Baffi, the restaurant in Rome would experience few, if any, negative effects from the use of its trademarked name in Kansas City because it is so far away and because so few people would be potential customers of both restaurants. Thus, the effects of the trademark infringement would be controlled by Italian law because of the limited range within which such an infringement has an effect.

The characteristics of laws are determined by the local culture's acceptance or rejection of various kinds of effects. For example, certain communities in the United States require that houses be built on lots that are at least 5 acres. Other communities prohibit outdoor advertising of various kinds. The local cultures in these communities make the effects of such restrictions acceptable.

Once businesses began operating online, they found that traditional effects-based measures did not apply as well and that the laws based on these measures did not work well either. For example, France has a law that prohibits the sale of Nazi memorabilia. The effects of this law were limited to people in France and they considered it reasonable. U.S. laws do not include a similar prohibition because U.S. culture makes a different trade-off between the value of memorabilia (in general) and the negative cultural memory of Nazism. When U.S.-based online auction sites began hosting auctions of Nazi memorabilia, those sites were in compliance with U.S. laws. However, because of the international nature of the Web, these auctions were available to people around the world, including residents of France. In other words, the effects of U.S. culture and law were being felt in France. The French government ordered Yahoo! Auctions to stop these auctions. Yahoo! argued that it was in compliance with U.S. law, but the French government insisted that the effects of those Yahoo! Auctions extended to France and thus violated French law. To avoid protracted legal actions over the jurisdiction issue, Yahoo! decided that it would no longer carry such auctions.

LEGITIMACY

Most people agree that the legitimate right to create and enforce laws derives from the mandate of those who are subject to those laws. In 1970, the United Nations passed a resolution that affirmed this idea of governmental legitimacy. The resolution made clear that the people residing within a set of recognized geographic boundaries are the ultimate source of legitimate legal authority for people and actions within those boundaries. Thus, **legitimacy** is the idea that those subject to laws should have some role in formulating them.

Some cultures allow their governments to operate with a high degree of autonomy and unquestioned authority. China and Singapore are countries in which national culture permits the government to exert high levels of unchecked authority. Other cultures, such as those of the Scandinavian countries, place strict limits on governmental authority.

The levels of authority and autonomy with which governments of various countries operate vary significantly from one country to another. Online businesses must be ready to deal with a wide variety of regulations and levels of enforcement of those regulations as they expand their businesses to other countries. This can be difficult for smaller businesses that operate on the Web.

NOTICE

Physical boundaries are a convenient and effective way to announce the ending of one legal or cultural system and the beginning of another. The physical boundary, when crossed, provides **notice** that one set of rules has been replaced by a different set of rules. Notice is the expression of such a change in rules. People can obey and perceive a law or cultural norm as fair only if they are notified of its existence. Borders provide this notice in the physical world. The legal systems of most countries include a concept called constructive notice. People receive **constructive notice** that they have become subject to new laws and cultural norms when they cross an international border, even if they are not specifically warned of the changed laws and norms by a sign or a border guard's statement. Thus, ignorance of the law is not a sustainable defense, even in a new and unfamiliar jurisdiction.

This concept presents particular problems for online businesses because they may not know that customers from another country are accessing their Web sites. Thus, the concept of notice—even constructive notice—does not translate very well to online business. The relationship between physical geographic boundaries and legal boundaries in terms of these four elements is summarized in Figure 7-2.

Jurisdiction on the Internet

The tasks of defining, establishing, and asserting jurisdiction are much more difficult on the Internet than they are in the physical world, mainly because traditional geographic boundaries do not exist. For example, a Swedish company that engages in electronic commerce could have a Web site that is entirely in English and a URL that ends in ".com,"

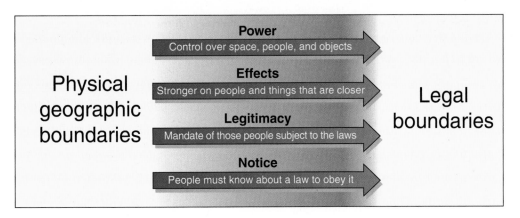

FIGURE 7-2   Physical geographic boundaries lead to legal boundaries

thus not indicating to customers that it is a Swedish firm. The server that hosts this company's Web page could be in Canada, and the people who maintain the Web site might work from their homes in Australia. If a Mexican citizen buys a product from the Swedish firm and is unhappy with the goods received, that person might want to file a lawsuit against the seller firm. However, the world's physical border-based systems of law and jurisdiction do not help this Mexican citizen determine where to file the lawsuit. The Internet does not provide anything like the obvious international boundary lines in the physical world. Thus, the four considerations that work so well in the physical world—power, effects, legitimacy, and notice—do not translate very well to the virtual world of electronic commerce.

Governments that want to enforce laws regarding business conduct on the Internet must establish jurisdiction over that conduct. A **contract** is a promise or set of promises between two or more legal entities—people or corporations—that provides for an exchange of value (goods, services, or money) between or among them. If either party to a contract does not comply with the terms of the contract, the other party can sue for failure to comply, which is called **breach of contract**. Persons and corporations that engage in business are also expected to exercise due care and not violate laws that prohibit specific actions (such as trespassing, libel, or professional malpractice). A **tort** is an intentional or negligent action (other than breach of contract) taken by a legal entity that causes harm to another legal entity. People or corporations that want to enforce their rights based on either contract or tort law must file their claims in courts with jurisdiction to hear their cases. A court has **sufficient jurisdiction** to hear a matter if it has both subject-matter jurisdiction and personal jurisdiction.

SUBJECT-MATTER JURISDICTION

Subject-matter jurisdiction is a court's authority to decide a particular type of dispute. For example, in the United States, federal courts have subject-matter jurisdiction over issues governed by federal law (such as bankruptcy, copyright, patent, and federal tax matters), and state courts have subject-matter jurisdiction over issues governed by state laws (such as professional licensing and state tax matters). If the parties to a contract are both located in the same state, a state court has subject-matter jurisdiction over disputes that arise from the terms of that contract. The rules for determining whether a court has subject-matter jurisdiction are clear and easy to apply. Few disputes arise over subject-matter jurisdiction.

PERSONAL JURISDICTION

Personal jurisdiction is, in general, determined by the residence of the parties. A court has personal jurisdiction over a case if the defendant is a resident of the state in which the court is located. In such cases, the determination of personal jurisdiction is straightforward. However, an out-of-state person or corporation can also voluntarily submit to the jurisdiction of a particular state court by agreeing to do so in writing or by taking certain actions in the state.

One of the most common ways that people voluntarily submit to a jurisdiction is by signing a contract that includes a statement, known as a **forum selection clause**, that the contract will be enforced according to the laws of a particular state. That state then has personal jurisdiction over the parties who signed the contract regarding any enforcement issue that arises from the terms of that contract. Figure 7-3 shows a typical forum selection clause that might be used on a Web site.

> These terms of use shall be governed by and construed in accordance with the laws of the State of Washington, without regard to its conflict of laws rules. Any legal action arising out of this Agreement shall be litigated and enforced under the laws of the State of Washington. In addition, you agree to submit to the jurisdiction of the courts of the State of Washington, and that any legal action pursued by you shall be within the exclusive jurisdiction of the courts of King County in the State of Washington.

FIGURE 7-3   A typical forum selection clause

In the United States, individual states have laws that can create personal jurisdiction for their courts. The details of these laws, called **long-arm statutes**, vary from state to state, but generally create personal jurisdiction over nonresidents who transact business or commit tortious acts in the state. For example, suppose that a company based in Arizona charges a customer in California for something she did not order. The company's tortious behavior in California could trigger California's long-arm statute and give its courts personal jurisdiction over the matter.

Companies should be aware of jurisdictional issues when conducting online business across state and international lines. In most states, the application of these laws to companies doing business is still evolving; however, the more business activities a company conducts in a state, the more likely a court will assert personal jurisdiction over that company using its long-arm statute.

An exception to the general rule for determining personal jurisdiction can arise in the case of tortious acts. A business can commit a tortious act by selling a product that causes harm to a buyer. The tortious act can be a **negligent tort**, in which the seller unintentionally provides a harmful product, or it can be an **intentional tort**, in which the seller knowingly or recklessly causes injury to the buyer. The most common business-related intentional torts involve defamation, misrepresentation, fraud, and theft of trade secrets. Courts tend to invoke their respective states' long-arm statutes much more often in cases of tortious acts than in breach of contract cases. If the case involves an intentional tort or a criminal act, courts will assert jurisdiction even more liberally.

JURISDICTION IN INTERNATIONAL COMMERCE

Jurisdiction issues that arise in international business are even more complex than the rules governing personal jurisdiction across state lines within the United States. The exercise of jurisdiction across international borders is governed by treaties between the countries engaged in the dispute. Some of the treaties that the United States has signed with other countries provide specific determinations of jurisdiction for disputes that might arise. However, in most matters, U.S. courts determine personal jurisdiction for foreign companies and people in much the same way that these courts interpret the long-arm statutes in domestic matters. Non-U.S. corporations and individuals can be sued in U.S. courts if they conduct business or commit tortious acts in the United States. Similarly, foreign courts can enforce decisions against U.S. corporations or individuals through the U.S. court system if those courts can establish jurisdiction over the matter.

Courts asked to enforce the laws of other nations sometimes follow a principle called **judicial comity**, which means that they voluntarily enforce other countries' laws or judgments out of a sense of comity, or friendly civility. However, most courts are reluctant to serve as forums for international disputes. Also, courts are designed to deal with weighing evidence and making findings of right and wrong. International disputes often require diplomacy and the weighing of costs and benefits. Courts are not designed to do cost–benefit evaluations and cannot engage in negotiation and diplomacy. Thus, courts (especially U.S. courts) prefer to have the executive branch of the government (primarily the State Department) negotiate international agreements and resolve international disputes.

The difficulties of operating in multiple countries are faced by many large companies that do business online. For example, eBay, which had invested more than $280 million in its Chinese operations, struggled to compete against Alibaba.com's TaoBao consumer auction unit and finally closed its operations in the country in 2006. Some observers believe that a Chinese cultural tendency to favor homegrown online services caused eBay's difficulties; however, others noted that Chinese laws favored Chinese companies and blocked eBay's PayPal unit from operating in China. Some have even accused the Chinese government of intentionally blocking access to eBay's site for a few minutes each day so that Chinese competitors (some of which were owned, in part or completely, by the Chinese government) would appear to be more reliable. Many argued that eBay, as a foreign company, was at a considerable disadvantage because of these government regulations.

The culture and government of China were also problematic for Google. In 2006, after going through the lengthy process of obtaining a government license to open a search engine site based in China (Google.cn; the company had operated Chinese language versions of Google.com for years), Google found its license revoked after less than three months of operations. The Chinese authorities questioned whether Google was operating a search engine (as permitted under the license) or a news service (under Chinese law, foreign owners are not permitted to operate online news services). Google worked hard to satisfy China's bureaucrats and was granted another operating license in 2007. After two years of operation under the new license, during which a number of conflicts arose between Google and the Chinese government over censorship, Google found that its computer systems in China had been hacked. Internal investigations concluded that the sophistication of the attack and its targets suggested that the Chinese government was involved in the attack. Specifically, the hackers had accessed the e-mail accounts of Chinese dissidents and human rights activists. In 2010, as a result of the attack and a general weariness with fighting with government censors, Google decided to close its operations in China.

Jurisdictional issues are complex and change rapidly. Any business that intends to conduct business online with customers or vendors in other countries should consult an attorney who is well versed in issues of international jurisdiction. However, there are a number of resources online that can be useful to nonlawyers who want to do preliminary investigation of a legal topic such as jurisdiction. The Harvard Law School's Berkman Center for Internet & Society Web site includes links to many current Internet-related legal issues and the Berkeley Technology Law Journal includes articles that analyze these topics.

Conflict of Laws

In the United States, business is governed by federal laws, state laws, and local laws. Sometimes, these laws address the same issues in different ways. Lawyers call this situation a **conflict of laws**. Because online businesses usually serve broad markets that span many localities and many states, they generally look to federal laws for guidance. On occasion, this can lead to problems with state and local laws.

One online business that faced a serious conflict of laws problem was the online wine sales industry. Since the repeal of national Prohibition in 1933, all U.S. states and most local governments have enacted a myriad of laws that heavily regulate all types of alcoholic beverage sales. These laws govern when and where alcoholic beverages of various kinds can be sold, who can purchase them, and where they can be consumed.

The U.S. Constitution's Commerce Clause prohibits the states from passing laws that interfere with interstate commerce. However, the states do have the right to regulate matters pertaining to the health and welfare of their citizens. Under this right, most states have laws that require alcoholic beverages be sold through a regulated system of producers, wholesalers, and retailers. Some states allowed producers (such as wineries) to sell directly to the public, but only within that state. When online wine stores wanted to sell their products across state lines, they encountered these laws. Some states allowed the sales, others allowed the sales if the online store delivered to a licensed retailer in the destination state, and some states prohibited all sales by online stores not located within the state. This situation resulted in a classic conflict of laws.

State and local laws regulate the sale of alcoholic beverages in the interest of the health and welfare of the state's citizens, yet those same laws give in-state producers an advantage over out-of-state producers (in some states, in-state producers could sell directly without adding the markup of a retailer; in other states, out-of-state producers could not compete at all). When a state law gives an in-state business an advantage over an out-of-state business, the free flow of interstate commerce is impeded and courts often rule in such cases that the U.S. Constitution's Commerce Clause is violated.

For years, the online wine industry worked to find a way to resolve these issues with the states, but did not have much success. Finally, wineries filed suit on the Commerce Clause violation issue. In 2005, the U.S. Supreme Court voted 5–4 to strike down Michigan and New York laws that barred out-of-state wineries from selling directly to consumers. Although the Supreme Court decision prohibits states from establishing laws that discriminate against out-of-state sellers, each state still can enforce laws limiting direct sales by all sellers and can specify that shipments originate within the state. You can learn more about the current state of legal challenges in this business at Free the Grapes, the Web site of a wine industry trade association that tracks developments in this area of online law.

Contracting and Contract Enforcement in Electronic Commerce

Any contract includes three essential elements: an offer, an acceptance, and consideration. The contract is formed when one party accepts the offer of another party. An **offer** is a commitment with certain terms made to another party, such as a declaration of willingness to buy or sell a product or service. An offer can be revoked as long as no payment, delivery of service, or other consideration has been accepted. An **acceptance** is the expression of willingness to take an offer, including all of its stated terms. **Consideration** is the agreed-upon exchange of something valuable, such as money, property, or future services. When a party accepts an offer based on the exchange of valuable goods or services, a contract has been created. An **implied contract** can also be formed by two or more parties that act as if a contract exists, even if no contract has been written and signed.

CREATING CONTRACTS: OFFERS AND ACCEPTANCES

People enter into contracts on a daily, and often hourly, basis. Every kind of agreement or exchange between parties, no matter how simple, is a type of contract. Every time a consumer buys an item at the supermarket, the elements of a valid contract are met, for example, through the following sequence of actions:

1. The store invites offers for an item at a stated price by placing it on a store shelf.

2. The consumer makes an offer by indicating a willingness to buy the product for the stated price. For example, the consumer might take the item to a checkout station and present it to a clerk with an offer to pay.

3. The store accepts the customer's offer and exchanges its product for the consumer's payment at the checkout station. Both the store and the customer receive consideration at this point.

Contracts are a key element of traditional business practice, and they are equally important on the Internet. Offers and acceptances can occur when parties exchange e-mail messages, engage in electronic data interchange (EDI), or fill out forms on Web pages. These Internet communications can be combined with traditional methods of forming contracts, such as the exchange of paper documents, faxes, and verbal agreements made over the telephone or in person. The requirements for forming a valid contract in an electronic commerce transaction are met, for example, through the following sequence of actions:

1. The Web site invites offers for an item at a stated price by serving a Web page that includes information about the item.

2. The consumer makes an offer by indicating a willingness to buy the product for the stated price by, for example, clicking an "Add to Shopping Cart" button on the Web page that displays the item.

3. The Web site accepts the customer's offer and exchanges its product for the consumer's credit card payment on its shopping cart checkout page. The Web site obtains consideration at this point and the customer obtains consideration when the product is received (or downloaded).

As you can see, the basic elements of a consumer's contract to buy goods are the same whether the transaction is completed in person or online. Only the form of the offer and acceptance are different in the two environments. The substance of the offer, acceptance, and the completed contract are the same.

When a seller advertises goods for sale on a Web site, that seller is not making an offer, but is inviting offers from potential buyers. If a Web ad were considered to be a legal offer to form a contract, the seller could easily become liable for the delivery of more goods than it has available to ship. A summary of the contracting process that occurs in an online sale appears in Figure 7-4.

When a buyer submits an order, which is an offer, the seller can accept that offer and create a contract. If the seller does not have the ordered items in stock, the seller has the option of refusing the buyer's order outright or counteroffering with a decreased amount. The buyer then has the option to accept the seller's counteroffer.

Making a legal acceptance of an offer is easy to do in most cases. When enforcing contracts, courts tend to view offers and acceptances as actions that occur within a particular context. If the actions are reasonable under the circumstances, courts tend to interpret those actions as offers and acceptances. For example, courts have held that a number of different actions—including mailing a check, shipping goods, shaking hands, nodding one's head, taking an item off a shelf, or opening a wrapped package—are each, in some circumstances, legally binding acceptances of offers. An excellent resource for many of the laws concerning contracts, especially as they pertain to U.S. businesses, is the Cornell Law School Web site, which includes the full text of the **Uniform Commercial Code (UCC)**.

CLICK-WRAP AND WEB-WRAP CONTRACT ACCEPTANCES

Most software sold today (either on CD or downloaded from the Internet) includes a contract that the user must accept before installing the software. These contracts, called **end-user license agreements (EULAs)**, often appear in a dialog box as part of the software installation process. When the user clicks the "Agree" button, the contract is deemed to be signed.

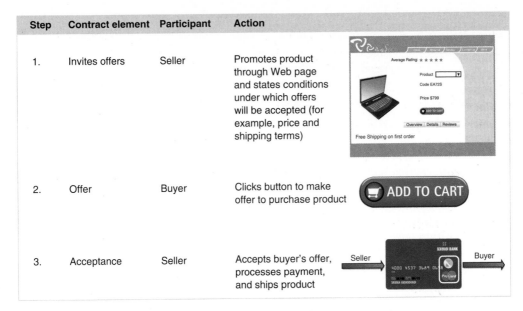

Step	Contract element	Participant	Action
1.	Invites offers	Seller	Promotes product through Web page and states conditions under which offers will be accepted (for example, price and shipping terms)
2.	Offer	Buyer	Clicks button to make offer to purchase product
3.	Acceptance	Seller	Accepts buyer's offer, processes payment, and ships product

FIGURE 7-4   Contracting process in an online sale

Years ago, when most software was sold in boxes that were encased in plastic shrink-wrap, EULAs were included on the box with a statement indicating that the buyer accepted the conditions of the EULA by removing the shrink-wrap from the box. This action was called a **shrink-wrap acceptance**. Today, a Web site user can agree to that site's EULA or its terms and conditions by clicking a button on the Web site (called a **click-wrap acceptance**) or by simply using the Web site (called a **Web-wrap acceptance** or **browser-wrap acceptance**).

Although many researchers and legal analysts have been critical of their use, U.S. courts have generally enforced the terms of EULAs to which users agreed using click-wrap or Web-wrap acceptances. Fewer cases have been adjudicated in the rest of the world. Although one case in Scotland (*Beta Computers v. Adobe Systems*) upheld a shrink-wrap acceptance, most European courts have not enforced contract terms considered to be abusive or suspect under the Unfair Contract Terms European Union Directive and the consumer protection laws of many European countries, even if the user had reasonable notice.

TERMS OF SERVICE AGREEMENTS

Many Web sites have stated rules that site visitors must follow, although most visitors are not aware of these rules. If you examine the home page of a Web site, you will often find a link to a page titled "Terms of Service," "Conditions of Use," "User Agreement," or something similar. If you follow that link, you find a page full of detailed rules and regulations, most of which are intended to limit the Web site owner's liability for what you might do with information you obtain from the site. These contracts are often called **terms of service (ToS)** agreements even when they appear under a different title. In most cases, a site visitor is held to the terms of service even if that visitor has not read the text or clicked a button to indicate agreement with the terms. The visitor is bound to the agreement by simply using the site, which is an example of the Web-wrap (or browser-wrap) acceptance discussed in the preceding section.

CREATING WRITTEN CONTRACTS ON THE WEB

In general, contracts are valid even if they are not in writing or signed. However, certain categories of contracts are not enforceable unless the terms are put into writing and signed by both parties. In 1677, the British Parliament enacted a law that specified the types of contracts that had to be in writing and signed. Following this British precedent, every state in the United States today has a similar law, called a **Statute of Frauds**. Although these state laws vary slightly, each Statute of Frauds specifies that contracts for the sale of goods worth more than $500 and contracts that require actions that cannot be completed within one year must be created by a signed writing. Fortunately for businesses and people who want to form contracts using electronic commerce, a writing does not require either pen or paper.

Most courts will hold that a **writing** exists when the terms of a contract have been reduced to some tangible form. An early court decision in the 1800s held that a telegraph transmission was a writing. Later courts have held that tape recordings of spoken words, computer files on disks, and faxes are writings. Thus, the parties to an electronic commerce contract should find it relatively easy to satisfy the writing requirement. Courts have been similarly generous in determining what constitutes a signature. A **signature** is any symbol executed or adopted for the purpose of authenticating a writing. Courts have held names on telegrams, telexes, faxes, and Western Union Mailgrams to be signatures. Even typed names or names printed as part of a letterhead have served as signatures. It is reasonable to assume that a symbol or code included in an electronic file would constitute a signature. Most countries now have laws that explicitly make digital signatures legally valid on contracts.

Firms conducting international electronic commerce do not need to worry about the signed writing requirement in most cases. The main treaty that governs international sales of goods, Article 11 of the United Nations Convention on Contracts for the International Sale of Goods (CISG), requires neither a writing nor a signature to create a legally binding acceptance. You can learn more about the CISG and related topics in international commercial law at the Pace University Law School CISG Database Web site.

IMPLIED WARRANTIES AND WARRANTY DISCLAIMERS ON THE WEB

Most firms conducting electronic commerce have little trouble fulfilling the requirements needed to create enforceable, legally binding contracts on the Web. One area that deserves attention, however, is the issue of warranties. Any contract for the sale of goods includes implied warranties. An **implied warranty** is a promise to which the seller can be held even though the seller did not make an explicit statement of that promise. The law establishes these basic elements of a transaction in any contract to sell goods or services. For example, a seller is deemed to implicitly warrant that the goods it offers for sale are fit for the purposes for which they are normally used. If the seller knows specific information about the buyer's requirements, acceptance of an offer from that buyer may result in an additional implied warranty of fitness, which suggests that the goods are suitable for the specific uses of that buyer. Sellers can also create explicit warranties by providing a detailed description of the additional warranty terms. It is also possible for a seller to create explicit warranties, often unintentionally, by making general statements in brochures or other advertising materials about product performance or suitability for particular tasks.

Sellers can avoid some implied warranty liability by making a warranty disclaimer. A **warranty disclaimer** is a statement declaring that the seller will not honor some or all implied warranties. Any warranty disclaimer must be conspicuously made in writing, which means it must be easily noticed in the body of the written agreement. On a Web page, sellers can meet this requirement by putting the warranty disclaimer in larger type, a bold font, or a contrasting color. To be legally effective, the warranty disclaimer must be stated obviously and must be easy for a buyer to find on the Web site. Figure 7-5 shows a portion of a sample warranty disclaimer for a Web site. The warranty disclaimer is printed in uppercase letters to distinguish it from other text on the page. This helps satisfy the requirement that the warranty disclaimer be easily noticed.

AUTHORITY TO FORM CONTRACTS

As explained previously in this section, a contract is formed when an offer is accepted for consideration. Problems can arise when the acceptance is issued by an imposter or someone who does not have the authority to bind the company to a contract. In electronic commerce, the online nature of acceptances can make it relatively easy for identity forgers to pose as others.

Fortunately, the Internet technology that makes forged identities so easy to create also provides the means to avoid being deceived by a forged identity. In Chapter 10, you will learn how companies and individuals can use digital signatures to establish identity in online transactions. If the contract is for any significant amount, the parties should require each other to use digital signatures to avoid identity problems. In general, courts will not hold a person or corporation whose identity has been forged to the terms of the contract; however, if negligence on the part of the person or corporation contributed to the forgery, a court may hold the negligent party to the terms of the contract. For example, if a company was careless about protecting passwords and allowed an imposter to enter the company's system and accept an offer, a court might hold that company responsible for fulfilling the terms of that contract.

Determining whether an individual has the authority to commit a company to an online contract is a greater problem than forged identities in electronic commerce. This issue, called **authority to bind**, can arise when an employee of a company accepts a contract and the company later asserts that the employee did not have authority to do so. For large transactions in the physical world, businesses check public information on file with the state of incorporation, or ask for copies of corporate certificates or resolutions, to establish the authority of persons to make contracts for their employers. These methods are available to parties engaged in online transactions; however, they can be time-consuming and awkward. You will learn about some good electronic solutions, such as digital signatures and certificates from a certification authority, in Chapter 10.

Disclaimers

WE DO NOT PROMISE THAT THIS WEB SITE OR ANY CONTENT, ELEMENT, OR FEATURE OF THIS SITE WILL BE ERROR-FREE OR UNINTERRUPTED, OR THAT ANY DEFECTS WILL BE CORRECTED, OR THAT YOUR USE OF THE SITE WILL PROVIDE SPECIFIC RESULTS. THE SITE AND ITS CONTENT ARE DELIVERED ON AN "AS-IS" BASIS. INFORMATION PROVIDED ON THE SITE IS SUBJECT TO CHANGE WITHOUT NOTICE. WE CANNOT ENSURE THAT ANY PROGRAMS, FILES OR OTHER DATA YOU DOWNLOAD FROM THE SITE WILL BE FREE OF VIRUSES OR DESTRUCTIVE FEATURES.

WE DISCLAIM ALL WARRANTIES, EXPRESS OR IMPLIED, INCLUDING ANY WARRANTIES OF ACCURACY, NON-INFRINGEMENT, MERCHANTABILITY AND FITNESS FOR A PARTICULAR PURPOSE. WE DISCLAIM ANY AND ALL LIABILITY FOR THE ACTS, OMISSIONS AND CONDUCT OF ANY THIRD PARTIES IN CONNECTION WITH OR RELATED TO YOUR USE OF THE SITE AND/OR ANY OF OUR SERVICES. YOU ASSUME TOTAL RESPONSIBILITY FOR YOUR USE OF THE SITE AND ANY LINKED SITES. YOUR SOLE REMEDY AGAINST US FOR DISSATISFACTION WITH THIS SITE OR ANY CONTENT CONTAINED ON THE SITE IS TO STOP USING THE SITE OR THE CONTENT. THIS LIMITATION OF RELIEF IS A PART OF THE BARGAIN BETWEEN THE PARTIES.

The above disclaimers apply to any damages, liability or injuries caused by any failure of performance, error, omission, interruption, defect of any kind, delay of operation or function, computer virus, communication failure, theft or destruction of or unauthorized access to, alteration of, or use, whether for breach of contract, tort, negligence or any other cause of action.

> warranty disclaimer text is capitalized for emphasis

FIGURE 7-5   A Web site warranty disclaimer

Use and Protection of Intellectual Property in Online Business

Online businesses must be careful with their use of intellectual property. **Intellectual property** is a general term that includes all products of the human mind. These products can be tangible or intangible. Intellectual property rights include the protections afforded to individuals and companies by governments through governments' granting of copyrights and patents, and through registration of trademarks and service marks. Depending on where they live, individuals may have a **right of publicity**, which is a limited right to control others' commercial use of an individual's name, image, likeness, or identifying aspect of identity. This right exists in most U.S. states but is limited by the provisions of the U.S. Constitution, specifically its First Amendment. Online businesses must take care to avoid deceptive trade practices, false advertising claims, defamation or product disparagement, and infringements of intellectual property rights by using unauthorized content on their Web sites or in their domain names. A number of legal issues can arise regarding the Web page content of electronic commerce sites. The most common concerns involve the use of intellectual property that is protected by other parties' copyrights, patents, trademarks, and service marks.

Copyright Issues

A **copyright** is a right granted by a government to the author or creator of a literary or artistic work. The right is for the specific length of time provided in the copyright law and gives the author or creator the sole and exclusive right to print, publish, or sell the work. Creations that can be copyrighted include virtually all forms of artistic or intellectual expression—books, music, artworks, recordings (audio and video), architectural drawings, choreographic works, product packaging, and computer software. In the United States, works created after 1977 are protected for the life of the author plus 70 years. Works copyrighted by corporations or not-for-profit organizations are protected for 95 years from the date of publication or 120 years from the date of creation, whichever is earlier.

The idea contained in an expression cannot be copyrighted. Only the particular form in which an idea is expressed creates a work that can be copyrighted. If an idea cannot be separated from its expression in a work, that work cannot be copyrighted. For example, mathematical calculations cannot be copyrighted. A collection of facts can be copyrighted, but only if the collection is arranged, coordinated, or selected in a way that causes the resulting work to rise to the level of an original work. For example, the Yahoo! Web Directory is a collection of links to URLs. These facts existed before Yahoo! selected and arranged them into the form of its directory. However, most copyright lawyers would argue that the selection and arrangement of the links into categories probably makes the directory a copyrightable expression of the facts.

In the past, copyright law in the United States (and in many other countries) required registration of copyrighted works. Today, a work that does not include the words "copyright" or "copyrighted," or the copyright symbol ©, but was created after 1989, is copyrighted automatically by virtue of the copyright law unless the creator expressly released the work into the public domain.

Most U.S. Web pages are protected by the automatic copyright provision of the law because they arrange the elements of words, graphics, and HTML tags in a way that creates an original work (in addition, many Web pages have been registered with the U.S. Copyright Office). This creates a potential problem because of the way the Web works. As you learned in Chapter 2, when a Web client requests a page, the Web server sends an HTML file to the client. Thus, a copy of the HTML file (along with any graphics or other files needed to render the page) resides on the Web client computer. Most legal experts agree that this copying is an allowable use of the copyrighted Web page.

The U.S. copyright law includes an exemption from infringement actions for certain allowable uses of copyrighted works; the term for such uses is "fair use." The **fair use** of a copyrighted work includes copying it to use in specific restricted ways in criticism, comment, news reporting, teaching, scholarship, or research. The law's definition of fair use is intentionally broad and can be difficult to interpret. Figure 7-6 shows the text of the U.S. law that creates the fair-use exception.

As you can see in the figure, the law includes four specific factors that a court will consider in determining whether a specific use qualifies as a fair use. The first factor gives nonprofit educational uses a better chance at qualifying than commercial uses. The second factor allows the court to consider a painting using different standards than a sound recording. The third factor is often used to allow small sections of a

---

Title 17, Chapter 1, § 107 of the United States Code

Limitations on exclusive rights: Fair use

Notwithstanding the provisions of sections 106 and 106A, the fair use of a copyrighted work, including such use by reproduction in copies or phonorecords or by any other means specified by that section, for purposes such as criticism, comment, news reporting, teaching (including multiple copies for classroom use), scholarship, or research, is not an infringement of copyright. In determining whether the use made of a work in any particular case is a fair use the factors to be considered shall include

(1) the purpose and character of the use, including whether such use is of a commercial nature or is for nonprofit educational purposes;
(2) the nature of the copyrighted work;
(3) the amount and substantiality of the portion used in relation to the copyrighted work as a whole; and
(4) the effect of the use upon the potential market for or value of the copyrighted work.

The fact that a work is unpublished shall not itself bar a finding of fair use if such finding is made upon consideration of all the above factors.

FIGURE 7-6   U.S. law governing the fair-use exception

work to qualify as fair use when the use of the entire work (or a substantial part of the work) might not qualify. The fourth factor, which is a deciding factor in most fair-use cases, allows the court to consider the amount of damage the use might cause to the value of the copyrighted work. The University of Texas Copyright Crash Course and the Stanford Copyright & Fair Use Web site are particularly helpful sources of information for making fair-use determinations. If you make fair use of a copyrighted work for a school assignment, you should provide a citation to the original work to avoid charges of plagiarism.

Copyright law has always included elements, such as the fair-use exemption, that make it difficult to apply. The Internet has made this situation worse because it allows the immediate transmission of exact digital copies of many materials. In the case of digital music, the original Napster site provided a network that millions of people used to trade music files that they had copied from their CDs and compressed into MPEG version 3 format files, commonly referred to as MP3s. This constituted copyright infringement on a grand scale, and a group of music recording companies sued Napster for facilitating the individual acts of infringement.

Napster argued that it had only provided the "machinery" used in the copyright infringements—much as electronics companies manufacture and sell VCRs that might be used to make illegal copies of videotapes—and had not itself infringed on any copyrights. Both the U.S. District Court and the Federal Appellate Court held that Napster was liable for vicarious copyright infringement, even though it did not directly infringe any music recording companies' copyrights. An entity becomes liable for **vicarious copyright infringement** if it is capable of supervising the infringing activity and obtains a financial benefit from the infringing activity. Because Napster failed to monitor its network and indirectly profited (by selling advertising on its Web site) from the infringement, the company was held liable even though it did not itself transfer any copies. The courts shut down Napster, and the company agreed to pay $26 million in copyright infringement damages before filing for bankruptcy. The **Napster** site that is owned and operated today by Best Buy offers legal music downloads to subscribers.

With the growth in popularity of portable music devices such as Apple's iPod, the demand for music in the MP3 (and similar) formats has continued to increase. The companies that sell music online today each have different rules and restrictions that come with the downloaded files. Some sites allow one copy to be installed on a portable music device. Others allow a limited number of copies to be installed. Still others allow unlimited copies, but only if the devices on which the copies are installed are owned by the person who downloaded the file.

The common practice of copying files from music CDs and placing those files on a portable music device, a smartphone, or a computer raises some interesting legal issues. This type of copying is governed in the United States by the fair-use provisions of the copyright laws, which you learned about earlier in this chapter. The fair-use provisions as they relate to copying music tracks are, at best, unclear and difficult to interpret. Some lawyers would argue that a person has the right under the fair-use provisions to make a backup copy of a music CD track, but other lawyers would disagree. A person who makes one copy for a portable music device, a second copy for a computer, and a third copy on a CD for backup purposes would be less likely to be protected under the fair-use provisions, but some lawyers would argue that all three uses should be protected.

Music that is purchased in digital form (as MP3 files, or through the Apple iTunes Store, for example) is often sold with specific restrictions on copying and sharing. Be sure to read and understand the terms under which you have purchased any digital music product before making copies, even for your own use.

Patent Issues

A **patent** is an exclusive right granted by the government to an individual to make, use, and sell an invention. In the United States, patents on inventions protect the inventor's rights for 20 years. An inventor can decide to patent the design of an invention instead of the invention itself, in which case the patent protects the design for 14 years. To be patentable, an invention must be genuine, novel, useful, and not obvious given the current state of technology. In the early 1980s, companies began obtaining patents on software programs that met the terms of the U.S. patent law. However, most firms that develop software to use in Web sites and for related transaction processing have not found the patent law to be very useful. The process of obtaining a patent is expensive and can take several years. Most developers of Web-related software believe that the technology in the software could become obsolete before the patent protection is secured, so they rely on copyright protection.

One type of patent has been of special interest to companies that do business online. A U.S. Court of Appeals ruled in 1998 that patents could be granted on "methods of doing business." The **business process patent**, which protects a specific set of procedures for conducting a particular business activity, is quite controversial. In addition to the Amazon. com patent on its 1-Click purchasing method (which you read about in Chapter 4), other Web businesses have obtained business process patents. The Priceline.com "name your own price" price-tendering system, About.com's approach to aggregating information from many different Web sites, and Cybergold's method of paying people to view its Web site have each received business process patents.

The ability of companies to enforce their rights under these patents is not yet clear. Many legal experts and business researchers believe that the issuance of business process patents grants the recipients unfair monopoly power and is an inappropriate extension of patent law. In 1999, Amazon.com sued Barnes & Noble for using a process on its Web site that was similar to the 1-Click method. The case was settled out of court in 2002, but the terms of the settlement were not disclosed.

The stakes in business process patent cases can be high. For example, a federal judge in 2007 ordered eBay to pay $30 million to MercExchange for infringement of some of its business process patents. MercExchange, a company that makes a business of buying patents and attempting to enforce them, had sued eBay for using a fixed price sales option that eBay calls "Buy It Now," arguing that several of its patents covered the business process of offering a fixed price option in an online auction. After winning the monetary damages, MercExchange continued to litigate the case, hoping to win an injunction that would prevent eBay from using the feature at all. In 2008, eBay agreed to buy three patents from MercExchange for an undisclosed sum to end the litigation.

Business process patents are common only in the United States. The intellectual property laws of most other countries do not permit patents to be issued for business processes. The appropriateness of business process patents is an issue that sparks intense debate among legal scholars and online business managers. Some business executives and lawyers argue that business process patents might be appropriate if their term were to be made shorter than other patents. There is some precedent for this position because current U.S. law already includes a provision for a shorter time period for design patents. A limited-term business process patent could be a logical extension of that policy. In 2014, the U.S. Supreme Court ruled in *Alice Corp. v. CLS Bank International* that the business process patented by Alice (which involved using a computer to confirm that a transaction was completed and authorizing payment) was a basic financial business concept that had been in common use for several hundred years. The Court concluded that adding a computer process was not a sufficient innovation to warrant patent protection. This ruling does not invalidate all business process patents, however, it does clarify that a business process will need to be more than just a technology-based implementation of an established business practice.

Most companies use their patents to protect intellectual property that they use in their businesses. However, a person or company can buy patents from the original inventors and then enforce the rights granted by the patents by suing others who use the patents without permission. These persons or companies, called **patent assertion entities**, or **patent trolls**, will often purchase patents that they believe are being infringed, then threaten to sue the infringers in the hopes of extracting a cash settlement. Many of these actions have been based on business process patents. For example, Microsoft paid patent-holder Eolas more than $100 million for infringing on patents that Eolas argued protected the concept of embedding interactive content in Web pages. Eventually, those patents were ruled invalid. A number of governments have introduced legislation designed to limit the power of patent trolls, but the results to date have been mixed.

Trademark Issues

A **trademark** is a distinctive mark, device, motto, or implement that a company affixes to the goods it produces for identification purposes. A **service mark** is similar to a trademark, but it is used to identify services provided. In the United States, trademarks and service marks can be registered with state governments, the federal government, or both. The name (or a part of that name) that a business uses to identify itself is called a **trade name**. Trade names are not protected by trademark laws unless the business name is the same as the product (or service) name. They are protected, however, under common law. **Common law** is the part of British and U.S. law established by the history of court decisions that has accumulated over many years. The other main part of British and U.S. law, called **statutory law**, arises when elected legislative bodies pass laws, which are also called statutes.

The owners of registered trademarks have often invested a considerable amount of money in the development and promotion of their trademarks. Web site designers must be very careful not to use any trademarked name, logo, or other identifying mark without the express permission of the trademark owner. For example, a company Web site that includes a photograph of its president who happens to be holding a can of Pepsi could be held liable for infringing on Pepsi's trademark rights. Pepsi can argue that the appearance of its trademarked product on the Web site implies an endorsement of the president or the company by Pepsi.

Domain Names and Intellectual Property Issues

Considerable controversy has arisen about intellectual property rights and Internet domain names. **Cybersquatting** is the practice of registering a domain name that is the trademark of another person or company in the hopes that the owner will pay huge amounts of money to acquire the URL. In addition, successful cybersquatters can attract many site visitors and, consequently, charge high advertising rates. Registering a generic name such as Wine.com with the hope that it might one day become valuable is not cybersquatting. It is completely legal speculation.

A related problem, called **name changing** (also called **typosquatting**), occurs when someone registers purposely misspelled variations of well-known domain names. These variants sometimes lure consumers who make typographical errors when entering a URL. For example, a person might easily type LLBaen.com instead of LLBean.com and end up at a spoofed Web site.

Since 1999, the U.S. Anticybersquatting Consumer Protection Act has prevented businesses' trademarked names from being registered as domain names by other parties. The law provides for damages of up to $100,000 per trademark. If the unauthorized registration of the domain name is found to be "willful," damages can be as much as $300,000.

Disputes that arise when one person has registered a domain name that is an existing trademark or company name are settled by the World Intellectual Property Organization (WIPO). WIPO began settling domain name disputes in 1999 under its Uniform Domain Name Dispute Resolution Policy (UDRP). The problems of international jurisdiction made enforcement by the courts of individual countries cumbersome and ineffective. As an international organization, WIPO can transcend borders and provide rulings that will be effective in a global online business environment.

Disputes can arise when a business has a trademark that is a common term. If a person obtains the domain name containing that common term, the owner of the trademark must seek resolution at WIPO. In more than 90 percent of its cases, WIPO rules in favor of the trademark owner, but a win is never guaranteed.

In one example, three cybersquatters made headlines when they tried to sell the URL barrydiller.com for $10 million. Barry Diller, then the CEO of USA Networks, won a WIPO decision (*Barry Diller v. INTERNTCO Corp.*) that ordered the domain name transferred to him. The ruling established that a famous person's own name is a common law service mark. The WIPO panel in the Barry Diller case found that the cybersquatters had no legitimate rights or interests in the domain name and that they had registered the name and were using it in bad faith.

In another example, Gordon Sumner, who has performed music for many years as Sting, filed a complaint with WIPO because a Georgia man obtained the domain name www.sting.com and offered to sell it to Sting for $25,000; however, in this case, WIPO noted that the word "sting" was in common and general use and had multiple meanings other than as an identifier for the musician. WIPO refused to award the domain to Sumner. After the WIPO decision, Sumner purchased the domain name for an undisclosed sum and now hosts his official Web site at www.sting.com.

Many critics have argued that the WIPO UDRP has been enforced unevenly and that many of the decisions under the policy have been inconsistent. One problem faced by those who have used the WIPO resolution service is that the WIPO decisions are not appealed to a single authority. Instead, the party losing in the WIPO hearing must find a court with jurisdiction over the dispute and file suit there to overturn the WIPO decision. No central authority maintains records of all WIPO decisions and appeals. This makes it very difficult for a trademark owner, a domain holder, or a lawyer for either party to anticipate how the UDRP will be interpreted in their specific cases.

Another example of domain name abuse is name stealing. **Name stealing** occurs when someone other than a domain name's owner changes the ownership of the domain name. A **domain name ownership change** occurs when owner information maintained by a public domain registrar is changed in the registrar's database to reflect a new owner's name and business address. Once the domain name ownership is changed, the name stealer can manipulate the site, post graffiti on it, or redirect online customers to other sites—perhaps to sites selling competing products. The main purpose of name stealing is to harass the site owner because the ownership change can be reversed quickly when the theft is discovered; however, name stealing can cut off a business from its Web site for several days.

Protecting Intellectual Property Online

Several methods can be used to protect copyrighted digital works online, but they only provide partial protection. One technique uses a **digital watermark**, which is a digital code or stream embedded undetectably in a digital image or audio file. The digital watermark can be encrypted (you will learn more about encryption in Chapter 10) to protect its contents, or simply hidden among the digital information that makes up the image or recording. **Verance** is a company that provides, among other products, digital audio watermarking systems to protect audio files on the Internet. Its systems identify, authenticate, and protect intellectual property. They also enable companies to monitor, identify, and control the use of their digital audio or video recordings. The company also makes products that can alert users when telephonic conversations, audiovisual transcripts, or depositions have been altered.

Blue Spike produces a watermarking system that authenticates copyright and provides copy control. **Copy control** is an electronic mechanism for limiting the number of copies that one can make of a digital work. **Digimarc** is another company that provides watermark intellectual property protection software. Its products embed a watermark that allows any works protected by its system to be tracked across the Web. In addition, the watermark can link viewers to commerce sites and databases and can control software and playback devices. Digimarc's watermark also stores copyright information and links to the image's creator, which enables nonrepudiation of a work's authorship and facilitates selling and licensing the work online.

Defamation

A **defamatory** statement is a statement that is false and that injures the reputation of another person or company. If the statement injures the reputation of a product or service instead of a person, it is called **product disparagement**. In some countries, even a true and honest comparison of products may give rise to product disparagement. Because the difference between justifiable criticism and defamation can be hard to determine, commercial Web sites should consider the specific laws in their jurisdiction (and consider consulting a lawyer) before making negative, evaluative statements about other persons or products.

Web site designers should be especially careful to avoid potential defamation liability by altering a photo or image of a person in a way that depicts the person unfavorably. In most cases, a person must establish that the defamatory statement caused injury. However, most states recognize a legal cause of action, called **per se defamation**, in which a court deems some types of statements to be so negative that injury is assumed. For example, the court will hold inaccurate statements alleging conduct potentially injurious to a person's business, trade, profession, or office as defamatory per se—the complaining party need not prove injury to recover damages. Thus, online statements about competitors should always be carefully reviewed before posting to determine whether they contain any elements of defamation.

An important exception in U.S. law exists for statements that are defamatory but that are about a public figure (such as a politician or a famous actor). The law allows considerable leeway for statements that are satirical or that are valid expressions of personal opinion. Other countries do not offer the same protections, so operators of Web sites with international audiences should be careful.

Also, recall that defaming or disparaging statements must be false. This protects Web sites that include unfavorable reviews of products or services if the statements made are not false. For example, if a person reads a book and believes it to be terrible, that person can safely post a review on Amazon.com that includes assessments of the book's lack of literary value. Such statements of personal opinion are true statements and thus neither defamatory nor disparaging. Finally, in many U.S. states, use of an individual's name, photo, or other elements of personal identity can violate that individual's right of publicity. A company that does business in a jurisdiction that recognizes this right must be careful to obtain permission for any use of an individual's name, photo, likeness, or identifying characteristics on their Web sites.

Deceptive Trade Practices

The ease with which Web site designers can edit graphics, audio, and video files allows them to do many creative and interesting things. Manipulations of existing pictures, sounds, and video clips can be very entertaining. If the objects being manipulated are trademarked, however, these manipulations can constitute infringement of the trademark holder's rights. Fictional characters can be trademarked or otherwise protected. Many Web pages include unauthorized use of cartoon characters and scanned photographs of celebrities; often, these images are altered in some way. A Web site that uses an altered image of Mickey Mouse speaking in a modified voice is likely to hear from the Disney legal team.

Web sites that include links to other sites must be careful not to imply a relationship with the companies sponsoring the other sites unless such a relationship actually exists. For example, a Web design studio's Web page may include links to company Web sites that show good design principles. If those company Web sites were not created by the design studio, the studio must be very careful to state that fact. Otherwise, it would be easy for a visitor to assume that the linked sites were the work of the design studio.

In general, trademark protection prevents another firm from using the same or a similar name, logo, or other identifying characteristic in a way that would cause confusion in the minds of potential buyers of the trademark holder's products or services. For example, the trademarked name "Visa" is used by one company for its credit card and another company for its synthetic fiber. This use is acceptable because the two products are significantly different and few consumers of credit cards or synthetic fibers would likely be confused by the identical names. However, the use of very well-known trademarks can be protected for all products if there is a danger that the trademark might be diluted. Various state laws define **trademark dilution** as the reduction of the distinctive quality of a trademark by alternative uses. Trademarked names such as "Hyatt," "Trivial Pursuit," and "Tiffany," and the shape of the Coca-Cola bottle have all been protected from dilution by court rulings. Thus, a Web site that sells gift-packaged seafood and claims to be the "Tiffany of the Sea" risks a lawsuit from the famous jeweler asserting damages caused by trademark dilution.

Advertising Regulation

In the United States, advertising is regulated primarily by the Federal Trade Commission (FTC). The FTC publishes regulations and investigates claims of false advertising. Its Web site includes a number of information releases that are useful to businesses and consumers. Any advertising claim that can mislead a substantial number of consumers in a material way is illegal under U.S. law. In addition to conducting its own investigations, the FTC accepts referred investigations from organizations such as the Better Business Bureau. FTC policies include information on what is permitted in advertisements and cover specific areas such as these:

- Bait advertising
- Consumer lending and leasing
- Endorsements and testimonials
- Energy consumption statements for home appliances
- Guarantees and warranties
- Prices

Other federal agencies have the power to regulate online advertising in the United States. These agencies include the Food and Drug Administration (FDA), the Bureau of Alcohol, Tobacco, and Firearms (BATF), and the Department of Transportation (DOT). The FDA regulates information disclosures for food and drug products. In particular, any Web site that is planning to advertise pharmaceutical products will be subject to the FDA's drug labeling and advertising regulations. The BATF works with the FDA to monitor and enforce federal laws regarding advertising for alcoholic beverages and tobacco products. These laws require that every ad for such products includes statements that use very specific language. Many states also have laws that regulate advertising for alcoholic beverages and tobacco products. The state and federal laws governing advertising and the sale of firearms are even more restrictive. Any Web site that plans to deal in these products should consult with an attorney who is familiar with the relevant laws before posting any online advertising for such products. The DOT works with the FTC to monitor the advertising of companies over which it has jurisdiction, such as bus lines, freight companies, and airlines.

Online Crime, Terrorism, and Warfare

In addition to the positive impacts the Internet has had, including providing a way for geographically distant people to communicate and get to know each other better and the creation of new business opportunities, the Internet has also been used for negative purposes. Some people in our world have found the Internet to be a useful tool for perpetrating crimes, conducting terrorism, and even waging war.

Online Crime: Jurisdiction Issues

Crime on the Web includes online versions of crimes that have been undertaken for years in the physical world, including theft, stalking, distribution of pornography, and gambling. Other crimes, such as commandeering one computer to launch attacks on other computers, are new.

Law enforcement agencies have difficulty combating many types of online crime. The first obstacle they face is the issue of jurisdiction. As you learned earlier in this chapter, determining jurisdiction can be tricky on the Internet. If the crime is theft of intellectual property (such as computer software or computer files), the questions of jurisdiction become even more complex. You can learn more about online crime issues at the U.S. Department of Justice Computer Crime & Intellectual Property Section Web site.

The prosecution of fraud perpetrators across international boundaries has always been difficult for law enforcement officials. The Internet has given new life to old fraud scams that count on jurisdictional issues to slow investigations of crimes. The advance fee fraud has existed in various forms for many years, and e-mail has made it inexpensive for perpetrators to launch large numbers of attempts to ensnare victims. In an **advance fee fraud**, the perpetrator offers to share the proceeds of some large payoff with the victim if the victim will make a "good faith" deposit or provide some partial funding first. The perpetrator then disappears with the deposit. In some online versions of this fraud, the perpetrator asks for identity information (bank account number, Social Security number, credit card number, and so on) and uses that information to steal the advance fee. Online advance fee frauds often victimize people who are less-sophisticated technology users and people who tend to trust unknown persons.

Enforcing laws against the distribution of pornographic material has also been difficult because of jurisdiction issues. The distinction between legal adult material and illegal pornographic material is, in many cases, subjective and often difficult to make. The U.S. Supreme Court has ruled that state and local courts can draw the line based on local community standards. This creates problems for Internet sales. For example, consider a case in which questionable adult content is sold on a Web site located in Oregon to a customer who downloads the material in Georgia. A difficult question arises regarding which community standards might apply to the sale.

A similar jurisdiction issue arises in the case of online gambling. Many gambling sites are located outside the United States. If people in California use their computers to connect to an offshore gambling site, it is unclear where the gambling activity occurs. Several states have passed laws that specifically outlaw Internet gambling, but the jurisdiction of those states to enforce laws that limit Internet activities is not clear.

In 2008, the United States Department of the Treasury and the Federal Reserve Bank jointly issued regulations that implement the Unlawful Internet Gambling Enforcement Act (UIGEA) of 2006. As a federal law, the UIGEA gives clearer jurisdiction to law enforcement officers than any state law could. The law prohibits gambling businesses from knowingly accepting payments in connection with unlawful Internet gambling, including payments made through credit cards, electronic funds transfers, and checks. Under the UIGEA regulations, "unlawful Internet gambling" includes making bets using the Internet that are unlawful under any federal or state law in the jurisdiction where the bet or wager is initiated, received, or otherwise made.

The first major enforcement action under the regulations occurred in 2009, when federal authorities seized the bank accounts of some 27,000 online poker players, which contained more than $34 million. In 2011, the FBI arrested the founders of three major poker sites with large U.S. audiences on criminal gambling, bank fraud, and money laundering charges. The defendants were alleged to have circumvented the UIGEA by tricking some small U.S. banks into processing payments for them and bribing others to do the same. After paying more than $780 million to settle the civil charges, the companies involved were merged into other gambling businesses or filed for bankruptcy. Several of the individuals charged went to prison under plea agreements.

Similar laws that restrict online gambling have been passed in other countries. However, some of these laws have been challenged as being discriminatory by the countries in which the online gambling companies operate. If a country's laws permit gambling within the country, but exclude foreign companies from providing gambling services (over the Internet), a basis exists for a discrimination complaint under the World Trade Organization's General Agreement on Trade in Services. The governments of Antigua and Barbados have each filed such complaints against the United States, arguing that the United States engaged in discriminatory trade practices by enforcing the UIGEA.

In 2011, the States of Illinois and New York proposed that they be permitted to use the Internet and out-of-state agents to sell lottery tickets to in-state adults. In response, the U.S. Department of Justice issued a memorandum opinion in which it reversed its long-held stand that virtually all forms of online gambling were illegal. The memorandum argued that state lotteries are not prohibited by federal law (specifically, the 1961 Wire Act, 18 U.S.C. 1084) because they do not involve wagering on sporting events. Because the underlying wagering is not illegal, the UIGEA (which requires the bets to be unlawful under federal or state law) does not apply. Gambling businesses and social networking sites welcomed the prospect of having locally sanctioned gambling on the Internet become legal and a number of state legislatures began drafting laws that would allow state governments and existing legal casinos to conduct nonsports gambling online.

New Types of Crime Online

As you learned in Chapter 6, the Internet made new types of business possible. The dark side of technological progress is that the Internet also made new types of crime possible. With these new types of crime, law enforcement officers often face difficulties when trying to apply laws that were written before the Internet became prevalent to criminal actions carried out on the Internet.

For example, most states have stalking laws that provide criminal penalties to people who harass, annoy, or alarm another person in a way that presents a credible threat. Many of these laws are triggered by physical actions, such as physically following the person targeted. The Internet gives a stalker the opportunity to use e-mail or chat room discussions to create the threatening situation. Laws that require physical action on the part of the stalker are not effective against online stalkers. Only a few states have passed laws that specifically address the problem of online stalking.

The Internet can amplify the effects of acts that, in the physical world, can be dealt with locally. For example, school playgrounds have long been the realm of bullying. Students who engaged in bullying were dealt with by school officials; only in extreme cases were such cases referred to law enforcement officials. Today, young people can use technology to harass, humiliate, threaten, and embarrass each other. These acts are called **cyberbullying**. Cyberbullying can include threats, sexual remarks, or pejorative comments transmitted on the Internet or posted on Web sites (social networking sites are often used for such postings). The perpetrator might also pose as the victim and post statements on media, such as photos or videos (often edited to cast the victim in an unfavorable light), that are intended to damage the victim's reputation. Because the Internet increases both the intensity and reach of these attacks, they are much more likely to draw the attention of law enforcement officials than bullying activities in the physical world.

Lawsuits against social media sites that host damaging content have been unsuccessful because such sites are generally not responsible for the content posted by individual members. Victims of online harassment can file civil suits against the perpetrators (if they can be identified) for defamation, negligent misrepresentation, invasion of privacy, and inflicting emotional distress. Criminal statutes in most jurisdictions have not kept up with technology and many forms of stalking and cyberbullying are difficult to prosecute under them; however, some U.S. states are starting to pass laws that address these online offenses. Florida's HB 609, enacted in 2013, covers cyberbullying of high school students and staff. In 2015, however, the U.S. Supreme Court ruled in *Elonis v. United States* that online statements must be made intentionally and with conscious intent to be threatening to be considered criminal violations. This type of intent can be difficult to prove and could make enforcement of laws against cyberbullying and other online threats more difficult.

The practice of sending sexually explicit messages or photos using a mobile phone is called **sexting**. Sexting is a crime in many jurisdictions, even if the message is sent to a friend or acquaintance. A number of politicians, athletes, and other celebrities have been embarrassed by sexting activity. When young persons under the age of 18 transmit an explicit photo of themselves, they can create serious criminal liability for themselves and their recipients. In the United States and many other countries, the mere possession (regardless of intent) of explicit photos of a minor is a felony punishable by prison sentences and requires offenders to register as a sex offender.

An increasing number of companies have reported attempts by competitors and others to infiltrate their computer systems with the intent of stealing data or creating disruptions in their operations. Smaller companies are easier targets because they generally do not have strong security in place (you will learn more about security in electronic commerce in Chapter 10), but larger organizations are not immune to these attacks. In 2004, lawyer and computer expert Myron Tereshchuk was convicted for criminal extortion. Over a period of two years, he threatened MicroPatent, a patent and trademark services company, with disclosure of confidential client information unless the company paid him $17 million. MicroPatent spent more than $500,000 on legal and technical consultants during the investigation and devoted significant internal resources to the effort. MicroPatent's sales managers also had to spend a tremendous amount of time with clients, reassuring them that their confidential information (details of their pending patent and trademark applications, for example) had not been compromised. MicroPatent's experience was not unusual. According to a recent Computer Security Institute survey of 634 companies, the average loss due to unauthorized data access was more than $300,000 and the average loss due to information theft was more than $350,000. Another survey by *InformationWeek*/Accenture found that 78 percent of surveyed companies believed that they were more vulnerable because attackers were getting more sophisticated.

In 2010, the National Retail Federation joined with eBay and the FBI to combat retail crime organizations that specialize in stealing in bulk from physical stores and then selling the stolen goods online. In recent years, shoplifters who try to return stolen goods for refunds have been thwarted by store policies that require a receipt or ask for identification (to track persons who have many returns). The Internet has opened up a new way for these criminals to profit by selling the stolen goods online. By working with retailers, eBay can use its data tracking technology to identify auctions that offer stolen items and alert law enforcement officials who can investigate suspicious activity.

Although the Internet has made the work of law enforcement more difficult in many cases, there are exceptions. As police agencies become more experienced in using the Web, they have found that it can help track down the perpetrators of crime in some cases. A number of cases have been solved because criminals have bragged about their crimes on social networking sites. From the Pennsylvania graffiti artists who posted photos of their vandalism in their social network profiles to the California teens who firebombed an airplane hangar and uploaded a video of themselves in action, criminals who use the Internet are making it easy for police to track them down. In other cases, criminals leave clues in their online profiles that police can use to corroborate other evidence, as in the case of the suspected murderer who described his favorite murder weapon in his online profile. Although privacy watchdog groups have expressed concern about law enforcement officers randomly surfing the Web looking for leads, anything posted online is public information and is subject to their scrutiny.

Online Warfare and Terrorism

Many Internet security experts believe that we are at the dawn of a new age of terrorism and warfare that could be carried out or coordinated through the Internet. A considerable number of Web sites currently exist that openly support or are operated by hate groups and terrorist organizations. Web sites that contain detailed instructions for creating biological weapons and other poisons, discussion boards that help terrorist groups recruit new members online, and sites that offer downloadable terrorist training films now number in the thousands. In recent years, the terrorist organization known as The Islamic State has used social networking to recruit supporters around the world, convincing them both to join their organized military actions in the Middle East and to attack targets in their own countries. Speeches distributed online by a radical imam were believed to have inspired the 2013 Boston Marathon bombers.

The U.S. Department of Homeland Security and international police agencies such as Interpol are devoting considerable resources to monitoring terrorist activities online. Historically, these agencies have not done a very good job of coordinating their activities around the world. The threat posed by global terrorist organizations motivated Interpol to update and expand its computer network monitoring skills and coordinate global antiterrorism efforts. State-sponsored attacks on other governments' agencies, military operations, or economic targets are generally assumed to be occurring, although the governments involved (both as victims and perpetrators go to great lengths to hide their identities). North Korea is believed to have launched multiple cyberattacks on U.S. government agencies and Sony Pictures in recent years, and the United States is believed to have responded with counterattacks.

The Internet provides an effective communications network on which many people and businesses have become dependent. Although the Internet was designed from its inception to continue operating while under attack, a sustained effort by a well-financed terrorist group or rogue state could slow down the operation of major transaction-processing centers. As more business communications traffic moves to the Internet, the potential damage that could result from this type of attack increases. You will learn more about security threats and countermeasures for those threats in Chapter 10.

Ethical Issues

Companies using Web sites to conduct electronic commerce should adhere to the same ethical standards that other businesses follow. If they do not, they will suffer the same consequences that all companies suffer: the damaged reputation and long-term loss of trust that can result in loss of business. In general, advertising or promotion on the Web should include only true statements and should omit any information that could mislead potential customers or wrongly influence their impressions of a product or service. Even true statements have been held to be misleading when the ad omits important related facts. Any comparisons to other products should be supported by verifiable information. The next section explains the role of ethics in formulating Web business policies, such as those affecting visitors' privacy rights and companies' Internet communications with children.

Ethics and Online Business Practices

Online businesses are finding that ethical issues are important to consider when they are making policy decisions. Recall from Chapter 3 that buyers on the Web often communicate with each other. A report of an ethical lapse that is rapidly passed among customers can seriously affect a company's reputation. In 1999, *The New York Times* ran a story that disclosed Amazon.com's arrangements with publishers for book promotions. Amazon.com was accepting payments of up to $10,000 from publishers to give their books editorial reviews and placement on lists of recommended books as part of a cooperative advertising program. When this news broke, Amazon.com issued a statement that it had done nothing wrong and that such advertising programs were a standard part of publisher–bookstore relationships. The outcry on Internet newsgroups and mailing lists was overwhelming. Two days later—before most traditional media outlets had even reported the story—Amazon.com announced that it would end the practice and offer unconditional refunds to any customers who had purchased a promoted book. Amazon.com had done nothing illegal, but the practice appeared to be unethical to many of its existing and potential customers.

Earlier the same year, eBay faced a similar ethical dilemma. Several newspapers had begun running stories about sales of illegal items, such as assault weapons and drugs, on the eBay auction site. At this point in time, eBay was listing about 250,000 items each day. Although eBay would investigate claims that illegal items were up for auction on its site, eBay did not actively screen or filter listings before the auctions were placed on the site.

Even though eBay was not legally obligated to screen the items auctioned, and even though screening would be fairly expensive, eBay decided that screening for illegal and copyright-infringing items would be in the best long-run interest of eBay. The team decided that such a decision would send a signal about the character of the company to its customers and the public in general. eBay also decided to remove an entire category—firearms—from the site. Not all of eBay's users were happy about this decision—the sale of firearms on eBay, when done properly, is completely legal. However, eBay again decided that its overall image as an open and honest marketplace was so important to its future success that the company chose to ban all firearms sales.

In 2009, a number of software developers complained that the Apple Apps Store (which you learned about earlier in this book) was slow to approve software to be sold on its Web site. Apple responded that it had a responsibility to protect its customers (the owners of its iPhone and iPad products) from unscrupulous software vendors who might try to sell applications for the devices that do not function properly, crash the phone or tablet, or install malware. Apple argued that its testing and approval program was necessary to maintain customer confidence in its products, even though it had no legal obligation to perform such testing on software provided by third-party developers and sold on the Apps Store Web site.

An important ethical issue that organizations face when they collect e-mail addresses from site visitors is how the organization limits the use of the e-mail addresses and related information. In the early days of the Web, few organizations made any promises to visitors who provided such information. Today, most Web sites state the organization's policy on the protection of visitor information, but many do not. In the United States, organizations are not legally bound to limit their use of information collected through their Web sites. They may use the information for any purpose, including the sale of that information to other organizations. This lack of government regulation that might protect site visitor information is a source of concern for many individuals and privacy rights advocates. These concerns are discussed in the next section.

Privacy Rights and Obligations

The issue of online privacy is continuing to evolve as the Internet and the Web grow in importance as tools of communication and commerce. Many legal and privacy issues remain unsettled and are hotly debated in various forums. The **Electronic Communications Privacy Act of 1986** is the main law governing privacy on the Internet today. Of course, this law was enacted before the general public began its wide use of the Internet. The law was written to update an existing law that prevented the interception of audio signal transmissions so that any type of electronic transmissions (including, for example, fax or data transmissions) would be given the same protections. In 1986, people were not using the Internet to transmit commercially valuable data in any significant amount, so the law was written to deal primarily with interceptions that might occur on leased telephone lines.

In the United States, a number of laws have been enacted that address online privacy issues, but none have survived constitutional challenges. In 1999, the FTC issued a report that examined how well Web sites were respecting visitors' privacy rights. Although the FTC found a significant number of sites without posted privacy policies, the report concluded that companies operating Web sites were developing privacy practices with sufficient speed and that no federal laws regarding privacy were required at that time. Privacy advocacy groups responded to the FTC report with outrage and calls for legislation. The Direct Marketing Association (DMA), a trade association of businesses that advertise their products and services directly to consumers using mail, telephone, Internet, and mass media outlets, has established a set of privacy standards for its members. Critics note that past efforts by the DMA to regulate its members' activities have been less than successful and continue to push for privacy laws. The DMA lobbies legislators on behalf of its members, who generally do not want any privacy laws that would interfere with their business activities.

Ethics issues are significant in the area of online privacy because laws have not kept pace with the growth of the Internet and the Web. The nature and degree of personal information that Web sites can record when collecting information about visitors' page-viewing habits, product selections, and demographic information can threaten the privacy rights of those visitors. This is especially true when companies lose control of the data they collect on their customers (and other people). Over the years, many companies have made news headlines because they allowed confidential information about individuals to be released without the permission of those individuals. Examples include incidents such as:

- In 2004, ChoicePoint (a company that compiles information about consumers) sold the names, addresses, Social Security numbers, and credit reports of more than 145,000 people to thieves who posed as legitimate businesses. More than 1000 fraud cases have been documented as a result of that privacy violation. ChoicePoint ended up paying a $10 million fine and set up a $5 million fund to compensate victims.
- In 2005, hackers broke into customer databases at DSW Shoe Warehouse and stole the credit card numbers, checking account numbers, and driver's license numbers of more than 1.4 million customers.
- In 2009, hackers breaching security at credit card processing company, Heartland Payment Systems, made off with more than 130 million card numbers issued by some 650 banks and other financial institutions.
- During the 2013 holiday shopping season, Target reported that hackers stole information including the names, credit card numbers, expiration dates, and security codes of more than 40 million of their retail customers by inserting malicious software into the company's point-of-sale terminals. In 2014, a similar attack gathered 56 million customers' credit card information from Home Depot.
- In 2015, there were several major security breaches that released millions of individuals' personal information (Anthem, CVS) and tax return data (IRS). Even the U.S. Office of Personnel Management found its records of personal and background check information on more than 22 million job applicants and current employees stolen.

Not all privacy compromises are the work of external agents. Sometimes, companies just lose things. Examples include incidents such as:

- In 2005, Ameritrade, Bank of America, and Time Warner each reported that they had lost track of shipments containing computer backup tapes that held confidential information for hundreds of thousands of customers or employees.

- In 2008, Horizon Blue Cross Blue Shield of New Jersey reported that an employee's laptop computer had been stolen. The laptop contained the personal information (including Social Security numbers) of more than 300,000 individuals.
- In 2013, an employee of the Kaiser Foundation Hospital in Anaheim lost a USB flash drive containing 49,000 patient records.

The number of security breaches leading to the loss of personal information continues to increase. For 2014, the Identity Theft Resource Center reported 783 confirmed incidents and projected that the upward trend in incidents will continue, also noting that a total of 675 individual records had been breached since it began tracking these incidents in 2005.

The Internet has also changed traditional assumptions about privacy because it allows people anywhere in the world to gather data online in quantities that would have been impossible a few years ago. For example, real estate transactions are a matter of public record in the United States. These transactions have been registered in county records for many years and have been available to anyone who wanted to go to the county recorder's office and spend hours leafing through large books full of handwritten records. Many counties have made these records available on the Internet, so now a researcher can examine thousands of real estate transaction records in hours without traveling to a single county office. Many privacy experts see this change in the ease of data access to be an important shift that affects the privacy rights of those who participate in real estate transactions. Because the Internet makes such data more readily available to a wider range of people, the privacy previously afforded to the participants in those transactions has been reduced.

Differences in cultures throughout the world have resulted in different expectations about privacy in electronic commerce. In Europe, for example, most people expect that information they provide to a commercial Web site will be used only for the purpose for which it was collected. Many European countries have laws that prohibit companies from exchanging consumer data without the express consent of the consumer. In 1998, the EU adopted a Directive on the Protection of Personal Data. This directive codifies the constitutional rights to privacy that exist in most European countries and applies them to all Internet activities. In addition, the directive prevents businesses from exporting personal data outside the EU unless the data will continue to be protected in accordance with provisions of the directive. The EU and its member countries have consistently exhibited a strong preference for using government regulations to protect privacy. The United States has exhibited an opposite preference. U.S. companies, especially those in the direct mail marketing industry, have consistently and successfully lobbied to avoid government regulation and allow the companies to police themselves. Companies that do business internationally must be aware of these differences. For example, a U.S. company that does business in the EU is subject to its privacy laws.

One of the major privacy controversies in the United States today is the opt-in versus opt-out issue. Most companies that gather personal information in the course of doing business on the Web would like to be able to use that information for any purpose of their own. Some companies would also like to be able to sell or rent that information to other companies. No U.S. law currently places limits on companies' use of such information. Companies are, in general, also free to sell or rent customer information. An increasing number of U.S. companies do provide a way for customers who would like to restrict use of their personal information to do so. The most common policy used in U.S. companies today is an opt-out approach. In an **opt-out** approach, the company collecting the information assumes that the customer does not object to the company's use of the information unless the customer specifically chooses to deny permission (that is, to opt out of having their information used). In the less common **opt-in** approach, the company collecting the information does not use the information for any other purpose (or sell or rent the information) unless the customer specifically chooses to allow that use (that is, to opt in and grant permission for the use). Figure 7-7 shows an example Web page that presents a series of opt-in choices to site visitors. The Web site will not send any of these three items to a site visitor unless that visitor opts in by checking one or more boxes.

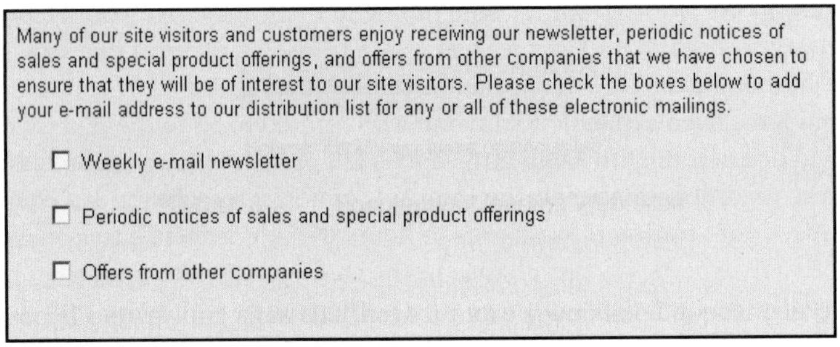

Many of our site visitors and customers enjoy receiving our newsletter, periodic notices of sales and special product offerings, and offers from other companies that we have chosen to ensure that they will be of interest to our site visitors. Please check the boxes below to add your e-mail address to our distribution list for any or all of these electronic mailings.

☐ Weekly e-mail newsletter

☐ Periodic notices of sales and special product offerings

☐ Offers from other companies

FIGURE 7-7   Example Web page showing opt-in choices

Figure 7-8 shows the opt-out approach. A Web site that uses the opt-out approach will send all three items to the site visitor unless the site visitor checks the boxes to indicate that the items are not wanted.

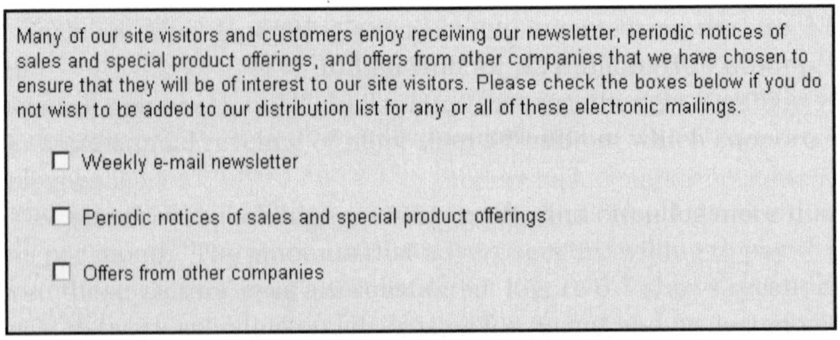

Many of our site visitors and customers enjoy receiving our newsletter, periodic notices of sales and special product offerings, and offers from other companies that we have chosen to ensure that they will be of interest to our site visitors. Please check the boxes below if you do not wish to be added to our distribution list for any or all of these electronic mailings.

☐ Weekly e-mail newsletter

☐ Periodic notices of sales and special product offerings

☐ Offers from other companies

FIGURE 7-8   Example Web page showing opt-out choices

As you can see, it is easy for site visitors to misread the text and make the wrong choice when deciding whether or not to check the boxes. Sites that use the opt-out approach are often criticized for requiring their visitors to take an affirmative action (checking the empty boxes) to prevent the site from sending items. Another approach to presenting opt-out choices is to use a page that includes checked boxes and instructs the visitor to "uncheck the boxes of the items you do not wish to receive." Most privacy advocates believe that the opt-in approach is preferable because it gives the customer privacy protection unless that customer specifically elects to give up those rights. Most U.S. businesses have traditionally taken the position that they have a right to use the information they collect unless the provider of the information explicitly objects. Some of these companies are changing to the opt-in approach, often at the prodding of privacy advocacy groups.

Until the legal requirements of privacy regulation become clearer, privacy advocates urge electronic commerce Web sites to be conservative in their collection and use of customer data. Many companies have adopted guidelines for use of customer data, in some cases adapted from EU law. In general, these guidelines acknowledge the organization's responsibility for respecting customer privacy and the importance of maintaining customers' trust. The most commonly used guidelines include:

1. Use data collected to provide improved service or other benefits to the customer.

2. Do not provide customer data to anyone outside your organization without the customer's express permission.

3. Give customers a description of what data is collected and provide clear explanations about how the data is used.

4. Give customers the right to have any of their data deleted.

5. Train employees in how to keep customer data safe and secure.

A number of organizations are active in promoting privacy rights. You can learn more about current developments in privacy legislation and practices throughout the world by following the links to these organizations' Web sites that appear under the heading Privacy Rights Advocacy Groups in the Web Links.

Communications with Children

An additional set of privacy considerations arises when Web sites attract children and engage in any form of communication with those children. Adults who interact with Web sites can read privacy statements and make informed decisions about whether to communicate personal information to the site. The communication of private information (such as credit card numbers, shipping addresses, and so on) is a key element in the conduct of electronic commerce.

The laws of most countries and most ethical frameworks consider children to be less capable than adults in evaluating information sharing and transaction risks. Thus, laws in the physical world prevent or limit children's ability to sign contracts, get married, drive motor vehicles, and enter certain physical spaces (such as bars, casinos, tattoo parlors, and racetracks). Children are considered to be less able (or unable) to make informed decisions about the risks of certain activities. Similarly, many people are concerned about children's ability to read and evaluate privacy statements and then consent to providing personal information to Web sites. Most social media sites use software that compares each registered participant against a database of known sex offenders and deletes the accounts of any it finds. Despite such safeguards, most experts agree that no technology will ever protect as well as parental involvement in their children's online activities.

LEARNING FROM FAILURES

DoubleClick

As you learned in Chapter 4, DoubleClick is one of the largest banner advertising networks in the world. DoubleClick arranges the placement of banner ads on Web sites. Like many other Web sites, DoubleClick uses cookies, which are small text files placed on Web client computers, to identify returning visitors.

Most visitors find the privacy risk posed by cookies to be acceptable. The Web servers at Amazon.com, for example, place Amazon.com cookies on the computers of visitors to the site so the visitors can be recognized when they return. This can be useful, for example, when a visitor who has placed several items in a shopping cart before being interrupted can return to Amazon.com later in the day and find the shopping cart intact. The Amazon.com Web server can read the client's Amazon.com cookie and find the shopping cart from the client's previous session. The Amazon.com server can read only its own cookies; it cannot read the cookies placed on the client computer by any other Web server.

There are two important differences between the Amazon.com scenario and what happens when DoubleClick serves a banner ad. First, the visitor usually does not know that the banner ad is coming from DoubleClick (and thus, does not know that the DoubleClick server could be writing a cookie to the client computer). Second, DoubleClick serves ads through Web sites owned by thousands of companies. As a visitor moves from one Web site to another, that visitor's computer can collect many DoubleClick cookies. The DoubleClick server can read all of its own cookies, gathering information from each one about which ads were served and the sites through which they were served. Thus, DoubleClick can compile a tremendous amount of information about a user's actions on the Web.

Even this amount of information collection would not trouble most people. DoubleClick can use the cookies to track a particular computer's connections to Web sites, but it does not record any identity information about the owner of that computer. Therefore, DoubleClick accumulates a considerable record of Web activity, but cannot connect that activity with a person.

In 1999, DoubleClick arranged a $1.7 billion merger with Abacus Direct Corporation. Abacus had developed a way to link information about people's Web behavior (collected through cookies such as those placed by DoubleClick's banner ad servers) to the names, addresses, and other information about those people that had been collected in an offline consumer database.

The reaction from online privacy protection groups was immediate and substantial. The FTC launched an investigation, the Internet's privacy issues-related virtual communities buzzed with furious conversation, and, in the end, DoubleClick abandoned its plans to integrate its cookie-generated data with the identity information in the Abacus database. Although DoubleClick is still one of the largest banner advertising networks, it had been counting on generating additional revenue by using the information in the combined database that it was unable to create.

When the FTC probe concluded two years later, DoubleClick was not charged with any violations of laws or regulations. The lesson here is that a company violates the Internet community's ethical standards at its own peril, even if the transgression does not break any laws.

Under the laws of most countries, people under the age of 18 or 21 are not considered adults. However, those countries that have proposed or passed laws that specify differential treatment for the privacy rights of children often define "child" as a person below the age of 12 or 13. This approach complicates the issue because it creates two classes of nonadults.

In the United States, the first attempts to regulate interactions between online business and children met with failure. In 2001, Congress enacted the Children's Internet Protection Act (CIPA), which required schools that receive federal funds to install filtering software (used to block access to adult content Web sites) on computers in their classrooms and libraries. In 2003, the Supreme Court held that CIPA was constitutional. In 1998, Congress enacted the Children's Online Protection Act (COPA) to protect children from "material harmful to minors." This law was immediately challenged and was held to be unconstitutional in 2009 because it unnecessarily restricted access to a substantial amount of lawful material, thus violating the First Amendment.

Congress was more successful with the **Children's Online Privacy Protection Act of 1998 (COPPA)**, which provides restrictions on data collection that must be followed by electronic commerce sites aimed at children. This law does not regulate content, as COPA attempted to do, so it has not been successfully challenged on First Amendment grounds.

Companies with Web sites that appeal to young people must be careful to comply with the laws governing their interactions with these young visitors. Companies that present online content intended for children usually have specific safeguards in place. For example, Disney requires a parent's (or teacher's) e-mail address and solicits consent before allowing children 12 or under to log in to the site. Disney also builds automated filters into children's activities that attempt to detect when a child has disclosed personal information when creating a drawing or a song or communicating with others on the site. Other sites that appeal to a young audience use similar techniques to limit unsupervised access to their Web pages. For example, Sanrio (the company that produces Hello Kitty and related products) asks for a birth date before allowing access to its English-language site that is directed at U.S. customers, **Sanriotown**. As shown in Figure 7-9, the site encourages visitors to notify the company that operates the site if they know a child who has gained access to the site in violation of COPPA.

Sanriotown.com does not collect personal information from persons under the age of 13. In order to ensure adherence to this policy, the opening page of our website asks for the date, month and year of birth of each visitor and denies further access to visitors whose birth date shows that they are under 13 years of age. If you believe that a child under 13 has gained access to the sanriotown.com site, or if you have any questions concerning sanriotown.com's privacy policy and practices, please contact us at:

Sanrio Digital (HK) Ltd
Unit 1109, Level 11, Cyberport 2
100 Cyberport Road
Hong Kong
Email: info@sanriotown.com

Source: http://www.sanriotown.com/login/privacy_us.php

FIGURE 7-9   Sanrio's approach to COPPA compliance

336

In 2013, the FTC issued a set of rules that clarified existing requirements under COPPA and added some specific new requirements. Under the new rules, operators of commercial Web sites and online services (including mobile device apps) directed to children under 13 that collect information from those children must comply with the following:

- Post a clear and comprehensive online privacy policy describing their information practices for personal information collected online from children;
- Provide direct notice to parents and obtain verifiable parental consent, with limited exceptions, before collecting personal information online from children;
- Give parents the choice of consenting to the operator's collection and internal use of a child's information, but prohibiting the operator from disclosing that information to third parties (unless disclosure is integral to the site or service, in which case, this must be made clear to parents);
- Provide parents access to their child's personal information to review and/or have the information deleted;
- Give parents the opportunity to prevent further use or online collection of a child's personal information;
- Maintain the confidentiality, security, and integrity of information they collect from children, including by taking reasonable steps to release such information only to parties capable of maintaining its confidentiality and security.

Companies that interact with children under 13 online should continually monitor government regulations that govern their activities because these rules are likely to be changed from time to time. Even companies that do not focus on younger customers need to be aware of COPPA provisions. As Yelp, the company that collects and publishes user reviews of restaurants, hotels, and other businesses learned in 2014 when it found itself settling with the FTC for COPPA violations. Yelp asks users to provide a birth date when they register; however, the company did not use that information to prevent users younger than age 13 from contributing reviews or providing personal information (such as their location). The FTC levied a civil penalty of $450,000 on Yelp and required the company to delete all information it had collected from those users.

Taxation and Electronic Commerce

Companies that do business on the Web are subject to the same taxes as any other company. However, even the smallest Web business can become instantly subject to taxes in many states and countries because of the Internet's worldwide scope. Traditional businesses may operate in one location and be subject to only one set of tax laws for years. By the time those businesses are operating in multiple states or countries, they have developed the internal staff and record-keeping infrastructure needed to comply with multiple tax laws. Firms that engage in electronic commerce must comply with these multiple tax laws from their first day of existence.

An online business can become subject to several types of taxes, including income taxes, transaction taxes, and property taxes. **Income taxes** are levied by national, state, and local governments on the net income generated by business activities. **Transaction taxes**, which include sales taxes, use taxes, and excise taxes, are levied on the products or services that the company sells or uses. Transaction taxes are also called **transfer taxes** because they arise when the ownership of a property or service is transferred to from one person or entity to another. **Property taxes** are levied by states and local governments on the personal property and real estate used in the business. In general, the taxes that cause the greatest concern for Web businesses are income taxes and sales taxes.

Nexus

A government acquires the power to tax a business when that business establishes a connection with the area controlled by the government. For example, a business that is located in Kansas has a connection with the state of Kansas and is subject to Kansas taxes. If that company opens a branch office in Arizona, it forms a connection with Arizona and becomes subject to Arizona taxes on the portion of its business that occurs in Arizona. This connection between a tax-paying entity and a government is called **nexus**. The concept of nexus is similar in many ways to the concept of personal jurisdiction discussed earlier in this chapter. The activities that create nexus in the United States are determined by state law and thus vary from state to state. Nexus issues have been frequently litigated, and the resulting common law is fairly complex. Determining nexus can be difficult when a company conducts only a few activities in or has minimal contact with the state. In such cases, it is advisable for the company to obtain the services of a professional tax advisor.

Companies that do business in more than one country face national nexus issues. If a company undertakes sufficient activities in a particular country, it establishes nexus with that country and becomes liable for filing tax returns in that country. The laws and regulations that determine national nexus are different in each country. Companies that sell through their Web sites do not, in general, establish nexus everywhere their goods are delivered to customers. Usually, a company can accept orders and ship from one state to many other states and avoid nexus by using a contract carrier such as FedEx or UPS to deliver goods to customers. Again, companies will find the services of a professional tax lawyer or accountant who has experience in international taxation to be valuable.

U.S. Income Taxes

The Internal Revenue Service (IRS) is the U.S. government agency charged with administering the country's tax laws. A basic principle of the U.S. tax system is that any verifiable increase in a company's wealth is subject to federal taxation. Thus, any company whose U.S.-based Web site generates income is subject to U.S. federal income tax. Furthermore, a Web site maintained by a company in the United States must pay federal income tax on income generated outside the United States. To reduce the incidence of double taxation of foreign earnings, U.S. tax law provides a credit for taxes paid to foreign countries. Most U.S. states levy an income tax on business earnings. If a company conducts activities in several states, it must file tax returns in all of those states and apportion its earnings in accordance with each state's tax laws. In some states, the individual cities, counties, and other political subdivisions within the state also have the power to levy income taxes on business earnings. Companies that do business in multiple local jurisdictions must apportion their income and file tax returns in each locality that levies an income tax. The number of taxing authorities (which includes states, counties, cities, towns, school districts, water districts, and many other governmental units) in the United States exceeds 30,000.

U.S. State Sales Taxes

Most U.S. states levy a transaction tax on goods sold to consumers. This tax is usually called a sales tax. Businesses that establish nexus with a state must file sales tax returns and remit the sales tax they collect from their customers. If a business ships goods to customers in other states, it is not required to collect sales tax from those customers unless the business has established nexus with the customer's state. However, the customer in this situation is liable for payment of a use tax in the amount that the business would have collected as sales tax if it had been a local business.

A **use tax** is a tax levied by a state on property used in that state that was not purchased in that state. Most states' use tax rates are identical to their sales tax rates. In addition to property purchased in another state, use taxes are assessed on property that is not "purchased" at all. For example, lease payments on vehicles are subject to use taxes in most states. The leased vehicle is not purchased (in any state) but when it is used in the lessee's state, it incurs that state's use tax. In the past, few consumers filed use tax returns and few states enforced their use tax laws with regularity. However, an increasing number of states are providing a line on their individual income tax returns that asks people to report and pay their use tax for the year along with their state income taxes. Some states allow taxpayers to estimate their use tax liability; others require an exact statement of the use tax amount.

Larger businesses use complex software to manage their sales tax obligations. Not only are the sales tax rates different in the approximately 7500 U.S. sales tax jurisdictions (which include states, counties, cities, and other sales tax authorities), but the rules about which items are taxable also differ. For example, New York's sales tax law provides that large marshmallows are taxable (because they are "snacks"), but small marshmallows are not taxable (because they are "food").

Some purchasers are exempt from sales tax, such as certain charitable organizations and businesses buying items for resale. Thus, to determine whether a particular item is subject to sales tax, a seller must know where the customer is located, what the laws of that jurisdiction say about taxability and tax rate, and the taxable status of the customer.

The sales tax collection process in the United States is largely regarded as a serious problem. Even the Supreme Court, in one of its sales tax decisions (*Quill v. North Dakota*, 1992), stated that the situation is needlessly confusing and encouraged Congress to act. Although a number of bills have been introduced since the *Quill* decision, none has become law.

A few states have enacted laws that require online retailers to collect and remit sales taxes on sales they make in their states, even though the online retailers do not have nexus with the state. Many more states have proposed or are considering such laws.

These statutes are often called **Amazon laws** because they are directed at large online retailers, such as Amazon.com. The idea behind these laws is that online retailers have an unfair pricing advantage over local stores because they are not required to collect sales tax (although the purchasers are required to file and pay a use tax, such taxes are widely avoided and it is costly for states to pursue the violators). The laws are designed to remove the unfair advantage and collect sales tax revenue, which many states need to balance their budgets. In 2013, Amazon began collecting sales tax voluntarily in most jurisdictions. As part of its long-term product distribution strategy, Amazon is building warehouses in many different states. Because these locations create nexus (Amazon owns or rents the warehouses in the state) for sales tax collection wherever they are built, Amazon no longer advocates actively against state sales tax laws. To protect the interests of its many small sellers, however, eBay has taken up the fight and is arguing that any sales tax compliance law exclude small merchants (usually considered to be online businesses with sales of less than $1 million per year).

In 2013, the Supreme Court refused to hear a case challenging the constitutionality of these state sales tax enforcement laws. Many observers believe that this will pave the way for federal legislation that replaces the patchwork of state laws and lower court decisions, many of which conflict with each other.

Many of the states have joined together to create the **Streamlined Sales and Use Tax Agreement (SSUTA)**. The SSUTA would simplify state sales taxes by making the various state tax codes more congruent with each other while allowing each state to set its own rates. Each state must adopt the agreement, and once a state does adopt it, companies in the state can choose one of several simple procedures for collecting and remitting sales taxes nationwide. Most states have not yet adopted this agreement. Legislation is proposed periodically in the U.S. Congress to resolve the issue, however, consensus is difficult to achieve since the interests of state governments, online retailers, traditional retailers, and consumers are complex and conflicting. At this point, it is difficult to see a clear path to legislative resolution of these issues anytime soon.

Import Tariffs

All countries in the world regulate the import and export of goods across their borders. In many cases, goods can only be imported into a country if a tariff is paid. A **tariff**, also called a **customs duty** or **duty**, is a tax levied on products as they enter the country. Countries have many reasons for imposing tariffs, and a complete discussion of tariffs and the role they play in international economics and foreign trade policy is beyond the scope of this book. Goods that are ordered online are subject to tariffs when they cross international borders. Even products that are delivered online (such as downloaded software) can be subject to tariffs. Many online shoppers have been surprised when an item they ordered from another country arrives with a bill from their government for the tariff.

European Union Value Added Taxes

The United States raises most of its revenue through income taxes. Other countries, especially those in the EU, use transaction taxes to generate most of their revenues. The

Value Added Tax (VAT) is the most common transaction tax used in these countries. A VAT is assessed on the amount of value added at each stage of production. For example, if a computer keyboard manufacturer purchased keyboard components for $20 and then sold finished keyboards for $50, the value added would be $30. VAT is collected by the seller at each stage of the transaction. A product that goes through five different companies on its way to the ultimate consumer would have VAT assessed on each of the five sales. In most countries, VAT is calculated at the time of each intermediate sale and remitted to the country in which that sale occurs.

The EU enacted legislation concerning the application of VAT to sales of digital goods that became effective in 2003. Companies based in EU countries must collect VAT on digital goods, no matter where in the EU the products are sold. This legislation has attracted the attention of companies based outside the EU that sell digital goods to consumers based in one or more EU countries. Under the law, non-EU companies that sell into the EU must now register with EU tax authorities and levy, collect, and remit VAT if their sales include digital goods delivered into the EU.

In 2015, new VAT rules became effective that require non-EU sellers to collect VAT at the rate levied in the buyer's country. There are currently 28 countries in the EU and most of them have different VAT rates, ranging from 17 percent (Luxembourg) to 27 percent (Hungary). Also, just as with U.S. sales taxes, many EU countries have multiple classifications of goods (such as food, medicine, and books) subject to the VAT at different rates. These multiple rates and categories can create an administrative nightmare for non-EU firms wishing to do business in the EU. EU-based firms, however, have the right to sell to customers anywhere in the EU and charge only the VAT rates applicable in the seller's country. This has prompted many non-EU firms to sell their digital goods to an EU distributor who then resells the products to EU customers.

Summary

As companies move business transactions and operations online, they can become subject to new laws and regulations, often without being aware of it. Some basic legal concepts, such as jurisdiction, remain unclear and ill-defined in online settings. The relationship between geographic boundaries and legal boundaries is based on the elements of power, effects, legitimacy, and notice. Although these elements have helped governments develop the concept of jurisdiction in the physical world, they exist in somewhat different forms on the Internet, so the jurisdiction rules that work well in the physical world do not always do so in the online world.

Conflict of laws issues can arise in new and interesting ways online. Contracts online are established through various types of offers and acceptances. Any contract for the electronic sale of goods or services includes implied warranties. Many companies include contracts or rules on their Web sites in the form of end-user license agreements and terms of service agreements.

The use and protection of intellectual property are major issues for online businesses, which must be careful to avoid infringement of trademarks, copyrights, or patents; defamation; and violation of publicity or privacy rights. Domain name disputes can be resolved through an international administrative mechanism that largely reduces the need for litigation. Online businesses must avoid implying relationships that do not exist and making negative evaluative statements about entities, even when true, given the subjective nature of defamation and product disparagement.

Unfortunately, the Internet is used by some to perpetrate crimes, advocate terrorism, and even wage war. Law enforcement agencies have found it difficult to combat many types of online crime, and governments are working to create adequate defenses for online war and terrorism.

Online businesses find it easy to track customer information, including online behavior and the use of such data has led to questions of ethics regarding online privacy. Some countries restrict information collection to a much greater degree than others. Companies that collect personal information can use an opt-in policy or an opt-out policy. Opt-in policies are more protective of customers' privacy rights. The number of data breaches that expose customer and employee data has continued to increase, leading many companies to increase security and threat testing. Online businesses must be careful when communicating with children. The laws of most countries require that parental consent be obtained before information is collected from children under the age of 13.

Online businesses are subject to the same laws and taxes as other companies, but the nature of doing business line can expose companies to a large number of laws and taxes sooner and in unexpected ways. The international nature of all online business can complicate a firm's tax obligations. The large number of government agencies that have jurisdiction and the power to tax makes it essential that companies doing business online understand the potential liabilities of doing business with customers in those jurisdictions.

Key Terms

acceptance	Amazon laws
advance fee fraud	authority to bind

breach of contract

browser-wrap acceptance

business process patent

click-wrap acceptance

common law

conflict of laws

consideration

constructive notice

contract

cookies

copy control

copyright

customs duty

cyberbullying

cybersquatting

defamatory

digital watermark

domain name ownership change

duty

end-user license agreements (EULAs)

fair use

forum selection clause

implied contract

implied warranty

income taxes

intellectual property

intentional tort

judicial comity

jurisdiction

legitimacy

long-arm statutes

name changing

name stealing

negligent tort

nexus

notice

offer

opt-in

opt-out

patent

patent assertion entity

patent troll

per se defamation

personal jurisdiction

power

product disparagement

property taxes

right of publicity

service mark

sexting

shrink-wrap acceptance

signature

Statute of Frauds

statutory law

Streamlined Sales and Use Tax Agreement
  (SSUTA)

subject-matter jurisdiction

sufficient jurisdiction

tariff

terms of service (ToS)

tort

trade name

trademark

trademark dilution

transaction taxes

transfer taxes

typosquatting

use tax

vicarious copyright infringement

warranty disclaimer

Web-wrap acceptance

writing

Review Questions

1. Briefly explain the role borders play in determining jurisdiction.
2. What is jurisdiction?
3. Briefly explain the difference between notice and constructive notice.
4. What is the difference between a breach of contract and a tort?
5. What is the difference between subject-matter jurisdiction and personal jurisdiction?
6. What is a long-arm statute?
7. What is the difference between a negligent tort and an intentional tort?
8. What is judicial comity?
9. Under what conditions might a conflict of laws occur?
10. What are the three key elements of a contract?
11. What is an implied contract?
12. What is the body of U.S. law that concerns contracts called?
13. How do most U.S. Web sites obtain a user's agreement to its end-user license agreement (EULA)?
14. What is an implied warranty?
15. What is a warranty disclaimer and when might an online business use one?
16. What is a right of publicity?
17. Briefly explain the differences between copyrights and patents.
18. Briefly explain the differences among trademarks, service marks, and trade names.
19. What is fair use under U.S. copyright law?
20. What is vicarious copyright infringement?
21. What is a patent troll?
22. What is the difference between common law and statutory law?
23. What is a digital watermark?
24. What is product disparagement?
25. What is cyberbullying?
26. Briefly explain the concept of nexus as it relates to taxation generally.
27. What is a use tax?

Exercises

1. In about 100 words, explain how the concepts of power, effects, and jurisdiction are related to each other.
2. The levels of authority and autonomy with which governments of various countries operate vary significantly from one country to another. In about 100 words, explain how different cultures allow these variations yet still perceive their own government to be legitimate.
3. In about 100 words, explain why constructive notice in international transactions can often be less effective when those transactions are completed online.

4. In the past, geographic borders have helped governments assert jurisdiction effectively. In about 100 words, describe one way the Internet has changed the role borders play in the determination of jurisdiction.

5. Online businesses are capable of committing a crime, breaching a contract, or engaging in a tortious action. In about 200 words, provide a specific example of each in an online commercial setting. In your answer, explain why each action you describe is either a crime, a breach of contract, or a tort.

6. Write a paragraph in which you outline the reasons an online business might want to use a forum selection clause in its terms of service statement.

7. To be enforceable, every contract must include an offer and an acceptance. Consider a typical online retail transaction in which an item is ordered and paid for online by a purchaser and shipped by the seller. In two or three paragraphs, identify specifically and describe the actions that constitute the offer and the acceptance.

8. In the United States, Great Britain, and many other countries, contracts of certain types must comply with the Statute of Frauds to be enforceable. In about 100 words, describe the specific elements a contract must include to comply with the Statute of Frauds. In your answer, provide one or two examples of how each required element could be satisfied.

9. Assume you have downloaded an app for your smartphone. In one or two paragraphs, describe how you and the app's seller have each obtained consideration in the completion of the transaction.

10. In one or two paragraphs, outline the key factors that determine fair use of copyrighted text under U.S. law.

11. The merits of allowing companies to patent their business processes have been debated by legal scholars and business experts. One proposed solution to this debate would allow the issuance of business patents, but restrict the patent protection period to a short time, perhaps two or three years. In about 200 words, present logical and factual arguments that support the issuance of limited-term business process patents. Conclude your arguments with a policy recommendation.

12. Use your favorite Web search engine to obtain a list of Web pages that include the words "privacy statement." Visit the Web pages on the search results list until you find a page that includes the text of a privacy statement. Print the page and turn it in with a report of about 200 words in which you answer the following questions:

   a. Does the site follow an opt-in or opt-out policy (or is the policy not stated clearly in the privacy statement)?

   b. Does the privacy statement include a specific provision or provisions regarding the collection of information from children?

   c. Does the privacy statement describe what happens to the collected personal information if the company goes out of business or is sold to another company? (List these provisions, if any.)

   Close your report with one paragraph in which you evaluate the overall clarity of the privacy statement.

13. The Good Grow Seed Company sells vegetable and flower seeds to home gardeners online and has noticed that many of its customers order the same types of seeds each year when they plant their gardens. The company would like to send e-mails to customers who have purchased seeds in the past. These e-mails would use information about the types of seeds

customers have purchased in the past and would offer them discounts on seeds for new varieties. Write a memo of about 200 words in which you attempt to convince Good Grow's marketing manager that the company should use an opt-in statement to request permission to send such e-mails.

14. In about 100 words, explain how a value-added tax (VAT) is calculated and collected. In your answer, contrast the use of a VAT with the use of a combined system of sales taxes and income taxes.

Cases

C1. Airbnb and Uber

Companies that use Internet technologies to change the structure of the industry in which they operate can create new legal questions, especially in businesses that are subject to governmental regulation. As you learned earlier in this chapter, Ride brokering services such as Lyft and Uber have created questions about the regulation of the vehicle-for-hire business. Laws in various jurisdictions require taxi and bus companies to hold specific types of licenses, to buy permits to operate in certain geographic areas, to carry specific types of insurance, and often to keep trip records. These laws can require specific standards for the companies' employees who drive the vehicles and for the vehicles themselves and are intended to provide for a certain basic level of competence and safety for passengers. In large metropolitan areas, such as New York City, the number of vehicles for hire is carefully managed and there have been disputes between government regulators and these new businesses regarding allegations that they increase traffic congestion. The larger question of whether the ride brokers or the vehicle drivers/owners are subject to various specific laws and regulations remains unresolved in many jurisdictions around the world.

Airbnb has created similar issues in the lodging industry. An online room-booking service that does not own any hotels or other properties itself, Airbnb has found itself in the same kind of unclear regulatory zone as it tries to operate legally in multiple jurisdictions around the world. In many cases, local laws regulate the commercial provision of lodging. Hotel companies work with those laws and often make a substantial investment in learning how to comply with new laws whenever they open a property in a new location. In general, Airbnb's hosts bear the responsibility for complying with local laws related to lodging. For example, many jurisdictions impose lodging taxes that must be collected and remitted by those who rent overnight accommodations. These laws and taxes vary widely even within a single country or state.

REQUIRED

1. Using your favorite search engine, the resources of your library, and information available on the Airbnb Web site, identify and evaluate risks to which Airbnb hosts are exposed and the protections provided them by Airbnb. Summarize your findings in a report of about 300 words.

2. Using your favorite search engine and the resources of your library, identify and evaluate risks to which Airbnb guests are exposed and the protections provided them by Airbnb. Summarize your findings in a report of about 200 words.

3. Using your favorite search engine, the resources of your library, and information available on the Uber Web site, identify and evaluate the protections provided to riders who use the service. Summarize your findings in a report of about 200 words.

4. New York City has engaged in negotiations with Uber and other online ride-for-hire brokers to find reasonable solutions to both safety and rider safety concerns in recent years. Using your favorite search engine and the resources of your library, identify and summarize the specific issues discussed in a report of about 100 words. Conclude your report with a summary of any implications you see for other large cities as they face these issues.

Note: Your instructor might assign you to a group to complete this case, and might ask you to prepare a formal presentation of your results to your class.

C2. Ellasaurus Products Enterprises

Ellen Carson is the author and illustrator of a successful series of children's books that chronicle the adventures of Ellasaurus, a four-year-old orange dinosaur. Ellen has done well with the books, but decided she could earn considerably more money by creating a merchandising business around the Ellasaurus character. Thus, she recently created Ellasaurus Products Enterprises (EPE), a company that develops and markets Ellasaurus toys, stuffed animals, coloring books, pajamas, and Halloween costumes from its location in Flint, Michigan.

EPE has been able to get some major retailers to stock the Ellasaurus product line, but others have been willing to take on a new and unproven product line. Ellen has decided to sell the Ellasaurus merchandise online directly to customers. She also sees an online presence as a great way to build and maintain customer loyalty. Ellen envisions a Web site with a number of virtual community features in addition to the product store. For example, she would like to offer online games, discussion areas, interactive stories, and other activities that would promote EPE products and her books.

The Ellasaurus book series is targeted to children who are between four and six years old. Ellen expects the EPE product line to appeal to a similar demographic. Ellen has visited sites such as Hello Kitty and Nick Jr., which appeal to similar age groups, to get ideas for the site. She would like the site to be appealing to her main audience, but she would like to obtain registration information from site visitors so EPE can send marketing e-mails and facilitate social networking activities among her customer base.

Ellen plans to sell merchandise to U.S. residents only at first, but she would like to sell internationally within a few years. The site will allow visitors from any country to register and participate in the virtual community features.

REQUIRED

1. Ellen will use some copyrighted illustrations from her books on the Web site. She will also include themes from the story lines of her books in some of the games that will be available (free) on the site to registered visitors. Prepare a report of about 300 words in which you discuss at least two intellectual property issues that might arise in the operation of the Web site.

2. Children are using smartphones and tablet devices at increasingly younger ages today. In about 100 words, outline the type of mobile app or apps that might work for Ellen.

3. In about 200 words, describe the ethical issues that Ellen faces because of the ages of her intended audience members. Be sure to deal specifically with advertising issues as well as issues that might arise in managing the virtual community elements on the Web site.

4. In about 300 words, outline the laws with which the site must comply when it registers site visitors under the age of 13. Include recommendations regarding how Ellen can best comply with those laws.

5. What concerns will arise as Ellen expands the scope of product sales internationally in a few years? In your response of about 300 words, include specific discussion of laws, ethics, privacy, culture, taxes, and customs tariffs.

Note: Your instructor might assign you to a group to complete this case, and might ask you to prepare a formal presentation of your results to your class.

For Further Study and Research

Abelson, R. and J. Creswell. 2015. "Data Breach at Anthem May Forecast a Trend," *The New York Times*, February 7, B1.

Alino, N. and G. Schneider, 2012. "Consumption Taxes on Digital Products in the European Union," *Journal of Legal, Ethical, and Regulatory Issues*, 16(2), 1–8.

Angwin, J. and D. Bank. 2005. "Time Warner Alerts Staff to Lost Data: Files for 600,000 Workers Vanish During Truck Ride," *The Wall Street Journal*, May 3, A3.

Apple, Inc. 2015. "App Store Rings in 2015 with New Records," Press Release, January 8. https://www.apple.com/pr/library/2015/01/08App-Store-Rings-in-2015-with-New-Records.html

Barnes, B. 2007. "Web Playgrounds of the Very Young," *The New York Times*, December 31. http://www.nytimes.com/2007/12/31/business/31virtual.html

Barry Diller v. INTERNETCO Corp. 2001. WIPO Case No. D2000–1734, March 9. http://www.wipo.int/amc/en/domains/decisions/html/2000/d2000-1734.html

Baturin, H. 2015. "The Marketplace Fairness Act: Potential Solutions to an Imperfect Law," *Georgetown Public Policy Review*, May 12. http://gppreview.com/2015/05/12/the-marketplace-fairness-act-potential-solutions-to-an-imperfect-law/

Beta Computers (Europe), Ltd. v. Adobe Systems (Europe), Ltd. 1996 SLT 604; 1996 SCLR 587.

Carver, B. 2010. "Why License Agreements Do Not Control Copy Ownership: First Sales and Essential Copies," *Berkeley Technology Law Journal*, 25, 1886–1954.

Classen, H. 2014. *A Practical Guide to Software Licensing for Licensees and Licensors.* Washington, DC: American Bar Association.

Clifford, C. 2013. "Entrepreneurs Want Patent Trolls Gone, But Current Legislation Is Sloppy," *Entrepreneur*, December 4. http://www.entrepreneur.com/article/230232

Costello, A. 2010. "Facebook Lawsuit Dismissed," *Long Island Herald*, August 11. http://www.liherald.com/stories/Facebook-lawsuit-dismissed,26966

DelBianco, S. 2015. "Chaffetz Internet Sales Tax Bill Is Too Costly and Complex," *CIO*, July 22. http://ww2.cfo.com/tax/2015/07/chaffetz-internet-sales-tax-bill-costly-complex/

Digital Millennium Copyright Act. 1998. Public Law No. 105–304, 112 Statutes 2860.

Direct Marketing. 2001. "FTC Closes DoubleClick Investigation," 63(12), April, 18.

The Economist. 2015. "Uber Handed Another Setback, This Time in Italy," May 30, 9.

The Economist. 2015. "Speak No Evil: The Justices Toss Out a Man's Conviction for Writing Violent Facebook Posts," June 6, 22.

Fairless, T. 2015. "Uber Files Complaints Against European Governments Over Bans," *The Wall Street Journal*, April 1. http://www.wsj.com/articles/uber-files-complaints-against-european-governments-over-bans-1427885946

Fidler, S. 2007. "Terrorism Fight 'in Wrong Century,' " *Financial Times*, July 10, 4.

Flegenheimer, M. 2015. "Ending Fight, for Now, City Hall Drops Plan for Uber Cap," *The New York Times*, July 23, A20.

Foege, A. 2005. "Extortion.com," *Fortune Small Business*, September 1.

Foster, A. 2002. "Computer-Crime Incidents at 2 California Colleges Tied to Investigation Into Russian Mafia," *Chronicle of Higher Education*, June 24.

Gertz, B. 2015. "Intel Assessment: Weak Response to Breaches Will Lead to More Cyber Attacks," *The Washington Free Beacon*, July 28. http://freebeacon.com/national-security/intel-assessment-obama-admin-response-to-cyber-encourages-more-attacks/

Gillette, F. and S. Kolhatkar. 2014. "Room With a Feud: Airbnb's Battle for New York," *Bloomberg BusinessWeek*, June 19, 54–58.

Granholm v. Heald, 544 U.S. 460 (2005).

Hale, K. and R. McNeal. 2011. "Technology, Politics, and E-commerce: Internet Sales Tax and Interstate Cooperation," *Government Information Quarterly*, 28(2), 262–270.

Harris, A. 2013. "PokerStars' Scheinberg to Pay $50 Million to End U.S. Probe," *Bloomberg BusinessWeek*, June 12. http://www.businessweek.com/news/2013–06-12/pokerstars-scheinberg-to-pay-50-million-to-end-u-dot-s-dot-probe-1

Hemphill, T. 2000. "DoubleClick and Consumer Online Privacy: An E-Commerce Lesson Learned," *Business & Society Review*, 105(3), Fall, 361–372.

Higgins, K. 2013. "Feds Indict Five in Massive Credit Card Data Breach Scheme," *Dark Reading*, July 25. http://www.darkreading.com/attacks-breaches/feds-indict-five-in-massive-credit-card-data-breach-scheme/d/d-id/1140189

Hulme, G. 2005. "Extortion Online," *InformationWeek*, September 13, 24–25.

Identity Theft Resource Center (ITRC). 2015. *Identity Theft Resource Center Breach Report Hits Record High in 2014*. San Diego: ITRC. http://www.idtheftcenter.org/ITRC-Surveys-Studies/2014databreaches.html

Kendall, B. 2013. "Supreme Court Won't Review N.Y. Sales-Tax Law for Online Retailers: High Court Rejects Legal Challenge by Amazon," *The Wall Street Journal*, December 2. http://online.wsj.com/news/articles/SB10001424052702303670804579233960044617496

King, R. 2009. "Lessons from the Data Breach at Heartland," *Bloomberg BusinessWeek*, July 6. http://www.bloomberg.com/bw/stories/2009-07-06/lessons-from-the-data-breach-at-heartlandbusinessweek-business-news-stock-market-and-financial-advice

Lee, J-A., C-Y Liu, and W. Li. 2013. "Searching for Internet Freedom in China: A Case Study on Google's China Experience," *Cardozo Arts & Entertainment Law Journal*, 31, 405–434.

Lee, T. 2013."Here's Why the House Patent Bill Won't Put a Stop to Patent Trolling," *The Washington Post*, December 6. http://www.washingtonpost.com/blogs/the-switch/wp/2013/12/06/heres-why-the-house-patent-bill-wont-put-a-stop-to-patent-trolling/

Levine, G. 2011. "Chances of Winning and Losing Domain Name Disputes," *UDRPCommentaries.com*, December 20. http://www.udrpcommentaries.com/chances-of-winning-and-losing-domain-name-disputes/

Levy, S. 2011. *In the Plex: How Google Thinks, Works, and Shapes Our Lives*. New York: Simon & Schuster.

Lieber, R. 2015. "Moral of Airbnb Horror Story: Beware," *The New York Times*, August 15, B1.

Macdonald, E. 2011. "When is a Contract Formed by the Browse-wrap process?" *International Journal of Law and Information Technology*. http://ijlit.oxfordjournals.org/content/early/2011/07/27/ijlit.ear009.short

Magid, L. 2013. "FTC Clarifies Children's Online Privacy Law (COPPA)," *Forbes*, April 25. http://www.forbes.com/sites/larrymagid/2013/04/25/ftc-clarifies-childrens-online-privacy-law-coppa/

Mangalindan, M. 2007. "EBay Is Ordered to Pay $30 Million in Patent Rift," *The Wall Street Journal*, December 13, B4.

Mazzetti, M. and D. Sanger. 2015. "U.S. Fears Data Stolen by Chinese Hacker Could Identify Spies," *The New York Times*, July 25, A1.

Minor, R. and C. Gartner. 2012. *VAT on Electronically Supplied Services to EU Consumers—A Practical Compliance Guide for Cross-Border Suppliers*. Luxembourg: Spitze.

Mitchell, K., D. Finkelhor, L. Jones, and J. Wolak. 2012. "Prevalence and Characteristics of Youth Sexting: A National Study," *Pediatrics*, 129(1), January 1, 13–20.

Morrison, K. 2014. "Yelp Pays $450,000 FTC Fine For COPPA Violation," *Ad Week*, September 22. http://www.adweek.com/socialtimes/yelp-pays-450000-ftc-fine-coppa-violation/204977

Nakashima, E. 2015. "Hacks of OPM Databases Compromised 22.1 Million People, Federal Authorities Say," *The Washington Post*, July 9. http://www.washingtonpost.com/blogs/federal-eye/wp/2015/07/09/hack-of-security-clearance-system-affected-21-5-million-people-federal-authorities-say/

The New York Times. 2013. "A Season for Sales Taxes," December 10, A30.

Nigro, D. 2005. "Supreme Court Lifts Shipping Bans," *Wine Spectator*, 30(6), July 31, 12.

Novak, J. 2014. "European VAT: Ten Things Online Sellers Need To Know About Taxes On Digital Goods And Services," *Forbes*, May 15. http://www.forbes.com/sites/janetnovack/2014/05/15/european-vat-10-things-online-sellers-need-to-know-about-taxes-on-digital-goods-and-services/

O'Connor, J. 2013. "Read Florida's New Law Targeting Online Bullying," *NPR StateImpact*, June 3. http://stateimpact.npr.org/florida/2013/06/03/read-floridas-new-law-targeting-online-bullying/

Overly, M. and M. Karlyn. 2013. *A Guide to IT Contracting: Checklists, Tools, and Techniques*. New York: CRC Press.

Pasahow, M. 2006. "Granholm v. Heald: Shifting the Boundaries of California Reciprocal Wine Shipping Law," *Berkeley Technology Law Journal*, January, 21(1), 569–584.

Perlroth, N. 2013. "Target Struck in the Cat-and-Mouse Game of Credit Theft," *The New York Times*, December 20, B1.

Preston, R. 2014. "Supreme Court Toughens Business Process Patent Test," *InformationWeek*, June 20. http://www.informationweek.com/software/enterprise-applications/supreme-court-toughens-business-process-patent-test/a/d-id/1278736

Puzzanghera, J. 2011. "Justice Department Opinion Allows States to Offer Online Gambling," *Los Angeles Times*, December 27. http://latimesblogs.latimes.com/money_co/2011/12/online-gambling-states-justice.html

Quill Corp. v. North Dakota, 504 U.S. 298 (1992).

Rader, R., C. Chien, and D. Hricik. 2013. "Make Patent Trolls Pay in Court," *The New York Times*, June 4. http://www.nytimes.com/2013/06/05/opinion/make-patent-trolls-pay-in-court.html

Roettgers, J. 2015. "Apple Music Under Investigation Over App Store 'Tax'," *Variety*, July 22. http://variety.com/2015/digital/news/apple-music-under-investigation-over-app-store-tax-1201546263/

Rustad, M. and M. V. Onufrio, 2010. "The Exportability of the Principles of Software: Lost in Translation?" *Hastings Science and Technology Law Journal*, 2(25), 25–80.

Sage, A. 2010. "Ebay, NRF to Take on Organized Retail Crime," *Reuters*, March 22. http://www.reuters.com/article/idUSTRE62L0OR20100322

Sang-Hum, C. 2013. "Computer Networks in South Korea Are Paralyzed in Cyberattacks," *The New York Times*, March 21, A5.

Sanger, D. and M. Fackler. 2015. "Tracking the Cyberattack on Sony to North Koreans," *The New York Times*, January 19, A1.

Samuelson, P. 2009. "Legally Speaking: When is a License Really a Sale?" *Communications of the ACM*, 52(3), March, 27–29.

Schmidt, M. 2015. "F.B.I. Still Lags in Countering Evolving Terrorist Threats, Report Says," *The New York Times*, March 26, A12.

350

Schneider, G., L. Barkacs, and C. Barkacs. 2006. "Software Errors: Recovery Rights Against Vendors," *Journal of Legal, Ethical and Regulatory Issues*, 9(2), 61–67.

Schultz, E. 2011. "Success in a Bottle: Wine Sites Finally Start to Win Over Web," *Advertising Age*, July 25. http://adage.com/article/news/wine-websites-find-success-states-open-borders/228867

Schwanhausser, M. 2008. "EBay Patent Case Settled: It Owns 'Buy It Now' After Six-Year Battle," *San Jose Mercury News*, February 29.

Seidenberg, S. 2015. "Business-method and Software Patents May Go Through the Looking Glass After Alice Decision," *ABA Journal*, February 1. http://www.abajournal.com/magazine/article/business_method_and_software_patents_may_go_through_the_looking_glass_after

Sengupta, S. 2013. "The Information-Gathering Paradox," *The New York Times*, October 26, SR4.

Sherman, M. 2011. "Sixteen, Sexting, and a Sex Offender: How Advances in Cell Phone Technology Have Led to Teenage Sex Offenders," *Boston University Journal of Science and Technology Law*, 17(1), 138–161.

Sidel, R. 2014. "Home Depot's 56 Million Card Breach Bigger Than Target's," *The Wall Street Journal*, September 18. http://www.wsj.com/articles/home-depot-breach-bigger-than-targets-1411073571

Singer, P. and A. Friedman. 2014. *Cybersecurity and Cyberware: What Everyone Needs to Know*, Oxford: Oxford University Press.

Smith, D. 2014. "Apple Settles with FTC After Kids Blow Millions on the App Store," *Readwrite*, January 15. http://readwrite.com/2014/01/15/apple-settles-ftc-after-kids-millions-parents-dollars-app-store-purchases

Smith, J. 2015. "I.R.S. Breach Exposes Data of Taxpayers," *The New York Times*, May 27, B1.

Sorkin, A. 2013. "In Tax Fight, Amazon Hands Baton to eBay," *The New York Times*, April 23. http://dealbook.nytimes.com/2013/04/22/in-tax-fight-amazon-hands-baton-to-ebay/

Stone, M. 2001. "Court Dismisses Class Action Against eBay," *BizReport*, January 19. http://www.bizreport.com/daily/2001/01/20010119–4.htm

Terhune, C. 2013. "Kaiser Permanente Reports Privacy Breach to 19,000 Patients," *The Los Angeles Times*, December 10, B1.

Thomas, K. and C. McGee. 2012. "The Only Thing We Have to Fear Is … 120 Characters," *TechTrends*, 56(1), January–February, 19–33.

United Nations. 1970. "Declaration on Principles of International Law Concerning Friendly Relations and Cooperation Among States in Accordance with the Charter of the United Nations," *General Assembly Resolution*, #2625, 35th Session.

Van Alstine, P. 2004. "Federal Common Law in an Age of Treaties," *Cornell Law Review*, 89(892), 917–927.

Van Name, M. and B. Catchings. 1998. "Practical Advice About Privacy and Customer Data," *PC Week*, 15(27), July 6, 38.

Vara, V. and L. Chao. 2006. "EBay Steps Back From Asia, Will Shutter China Site," *The Wall Street Journal*, December 19. http://online.wsj.com/article/SB116647579560853680.html

Vernor, Timothy S. v. Autodesk, Inc. 2011. No. 09–3596, Order (9th Cir. Jan 18).

Vinton, K. 2015. "CVS Investigates Credit Card Breach at its Online Photo Service," *Forbes*, July 17. http://www.forbes.com/sites/katevinton/2015/07/17/cvs-investigates-credit-card-breach-at-its-online-photo-service/

Ward, B. and J. Sipior. 2011. "The Battle Over E-commerce Sales Taxes Heats Up," *Information Systems Management*, 28(4), 321–326.

World Intellectual Property Organization. 2011. "The Uniform Domain Name Dispute Resolution Policy and WIPO," August. http://www.wipo.int/export/sites/www/amc/en/docs/wipointaudrp.pdf

Wyatt, E. 2012. "U.S. Penalizes Online Company in Sale of Personal Data," *The New York Times*, June 13, B2.

Wyatt, E. 2014. "Government and Apple Settle Children's App Purchase Inquiry," *The New York Times*, January 15. http://www.nytimes.com/2014/01/16/technology/government-and-apple-settle-childrens-app-purchase-inquiry.html?hp

Zelinsky, E. 2011. "Lobbying Congress: Amazon Laws in the Lands of Lincoln and Mt. Rushmore," *State Tax Notes*, 60, 557–581.

PART 3

Technologies for Electronic Commerce

Blend Images Photography/Veer

Web Server Hardware and Software

LEARNING OBJECTIVES

In this chapter, you will learn:

- How a Web server performs its basic functions
- What operating system and server software is used on Web servers
- How to identify and manage e-mail and spam control issues
- How commonly used Internet and Web site utility programs work
- What hardware online businesses use to power their Web sites
- How cloud computing and content delivery networks are providing new Web infrastructure options for online businesses

INTRODUCTION

Channel 2 News is an organization that produces news content for the daily evening television news program on Israel's Channel 2. It also provides news and current affairs programming for other Channel 2 shows, Web sites, and its mobile device app. Both the Web sites and the mobile app offer significant numbers of high-resolution photographs and video clips. This type of content, as you will learn in this chapter, requires the transmission of much larger files over the Internet than the text and simple graphics that make up many Web pages.

More than many other types of business, the operation of an online news organization faces wide variation in user interest levels and the accompanying need for Internet bandwidth. There are often slow news days, with not much occurring in the local area or the world, but unexpected events can happen around the world all at once. When this happens, large percentages of the Channel 2 audience will want information at the same time. Moreover, as a news story is breaking, many Channel 2 customers will check in for updates repeatedly, especially on the Web site and the mobile app. The effect is magnified because highly interesting breaking news stories often come with many different video clips and large graphics. The mobile app allows users to specify that Channel 2 notify them when specific news events are occurring. This made the demand on Channel 2's Web servers even greater.

When users overloaded the system with multiple requests for these items, they would often experience delays or pauses in video playback on their devices. These delays would inevitably occur just when users felt they needed Channel 2 to provide information the most, and audience members often became frustrated with the quality of service being provided.

This wide variation in the volume of Internet traffic made planning for and implementing an optimal Web server configuration difficult. Unlike a business that has regular peak periods, such as a florist or a toy retailer, the peak periods in the news business are largely unpredictable.

To solve this problem, Channel 2 contracted with Google Cloud Computing to store its content on their Web servers. As you will learn in this chapter, cloud computing services provide a way for companies with wide variations in their Internet traffic to buy availability on the service provider's servers, avoiding making an investment in their own servers that would be unused most of the time.

Web Server Basics

As you learned in Chapter 2, Web servers are computers that are designed to provide public access to files that are rendered as Web pages on visitors' computers. In this chapter, you will learn about these computers and the software they use to deliver Web sites. Web sites that have many visitors must use a large number of these Web server computers to deliver Web page files efficiently. Operating large numbers of computers requires synchronization of their activities, dividing the workload that each computer must carry. You will learn about these elements of Web site operation in this chapter as well.

When people use Web browser software to become part of the Web, their computers become Web client computers on a worldwide client/server network. Client/server architectures are used in LANs, WANs, and the Web. In a client/server architecture, the client computers typically request services, such as printing, information retrieval, and database access, from the server, which processes the clients' requests. The computers that perform the server function usually have more memory and larger, faster disk drives than the client computers they serve. Recall from Chapter 2 that Web browser software enables computers to function as Web clients. Thus, a Web browser is also called Web client software.

The Internet connects many different types of computers and other devices, each running different types of operating system software. The ability of a network to connect devices that use different operating systems is called **platform neutrality**. Because Web software is platform neutral, it enables all of the devices it interconnects to communicate with each other easily and effectively. Platform neutrality was a critical factor in the rapid spread and widespread acceptance of the Internet and the Web. Before the Internet, computers that were connected to each other using leased phone lines either had to run the same operating system software or needed specifically configured translation software installed on each computer to communicate with each other. Figure 8-1 shows how the Web's platform neutrality provides multiple interconnections among a wide variety of client and server computers.

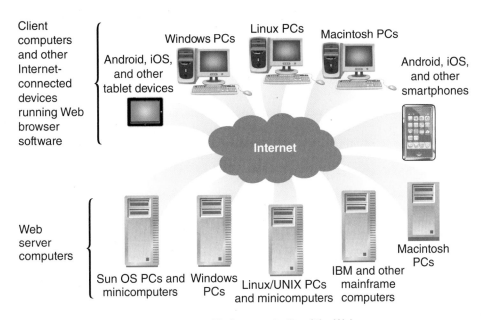

FIGURE 8-1   Platform neutrality of the Web

The job of a Web server is to respond to requests from Web client computers. The three elements of a Web server are the hardware (computers and related components), operating system software, and Web server software. In the early days of electronic commerce, Web sites were collections of individual pages about the site's product or service offerings. Today, most Web sites regularly deliver customized pages in response to customers' specific needs. You will learn how sites do that in the next section.

Dynamic Content Generation

A **static page** is an unchanging Web page composed of a set of files stored on a Web server. A **dynamic page** is a Web page whose content is created by software in response to user requests. Dynamic pages allow a Web server to provide customized pages in response to specific queries from site visitors. These customized pages are called **dynamic content**. Dynamic content can give the user an interactive experience with the Web site. Individual Web page elements, such as text, graphics, form fields, and video can change in response to user input or other variables. For example, customers who enter their order numbers can receive dynamic Web pages that show the details of their orders. Most online business sites generate thousands of dynamic Web pages every minute in response to requests from site users' Web browsers.

Web site designers can incorporate dynamic content using two basic approaches. The first approach is called **client-side scripting**, in which software operates within the Web browser to change what is displayed on the Web page in response to a user's actions (such as mouse clicks or keyboard text input). In client-side scripting, changes are generated within the browser using scripts written in languages such as JavaScript or Adobe Flash. The Web browser retrieves a file from the Web server that includes the script's code. Then the code, using input from the user (boxes checked, form fields filled out, and so on), instructs the Web browser to request specific page elements from the Web server and specifies how they will be displayed in the Web browser.

In the second approach, called **server-side scripting**, a program running on the Web server creates a Web page using specific information collected from the user's Web browser, including that user's input (boxes checked, form fields filled out, and so on). The content of the request can also include information such as the type of Web browser making the request, or even simply the passage of time. For example, if a customer is logged into an online banking site and does not enter any text or click anywhere on the page for a few minutes, the Web server could automatically terminate the connection and send a page to the Web browser indicating that "your session has expired." In all server-side dynamic page-generation activities, server-side scripts are mixed with HTML-tagged text to create the dynamic Web page.

The most common software tools used to create dynamic Web pages include Microsoft's ASP.Net (often included in a program written in a standard language such as C#, C++, or Visual Basic), Apache Software Foundation's **Hypertext Preprocessor (PHP)**, or Adobe's ColdFusion. Although JavaScript is used extensively for client-side scripting, it can also be used for server-side scripting. The Java programming language is another tool used to create server-side scripts. AJAX (asynchronous JavaScript and XML) is a newer framework used to create interactive Web sites that look like applications running in a Web browser.

Most dynamic Web pages must reload in their entirety if any page content changes. AJAX lets programmers create Web pages that will update asynchronously by exchanging small amounts of data with the server while the rest of the Web page continues to be displayed in the browser. Because the entire Web page does not reload with every change, the user experiences faster responses. Ruby on Rails, Python, and Scala are also newer Web development frameworks that are used to accomplish the same objectives as AJAX.

As these development frameworks and languages evolve, sites sometimes switch from one to the other. For example, Twitter originally used Ruby on Rails to generate dynamic Web pages, but switched to Java in 2011 because its staff believed Java would handle high user volumes better. Many Web sites use more than one language and/or development framework to accomplish specific objectives.

Multiple Meanings of "Server"

As you learned in Chapter 2, computers that are connected to the Internet and make some of their contents publicly available using the HTTP protocol are called Web servers. Unfortunately, the term "server" is used in many different ways by information systems professionals, which can be confusing. You are likely to encounter a number of different uses of the word "server."

A **server** is any computer used to provide (or "serve") files or make programs available to other computers connected to it through a network (such as a LAN or a WAN). The software that the server computer uses to make these files and programs available to the other computers is often called **server software**. Sometimes this server software is included as part of the operating system that is running on the server computer. Thus, some information systems professionals informally refer to the operating system software on a server computer as server software, a practice that adds considerable confusion to the use of the term "server."

Some servers are connected through a router to the Internet. As you learned in Chapter 2, these servers can run software, called Web server software, that makes files on those servers available to other computers on the Internet. When a server computer is connected to the Internet and is running Web server software (usually in addition to the server software it runs to serve files to client computers on its own network), it is called a Web server.

Similar terminology issues arise for server computers that perform e-mail processing and database management functions. Recall that the server computer that handles incoming and outgoing e-mail is usually called an **e-mail server**, and the software that manages e-mail activity on that server is frequently called e-mail server software. The server computer on which database management software runs is often called a **database server**. The computer on which a company runs its accounting and inventory management software is sometimes called a **transaction server**.

Thus, the word "server" is used to describe several types of computer hardware and software, all of which might be found in a typical electronic commerce operation. The only way to determine which server people are talking about when they use the term is from the context or by asking a clarifying question. If you hear a computer technician say, "The server is down today," the problem might be in the hardware, the software, or a combination of the two.

Web Client/Server Architectures

In Chapter 2, you learned that the Web is software that runs on the Internet. In this section, you will learn more about how Web client and Web server software work. When a person uses a Web browser to visit a Web site, the Web browser (also known as a Web client) requests files from the Web server at the company or organization that operates the Web site. Using the Internet as the transportation medium, the request is formatted by the browser using HTTP and sent to the server computer. When the server receives the request, it retrieves the files containing the HTML text and other files that contain Web page elements, formats them using HTTP, and sends them back to the Web browser over the Internet.

When the HTTP-formatted files (one containing the HTML-marked text and one for each separate graphic, photo, or other file) arrive at the client computer, the Web browser formats the information contained in the files as a Web page on the client computer. This process repeats as the client requests, the server responds, and the client displays the result. Sometimes, a single client request results in dozens or even hundreds of separate server responses to locate and deliver information. A Web page containing many graphics and other objects can be slow to appear in the client's Web browser window because each page element requires a separate request and response.

The basic Web client/server model is a two-tier model because it has only one client and one server. All communication takes place on the Internet between the client and the server. Of course, other computers are involved in forwarding packets of information across the Internet, but the messages are created and read only by the client and the server computers in a **two-tier client/server architecture**. Figure 8-2 shows how a Web client and a Web server communicate with each other in a two-tier client/server architecture.

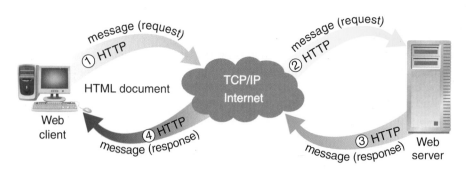

FIGURE 8-2   Message flows in a two-tier client/server network

The message that a Web client sends to request a file or files from a Web server is called a **request message**. A typical request message from a client to a server consists of three major parts:

- Request line
- Optional request headers
- Optional entity body

The **request line** contains a command, the name of the target resource (a filename and a description of the path to that file on the server), and the protocol name and version number. Optional **request headers** can contain information about the types of files that the client will accept in response to this request. Finally, an optional **entity body** is sometimes used to pass bulk information to the server.

When the server receives the request message, it executes the command included in the message (in this case, it sends a particular Web page file back to the client). The server does this by retrieving the Web page file from its disk (or another disk on a network to which it is connected) and then creating a properly formatted **response message** to send back to the client. A server's response consists of three parts that are identical in structure to a request message: a response header line, one or more response header fields, and an optional entity body. In the response, however, each part has a slightly different function than it does in the request. The **response header line** indicates the HTTP version used by the server, the status of the response (whether the server found the file that the client wanted), and an explanation of the status information. Response header fields follow the response header line. A **response header field** returns information describing the server's attributes. The entity body returns the HTML page requested by the client machine.

Although the two-tier client/server architecture works well for the delivery of Web pages, a Web site that delivers dynamic content and processes transactions must do more than respond to requests for Web pages. A **three-tier architecture** extends the two-tier architecture to allow additional processing (for example, collecting the information from a database needed to generate a dynamic Web page) to occur before the Web server responds to the Web client's request. The third tier often includes databases and related software applications that supply information to the Web server. The Web server can then use the output of these software applications when responding to client requests, instead of just delivering a Web page.

A good example of services supported by a database in a three-tier architecture is a catalog-style Web site with search, update, and display functions. Assume that a user requests a display of an online specialty food store's exotic fruit selections. The client request is formulated into an HTTP message by the Web browser (tier 1), sent over the Internet to the Web server, and examined by the Web server. The Web server (tier 2) analyzes the request and determines that responding to the request requires the help of the server's database. The server sends a request to the database management software (tier 3) to search for, retrieve, and return all information about exotic fruit in the company's catalog database. The database information flows back through the database management software system to the server, which formats the response into an HTML document and sends that document inside an HTTP response message back to the client over the Internet. Figure 8-3 shows an overview of information flows in a three-tier architecture. Numbers on the flow arrows indicate the order in which the messages flow over the indicated paths.

Architectures that have four, five, or even more tiers divide into separate tiers the software applications and the databases and database management programs that work with those software applications. Also, some sites have software applications that generate information (a fourth tier) that feeds into other software applications or databases (in the third tier) that in turn generate information for the Web server to turn into Web pages (in

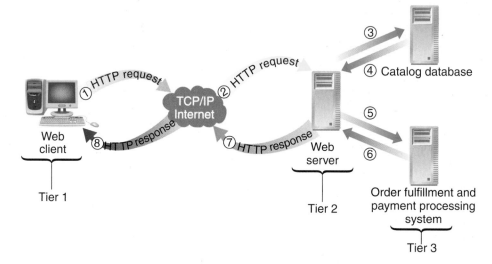

FIGURE 8-3   Message flows in a three-tier client/server network

the second tier), which then go to the requesting client (in the first tier). Architectures that have more than three tiers are often called **n-tier architectures**. N-tier systems can track customer purchases stored in shopping carts, look up sales tax rates, keep track of customer preferences, update in-stock inventory databases, and keep the product catalog current.

Software for Web Servers

Some Web server software can run on only one computer operating system, while some can run on several operating systems. In this section, you will learn about the operating system software used on most Web servers and the Web server software itself. You also will learn about other programs, such as Internet utilities and e-mail software, that companies often run on Web servers or other computers as part of electronic commerce operations.

Operating Systems for Web Servers

Operating system tasks include running programs and allocating computer resources such as memory and disk space to those programs. Operating system software also provides input and output services to devices connected to the computer, including keyboards, mice, monitors, touch screens, scanners, and printers. For large systems, the operating system must also keep track of multiple users logged on to the system and ensure that they do not interfere with one another.

Most Web server software runs on Microsoft Windows Server products, Linux, or other UNIX-based operating systems such as FreeBSD. Some companies believe that Microsoft products are simpler for their information systems staff to learn and use than UNIX-based systems. Other companies worry about the security weaknesses caused by the tight integration between application software and the operating system in Microsoft products.

UNIX-based Web servers are more widely used, and many industry experts believe that UNIX is a more secure operating system on which to run a Web server.

Linux is an open-source operating system that is fast, efficient, and easy to install. An increasing number of companies that sell computers intended to be used as Web servers include the Linux operating system in default configurations. Although Linux can be downloaded free from the Web, most companies buy it through a commercial distributor. These commercial distributions of Linux include additional software, such as installation utilities, and a support contract for the operating system. Commercial Linux distributors that sell versions of the operating system with utilities for Web servers include Red Hat, and SUSE Linux Enterprise. Canonical sells technical support and services for the Ubuntu Linux distribution. Oracle sells Web server hardware along with its UNIX-based operating system, Solaris. You can learn more about open-source software in general at the Open Source Initiative Web site.

Web Server Software

This section describes the two most commonly used Web server programs, Apache HTTP Server and Microsoft Internet Information Server (IIS). Other Web server software products are used by online businesses, including nginx (pronounced "engine-x") and lighttpd (pronounced "lighty"). Some large online businesses have written their own Web server software; for example, Google runs Google Web Server with the Linux operating system on its millions of server computers. Netcraft, a British network consulting firm, conducts continual surveys to tally the number of Web sites in existence and track which Web server software each uses. Figure 8-4 shows the use of Web server software by active sites in August, 2015.

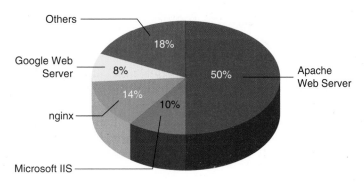

Source: Netcraft Web Surveys for August, 2015 (http://www.netcraft.com).

FIGURE 8-4   Percent of active Web sites that use major Web server software products

The Netcraft Web server surveys show that the market shares of Web server software have been moving a bit after several years of stability. Apache currently holds about half of the market. Microsoft IIS held between 15 and 20 percent of the market for a number of years, but has recently declined to a 10 percent share. The open source nginx (pronounced "engine ex") software has been growing steadily and now holds a 14 percent share. Because Google operates so many server computers, Google Web Server accounts for 8 percent of the market, even though Google is the only company that uses it.

APACHE HTTP SERVER

In 1994, Rob McCool was a student at the University of Illinois working in the National Center for Supercomputing Applications (NCSA) on campus. He was part of the programming team that developed Mosaic, an early NCSA Web browser. McCool and his fellow NCSA developers formed an e-mail discussion group to keep track of what everyone was doing on their project, which was Web server software. Programmer's fixes or improvements to a program are called software patches, and there were so many fixes and improvements made to this Web server software by so many programmers that it became known as "a patchy server." The name stuck and the software became known as "Apache Web Server." As each patch improved the software, it was made available for distribution to anyone who wanted to use it as open-source software (about which you learned in earlier chapters).

Apache HTTP Server has been the dominant Web server software since 1996 because it is available at no cost and it is supported collectively by a large base of technically proficient users who contribute technical advice to online discussion forums, wikis, and blogs. It is often cited as the most successful open-source software of all time. Apache runs on many operating systems (including FreeBSD-UNIX, HP-UX, Linux, Microsoft Windows, SCO-UNIX, and Solaris). A number of companies sell support services for Apache for organizations that want the additional security; however, many Apache installations are supported by the organization's own technical staff using the free online help that is available.

MICROSOFT INTERNET INFORMATION SERVER

Microsoft Internet Information Server (IIS) comes bundled with current versions of Microsoft Windows Server operating systems. IIS is used on many corporate intranets because many companies have adopted Microsoft products as their standard products. Small sites running personal Web pages also use IIS, as do some of the largest online business sites. IIS itself is free; however, the Microsoft Windows Server operating system software with which it is packaged can range in cost from under $1000 for a small business running one or two servers to many thousands of dollars for large organizations running many servers (the details are complicated; Microsoft Windows Server pricing guides often fill documents of more than 50 pages).

Electronic Mail (e-mail)

Although the Web, with its interactions between Web servers and clients, is the most important technology used in electronic commerce today, many buyers and sellers also use e-mail to gather information, execute transactions, and perform other online business tasks. In this section, you will learn more about e-mail and the technologies used to implement it on the Internet.

E-Mail Benefits

Not only was e-mail one of the first Internet applications, it was also one reason that many people were originally attracted to the Internet. E-mail conveys messages from one destination to another in a few seconds. Messages can contain character formatting similar to word-processing programs and can include documents, pictures, audio, movies, worksheets, or other files. These **attachments** can be the most important part of the message. Today, e-mail is the most popular form of business communication—far surpassing the telephone, conventional mail, and fax in volume.

E-Mail Drawbacks

Despite its many benefits, e-mail does have some drawbacks. One annoyance associated with e-mail is the amount of time that businesspeople spend answering their e-mails today. Researchers have found that most managers can deal with e-mail messages at an average rate of about five minutes per message. Some messages can be deleted within a few seconds, but those are balanced by the e-mails that require the manager to spend considerable time finding facts, checking files, and doing other tasks as part of answering e-mail. Researchers have found that most people (not including those who answer e-mails as their full-time job) feel e-mail is overly burdensome when they are getting 20 or 30 messages a day—which takes about two hours out of their day to answer, research, or otherwise handle.

A second major irritation brought by e-mail is the **computer virus**, more simply known as a **virus**, which is a program that attaches itself to another program and can cause damage when the host program is activated. E-mail attachments can be or can contain viruses. Using virus protection software and dealing with e-mailed security threats is a cost that comes with e-mail use. You will learn more about computer viruses and other threats that can be transmitted through e-mail (and how to control them) in Chapter 10. As you learned in Chapter 2, the most frustrating and expensive problem associated with e-mail today is the issue of unsolicited commercial e-mail, also known as UCE or **spam**. This nagging problem is discussed in the next section.

Spam

Figure 8-5 shows the proportion of all e-mails entering business e-mail servers that has been spam during the years in which e-mail has been widely used. The magnitude of the spam problem is substantial. During one 24-hour period in 2009 (the peak year for spam), researchers estimated that 220 billion spam e-mail messages were sent.

Researchers who track spam believe that spam growth has peaked and that legal measures and technical solutions will continue to reduce the amount of spam as a percentage of total e-mail traffic in the future, as discussed in the next several sections of this chapter.

Solutions to the Spam Problem

As long as it remains inexpensive to send e-mails (and thus, spam), the benefits reaped by spammers will remain sufficient to make sending spam a potentially profitable enterprise.

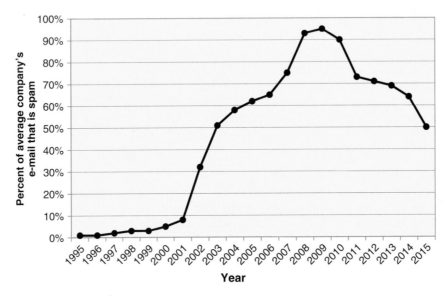

Sources: Symantec *Intelligence Reports, Spam and Phishing Reports,* and *Spam Reports;* www.symantec.com

FIGURE 8-5   Spam as a proportion of all business e-mail

The methods used to limit spam and its effects have taken various forms. Some of these approaches require the passing of laws, and some require technical changes in the mail-handling systems of the Internet. Other approaches can be implemented under existing laws and with current technologies, but only if large numbers of organizations and businesses cooperate. A few tactics that reduce spam can be undertaken by individual e-mail users. In the sections that follow, you will learn more about each of these approaches to controlling the spam problem.

INDIVIDUAL USER ANTISPAM TACTICS

One way individuals can limit spam is to reduce the likelihood that a spammer can automatically generate their e-mail addresses. Many organizations create e-mail addresses for their employees by combining elements of each employee's first and last names. For example, many companies often combine the first letter of an employee's first name with the entire last name to generate e-mail addresses for all employees. Larger companies often use employees' entire first and last names because they are likely to have both a Jane Smith and a Judy Smith working for them. A spam sender able to obtain an employee list can generate potential e-mail addresses using the names on the list. Or the spam sender might simply generate logical combinations of first initials (or names) and common last names. The cost of sending e-mail is so low that a spammer can afford to send thousands of e-mails to randomly generated addresses in the hope that a few of them are valid. By using an e-mail address that is more complex, such as xq7yy23@mycompany .com, individuals can reduce the chances that a spammer can randomly generate his or her address. Of course, such an address is hard to remember, which somewhat defeats the purpose of e-mail as a convenient way to communicate.

A second way to reduce spam is to control the exposure of an e-mail address. Spammers use software robots to search the Internet for character strings that include the @ character, which appears in every e-mail address. These robots search Web pages, discussion boards, chat rooms, and any other online source that might contain e-mail addresses. Again, the spammer can afford to send thousands of messages to e-mail addresses gathered in this way. Even if only one or two people respond, the spammer can earn a profit because the cost of sending e-mail messages is so low.

Some individuals maintain multiple e-mail addresses to thwart spam. They use one address for display on a Web site, another to register for access to Web sites, another for shopping accounts, and so on. If a spammer starts using one of these addresses, the individual can stop using it and switch to another. Many Web hosting services include a large number (often 100 to 200) of e-mail addresses as part of their service, so this can be a useful tactic for people or small businesses with their own Web sites.

These three strategies focus on limiting spammers' access to or use of an e-mail address. Other approaches use one or more techniques that filter e-mail messages based on their contents.

BASIC CONTENT FILTERING

All content-filtering solutions require software that identifies content elements in an incoming e-mail message that indicate the message is (or is not) spam. The content-filtering techniques differ in which content elements they examine, whether they look for indications that the message is (or is not) spam, and how strictly they apply the rules for classifying messages. Most basic content filters examine the e-mail headers (From, To, Subject) and look for indications that the message might be spam. The software that performs the filtering task can be placed on individual users' computers (called **client-level filtering**) or on mail server computers (called **server-level filtering**). Server-level filtering can be implemented on an ISP's mail server, an individual company's mail server, or both. Also, many individuals that have ISP and/or company mail servers that filter their e-mail also install client-level filters on their computers. Spam that gets through one filter can be trapped by another filter.

The most common basic content-filtering techniques are black lists and white lists. A **black list spam filter** looks for From addresses in incoming messages that are known to be spammers. The software can delete the message or put it into a separate mailbox for review. A black list spam filter can be implemented at the individual, organization, or ISP level. Several organizations, such as the Spam and Open Relay Blocking System collect black lists and make them available to ISPs and company e-mail administrators. Other groups, such as the Spamhaus Project, track known spammers and publish lists of the mail servers they use. Some of these are free services; others charge a fee. The biggest drawback to the black list approach is that spammers frequently change their e-mail servers, which means that a black list must be continually updated to be effective. This updating requires that many organizations cooperate and communicate information about known spammers. In addition to its black list, the Spamhaus Project maintains a list of known spammers on its site. These are individuals and companies who have had their services terminated by an ISP for spam-related violations of an acceptable use policy more than three times. The Spamhaus Project provides detailed information about those on this list to law enforcement agencies.

A **white list spam filter** examines From addresses and compares them to a list of known good sender addresses (for example, the addresses in an individual's address book). A white list filter is usually applied at the individual user level, although it is possible to do the filtering at the organization level if the e-mail administrator has access to all individuals' address books (some companies mandate such access for security purposes). The main drawback to this approach is that it filters out any incoming messages sent by unknown parties, not just spam. Because the number of **false positives** (messages that are rejected but should not have been) can be very high for white list filters, the rejected e-mails are always placed into a review mailbox instead of being deleted.

White list and black list approaches can be used in client-level or server-level filters, but both have serious drawbacks. To overcome these drawbacks, the two approaches are often used together or with other content-filtering approaches to achieve an acceptable level of filtering without an excessive false positive rate.

CHALLENGE-RESPONSE CONTENT FILTERING

One content-filtering technique uses a white list as the basis for a confirmation procedure. This technique, called **challenge-response**, compares all incoming messages to a white list. If the message is from a sender who is not on the white list, an automated e-mail response is sent to the sender. This message (the challenge) asks the sender to reply to the e-mail (the response). The reply must contain a response to a challenge presented in the e-mail.

These challenges are designed so that a human can respond easily, but a computer would have difficulty formulating the response. For example, a challenge might include a picture of a fruit bowl and would ask the sender to respond with the number of apples in the bowl. This prevents a spammer from setting up a computer that receives challenges and answers them (the program would have difficulty identifying and counting the number of apples). It would be inefficient for a spammer to hire a human to respond to thousands of challenges. Most implementations also include an audio alternative for visually impaired users. To learn more about this technique, you can visit the CAPTCHA Project site at Carnegie Mellon University. An example of a challenge that uses distorted letters and numbers (in this case, 5BM6HW3F) is shown in Figure 8-6.

The major drawback to challenge-response systems is that they can be abused. For example, a perpetrator could send out thousands of e-mails to recipients that use challenge-response systems. If the perpetrator includes the victim's e-mail as the From address in those e-mails, the victim will be bombarded by the automated challenges sent out by the challenge-response systems of the recipients. The potential damage of this tactic becomes greater as more e-mail servers install challenge-response systems.

Because challenge-response systems require users to change their behavior, and because they do not provide an immediate and significant benefit (the benefit is spam reduction over time), these systems have not become very widely used.

Type the code shown

FIGURE 8-6   Example of a challenge that uses distorted letters and numbers

ADVANCED CONTENT FILTERING

Advanced content filters that examine the entire e-mail message can be more effective than basic content filters that only examine the message headers or the IP address of the e-mail's sender. However, creating effective content filters can be challenging. For example, a company might think it good to delete any e-mail message that includes the word "sex," but the company could unintentionally delete all e-mails from customers in the town of Essex.

Many advanced content filters operate by looking for spam indicators throughout the e-mail message. When the filter identifies an indicator in a message, it increases that message's spam "score." Some indicators increase the score more than others. Indicators can be words, word pairs, certain HTML codes (such as the code for the color white, which makes part of the message invisible in most e-mail clients), and information about where a word occurs in the message. Unfortunately, as soon as spam filter vendors identify a good set of indicators, spammers stop including those indicators in their messages.

One type of advanced content filter that is based on a branch of applied mathematics called Bayesian statistics shows some promise of staying one step ahead of the spammers. **Bayesian revision** is a statistical technique in which additional knowledge is used to revise earlier estimates of probabilities. In software that contains a **naïve Bayesian filter** (the most common type in use today), the software begins by not classifying any messages. The user reviews messages and indicates to the software which messages are spam and which are not. The software gradually learns (by revising its estimates of the probability that a message element appears in a spam message) to identify spam messages.

After seeing a few dozen messages classified, the naïve Bayesian filter can identify spam messages about 80 percent of the time. As the filter continues to work, the user reviews its classifications and tells the software when it makes a mistake. After classifying a few hundred messages (and being corrected by the user when it errs), a naïve Bayesian filter can spot spam about 95 percent of the time. Although these filters are highly effective and have low false positive rates, they must be trained, which takes time. The training is best done by each individual user because one person's spam can be another person's important message. This need for every user to train the software limits the use of naïve Bayesian filters. However, naïve Bayesian filters can be installed on computers used by people who receive large amounts of e-mail in organizations that also use other techniques at the server level. POPFile is a good example of an open-source program that runs naïve Bayesian filters on individual client computers.

LEGAL SOLUTIONS

A number of U.S. jurisdictions have passed laws that provide penalties for the sending of spam. In January 2004, the U.S. CAN-SPAM law (the law's name is an acronym for "Controlling the Assault of Non-Solicited Pornography and Marketing") went into effect. Researchers noted a drop in spam for two months after the law's effective date, but by the third month spam was back to its earlier levels. Observers noted that spammers likely slowed down their activities when the law took effect but went back to work when widespread prosecutions under the law did not materialize.

The CAN-SPAM law regulates all e-mail messages sent for the primary purpose of advertising or promoting a commercial product or service. The law's main provisions include:

- *Misleading address header information*: E-mail headers and routing information, including the originating domain name and e-mail address, must be accurate and must identify the person who sent the e-mail.
- *Deceptive subject headers*: The e-mail's subject line cannot mislead the recipient about the contents or subject matter of the message.
- *Clear and conspicuous notice of message nature*: The e-mail must contain a clear and conspicuous notice that the message is an advertisement or solicitation and that the recipient can opt out of receiving further commercial e-mail from the sender.
- *Physical postal address*: The e-mail must include the sender's valid physical postal address.
- *Mandatory provision of an opt-out mechanism*: The e-mail must include a return e-mail address or another Internet-based response mechanism that allows a recipient to ask not to be sent future e-mail messages. These requests must be honored. The message may include a menu of choices that allows a recipient to opt out of certain types of messages, but one option on the menu must be an option to stop sending all commercial messages of any type.
- *Effectiveness of opt-out mechanism*: Opt-out requests must be honored within 10 business days. Any opt-out mechanism offered must be able to process opt-out requests for at least 30 days after the e-mail is sent. Once an opt-out request has been received, the sender is prohibited from helping any other entity send e-mail to the opt-out address or from having another entity send e-mail on the sender's behalf to that address.
- *Transfer of e-mail addresses*: Once a recipient has submitted an opt-out request, the sender is prohibited from selling or transferring that e-mail address to any other entity.

The law also prohibits misleading address header information in transaction-related e-mail messages. For example, an e-mail that facilitates a transaction or that updates a customer regarding a business transaction would fall under this provision. Each violation of a provision of the law is subject to a fine of up to $11,000. Additional fines are assessed for those who violate one of the preceding provisions and do one or more of the following:

- Harvest e-mail addresses from Web sites or Web services that have published a notice prohibiting the transfer of e-mail addresses for the purpose of sending e-mail.
- Send e-mail messages to addresses that have been generated by combining names, letters, or numbers into multiple combinations and permutations.
- Use scripts or other automated tools to register for multiple e-mail or user accounts that are then used to send commercial e-mail.
- Relay e-mails through a computer or network without the permission of the computer's or network's owner.

Thus, a successful prosecution could cost the convicted spammer a considerable amount of money. The law further provides for criminal penalties, including imprisonment, for commercial senders of e-mail who do or conspire to do any of the following:

- Use another person's or entity's computer to send commercial e-mail from or through it without the computer owner's permission.
- Use a computer to relay or retransmit multiple commercial e-mail messages with the intent to deceive or mislead recipients or an Internet access service about the origin of the messages.
- Send multiple e-mail messages that contain false header information.
- Present false identification when registering for multiple e-mail accounts or domain names.
- Falsely represent themselves as owners of multiple IP addresses that are used to send commercial e-mail messages.

The CAN-SPAM law has allowed U.S. prosecutors to bring a number of successful cases against spammers, including cases in which damages were assessed in the hundreds of millions of dollars. Some of the more notorious spammers have been sent to prison. Spammers' appeals of these decisions, usually based on the argument that spam is protected speech under the First Amendment, have been consistently rejected by the courts.

These successes have helped stem the tide of spam over the past few years. However, many spammers use mail servers located in countries that do not have (and that are unlikely to adopt) antispam laws. As you learned in Chapter 7, the issues of jurisdiction can be unclear for businesses that operate online. Even if a plaintiff is successful in court, enforcement of court-ordered fines or collection of damages can be difficult. Spammers can also evade cease-and-desist orders because they can move their operations from one server to another in minutes. Many spammers forward mail through servers that they have hijacked (you will learn more about security threats to servers in Chapter 10).

In a decision that disappointed many in the information technology community, the FTC refused to create a do-not-spam list that would have been modeled after its do-not-call list, which has been reasonably successful in limiting marketers' phone calls.

Legal solutions to the spam problem have achieved only limited success in reducing spam because it is expensive for governments to prosecute spammers. To become cost effective, prosecutors must be able to identify spammers easily (to reduce the cost of bringing an action against them) and must have a greater likelihood of winning the cases they file (or must see a greater social benefit to winning). The best way to make spammers easier to find has been to make technical changes in the e-mail transport mechanism in the Internet's infrastructure.

TECHNICAL SOLUTIONS

The Internet was not designed originally to do many of the things it does today. For example, it was not designed to be secure, to process transactions, or to handle billions of e-mail messages. As you learned in Chapter 2, Internet e-mail was an incidental afterthought in a system created to transfer large files from one researcher to another. The Internet's original design did not include any mechanisms for ensuring that the identity of an e-mail sender would always be known to the e-mail's recipient.

At least one technical strategy for fighting spam exploits a weakness in the original design of the Internet. The Internet protocol that governs communication among servers on the Internet (including e-mail servers) was designed to be a polite set of rules. When one computer on the Internet sends a message to another computer, it will wait to receive an acknowledgment that the message has been received before sending more messages. In the ordinary course of Internet communications, the acknowledgment messages come back in far less than a second. If a computer is set to send the acknowledgment back more slowly, the originating computer will slow down because it must continue to scan for the acknowledgment (which consumes some of its processing power) and it will not send any more messages to that address until it does receive the acknowledgment.

To use this characteristic of the Internet messaging rules to counter spam, the defending company must develop a way to identify computers that are sending spam. Some vendors, such as IBM, sell software and access to a large database that tracks such computers continually. Other vendors sell software that identifies multiple e-mail messages coming from a single source in rapid succession (as would happen if a spammer were sending spam to everyone at a particular company). Once the spamming computer is identified, the software waits to send the message acknowledgments. It can also launch a return attack, sending e-mail messages back to the computer that originated the suspected spam. This practice is called **teergrubing**, which is from the German word for "tar pit." The objective is to ensnare the spam-sending computer in a trap that drags down its ability to send spam. Although many organizations use teergrubing as part of their spam defense strategy, some are concerned that launching a counterattack might violate laws that were enacted, ironically enough, to punish spammers.

Most industry observers agree that an ultimate solution to the spam problem could come from new e-mail protocols that provide absolute verification of the source of each e-mail message. An Internet Engineering Task Force (IETF) working group released the first proposed standard for a message header field that indicates an e-mail's authentication status in 2015.

The most effective technical solutions to the spam problem have been the coordinated efforts of large Internet users to identify the sources of spam and to block them. As more and more spamming activity moves to countries that have lax regulations regarding spam, it has become easier to identify and block these users. The recent substantial reductions in the level of spam are most likely a result of these efforts combined with more effective enforcement of laws in multiple jurisdictions.

Web Site Utility Programs

In addition to Web server software, people who develop Web sites work with a number of utility programs, or tools. Some of these programs run on the Web server itself, while others run on the client computers that Web developers use when they are creating Web sites. E-mail was one of the earliest Internet utility programs and it has become one of the most important. In earlier chapters, you learned how companies are using e-mail as a key element in their electronic commerce strategies. You will learn about several of these programs and see examples of how they work.

Tracert and Other Route-Tracing Programs

Tracert (TRACE RouTe) sends data packets to every computer on the path (Internet) between one computer and another computer and clocks the packets' round-trip times. This provides an indication of the time it takes a message to travel from one computer to another and back, ensures that the remote computer is online, and pinpoints any data traffic congestion. Route-tracing programs also calculate and display the number of hops between computers and the time it takes to traverse the entire one-way path between machines. Figure 8-7 shows a route traced from a Cox Cable network in Connecticut to one of the BBC's Web servers in London using the Tracert program on a Windows PC.

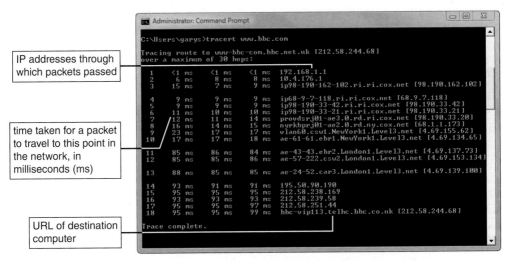

FIGURE 8-7   Tracing a path between two computers on the Internet

By looking at the first column in the figure, you can see that the route included 18 hops and took just under one-tenth of a second (which is 100 milliseconds) to travel the

374

entire length of the transmission path. The Windows Tracert program sends three test packets; the speeds for each packet are shown in milliseconds in the second, third, and fourth columns in the figure. The last column shows either the URL or the IP address of each computer through which the packets passed.

Telnet and FTP Utilities

Telnet is a program that allows a person using one computer to access files and run programs on a second computer that is connected to the Internet. This remote login capability can be useful for running older software that does not have a Web interface. Telnet lets a client computer give commands to programs running on a remote host, allowing for remote troubleshooting or system administration. As more companies place information on Web pages, which are accessible through any Web browser, the use of Telnet will continue to decrease.

The **File Transfer Protocol (FTP)** is the part of the TCP/IP rules that defines the formats used to transfer files between TCP/IP-connected computers. Although many FTP file transfers and file management operations can be conducted directly through a Web browser, most people today use software such as FileZilla or CuteFTP to perform these tasks.

Indexing and Searching Utility Programs

Search engines and indexing programs are important elements of many Web servers. Search engines or search tools search either a specific site or the entire Web for requested documents. An indexing program can provide full-text indexing that generates an index for all documents stored on the server. When a browser requests a Web site search, the search engine compares the index terms to the requester's search term to see which documents contain matches for the requested term or terms. More advanced search engine software (such as that used by the popular search engine site Google) uses complex relevance ranking rules that consider things such as how many other Web sites link to the target site. Many Web server software products also contain indexing software. Indexing software can often index documents stored in many different file formats.

Data Analysis Software

Web servers can capture visitor information, including data about who is visiting a Web site (the visitor's URL), how long the visitor's Web browser viewed the site, the date and time of each visit, and which pages the visitor viewed. This data is placed into a Web **log file**. As you can imagine, the file grows very quickly—especially for popular sites with thousands of visitors each day. Careful analysis of the log file can reveal many useful facts about site visitors and their preferences. To make sense of a log file, you must run third-party Web log file analysis programs. These programs summarize log file information by querying the log file and either returning gross summary information, or accumulating details that reveal how many visitors came to the site per day, hour, or minute, or which hours of the day were peak loading times. Popular Web log file analysis programs include products by Adobe Analytics, Google Analytics, and WebTrends.

Link-Checking Utilities

Over time, the Web sites to which a given page links can change their URLs or even disappear. A **dead link**, when clicked, displays an error message rather than a Web page. Sites that have many dead links are sometimes said to have **link rot**. A **link checker** utility program examines each page on the site and reports any URLs that no longer exist. It can also identify **orphan files**, which are files on the Web server that are not linked to any Web page. Other important site management features include script checking and HTML validation. Some management tools can locate error-laden pages and code, list broken links, and e-mail maintenance results to site managers. Some Web site development and maintenance tools, such as Adobe's Dreamweaver, include link-checking features. Freestanding link-checking programs, such as Elsop LinkScan, and LinxCop are available as well.

Remote Server Administration

With **remote server administration** software, a Web site administrator can control a Web site from any Internet-connected computer. It is convenient for an administrator to be able to monitor server activity and manipulate the server from wherever he or she happens to be. LabTech Software sells software that includes remote administration functions along with link-checking, HTML troubleshooting, site-monitoring, and other utility programs that can be useful in managing the operation of a Web site.

Web Server Hardware

Organizations use a wide variety of computer brands, types, and sizes to host their online operations. Small companies can run Web sites on desktop PCs, but most online business operations are operated on computers designed specifically for the task of Web site hosting. Businesses select the specific hardware and software elements for a given Web site based on the site's functionality, the quantity of visitors expected to use the site, the number of pages those visitors will view during an average visit, the size of those pages (including graphics and other page elements), and the likely maximum number of simultaneous visitors. Some companies provide help in determining server size and capabilities online, including the Intel Server Sizing Tool.

Web Server Computers

Web server computers generally have more memory, larger (and faster) hard disk drives, and faster processors than the typical desktop computer. Many Web server computers use multiple processors; very few desktop PCs have more than one processor. Because Web server computers use faster and higher-capacity hardware elements (such as memory and hard disk drives) and use more of these elements, they are usually much more expensive than workstation PCs. Today, a high-end desktop PC costs between $500 and $1200. A company might be able to buy a low-end Web server computer for about the same amount of money, but most companies spend between $2000 and $50,000 on an individual Web server. Large organizations that use thousands of servers can spend millions of dollars on their server hardware. Companies that sell Web server hardware, such as Dell,

LEARNING FROM FAILURES

Web Servers at eBay

The online auction site eBay is very popular, as you have learned in earlier chapters. Indeed, it is so popular that its Web servers deliver hundreds of millions of pages per day. These pages are a combination of static HTML pages and dynamically generated Web pages. The dynamic pages are created from queries run against eBay's Oracle database, in which it keeps all of the information about all auctions that are under way or have closed within the most recent 30 days. With millions of auctions under way at any moment, this database is extremely large. The combination of a large database and high-transaction volume makes eBay's Web server operation an important part of the company's success and a potential contributor to its failure. The servers at eBay failed more than 15 times during the first five years (1995–2000) of the company's life. The worst series of failures occurred during May and June of 2000, when the site went down four times. One of these failures kept the site offline for more than a day—a failure that cost eBay an estimated $5 million. The company's stock fell 20 percent in the days following that failure.

At that point, eBay decided it needed to make major changes in its approach to Web server configuration. Many of eBay's original technology staff had backgrounds at Oracle, a company that has a tradition of selling large databases that run on equally large servers. Further, the nature of eBay's business—any visitor might want to view information about any auction at any time—led eBay management initially to implement a centralized architecture with one large database residing on a few large database server computers. It also made sense to use similar hardware to serve the Web pages generated from that database.

In mid-2000, following the worst site failure in its history, eBay decided to move to a decentralized architecture. This was a tremendous challenge because it meant that the single large auction information database had to be replicated across groups, or clusters, of Web and database servers. However, eBay realized that using just a few large servers had made it too vulnerable to the failure of those machines. Once eBay completed the move to decentralization, it found that adding more capacity was easier. Instead of installing and configuring a large server that might have represented 15 percent or more of the site's total capacity, clusters of six or seven smaller machines could be added that represented less than 1 percent of the site's capacity. Routine periodic maintenance on the servers also became easier to schedule.

The lesson from eBay's Web server troubles is that the architecture should be carefully chosen to meet the needs of the site. Web server architecture choices can have a significant effect on the stability, reliability, and, ultimately, the profitability of an electronic commerce Web site.

Hewlett-Packard, and Oracle, all have configuration tools on their Web sites that allow visitors to design their own Web servers.

Although some Web server computers are housed in freestanding cases, most are installed in equipment racks. These racks are usually about 6 feet tall and 19 inches wide. They can each hold between 10 and 20 midsized servers. An increasingly popular server configuration involves putting small server computers on a single computer board and then installing many of those boards into a rack-mounted frame. These servers-on-a-card are called **blade servers**, and more than 300 of them can be installed in a single 6-foot rack. Each blade server costs between $500 and $5000, depending on its components. Figure 8-8 shows a set of rack-mounted blade servers.

Amy Walters/iStock/Thinkstock

FIGURE 8-8   Rack-mounted blade servers

Web Servers and Green Computing

The use of large collections of computers, especially powerful computers such as Web servers, requires significant amounts of electrical power to operate. Although much of this electrical power is used to operate the servers themselves, a substantial portion of it is used to cool the rooms in which the servers reside. Large computers generate tremendous amounts of heat. Efforts to reduce the environmental impact of large computing installations are called **green computing**. Companies that operate large numbers of Web server computers are finding some very interesting ways to minimize the impact of using so much electricity and the heat that it generates.

In 2009, Google opened a server facility in Finland in a building that was previously used as a paper mill. This installation is located near the coastline and is built over granite tunnels that draw in seawater that Google uses instead of electric-powered air conditioning to dissipate the heat generated by the servers. The low average temperatures in Finland reduce the overall need for cooling as well.

Facebook operates a Web server facility in Lulea, Sweden (which is just 60 miles south of the Arctic Circle) that uses the outside air to cool its servers. A nearby river has a dam with hydroelectric power generators that provide inexpensive electricity to operate the servers themselves.

Hewlett-Packard uses cool air available in the high altitudes of the Rocky Mountains in its Fort Collins, Colorado, server facility. FedEx and Harris Corporation have also used natural cooling in their U.S. Web server installations.

All of these efforts reduce the impact that online businesses have on the planet's limited energy resources. They can also provide substantial energy cost savings for the companies that use these strategies.

Web Server Performance Evaluation

Benchmarking Web server hardware and software combinations can help in making informed decisions for a system. **Benchmarking**, in this context, is testing that is used to compare the performance of hardware and software.

Elements affecting overall server performance include hardware, operating system software, server software, connection bandwidth, user capacity, and type of Web pages being delivered. The number of users the server can handle is also important. This can be difficult to measure because both the bandwidth of the Internet connection and the sizes of the Web pages delivered can affect that number. Two factors to evaluate when measuring a server's Web page delivery capability are throughput and response time. **Throughput** is the number of HTTP requests that a particular hardware and software combination can process in a unit of time. **Response time** is the amount of time a server requires to process one request.

One way to choose Web server hardware configurations is to run tests on various configurations, which can be difficult for equipment not yet purchased. Independent testing labs such as Mindcraft test software, hardware systems, and network products for users. Its site contains reports that compare combinations of application server platforms, operating systems, and Web server software products. A not-for-profit company that develops benchmarks for servers is the Standard Performance Evaluation Corporation.

Companies that operate more than one Web server must decide how to configure servers to provide the best service possible. The various ways that servers can be connected to each other and to related hardware, such as routers and switches, are called **server architectures**.

Web Server Hardware Architectures

Earlier in this chapter, you learned that electronic commerce Web sites can use two-tier, three-tier, or n-tier architectures to divide the work of serving Web pages, administering databases, and processing transactions. Many electronic commerce sites require more than one computer within each tier.

Large online businesses use hundreds or even thousands of Web server computers. Large collections of servers are called **server farms** because the servers are often lined up in rows, like crops in a field. One approach to designing a large site's operations, sometimes called a **centralized architecture**, is to use a few very large and fast computers. A second approach is to use a large number of less-powerful computers and divide the workload among them. This is sometimes called a **distributed architecture** or, more commonly, a **decentralized architecture**. These two different approaches to Web site architecture are shown in Figure 8-9.

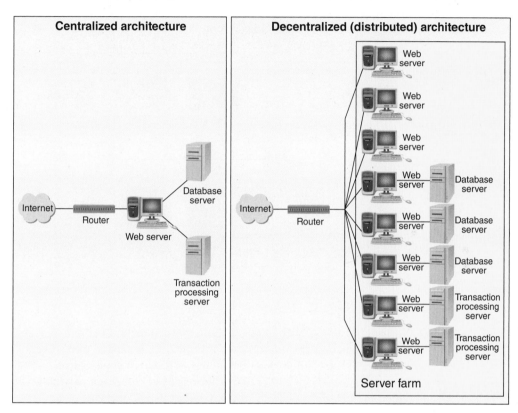

FIGURE 8-9   Centralized and decentralized Web site architectures

The centralized approach requires expensive computers and is more sensitive to technical problems. If one of the few servers becomes inoperable, a large portion of the site's capability is lost. The decentralized architecture spreads failure risk over a large number of servers. If one server becomes inoperable, the site can continue to operate without much degradation in capability. The smaller servers used in the decentralized architecture are less expensive than the large servers used in the centralized approach. That is, the total cost of 100 small servers is usually less than the cost of one large server with the same capacity as the 100 small servers. However, the decentralized architecture does require additional hardware to connect the servers to each other. Most large decentralized sites use load-balancing systems, which cost additional money, to assign the workload efficiently. Load-balancing systems are described in the next section of this chapter.

LOAD-BALANCING SYSTEMS

A **load-balancing switch** is a piece of network hardware that monitors the workloads of servers attached to it and assigns incoming Web traffic to the server that has the most available capacity at that instant in time. In a simple load-balancing system, the traffic that enters the site from the Internet through the site's router encounters the load-balancing switch, which then directs the traffic to the Web server best able to handle the traffic. Figure 8-10 shows a basic load-balancing system.

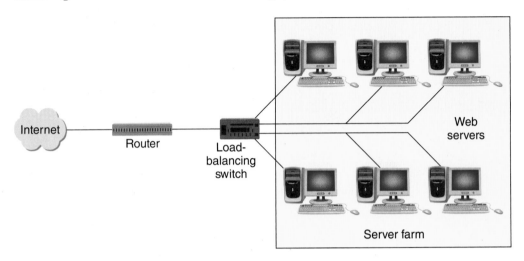

FIGURE 8-10   Basic load-balancing system

In more complex load-balancing systems, the incoming Web traffic, which might enter from two or more routers on a larger Web site, is directed to groups of Web servers dedicated to specific tasks. In the complex load-balancing system that appears in Figure 8-11, the Web servers have been gathered into groups of servers, each of which handles a specific function, including: delivery of static HTML pages, querying of an information database, generating and delivering dynamic Web pages, and processing transactions.

Load-balancing switches and the software that helps them do their work usually cost about $2000 for a simple system. Larger and more complex systems usually cost $15, 000 to $40,000.

Cloud Computing

As you have learned from Chapter 2 and this chapter, setting up and operating a Web server can be a complex and expensive proposition, even when parts of the task are outsourced to an Internet service provider. To avoid the cost and effort of planning and installing the hardware and software required to go online, many smaller businesses and an increasing number of larger businesses have chosen to outsource their entire computing networks by using cloud computing. **Cloud computing** is a service that allows multiple organizations to share a network of server computers and the software that runs on those computers. This strategy gives businesses access to a large array of computers,

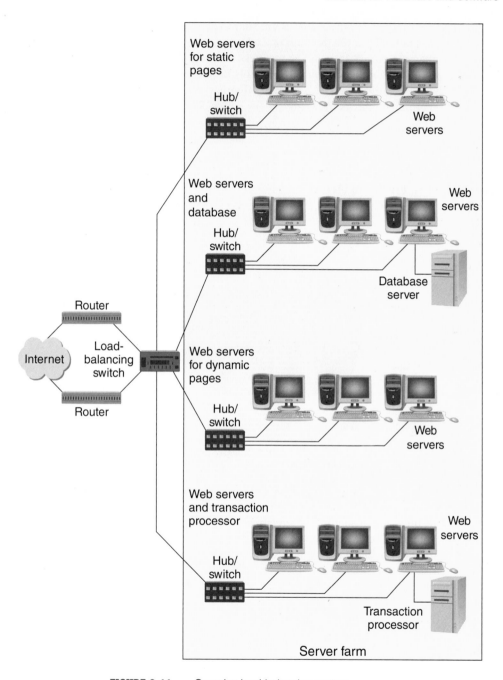

FIGURE 8-11 Complex load-balancing system

with the related storage and backup facilities, at a lower cost than they could purchase the same amount of computer power themselves. Cloud computing is sometimes called **infrastructure as a service (IaaS)** or **platform as a service (PaaS)**.

Because cloud computing resources are shared across multiple users, they can be reallocated dynamically as the demand of each user changes. Instead of buying more servers during a temporary increase in business activity, a cloud user can arrange for the cloud provider to make more resources available as needed. Since cloud computing can be done worldwide over the Internet, even daily fluctuations in computer use can be averaged across users. For example, as the business day winds down in the Western hemisphere, business activity picks up in the Eastern hemisphere. A worldwide cloud computing provider can serve both geographic areas with far less equipment than would be needed to handle peak capacity in one geographic area alone. This approach also consumes less electricity, heating and cooling cost, and physical space, saving even more money.

The largest cloud computing service providers include Amazon, Microsoft, IBM, and Google, but many smaller companies offer these services and collectively make up a large part of the total market, as shown in Figure 8-12.

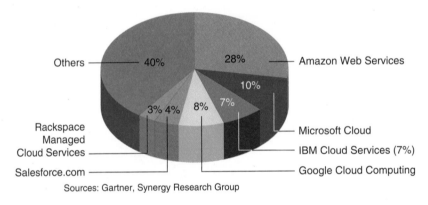

Sources: Gartner, Synergy Research Group

FIGURE 8-12　　Cloud computing provider global market shares, 2015

Some large companies use more than one cloud service provider so that they have a reliable backup and do not become dependent on one source. Many companies have wrestled with the issue of security when considering the move to a cloud computing approach. Smaller companies often conclude that the security provided by a large cloud computing provider is likely superior to what they could create in their own systems, however, larger companies are less likely to reach that conclusion. Some larger firms have used a strategy called **hybrid cloud computing** in which they move their large-volume and routine work to a cloud provider, but retain their more sensitive data and process on internal servers.

Content Delivery Networks

One of the most important goals of any online business Web site is to provide continual, reliable connections with customers. In the early days of the Web, when Web sites were mostly text, the Internet easily provided sufficient bandwidth for the communications conducted between companies' Web servers and customers' Web browsers. As Web sites added graphic images and files (documents, reports, spreadsheets), the demand on the

Internet communications channel increased, but the technologies used in the Internet's backbone network were sufficient to handle the increased traffic load.

Beginning about 2008, however, Web traffic began to include substantial numbers of audio and video files. A Web page with a mix of text and graphics is usually less than 1 MB in size, but a typical popular song recorded in MP3 format is between 3 and 5 MB and a compressed video file can be anywhere from a few MB to several GBs in size, and high-definition video files containing a single feature-length film can be 4–8 GB. Current estimates are that between 40 and 55 percent of all Internet traffic worldwide consists of YouTube and Netflix video files. Since these video files are each as much as 8000 times larger than the average Web page download, the rapid recent growth in Internet traffic shown in Figure 8-13 is not surprising.

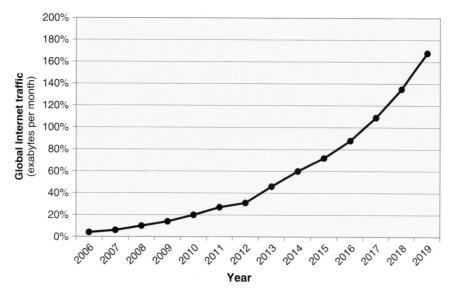

Sources: Cisco *Visual Networking Index*, 2015; Minnesota Internet Traffic Studies, 2009

FIGURE 8-13   Growth of Internet traffic, actual and projected

Although the Internet backbone is sufficient to handle this traffic, making sure that everything gets transmitted efficiently to every Web browser making requests can be challenging. As you learned in Chapter 2, the Internet is a packet-switched network, which means that it breaks up large files into many small packets and routes those packets through interconnected multiple servers. This break-down-and-rebuild process requires additional communication in the network, which increases as average file sizes increase. If you have ever played a video that paused while playing, you have witnessed the delay in transmission caused by the inability of the network to handle the full traffic load momentarily. This delay is called **latency** and can be a problem for businesses that rely on the Internet to deliver large audio and video files to customers.

To prevent their customers from experiencing latency, online businesses have turned to companies, called **content delivery networks (CDNs)**, that provide a service in which they store large file contents on multiple servers located throughout the Internet. When a customer's Web browser requests a large file, that request is routed to the server nearest to them that has a stored copy of the file. Major CDNs, such as Akamai, Level 3, Limelight, and Tata Communications, place their servers in the data centers of large companies, Internet service providers, universities, and other large organizations so they can locate files close to as many potential users as possible.

Large businesses that sell or otherwise provide content that includes large files pay a fee to a CDN to have their large files stored in multiple locations around the world. Smaller businesses can purchase CDN services through their Internet service providers, who in turn contract with one or more of the larger CDNs. For example, Rackspace resells Akamai's CDN service to its customers for about 10 cents per GB. Some companies that provide large numbers of media files to customers, such as Apple, have created their own CDNs.

Summary

The platform neutral nature of the Internet allows the Web to use a simple two-tier client/server architecture in which Web browsers (the clients) request files from Web servers and then render them into Web pages to be displayed. To accomplish more complex activities, such as transaction processing and dynamic Web page generation, online businesses use three-tier or higher (n-tier) architectures that integrate databases and payment-processing software with shipping and inventory control software.

Web server computers use a variety of operating systems, including Microsoft systems and UNIX-based operating systems such as Linux. The most widely used Web server programs are the open source Apache HTTP Server and nginx, along with Microsoft Internet Information Server.

The problem of unsolicited commercial e-mail (spam) peaked in 2009 and has been declining since then. Content filters, particularly naïve Bayesian filters, provide some protection and laws designed to punish spammers have had some effect. Technical strategies that identify the source of spam e-mails and block those sources have also helped stem the tide of spam.

Web server computers also run a variety of utility programs such as Tracert, Telnet, and FTP. Many Web administrators also use software that helps with link checking and remote server administration tasks.

The operating system, connection bandwidth, user capacity, and the type of pages that the site serves affect overall Web server performance. Benchmarking software and consulting firms that use it can help companies evaluate specific combinations of Web server hardware, software, and operating systems.

Web server hardware is also an important consideration in the design of an online business site. Server computers must be chosen and configured carefully. Large Web sites that have many Web server computers use load-balancing hardware and software to manage their high-activity volumes.

Cloud computing, including hybrid cloud strategies, can help online businesses make their Web server infrastructure more flexible and can provide backup security. Many online businesses contract with content delivery networks, sometimes indirectly, to reduce the latency that their customers might otherwise experience when receiving large files, including music and video content.

Key Terms

attachments

Bayesian revision

benchmarking

black list spam filter

blade servers

centralized architecture

challenge-response

client-level filtering

client-side scripting

cloud computing

computer virus

content delivery network (CDN)

database server

dead link

decentralized architecture

distributed architecture

dynamic content

dynamic page

e-mail server

entity body

false positives

File Transfer Protocol (FTP)

green computing

hybrid cloud computing

Hypertext Preprocessor (PHP)

infrastructure as a service (IaaS)

latency

link checker

link rot

load-balancing switch

log file

naïve Bayesian filter

n-tier architectures

orphan file

platform as a service (PaaS)

platform neutrality

remote server administration

request headers

request line

request message

response header field

response header line

response message

response time

server

server architectures

server farms

server software

server-level filtering

server-side scripting

spam

static page

teergrubing

Telnet

three-tier architecture

throughput

Tracert

transaction server

two-tier client/server architecture

virus

white list spam filter

Review Questions

1. What is platform neutrality?
2. What is a static Web page?
3. What is dynamic Web page content?
4. Name and briefly define the different types of server computers that might be used in an online business.
5. List the main tasks performed by a Web server computer.
6. What is the function of a request message in a two-tier client-server architecture.
7. What is included in a response header line?
8. What is the relationship between UNIX and Linux?
9. What is open source software?
10. Name one specific concern that business organizations have about e-mail attachments.

11. Briefly explain the difference between client-level and server-level spam filtering.

12. What problem is created by false positives in white list spam filters?

13. Briefly explain how a challenge-response system works to reduce spam.

14. What is Bayesian revision?

15. What is teergrubing?

16. Briefly describe the information that can be provided by a route-tracing program.

17. Provide one example of the type of information that might be included in a Web log file.

18. What is an orphan file on a Web server?

19. What is remote server administration?

20. In a Web server, what is throughput?

21. What is a load-balancing switch?

22. What is cloud computing?

23. What is a content delivery network?

24. What is latency?

Exercises

1. In about 200 words, describe the technologies Web servers use to tailor customized Web pages that respond to users' requests. In your answer, include a comparison of client-side and server-side approaches and outline the advantages of each.

2. In about 100 words, describe how an n-tier architecture might be used by an online business. Include in your answer an outline of the functions that would likely be performed by computers configured in this way.

3. Using your favorite search engine, find at least two companies that provide technical support for users of the Apache Web Server software. Learn what services they provide and, if possible, what they charge. Review their Web sites to learn more about the companies and summarize your findings in a report of about 200 words.

4. In about 200 words, distinguish between white-list and black-list spam filters, then outline the advantages and disadvantages of each.

5. In about 100 words, explain why laws designed to limit spam can be ineffective against many perpetrators.

6. The CAN-SPAM law prohibits a business from including misleading information in an e-mail header if the message is related to a transaction. In about 100 words, explain why the drafters of the law considered this to be a serious issue.

7. Use W3C Link Checker or Elsop LinkScan Quick Check to check the links on any Web site of your choice. Print a few pages of the report and be prepared to turn them in to your instructor. Be patient. These programs can take some time to complete their work—especially on a Web page that has a large number of links.

8. In about 100 words, describe the key characteristics of a blade server and outline reasons that an online business might prefer to use blade servers for Web server applications.

9. Large computing installations (such as server farms) can have significant impacts on the environment. In about 100 words, summarize these impacts and recommend measures that can be taken to reduce them.

10. In about 100 words, outline the benefits and costs of using a decentralized instead of a centralized server architecture for an online business operation.

Cases

C1. City of Asheville

Asheville is a steadily growing, prosperous city in Western North Carolina with a metropolitan area population of about 250,000 and an annual operating budget of more than $150 million. The city operates a Web site with information about the city and links to a variety of online services. Asheville also has a mobile app for citizen services requests that is very popular.

When Jonathan Feldman became the city's chief information officer, he conducted a review of its information infrastructure to establish priorities for his staff. One of the items on his list of concerns was the city's disaster recovery infrastructure. Having had some involvement in the Hurricane Katrina recovery, Feldman was worried about what he found. Asheville did have a disaster recovery facility, but it was located just two blocks away from the city's main data center. Further, the switchover from the main data center to the backup servers in an emergency would take more than a day to accomplish. As he considered the increased needs of citizens to gain information about city services should an emergency occur, Feldman was concerned that the city's Web servers would be offline for such an extended period, especially those servers that supported the mobile app.

Operating a disaster recovery facility can be expensive. In addition to replicating the regular data center's servers, storage devices, and software, the facility needs to have reliable dual backup power supplies. In addition, the physical facility itself must be reinforced to withstand forces of nature threats such as hurricanes, high winds, and floods. And to be truly effective, the recovery facility should be located far enough from the main data center so that a threat that affects one will not threaten the other. Feldman knew from experience that convincing a city council to spend substantial funds on computer equipment that might never be used can be a challenge.

REQUIRED

1. Using your favorite search engine and the resources of your library, develop a set of recommendations regarding the possible use of cloud computing services to operate the City of Asheville mobile app server. In about 200 words, outline pros and cons of this solution to Feldman's concerns.

2. Many companies use a hybrid cloud approach for their entire information technology infrastructure by storing highly sensitive data and programs in their own data center and moving routine operations to the cloud. Using your favorite search engine and the resources of your library to review hybrid cloud options and write about 200 words in which you recommend a hybrid cloud strategy for the City of Asheville's information technology infrastructure, including its Web servers, mobile app server, and disaster recovery servers.

Note: Your instructor might assign you to a group to complete this case, and might ask you to prepare a formal presentation of your results to your class.

C2. Random Walk Shoes

Amy Lawrence, the owner of Random Walk Shoes, has asked you to help her as she launches her company's first Web site. In college, Amy was a business major with an artistic bent. She helped to pay her way through college by decorating sneakers with her hand-painted designs. Her business grew through word of mouth and through her participation in crafts fairs. By the time she earned her degree, Amy was running a successful business from her dorm room.

Amy expanded her sales efforts to include crafts fairs in nearby towns. She hired two college students to work for her, and she convinced several area gift shops to stock samples of her merchandise. The gift shops were not an ideal retail outlet for her products, however, since most people who want to buy decorated sneakers want to choose specific designs or have special designs created just for them. Customers also want to choose the specific shoes on which the design is placed. One of Amy's student workers suggested that she consider selling her products on the Web.

Realizing that the Web would give Random Walk Shoes a chance to reach a much wider audience and would allow customers to choose design-shoe combinations, Amy began gathering information and developing estimates about her planned Web activity. Using her digital camera, she took several hundred pictures of shoes, designs, and shoe-design combinations. She then hired a local Web designer to create sample pages for the Web site, including catalog pages that contained the digital images. She also created a number of videos showing the customized sneakers in action.

When the Web designer had completed a prototype of the site, Amy worked with the designer to calculate page sizes (including the images). The average page size was 1 MB. She also calculated the average size of a video to be 800 MB. Amy and her employees then navigated the prototype site several hundred times to develop an estimate of how many pages an average visitor would download and how many videos they would watch. They concluded that an average site visitor would visit 23 pages and watch one video during each visit. Amy worked with the Web designer to develop estimates of the activity they expect to occur on the Web site during its first two years of operation. These estimates include:

- The database of Web page information (including the images and the videos) will require about 1 TB of disk space.
- The database management software itself will require about 500 MB of disk space.
- The shopping cart software will require about 300 MB of disk space.
- About 8000 customers will visit the site during the first month, and site traffic will grow about 20 percent each month during the first two years.
- The site should accommodate a peak traffic load of 1000 visitors at one time.

Amy wants to include features on the site that are similar to those found on competing sites (a list of links to businesses that sell customized shoes on the Web is included in the Web Links for your reference). Amy wants the site to provide a good experience for visitors. If the site is successful, it will generate sufficient revenue to allow an upgrade after two years. However, she does not want to spend more money than is necessary to get the site up and keep it running for the next two years.

REQUIRED

1. Determine the features and capacities (RAM, disk storage, processor speed) that Amy should include in the Web server computer she will need for her site. Summarize your purchase recommendation in a one-page memorandum to Amy. You may include information

from vendors' sites (such as Dell, HP Servers, or Oracle Enterprise Servers) as an appendix to your memorandum.

2. Consider the advantages and disadvantages of using open source Web server software (such as Apache Web Server) on the new computer. In a one-page memorandum to Amy, make a specific recommendation and support it with facts and a logical argument.

3. Evaluate whether Amy should consider using a content delivery network service. Outline the pros and cons of doing so in about 100 words.

Note: Your instructor might assign you to a group to complete this case and might ask you to prepare a formal presentation of your results to your class.

For Further Study and Research

Akamai Technologies, Inc. 2014. *State of the Internet*. Cambridge, MA: Akamai.

Bacic, H. 2015. "Are You Using a Content Delivery Network for Your Website Yet? You Should Be," *Forbes*, March 16. http://www.forbes.com/sites/allbusiness/2015/03/16/are-you-using-a-content-delivery-network-for-your-website-yet-you-should-be/

Boyle, J. 2015. "Just How Big Will Asheville Get?" *The Citizen-Times*, January 30. http://www.citizen-times.com/story/news/local/2015/01/29/just-big-will-asheville-get/22539563/

Cisco Systems, Inc. 2015. *Cisco Visual Networking Index*. San Jose, CA: Cisco.

The Computer & Internet Lawyer. 2009. "Court Orders Spammers to Give Up $3.7 Million in US SAFE Web Case," 26(9), September, 26–27.

Forrest, C. 2015. "The State of Cloud Computing: Ten Things You Need to Know," *TechRepublic*, August 11. http://www.techrepublic.com/article/the-state-of-cloud-computing-10-things-you-need-to-know/

Fung, B. 2015. "Netflix Now Accounts for Almost 37 Percent of Our Internet Traffic," *The Washington Post*, May 28. https://www.washingtonpost.com/news/the-switch/wp/2015/05/28/netflix-now-accounts-for-almost-37-percent-of-our-internet-traffic/

Graham, P. 2003. "Better Bayesian Filtering," *Paul Graham*, January. http://www.paulgraham.com/better.html

Gross, G. 2004. "Judge Awards ISP $1 Billion in Spam Damages," *Computerworld*, December 20. http://www.computerworld.com/governmenttopics/government/legalissues/story/0,10801,98421,00.html

Howell, D. 2015. "How to Choose the Right Server for Your Business," *TechRadar Pro*, August 14. http://www.techradar.com/news/computing/servers/how-to-choose-the-right-server-for-your-business-1092468

Ibrahim, A. and I. Osman. 2012. "A Behavioral Spam Detection System," *Future Computer, Communication, Control and Automation*, 119, 77–81.

Kepes, B. 2014. "A Good Hybrid Cloud Case Study—Asheville Shows How Hybrid Should Be Done," *Forbes*, November 26. http://www.forbes.com/sites/benkepes/2014/11/26/a-good-hybrid-cloud-case-study-asheville-shows-how-hybrid-should-be-done/

Krill, P. 2015. "A Developer's Guide to the Pros and Cons of Python," *InfoWorld*, February 24. http://www.infoworld.com/article/2887974/application-development/a-developer-s-guide-to-the-pro-s-and-con-s-of-python.html

Metz, C. 2013. "The Second Coming of Java: Clinton-Era Relic Returns to Rule Web," *Wired*, September 25. http://www.wired.com/wiredenterprise/2013/09/the-second-coming-of-java/

Mlot, S. 2015. "Report: Apple Building High-Speed Content Delivery Network," *PC Magazine*, June 8. http://www.pcmag.com/article2/0,2817,2485590,00.asp

PC World, 2005. "Spam Law Test," *23*(1), January, 20–22.

Richter, F. 2014. "Netflix and YouTube Are America's Biggest Traffic Hogs," *Statistica*, November 24. http://www.statista.com/chart/1620/top-10-traffic-hogs/

Smalley, E. 2011. "2011: The Year Data Centers Turned Green," *Wired*, December 30. http://www.wired.com/wiredenterprise/2011/12/green-data-centers-of-2011/

Stone, B. 2009. "Spam Back to 94% of All E-mail," *The New York Times*, March 31. http://bits.blogs.nytimes.com/2009/03/31/spam-back-to-94-of-all-e-mail/

Synergy Research Group. 2015. "AWS Market Share Reaches Five-Year High Despite Microsoft Growth Surge," February 12. https://www.srgresearch.com/articles/aws-market-share-reaches-five-year-high-despite-microsoft-growth-surge

University of Minnesota. 2009. *Minnesota Internet Traffic Studies*. Minneapolis: University of Minnesota. http://www.dtc.umn.edu/mints/home.php

Verge, J. 2015. "Gartner: AWS Pulls Further Ahead of Others in IaaS Cloud Market," *Data Center Knowledge*, May 28. http://www.datacenterknowledge.com/archives/2015/05/28/gartner-aws-pulls-further-ahead-in-iaas-cloud-market/

Wagner, M. and T. Kemp. 2001. "What's Wrong with eBay?" *InternetWeek*, January 15, 1–2.

Waterson, D. 2015. "Back to the Server: Server-Side JavaScript On The Rise, *Mozilla Developer Network*, July 1. https://developer.mozilla.org/en-US/docs/Archive/Web/Server-Side_JavaScript/Walkthrough

Wayner, P. 2014. "Nine Cutting-edge Programming Languages Worth Learning Now," *InfoWorld*, November 3. http://www.infoworld.com/article/2840235/application-development/9-cutting-edge-programming-languages-worth-learning-next.html

Wodehouse, C. 2015. "Server-Side Scripting: Back-End Web Development Technology," *Upwork*, May 5. https://www.upwork.com/hiring/development/server-side-scripting-back-end-web-development-technology/

Electronic Commerce Software

LEARNING OBJECTIVES

In this chapter, you will learn:

- How to find and evaluate Web-hosting services for online business operations
- What functions are performed by electronic commerce software
- How electronic commerce software works with database and ERP software
- What enterprise application integration and Web services are and how they can be used with electronic commerce software
- Which types of electronic commerce software are used by small, medium, and large businesses
- How electronic commerce software works with customer relationship management, knowledge management, and supply chain management software

INTRODUCTION

Online businesses know that it is important to process and ship orders quickly all the time, but it is harder to accomplish that goal during times of high demand for specific products. Although demand can be hard to predict, there are times when planning ahead is possible and it can be important to antici-pate those situations. When e-commerce manager Anna Sims at pet products retailer Harry Barker found that the store's products would be featured on a segment of ABC's *Good Morning America* show, she knew that it could generate a sudden influx of online orders. If the company's Web site became overloaded by the bump in traffic or the resulting orders were not fulfilled promptly and accurately, the value of the publicity could go from positive to negative very quickly.

The company took three steps to increase its order-handling capacity well before the air date of the segment. First, it added an extra Web server that it dedicated to processing incoming customer orders. Second, it hired additional temporary staff at its call center, to handle a higher volume of customer phone and e-mail inquiries, and at its warehouse to process a large number of orders efficiently. Finally, it made plans to batch the orders as they came in and send them to the warehouse 30 at a time instead of individually.

When the show aired, Harry Barker provided a special URL that took customers to a separate Web page created just for them. The page included discounts for viewers of the program as an inducement to draw them to this page rather than the regular Harry Barker home page. The page included text that explained the publicity from the show was expected to generate a large volume of orders and that it could take up to 10 days for customers to receive their merchandise.

The company also followed up with e-mail surveys and monitored social media to measure how well it met all of these new customers' expectations. In this chapter, you will learn about the kinds of software that sites like Harry Barker use to make their revenue models work, including software that enables catalog display of goods, shopping cart functions, and transaction processing activities.

Web Hosting Alternatives

In Chapter 8, you learned how companies can do business online using their own servers and server software, an approach called **self-hosting**. Some companies, especially midsize and smaller companies, use a third-party Web-hosting service instead of self-hosting. A third-party host can provide both Web hosting and software that performs other electronic commerce functions.

As you learned in Chapter 2, Internet service providers (ISPs) provide Internet access to companies and individuals. Virtually all of these companies also offer Web-hosting services and sometimes call themselves **commerce service providers (CSPs)**. These firms, which often offer Web server management and rent application software (such as databases, shopping carts, and content management programs) to businesses, sometimes call themselves **managed service providers (MSPs)** or **application service providers (ASPs)**. Today, most ISPs, CSPs, MSPs, and ASPs offer similar services and the acronyms are used interchangeably.

The main categories of Web-hosting services offered by these providers include shared hosting, dedicated hosting, and co-location. **Shared hosting** means that the client's Web site is on a server that hosts other Web sites simultaneously. With **dedicated hosting**, the service provider makes a Web server available to the client, but the client does not share the server with other clients of the service provider. In both shared hosting and dedicated hosting, the service provider owns the server hardware and leases it to the client. The service provider maintains the Web server hardware and software, and provides the connection to the Internet through its routers and other network hardware. In a **co-location** (also spelled **collocation** and **colocation**) service, the service provider rents a physical space to the client to install its own server hardware. The client installs its own software and maintains the server itself, but the service provider furnishes a reliable power supply (with backup provisions in case of a natural disaster or other power outage) and a connection to the Internet.

When making Web server-hosting decisions, a company should ask whether the hardware platform and software combination can be upgraded when the traffic on its Web site increases. Many hosting services provide Web server hardware and software combinations that are **scalable**, which means they can be adapted to meet changing requirements when their clients grow.

Basic Functions of Electronic Commerce Software

Because electronic commerce sites vary in size, purpose, audience, and other factors, a range of software and hardware products are available for building electronic commerce sites, but all electronic commerce software must provide the following elements:

- Catalog display
- Shopping cart capabilities
- Transaction processing

Larger and more complex electronic commerce sites need software that adds other features and capabilities to the basic set of commerce tools. These additional software components can include:

- Middleware that integrates the electronic commerce system with existing company information systems that handle inventory control, order processing, and accounting
- Enterprise application integration
- Web services
- Integration with enterprise resource planning (ERP) software
- Supply chain management (SCM) software
- Customer relationship management (CRM) software
- Content management software
- Knowledge management software

The basic elements required to do business online are described in the following sections. The more advanced functions used by larger, more comprehensive sites are covered later in this chapter.

Catalog Display Software

A **catalog** is an organized listing of goods or services offered for sale. To further organize its offerings, a retailer may break them down into departments. As in a physical store, merchandise in an online store can be grouped within logical departments to make locating an item, such as a camping stove, simpler. Web stores often use the same department names as their physical counterparts. In most physical stores, each product is kept in only one place. A Web store has the advantage of being able to include a single product in multiple categories. For example, running shoes could be listed as both footwear and athletic gear.

A small online business site can have a very simple static catalog. A **static catalog** is a simple list, tagged with HTML codes, that can be displayed on a single Web page or a series of related Web pages. This simple list approach can provide a short description and perhaps a photo of each item offered for sale. To add an item, delete an item, or change an item's listing, the company must edit the HTML-tagged text in one or more files. Since this can become a cumbersome process when the number of items grows beyond a few hundred, most online businesses use a dynamic catalog.

A **dynamic catalog** stores the information about items in a database, usually on a separate computer, which is accessible to the server that is running the Web site itself. A dynamic catalog can feature multiple photos of each item, detailed descriptions, and can include a search tool that allows customers to search for an item and determine its availability. Dynamic catalog software is often included in the more comprehensive electronic commerce software packages; however, some companies write their own software to link their existing databases of product information to their Web sites. Both types of catalog functions (static and dynamic) are located in the third tier of the three-tier Web site architecture that you learned about in Chapter 8.

As you learned in Chapter 3, good sites give buyers multiple different ways to find products. Besides offering a well-organized catalog, most sites with many products provide an **internal search engine**, which is a software that allows customers to enter descriptive search terms, such as "men's shirts," so they can quickly find the Web page containing what they want to purchase.

Shopping Cart Software

In the early days of electronic commerce, shoppers selected items they wanted to purchase by filling out online forms, a process that required a shopper to type in product descriptions and item numbers, along with other information, into online ordering systems. This was awkward to use and error-prone for customers ordering more than one or two items at a time. Today, shopping carts are the standard method for processing sales online. As you learned in Chapter 4, a shopping cart, also called a shopping bag or shopping basket, keeps track of the items customers have selected and allows customers to view the contents of their carts, add new items, or remove items. To order an item, the customer simply clicks a button or link near the item's description that indicates "add to cart" or similar language. All of the details about the item, including its price, product number, and other identifying information, are stored automatically in the cart. A good shopping cart allows the customer to view the cart's contents and remove the unwanted items at any time during the session by providing a link to the cart on every page displayed during the shopping process. When the customer is ready to conclude the shopping session, the click of a button takes the customer to a series of checkout screens that lead to execution of the purchase transaction. Figure 9-1 shows a typical shopping cart page at a site that sells tools.

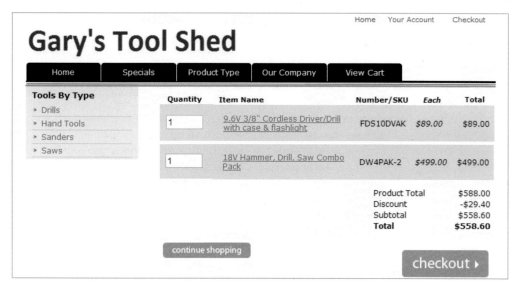

FIGURE 9-1   Typical shopping cart page

Clicking the checkout button usually displays a screen that asks for billing and shipping information and that confirms the order. As you can see from the figure, the shopping cart software keeps a running total of each type of item. The shopping cart calculates a total as well as sales tax and shipping costs along with any discounts.

Some shopping cart software allows the customer to fill a shopping cart with purchases, put the cart in virtual storage, and come back days later to confirm and pay for the purchases. Shopping cart software products, such as **BigCommerce**, **SalesCart**, and **Volusion**, include a variety of useful features. Some shopping cart software is sold for one-time licensing fee that can range from a few hundred to a few thousand dollars, but most of these packages are sold on a subscription license basis with a fee that ranges from $15 to $300 per month plus, in some cases a transaction fee assessed as a percentage of sales.

HTTP messaging, which is the foundation of the Web, is a **stateless system** (it does not retain information from one transmission or session to another), thus shopping cart software must store information about specific shoppers and their purchases. One way that shopping cart software does this is to create cookies; which, as you learned in Chapter 7, are bits of information stored on a client computer (you will learn more about cookies in Chapter 10). When a customer returns to the shopping site that issued a particular cookie, the shopping cart software reads the cookie from the customer's computer and uses the information stored there to retrieve the customer's shopping information from the seller's server computer.

Some shoppers configure their Web browser software to refuse cookies, so many sites use another method to preserve shopping cart information from one browser session to another. Some shopping cart software packages, such as **ShopSite**, do this by assigning each shopper a temporary identifying number. This number is added to the end of the URL that appears in the browser's address bar and persists as the shopper navigates from one Web site to another. When the customer returns, the URL still includes the identifying number, which the Web server uses to reinstate the customer's shopping cart information. When the shopper closes the browser, the temporary number is discarded and is no longer available, even if the customer later reopens the browser and returns to the same Web site. Thus, this approach works only as long as the shopper continues to keep the browser software open.

The higher-priced shopping cart software options often include additional services along with the basic functions described above. These include dynamic pricing management, promotion management, integration of fulfillment services, product review management, product recommendation triggers, abandoned cart management, sales tax calculations, and credit card processing. In an online business, **dynamic pricing management** software can adjust pricing in real time based on customer category, past purchase volume (in units or dollars), order size, or any other variable the seller chooses. **Promotion management** software allows sellers to create special offers (promotions) on specific products in response to variations in customer demand, seasonal preferences, introduction of new product varieties or package sizes, and any other variable chosen. Many online sellers use third-party fulfillment services to deliver their products. **Fulfillment integration** software can connect a seller's shopping cart directly to the fulfillment service provider's computers so that shipping can be triggered by the shopping cart software automatically when the sale transaction is completed. **Product review management** software allows customers to post reviews of products. Features in such software allow the seller to edit or delete these postings and to respond to them efficiently. **Product recommendation triggers** are software tools that respond to a customer's product selection with suggestions for related products or refills for products that have consumable elements (such as blades for a razor). These triggers can also be set to remind a customer after a specified amount of time has passed since that customer purchased a consumable product. For example, a customer that buys a 60-day supply of a certain vitamin will see a reminder to buy that item again 60 days after their purchase. **Abandoned cart management** software enables the shopping cart to retain a record of what customers have added to their shopping carts when their session is terminated for some reason. This allows customers to pick up where they left off when they return to the site after an interruption. In some cases, these tools include the ability to send a reminder e-mail to customers when they have left the site with items in their cart. Often, this friendly reminder will bring customers back to the site to complete their purchase transaction. As you learned in Chapter 7, the calculation and payment of sales taxes (and value-added taxes for businesses that sell into European and South American countries) can be a complex affair. Some shopping cart software includes tools for calculating and, in some cases, remitting these taxes to the appropriate governments. You will learn more about credit card payment processing in Chapter 11; however, a number of the more costly shopping cart software tools do either provide credit card payment processing or include links to third-party payment processing services.

Transaction Processing

Transaction processing occurs when the shopper proceeds to the virtual checkout counter by clicking a checkout button. Then the electronic commerce software performs any necessary calculations, such as volume discounts, sales tax, and shipping

LEARNING FROM FAILURES

PDG Software

PDG Software is a company based in Tucker, Georgia, that sells electronic commerce software to companies that operate small and midsize electronic commerce Web sites. PDG sells shopping cart software, auction software, and a number of other packages. Although it sells some of its software directly to the companies that use it, most of its sales are through resellers—firms that use PDG software as part of Web sites that they design, build, and deliver to customers as complete units.

An attacker discovered a vulnerability in the PDG software that would allow intruders to gain access to PDG shopping cart software installed on a retailer's Web site and open the file that contained customer names, contact information, and credit card numbers. PDG developed a patch that its customers could use to repair the software the same day it found out about the intrusions. PDG posted the patch on its Web site so that companies using the software could download and install the patch. Both PDG and the FBI issued press releases immediately to warn users of the problem with the shopping cart software and encourage them to obtain the patch. Unfortunately, many users of PDG shopping cart software had purchased it as part of a complete electronic commerce Web site. These users were, in many cases, unaware

that they were running the PDG shopping cart software.

Because it took so long—several months, in some cases—to find and contact the companies using the software, online offenders were able to exploit this vulnerability and collect thousands of credit card numbers. In most cases such as this, the difficulty of finding the sites that are running the vulnerable software helps slow down the attackers. Unfortunately, in this case, the intruder who discovered the opening also found that entering a specific word in a search engine's search expression would instantly return a list of the thousands of sites running the PDG software.

Most of the Web sites found out about the problem when their customers called them, suspicious because their credit card information had been compromised. The lesson from this failure is that companies that operate electronic commerce Web sites must know the source of the software used in creating and maintaining their sites and must monitor news about the security of that software.

costs. At checkout, the customer's Web browser software and the seller's Web server software both switch into a secure state of communication. You will learn more about how Web clients and servers establish these secure communication states in Chapter 10. Figure 9-2 shows how the three key functions of a basic electronic commerce Web site (catalog display, shopping cart, and transaction processing) are combined in the site's architecture.

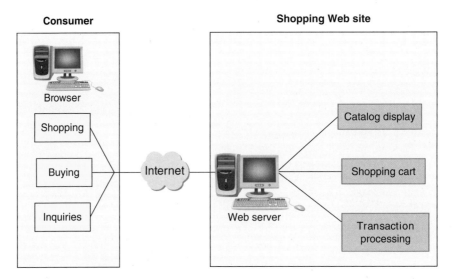

FIGURE 9-2   Basic electronic commerce site architecture

Although a basic online store's electronic commerce software can generate reports that summarize sales and inventory shipped, most midsize and larger companies use an accounting software package to record sales and inventory movements. To integrate effectively with accounting software, the electronic commerce software must communicate with that accounting software, which typically runs on other computers in the seller's network. When an item is sold online, the electronic commerce software must communicate that fact to both the sales and inventory management modules in the accounting software.

Computing sales taxes and shipping costs are also important parts of online sales. Sales tax rates and shipping rates can change often, so Web site managers must either monitor and update the rates continually or use software that updates the rates automatically. Shipping companies such as FedEx and UPS offer software to shippers that integrates with electronic commerce software to ensure that the rates they have are current. Other calculation complications include provisions for coupons, special promotions, and time-sensitive offers; for example, "purchase a round-trip ticket before the end of the month and receive a 50 percent discount."

In larger companies, the integration of the Web site's transaction processing into the accounting and operation-control systems of the company can be very complex. The next section discusses some of the advanced functions that larger companies look for in electronic commerce software.

How Electronic Commerce Software Works With Other Software

In this section, you will learn about the features that larger companies need in their electronic commerce software. Although there are exceptions, such as Amazon.com and Buy.com, most large companies that have electronic commerce operations also have substantial business activity that is not related to electronic commerce. Thus, integrating electronic commerce activities into the company's other operations is very important. A basic element of any large company's information system is its collection of databases.

Databases

A **database** is a collection of information that is stored on a computer in a highly structured way. The rules a business establishes about its database structure are carefully thought out and take into account how the company does business (its **business rules**) and how the company can reduce the likelihood that errors and inconsistencies will develop in the database.

A **database manager** (or **database management software**) is a software that makes it easy for users to enter, edit, update, and retrieve information in the database. The most commonly used low-end database manager is Microsoft Access. More complex database managers that can handle larger databases and can perform more functions at higher speeds include IBM DB2, Microsoft SQL Server, and Oracle. Large companies that have operations in many locations must make most (or all) of their data available to users in those locations. Large information systems that store the same data in many different physical locations are called **distributed information systems**, and the databases within those systems are called **distributed database systems**.

Most companies use commercial database products; however, an increasing number of companies and other organizations are using MySQL, which was developed and is maintained by a community of programmers on the Web. Similar to the Linux operating system you learned about in earlier chapters, MySQL is an open-source software, even though it was developed by a Swedish company, MySQL AB, which is now owned by Oracle. Oracle sells annual subscriptions for MySQL support and maintenance services.

Online stores that sell many different products use databases that store product information, including size, color, type, and price details. Most companies that have both online and physical operations use the same database for all functions of their businesses. The details of database design and operation can become quite complex and are beyond the scope of this book. You can learn more about databases by taking courses in database design and implementation.

Middleware

Larger companies usually establish connections between their electronic commerce software (that is, their catalog display, shopping cart, and transaction processing software) and their accounting and inventory management databases or applications by using middleware. **Middleware** is software that takes information about sales and inventory shipments from the electronic commerce software and transmits it to accounting and inventory management software in a form that these systems can read. For example, the sales module of an accounting system might be designed to accept the input of a telephone salesperson. The salesperson enters the product numbers, quantities, and shipping method into the sales module by using a keyboard while talking to the customer on the phone. Middleware would extract information about a sale from the Web site's shopping cart software and enter it directly into the accounting software's sales module without requiring that a person reenter the information.

Some larger companies have sufficient IT staff to write their own middleware; however, most companies purchase middleware that is customized for their businesses by the software vendor or a consulting firm. Thus, most of the cost of middleware is not the software itself, but the cost of customizing it to work in a given company. Making a company's information systems work together is called **interoperability** and is an important goal of companies when they install middleware. The total cost of a middleware implementation can range from $10,000 to several million dollars, depending on the complexity of the company's underlying operations and its existing information systems. Major middleware vendors include Broadvision, IBM Tivoli Software, and Informatica.

Enterprise Application Integration

A program that performs a specific function, such as creating invoices, calculating payroll, or processing payments received from customers, is called an **application program**, **application software**, or, more simply, an **application**. An **application server** is a computer that takes the request messages received by the Web server and runs application programs that perform some kind of action based on the contents of the request messages. The actions that the application server software performs are determined by the rules used in the business. These rules are called **business logic**. An example of a business rule is the following: When a customer logs in, check the password entered against the password file in the database.

In many organizations, the business logic is distributed among many different applications that are used in different parts of the organization. In recent years, many IT departments have devoted significant resources to the creation of links among these scattered applications so that the organization's business logic can be interconnected. The creation and management of these links are called **enterprise application integration**. The integration is accomplished by programs that transfer information from one application to another. For example, a program might transfer information from order entry systems in several different divisions to a single accounts receivable and sales system that integrates all enterprise-wide sales activity. Data formats in the various programs are often different, requiring the transfer programs to edit and reformat the data before transferring it. Many systems use XML data feeds to move data from one application to another in these implementations.

Application servers are usually grouped into two types: page-based and component-based systems. **Page-based application systems** return pages generated by scripts that include the rules for presenting data on the Web page with the business logic.

Scripting tools used in page-based application systems include Adobe ColdFusion, JavaServer Pages (JSP), Microsoft Active Server Pages (ASP), and Hypertext Preprocessor (PHP). Because page-based systems combine presentation and business logic, they are hard to revise and update.

To avoid this problem, an increasing number of businesses use a **component-based application system** that separates the presentation logic from the business logic. Each component of logic is created and maintained separately, which makes updating and changing elements of the system much easier. The most common component-based systems used on the Web are Enterprise JavaBeans (EJBs), Microsoft COM, and the Object Management Group's Common Object Request Broker Architecture (CORBA).

Integration with ERP Systems

Many B2B Web sites must be able to connect to complex existing information systems such as enterprise resource planning software. **Enterprise resource planning (ERP)** software packages are business systems that integrate all facets of a business, including accounting, logistics, manufacturing, marketing, planning, project management, and treasury functions.

The two major ERP vendors are Oracle and SAP. A typical installation of ERP software costs $1 million to $10 million in a midsize company (larger companies often spend more than $100 million); thus, companies that are already running these systems have made a significant investment in them and require that their online operations integrate with them. Figure 9-3 shows a typical architecture for a B2B Web site in a company that has an ERP system and uses EDI to connect to its trading partners.

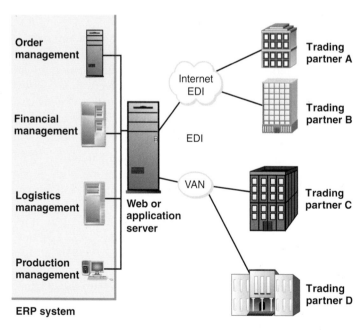

FIGURE 9-3   ERP system integration with EDI

Often, smaller online businesses cannot afford to buy a full ERP software implementation; however, they can purchase products such as **NetSuite** that offer subscriptions to ERP software for all sizes of businesses. Instead of installing and customizing ERP software on their own computer network, the business uses a Web browser to access the ERP software on the vendor's site. This practice of offering software use online is called **software as a service (SaaS)**. Although the ERP systems provided in this manner are not perfectly customized to each business, the software does allow some customization and many businesses find that they work very well.

Web Services

Companies are using the Internet to connect software applications at one organization directly to software applications at other organizations. The W3C defines **Web services** as software systems that support interoperable machine-to-machine interaction over a network. In other words, a Web service is a set of software and technologies that allow computers to use the Web to interact with each other directly, without human operators directing the specific interactions. An SaaS product provides a complete software package through a Web browser and generally includes interaction with human beings. Web services are designed to automate narrow, specific functions in the background and generally do not include interaction with human beings.

A general name for the ways programs interconnect with each other is **application program interface (API)**. When the interaction is done over the Web, the techniques are called **Web APIs**. Web services use Web APIs of various types, as you will learn later in this section.

WHAT WEB SERVICES CAN DO

Companies use Web services to offer improved customer service and reduce costs in a variety of ways. Some companies use Web services to transmit XML-tagged data from one application to another to accomplish enterprise application integration. In other applications, Web services provide continuous data feeds between two different companies. Many companies have found Web services to be less expensive and more easily implemented alternatives to installing multiple middleware software programs. Examples of specific Web services implementations include:

- J.P. Morgan Chase & Co., a major investment bank, uses Web services in its investment information portal to pull information, such as general economic forecasts, financial analyses of specific companies, industry forecasts, and financial markets results, into online reports available to customers on the company's portal site.
- Nationwide Building Society, a mortgage company in Swindon, England, uses Web services to communicate automatically with mortgage application service companies. These service companies obtain information from consumers who want mortgages and then forward the information in a prescribed XML format to Nationwide, where its Web services software reformats the submission and enters it into Nationwide's enterprise computer system. When Nationwide makes its lending decision, the

Web service sends the decision back to the mortgage application service company's computer. Using Web services has reduced costs and turnaround time for these loan decisions, simultaneously saving money and giving customers better service.

- CUNA Mutual Group sells services to credit unions throughout the United States. Many of these services, such as check clearing, do not change much over time, so CUNA performs them running programs on old computer systems that they have been using for many years. Instead of reprogramming everything to be accessible on the Web, CUNA created a Web services layer that takes information from the old computer systems and generates Web pages that its customers can use to obtain those services.

- The MSN Money site buys stock quotes and other information from Morningstar, Inc., which delivers them, computer-to-computer, using Web services. If you view an MSN Money stock quote page, you can see the acknowledgement for those stock quotes (along with those of other Web services providers that contributed to the page) near the bottom of the Web page under the heading "Data Providers."

HOW WEB SERVICES WORK

A key element of the Web services approach is that programmers can write software that accesses units of business application logic without knowing the details of how each unit is implemented. Web services can be combined with other Web services to execute a complex business transaction. Thus, Web services allow programs written in different languages on different platforms to communicate with each other and accomplish transaction processing and other business tasks.

The common format of this machine-to-machine communication was originally HTML; however, most Web services implementations now use XML. As you learned in Chapter 2, organizations can use XML to mark up content with agreed-upon sets of descriptive tags.

The first Web services were just sources of information that programmers could incorporate into software applications. For example, a company that wanted to collect all its financial management information into one spreadsheet could use Web services to obtain information about bank account and loan balances, stock portfolio holdings, and current interest rates on financial instruments from many different sources. The spreadsheet model could use the information supplied by those Web services to update itself automatically.

For a more advanced example, consider a company that implements Web services in its purchasing function to obtain price information from a variety of vendors. After a purchasing agent reviews the price and delivery information and authorizes the transaction, the Web service can submit the order directly to the vendor's computer and track it (through its connection to the shipper's computer system) until the shipment is received. As Web services systems become more sophisticated, they can often make the decisions themselves.

WEB SERVICES SPECIFICATIONS

The first widely used approach to Web services was **Simple Object Access Protocol (SOAP)**, which is a message-passing protocol that defines how to send marked-up data from one software application to another across a network. Implementing SOAP uses three rule sets (usually called protocols or specifications) that let programs work with formatted (using XML or HTML) data flows. The communication rules are included in the SOAP specification. Two other commonly used specifications are the **Web Services Description Language (WSDL)**, which is used to describe the logic unit characteristics of each Web service, and the **Universal Description, Discovery, and Integration Specification (UDDI)**, which works as a sort of address book to identify the locations of Web services and their associated WSDL descriptions. After using the UDDI "address book" to find the WSDL that describes a particular Web service, programmers can use the information contained in the WDSL to connect application programs to that Web service (some programs can even configure themselves using the information in the WSDL descriptions).

REST AND RESTFUL DESIGN

Although SOAP protocols continue to be used widely to implement Web services, another approach that uses a simpler structure has become more common in Web services implementations. In 2000, Roy Fielding outlined a principle called **Representational State Transfer (REST)**, that describes the way the Web uses networking architecture to identify and locate Web pages and the elements (graphics, audio clips, and so on) that make up those Web pages. Some Web services designers who found SOAP to be overly complex for their applications turned to Fielding's REST idea and used it to structure their work.

Web services that are built on the REST model are said to use **RESTful design** and are sometimes called **RESTful applications**. A RESTful application transfers structured information from one Web location to another. This structured information is most often an XML- or XHTML-tagged data set. The Web service is made available at a specific address (much as a Web page is made available at its URL) and can be accessed by any other computer that has a Web browser function. More than half of all Web services today are RESTful applications. The most widely used is the Atom Publishing Protocol, which simplifies blog publishing. You can see examples of Web services that use RESTful design at ProgrammableWeb.

Electronic Commerce Software for Small and Midsize Companies

In this section, you will learn about software that small and midsize businesses can use to implement online business Web sites. In most cases, these companies can create a Web site that stands alone in its business activities (primarily promotion and sales activities) and does not need to be coordinated completely with the business's other activities, which would include human resources, purchasing, and so on.

Basic CSPs

Using a service provider's shared or dedicated hosting services instead of building an in-house server or using a co-location service means that the staffing burden shifts from the company to the Web host. The operating costs of a large Web site are shared by all of the businesses hosted by the service. The host provider is responsible for keeping the servers working through power outages.

CSPs offer free- or low-cost electronic commerce software for building online business sites hosted on the CSP's server. Services in this category can cost less than $20 per month, and the software is built into the CSP's site, allowing companies to create an online presence quickly using the Web interface of the software. Gate.com, ProHosting. com, and 1&1 Internet are examples of service providers that cater to small and midsize companies. Yahoo! offers its electronic commerce services, which include site design, an online payment function, order processing and shipping, and marketing programs, as described on its Yahoo! Small Business Ecommerce Web page.

Mall-Style CSPs

Mall-style CSPs provide small businesses with a basic Web site, online store design tools, storefront templates, and an easy-to-use interface. These service providers charge a low monthly fee and may also charge one-time setup fees (similar to basic CSPs); however, others also charge a percentage of or fixed amount for each customer transaction. Mall-style CSPs provide shopping cart software or the ability to use another vendor's shopping cart software. They also provide payment-processing services so the online store can accept credit cards.

In the early days of the Web, there were many different mall-style CSPs, some of which provided free Web site hosting in exchange for displaying ads on the sites. Today, the two main mall-style CSPs that remain in business are Amazon Services (through its "Professional Sellers" and "Individual Sellers" programs) and eBay Stores. These services give individuals and smaller companies a way to launch an online business (or add online sales to an existing business operation) easily without making a long-term commitment or a substantial up-front investment.

Estimated Operating Expenses for a Small Web Business

A small business owner who wants to take some commerce activity online would normally expect to spend between $400 and $8200 to become operational using either a basic CSP or a mall-style CSP. These estimates assume that the business will offer fewer than 100 items for sale and that the business already owns a computer and has Internet access for that computer. Figure 9-4 shows ranges of estimates for first-year expenses that a small business owner might incur to put this type of store on the Web.

The costs shown are average low and high estimates for each item. Depending on which CSP and electronic commerce software options are chosen, the actual costs could be somewhat lower or considerably higher. For example, some CSPs include free registration for several domains when a store signs up for a one-year or longer contract for services. The estimates shown in the figure omit ongoing payment-processing charges, which might average 0–50 cents per transaction and 2–4 percent of each sale's total. Most

	Cost Estimates	
Operating Costs	Low	High
Initial site setup fee	$ 0	$ 200
Annual CSP maintenance fee (12 x $20 to $300)	240	3600
Domain name registrations	0	300
Scanner for photo conversion or digital camera	60	2000
Photo editing software	0	800
Occasional HTML and site design help	100	1100
Merchant credit card setup fees	0	200
Total first-year costs	$400	$8200

FIGURE 9-4   Approximate costs to put a small store online

new merchants estimate that payment processing overall will cost roughly 3–6 percent of dollar sales. You will learn more about payment-processing options for online businesses in Chapter 11.

Contrast the preceding costs with comparable estimated costs for self-hosting a Web site. Setup and Web site maintenance costs include equipment, communications, physical location, and staff. Equipment such as a basic server and a router would have a one-time cost ranging from $2000–$10,000. A basic business-class Internet connection (see Chapter 2) could run $480–$1800 per year. A server must be housed in a room that is both secure and convenient to communications access. The cost to secure a small room, properly air-condition it, and install a chemical fire extinguishing system could easily reach $5000 a year. A self-hosted system requires an information technology staff that is familiar with Web programming and scripting languages, electronic commerce packages, and database management systems. Technicians will likely be required to monitor and maintain equipment. Staff costs could range from $50,000 to $100,000 annually. In total, annual operating costs for self-hosting will generally run between $60,000 and $100,000. Companies should carefully compare their estimates of self-hosting costs with the fees charged by hosting services that provide similar capabilities.

Costs for larger sites are much more difficult to estimate. The cost of integrating the Web site and related software (such as shopping cart, order-processing, and inventory control) with existing systems can be the largest cost. You will learn more about managing the costs of Web site implementation and operation for midsize and large organizations in Chapter 12. Next, you will learn about midrange electronic commerce software packages that are suitable for running larger businesses.

Electronic Commerce Software for Midsize Businesses

This section includes a discussion of software that midsize companies can use to implement online business activities. It also includes an outline of Web site development tools that can be used for that purpose and an overview of midrange electronic commerce software products that are representative of the types of products available.

Web Site Development Tools

Although they are more often used for creating small business sites, it is possible to construct the elements of a midrange electronic commerce Web site using the Web page creation and site management tools you learned about in Chapter 2. After creating the Web site with these tools, the designer can add purchased software elements, such as shopping carts and content management software, to the site. The final step is to create the middleware that connects the site to the company's existing product and transaction-processing databases.

Midrange Electronic Commerce Software

Midrange electronic commerce software typically costs between $5000 and $200,000, with annual operating costs ranging from $1000 to $30,000. Almost all software in this category offers connectivity to database or ERP systems that store inventory information. Because most of these products are customized for each installation, they are often sold either as components that can be assembled in different configurations or in multiple versions designed for specific types of business.

Intershop sells a series of midrange electronic commerce software packages for specific types of online businesses, including B2B, B2C, mobile commerce, and software services. Each package provides specific search and catalog capabilities, electronic shopping carts, online credit card transaction processing, and the ability to connect to existing back-end business systems and databases to work with each type of business. Intershop products include setup wizards, catalog tools, and data management functions. The B2C and mobile commerce products include many built-in storefront template choices. Users of Intershop can manage and edit the storefronts using a Web browser interface. In the B2B and B2C products, users can track inventory levels, view the quantity of items available, create lists of inventory transactions, and add new products into the inventory. A database management system is included, but Intershop software can work with DB2 (IBM's relational database) or Oracle databases. The software can generate a variety of Web site traffic and customer activity reports.

IBM produces WebSphere Commerce Professional, which is also a family of electronic commerce packages. IBM WebSphere software components include catalog templates, setup wizards, and catalog management tools for both B2B and B2C operations. These components link to existing corporate systems, such as inventory databases and procurement systems.

Customizing WebSphere requires programmers with JavaScript, Java, or C++ expertise. WebSphere components can connect to existing DB2 or Oracle databases. A single store or several different stores can be administered from the same browser-based interface. A large number of midrange electronic commerce sites use WebSphere software. The system has all the standard electronic commerce features, including tools for a shopping cart, e-mail notifications upon sale completion, secure transaction support, promotions and discounting, shipment tracking, links to accounting systems, and browser-based local and remote administration. A typical installation of WebSphere Commerce Professional edition costs between $50,000 and $300,000, depending on how many servers will be running the product and which options are purchased with the software.

Electronic Commerce Software for Large Businesses

Larger businesses require many of the same advanced capabilities as midsize firms, but the larger firms need to handle higher transaction loads. In addition, they need dedicated software applications to deal with specific elements of their online business. In this section, you will learn about electronic commerce software that has higher transaction-load capability, and you will learn about software that accomplishes specific tasks in large businesses, such as customer relationship management, supply chain management, content management, and knowledge management.

Software used in large online business operations is sometimes called **enterprise-class software**. The term "enterprise" is used in information systems to describe a system that serves multiple locations or divisions of one company and encompasses all areas of the business or enterprise. Enterprise-class electronic commerce software typically provides tools for both B2B and B2C commerce and interacts with a wide variety of existing systems, including database, accounting, and ERP systems. As electronic commerce has become more sophisticated, large companies have demanded that their Web sites and supporting information infrastructure do more things. The cost of these enterprise systems for large companies ranges from $200,000 for basic systems to $10 million and more for comprehensive customized packages.

Enterprise-Class Electronic Commerce Software

Enterprise-class electronic commerce software running large online organizations usually requires several dedicated computers—in addition to the Web server system and any necessary firewalls. Examples of enterprise-class products that can be used to run a large online business with high transaction rates include IBM WebSphere Commerce Enterprise, Oracle E-Business Suite, and several products from Broadvision.

Enterprise-class software typically provides tools for linking to and supporting supply and purchasing activities. For example, a large part of B2B commerce is ordering supplies from trading or business partners and issuing the appropriate documents (or EDI transaction sets), such as purchase orders. Large sales firms require secure transaction processing and fulfillment, connections to the firm's inventory system to issue purchase orders automatically when needed, and the ability to generate entries for the accounting or ERP systems. In contrast, both basic and midrange electronic commerce packages usually require an administrator to check inventory manually and place orders explicitly for items that need to be replenished.

For electronic goods (software, videos, music, and so on), this software allows customers to download directly from the site. Databases connected to enterprise electronic commerce software can contain millions of rows of information about products, prices, inventory, user profiles, and user purchasing history. The history provides a way to recommend to a user on a return visit related items that he or she might want to purchase. Figure 9-5 shows a typical enterprise-class electronic commerce architecture.

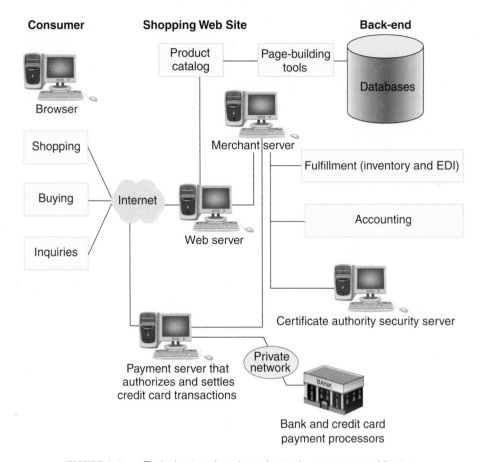

FIGURE 9-5   Typical enterprise-class electronic commerce architecture

As you learned in Chapter 5, companies are using the Web to integrate their supply chains. As a result, enterprise-class commerce Web sites must include or work with supply chain management software.

In Chapter 6, you learned about companies that were building social networking elements into their sites to engage their customers and suppliers. A part of that strategy is providing useful, fresh content to attract site visitors. This need has given rise to software that automatically manages and rotates content on Web sites. Some companies have even developed software that helps them manage the knowledge that exists in their businesses.

In Chapters 3 and 4, you learned that companies are storing data about site visitors in large databases and analyzing it to improve their relationships with those customers. These clickstreams track the path a visitor takes through a Web site, including which pages were viewed, the amount of time spent on each page, and the sequence in which pages were viewed. Thus, large electronic commerce sites must include customer relationship management software.

An enterprise-class Web site often includes several of these types of software packages in its design. The next sections of this chapter discuss software that works with electronic commerce software in large companies to help those companies achieve all of their electronic commerce objectives.

Content Management Software

Content management software helps companies control the large amounts of text, graphics, and media files that have become crucial to doing business. Most content management software includes tools that help companies manage information that was once stored in paper reports, schedules, analyses, and memos. In addition to the text and numbers stored in traditional databases, content management systems facilitate the storage of and access to all types of information, including images, technical drawings, geographic information, videos, audio files, and so on. The increased use of social media and networking as part of online business operations (which you learned about in Chapter 6) has made content management even more important as all kinds of Web sites now put content online. Content management systems help them organize, control, and move this information to and from their Web sites.

Before committing to a content management program, companies should perform testing to ensure that company employees find the software's procedures for performing regular maintenance (for example, adding new categories of products and new items to existing product pages) to be straightforward. The software should also facilitate typical content creation tasks, such as adding sale-item specials.

Companies that need many different ways to access corporate information—for example, product specifications, drawings, photographs, or lab test results—often choose to manage the information and access to that information using content management software. The leading providers of content management software include IBM and Oracle, which provide the software as components in other enterprise software packages, and several smaller companies that provide stand-alone content management software. Content management software generally costs between $50,000 and $500,000, but it can cost three or four times that much to customize, configure, and implement.

Knowledge Management Software

Large companies use content management systems to organize their information, but an increasing number of them have begun to understand that the true value of those documents is the collective knowledge they contain. Thus, they are using systems that help them manage the knowledge itself, rather than the documentary representations of that knowledge. The software that has been developed to meet that goal is called **knowledge management (KM) software**.

KM software helps companies do four main things: collect and organize knowledge, share the knowledge among users, enhance the ability of users to collaborate, and preserve the knowledge gained through the use of information so that future users can benefit from the learning of current users. KM software includes tools that read electronic documents (in formats such as Microsoft Word or Adobe PDF), scanned paper documents, e-mail messages, and Web pages. KM software often includes powerful search tools that use proprietary semantic and statistical algorithms to help users find the content, human experts, and other resources that can aid them in their research and decision-making tasks. Early KM systems often disrupted the flow of users' work. Today, KM systems collect knowledge elements by extracting them from the normal interactions users have with information.

The major software vendors have KM software offerings, including IBM and Microsoft SharePoint. Total costs for a KM software implementation, including hardware, software licenses, and consultant fees, can range from $10,000 to $1 million or more.

Supply Chain Management Software

Supply chain management (SCM) software helps companies to coordinate planning and operations with their partners in the industry supply chains of which they are members. SCM software performs two general types of functions: planning and execution. Most companies that sell SCM software offer products that include both components, but the functions are quite different. SCM planning software helps companies develop coordinated demand forecasts using information from each participant in the supply chain. SCM execution software helps with tasks such as warehouse and transportation management. Two companies that sell SCM software are JDA and Logility.

Common SCM software components include those that manage demand planning, supply planning, and demand fulfillment. Demand planning components examine customers' buying patterns and generate continually updated forecasts. The supply planning component coordinates distribution logistics, inventory-level forecasting, collaborative procurement, and supply allocations. The demand fulfillment component handles execution activities, including order management, customer verification, backlog control, and order fulfillment.

The cost of SCM software implementations varies tremendously depending on how many locations (retail stores, wholesale warehouses, distribution centers, and manufacturing plants) are in the supply chain. For example, a retailer with 500 stores might pay between $1 million and $5 million for an SCM package that includes both planning and execution functions, but a wholesaler with only three or four distribution centers might be able to install an SCM product for under $300,000.

Customer Relationship Management Software

You learned about the philosophy and techniques of customer relationship management (CRM) in Chapter 4. The goal of CRM is to understand each customer's specific needs and then customize a product or service to meet those needs. The idea is that a customer whose needs are being met exactly is willing to pay more for the goods or services that they need. Although companies of all sizes can practice CRM techniques, large companies can afford to buy and implement software products that automate many CRM functions.

Customer relationship management (CRM) software must obtain data from operations software that conducts activities such as sales automation, customer service center operations, and marketing campaigns. The software must also gather data about customer activities on the company's Web site and any other points of contact the company has with its existing and potential customers. CRM software uses this data to help managers conduct analytical activities, such as gathering business intelligence, planning marketing strategies, customer behavior modeling, and customizing the products and services to meet the needs of specific customers or categories of customers.

In its most basic form, CRM uses information about customers to sell them more (or more profitable) goods or services. More advanced CRM is about delivering extremely attractive and positive experiences regularly to customers. CRM can be very important in maintaining customer loyalty in businesses where the purchase process is long and complex. Companies that design and install custom machinery, software products, or office workflow systems often find themselves involved in these types of long and complex processes. CRM software can help maintain positive and consistent contacts with multiple employees at the purchasing company.

In the early years of CRM software implementation (approximately 1996 to 2000), companies often spent millions of dollars to buy CRM systems and undergo complete restructurings of their customer-interaction strategies. After learning that a single large-scale CRM implementation was not going to solve all of their problems in one fell swoop, companies gradually stopped thinking of CRM software as a tool for changing their overall customer strategy and instead began using CRM software to solve smaller and more specific problems. For example, a cable company might use CRM to track service outages and repair team responses in real time, but would not expect the CRM system to calculate the ongoing profitability of on-demand video services.

One of the most popular targets for focused CRM applications has been call center operations. By examining problems that arise in their call centers, many companies have identified specific applications where CRM software can improve response times, accuracy, and effectiveness. Today, most online businesses use small, precisely focused CRM software to address specific problems. For example, monitoring metrics such as shopping cart abandonments, product returns, product page views, and user session characteristics, companies can examine specific elements of their customers' experiences and make changes to their Web sites that can increase their effectiveness and profitability.

The implementation of a CRM system requires an integration of multiple data sources that have been cleaned and aggregated with an analytic engine that can make sense of the data using models that are continually revised to generate strategies for customized pricing, marketing campaigns, Web site special offers, and even catalog mailings that are synchronized with the online marketing effort. Figure 9-6 shows a general outline of the elements in a CRM system.

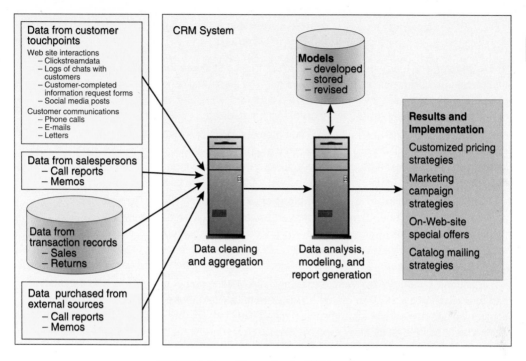

FIGURE 9-6   Elements of a CRM system

Some companies create their own CRM software using outside consultants and their own IT staffs but most companies today are more likely to buy a CRM software package rather than create their own. Siebel Systems was the first company to specialize in CRM software and it had gained a large share of the market. In 2005, Oracle bought Siebel and merged its operations into its existing CRM business, called Oracle CRM On Demand. Other major software firms have created products in this market, including SAP CRM. Prices for these systems start at around $20,000 (on average, about $1000 per user); large implementations can cost millions of dollars. Salesforce.com is a CRM software vendor and was one of the first companies to offer any type of software as an SaaS. Salesforce.com has been successful in selling its CRM SaaS products to a variety of businesses, including a number of small- and medium-sized online firms.

Summary

In this chapter, you learned about electronic commerce software for small, midsize, and large businesses and the functions provided by each. The electronic commerce software a company chooses depends on its size, objectives, and budget. A company can host its own site or contract with a service provider for shared hosting, dedicated hosting, or co-location.

Another option is to contract with a commerce service provider that can provide, in addition to hosting services, all of the other services that an online business needs, including: catalog display and management, databases, shopping carts, content management, Web analytics, and payment processing. Smaller online businesses often choose a commerce service provider.

Shopping cart software is available alone or in combination with commerce services, and can include a number of management tools that help businesses monitor and increase their online sales. These tools include dynamic pricing management, promotion management, integration of fulfillment services, product review management, product recommendation triggers, abandoned cart management, sales tax calculations, and credit card processing.

Electronic commerce software must work with existing company systems and databases. Larger firms often purchase or create middleware to facilitate these interfaces. Alternatively companies can use enterprise application integration software that is easier page-based or component-based to tie its other systems into its Web site. Companies can use Web services to get their information systems to work across organizational boundaries.

Electronic commerce software for larger businesses often includes customer relationship management, supply chain management, content management, and knowledge management functions or, alternatively, work with dedicated software that performs these functions.

Key Terms

abandoned cart management

application

application program

application program interface (API)

application server

application service providers (ASPs)

application software

business logic

business rules

catalog

collocation

colocation

co-location

commerce service providers (CSPs)

component-based application system

content management software

customer relationship management (CRM) software

database

database management software

database manager

dedicated hosting

distributed database systems

distributed information systems

dynamic catalog

dynamic pricing management

enterprise application integration

enterprise resource planning (ERP)

enterprise-class software

fulfillment integration

internal search engine

interoperability

knowledge management (KM) software

mall-style CSPs

managed service providers (MSPs)

middleware

page-based application systems

product recommendation trigger

product review management

promotion management

Representational State Transfer (REST)

RESTful applications

RESTful design

scalable

self-hosting

shared hosting

simple Object Access Protocol (SOAP)

software as a service (SaaS)

static catalog

stateless system

supply chain management (SCM) software

transaction processing

Universal Description, Discovery, and Integration Specification (UDDI)

Web APIs

Web services

Web Services Description Language (WSDL)

Review Questions

1. What are the main functions of a commerce service provider?

2. How does Web server co-location differ from a shared Web server?

3. Why might an online retailer choose to use a dynamic catalog rather than a static catalog?

4. Why is the stateless nature of the Internet a problem for shopping cart software?

5. How might a dynamic pricing management program increase sales?

6. Outline the function of a fulfillment integration provider.

7. What is a product recommendation trigger?

8. What is shopping cart abandonment?

9. Name the main functions of shopping cart software.

10. Why is the calculation of sales taxes a complex matter?

11. List the steps that must occur to process an online retail sales transaction.

12. Why would database management software be an important component of an online business Web site's technology?

13. What is middleware?

14. What is business logic?

15. Why is application integration an important part of running an online business?

16. Which business functions are integrated in a typical ERP system?

17. What is the difference between software as a service (SaaS) and Web services?

18. Briefly describe one example of a Web service that might be a useful part of an online business Web site.

19. What are the key differences between a basic commerce service provider (CSP) and a mall-style CSP?

20. What is the key function of a content management system as used in an online business?

21. Name four types of information that might be useful inputs to a customer relationship management (CRM) system.

22. In about 100 words, summarize the advantages and disadvantages of using a mall-style commerce service provider such as eBay Stores or Amazon.com's Pro Merchant program instead of operating a stand-alone electronic commerce site.

23. In one or two paragraphs, explain the functions of supply chain management software.

24. Write a paragraph in which you explain the purpose of cloud computing.

Exercises

1. In one or two paragraphs, outline the differences between shared and dedicated hosting.

2. In about 100 words, outline the key elements that should be a part of any electronic commerce software package.

3. Giving online customers alternative paths that lead to products in which they might be interested is important. In about 100 words, explain how static and dynamic catalogs could either facilitate or inhibit customers as they try to find a particular product on a company's Web site.

4. In about 200 words, explain why shopping cart abandonment could be a problem for an online retailer and describe at least two measures that can be taken to reduce its occurrence.

5. In two or three paragraphs, explain the difference between page-based application and component-based application systems. In your answer, be sure to outline which is preferable in an online business system design and explain why.

6. In a paragraph or two, describe the goals of enterprise application integration and explain why XML is often used in such efforts.

7. In about 100 words, describe the idea behind software as a service (SaaS). In your answer, include at least three examples of electronic commerce software packages or components that are offered as an SaaS.

8. In about 200 words, outline the difference between the Simple Object Access Protocol (SOAP) and the Representational State Transfer (REST) principle as they are used in the creation of Web services. In your answer, discuss the advantages and disadvantages of each.

9. Electronic commerce software must summarize sales and shipments. In about 100 words, explain how software for a small online store might accomplish this task and contrast it with how software for a large enterprise might do so.

10. In two or three paragraphs, outline the differences between knowledge management software and content management software. Include a description of at least one application of each that might be useful in an online business.

11. In two or three paragraphs, explain how database software could be an important part of a customer relationship management system as used in an online business.

Cases

C1. Moss Bros.

Since 1851, Moss Bros. has been selling quality menswear to the best-dressed gentlemen of London. Started in a corner of the Covent Garden area by Moses Moss, the retailer and formal wear rental business operates more than 130 stores throughout England and Ireland. The company also sells online in the United Kingdom and the United States. With sales over $150 million ($10 million of which are online), the firm has come a long way from its humble beginnings.

For many years, Moss Bros. has kept meticulous records of its customers' preferences, sizes, and past purchases. In 2013, the firm's e-commerce director Neil Sansom began an 18-month initiative to capitalize on its extensive customer records to increase sales, in particular, online sales. Sansom called the customer data its "golden records" and set mining them. Beginning with its most frequent customers, Moss Bros. built profiles and tracked their transactions to identify what prompted them to make purchases. Then, using that information, they developed personalized marketing messages and sent them in e-mails that were carefully timed to appeal to customers at just the right moment.

Although the implementation of the system is in its early stages, the firm has found that the basic promotional message targeting that it can do at this point has already doubled their rate of success achieved with e-mail promotions. The more the firm learns about its customers, the more it believes it will be able to turn that new knowledge into additional sales and it is looking forward to even better results once it extends its analytics to include all customers.

REQUIRED

1. In about 100 words, describe at least two specific examples of the type of marketing strategies that Moss Bros. might expect to see as output of their CRM system.

2. Draft a diagram that shows how you believe Moss Bros. might best connect its various data sources and use them to manage their customer relationships. You can use Figure 9-6 as a general guide. In an accompanying memo of about 200 words, explain how information flows through your diagram and provide details of the specific sources of each type of data you included.

3. In England, formal attire is expected at school proms, weddings, and at many entertainment events such as classical music concerts, the opera, and even certain horse races. In about 100 words provide at least two specific examples of how Moss Bros. might use social media to target e-mails to its customers promoting its formal wear rental services.

Note: Your instructor might assign you to a group to complete this case, and might ask you to prepare a formal presentation of your results to your class.

C2. Annette's Crafts

Annette Jackson owns a small crafts store in central Missouri where she sells handmade craft items produced by local artisans. She wants to expand her store's reach outside the region by selling online. She has asked you to help her estimate how much it might cost in the first year to create and operate the online store.

She plans to start the online store with a catalog of about 100 items, each of which will include several photographs of the item. She expects to have about 20 transactions per day on average during the first few months, but does expect the volume to grow about 50 percent in the second year of operation. After that, she hopes for a smaller annual increase of about 10–20 percent.

Annette wants you to investigate two CSP offerings and report back to her what you find. Since she is selling locally produced items, the store will not need a third-party fulfillment provider, but she will need payment-processing services and would like to use a CSP that provides them if possible.

Annette would like to consider the following information for the two CSP offerings:

- Costs: initial setup fee, monthly fee, and transaction fees
- Amount of disk space the CSP would provide
- Promotion and marketing opportunities
- Customer communications capabilities, such as automated e-mail confirmation of orders
- Shopping cart or other order entry mechanism
- Storefront-building wizards for creating a new store
- Web analytics reports available from the CSP with information about site visitors, number of hits to the Web site, shopping cart abandonment statistics, and similar metrics.
- Payment-processing services offered by the CSP

REQUIRED

1. Use your favorite search engine to find basic CSPs that might meet Annette's needs. Analyze the features of each CSP's offering to gather information that might be useful to Annette, then summarize your findings in a report of about 400 words. Use the list of information above as a guide to organizing your report. Conclude by recommending one of the CSPs you identified.

2. Another option for Annette's online store would be to use a mall-style CSP. Examine the mall-style CSP offerings of Amazon Services (through its "Professional Sellers" and "Individual Sellers" programs) and eBay Stores. In a 100-word report to Annette, outline the advantages and disadvantages of using a mall-style CSP rather than one of the basic CSP options you reviewed in your answer to the previous requirement.

Note: Your instructor might assign you to a group to complete this case, and might ask you to prepare a formal presentation of your results to your class.

For Further Study and Research

Alton, L. 2015. "Seven Ways Big Data Redefines Supply Chain Management," *Small Business Computing*, August 7. http://www.smallbusinesscomputing.com/biztools/7-ways-big-data-redefines-supply-chain-management.html

Babcock, C. 2015. "Salesforce Polishes Its CRM Interface With Lightning," *InformationWeek*, August 25. http://www.informationweek.com/cloud/software-as-a-service/salesforce-polishes-its-crm-interface-with-lightning/d/d-id/1321887

Barrett, V. 2010. "Salesforce.com: The Web's Big Upstart," *Forbes*, December 6, 1–3.

Birman, K. 2012. "CORBA: The Common Object Request Broker Architecture," 249–269. In Berman, K., ed., *Guide to Reliable Distributed Systems*. London: Springer.

Blair, G. and P. Grace. 2012. "Emergent Middleware: Tackling the Interoperability Problem," *IEEE Internet Computing*, 16(1), 78–82.

Bruno, E. 2007. "SOA, Web Services, and RESTful Systems," *Dr. Dobb's Journal*, 32(7), July, 32–37.

Bucholz, C. 2012. "One Customer Relationship Style Does Not Fit All," *CRM Buyer*, March 1. http://www.crmbuyer.com/story/74540.html

Corredor, I., J. Martinez, M. Familiar, and L. Lopez. 2012. "Knowledge-aware and Service-oriented Middleware for Deploying Pervasive Services," *Journal of Network and Computer Applications*, March, 35(2), 562–576.

Demery, P. 2012. "When It's Monday and Christmas Is Tuesday, Will You Know Where Your Web Orders Are?" *Internet Retailer*, June, 96–100.

Dusto, A. 2015. "Amping Up Tech Spending," *Internet Retailer*, August, 22–26.

eMarketer. 2015. "Social Integration Tops CRM Users' Wish Lists," August 12. http://www.emarketer.com/Article/Social-Integration-Tops-CRM-Users-Wish-Lists/1012847

Enright, A. 2014. "Moss Bros. Is Poised to Hyper-personalize Its Interactions With Consumers," *Internet Retailer*, December 30. https://www.internetretailer.com/2014/12/30/moss-bros-will-hyper-personalize-its-consumer-interactions

Ferguson, G. 2002. "Have Your Objects Call My Objects," *Harvard Business Review*, 80(6), June, 138–143.

Karande, A., V. Chunekar, and B. Meshram. 2011. "Working of Web Services Using BPEL Workflow in SOA," *Advances in Computing, Communication, and Control*, 125, 143–149.

Karpinski, R. 2008. "Web Services in Action," *Telephony*, 248(4), March 17, 6.

Kay, R. 2007. "Representational State Transfer (REST)," *Computerworld*, 41(32), August 6, 40.

Payne, A. and P. Frow. 2005. "A Strategic Framework for Customer Relationship Management," *Journal of Marketing*, 69(4), October, 167–176.

Rashid, F. 2015. "The Best Online Shopping Cart Software for 2015," *PC Magazine*, May 26. http://www.pcmag.com/article2/0,2817,2484670,00.asp

Sharma, R. and M. Sood. 2011. "A Model-driven Approach to Cloud SaaS Interoperability," *International Journal of Computer Applications*, 30(8), September, 1–8.

Sheldon, P. and A. Hoar. 2013. *The Forrester WaveTM : B2B Commerce Suites, Q4 2013*. Cambridge, MA: Forrester.

Wang, W. and W. Liu. 2011. "Study on the Integration of ERP and APS Based on CORBA Static Invocation," *IEEE International Conference on Service Operations, Logistics, and Informatics*, Beijing, July, 172–176.

Waxer, C. 2009. "Bluefly's Bug Zapper," *CIO Magazine*, December 1, 22.

Woodward, K. 2012. "Fighting the Web With the Web," *Internet Retailer*, June, 91–94.

Zhu, Y., K. Chen, X. Guo, and Y. He. 2011. "Management Information Ontology Middleware and Its Needs Guidance Technology," *Recent Advances in Computer Science and Information Engineering*, 125, 415–421.

Electronic Commerce Security

Blend Images Photography/Veer

LEARNING OBJECTIVES

In this chapter, you will learn:

- What security risks arise in online business and how to manage them
- How to create a security policy
- How to implement security on Web client computers
- How to implement security in the communication channels between computers
- How to implement security on Web server computers
- What organizations promote computer, network, and Internet security

INTRODUCTION

As you will learn in this chapter, an important element in maintaining security over individual and company online assets is the proper use of password protection. Experts agree that long and complex passwords are best and that a different password should be used for each online activity. Further, these experts note that all passwords should be changed regularly. In theory, this is fine, but in practice, most people with active online lives shop at multiple stores, use multiple social media tools, use multiple online services, and often have multiple e-mail and bank accounts. Remembering dozens of complex passwords and changing them regularly is simply not something that most people are willing to do.

One solution is offered by companies that sell password management tools. This software can create and store a large number of suitably complex passwords, one for each online activity, and can enter them when a user needs to access a site. Further, it can regenerate and reset those passwords on a regular schedule automatically. So that these tools are convenient to use, they are usually available online, so users can access their passwords from different locations using any of their Internet-connected devices. To maintain security over the password manager itself, the user simply needs to remember one master password.

This is an appealing solution and many people now use password managers. However, the approach does have one weak link, which is the master password. If a user's master password becomes compromised, it opens the door to every single password and login stored in the password manager. **LastPass**, a company that provides password manager services, was hacked in 2015. The hacker was able to obtain users' master passwords, e-mail addresses, and the hints that users had created to remind them of their master passwords in case they forgot them. Fortunately, LastPass had stored the master passwords in an encrypted form, a security procedure you will learn about in this chapter. When it discovered the hack, it reset all users' master passwords and required them to verify their identity by e-mail before allowing them to access their passwords.

The elapsed time between when the hack occurred and when LastPass changed the master passwords (and notified their users, law enforcement, and the media) was important because a hacker could use decryption tools to discover the passwords. Depending on how long and complex user passwords were, it is possible that the hacker could have extracted some master passwords and used them before they were changed. In this chapter, you will learn more about threats to online security and the methods used to reduce the risk of loss due to those threats.

Online Security Issues Overview

Individuals and businesses have been concerned about security online ever since the Internet became a communications tool for business activities. Those concerns have grown every year with the steady increase in all types of sales and financial transactions. Today, security is a concern for everyone engaging in online transactions or communication regarding economic activities of any kind.

As you learned in Chapter 7, people have become increasingly concerned about the willingness and ability of online businesses to keep personal information confidential. This chapter outlines key security problems and presents some solutions to those problems.

Origins of Security on Interconnected Computer Systems

Many computer security techniques were developed by the U.S. Department of Defense, including *Trusted Computer System Evaluation Criteria* (known as the "Orange Book" because its cover was orange), first issued in the late 1970s. It spelled out rules for access control; including the separation of confidential, secret, and top secret information; and established criteria for certification levels for computers ranging from D (not trusted to handle multiple levels of classified documents at once) to A1 (the most trustworthy level).

When businesses began using computers, they adopted these military security methods, which included physical controls over access to computers such as alarmed doors, guards, security badges, and surveillance cameras. Back then, people used terminals to access large computers and there were few computer networks. Networks that did exist did not extend outside the organization to which they belonged. Thus, computer security could be accomplished by managing the activities of the few people who had access to terminals or the computer room. Today, the population of computer users and the number of ways those users access computing resources have increased tremendously. Furthermore, computers are now transmitting valuable information such as electronic payments, purchase orders, order confirmations, and authorization for large financial transactions. All of these factors have made the need for comprehensive security risk controls more important than ever.

Computer Security and Risk Management

Computer security is the protection of assets from unauthorized access, use, alteration, or destruction. There are two general types of security: physical and logical. **Physical security** includes tangible protection devices, such as alarms, guards, fireproof doors, security fences, safes or vaults, and bombproof buildings. Protection of assets using nonphysical means is called **logical security**. Any act or object that poses a danger to computer assets is known as a **threat**. A **countermeasure** is a procedure that recognizes, reduces, or eliminates a threat. The extent and expense of countermeasures can vary, depending on the importance of the asset at risk.

Threats that are unlikely to occur (that is, have a low probability of occurrence) can be ignored when the cost to protect against the threat exceeds the value of the protected

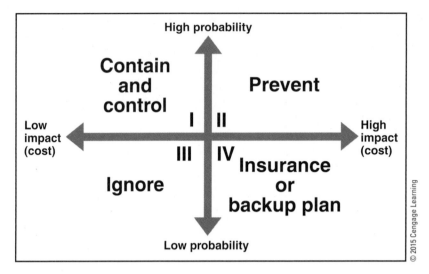

FIGURE 10-1   Risk management model

asset. For example, it would make sense to protect from tornadoes a computer network in Oklahoma, where there is significant and regular tornado activity. However, a similar network located in Maine would not require the same protection because tornadoes are extremely rare in Maine. The risk management model shown in Figure 10-1 illustrates four general actions that an organization could take, depending on the impact (cost) and the probability of the physical threat. In this model, a tornado in Oklahoma would be in quadrant II, whereas a tornado in Maine would be in quadrant IV.

The same sort of risk management model applies to protecting Internet and electronic commerce assets from both physical and electronic threats. Examples of the latter include impostors, eavesdroppers, and thieves. An **eavesdropper**, in this context, is a person or device that can listen in on and copy Internet transmissions. People who write programs or manipulate technologies to obtain unauthorized access to computers and networks are called **crackers** or **hackers**.

A cracker is a technologically skilled person who uses his or her skills to obtain unauthorized entry into computers or network systems—usually with the intent of stealing information or damaging the information, the system's software, or even the system's hardware. Originally, the term hacker was used to describe a dedicated programmer who enjoyed writing complex code that tested the limits of technology. Although the term hacker is still used in a positive way by computer professionals who make a strong distinction between the terms hacker and cracker, the media and the general public usually use the term to describe those who use their skills for ill purposes. Some people also use the terms **white hat hacker** and **black hat hacker** to make a distinction between good hackers and bad hackers.

To implement an effective security scheme, organizations must identify risks, determine how to protect threatened assets, and calculate how much to spend to protect those assets. In this chapter, you will learn how organizations manage risk by identifying threats and determining how to protect assets from those threats.

Elements of Computer Security

Computer security includes three main elements: secrecy, integrity, and necessity (also known as denial of service). **Secrecy** refers to protecting against unauthorized data disclosure and ensuring the authenticity of the data source. **Integrity** refers to preventing unauthorized data modification. **Necessity** refers to preventing data delays or denials (removal). Integrity threats are reported less frequently and are less well known to the general public. An **integrity violation** occurs, for example, when an e-mail message is intercepted and its contents are changed before it is forwarded to its original destination. That is, the integrity of the message has been violated. In this particular exploit, which is called a **man-in-the-middle exploit**, the contents of the e-mail are often altered in a way that changes the message's original meaning.

Necessity violations involve preventing or delaying access to data. For example, an online attacker could delay a message containing a buy order for shares of stock. If the stock price increases during the delay, the sender loses the value of that price increase. Other necessity violations include activities such as overwhelming a business Web site with inquiries from automated fake customers so that genuine customers cannot access the Web site.

Establishing a Security Policy

Any organization concerned about protecting its electronic commerce assets should have a **security policy** in place. A security policy is a written statement describing which assets to protect and why they are being protected, who is responsible for that protection, and which behaviors are acceptable and which are not. A security policy should address physical security, network security, access authorizations, virus protection, and disaster recovery and should be a living document that is regularly reviewed and updated.

Organizations must protect assets from unauthorized disclosure, modification, or destruction. A corporate security policy concerning confidential information could be as simple as "do not reveal confidential company information to anyone outside the company." Most organizations follow a four-step process when creating a security policy. These steps include:

1. Determine which assets must be protected from which threats. For example, a company that stores customer credit card numbers might decide that those numbers are an asset that must be protected.

2. Determine who needs access to various parts of the system or specific information assets. Some of those users might be located outside the organization (for example, suppliers, customers, and strategic partners).

3. Identify resources available or needed to protect the information assets while ensuring access by those who need it.

4. Using the information gathered in the first three steps, the organization develops a written security policy.

Requirement	Meaning
Secrecy	Prevent unauthorized persons from reading messages and business plans, obtaining credit card numbers, or deriving other confidential information.
Integrity	Enclose information in a digital envelope so that the computer can automatically detect messages that have been altered in transit.
Availability	Provide delivery assurance for each message segment so that messages or message segments cannot be lost undetectably.
Key management	Provide secure distribution and management of keys needed to provide secure communications.
Nonrepudiation	Provide undeniable, end-to-end proof of each message's origin and recipient.
Authentication	Securely identify clients and servers with digital signatures and certificates.

FIGURE 10-2   Requirements for secure electronic commerce

Once the security policy is written and approved by management, the organization commits resources to building or buying software, hardware, and physical barriers that implement the security policy.

A comprehensive plan for security should protect a system's privacy, integrity, and availability (necessity) and authenticate users. When these goals are used to create a security policy for an electronic commerce operation, they should be selected to satisfy the list of requirements shown in Figure 10-2. These requirements provide a minimum level of acceptable security for most electronic commerce operations.

Security measures must be designed to work together to prevent unauthorized disclosure, destruction, or modification of assets. A good security policy should address the following:

- *Authentication*: Who is trying to access the site?
- *Access control*: Who is allowed to log on to and access the site?
- *Secrecy*: Who is permitted to view selected information?
- *Data integrity*: Who is allowed to change data?
- *Audit*: Who or what causes specific events to occur, and when?

In this chapter, you will learn how these security policy issues apply to online business activities. The topics in this chapter are organized to follow the transaction-processing flow, beginning with the consumer and ending with the Web server (or servers) at the electronic commerce site. Each logical link in the process includes assets that must be protected to ensure security: client devices, the communication channel on which the messages travel, and the Web servers, including any other computer connected to the Web servers.

Security for Client Devices

Client computers, smartphones, and tablet devices need protection from threats that originate in software and data that are downloaded from the Internet. In this section, you will learn how downloaded active content can threaten client devices. You will also learn how client devices can be threatened by servers masquerading as legitimate Web sites. This section describes these threats and outlines how to prevent or reduce the threats they pose.

Cookies and Web Bugs

As you learned earlier in this book, communications between Web clients and servers are accomplished using multiple independent transmissions; that is, no continuous connection (sometimes called an **open session**) is maintained between the client and the server. You have also learned that cookies are small text files that Web servers place on Web client computers to identify returning visitors. Cookies also allow Web servers to maintain some types of shopping cart and payment processing functions without creating an open session by saving information about a Web user from one set of independent server–client message exchanges to another.

There are two ways of categorizing cookies: by time duration and by source. The two kinds of time-duration cookie categories include **session cookies**, which exist until the Web client ends the connection (or "session"), and **persistent cookies**, which remain on the client computer indefinitely. Electronic commerce sites use both kinds of cookies. For example, a session cookie might contain information about a particular shopping visit and a persistent cookie might contain login information that can help the Web site recognize visitors when they return to the site on subsequent visits. Each time a browser moves to a different part of a merchant's Web site, the merchant's Web server asks the visitor's computer to send back any cookies that the Web server stored previously on the visitor's computer.

Another way to categorize cookies is by their source. Cookies can be placed on the client computer by the Web server site, in which case they are called **first-party cookies**, or they can be placed by a different Web site, in which case they are called **third-party cookies**. A third-party cookie originates on a Web site other than the site being visited. These third-party Web sites usually provide advertising or other content that appears on the Web site being viewed. The third-party Web site providing the advertising is often interested in tracking responses to their ads by visitors who have already seen the ads on other sites. If the advertising Web site places its ads on a large number of Web sites, it can use persistent third-party cookies to track visitors from one site to another. Earlier in this book, you learned about DoubleClick and similar online ad placement services that perform this function.

The most complete way for Web site visitors to protect themselves from revealing private information or being tracked by cookies is to disable cookies entirely. The problem with this approach is that useful cookies are blocked along with the others, requiring visitors to enter information each time they revisit a Web site. The full resources of some sites are not available to visitors unless their browsers are set to allow cookies.

For example, most distance learning software used by schools to deliver online courses does not work properly in student Web browsers unless cookies are enabled.

Web users can accumulate large numbers of cookies as they browse the Internet. Most Web browsers have settings that allow the user to refuse only third-party cookies or to review each cookie before it is accepted. Figure 10-3 shows the dialog box that can be used to manage stored cookies in the Mozilla Firefox Web browser.

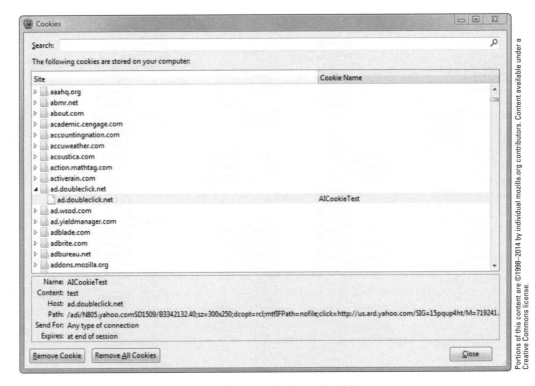

FIGURE 10-3   Mozilla Firefox dialog box for managing stored cookies

You can learn more about cookies at the Cookie Central Web site, which includes current news on cookie developments and answers common questions about cookies. Most of the electronic commerce software packages you learned about in Chapter 9 include features Web site managers can use to analyze Internet traffic at their sites. These services also provide information to Web sites about who visits their sites and what sites the visitors came from.

Some advertisers send images (from their third-party servers) that are included on Web pages but are too small to be visible. A **Web bug** (also called a **Web beacon**) is a tiny graphic that a third-party Web site places on another site's Web page. When a site visitor loads the Web page, the Web bug is delivered by the third-party site, which can then place a cookie on the visitor's computer. A Web bug's only purpose is to provide a way for a third-party Web site (the identity of which is unknown to the visitor) to place cookies from that third-party site on the visitor's computer. The Internet advertising community sometimes calls Web bugs "clear GIFs" or "1-by-1 GIFs" because the graphics can be created in the GIF format with a color value of "transparent" and can be as small as 1 pixel by 1 pixel.

Active Content

Recall that many Web sites use dynamic Web pages to customize content for each user. Another way to customize content is to embed programs into Web pages. These programs run when a client device loads the Web page and are called **active content**. Active content programs can display moving graphics, download and play audio, or implement Web-based spreadsheet programs. Active content can also place items into a shopping cart and compute a total invoice amount, including sales tax, handling, and shipping costs. Active content moves some processing work from the server to the client device. Unfortunately, because active content elements are programs that run on the client device, they can damage it. Thus, active content can pose a threat to the security of client devices.

Cookies, graphics, Web browser plug-ins, Java applets, **JavaScript**, VBScript, and ActiveX controls can be used to deliver active content. Active content can also be delivered as an e-mail attachment. Most Web browsers allow the user to disable both Java and JavaScript individually or together; however, many Web sites use these active content tools to provide important functionality. This makes many users reluctant to disable them. JavaScript and VBScript are **scripting languages**; they provide scripts, or commands, that are executed on the client. An **applet** is a small application program. Applets typically run within the Web browser and are most often written in the Java programming language. Active content is launched in a Web browser automatically when that browser loads a Web page containing active content. The applet downloads automatically with the page and begins running. Most browsers allow users to limit the actions taken by Java applets and scripting languages by running them in a **sandbox**, which is a functional subset of the full browser. When scripting languages are run in a sandbox, active content tools do not have full access to the client device. For example, Java applets operating in the sandbox cannot perform file input, output, or delete operations. This prevents secrecy (disclosure) and integrity (deletion or modification) violations.

An **ActiveX** control is an object that contains programs and properties that Web designers place on Web pages to perform particular tasks. Unlike Java or JavaScript code, ActiveX controls run only on computers with Windows operating systems. The security danger with ActiveX controls is that once they are downloaded, they execute like any other program on a client computer. They have full access to all system resources, including operating system code. An ill-intentioned ActiveX control could reformat a user's hard disk, rename or delete files, send e-mails to all the people listed in the user's address book, or simply shut down the computer. Because ActiveX controls have full access to client computers, they can cause secrecy, integrity, or necessity violations. Most Web browsers can be configured to provide a warning that allows the user to avoid downloading ActiveX controls.

Because active content modules are embedded in Web pages, they can be completely invisible when you visit a page containing them. Crackers intent on doing mischief to client computers can embed malicious active content in these seemingly innocuous

Web pages. This delivery technique is called a Trojan horse. A **Trojan horse** is a program hidden inside another program or Web page that masks its true purpose. The Trojan horse could snoop around a client computer and send back private information to a cooperating Web server—a secrecy violation. The program could alter or erase information on a client computer—an integrity violation. Zombies are equally threatening. A **zombie** is a Trojan horse that secretly takes over another computer for the purpose of launching attacks on other computers. The computers running the zombie are also sometimes called zombies. When a Trojan horse (or other type of virus) has taken over a large number of computers (and thus made them into zombies), the person who planted the virus can take control of all the computers and form a **botnet** (short for **robotic network**, also called a **zombie farm** when the computers in the network are zombies) that can act as an attacking unit, sending spam or launching denial-of-service attacks against specific Web sites.

Graphics and Plug-Ins

Some graphics file formats allow for the inclusion of instructions that tell a browser how to render a graphic. Thus, any Web page containing such a graphic could pose a threat if the embedded code were written to cause harm to a client computer. Similarly, browser **plug-ins**, which are small programs that enhance the capabilities of browsers, can expose client computers to risks. Plug-ins help a browser perform useful tasks, such as playing audio or video; however, plug-ins can also execute commands buried within the media files. These hidden commands could damage a client computer by, for example, erasing files.

Viruses, Worms, and Antivirus Software

Most users know that e-mail attachments can pose security risks to client devices. These attachments can contain virtually any type of file (documents, spreadsheets, databases, images, and so on). Most programs, including Web browser e-mail clients, display attachments by automatically executing an associated program; for example, the recipient's Excel program reads an attached Excel workbook file and opens it, or Word opens and displays a Word document. Although this activity itself does not cause damage, Word and Excel macro viruses inside the loaded files can do damage to a client device or its contents when those files are opened.

A virus is software that attaches itself to another program and can cause damage when the host program is activated. A **worm** is a type of virus that replicates itself on the computers that it infects. Worms can spread quickly through the Internet. A **macro virus** is a type of virus that is coded as a small program, called a macro, and is embedded in a file formatted for use in a program, such as Microsoft Word or Excel, that can run the macro. The history of viruses, worms, and similar malware dates back to the 1980s. Figure 10-4 lists some of these early instances and describes the nature of their attacks.

The first virus to become major news was the ILOVEYOU virus, also known as the "love bug," and its variants in 2000. The ILOVEYOU virus was eventually traced to a 23-year-old computer science student who lived in the Philippines. The virus spread rapidly through the Internet attached to e-mail messages. It infected the computer of anyone who opened the e-mail attachment and clogged e-mail systems with thousands of copies of the useless e-mail message. The virus spread quickly because it compromised

Year	Name	Type	Description
1986	Brain	Virus	Written in Pakistan, this virus infected floppy disks used in personal computers at that time. It consumed empty space on the disks, preventing it from being used to store data or programs.
1988	Internet Worm	Worm	Robert Morris, Jr., a graduate student at Cornell University, wrote this experimental, self-replicating, self-propagating program and released it onto the Internet. It replicated faster than he had anticipated and crashed computers at universities, military sites, and medical research facilities throughout the world.
1991	Tequila	Virus	Tequila writes itself to a computer's hard disk and runs any time the computer is started. It also infects programs when they are executed. Tequila originated in Switzerland and was mostly transmitted via Internet downloads.
1992	Michelangelo	Trojan Horse	Set to activate on March 6 (Michelangelo's birthday), this Trojan Horse would overwrite large portions of the infected computer's hard disk.
1993	SatanBug	Virus	Infects programs when they run, causing them to fail or perform incorrectly. SatanBug was designed to interfere with antivirus programs so they could not detect it.
1996	Concept	Virus Worm	One of the first viruses to be written in Microsoft Word's macro language, Concept travels with infected Word document files. When an infected document is opened, Concept places macros in Word's default document template, which infects any new Word documents created on that computer.
1999	Melissa	Virus Worm	A Microsoft Word macro virus that spreads by e-mailing itself automatically from one user to another. It inserts comments from "The Simpsons" television show and confidential information from the infected computer. Melissa spread throughout the world in a few hours. Many large companies were inundated by Melissa. For example, Microsoft closed down its e-mail servers to prevent the spread of this virus within the company.

FIGURE 10-4   Early computer viruses, worms, and Trojan horses

Microsoft Outlook, a widely used e-mail client software product. The virus could automatically send itself to as many as 300 addresses stored in a computer's Microsoft Outlook address book. Besides replicating itself explosively through e-mail, the virus caused other harm, such as destroying music and photo files stored on the target computers. The ILOVEYOU virus also searched for other users' passwords and forwarded that information to the original perpetrator. Within days, the virus spread to 40 million computers in more than 20 countries and caused an estimated $9 billion in damages—most of it in lost worker productivity.

In 2001, the incidences of virus and worm attacks increased. With more than 40,000 reported security violations occurring that year, the parade of attacks included Code Red and Nimda virus–worm combinations, each affecting millions of computers and costing billions of dollars to clean up. Both Code Red and Nimda are examples of a **multivector virus**, so-called because they can enter a computer system in several different ways (vectors). Even though Microsoft issued security patches that should have stopped the Code Red virus–worm, it continued to propagate throughout the Internet in 2002. Both the original Code Red virus and a variant called Code Red 2 infected thousands of new computers during the year.

A new version of the Code Red virus called Bugbear appeared in 2003. Bugbear was spread through Microsoft Outlook e-mail clients. The person receiving the e-mail did not even have to click an attachment to run the malicious code—Bugbear started itself through a security loophole in the connection between Outlook and the Internet Explorer browser. Of course, Microsoft issued a security patch for the browser, but many users did not install the patch. When launched, Bugbear first checked to see if the computer was running antivirus software. **Antivirus software** detects viruses and worms and either deletes them or isolates them on the client computer so they cannot run. If antivirus software existed on the system, Bugbear attempted to destroy it. Then it installed a Trojan horse program on the computer that let attackers access the computer through the Internet and upload or download files at will. Bugbear would then send out e-mail messages with attachments that would infect the recipients. It did not create its own e-mail messages but took previously sent e-mail messages that were on the computer and resent them to different addresses. This often fooled recipients because the e-mail messages had subject headers that seemed normal and gave no hint that the e-mail might contain a virus. Bugbear was difficult to eliminate from an infected computer because it gave its own files randomly generated names; thus, the virus files had different names on every infected computer. Figure 10-5 summarizes these and other viruses, worms, and Trojan horses that spread throughout the world during the 2000–2007 time period.

Beginning in 2008, a similar virus named Conficker emerged and spread widely. Conficker is believed to have infected nearly 15 million computers and continues to be a concern because the virus can reinstall itself after it has been removed. The size of the ongoing infection caused great concern, and Internet service providers, computer security firms, and online businesses formed a working group to monitor the virus. The working group remained active for over a year until the number of computers infected worldwide was reduced substantially.

In 2010, a new use of the Trojan horse–worm combination attack was introduced with the Stuxnet. For the first time, a Trojan horse that spread through a computer operating

Year	Name	Type	Description
2000	ILOVEYOU	Virus Worm	Arrives attached to an e-mail message with the subject line "ILOVE YOU" and infects any computer on which the attachment is opened. It sends itself to addresses in any Microsoft Outlook address book it finds on the infected computer and can destroy music and photo files stored on infected computers. When launched, it clogged e-mail servers in many large organizations and slowed the operation of the entire Internet.
2001	Code Red	Virus Worm Trojan Horse	Code Red can infect Web servers and personal computers. It defaces Web pages and can be transmitted from Web servers to personal computers. It can give hackers control over Web server computers. Code Red can reinstall itself from hidden files after it is removed.
2001	Nimda	Virus Worm	Nimda modifies Web documents and certain programs on the infected computer. It also creates multiple copies of itself using various file names. It can be transmitted via e-mail, a LAN, or from a Web server to a Web client.
2002	BugBear	Virus Worm Trojan Horse	BugBear is spread through e-mail and through local area networks. It identifies antivirus software and attempts to disable it. BugBear can log keystrokes and store them for later transmission through a Trojan Horse program that it installs on the infected computer. This program gives hackers access to the computer and allows file uploads and downloads.
2002	Klez	Virus Worm	Klez is transmitted as an e-mail attachment and overwrites files, creates hidden copies of the original files, and attempts to disable antivirus software.
2003	Slammer	Worm	Slammer's primary purpose was to demonstrate how rapidly a worm could be transmitted on the Internet. It infected 75,000 computers in its first ten minutes of propagation.
2003	Sobig	Trojan Horse	Sobig turns infected computers into spam relay points. Sobig transmits mass e-mails with copies of itself to potential victims.
2004	MyDoom	Worm Trojan Horse	MyDoom turns the infected computer into a zombie that will participate in a denial of service attack on a specific company's Web site.

FIGURE 10-5   Computer viruses, worms, and Trojan horses: 2000–2007

(Continued)

Year	Name	Type	Description
2004	Sasser	Virus Worm	Written by a German high school student, Sasser finds computers with a specific security flaw and then infects them. The infected computers are slowed by the virus, often to the point that they must be rebooted.
2005	Zotob	Worm Trojan Horse	Zotob peforms port scans and infects computers that appear to have a specific security flaw. Once installed on a target computer, Zotob can log keystrokes, capture screens, and steal authentication credentials and CD software keys. Infected computers can also be used as zombies for mass mailing or attacking other computers.
2006	Nyxem	Worm Trojan Horse	Nyxem disables security and file sharing software, destroys files created by Microsoft Office programs. It activates on the third of each month and spreads itself by mass mailing.
2006	Leap	Worm Virus	Leap (also called Oompa-Loompa) infects programs that run on the Macintosh OS-X operating system. Delivered over the iChat instant messaging system, it can only spread within a specific network.
2007	Storm	Worm Trojan Horse	Storm gathers infected computers into a botnet from which it launches spam. Spread as an e-mail containing phony news clips with an attachment that it alleges is a news film.

FIGURE 10-5   (Continued)

system (in this case, Microsoft Windows) was designed to target industrial equipment. The specific target in this case was control systems made by German industrial giant Siemens. These systems were used in many different industrial settings, but the target of the 2010 attack appeared to be systems that controlled Iranian uranium enrichment operations.

In 2011, two existing Trojan horse–worm exploits, Zeus and SpyEye, were combined to create a series of new variants that targeted bank account information stored on computers. These new variants hide their files from regular Windows Explorer searches and hide their registry keys, which makes them difficult to detect. They can intercept credit card or online banking data entered into a Web browser and transmit it to the perpetrator.

Cryptolocker, a Trojan that attacks computers running Windows operating systems, became widespread in late 2013. As **ransomware**, a Trojan that encrypts files on the victim computer and demands a payment for the key to unlock them, Cryptolocker presents yet another type of threat to Internet users and is typically installed from an e-mail attachment, although it is multivector and can enter individual computers through Web pages or other devices on the same network. In 2014, several computer security firms and antivirus software vendors posted free decryption keys for Cryptolocker on their Web sites, but not before the perpetrators had walked away with more than $3 million in ransom payments. Also, once the decryption keys had been posted, a more advanced variation of the exploit named Cryptowall appeared, which required the development of new decryption keys.

Regin, a Trojan–worm combination, is believed to have been developed by a spy agency in 2011 or 2012. It became widespread by victims' visits to spoofed Web pages in 2014. It can be difficult for antivirus software to remove because it continually downloads and installs multiple versions of itself. Regin is intended to remain on the victim's computer for a long time, reporting summaries of the user's activity, logins, and passwords to the perpetrator.

In 2015, a Cryptolocker variant named TeslaCrypt became widespread. TeslaCrypt seeks out computer game software on the victim computer and encrypts those files, demanding a ransom payment for the key to unlock the games. Within a few months of its wide appearance, Cisco's Talos Group posted a decryption tool for TeslaCrypt that victims can download at no cost. Figure 10-6 summarizes malware activity from 2008 to 2015.

Symantec and McAfee, among other companies, keep track of viruses and sell antivirus software. You can follow the Web Links (**Symantec Security Response** and **McAfee Virus Information**) to find descriptions of thousands of viruses. Antivirus software is only effective if the antivirus data files are kept current. The data files contain virus-identifying information that is used to detect viruses on a client computer. Because new viruses appear regularly, users must be vigilant and update their antivirus data files regularly so that the newest viruses are recognized and eliminated. Some Web e-mail systems, such as Gmail and Yahoo! Mail, automatically scan attachments using antivirus software before downloading e-mail. In these cases, the antivirus software is run by the Web site and the user does not need to take any action to keep the software updated.

Digital Certificates

One way to control threats from active content is to use digital certificates. A **digital certificate** is an attachment to an e-mail message or a program embedded in a Web page that verifies the identity of the e-mail's sender or the Web site. A digital certificate also contains the means to send an encrypted communication to the Web page or e-mail message. Digital certificates for downloaded programs identify the software publisher (thus ensuring that the identity of the software publisher matches the certificate) and indicates whether the certificate has expired or is still valid. The digital certificate is an example of **signed code**. Signed code serves the same function as a photo on a driver's license or passport. It provides proof that the holder is the person or organization identified by the certificate. A certificate supplies a level of assurance that the software is genuine and was created by a specific company, but does not imply anything about either the usefulness or quality of the downloaded program. The idea behind certificates is that if the user trusts the software developer, signed software can be trusted because, as proven by the certificate, it came from that trusted developer.

Digital certificates are used to execute online transactions, send encrypted e-mail, and make electronic funds transfers. A digital certificate can verify the true identity of a Web

Year	Name	Type	Description
2008	Conficker	Worm Trojan Horse	Conficker can reinstall itself when removed and remains on more than 7 million computers. Can launch a barrage of spam e-mail or a crippling denial-of-service attack on any Web site.
2009	Clampi	Worm Trojan Horse	Activated in 2009 after laying dormant for years. Captures usernames and passwords for more than 4000 financial institution Web sites. Perpetrators can this information to make purchases or transfer funds from victim accounts.
2009	URLzone	Worm Trojan Horse	Monitors user activity and hijacks session when victim logs into a financial institution Web site that it is programmed to recognize. Transfers money from victim's accounts to confederates, who take their cut, then buy goods shipped to a foreign address used by the perpetrator.
2010	Stuxnet	Worm Trojan Horse	Spreads through Microsoft Windows, but targets industrial software and equipment built by Siemens. The first worm designed to attack such systems, experts believe it was created to damage Iranian uranium enrichment systems.
2010	VBManie	Virus Trojan Horse	Transmitted by e-mail messages with the subject header "here you have." The message states that the attachment is "The Document I told you about."
2011	Antispyware 2011	Virus Trojan Horse	Posing as an antivirus program, it disables antivirus programs already installed on the victim computer. It also blocks Internet access so the disabled antivirus program cannot obtain updates that might restore it.
2011	ZeuS/SpyEye variants	Worm Trojan Horse	These two Trojans were merged to create a series of new variants designed to attack mobile banking information stored on computers.
2013	Cryptolocker	Worm Trojan Horse	Encrypts files on the attacked computer and demands a ransom payment for the key needed to unlock the files.
2014	Regin	Worm Trojan Horse	Infection occurs by visiting a spoofed Web page that installs Regin, which in turn installs additional versions of itself, making detection difficult. It spies on user operations and is intended for long-term monitoring of the target computer.
2015	TeslaCrypt	Worm Trojan Horse	A Cryptolocker variant that identifies game software installed on the attacked computer, encrypts the game files, and demands a ransom payment for the decryption key.

FIGURE 10-6   Computer viruses, worms, and Trojan horses: 2008–2015

LEARNING FROM FAILURES

Microsoft Internet Information Server

As you learned in Chapter 8, Internet Information Server (IIS) is Microsoft's Web server software. Microsoft supplies IIS with the versions of its Windows server operating systems that are suitable for use in operating electronic commerce Web sites.

In August 2001, Microsoft faced an uncomfortable situation that many U.S. manufacturing companies have experienced with recalled, defective products. Microsoft executives stood by at a news conference while a U.S. government official announced to reporters that there was a serious flaw in a Microsoft product. The director of the FBI's National Infrastructure Protection Center was warning reporters that the Code Red worm, which was spreading through the Internet for the third time in as many weeks, was a serious threat to the continued operation of the Internet.

The Code Red worm exploits a vulnerability in the Microsoft IIS Web server software. When the worm was first identified, Microsoft quickly made a patch available on its Web site. Microsoft also announced that Web server installations that had kept current with all of the updates and patches that Microsoft had issued would not be subject to attack by the worm.

Many Microsoft customers were outraged by these statements, noting that Microsoft had issued more than 40 software patches in the first half of 2001 and 100 or more patches in each of several prior years. IIS users complained that keeping the software current was virtually impossible and called for Microsoft to deliver software that was more secure when first installed.

Many IIS users began to consider switching to other Web server software. Gartner, Inc., a major IT consulting firm, recommended to its clients that they seriously consider alternatives to IIS for their critical Web server installations. Many industry observers and software engineers agree that Microsoft was a victim of its own success. It had created a very popular and complex piece of software. It is extremely difficult to ensure that no bugs exist in complex software products, and the popularity of the software made it an attractive target for crackers—one worm could bring down many of the servers operating on the Internet. These two factors, plus the likelihood that many IIS servers would not have all of the available security upgrades installed, combined to make it an irresistible target for a worm creator.

Microsoft has struggled to gain the confidence of large corporate IT departments. The company has worked hard to convince users that its operating system software is reliable and trustworthy. For example, when Microsoft introduced version 7 of IIS in 2008, it announced that its architecture had been changed so that users could install only the modules they needed to reduce the software's "attack surface."

The Code Red worm attack on its Web server software was a major setback in its reputation-building effort. Since that attack, a number of security weaknesses have been identified in IIS and patched by Microsoft. The news reports that inevitably accompany these patches have created a continuing public relations issue for the company. You can visit the **Microsoft Safety & Security Center** through this book's Web Links to see how Microsoft deals with ongoing concerns that its software is secure in the face of regular and frequent attacks.

site to a shopper and can similarly verify a shopper's identity to a Web site. Web browsers exchange digital certificates automatically and invisibly when requested to validate the identity of each party involved in a transaction.

Digital certificates are issued to organizations or individuals by a **certification authority (CA)**. A CA requires entities applying for digital certificates to supply appropriate proof of identity. Once the CA is satisfied, it issues a certificate. Then, the CA signs the certificate, and its stamp of approval is affixed in the form of a public encryption key (you will learn more about encryption later in this chapter). The public encryption key unlocks the certificate for anyone who receives the certificate attached to the publisher's code. A digital certificate includes six main elements:

- Certificate owner's identifying information, such as name, organization, address, and so on
- Certificate owner's public encryption key
- Dates between which the certificate is valid
- Serial number of the certificate
- Name of the certificate issuer
- Digital signature of the certificate issuer

A **key** is a number—usually a long binary number—that is used with the encryption algorithm to lock the characters of the message being protected so that they are undecipherable without the key. Longer keys usually provide significantly better protection than shorter keys. In effect, the CA is guaranteeing that the individual or organization that presents the certificate is who or what it claims to be.

Identification requirements vary from one CA to another. One CA might require a driver's license for individuals' certificates; others might require a notarized form or fingerprints. CAs usually publish identification requirements so that any Web user or site accepting certificates from each CA understands the stringency of that CA's validation procedures. Only a small number of CAs exist because the certificates issued are only as trustworthy as the CA itself, and only a few companies have decided to build the reputation needed to be a successful seller of digital certificates. Two leading CA providers today are Thawte and Symantec Enterprise (which purchased Verisign's CA business for $1.28 billion in 2010), but other companies such as Comodo, DigiCert, Entrust Datacard, and GeoTrust also offer CA services.

After news reports that hackers had been able to obtain falsified digital certificates from CAs, concerns grew that CAs might be performing insufficient verification on certificate applicants before issuing the certificates. These concerns led a group of CAs to develop a more stringent set of verification steps and, in 2008, stricter criteria were adopted and steps were taken to assure the consistent application of verification procedures. CAs that followed these more extensive verification procedures were permitted to issue a new type of certificate called a **Secure Sockets Layer-Extended Validation (SSL-EV) digital certificate**. To issue an SSL-EV certificate, a certification authority must confirm the legal existence of the organization by verifying the organization's registered legal name, registration number, registered address, and physical business address. The CA must also verify the organization's right to use the domain name and that the organization has authorized the request for an SSL-EV certificate.

Annual fees for digital certificates range from about $100 to more than $1000, depending on the features they include (such as encryption strength, or the SSL-EV designation) and whether they are purchased alone or with certificates for other Web sites owned by the same company. Digital certificates expire after a period of time (usually one year). This built-in limit provides protection because certificate holders must submit their credentials for reevaluation periodically. Certificates become invalid on their expiration dates or when they are revoked by the CA. If the CA determines that a Web site has violated the terms to which it agreed, the CA will refuse to issue new certificates to that site and revoke existing certificates.

You can tell if you are visiting a Web site that has an SSL-EV certificate by looking at the address window of your browser. In Chrome and Firefox, the site's verified organization name appears in the address window to the left of the URL in green text and a lock symbol displays. In Internet Explorer, the background of the address window turns green and the verified name of the organization appears to the right of the URL along with a lock symbol.

In 2015, the online security and antivirus firm Kaspersky was the victim of hackers who used a stolen digital certificate to install malware on a Kaspersky server. The digital certificate was owned by Foxconn, a large electronics manufacturer in Taiwan. To accomplish the attack on Kaspersky, the hackers had to first attack Foxconn to obtain the digital certificate. The malware they installed on the Kaspersky server was part of a large attack that involved multiple exploits and, before it was discovered, had infected a number of servers on Kaspersky's internal networks.

Getting and maintaining a digital certificate can be an involved process that can take a Web site administrator many hours to complete. And, since digital certificates expire, the process must be repeated whenever it is time to renew. In 2014, a group including the Electronic Frontier Foundation, Mozilla, Cisco, Akamai, IdenTrust, and researchers at the University of Michigan formed and devoted its initial efforts to making digital certificates publicly available at no cost. This group, called the Internet Security Research Group (ISRG) wants to make secure communications using HTTPS (rather than the Web's original, insecure HTTP protocol) the standard way of handling information flows between Web browsers and Web servers. To do this, the group believes that digital certificates should be available at no cost and should be easy to obtain. They have created automated client software that facilitates the process and launched their effort in 2015. You can learn more about this effort at the project's **Let's Encrypt** Web site.

Steganography

The term **steganography** describes the process of hiding information (a command, for example) within another piece of information. This information can be used for malicious purposes. Frequently, computer files contain redundant or insignificant information that can be replaced with other information. This other information resides in the background and is undetectable by anyone without the correct decoding software. Steganography provides a way of hiding an encrypted file within another file so that a casual observer cannot detect that there is anything of importance in the container file. In this two-step process, encrypting the file protects it from being read, and steganography makes it invisible.

Many security analysts believe that the terrorist organization Al Qaeda used steganography to hide attack orders and other messages in images that its confederates posted on Web sites in preparation for the attacks of September 11, 2001. Messages hidden using steganography are extremely difficult to detect. This fact, combined with the fact that there are millions of images on the Web, makes the use of steganography by global terrorist organizations a deep concern for governments and security professionals. You can learn more about steganography at the Information Hiding: Steganography & Digital Watermarking Web site.

Physical Security for Client Devices

In the past, physical security was a major concern for large computers that ran important business functions such as payroll or billing; however, as networks (including intranets and the Internet) have made it possible to control important business functions from client computers, concerns about physical security for client computers have become greater. Many of the physical security measures used today are the same as those used in the early days of computing; however, some interesting new technologies have been implemented as well.

Devices that read fingerprints are now available for personal computers. These devices, which cost less than $100, provide much stronger protection than traditional password approaches. In addition to fingerprint readers, companies can use other biometric security devices that are more accurate and, of course, cost more. A **biometric security device** is one that uses an element of a person's biological makeup to perform the identification. These devices include writing pads that detect the form and pressure of a person writing a signature, eye scanners that read the pattern of blood vessels in a person's retina or the color levels in a person's iris, and scanners that read the palm of a person's hand (rather than just one fingerprint) or that read the pattern of veins on the back of a person's hand.

Client Security for Mobile Devices

As more and more people use mobile devices, such as smartphones and tablets, to access the Internet, concern for the security of these devices increases proportionally. Security issues related to mobile client devices can be simple, such as the physical threat of losing a phone or tablet device. They can also be more complex, such as an attack by a Trojan horse, a virus, or an app that shares your personal information.

The first step to take in securing a mobile device is to set up a password for access to the phone. This can prevent or at least delay a thief who has stolen your device from obtaining private information you have stored on it.

Almost all mobile devices include software that allows the owner to initiate a remote wipe if the device is stolen. A **remote wipe** clears all of the personal data stored on the device, including e-mails, text messages, contact lists, photos, videos, and any type of document file. If a mobile device does not include remote wipe software, it can be added as an app. Most corporate e-mail servers include the ability to do a remote wipe of any employee's mobile devices through the e-mail synchronization software installed on the devices.

Web sites that contain malware can infect mobile devices just as easily as they can client computers. Text messages and e-mails with attached viruses and Trojan horses can infect smartphones and tablet devices. Thus, an increasing number of users are installing antivirus software on their mobile devices.

Apps that contain malware or that collect information from the mobile device and forward it to perpetrators are called **rogue apps**. To weed out rogue apps, the Apple App Store tests apps before they are authorized for sale. The Android Market does not screen for rogue apps as extensively as Apple; however, all Android apps must request permission from the user to access any specific information stored on the device. The app will request these permissions when the user installs the app. To avoid rogue Android apps, experts advise mobile device users to read reviews of apps before installing them and not to be in a rush to install new apps with few reviews. They also recommend avoiding app stores other than the Android Market.

Communication Channel Security

The Internet serves as the electronic connection between buyers (in most cases, clients) and sellers (in most cases, servers). The most important thing to remember as you learn about communication channel security is that the Internet was not designed to be secure. Although the Internet has its roots in a military network, that network was not designed to include any significant security features. It was designed to provide redundancy in case one or more communications lines were cut. In other words, the goal of the Internet's packet-switching design was to provide multiple alternative paths on which critical military information could travel. The military always sends sensitive information in an encrypted form so that the content of messages traveling over any network— even if intercepted—remains secret. The security of messages traversing the military predecessors to the Internet was provided by software that operated independently of the network to encrypt messages. As the Internet developed, it did so without any significant security features that became a part of the network itself.

Today, the Internet remains largely unchanged from its original, insecure state. Message packets on the Internet travel an unplanned path from a source node to a destination node. A packet passes through a number of intermediate computers on the network before reaching its final destination. The path can vary each time a packet is sent between the same source and destination points. Because users cannot control the path and do not know where their packets have been, it is possible that an intermediary can read the packets, alter them, or even delete them; that is, any message traveling on the Internet is subject to secrecy, integrity, and necessity threats. This section describes these problems in more detail and outlines several solutions for those problems.

Secrecy Threats

Secrecy is the security threat that is most frequently mentioned in articles and the popular media. Closely linked to secrecy is privacy, which also receives a great deal of attention. Secrecy and privacy, though similar, are different issues. Secrecy is the prevention of unauthorized information disclosure. **Privacy** is the protection of individual rights to nondisclosure. The Privacy Council, which helps businesses implement smart privacy and data practices, created an extensive Web site that addresses privacy—covering both business and legal issues. Secrecy is a technical issue requiring sophisticated physical and logical mechanisms, whereas privacy protection is a legal matter. A classic example of the difference between secrecy and privacy is e-mail.

A company might protect its e-mail messages against secrecy violations by using encryption. Secrecy countermeasures protect outgoing messages. E-mail privacy issues address whether company supervisors should be permitted to read employees' messages randomly. Disputes in this area center around who owns the e-mail messages the company or the employees who sent them. The focus in this section is on secrecy, preventing unauthorized persons from reading information they should not be reading.

One significant threat to electronic commerce is theft of sensitive or personal information, including credit card numbers, names, addresses, and personal preferences. This kind of theft can occur any time anyone submits information over the Internet because it is easy for an ill-intentioned person to record information packets (a secrecy violation) from the Internet for later examination. The same problems can occur in e-mail transmissions. Software applications called **sniffer programs** provide the means to record information that passes through a computer or router that is handling Internet traffic. Using a sniffer program is analogous to tapping a telephone line and recording a conversation. Sniffer programs can read e-mail messages and unencrypted Web client–server message traffic, such as user logins, passwords, and credit card numbers.

Periodically, security experts find electronic holes, called backdoors, in electronic commerce software. A **backdoor** is an element of a program (or a separate program) that allows users to run the program without going through the normal authentication procedure for access to the program. Programmers often build backdoors into programs while they are building and testing them to save the time it would take to enter a login and password every time they open the program. Sometimes programmers forget to remove backdoors when they are finished writing the program; other times, programmers intentionally leave a backdoor in place.

A backdoor allows anyone with knowledge of its existence to cause damage by observing transactions, deleting data, or stealing data. For example, a security consulting firm found that Cart32, a widely used shopping cart program, had a backdoor through which credit card numbers could be obtained by anyone with knowledge of the backdoor. This backdoor resulted from a programming error and not an intentional effort (and Cart32 provided a software patch that closed the backdoor immediately), but customers of the merchants who used Cart32 had their credit card numbers exposed to hackers around the world until those merchants applied the patch.

Credit card number theft is an obvious problem, but proprietary corporate product information or prerelease product data can be intercepted and passed along easily, too. Confidential corporate information can be considerably more valuable than information about credit cards, which usually have spending limits. Stolen corporate information, such as blueprints, product formulas, or marketing plans, can be worth millions of dollars.

Here is an example of how an online eavesdropper might obtain confidential information. Suppose a user logs on to a Web site that contains a form with text boxes for name, address, and e-mail address. When the user fills out those text boxes and clicks the submit button, the information is sent to the Web server for processing. Some Web servers obtain and track that data by collecting the text box responses and placing them at the end of the server's URL (which appears in the address box of the user's Web browser). This long URL (with the text box responses appended) is included in all HTTP request and response messages that travel between the user's browser and the server.

So far, no violations have occurred. Suppose, however, that the user decides not to wait for a response from the server. Instead, the user visits another Web site. The server at this second Web site can capture the URL from which the user just came by copying it from the HTTP request message that the browser sends. Web sites use this URL logging technique for the completely legitimate purpose of identifying sources of customer traffic. However, any employee at the second site who has access to the server log can read the part of the URL that includes the information entered into those text boxes on the first site, thus obtaining that user's confidential information.

In 2013, a major man-in-the-middle exploit occurred. A vulnerability in the Border Gateway Protocol used to route Internet traffic that had been identified five years earlier by security researchers was used more than 38 times to hijack Internet traffic heading to U.S. government agencies, corporate offices, and other destinations. The perpetrators were never identified, but the hijacked traffic was delayed and routed through computers in London, Moscow, Tehran, and other locations. In one case, a packet going from one address in Denver to another address in Denver was routed through Iceland. The Internet security firm that identified these exploits could not determine whether any of the hijacked packets were modified or destroyed. The protocol involved has been patched to prevent future exploits of this type.

Web users continually reveal information about themselves when they use the Web. This information includes IP addresses and the type of browser being used. Such data exposure is a secrecy breach. Several companies and organizations offer **anonymous Web services** that hide personal information from sites visited. These services provide a measure of secrecy to Web surfers who use them by replacing the user's IP address with the IP address of the anonymous Web service on the front end of any URLs that the user visits. When the Web site logs the site visitor's IP address, it logs the IP address of the anonymous Web service rather than that of the visitor, which preserves the visitor's privacy.

Using such a service can make anonymous Web surfing possible, but tedious, because each URL that the user wants to visit must be typed into the text box on the anonymous Web service's home page. To make the process easier, companies such as Anonymizer provide browser plug-in software that users can download and install for an annual subscription fee. ShadowSurf.com provides a free anonymous browser service online. Tor is free software that allows users to use its network to protect themselves from network surveillance. Tor randomly reroutes Internet traffic through its worldwide network of more than 5000 computers in a way that conceals the users' online activity from government and private monitors. Interest in and use of these services increased in 2013 following disclosures that described the U.S. government's broad programs for gathering information about individuals' online activities around the world.

Integrity Threats

An integrity threat, also known as **active wiretapping**, exists when an unauthorized party can alter a message stream of information. Unprotected banking transactions, such as deposit amounts transmitted over the Internet, are subject to integrity violations. Of course, an integrity violation implies a secrecy violation because an intruder who alters information can read and interpret that information. Unlike secrecy threats, where a viewer simply sees information he or she should not, integrity threats can cause a change in the actions a person or corporation takes because a mission-critical transmission has been altered.

Cybervandalism is an example of an integrity violation. **Cybervandalism** is the electronic defacing of an existing Web site's page. The electronic equivalent of destroying property or placing graffiti on objects, cybervandalism occurs whenever someone replaces a Web site's regular content with his or her own content. Recently, several cases of Web page defacing involved vandals replacing business content with pornographic material and other offensive content.

Masquerading or **spoofing**—pretending to be someone you are not, or representing a Web site as an original when it is a fake—is one means of disrupting Web sites. **Domain name servers (DNSs)** are the computers on the Internet that maintain directories that link domain names to IP addresses. Perpetrators can use a security hole in the software that runs on some of these computers to substitute the addresses of their Web sites in place of the real ones to spoof Web site visitors.

For example, a hacker could create a fictitious Web site masquerading as www. widgets.com by exploiting a DNS security hole that substitutes the hacker's fake IP address for Widgets.com's real IP address. All subsequent visits to Widgets.com would be redirected to the fictitious site. There, the hacker could alter any orders to change the number of widgets ordered and redirect shipment of those products to another address. The integrity attack consists of intercepting and altering an order and then passing it to the real company's Web server. The Web server is unaware of the integrity attack and simply verifies the consumer's credit card number and passes on the order for fulfillment.

Major electronic commerce sites that have been the victims of masquerading attacks in recent years include Amazon.com, AOL, eBay, and PayPal. Some of these schemes combine spam with spoofing. The perpetrator sends millions of spam e-mails that appear to be from a legitimate company. The e-mails contain a link to a Web page that is designed to look exactly like the company's site. The victim is encouraged to enter username, password, and sometimes even credit card information. These exploits, which capture confidential customer information, are called **phishing expeditions**. The most common victims of phishing expeditions are users of online banking and payment system (such as PayPal) Web sites. You will learn more about the phishing problem and the measures banks and other companies are taking to combat it in Chapter 11.

Necessity Threats

The purpose of a **necessity threat**, which usually occurs as a **delay attack**, **denial attack**, or **denial-of-service (DoS) attack**, is to disrupt normal computer processing, or deny processing entirely. For example, slowing down the response time of any Web site could drive customers to competitors' sites and discourage them from ever returning. The Internet Worm attack of 1998, which disabled thousands of computer systems that were connected to the Internet, was the first recorded example of a DoS attack.

Attackers can use the botnets you learned about earlier in this chapter to launch a simultaneous attack on a Web site (or a number of Web sites) from all of the computers in the botnet. This form of attack is called a **distributed denial-of-service (DDoS) attack**. The attack on U.S. and South Korean government and business Web sites you learned about at the beginning of this chapter was a DDoS attack.

DoS attacks can remove information from a transmission or file. One denial attack targeted PCs that have Quicken (an accounting program) installed. The perpetrator's computer was able to take control of the Quicken software and use that program's electronic payment capability to divert money from the victims' bank accounts to the perpetrator's bank account. In another DoS attack against high-profile sites such as Amazon.com and Yahoo!, the attackers used a botnet to send a flood of data packets to the sites. This overwhelmed the sites' servers and choked off legitimate customers' access. Prior to the attack, perpetrators located vulnerable computers and loaded them with the software that launched simultaneous attacks from all of those computers.

Threats to the Physical Security of Internet Communications Channels

The Internet was designed from its inception to withstand attacks on its physical communication links. Recall from Chapter 2 that one purpose of the U.S. government research project that led to the development of the Internet was to provide an attack-resistant technology for coordinating military operations. Thus, the Internet's packet-based network design precludes it from being shut down by an attack on a single communications link on that network.

Despite this security feature, an individual user's Internet service could be interrupted by destruction of that user's link to the Internet because few individual users have multiple connections to an ISP. However, larger companies and organizations (and ISPs themselves) often have multiple links to the Internet backbone, each through a different access provider. If one link becomes overloaded or unavailable, the service provider can switch traffic to another network access provider's link to keep the company, organization, or ISP (and its customers) connected to the Internet.

Threats to Wireless Networks

As you learned in Chapter 2, networks can use wireless access points (WAPs) to provide network connections to computers and other mobile devices within a range of several hundred feet. If not protected, a wireless network allows anyone within that range to log in and have access to any resources connected to that network. Such resources might include any data stored on any computer connected to the network, networked printers, messages sent on the network, and, if the network is connected to the Internet, free access to the Internet. The security of the connection depends on the **Wireless Encryption Protocol (WEP)**, which is a set of rules for encrypting transmissions from the wireless devices to the WAPs.

Companies that have large wireless networks are usually careful to turn on WEP in devices, but smaller companies and individuals who have installed wireless networks in their homes often do not turn on the WEP security feature. Many WAPs are shipped to buyers with a default login and password already set. Companies that install these WAPs sometimes fail to change that login and password. This has given rise to a new avenue of entry into networks.

In some cities that have large concentrations of wireless networks, attackers drive around in cars using their wireless-equipped laptop computers to search for accessible networks. These attackers are called **wardrivers**. When wardrivers find an open network (or a WAP that has a common default login and password), they sometimes place a chalk mark on the building so that other attackers will know that an easily entered wireless network is nearby. This practice is called **warchalking**. Some warchalkers have created Web sites that include maps of wireless access locations in major cities around the world. Companies can avoid becoming targets by simply turning on WEP in their access points and changing the logins and passwords to something other than the manufacturers' default settings.

An early victim of a wireless attack, Best Buy was using wireless point-of-sale (POS) terminals in some of its stores. The wireless POS terminals could be moved easily from one area of the store to another, and they helped Best Buy handle large customer flows better than it could using only fixed POS terminals. Unfortunately, Best Buy had not enabled WEP on these terminals. A customer who had just purchased a wireless card for his laptop decided to launch a sniffer utility program on the laptop in his car in the parking lot. The customer was able to intercept data from the POS terminals, including transaction details and what he said looked like credit card numbers. Best Buy stopped using the wireless POS terminals when the story appeared in the news.

Encryption Solutions

Encryption is the coding of information by using a mathematically based program and a secret key to produce a string of characters that is unintelligible. The science that studies encryption is called **cryptography**. Cryptography is different from steganography, which makes text undetectable to the naked eye. Cryptography does not hide text; it converts it to other text that is visible but does not appear to have any meaning. What an unauthorized reader sees is a string of random text characters, numbers, and punctuation.

ENCRYPTION ALGORITHMS

A program that transforms normal text, called **plain text**, into **cipher text** (the unintelligible string of characters) is called an **encryption program**. The logic behind an encryption program that includes the mathematics used to do the transformation from plain text to cipher text is called an **encryption algorithm**.

Messages are encrypted just before they are sent over a network or the Internet. Upon arrival, each message is decoded, or **decrypted**, using a **decryption program**—a type of encryption-reversing procedure. Encryption algorithms are considered so vitally important to preserving security within the United States that the National Security Agency has control over their dissemination. Some encryption algorithms are considered so important that the U.S. government has banned publication of details about them. Currently, it is illegal for U.S. companies to export some of these encryption algorithms.

The Freedom Forum Online contains a number of articles on lawsuits and legislation surrounding encryption export laws. Critics consider publication restrictions a freedom of speech issue. If you are interested in reading more about the latest arguments in the ongoing debates over freedom of speech and export law, search the Freedom Forum using the keyword "encryption" as the search term.

One property of encryption algorithms is that someone can know the details of the algorithm and still not be able to decipher the encrypted message without knowing the key that the algorithm used to encrypt the message. The resistance of an encrypted message to attack attempts depends on the size (in bits) of the key used in the encryption procedure. Most security experts today believe that a 128-bit key provides adequate security for data transmission, but 192-bit and 256-bit encryption keys are also in common use. For digital certificates, most sites now use 2048-bit encryption; however, a number of sites are moving to 4096-bit encryption. A sufficiently long key can help make the encryption unbreakable.

The type of key and associated encryption program used to lock a message, or otherwise manipulate it, subdivides encryption into three functions: hash coding, asymmetric encryption, and symmetric encryption. The next three sections describe each of these approaches to encryption.

HASH CODING

Hash coding is a process that uses a **hash algorithm** to calculate a number, called a **hash value**, from a message of any length. It is a fingerprint for the message because it is almost certain to be unique for each message. Hash coding can indicate whether a message has been altered in transit because its original hash value and the hash value computed by the receiver will not match after a message is altered.

ASYMMETRIC ENCRYPTION

Asymmetric encryption, or **public-key encryption**, encodes messages by using two mathematically related numeric keys. In 1977, MIT professors Ronald Rivest, Adi Shamir, and Leonard Adleman invented the RSA Public Key Cryptosystem. In their system, one key of the pair, called a **public key**, is freely distributed to anyone interested in communicating securely with the holder of both keys. The public key is used to encrypt messages using one of several different encryption algorithms. The second key, called a **private key**, is kept by the key owner. The owner uses the private key to decrypt all messages received.

Here is an example showing how asymmetric encryption works: If Herb wants to send a message to Allison, he obtains Allison's public key from any of several public places. Then, he encrypts his message to Allison using that public key. Only Allison can read the encrypted message by decrypting it with her private key. Because the keys are unique, only one private key can open the message encrypted with a corresponding public key, and vice versa. Reversing the process, Allison can send a private message to Herb using Herb's public key to encrypt the message. When he receives Allison's message, Herb uses his private key to decrypt the message. If they are sending e-mail to one another, the message is secret only while in transit. Once a message is downloaded from the mail server and decoded, it is stored in plain text on the recipient's machine.

One of the most popular technologies used to implement public-key encryption today is called **Pretty Good Privacy (PGP)**. PGP was invented in 1991 by Phil Zimmerman, who charged businesses to use it but allowed individuals to use it at no cost. PGP can use several different algorithms to perform public-key encryption. Today, individuals can download free versions of PGP for personal use from the PGP International site and businesses can buy licenses for the product from Symantec (which bought the original PGP Corporation).

SYMMETRIC ENCRYPTION

Symmetric encryption, also known as **private-key encryption**, encodes a message with an algorithm that uses a single numeric key, such as 456839420783, to encode and decode data. Because the same key is used, both the message sender and the message receiver must know the key. Encoding and decoding messages using symmetric encryption is very fast and efficient. However, the key must be guarded. If the key is made public, then all messages sent previously using that key become vulnerable, and the keys must be changed.

It can be difficult to distribute new keys to authorized parties while maintaining security and control over the keys because transmitting anything privately (including a new secret key) requires that it be encrypted. Private keys do not work well in large environments such as the Internet because each pair of users that want to share information privately must have their own private key. That requires a prohibitively large number of keys.

In highly secure environments such as banking or the military, private-key encryption is commonly used. Distribution of the private keys requires guards (two-person control) and secret transportation plans. The **Data Encryption Standard (DES)** was the U.S. government's primary method of private-key encryption from 1976 through 1999. As faster computers became available, the size (bit length) of the keys had to be increased regularly, and the U.S. government moved to a stronger version of DES, called **Triple Data Encryption Standard (Triple DES or 3DES)**. In 2001, the U.S. government developed a more secure encryption standard called the **Advanced Encryption Standard (AES)**. Today, most U.S. government agencies and high-security business environments use AES 128-bit or 256-bit key lengths. As you will learn in the next section, the Web uses a combination of public- and private-key encryption to establish secure connections between servers and Web browsers.

COMPARING ASYMMETRIC AND SYMMETRIC ENCRYPTION SYSTEMS

Public-key (asymmetric) systems provide several advantages over private-key (symmetric) encryption methods. First, the combination of keys required to provide private messages between enormous numbers of people is small. If n people want to share secret information with one another, then only n unique public-key pairs are required—far fewer than an equivalent private-key system. Second, key distribution is not a problem. Each person's public key can be posted anywhere and does not require any special handling to distribute. Third, public-key systems make implementation of digital signatures possible. This means that an electronic document can be signed and sent to any recipient with nonrepudiation. That is, with public-key techniques, it is not possible for anyone other than the signer to produce the signature electronically; in addition, the signer cannot later deny signing the electronic document.

Public-key systems have disadvantages. One disadvantage is that public-key encryption and decryption are significantly slower than private-key systems. This extra time can add up quickly as individuals and organizations conduct commerce on the Internet. Public-key systems do not replace private-key systems but serve as a complement to them. Public-key systems are used to transmit private keys to Internet participants so that additional, more efficient communication can occur in a secure Internet session. Figure 10-7 shows a graphical comparison of the hash coding, private-key, and public-key encryption methods: Figure 10-7a shows hash coding; Figure 10-7b depicts private-key encryption; and Figure 10-7c illustrates public-key encryption.

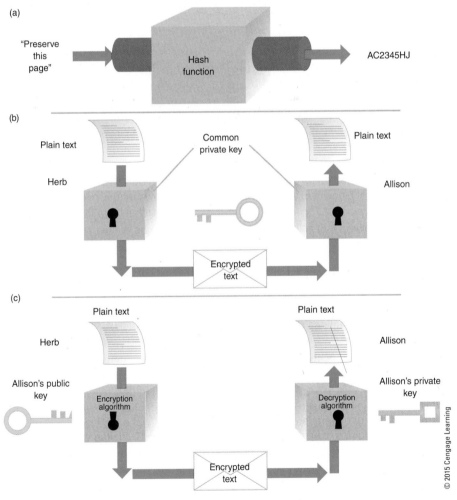

FIGURE 10-7   Comparison of (a) hash coding, (b) private-key, and (c) public-key encryption

Encryption in Web Browsers

Two encryption approaches are used to establish secure connections between Web servers and clients—the **Secure Sockets Layer (SSL)** system developed by Netscape Communications and the **Secure Hypertext Transfer Protocol (S-HTTP)** developed by CommerceNet. SSL and S-HTTP allow both the client and server computers to manage encryption and decryption activities between each other during a secure Web session; however, SSL and S-HTTP have different goals. SSL secures connections between two computers, and S-HTTP establishes security for each individual message.

SECURE SOCKETS LAYER (SSL) PROTOCOL

SSL provides a security "handshake" in which the client and server computers exchange a brief burst of messages. In those messages, the client and server agree on the level of security to be used for exchange of digital certificates and other tasks. Each computer identifies the other. After identification, SSL encrypts and decrypts information flowing between the two computers. This means that information in both the HTTP request and any HTTP response is encrypted. Encrypted information includes the URL the client is requesting, any forms containing information the user has completed (which might include sensitive information such as a login, a password, or a credit card number), and HTTP access authorization data, such as usernames and passwords. In short, *all* communication between SSL-enabled clients and servers is encoded. When SSL encodes everything flowing between the client and server, an eavesdropper receives only unintelligible information.

SSL can secure many different types of communication between computers in addition to HTTP. For example, SSL can secure FTP sessions, enabling private downloading and uploading of sensitive documents, spreadsheets, and other electronic data. SSL can secure Telnet sessions in which remote computer users can log on to corporate host machines and send their passwords and usernames. The protocol that implements SSL is HTTPS. By preceding the URL with the protocol name HTTPS, the client is signifying that it would like to establish a secure connection with the remote server.

Secure Sockets Layer allows the length of the private session key generated by every encrypted transaction to be set at a particular bit length (such as 128-bit or 256-bit). A **session key** is a key used by an encryption algorithm to create cipher text from plain text during a single secure session. The longer the key, the more resistant the encryption is to attack. A Web browser that has entered into an SSL session indicates that it is in an encrypted session (most browsers use an icon in the browser status bar). Once the session is ended, the session key is discarded permanently and not reused for subsequent secure sessions.

In an SSL session, the client and server agree that their exchanges should be kept secure because they involve transmitting credit card numbers, invoice numbers, or verification codes. To implement secrecy, SSL uses a combination of public-key (asymmetric) encryption and private-key (symmetric) encryption.

In SSL, the browser generates a private key, and then encrypts it using the server's public key. The server's public key is stored in the digital certificate that the server sent to the browser during the authentication step. Once the key is encrypted, the browser sends it to the server. The server, in turn, decrypts the message with its private key and exposes the shared private key.

Here is how SSL works with an exchange between a browser (SSL client) and a Web server (SSL server):

1. When a client browser sends a request message to a server's secure Web site, the server sends a hello request to the browser (client). The browser responds with a client hello. The exchange of these greetings, or the handshake, allows the two computers to determine the compression and encryption standards that they both support.

2. Next, the browser asks the server for a digital certificate as a proof of identity. In response, the server sends to the browser a certificate signed by a recognized certification authority.

3. The browser checks the serial number and certificate fingerprint on the server certificate against the public key of the CA stored within the browser. Once the CA's public key is verified, the endorsement is verified. That action authenticates the Web server. The browser responds by sending its client certificate and an encrypted private session key to be used. When the server receives this information, it initiates the session, which uses the private key now shared between the browser and the Web server.

4. With the session established as secure, request messages from the browser are accepted by the Web server, which sends the necessary responses. In this secure session, the browser user can make purchases, pay bills, or trade securities without worrying about threats to the security of the information passing between the two computers.

From this point on in the session, public-key encryption is no longer used; the transmission is protected by private-key encryption. All messages sent between the client and the server are encrypted with the shared private key, also known as the session key. When the session ends, the session key is discarded.

Any new connection between a client and a secure server starts the entire process all over again, beginning with the handshake between the client browser and the server. Figure 10-8 illustrates the SSL handshake that occurs before a client and server exchange private-key-encoded business information for the remainder of the secure session.

SECURE HTTP (S-HTTP)

Secure HTTP (S-HTTP) is an extension to HTTP that provides a number of security features, including client and server authentication, spontaneous encryption, and request/response nonrepudiation. S-HTTP provides symmetric encryption for maintaining secret communications and public-key encryption to establish client/server authentication. S-HTTP security is established during the initial session between a client and a server. Either the client or the server can specify that a particular security feature be required, optional, or refused. This process of proposing and accepting (or rejecting) various transmission conditions is called **session negotiation**.

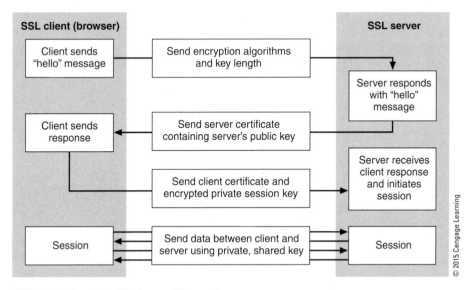

FIGURE 10-8   Establishing an SSL session

S-HTTP establishes a secure session with a client–server handshake exchange (similar to SSL's procedure), but S-HTTP includes security details in its packet headers. The headers define the type of security techniques, including the use of private-key encryption, server authentication, client authentication, and message integrity. Once the client and server agree to security implementations enforced between them, all subsequent messages between them during that session are wrapped in a secure container, sometimes called an envelope. This **secure envelope** encapsulates and encrypts the message, which provides secrecy, integrity, and client/server authentication. S-HTTP is still used by some Web servers; however, SSL has largely replaced it.

You have learned how encryption provides message secrecy and confidentiality, and you have learned how digital certificates serve to authenticate a server to a client, and vice versa. In the next section, you will learn how to implement message integrity, which prevents an interloper from changing a message in transit.

Hash Functions, Message Digests, and Digital Signatures

Although it is difficult to prevent a perpetrator from altering a message, one technique can detect when a message has been altered. To detect message alteration, a hash algorithm is applied to the message content to create a **message digest**, which is a number that summarizes the encrypted information. The computer receiving the message can calculate the message digest value independently and compare that value with the message digest computed using the hash algorithm. If the two message digest values match, the encrypted message was not altered in its transmission. If they do not match, the receiver can ask the sender to resend the message.

Hash functions are not ideal because the hash algorithm is public and widely known. For example, a message containing a purchase order could be intercepted, the shipping address and quantity ordered could be altered, the message digest could be regenerated, and the new message and its accompanying message digest could be sent on to the merchant. Upon receipt, the merchant would calculate the message digest value and confirm that the two message digest values match. The merchant would conclude (incorrectly) that the message had not been altered. To prevent this type of fraud, the sender can encrypt message digests using a private key.

An encrypted message digest created using a private key is called a **digital signature**. A purchase order accompanied by a digital signature provides the merchant with positive identification of the sender and assurance that the message was not altered. Because the message digest is encrypted using a public key, only the owner of the public/private key pair could have encrypted the message digest. Thus, when the merchant decrypts the message with the user's public key and calculates a matching message digest value, the sender is authenticated. Only the true sender could have authored the message because only the sender's private key would yield an encrypted message that could be decrypted successfully by an associated public key. As you learned in Chapter 5, this kind of nonrepudiation is especially important in B2B transactions online. Figure 10-9 illustrates how a digital signature and a signed message are created and sent.

Encrypting both the digital signature and the message itself guarantees message secrecy. Used together, public-key encryption, message digests, and digital signatures provide a high level of security for Internet transactions. As you learned in Chapter 7, digital signatures have the same legal status as written signatures in most countries today.

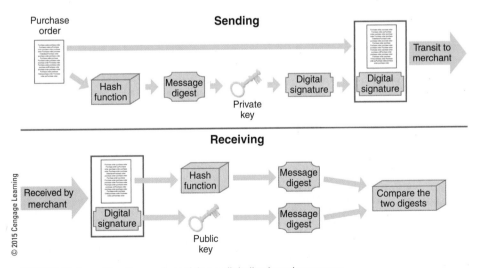

FIGURE 10-9   Sending and receiving a digitally signed message

Security for Server Computers

The server is the third link in the client–Internet–server electronic commerce path between the user and a Web server. The Web server administrator's job is to make sure that security policies are documented and implemented to minimize the impact of Web server threats.

Password Attack Threats

One of the most sensitive files on a Web server is the file that holds Web server username–password pairs. An intruder who can access and read that file can enter privileged areas masquerading as a legitimate user. To reduce this risk, most Web servers store user authentication information in encrypted files.

The passwords that users select can be the source of a threat. Users sometimes select passwords that are guessed easily, such as their mother's maiden name, the name of a child, or their telephone number. **Dictionary attack programs** cycle through an electronic dictionary, trying every word and common name as a password.

User passwords, once compromised, provide an opening for entry into a server that can remain undetected for a long time. Many organizations now require users to create strong passwords that contain a combination of letters, numbers, and special characters that are unlikely to appear in an attack program's dictionary. Other organizations use their own dictionary check as a preventive measure. When a user selects a new password, the password assignment software checks the password against its dictionary and, if it finds a match, refuses to allow the use of that password. Good password assignment software checks against common words, names (including common pet names), acronyms that are commonly used in the organization, and words or characters (including numbers) that have some meaning for the user requesting the password (for example, employees might be prohibited from using their employee numbers as passwords). Figure 10-10 shows examples of passwords that range from very weak to very strong.

There are a number of online resources that can help you create very strong passwords. One of the most respected of these is the Gibson Research Corporation's Ultra High Security Password Generator.

Some security experts recommend the use of a passphrase instead of or in the creation of a complex password. A **passphrase** is a sequence of words or text that is easy to remember, but is complex enough to serve as either a good password itself or as a prompt to remember a good password. For example, a U.S. user might find it easy to remember the opening words to the country's national anthem and create the passphrase, "OSay,CanYouSee,ByTheDawn'sEarlyLight." This passphrase would be a long password, and it could be improved by making a few substitutions to increase the variety of characters it uses, yet still be easy to remember, for example: "0$ay,CanYou$ee,ByTheDawn'$EarlyL1ght." A password constructed using the initial letters of the words, including punctuation and these substitutions, would not be as long yet could still be effective and remain easy to remember, for example: "0$,Cy$,Btdel."

Another solution to the password issue is to use a password manager, such as the LastPass program you learned about in the opening to this chapter. A **password manager** is software that stores securely all of a person's passwords. Instead of having to remember

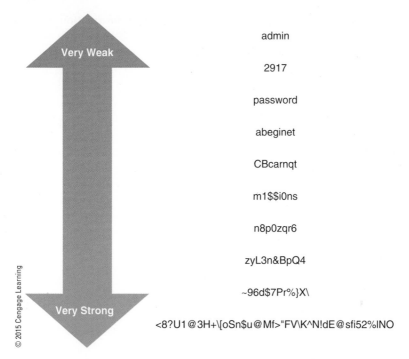

admin

2917

password

abeginet

CBcarnqt

m1$$i0ns

n8p0zqr6

zyL3n&BpQ4

~96d$7Pr%}X\

<8?U1@3H+\[oSn$u@Mf>"FV\K^N!dE@sfi52%INO

© 2015 Cengage Learning

FIGURE 10-10   Examples of passwords, from very weak to very strong

a separate password for every online account, the password manager users need only remember one master password to obtain access to the password manager program. Most password manager programs operate automatically. When a user opens a Web page, the password manager checks to see if the login and password are already stored in it. If so, the password manager enters them into the appropriate fields of the Web page. The main concern of password manager users is being sure that the master password used to access the software is as long and complex as possible. As you learned in the chapter opener, an attack that obtains the master password will instantly give the hacker access to all of the user's online accounts.

Database Threats

Electronic commerce systems store user data and retrieve product information from databases connected to the Web server. Besides storing product information, databases connected to the Web contain valuable and private information that could damage a company irreparably if disclosed or altered. Most database management systems include security features that rely on usernames and passwords. Once a user is authenticated, specific parts of the database become available to that user. However, some databases either store username/password pairs in an unencrypted table, or they fail to enforce security at all and rely on the Web server to enforce security. If unauthorized users obtain user authentication information, they can masquerade as legitimate database users and reveal or download confidential and potentially valuable information. Trojan horse programs hidden within the database system can also reveal information by changing the access rights of various user groups. A Trojan horse can even remove access controls within a database, giving all users complete access to the data—including intruders.

Other Software-Based Threats

Web server threats can arise from programs executed by the server. Java or C++ programs that are passed to Web servers by a client, or that reside on a server, frequently make use of a buffer. A **buffer** is an area of memory set aside to hold data read from a file or database. A buffer is necessary whenever any input or output operation takes place because a computer can process file information much faster than the information can be read from input devices or written to output devices. Programs filling buffers can malfunction and overfill the buffer, spilling the excess data outside the designated buffer memory area. This is called a **buffer overrun** or **buffer overflow** error. Usually, this occurs because the program contains an error or bug that causes the overflow. Sometimes, however, the buffer overflow is intentional. The Internet Worm of 1988 was such a program. It caused an overflow condition that eventually consumed all resources until the affected computer could no longer function.

A more insidious version of a buffer overflow attack writes instructions into critical memory locations so that when the intruder program has completed its work of overwriting buffers, the Web server resumes execution by loading internal registers with the address of the main attacking program's code. This type of attack can open the Web server to severe damage because the resumed program—which is now the attacker program—may regain control of the computer, exposing its files to disclosure and destruction by the attacking program. Good programming practices can reduce the potential damage from buffer overflows, and some computers include hardware that works with the operating system to limit the effects of buffer overflows that are intentionally programmed to create damage.

A similar attack, one in which excessive data is sent to a server, can occur on mail servers. Called a **mail bomb**, the attack occurs when hundreds or even thousands of people each send a message to a particular address. The attack might be launched by a large team of well-organized hackers, but more likely the attack is launched by one or a few hackers who have gained control over others' computers using a Trojan horse virus or some other method of turning those computers into zombies. The accumulated mail received by the target of the mail bomb exceeds the allowed e-mail size limit and can cause e-mail systems to malfunction.

Threats to the Physical Security of Web Servers

Web servers and the computers that are networked closely to them, such as the database servers and application servers used to supply content and transaction-processing capabilities to electronic commerce Web sites, must be protected from physical harm. For many companies, these computers have become repositories of important data (information about customers, products, sales, purchases, and payments). They have also become important parts of the revenue-generating function in many businesses. As key physical resources, these computers and related equipment warrant high levels of protection against threats to their physical security. As you learned in Chapter 9, many companies outsource the hosting of their Web servers to companies that can maintain stronger protection over the servers than the company could provide for computers maintained at its own location.

Many companies maintain backup copies of their servers' contents at a remote location. If the Web server operation is critical to the continuation of the business, a company can maintain a duplicate of the entire Web server physical facility at a remote location. In the case of a system failure, the company's Web operations can be switched over to the backup location in less than a second. Examples of mission-critical Web servers that would warrant such a comprehensive (and expensive) level of physical security include airline reservation systems, stock brokerage firm trading systems, and bank payment clearing systems.

Some companies rely on their Internet service providers for Web server security, which is often offered as an add-on service in the hosting contract. Other companies hire smaller, specialized security service providers to handle security. Having a service provider handle security can add an additional $200 to $2000 per month to the provider's standard bandwidth charges.

Access Control and Authentication

Access control and authentication refer to controlling who and what has access to the Web server. Most people who work with Web servers access the server from a client computer, which can be at a remote location. Recall that authentication is verification of the identity of the entity requesting access to the computer. Just as users can authenticate servers with which they are interacting, servers can authenticate individual users. When a server requires positive identification of a user, it requests that the client send a certificate.

Servers can authenticate users in several ways. First, if the server cannot decrypt the user's digital signature contained in the certificate using the user's public key, it can conclude that the certificate did not come from the true owner and can deny access. Second, servers can check the time stamp on the certificate to ensure that it has not expired. A server will not allow access by a user with an expired certificate. Third, servers can use a callback system in which the server software checks the user's client computer name and address against a list of authorized client computers before "calling back" to establish a connection.

Usernames and passwords can also provide protection. To authenticate users using passwords and usernames, the server must acquire and store a database containing users' passwords and usernames. Many Web servers store usernames in plain text and encrypt passwords. With the plain text username and encrypted password stored, the system can validate users when they log on by checking the usernames they enter against the list of usernames stored in the database. The password that a user enters is checked against the encrypted password stored in the database. If the two passwords match, the login is accepted. That is why even a system administrator cannot tell you what your forgotten password is on most systems. Instead, the administrator must assign a new temporary password that the user can change to another password.

Usernames and passwords can be saved in a cookie on the client computer, which allows access to subscription areas of the site without entering the username and password on subsequent site visits. However, cookie information can be stored on the client computer as plain text. If the cookie contains login and password information, then that information is visible to anyone who has access to the user's computer.

Web servers often provide access control list security to restrict file access to selected users. An **access control list (ACL)** is a list or database of files and other resources and the usernames of people who can access the files and other resources. Each file has its own access control list. When a client computer requests Web server access to a file or document that has been configured to require an access check, the Web server checks the resource's ACL file to determine if the user is allowed to access that file. This system is especially convenient to restrict access of files on an intranet server so that individuals can only access selected files on a need-to-know basis. The Web server can exercise fine control over resources by further subdividing file access into the activities of read, write, or execute. For example, some users may be permitted to read the corporate employee handbook but not allowed to update or write to the file. Only the human resources (HR) manager would have write access to the employee handbook, and that access privilege is stored along with the HR manager's ID and password in an ACL.

Firewalls

A **firewall** is software or a hardware–software combination that is installed in a network to control the packet traffic moving through it. Most organizations place a firewall at the Internet entry point of their networks. The firewall provides a defense between a network and the Internet or between a network and any other network that could pose a threat. Firewalls all operate on the following principles:

- All traffic from inside to outside and from outside to inside the network must pass through it.
- Only authorized traffic, as defined by the local security policy, is allowed to pass through it.
- The firewall itself is immune to penetration.

Those networks inside the firewall are often called **trusted**, whereas networks outside the firewall are called **untrusted**. Acting as a filter, firewalls permit selected messages to flow into and out of the protected network. For example, one security policy a firewall might enforce is to allow all HTTP (Web) traffic to pass back and forth but disallow FTP or Telnet requests either into or out of the protected network. Firewalls can separate corporate networks from one another and prevent personnel in one division from accessing information from another division of the same company. Using firewalls to segment a corporate network into secure zones serves as a coarse need-to-know filter.

Large organizations that have multiple sites and many locations must install a firewall at each location that has an external connection to the Internet. Such a system ensures an unbroken security perimeter that is effective for the entire corporation. In addition, each firewall in the organization must follow the same security policy. Otherwise, one firewall might permit one type of transaction to flow into the corporate network that another excludes. Without a consistent policy, an unwanted access that occurs through a breach in one firewall can expose the information assets of the entire corporation to the threat.

Organizations should remove any unnecessary software from their firewalls. Having fewer software programs on the system reduces the chances for software security breaches. Access to a firewall should be restricted to a console physically connected directly to the firewall machine. Managers should forbid remote administration of the firewall to avoid the threat of an outside attacker gaining access to the firewall by posing as an administrator.

Firewalls are classified into the following categories: packet filter, gateway server, and proxy server. **Packet-filter firewalls** examine all data flowing back and forth between the trusted network (within the firewall) and the Internet. Packet filtering examines the source and destination addresses and ports of incoming packets and denies or permits entrance to the packets based on a preprogrammed set of rules.

Gateway servers are firewalls that filter traffic based on the application requested. Gateway servers limit access to specific applications such as Telnet, FTP, and HTTP. Application gateways arbitrate traffic between the inside network and the outside network. In contrast to a packet-filter technique, an application-level firewall filters requests and logs them at the application level, rather than at the lower IP level. A gateway firewall provides a central point where all requests can be classified, logged, and later analyzed. An example is a gateway-level policy that permits incoming FTP requests but blocks outgoing FTP requests. That policy prevents employees inside a firewall from downloading potentially dangerous programs from the outside.

Proxy server firewalls are firewalls that communicate with the Internet on the private network's behalf. When a browser is configured to use a proxy server firewall, the firewall passes the browser request to the Internet. When the Internet sends back a response, the proxy server relays it back to the browser. Proxy servers are also used to serve as a huge cache for Web pages.

Organizations today often have telecommuting workers and other people with remote access. This increases the number of computers that must be protected by the firewall. This **perimeter expansion** problem is particularly troublesome for companies that have employees or subcontractors using laptop computers to access confidential company information from all types of networks at customer locations, vendor locations, and even public locations, such as airports.

Crackers spend a great deal of time and energy trying to enter the servers of organizations. Organizations often install intrusion detection systems as part of their firewalls. **Intrusion detection systems** are designed to monitor attempts to log into servers and analyze those attempts for patterns that might indicate a cracker's attack is under way.

Once the intrusion detection system identifies an attack, it can block further attempts that originate from the same IP address until the organization's security staff can examine and analyze the access attempts and determine whether they are an attack.

As more organizations rely on cloud computing for crucial production systems, the need for security in cloud environments is increasing. The development of firewalls that work with cloud computing is advancing rapidly but has lagged behind the need for these products. Instead of establishing security policies for each server, these firewalls must enforce a single set of policies across all of the servers in the cloud. One problem in cloud environments is that the servers and databases in the cloud are started up and wound down as needed. Thus, the type of identifiable servers that most firewall products are designed to protect does not exist in the same form in cloud server environments.

In addition to firewalls installed on organizations' networks, it is possible to install software-only firewalls on individual client computers. These firewalls are often called **personal firewalls**. The use of personal firewalls has become an important tool in the protection of expanded network perimeters for many companies. You can learn more about firewall protection for home computers at the Gibson Research Shields Up! Web site.

Organizations That Promote Computer Security

Following the occurrence of the Internet Worm of 1988, a number of organizations were formed to share information about threats to computer systems. These organizations are devoted to the principle that sharing information about attacks and defenses for those attacks can help everyone create better computer security. Some of the organizations began at universities; others were launched by government agencies. In this section, you will learn about some of these organizations and their resources.

CERT

In 1988, a group of researchers met to study the infamous Internet Worm attack soon after it occurred. They wanted to understand how worms worked and how to prevent damage from future attacks of this type. The National Computer Security Center, part of the National Security Agency, initiated a series of meetings to figure out how to respond to future security breaks that might affect thousands of people. Soon after those meetings, the U.S. government created the Computer Emergency Response Team and housed it at Carnegie Mellon University in Pittsburgh.

The organization is now operated as part of the federally funded Software Engineering Institute at Carnegie Mellon, and it has changed its legal name from the Computer Emergency Response Team (which had been abbreviated to "CERT" by most people who wrote and talked about it) to CERT. CERT still maintains an effective and quick communications infrastructure among security experts so that security incidents can be avoided or handled quickly.

Today, CERT responds to thousands of security incidents each year and provides a wealth of information to help Internet users and companies become more knowledgeable about security risks. CERT posts alerts to inform the Internet community about security events, and it is regarded as a primary authoritative source for information about viruses, worms, and other types of attacks.

Other Organizations

CERT is the most prominent of these organizations and has formed relationships, such as the Internet Security Alliance, with other industry associations. However, CERT is not the only computer security resource. In 1989, one year after CERT was formed, a cooperative research and educational organization called the Systems Administrator, Audit, Network, and Security Institute was launched. Now known as the SANS Institute, this organization includes thousands of members who work in computer security consulting firms and information technology departments of companies as auditors, systems administrators, and network administrators.

Many SANS education and research efforts yield resources such as news releases, research reports, security alerts, and white papers that are available on the Web site at no cost. SANS also sells publications to generate funds that it uses for research and educational programs. The SANS Institute operates the Infocon Internet Storm Center, a Web site that provides current information on the location and intensity of computer attacks throughout the world.

Purdue University's Center for Education and Research in Information Assurance and Security (CERIAS) is a center for multidisciplinary research and education in information security. The CERIAS Web site provides resources in computer, network, and communications security and includes a section on information assurance.

The Center for Internet Security is a not-for-profit organization devoted to helping companies that operate electronic commerce Web sites reduce the risk of disruptions from technical failures or deliberate attacks on their computer systems. It also provides information to auditors who review such systems and to insurance companies that provide coverage for companies who operate such systems.

For current information about computer security, you can visit CSO Online, which carries articles that have appeared in *CSO Magazine* along with other news items related to computer security. A British publication, Infosecurity, is available online and includes articles about all types of online security issues.

Computer Forensics and Ethical Hacking

A small number of specialized consulting firms engage in the unlikely enterprise of breaking into servers and client computers at the request of the organizations that own those computers. Called **computer forensics experts** or **ethical hackers**, these computer sleuths are hired to probe PCs and locate information that can be used in legal proceedings. The field of **computer forensics** is responsible for the collection, preservation, and analysis of computer-related evidence. Ethical hackers are often hired by companies to test their computer security safeguards. They are also hired by law enforcement agencies investigating crimes and by law firms undertaking investigations on behalf of their clients.

Summary

Online businesses today face substantial security risks and must manage them effectively. Most online firms create a formal security policy document that identifies risks and the countermeasures that can reduce those risks to an acceptable level. Online security elements include secrecy, integrity, and necessity. These three elements are each enforced in the three components of online business transactions, including client devices, the communication channel, and Web server computers.

Client devices can be threatened by active content in browser plug-ins, by attacks (including viruses, Trojan horses, and worms) delivered through Web browsing activity or e-mail, or by attacks launched through other devices on the same network. Antivirus software is an important element in the protection of client computers.

The Internet itself, which is the primary communication channel used in online business, is especially vulnerable to attacks. Encryption can provide secrecy and integrity protection against many of these attacks and can be implemented with private keys, public keys, or a combination of techniques. Digital certificates provide both integrity and user authentication, which can provide nonrepudiation in online transactions. Specific Internet protocols can provide secure Web browser connections. Wireless networks are subject to threats of signal interception, but these threats can be reduced by a secure form of wireless encryption. The increasing use of mobile devices in online business also exposes communications to additional threats.

Web servers must be protected from both physical threats and Internet-based attacks on their software. Server protection methods include access control and authentication, which are provided by username and password login procedures and client certificates. Firewalls can be used to separate trusted inside networks and clients from untrusted outside networks, including other divisions of a company's enterprise network system and the Internet.

A number of organizations have been formed to share information about computer security threats and defenses. When major security outbreaks occur, these organizations can facilitate the location and elimination of the threat. Computer forensics firms that undertake attacks against their clients' computers can play an important role in helping to identify security weaknesses.

Key Terms

access control list (ACL)	biometric security device
active content	black hat hacker
active wiretapping	botnet
ActiveX	buffer
Advanced Encryption Standard (AES)	buffer overflow
anonymous Web services	buffer overrun
antivirus software	certification authority (CA)
applet	cipher text
asymmetric encryption	computer forensics
backdoor	computer forensics experts

computer security

countermeasure

crackers

cryptography

cybervandalism

Data Encryption Standard (DES)

decrypted

decryption program

delay attack

denial attack

denial-of-service (DoS) attack

dictionary attack programs

digital certificate

digital signature

distributed denial-of-service (DDoS) attack

domain name servers (DNSs)

eavesdropper

encryption

encryption algorithm

encryption program

ethical hackers

firewall

first-party cookies

gateway servers

hackers

hash algorithm

hash coding

hash value

integrity

integrity violation

intrusion detection systems

JavaScript

key

logical security

macro virus

mail bomb

man-in-the-middle exploit

masquerading

message digest

multivector virus

necessity

necessity threat

open session

packet-filter firewalls

passphrase

password manager

perimeter expansion

persistent cookies

personal firewalls

phishing expeditions

physical security

plain text

plug-ins

Pretty Good Privacy (PGP)

privacy

private key

private-key encryption

proxy server firewalls

public key

public-key encryption

ransomware

remote wipe

robotic network

rogue apps

sandbox

scripting languages

secrecy

secure envelope

Secure Hypertext Transfer Protocol (S-HTTP)

Secure Sockets Layer (SSL)

Secure Sockets Layer-Extended Validation
    (SSL-EV) digital certificate security policy

session cookies

session key

session negotiation

signed code

sniffer programs

spoofing

steganography

symmetric encryption

third-party cookies

threat

Triple Data Encryption Standard (Triple DES or 3DES)

Trojan horse

trusted

untrusted

warchalking

wardrivers

Web bug (Web beacon)

white hat hacker

Wireless Encryption Protocol (WEP)

worm

zombie

zombie farm

Review Questions

1. Briefly explain the difference between physical and logical security.
2. What is a countermeasure?
3. What is a white hat hacker?
4. Briefly explain what secrecy, integrity, and necessity are in the context of computer security.
5. What is a man-in-the-middle exploit?
6. What is a security policy?
7. Provide one example of an integrity violation.
8. What is a session cookie?
9. What is a third-party cookie?
10. What is a Web bug?
11. What is active content?
12. What is a scripting language?
13. What is a zombie?
14. What is a macro virus?
15. How is a multivector worm or virus a more severe threat than other worms or viruses?
16. Why is an SSL-EV digital certificate superior to an ordinary digital certificate
17. What is ransomware?
18. What is signed code?
19. What is steganography?
20. What is a biometric security device?
21. What is a backdoor?
22. Who are most likely to be victimized by a phishing expedition?
23. Briefly describe what occurs in a denial-of-service attack.
24. What is a hash algorithm and when might it be used?
25. What is a message digest?
26. What is a dictionary attack?
27. How does a packet-filter firewall work?
28. What is computer forensics?

Exercises

1. Refer to Figure 10-1. In two paragraphs, identify and briefly describe two threats that you would place in Quadrant III and explain why you would classify them as Quadrant III threats.

2. Best Cutting Boards (BCB) makes and sells handcrafted wood cutting boards online. BCB offers about 100 different products for sale on its Web site, which sees about 9000 visitors per month. The average transaction amount is $112 and it makes an average of 150 sales per day. BCB accepts four different credit cards and PayPal and has more than 100,000 registered customers in its database, which is stored along with all transaction data on its own Web server at the company's offices in Des Moines, Iowa. In about 300 words, outline a draft security policy for the company's Web server. Be sure to consider any threats that exist because the company stores customer credit card numbers, the customer database, and transaction information on the same computer. You can use the Web Links for this exercise to find samples of security policies and detailed guidelines for creating them.

3. In about 100 words, explain the difference between session cookies and persistent cookies. In your answer, be sure to include how each type of cookie is used.

4. Write a paragraph in which you explain the concept of a sandbox and describe how it can be used to reduce security risks in client computers.

5. In a paragraph or two, explain what a botnet is and how it could cause more damage than a single Trojan horse attack.

6. In about 100 words, explain what assurances a certification authority (CA) provides to a business that purchases one of its digital certificates. In your answer, describe what general procedures a CA typically follows before issuing a digital certificate.

7. Write a paragraph in which you explain how remote wipe software can increase security for the user of a mobile device.

8. In a paragraph or two, describe the purpose and use of a sniffer program.

9. In about 100 words, describe the function of an anonymous Web service and explain why an individual or company might want to use such a service.

10. In about 200 words, explain the differences between private-key encryption and public-key encryption. In your answer, include examples of when and why each might be used.

11. Using your favorite search engine or the resources of your library, identify firewall issues that might arise for a company that uses cloud computing in its online sales system. In about 100 words, summarize your findings in terms of the perimeter expansion problem.

Cases

C1. Adobe Analytics

Adobe Analytics offers a number of software products and tools that companies can use to generate detailed reports for online business managers about the amount and nature of their Web site traffic. This software can tell Web site owners not only how many unique computers logged on to their sites, but can provide detailed information about which pages they viewed, how long and in what order they viewed those pages, from which Web site they arrived, and to which Web site they went when they left. Many online businesses find the information in Adobe Analytics reports to be valuable and they subscribe to one of the company's services, which include not only the reports but also various levels of consultation with their marketing and Web operations managers.

Adobe Analytics software can also generate a list of sites a visitor has viewed in the past. The software accomplishes this by placing cookies on client computers and by having their clients include Web bugs (the company calls them "Web beacons") in the pages their Web servers deliver to site visitors' browsers and in marketing e-mail messages they send. This information is extremely valuable to Adobe Analytics clients because it can tell them if visitors to their site have, for example, looked at several different sites that offer similar products before entering their Web site.

Individuals can examine the cookies stored by their Web browsers to learn more about which companies have placed cookies on their computers. Cookies shown as having been placed by either the 2o7.net or omtrdc.net domains are Adobe Analytics cookies (these are the domains where its cookie-placing servers are located) and the company uses information about previous visits to individual Web sites to make its reports to and consultations with clients even more valuable. The cookies that Adobe Analytics places generally do not expire for several years.

Adobe Analytics offers consumers a way to avoid having 2o7.net or omtrdc.net cookies placed on their computers. To do so, persons must find the right page on the company's Web site and then must elect to have a specific opt out cookie installed on their computers. This cookie will instruct Adobe Analytics servers not to place any more cookies on their computers.

REQUIRED:

1. Using your favorite search engine or the Web Links for this book, locate and read Adobe's privacy statement on its Web site. In about 200 words, evaluate how easy it is to find the company's policies on cookies, how clearly it presents the options and how well you think the company protects the privacy of those who own computers on which the company has placed cookies. Be sure to discuss the range of options that Adobe provides and comment on whether you found them to be clearly stated and easy to use.

2. Given that Adobe Analytics provides a valuable service to online businesses that want to learn more about potential customers who visit their sites, discuss the ethical issues arise for the company and its clients when the cookies are placed on customers' computers. In your discussion (of about 300 words), be sure to consider the following: site visitors generally do not know that cookies are being placed on their computers, the cookies are identified only as being placed by the 2o7.net or omtrdc.net domains (neither Adobe Analytics nor the client who will use the cookie information is identified), and that the cookies have a life of several years.

3. NBC Sports used several analytics tools from various companies to capture comprehensive cross-platform audience measurement statistics for its coverage of the Vancouver Olympic Winter Games. NBC was broadcasting part of its Olympic game coverage on its Web site for the first time, so it wanted to track and analyze the effectiveness of its advertising in that medium. In about 200 words, describe the ethical issues that you believe might exist for companies such as Adobe Analytics as a result of their contracts with NBC Sports or their interactions with the other companies involved (those companies provide primarily television audience tracking services).

Note: Your instructor might assign you to a group to complete this case, and might ask you to prepare a formal presentation of your results to your class.

C2. Materials Equipment

You are an information technology (IT) consultant to Materials Equipment, Inc. (MEI), a major industrial equipment distributor. Its products include materials-handling machinery for assembly lines and product-packaging areas. Although a number of MEI customers have product lines that require moving fluids, MEI has not expanded into that business. Instead, it works with another supplier that specializes in fluid-related products. MEI has been in business for more than 70 years and sells more than $200 million worth of parts and equipment each year to its 3000 customers. MEI's customers are located all over the world, but most are in the United States, Mexico, Malaysia, China, and Singapore.

Joe Everson, MEI's director of sales, has hired you to help him as he begins planning for a new Web site that MEI would operate with two other companies that sell products (such as bearings, seals, hoses, and hose fittings used in moving fluids) and services (design, layout, and installation of materials-handling equipment) that are complementary to MEI's products. The Web site would provide MEI customers a single destination where they could buy MEI products along with the products and services of the MEI's strategic partners. The site would also offer information about current trends in industrial equipment technologies and the application of those technologies along with a used equipment marketplace in which MEI customers could list equipment for sale. Joe believes that giving customers a convenient way to liquidate old equipment will make it easier for his sales representatives to sell new equipment to those customers.

Joe has put together an internal team to examine the feasibility of the Web site, including key employees from MEI's Sales, Finance, Product Engineering, and IT Services departments. The team has identified several security issues that they want to resolve before they move forward with the Web site design. Joe would like you to help the team understand encryption and digital certification technologies and how they might be used in the new Web site.

REQUIRED:

1. Write a 200-word briefing report on how Web sites use encryption. Explain the technology, how it is used, and describe one or two common applications.

2. In a report of about 200 words, outline how and why MEI might use encrypted e-mail in communicating with its strategic partners and with its customers.

3. In about 300 words, explain what digital certificates are and how they might be useful to MEI, its strategic partners, and their customers if they were to be used in the operation of the new Web site. Be sure to discuss which parts of the site or communications among MEI, its strategic partners, and their customers might benefit from extended validation certificates and consider the potential cost of acquiring digital certificates of any type in your evaluation of their benefits.

Note: Your instructor might assign you to a group to complete this case, and might ask you to prepare a formal presentation of your results to your class.

For Further Study and Research

Baldoni, R. and G. Chockler. 2012, *Collaborative Financial Infrastructure Protection: Tools, Abstractions, and Middleware*. New York: Springer.

Chow, R., M. Jakobsson, and J. Molina. 2012. "The Future of Authentication," *IEEE Security & Privacy*, 10(1), January/February, 22–27.

Connell, S. 2004. "Security Lapses, Lost Equipment Expose Students to Possible ID Theft Loss," *The Los Angeles Times*, August 29, B4.

Creighton, D. 2004. "Chronology of Virus Attacks," *The Wall Street Journal*, May 13. http://online.wsj.com/article/0,,SB108362410782000798,00.html

Curran, K., J. Doherty, A. McCann, and G. Turkington. 2011. "Good Practices for Strong Passwords," *EDPACS: The EDP Audit, Control, and Security Newsletter*, 44(5), 1–13.

DeFigueiredo, D. 2011. "The Case for Mobile Two-Factor Authentication," *IEEE Security and Privacy*, 9(5), September/October, 81–85.

DoD Directive 5215.1 CSC-STD-001–83. 1983. *Department of Defense Trusted Computer System Evaluation Criteria* (the "Orange Book"), Washington, DC.

Eckersley, P. 2014. "Launching in 2015: A Certificate Authority to Encrypt the Entire Web," *Electronic Frontier Foundation*, November 18. https://www.eff.org/deeplinks/2014/11/certificate-authority-encrypt-entire-web

Electronic Frontier Foundation. 2015. *Surveillance Self-Defense: An Introduction to Threat Modeling*, January 12. https://ssd.eff.org/en/module/introduction-threat-modeling

Goldsborough, R. 2012. "Computer Disasters: Preparing for the Worst," *Tech Directions*, 71(6), 14.

Gorman, S. 2009. "FBI Suspects Terrorists Are Exploring Cyber Attacks," *The Wall Street Journal*, November 18, A4.

Gorman, S., E. Ramstad, J. Solomon, Y. Dreazen, R. Smith, and R. Sidel. 2009. "Cyber Blitz Hits U.S., Korea," *The Wall Street Journal*, July 9, A1, A4.

Greenberg, A. 2015. "Hack Brief: Password Manager LastPass Got Breached Hard," *Wired*, June 15. http://www.wired.com/2015/06/hack-brief-password-manager-lastpass-got-breached-hard/

Happich, J. 2014. "Data Encryption: Seeking New Levels of Security," *EET India*, January 30. http://www.eetindia.co.in/ART_8800694674_1800006_NT_1a2ad299.HTM

Jakobsson, M., R. Chow, and J. Molina. 2012. "Authentication—Are We Doing Well Enough?" *IEEE Security & Privacy*, 10(1), January/February, 19–21.

King, R. 2011. "Many Mobile Users Are Uneasy About Smartphone Security," *ZDNet*, October 31. http://www.zdnet.com/blog/btl/many-mobile-users-are-uneasy-about-smartphone-security-survey/62145

Langner, R. 2011. "Stuxnet: Dissecting a Cyberwarfare Weapon," *IEEE Security and Privacy*, 9(3), May/June, 49–51.

Lawrence, D. 2014. "Spy vs. Spy: The U.S. Government Designed and Funds the Best Defense Against Its Own Surveillance," *Bloomberg Businessweek*, January 27, 42–47.

Lee, C. 2008. "GAO Finds Data Protection Lagging," *The Washington Post*, February 26, A15.

Lyne, J. 2013. "Computer Virus Spreading That Means You Never Get to See Your Files Again," *Forbes*, October 22. http://www.forbes.com/sites/jameslyne/2013/10/22/computer-virus-spreading-that-means-you-never-get-to-see-your-files-again/

McCarthy, N. 2012. *The Computer Incident Response Planning Handbook: Executable Plans for Protecting Information at Risk*. New York: McGraw-Hill Osborne.

McCracken, H. 2004. "Microsoft's Security Problem—and Ours," *PC World*, 22(1), January, 25.

McMillan, R. 2010. "After One Year, Seven Million Conficker Infections," *PC World*, January, 44.

Network Security. 2013. "CryptoLocker Runs Rampant, But Drops Ransom Price," December, 2.

The New York Times. 2009. "Hackers Steal South Korean, U.S. Military Secrets," December 18.

Pereira, J. 2008. "Data Theft Carried Out on Network Thought Secure," *The Wall Street Journal*, March 31, B4.

Perlroth, N. 2015. "I.R.S. Breach Demonstrates the Need to Guard Personal Data," *The New York Times*, May 28, B2.

Petreley, N. 2001. "The Cost of Free IIS," *Computerworld*, 35(43), October 22, 49.

Pocock, D. 2013. "RSA Key Sizes: 2048 or 4096 Bits? *DanielPocock.com*, June 18. http://danielpocock.com/rsa-key-sizes-2048-or-4096-bits

Rashid, F. 2011. "ZeuS Trojan Merger with SpyEye, Other Banking Malware Worry Researchers," *eWeek*, November 29. http://www.eweek.com/c/a/Security/Zeus-Trojan-Merger-with-SpyEye-Other-Banking-Malware-Worry-Researchers-648865/

Regan, K. 2001. "Hack Victim Bibliofind to Move to Amazon," *E-Commerce Times*, April 6. http://www.ecommercetimes.com/story/8768.html

Ren, K., C. Wang, and Q. Wang. 2012. "Security Challenges for the Public Cloud," *IEEE Internet Computing*, 16(1), January, 69–73.

Rivest, R. 1992. *The MD5 Message-Digest Algorithm*, IETF RFC 1321.

Sang-Hun, C. and J. Markoff. 2009. "Cyberattacks Jam Government and Commercial Web Sites in U.S. and South Korea," *New York Times*, July 7, 4.

Saraswat, P. and R. Gupta. 2012. "A Review of Digital Steganography," *Journal of Pure and Applied Science & Technology*, 2(1), January, 98–106.

Schneier, B. 2013. "The Spooks Need New Ways to Keep Their Secrets Safe," *Financial Times*, September 6, 7.

Schneier, B. 2014. "The Internet of Things Is Wildly Insecure," *Wired*, January 6. http://www.wired.com/opinion/2014/01/theres-no-good-way-to-patch-the-internet-of-things-and-thats-a-huge-problem/

Shipley, G. 2001. "Growing Up with a Little Help from the Worm," *Network Computing*, 12(20), October 1, 39.

Smith, A. 2014. "Newly Discovered Sophisticated Malware Has Been Spying on Computers for Six Years," *Newsweek*, November 24. http://europe.newsweek.com/new-sophisticated-malware-has-been-spying-computers-six-years-286640

Thompson, J. 2012. "Smartphone Security: What You Need to Know," *TechRadar.com*, February 5. http://www.techradar.com/news/phone-and-communications/mobile-phones/smartphone-security-what-you-need-to-know-1056995

Tiwari, R. 2011. "Microsoft Excel File: A Steganographic Carrier File," *Digital Crime and Forensics*, 3(1), 37–52.

U.S. National Institute of Standards and Technology. 1993. *Data Encryption Standard (DES): Federal Information Processing Standards Publication 46–2*. Gaithersburg, MD: U.S. Computer Systems Laboratory.

Vamosi, R. 2010. "New Banking Trojan Horses Gain Polish," *PC World*, January, 41–42.

Vaughan-Nichols, S. 2015. "Securing the Internet: Let's Encrypt to Release First Security Certificates September 7," *ZDNet*, August 24. http://www.zdnet.com/article/securing-the-internet-lets-encrypt/

Villeneuve, N. 2015. "TeslaCrypt: Following the Money Trail and Learning the Human Costs of Ransomware," May 15. https://www.fireeye.com/blog/threat-research/2015/05/teslacrypt_followin.html

Vishwakarma, D., S. Maheshwari, and S. Joshi. 2012. "Efficient Information Hiding Using Steganography," *International Journal of Emerging Technology and Advanced Engineering*, 2(1), January, 154–159.

Wheeler, E. 2011. *Security Risk Management: Building an Information Security Risk Management Program from the Ground Up*. Waltham, MA: Syngress.

Wilshusen, G. and D. Powner. 2009. "Cybersecurity: Continued Efforts Are Needed to Protect Information Systems from Evolving Threats," *GAO Reports*, November 17, 1–20.

Zetter, K. 2013. "Someone's Been Siphoning Data Through a Huge Security Hole in the Internet," *Wired*, December 13. http://www.wired.com/threatlevel/2013/12/bgp-hijacking-belarus-iceland/

Zetter, K. 2015. "Attackers Stole Certificate from Foxconn to Hack Kaspersky with Duqu 2.0," *Wired*, June 15. http://www.wired.com/2015/06/foxconn-hack-kaspersky-duqu-2/

Zissis, D. and D. Lekkas. 2012. "Addressing Cloud Computing Security Issues," *Future Generation Computer Systems*, 28(3), March, 583–592.

Payment Systems for Electronic Commerce

LEARNING OBJECTIVES

In this chapter, you will learn:

- What the most common online payment systems are and how they function
- How payment cards are used in online retail transactions
- What stored-value cards are and how they are used in electronic commerce
- What challenges and opportunities are presented by the use of digital cash
- How digital wallets facilitate online transactions through computers and mobile devices
- How the banking industry uses Internet technologies

INTRODUCTION

The global financial services industry has come a long way in the past 50 years. For most of the twentieth century, banking was a conservative and possibly even sleepy industry. One old joke about banking termed it the "5-4-3 business"; that is, you could succeed by simply lending money at 5 percent that you had borrowed from your customers at 4 percent and be on the golf course by 3 p.m. Today, the financial services industry is no longer simple and is often not conservative, as those who suffered through the savings and loan crisis of the 1980s and the global financial crisis of the late 2000s can attest.

The complexity of today's many different kinds of financing arrangements and investment opportunities has given birth to a branch of the industry often called financial technology. **Financial technology** (or **fintech**) is the use of powerful computers connected through the Internet that use tools such as Web services (which you learned about in Chapter 9) to improve the quality while reducing the costs of existing financial services and, more importantly, to create entirely new types of financial products and services.

Payment services that are not operated by banks at all are one of these new products. These services include PayPal, the pioneer, and later variations such as Amazon Payments, Android Pay, Apple Pay, Google Wallet, Square, Venmo, among many others. In addition to allowing users to pay for online purchases easily, these services enable cash transfers among individuals for loans, gifts, or expense sharing. They offered more convenience than the banking system's checking accounts did and have been widely adopted, especially as Internet-connected mobile devices became widespread.

In addition to changing the way payments are made, financial technology has revolutionized lending. Online loan facilitators such as Lending Club and Funding Circle take banks out of the industry value chain for loan services by matching pools of lenders with borrowers directly. By collecting large amounts of data from social networks and other online sources about potential borrowers, loan facilitators such as OnDeck can reduce lenders' risk. All of these firms reduce costs; according to one 2015 report in *The Economist*, their operating expenses run about 2 percent of their total outstanding loan balances compared with 5–7 percent at traditional banks.

In this chapter, you will learn how these financial technologies operate in online payment systems and in stored-value cards. You will also learn how existing forms of payment, such as credit cards, are used in online business.

Common Online Payment Methods

An important element of electronic commerce is the need for online payments. As you learned in Chapter 5, many B2B transactions are completed using electronic funds transfers (EFTs). In this chapter, you will learn about other online payment systems used by both businesses and individual consumers.

Cash, checks, credit cards, and debit cards are the four most common methods used in the world by consumers to pay for purchases overall (that is, including both online and in physical stores). These four payment methods account for more than 90 percent of all consumer payments in the United States today. Only a small percentage of consumer payments are made by electronic transfer of any kind, with most of those being automated payments for auto loans, insurance, and home mortgages that are made from consumers' checking accounts.

Cash and checks are difficult to use online, so more than 60 percent of B2C online payments in the United States are made using credit or debit cards, with alternative payment systems (predominantly PayPal) accounting for most of the remainder. Most industry analysts expect that the use of credit and debit cards will continue to decrease as the use of alternative payment systems grows. An increasing proportion of all of these payments are made using mobile devices. Figure 11-1 shows forecasted forms of U.S. B2C online payments for 2018.

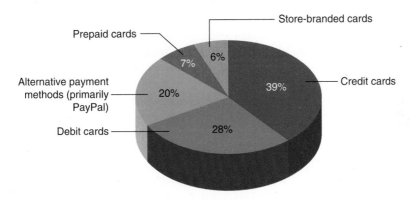

FIGURE 11-1   Forms of payment for U.S. B2C transactions, estimates for 2018

Source: Adapted from forecasts by *Internet Retailer*, Javelin Strategy & Research and *The Nilson Report.*

Online payments can be convenient for customers and can save companies money. Estimates of the cost of billing one person by mail range between $1 and $1.50. Sending bills and receiving payments over the Internet can drop the transaction cost to an average of 50 cents per bill. The total savings is huge when the unit cost is multiplied by the number of customers who could pay online. For example, a telephone company in a major metropolitan area might have 5 million customers, each of whom receives a bill every month. In one year, a savings of 50 cents on each of those 60 million bills adds up to about $30 million. The environmental impact is also significant. Those 60 million paper bills weigh about 1.7 million pounds. It takes 2200 trees to make that much paper—in addition to the energy consumed and the wastes generated in the paper-making process.

Electronic Bill Presentment and Payment Systems

Paying bills online saves money and can be convenient for customers if the process does not require them to change their behavior very much. **Electronic bill presentment and payment (EBPP) systems** are designed to deliver bills and accept payment for them online. To be successful, they must be easier to use and less time consuming for customers than opening a bill received in the mail, writing a check, and mailing that check back to the biller. The Internet provides a good way to accomplish this.

Since online bill payments were first introduced in the early 2000s, the proportion of consumers that choose this option has been steadily increasing. Industry experts estimate that some 70 percent of all consumer bills that were once paid using paper checks are now paid electronically. Online billing and payment systems generate huge savings in postage and paper costs, but billers also receive remittances 3–12 days faster, which can dramatically improve their cash flow.

There are two types of EBPP systems currently in use. The first, called **biller-direct EBPP systems**, are used by large companies who want to manage and maintain their own systems. Utilities, telephone companies, and financial services companies (for payments on credit cards, mortgage and auto loans, and so on) are the primary users of biller-direct systems. Companies that want to implement a biller-direct system can develop their own software or buy software already designed for the purpose. Another option is to contract with a service provider who will operate its biller-direct system on the company's Web site.

The second type of system is called a **consolidator EBPP system**, in which a separate company (the consolidator) aggregates all of a customer's bills on its system. That system can be delivered on the consolidator's Web site or, more often, delivered on the Web site of the customer's financial institution (for example, a bank or credit union). Consolidator systems are not as attractive to billers as bill-direct systems because the consolidator providing the service must be paid a fee and a delay (although not as long as the delay when using paper) is introduced into the system.

Bill payers are generally unwilling to incur a fee to pay bills online and are unlikely to trust a financial service provider that is not known to them, so consolidators have not had much success in marketing their services to the general public. Most consolidator EBPP systems are operated by banks or credit unions as a service to their customers. Leading firms that offer software and service options for EBPP include Intuit (for biller-direct systems), Yodlee (for consolidator systems), and Fiserv (for both types of systems).

Micropayments and Small Payments

Internet payments for items costing from a few cents to approximately a dollar are called **micropayments**. One issue with micropayments is a matter of human psychology. Researchers have found that many people prefer to buy small-value items by making regular fixed-amount payments rather than by making small payments in varying amounts, even when the small varying payments would cost less money overall. An example of this behavior is the preference most mobile telephone users have for fixed monthly payment plans over charges based on minutes used. They prefer the predictability of knowing exactly what their monthly payments will be to the possibility that they will pay less in some months because their usage is lower.

Many companies have tried to establish successful systems to process micropayments. Millicent, DigiCash, Yaga, and BitPass were among the companies that entered this business and failed. Industry observers see a need for a micropayments processing system on the Web, but no company has gained broad acceptance of its system. The companies who entered this market used systems that either accumulated micropayments and charged them periodically to a credit card or accepted a deposit and charged the micropayments against that deposit. Some companies that offer digital cash and bill paying services do provide micropayment capabilities as part of their services, but no company is currently devoted solely to offering micropayment services.

Payments between $1 and $10 do not have a generally accepted name (some industry observers use the term micropayment to describe any payment of less than $10); in this book, the term **small payments** is used to describe all payments of less than $10. Mobile telephone carriers are currently the most widely used small payments services. Buyers make their purchases using their mobile phones and the charges appear on the buyers' monthly mobile phone bill. The use of this micropayment system has been held back by the mobile carriers' substantial charges for providing the service, which can amount to 30 percent of each transaction. The company that offers the service typically takes another 5 percent, thus the buyer can end up paying substantially more than the actual value of the purchase. One of the largest small payments markets today is for music downloads. Most of the music and smartphone software downloads sold by Amazon and Apple (iTunes) are paid by credit card. Sales through the Google Play store are primarily paid as charges on the customer's monthly mobile phone bill.

In the following sections, you will learn about four payment technologies: payment cards, digital cash, software wallets, and stored-value cards. Each technology has unique properties, costs, advantages, and disadvantages.

Payment Cards

Businesspeople often use the term **payment card** as a general term to describe all types of plastic cards that consumers (and many businesses) use to make purchases. The main categories of payment cards are credit cards, debit cards, charge cards, prepaid cards, and gift cards.

A **credit card**, such as a Visa or MasterCard, has a spending limit based on the user's credit history; a user can pay off the entire credit card balance or pay a minimum amount each billing period. Credit card issuers charge interest on any unpaid balance. Many consumers already have credit cards, or are at least familiar with how they work. Credit cards are widely accepted by merchants around the world and provide assurances for both the consumer and the merchant. A consumer is protected by an automatic 30-day period in which he or she can dispute an online credit card purchase. Online credit card purchases are similar to telephone purchases in that the card holder is not present and cannot provide proof of identity as easily as he or she can when standing at the cash register. Online and telephone purchases are often called **card not present transactions** and both include an extra degree of risk for merchants and banks.

A debit card looks like a credit card, but it works quite differently. Instead of charging purchases against a credit line, a **debit card** removes the amount of the sale from the cardholder's bank account and transfers it to the seller's bank account. Debit cards are also called **electronic funds transfer at point of sale (EFTPOS) cards**, especially outside the United States. Debit cards are issued by the cardholder's bank and usually carry the name of a major credit card issuer, such as Visa or MasterCard, by agreement between the issuing bank and the credit card issuer. By branding their debit cards (with the Visa or MasterCard name), banks ensure that their debit cards will be accepted by merchants who recognize the credit card brand names.

A **charge card**, offered by companies such as American Express, carries no spending limit, and the entire amount charged to the card is due at the end of the billing period. Charge cards do not involve lines of credit and do not accumulate interest charges. (*Note:* In addition to its charge card products, American Express also offers credit cards, which do have credit limits and which do accumulate interest on unpaid balances.) In the United States, many retailers, such as department stores and oil companies that own gas stations, issue their own charge cards. Cards issued by a specific retailer, such as Exxon fuel stations or Kohl's department store, are sometimes called **store charge cards** or **store-branded cards**. The purchasing cards (or p-cards) that you learned about in Chapter 5 can be either credit cards or charge cards.

Many retailers offer cards that can be redeemed by anyone for future purchases. They can also be used to make small purchases that would be expensive for a merchant to process as credit card sales. More often, they are given to third parties as gifts. Prepaid cards sold with the intention that they be given as gifts are called **gift cards**. Gift cards are available for a range of merchants, from Starbucks to Lowe's to the Apple iTunes store. These **prepaid cards** are sometimes used by people who do not want to be tempted by a credit card to purchase more than they can afford.

To address consumer concerns about providing their payment card numbers online, several payment card companies have offered cards with disposable numbers. These cards, sometimes called **single-use cards**, gave consumers a unique card number that was valid for one transaction only. Most of these card issuers found that people did not use them and withdrew them from the market. Single-use cards required consumers to behave differently and not enough consumers saw a clear benefit to justify their learning how to use this new product.

Advantages and Disadvantages of Payment Cards

Payment cards have several features that make them a popular choice for both consumers and merchants in online and offline transactions. For merchants, payment cards provide fraud protection. When a merchant accepts payment cards for online payment or for orders placed over the telephone, the merchant can authenticate and authorize purchases using an interchange network. An **interchange network** is a set of connections between banks that issue credit cards, the associations that own the credit cards (such as MasterCard or Visa), and merchants' banks. You will learn more about interchange networks and how this system operates later in this chapter. For U.S. consumers, the Consumer Credit Protection Act limits the cardholder's liability to \$50 if the card is used fraudulently. Once the cardholder notifies the card's issuer of the card theft, the cardholder's liability ends. Frequently, the payment card's issuer waives the \$50 liability when a card is used fraudulently. Some other countries have similar laws, but this type of protection is not widespread outside the United States.

Payment card service companies do charge merchants per-transaction fees and monthly processing fees for processing payments, however, merchants consider them as a necessary cost of doing business. The consumer pays no per-transaction fees for using payment cards, but the prices of goods and services are slightly higher than they would be in an environment free of payment cards. Some credit cards and a few debit cards and charge cards assess consumers an annual fee.

Payment Acceptance and Processing

In a physical store, the customer or a sales clerk runs the card through the online payment card terminal and the card account is charged immediately. In this type of in-person transaction, customers walk out of the store with purchases in their possession, so charging and shipment occur nearly simultaneously. Online stores and mail order stores in the United States must ship merchandise within 30 days of charging a payment card. Because the penalties for violating this law can be significant, most online and mail order merchants do not charge payment card accounts until they ship merchandise.

Processing a payment card transaction online involves two general processes, the acceptance of payment and clearing the transaction. Payment acceptance includes the steps necessary to determine that the card is valid and that the transaction will not exceed any credit limit that might exist for the card. Clearing the transaction includes all of the steps needed to move the funds from the card holder's bank account into the merchant's bank account. This section outlines the steps involved in both of these processes.

OPEN AND CLOSED LOOP SYSTEMS

In some payment card systems, the card issuer pays the merchants that accept the card directly and does not use an intermediary, such as a bank or clearinghouse system. These types of arrangements are called **closed loop systems** because no other institution is involved in the transaction. American Express and Discover Card are examples of closed loop systems. Figure 11-2 shows the basic interactions among the entities involved in a closed loop payment card system.

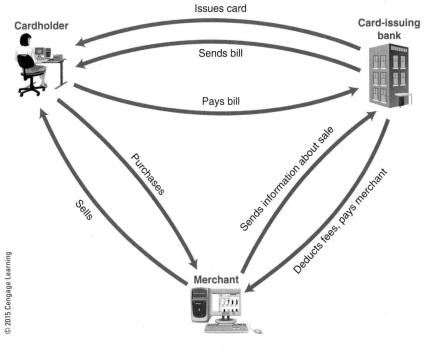

© 2015 Cengage Learning

FIGURE 11-2   Closed loop payment card system

Open loop systems add additional payment processing intermediaries to the structure of a closed loop system. Suppose an Internet shopper uses a Visa card issued by the First Bank of Woodland to purchase an item from Web Wonders, whose merchant account is at the Hackensack Commerce Bank. The banking system includes one or more intermediaries (banks or other types of payment processing companies) that coordinate the transfer of funds from the First Bank of Woodland to the Hackensack Commerce Bank. Whenever additional parties, such as the intermediaries in this example, are included in payment card transaction processing, the system is called an **open loop system**. Visa and MasterCard are two of the most widely known examples of open loop systems. Many banks issue both of these cards.

Unlike American Express or Discover, neither Visa nor MasterCard issues cards directly to consumers. Visa and MasterCard are **credit card associations** that are operated by the banks who are members in the associations. These member banks, which are called **customer issuing banks** or **issuing banks**, issue credit cards to individual consumers. The issuing banks are responsible for evaluating their customers' credit standings and establishing appropriate individual credit limits. If a cardholder does not pay, the issuing bank absorbs the loss. Figure 11-3 shows the basic interactions among the entities involved in an open loop payment card system.

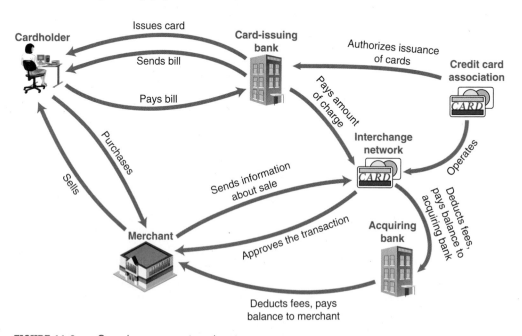

FIGURE 11-3   Open loop payment card system

MERCHANT ACCOUNTS

An **acquiring bank** is a bank that does business with sellers (both Internet and non-Internet) that want to accept payment cards. To process payment cards for Internet transactions, a business must set up a **merchant account** with an acquiring bank.

One type of merchant account is similar to a regular business checking account; the merchant's acquiring bank collects credit card receipts on behalf of the merchant from the payment card-issuing bank and credits their value, net of processing fees, to the merchant's account. More commonly, a merchant account is set up to operate as a credit line rather than as a checking account; that is, the acquiring bank makes what is essentially a non-interest-bearing loan to the merchant in the amount of the net credit card receipts each day. As the acquiring bank collects the proceeds of the transactions from the issuing bank, the acquiring bank reduces the balance of the non-interest-bearing loan to the merchant.

A seller must provide information about its business operations to an acquiring bank before it will set up a merchant account. Typically, a new merchant must supply a business plan, details about existing bank accounts, and a business and personal credit history. The acquiring bank wants to be sure that the merchant has a good prospect of staying in business and wants to minimize its risk. If the merchant is new or is not doing well financially, the acquiring bank might ask for a deposit or personal guarantees of the owners or stockholders of the merchant. In some cases, the acquiring bank will demand that collateral (the owner's house, for example) be assigned.

The riskiness of the business also influences the acquiring bank's decision to provide a merchant account. Some types of businesses have a higher likelihood that customers will contest card charges than others. For example, a business that sells a guaranteed weight loss scheme—a business in which many customers might want their money back—might have difficulty finding an acquiring bank willing to provide a merchant account. The bank assesses the level of risk in the business based on the type of business and the credit information that is provided. Acquiring banks must estimate what percentage of sales are likely to be contested by cardholders. When a cardholder successfully contests a charge, the acquiring bank must retrieve the money it placed in the merchant account in a process called a **chargeback**. To ensure that sufficient funds are available to cover chargebacks, an acquiring bank might require a company to maintain funds on deposit in the merchant account. For example, a new or risky business that plans to make $100,000 in sales each month might be required to keep $50,000 or more on deposit in its merchant account.

In addition to chargeback deductions, the acquiring bank will deduct fees from the gross sales amount in determining the net amount to credit the merchant each day. These fees include **acquirer fees**, which are charged by the acquiring bank for providing the payment card processing service, and **interchange fees**, which are charged at rates that depend on the merchant's industry. Acquirer fees usually include a charge per month and per transaction and are set by the acquiring bank. The interchange fee rates are set by the card association itself (for example, Visa or MasterCard) and charged to the acquiring bank, which generally passes the cost along to the merchant.

One problem facing online businesses is that the level of fraud in online transactions is much higher than either in-person or telephone transactions of the same nature (that is, the same amount and the same type of good or service being purchased). Fewer than 15 percent of all credit card transactions are completed online, but those transactions are responsible for about 64 percent of the total dollar amount of credit card fraud.

According to a series of annual surveys conducted by credit card research company Cybersource, the proportion of online transactions that are fraudulent increased steadily every year from the inception of electronic commerce through 2008. Since 2008, that proportion has been trending gradually downward. Online fraud experts believe that this decline in fraud losses is a result of merchants' increased use of antifraud measures. These antifraud measures include the use of fraud scoring services that provide risk ratings for individual transactions in real time, shipping only to the card billing address, and requiring **card verification numbers (CVNs)** for card not present transactions. A CVN is a three- or four-digit number that is printed on the credit card, but is not encoded in the card's magnetic strip. Having a CVN establishes that the purchaser has the card (or has seen the card) and is more likely not to be using a stolen card number. The CVN is also known by a number of different names and acronyms, including **card security code (CSC)**, **card verification data (CVD)**, **card verification value (CVV or CV2)**, **card verification value code (CVVC)**, **card verification code (CVC)**, **verification code (V-Code or V Code)**, and **card code verification (CCV)**. The next section outlines payment card authorization and payment processing options for online businesses.

PAYMENT CARD TRANSACTION PROCESSING

Most online merchants accept both closed loop system cards (such as American Express and Discover) and open loop system cards (such as MasterCard and Visa), their internal payment processing systems must be able to work with both types of cards. In addition, some online merchants accept direct deductions from customers' checking accounts. These direct deduction transactions are done through a network of banks called the **Automated Clearing House (ACH)**. Issuing banks, interchange networks, and acquiring banks also use the ACH network to transfer funds to clear their card payment accounts with each other, so this network is an important part of online payment processing. The ACH provides a standardized funds transfer system and gives each participant a verified audit trail and nonrepudiation. These benefits are similar to those provided to EDI trading partners by a VAN, as you learned in Chapter 5. You can learn more about ACHs by following the Web Links to the EPN, NACHA—The Electronic Payments Association, and The Clearing House. The U.S. Federal Reserve Bank's FedACH Services site also has information about the operation of the ACH.

Processing payment card transactions that might be from a debit card or a credit card, that might need open loop or closed loop processing, or that might even involve the ACH directly is a complex task. Large online businesses have entire departments of highly skilled employees who build and maintain the systems needed to accomplish this work. Midsized online businesses often purchase software (separately or as part of an electronic commerce software package) that handles the processing, but they must hire skilled employees to manage the activity.

Small online businesses often do not have the resources to manage this function in-house, even with purchased software. They generally rely on a service provider either to assist them in processing payment card transactions or to handle the entire function for them. These service providers are called **payment processing service providers** or **payment processors** and are usually grouped into two general types, front-end processors and back-end processors.

A **front-end processor** obtains authorization for the transaction by sending the transaction's details to the interchange network and storing a record of the approval or denial (a process which usually takes less than a second). Front-end processors (or the hardware and software that they use to obtain transaction approvals) are often called **payment gateways**. A **back-end processor** takes the transactions from the front-end processor and coordinates information flows through the interchange network to settle the transactions. The back-end processor handles chargebacks and any other reconciliation items through the interchange network and the acquiring and issuing banks, including the ACH transfers.

Some payment processors, such as IPPay, Authorize.Net, Global Payments, and FirstData, handle all elements of payment processing, including the payment gateway function, front-end processing, and back-end processing. Other companies specialize in handling just one element of the process or in a particular industry. For example, Digital River specializes in providing payment processing services for online businesses that sell downloadable software and games.

Many payment processors work with electronic commerce software in ways that prevent a customer from realizing that a separate company is handling their credit card transactions. For online sellers with established reputations, this is beneficial because it prevents customers from worrying that another entity will be handling their credit card information. However, a number of payment processors open their Web sites in a new window to process the payment transaction. In these cases, the customer becomes aware that their payment transaction is being handled by a third party. Payment processors that operate this way include eBay's PayPal and BillMeLater services, Checkout by Amazon, Google Checkout, ClickandBuy, and Digital River's share*it! service. For smaller online sellers or new businesses that do not yet have a well-established reputation, using a payment processor with a well-known name like Amazon or Google to handle the card payment part of their transactions can help customers feel comfortable with providing their credit card information.

Stored-Value Cards

Today, most people carry a number of plastic cards—credit cards, debit cards, subway card, charge cards, driver's license, health insurance card, employee or student identification card, and others. These cards store information electronically using either a magnetic strip or a microchip that is embedded into the card. Most magnetic strip cards hold value that can be recharged by inserting them into the appropriate machines, inserting currency into the machine, and withdrawing the card; the card's strip stores the increased cash value. Magnetic strip cards are passive; that is, they cannot send or receive information, nor can they increment or decrement the value of cash stored on the card. The processing must be done on a device into which the card is inserted.

A **stored-value card** is a plastic card with an embedded microchip that can store information. The microchip can also include a tiny computer processor that can perform calculations and storage operations right on the card. Most of these cards incorporate **near field communication (NFC)** technology, which allows for contactless data transmission over short distances (generally less than about 25 inches), so the computer processor in the microchip can interact with readers and other devices.

A stored-value card can store more than 100 times the amount of information that a magnetic strip plastic card can store. Thus, a stored-value card can hold private user data, such as financial facts, encryption keys, account information, credit card numbers, health insurance information, medical records, and so on.

Stored-value cards are safer than magnetic strip credit cards because the information stored on a smart card can be encrypted. For example, conventional credit cards display the account number on the face of the card and the cardholder's signature on the back. The card number and a forged signature are all that a thief needs to purchase items on someone else's card. Stored-value cards make this type of theft much more difficult because the key to unlock the encrypted information is a PIN; there is no visible CVN on the card that a thief can identify, nor is there a physical signature on the card that a thief can see and use as an example for a forgery.

NFC-enabled stored-value cards have been in use since the late 1990s and became widely used in Europe and parts of Asia with consumers paying for telephone calls at public phones and television programs delivered to homes via cable. They have not been as successful in the United States. Stored-value cards became popular in Hong Kong, where many restaurant and retail store cash registers have built-in smart card readers. Hong Kong's transportation companies; including subways, buses, railways, trams, and ferries; joined together to create a stored-value card called the Octopus that let commuters use one card for all of their public transportation needs. The Octopus card, now owned and administered by an independent company, can be reloaded at any transportation location or at 7-Eleven stores throughout Hong Kong. Similar cards are now widely used in Europe and throughout Asia.

In the United States, stored-value card use has increased somewhat in recent years, but it is still not widespread. In San Francisco, the Bay Area Metropolitan Transportation Commission patterned its TransLink smart card system after the Octopus Card. A number of fuel companies have created their own smart cards that customers can swipe at the pump to pay for gasoline purchases. MasterCard has seen an increase in the use of its PayPass smart cards in the United States as well.

Digital Cash

Although credit cards dominate online payments today, digital cash shows some promise for the future. **Digital cash** (also called e-cash or electronic cash) is a general term that describes any value storage and exchange system created by a private (nongovernmental) entity that does not use paper documents or coins and that can serve as a substitute for government-issued physical currency. A successful electronic cash system will need common standards so that one issuer's digital cash can be accepted by another issuer. To date, each digital cash issuer has created its own standards; thus none of them has become widely accepted.

Digital cash can be held in online storage or offline storage. Online cash storage means that the consumer does not personally possess digital cash. Instead, a trusted third party, such as an online bank, coordinates all transfers of digital cash and holds the consumers' cash accounts. In an online storage system, the merchant must contact the consumer's bank to receive payment for a purchase. This helps prevent fraud by confirming that the consumer's cash is valid.

In the United States, most consumers have credit cards, debit cards, charge cards, and checking accounts. These payment alternatives work well for U.S. consumers in both online and offline transactions. In many other countries, especially in the developing world, consumers prefer to use cash. Because cash is difficult to use for online transactions, digital cash fills an important need for consumers in those countries as they conduct B2C electronic commerce. This type of need does not exist in the United States because U.S. consumers already use payment cards for traditional commerce, and these payment cards work well for electronic commerce.

The most well-known digital cash provider today is **Bitcoin**. In 2008, a person who remains anonymous created Bitcoin as a digital currency that was independent of banks and government control of any kind. Bitcoin uses an online ledger book in which each participant's balance is public information and transactions are recorded between anonymous individuals. Participants' network addresses are confirmed using public-key cryptography, which maintains their anonymity. Because Bitcoin is an encrypted form of currency, it is sometimes called a **cryptocurrency**.

Although some merchants (such as TigerDirect.com and WordPress online and local physical retailers, primarily in the San Francisco Bay area) accept Bitcoins as payment for purchases, a large proportion of Bitcoin transactions are used to make illegal purchases (such as drugs), or to engage in currency speculation (the traded value of Bitcoins has ranged from under $1 to over $1200). In 2014, about 90 percent of Bitcoins were held by speculators rather than by individuals who expect to use the digital currency to make purchases. As a currency that lacks stability and has no country's legal system to back it, Bitcoin is of limited use in everyday transactions. Experts disagree on the future viability of Bitcoin; however, some believe it has great potential for adoption around the world.

Although Bitcoin is the largest global provider of digital cash, other companies operate digital cash systems that are popular in specific geographic areas. For example, Ukash has been widely used in the United Kingdom and Paysafecard, based in Vienna, has been popular in much of Western Europe.

Concerns about digital cash include privacy and security, independence, portability, and convenience. Users of digital cash want to know whether transactions are vulnerable and whether the electronic currency can be copied, reused, or forged. Two characteristics of physical currency are important to have in any digital cash implementation. First, it must be impossible to spend digital cash more than once, just as with traditional currency. Second, digital cash ought to be anonymous, just as currency is. **Anonymous digital cash** is digital cash that, like bills and coins, cannot be traced back to the person who spent it. The digital cash transaction must occur between the two parties only, and the recipient must know that the electronic currency is not counterfeit or being used in two different transactions at the same time. Perhaps the most important characteristic of cash is convenience. If digital cash requires special hardware or software, it is not convenient for people to use. Chances are good that people will not adopt a digital cash system that is difficult to use.

The Double Spending Issue

Protection against fraud is still a concern, so either hardware or software must be used to prevent fraudulent spending or double spending. **Double spending** is spending a particular piece of digital cash twice by submitting the same electronic currency to two different vendors. When the electronic currency reaches the bank for clearance a second time, it is too late to prevent the fraudulent act. The main deterrent to double spending is the threat of detection and prosecution. Thus, digital cash must be traceable back to its origin. A two-part lock provides anonymous security but signals when someone is attempting to double spend cash. When a second attempted transaction is made with the same digital cash, the system must detect and prevent that transaction. Figure 11-4 shows a graphic representation of this double-spending detection process.

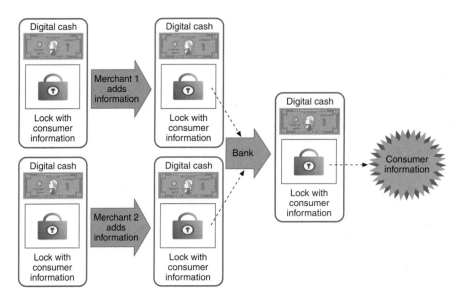

FIGURE 11-4   Detecting double spending of digital cash

Advantages and Disadvantages of Digital Cash

Digital cash transactions can be more efficient (and therefore less costly) than other payment methods because these transfers occur on the Internet, which is an existing infrastructure. Transferring digital cash on the Internet costs less than processing credit card transactions. Conventional money exchange systems require banks, bank branches, clerks, automated teller machines, and an electronic transaction system to manage, transfer, and dispense cash. In addition, digital cash does not require that one party obtain an authorization, as is required with credit card transactions.

Digital cash does have disadvantages, however, and they are significant. Using digital cash provides no audit trail; that is, digital cash is just like real cash in that it cannot be easily traced. Because true digital cash is not traceable, another problem arises: money laundering. **Money laundering** is a technique used by criminals to convert money that they have obtained illegally into cash that they can spend without having it identified as the proceeds of an illegal activity. Money laundering can be accomplished by purchasing goods or services with ill-gotten digital cash. The goods are then sold for physical cash on the open market.

Because no system of digital cash is not backed by a bank or a government (at least none has been thus far), users face some risks when using it that derive from that specific fact. For example, if a digital cash system does become widely used, it might then become the target of government regulatory actions designed to control it, stop its growth, or otherwise take away one or more of the reasons for its existence. In 2014, China required its banks to stop trading in Bitcoin; in the United States, the New York legislature considered a bill that would regulate Bitcoin (the bill did not become law).

Technological advances could allow a newer kind of digital cash to emerge one day that would render existing digital cash systems obsolete, making the digital cash worthless.

Digital Wallets

Many consumers have begun to tire of repeatedly entering detailed shipping and payment information each time they make online purchases. To simplify the online checkout process, many electronic commerce sites include a feature that allows a customer to store their name, address, and credit card information on the site. However, consumers must enter their information at each site with which they want to do business. A **digital wallet**, serving a function similar to a physical wallet, is an electronic device or software that can store credit card numbers, digital cash, owner identification, and owner contact information and provide that information to an online business at checkout. Digital wallets give consumers the benefit of entering their information just once, instead of having to enter their information at every site with which they want to do business.

Software-Based Digital Wallets

Software-based digital wallets fall into two categories, depending on where they are stored. A **server-side digital wallet** stores a customer's information on a remote server belonging to a particular merchant or wallet publisher.

The main weakness of server-side digital wallets is that a security breach could reveal thousands of users' personal information to unauthorized parties. Typically, server-side digital wallets employ strong security measures that minimize the possibility of unauthorized disclosure.

A **client-side digital wallet** stores information on the customer's computer. Many early digital wallets were client-side wallets that required users to download the wallet software. This need to download software onto every computer used to make purchases is a chief disadvantage of client-side wallets. Server-side wallets, on the other hand, remain on a server and thus require no download time or installation on a user's computer. Before a consumer can use a server-side wallet on a particular merchant's site, the merchant must enable that specific wallet. Each wallet vendor must convince a large number of merchants to enable its wallet before it will be accepted by consumers. Thus, only a few server-side wallet vendors will be able to succeed in the market.

A disadvantage of client-side wallets is that they are not portable. For example, a client-side wallet is not available when a purchase is made from a computer other than the computer on which the wallet resides. This removes the risk that an attack on a client-side digital wallet vendor's server could reveal the sensitive information. However, an attack on the user's computer could yield that information. Most security analysts agree that storing sensitive information on client computers is safer than storing that information on the vendor server because it requires attackers to launch many attacks on user computers, which are more difficult to identify (even though the user computers are less likely than a vendor server to have strong security features installed). Google Wallet, Microsoft Windows Live ID, and Yahoo! Wallet are the most widely used server-side digital wallets in use today.

Hardware-Based Digital Wallets

Smartphones and tablets, as mobile devices, can be used as **hardware-based digital wallets** that can store a variety of identity credentials (such as a driver's license, medical insurance card, store loyalty cards, and other identifying documents). The smartphone can transmit portions of this identity information on command using its Bluetooth or wireless transmission capability to nearby terminals. The NFC technology you learned about earlier in this chapter, which allows for contactless data transmission over short distances, can also be used if the smartphone is equipped with an NFC chip.

NFC chips have been used in the United States for a number of years on payment cards such as MasterCard's PayPass card. NFC chips embedded in mobile phones were first widely used in Japan, where the devices are called *Osaifu-Keitai*, which translates approximately to "mobile wallet."

In the United States, a number of hardware-based digital wallets for mobile devices have been released. Google Wallet, which uses the PayPass technology that MasterCard developed for its credit cards, became available for mobile devices in 2011. Google followed with a variation of that product, Android Pay, introduced in 2015. PayPal bought the digital wallet Venmo in 2013 and Apple Pay became available in 2014. Amazon announced a digital wallet in 2014, but quickly decided to let other companies compete for this market and discontinued its digital wallet in 2015. Some industry observers expect banks to enter the digital wallet business; however, others believe it might be too late for them to overcome the foothold established by companies such as Apple, Google, and PayPal.

Security is a major concern for users of mobile device digital wallets. The digital wallet stores information relating to one or more credit cards that the wallet owner uses to fund transactions. In some digital wallets, that information is stored on the device; however, it is more secure to store the credit card information (in encrypted files) on a server maintained by the digital wallet provider. Since mobile devices are easily lost or stolen, a good digital wallet must prevent unauthorized access. Apple Pay, which is designed for use only on Apple devices, uses the iPhone Touch ID button, which requires the owner's fingerprint for access. The NFC communication between the mobile device and the reader could be intercepted, so that should be encrypted and should not transmit credit card or other identity-related information.

Privacy is an issue with mobile device digital wallets as well. Banks record their customers' credit card transactions in detail and generate considerable revenue selling that information (or summaries of it) to other companies who are interested in what kind of consumers purchased what kind of products along with where and when the purchases occurred. The operator of a digital wallet system must decide whether to follow this tradition, which can invade customers' privacy, or not.

Internet Technologies and the Banking Industry

The largest dollar volume of payments in the world today is still made using paper checks. These paper checks are processed through the international banking system. The other major payment forms in use today also involve banks in one way or another. This section outlines how Internet technologies are providing new tools and creating new threats for the banking industry.

Check Processing

In the past, checks were processed physically by banks and clearinghouses. When a person wrote a check to pay for an item at a retail store, the retailer would deposit the check in its bank account. The retailer's bank would then send the paper check to a clearinghouse, which would manage the transfer of funds from the consumer's bank to the retailer's account. The paper check would then be transported to the consumer's bank, which might then send the cancelled check to the consumer. In recent years, many banks have stopped sending cancelled checks to their consumer account holders to save postage, instead providing access to PDF images of processed checks to account folders. Despite these savings, the cost of transporting tons of paper checks around the country has grown each year.

In addition to the transportation costs, another disadvantage of using paper checks is the delay that occurs between the time that a person writes a check and the time that check clears the person's bank. This delay (which is similar to the delay you learned about earlier in PayPal accounts, and which is also called **float**) makes it possible to write checks a few days before money is in the account to cover those checks. In effect, the bank's customer obtains the free use of funds for a few days and the bank loses the use of those funds for the same time period. Although the delay normally lasts only a few days, there are times when it can become significantly longer. Railroad and airline strikes, for example, have caused the float to be extended. The terrorist attacks of September 11, 2001, caused a significant increase in the float.

Banks have been working for years to develop technologies that will help them reduce the float. In 2004, a U.S. law went into effect that has done just that. This law, the Check Clearing for the 21st Century Act (usually referred to as **Check 21**), permits banks to eliminate the movement of physical checks entirely. Today, retailers can scan a customer's check. The scanned image is transmitted instantly through a clearing system and posts almost immediately to both accounts (that is, the withdrawal from the customer's account and the deposit to the retailer's account occur instantly), eliminating any float on the transaction. You can learn more about the Check 21 law and its implementation by following this book's Web Links to the Federal Reserve Financial Services - Check 21-Enabled Services pages or the American Bankers Association Check 21 Resource Center.

LEARNING FROM FAILURES

NetBank

CompuBank and NetBank were two of the first Internet banks to open in the United States. They were both pure Internet banks; that is, neither was founded by an existing bank with a physical presence. After four years of operation, CompuBank had about 50,000 accounts and $64 million of deposits and was losing more than $20 million per year. NetBank had done considerably better, with 160,000 accounts and $1 billion of deposits and 10 consecutive quarters of profitability.

In early 2001, CompuBank decided to close its operations and found NetBank to be a willing purchaser of its accounts. When a bank buys accounts from another bank, it performs a series of procedures called due diligence. These **due diligence** procedures include checking the new customers' credit histories and banking records. Due diligence is usually performed before the transaction is completed and before the closing bank's customers look to the buying bank as the institution that will handle their accounts.

For a number of reasons, not all of which are clear, the due diligence process was still under way on the date that the transfer of accounts was to take place. NetBank placed holds on many accounts and sent letters to many account holders explaining that they were not acceptable customers by NetBank standards. For any bank, this would have been a difficult situation, but the nature of the two banks as Internet-only operations made things considerably worse for everyone.

Press accounts of the fiasco included stories of the problems that between 4000 and 8000 CompuBank depositors experienced. Some of the problems were small—online bill payments did not occur, debit and credit cards were rejected at stores and restaurants, and ATMs would not yield cash—while others were much larger. One couple who had kept the money to cover closing costs on a house purchase in a CompuBank account found that NetBank had placed a hold on the money. Because they could not pay the closing costs, they were forced to find another mortgage lender. In the suit they filed against NetBank, the couple asserted that the increased rate on the mortgage loan would cost them tens of thousands of dollars. Other CompuBank customers were irritated that they lost access to their money for weeks. Some customers could not determine whether the bills they had set up to be paid automatically had, in fact, been paid.

NetBank admitted failures in customer service related to the incident. Many customers who called to complain or ask for explanations experienced 45-minute waits on hold and then were transferred to the bank's Security Department, where a recording answered and asked callers to leave their Social Security numbers and wait to be called back. None of the customers reported being called back. The timing of NetBank's notification was problematic, too. Many customers reported receiving a letter from NetBank indicating that there were problems with their accounts. The letter, dated April 30, was received by the customers on or after May 14. The letter included a telephone number to call for assistance, but that number had been disconnected on May 12. Many of the unhappy customers found each other on Internet discussion boards and compared notes.

NetBank has never disclosed the number of customers it lost by its handling of this transition; indeed, it may not know. CompuBank's customers were largely experienced Internet users who chose to be part of the leading edge in handling their financial affairs. Many of them, after this experience, have sworn that they will never again do business with a bank that does not have a physical presence. The lesson from NetBank's experience is that customer service and the ability to communicate with customers become extremely important for companies that process electronic payments or are responsible for their customers' finances.

Mobile Banking

In Chapter 6, you learned about new opportunities that are emerging for businesses that want to reach customers who use smartphones and other mobile devices to connect to the Internet. In recent years, banks have begun to explore the potential of mobile commerce in their businesses, too.

Most banks today offer mobile apps that allow customers using smartphones or tablet devices to obtain their bank balances, view their account statements, or find a nearby ATM.

Many banks' mobile apps enable customers to transact all types of banking business, including the option of taking a picture of a check with the smartphone's camera and depositing it into their bank accounts electronically. Several vendors, including Intuit GoPayment and Square, offer a tiny credit card reader that can be attached to a mobile device to make it a highly portable payment processing terminal. This allows businesses (or their employees) to process customer credit card payments virtually anywhere. These devices have become popular with residential service businesses (electricians, plumbers, and landscapers, for example) because they allow the employee to collect payment immediately after delivering the service.

Payment System Threats: Phishing and Identity Theft

Online payment systems offer criminals and criminal enterprises an attractive arena in which to operate. Consumers who engage in online payments can become easy prey for criminals. In Chapter 10, you learned about the phishing expedition, which is a technique for committing fraud against the customers of online businesses. Although phishing expeditions can be launched against all types of online businesses, they are of particular concern to financial institutions because their customers expect a high degree of security to be maintained over the personal information and resources that they entrust to their online financial institutions.

Phishing Attacks

The basic structure of a phishing attack involves an attacker who sends e-mail messages (such as the one shown in Figure 11-5) to a large number of recipients who might have an account at a targeted Web site. PayPal is the targeted site in the example shown in the figure.

The e-mail message tells the recipient that his or her account has been compromised and it is necessary for the recipient to log in to the account to correct the matter. The e-mail message includes a link that appears to be a link to the login page of the Web site. However, the link actually leads the recipient to the phishing attack perpetrator's Web site, which is disguised to look like the targeted Web site. The unsuspecting recipient enters his or her login name and password, which the perpetrator captures and then uses to access the recipient's account. Once inside the victim's account, the perpetrator can access personal information, make purchases, or withdraw funds at will.

When the e-mails used in a phishing expedition are carefully designed to target a particular person or organization, the exploit is called **spear phishing**. The spear phishing perpetrator must do considerable research on the intended recipient, but by obtaining detailed personal information and using it in the e-mail, the perpetrator can greatly increase the chances that the victim will open the e-mail and click the link to the phishing Web site. Spear phishers have launched attacks against employees of specific companies

Date: xx-xxx-xxx-xxx
From: xx-xxx-xxx-xxx
Subject: xx-xxx-xxx-xxx
To: xx-xxx-xxx-xxx

Dear valued **PayPal** member:

PayPal is committed to maintaining a safe environment for its community of
buyers and sellers. To protect the security of your account, PayPal employs
some of the most advanced security systems in the world and our anti-fraud
teams regularly screen the PayPal system for unusual activity.

Recently, our Account Review Team identified some unusual activity in your
account. In accordance with PayPal's User Agreement and to ensure that your
account has not been compromised, access to your account was limited. Your
account access will remain limited until this issue has been resolved. This
is a fraud prevention measure meant to ensure that your account is not compromised.

In order to secure your account and quickly restore full access, we may
require some specific information from you for the following reason:

We would like to ensure that your account was not accessed by an
unauthorized third party. Because protecting the security of your account
is our primary concern, we have limited access to sensitive PayPal account
features. We understand that this may be an inconvenience but please
understand that this temporary limitation is for your protection.

Case ID Number: xx-xxx-xxx-xxx

We encourage you to log in and restore full access as soon as possible.
Should access to your account remain limited for an extended period of
time, it may result in further limitations on the use of your account.

However, failure to restore your records will result in account suspension.
Please update your records within 48 hours. Once you have updated your account
records, your **PayPal** session will not be interrupted and will continue as normal.

To update your **Paypal** records click on the following link:
xx-xxx-xxx-xxx

Thank you for your prompt attention to this matter. Please understand that
this is a security measure meant to help protect you and your account. We
apologize for any inconvenience.

Sincerely,
PayPal Account Review Department

PayPal Email ID xxxxx

Accounts Management As outlined in our User Agreement, **PayPal** will
periodically send you information about site changes and enhancements.

Visit our Privacy Policy and User Agreement if you have any questions.
xx-xxx-xxx-xxx

FIGURE 11-5   Phishing e-mail message

that include jargon and acronyms that are frequently used in the company or its industry. By using familiar language and terms, the spear phisher gains the victim's trust and is more likely to convince the victim to click the phishing link.

Phishing perpetrators are quick to capitalize on new opportunities to practice their fraud. In 2008, the U.S. government enacted an economic stimulus law that paid millions of its citizens a rebate check. Within a week of the law's passage, phishing e-mails began appearing in inboxes throughout the country. The e-mails appeared to be from the Internal Revenue Service and promised an early rebate to responders who clicked the link (to the phishing Web site) and provided details such as bank account numbers, Social Security numbers, and passwords to online accounts.

The links in phishing e-mails are usually disguised. One common way to disguise the real URL is to use the @ sign, which causes the Web server to ignore all characters that precede the @ and only use the characters that follow it. For example, a link that displays:

https://www.paypal.com@218.36.41.188/fl/login.html

looks like it is an address at PayPal. However, the @ sign causes the Web server to ignore the "paypal.com" and instead takes the victim to a Web page at the IP address 218.36.41.188. In the e-mail shown in the figure, the link appears in the victim's e-mail client software as:

https://paypal.com/cgi-bin/webscr?cmd=_login-run

but when the victim clicks the link, the browser opens a completely different URL:

http://leasurelandscapes.com/snow/webscr.dll

Instead of the URL it shows in the e-mail client, the link in the phishing e-mail actually includes the following JavaScript code:

```
<A onmouseover="window.status='https://www.paypal.com/cgi-bin/webscr?
cmd=_login-run'; return true" onmouseout="window.status='https://
www.paypal.com/cgi-bin/webscr?cmd=_login-run'"href="http://
leasurelandscapes.com/snow/webscr.dll">https://www.paypal.com/
cgi-bin/webscr?cmd=_login-run</A>
```

This code is invisible in many e-mail clients, so the victim might never know that the Web browser has opened a phony site. Phishers use other tricks to hide URLs, including code that opens a pop-up window that displays the financial institution's URL and positions that window so it covers the browser's address bar. Phishing perpetrators often include graphics from the Web site of the victim's financial institution in the phishing e-mail to make it even more convincing. You can learn more about the details of phishing techniques by visiting the Web sites of the Conferences on Email and Anti-Spam and the Anti-Phishing Working Group (APWG).

Using Phishing Attacks for Identity Theft

Many perpetrators of phishing attacks are individuals working alone. However, the large amounts of illegal revenue that can be generated by combining phishing attacks with identity theft have drawn the attention of highly structured groups of criminals whose members possess a variety of specialized skills.

U.S. laws define **organized crime**, also called **racketeering**, as unlawful activities conducted by a highly organized, disciplined association for profit. The associations that engage in organized crime are often differentiated from less organized groups such as gangs and from organized groups that conduct unlawful activities for political purposes, such as terrorist organizations. Organized crime associations have traditionally engaged in criminal activities such as drug trafficking, gambling, money laundering, prostitution, pornography production and distribution, extortion, truck hijacking, fraud, theft, and insider trading. Often these activities are carried out simultaneously with legitimate business activities, which provide cover for the illegal activities.

The Internet has opened new opportunities for organized crime in its traditional types of criminal activities and in new areas such as generating spam (which you learned about in earlier chapters), phishing, and identity theft. **Identity theft** is a criminal act in which the perpetrator gathers personal information about a victim and then uses that information to obtain credit. After establishing credit accounts, the perpetrator runs up charges on the accounts and then disappears. Figure 11-6 includes a list of the types of personal information that identity thieves most want to obtain (listed in approximate order of usefulness to the criminal).

Social Security number
Driver's license number
Credit card numbers
Card verification numbers (CVNs)
Passwords (PINs)
Credit reports
Date of birth
ATM (or debit) card numbers
Telephone calling card numbers
Mortgage (or other loan) information
Telephone numbers
Home address
Employer name and address

FIGURE 11-6   Types of personal information most useful to identity thieves

Large criminal organizations can be highly efficient perpetrators of identity theft because they can exploit large amounts of personal information very quickly and efficiently. These organizations can use phishing attacks to gather personal information and then use it to perpetrate identity theft and other crimes. These criminal organizations often sell or trade information that they cannot use immediately to other organized crime entities around the world. Some of these criminal transactions are even conducted online. For example, a hacker who has planted zombie programs on a large number of computers (thus creating a **zombie farm**) might sell the right to use the zombie farm to an organized crime association that wants to launch a phishing attack (when a zombie farm is used this way, the attack is sometimes called a **pharming attack**). Individuals who commit these crimes have always posed a serious threat, but organized crime's entry into this activity increases the threat. There are two elements in phishing, the collection of the information (done by **collectors**) and the use of the information (done by **cashers**). The skills needed to perform these two activities are different. By facilitating transactions between collectors and cashers (and by participating as one or both), crime organizations have increased the efficiency and volume of phishing activity overall.

More than a million people fall victim to phishing attacks each year and as a group experience financial losses exceeding $1.5 billion. Although the overall incidence of phishing attacks is decreasing as Internet users become aware of them, experts believe that the proportion of all phishing attacks committed by organized crime associations will continue to increase because it is so profitable.

Phishing Attack Countermeasures

In Chapter 8, you learned that several groups are working on ways to improve the Internet's mail transport protocols so that spam senders can be identified. Because spam is a key element of phishing attacks, any protocol change that improves e-mail recipients' ability to identify the source of an e-mail message will also help to reduce the threat of phishing attacks.

The most important step that companies can take today, however, is to educate their Web site users. Most online banking sites continually warn their customers that the site never sends e-mails that ask for account information or that ask the recipient to log in to their Web site and make changes to his or her account information. PayPal occasionally interrupts its own login screen sequence to insert a page that provides information about phishing attacks.

Many companies, especially those that operate financial Web sites, have contracted with consulting firms that specialize in anti-phishing work. These consultants monitor the Web for new Web sites that use the company's name or logo and move quickly to shut down those sites. Most phishing perpetrators set up their entrapping Web sites (with the target company's name and logo) a few days before they launch their e-mail campaign, so this monitoring technique can be effective. Another anti-phishing technique is to monitor online chat rooms that are used by criminals. By watching for offers of stolen credit card information and other phishing exploits, consultants can identify phishing schemes that are under way.

The incidence of phishing attacks has grown rapidly over the past two years, and most industry analysts expect that phishing will be a problem that will plague online businesses for the near future. Phishing can be a profitable criminal activity and as more companies increase their defenses, analysts expect phishing perpetrators to become even better at working around those defenses.

Summary

Credit, debit, and charge cards (payment cards) are the most popular forms of payment on the Internet, but alternative payment systems, such as PayPal, are increasingly common. Electronic bill presentment and payment systems, both biller-direct and consolidator, continue to become more widely used as replacements for paper check payments. The issues presented by small payments and micropayments have been largely resolved by use of payment cards and prepaid accounts of various types.

Online businesses must establish a merchant account with an acquiring bank to process credit and debit card payments. The processing is then accomplished using either internally-developed payment processing software (large companies), purchased software, or contracted processing services (smaller companies).

Stored-value cards, including smart cards and magnetic strip cards, are physical devices that hold information, including cash value, for the cardholder. Magnetic strip cards have limited capacity. Smart cards can store greater amounts of data on an embedded microchip. Stored-value cards can incorporate near field communication technology and be used at touchless card readers to execute transactions.

Digital cash, a form of online payment that is portable and anonymous, offers a replacement for physical cash that can be attractive to users in countries that do not have an established infrastructure for handling card payments. Although some digital cash products claim freedom from government and banking regulation to be a benefit, that freedom can also be a liability.

Digital wallets, which can be software-based or hardware-based, provide a place where online shoppers can store their payment card information, digital cash, and personal identification data. Software-based digital wallets eliminate the need for consumers to reenter payment card and shipping information at each business's Web site. Hardware-based digital wallets are becoming widely used when installed on mobile devices and used for a variety of payment functions.

Banks still process most monetary transactions, and a significant portion of the total dollar volume of those transactions is still accomplished with paper checks; however, banks often use Internet technologies to process those checks and business transactions are moving to electronic funds transfer and online payments. Retail transactions and consumer payments on loans are largely electronic now in the United States. Banking using apps on mobile devices is growing and both small businesses and individuals are finding that portable card readers designed for use with mobile devices, such as Square, are convenient ways to accept card payments for transactions at a variety of locations. Phishing expeditions and identity theft pose a significant threat to online financial institutions and their customers.

Key Terms

acquirer fees	biller-direct EBPP systems
acquiring bank	card code verification (CCV)
anonymous digital cash	card not present transactions
automated Clearing House (ACH)	card security code (CSC)
back-end processor	card verification code (CVC)

card verification data (CVD)

card verification numbers (CVNs)

card verification value (CVV or CV2)

card verification value code (CVVC)

cashers

charge card

chargeback

Check 21

client-side digital wallet

closed loop systems

collectors

consolidator EBPP system

credit card

credit card associations

cryptocurrency

customer issuing banks

debit card

digital cash

digital wallet

double spending

due diligence

electronic bill presentment and payment system (EBPP)

electronic funds transfer at point of sale (EFTPOS) cards

financial technology

fintech

float

front-end processor

gift cards

hardware-based digital wallets

identity theft

interchange fees

interchange network

issuing banks

merchant account

micropayments

money laundering

near field communication (NFC)

open loop system

organized crime

payment card

payment gateways

payment processing service providers

payment processors

pharming attack

prepaid cards

racketeering

server-side digital wallet

single-use cards

small payments

spear phishing

store charge cards

store-branded cards

stored-value card

verification code (V-Code or V Code)

zombie farm

Review Questions

1. Name the most common forms of payment used in online transactions.
2. What types of companies are most likely to use biller-direct EBPP systems?
3. What types of companies are most likely to use consolidator EBPP systems?
4. What is a micropayment?
5. What is a debit card?
6. What is a store charge card and how is it different from a credit card?
7. What is a payment card interchange network?
8. What is a credit card association?

9. What is a merchant account?

10. What is a chargeback?

11. What is an acquirer fee and what services does it cover?

12. Name one factor that affects the rate charged as an interchange fee.

13. Why do online merchants often ask a customer to provide their credit card's CVN?

14. Name three types of businesses that might use an ACH network.

15. What is a payment gateway?

16. Briefly explain the key differences between a stored-value card that uses a magnetic strip and one that uses an embedded microchip.

17. What are the two types of storage available for digital cash?

18. Briefly describe the double spending issue with digital cash.

19. What is money laundering?

20. What is a digital wallet?

21. Why is privacy a concern for users of a digital wallet?

22. What is the meaning of "float" as the term is used in the financial services industry?

23. What is a phishing attack?

24. What is identity theft?

25. What is a zombie farm?

Exercises

1. In about 100 words, discuss issues that arise when processing small payments (under $10) for online transactions. Be sure to describe the solutions to any problems you identify, including the names of companies or products that provide such solutions.

2. In a paragraph, explain how payment processing is different for credit cards and debit cards.

3. In about 100 words, explain what a "card not present" transaction is and why it presents a greater risk than card present transactions for a retail business.

4. In one or two paragraphs, explain the difference between an open loop and a closed loop payment card processing system.

5. In one or two paragraphs, describe the role of an acquiring bank in processing online payment transactions.

6. In about 100 words, explain why an acquiring bank would normally evaluate the creditworthiness of a business before opening a merchant account to process credit card transactions for that business.

7. In about 200 words, explain what function is performed by payment processors and briefly describe how each of the two types of payment processors performs this function.

8. In about 100 words, explain why stored-value cards that are NFC enabled were slower to catch on in the United States than in Europe and Asia.

9. Bitcoin has fluctuated widely in value since its inception. In about 100 words, outline the reasons that a cryptocurrency might fluctuate to a greater degree than most other currencies.

10. Some anonymous digital cash products are touted as being free from the constraints of any banking system or government regulation. In about 100 words, evaluate this claim and outline how such a freedom might affect the usefulness of such a product.

11. In one or two paragraphs, explain what the Check 21 law facilitates and explain what it was intended to accomplish.

12. In about 100 words, explain how a phishing attack could be used to perpetrate identity theft. Include a brief description of countermeasures that might prove effective in thwarting such an attack.

Cases

C1. Digital Wallets on Mobile Devices: Apple and Google

One of the fastest-growing segments of the online payments business is mobile payments. U.S. mobile payments are expected to reach $140 billion by 2019 and purchases using mobile devices could account for half of all online retail sales by 2017.

Google introduced one of the first digital wallet products that would work on a mobile device in 2011 when it also introduced support for the operation of NFC chips in its Android mobile operating system. Google Wallet stores a MasterCard account for users that agree to maintain a cash balance with the card's issuing bank, so it operates essentially as a debit card. Google Wallet does not charge a fee to merchants or the MasterCard issuing banks, nor does it charge a transaction fee. Instead, it generates revenue from advertisers who pay to display ads, offer coupons or other promotions (specific ads are displayed based on the mobile device's proximity to the stores that are making the offers). Google Wallet has been slow to catch on with users.

In 2014, Apple introduced a digital wallet product for its mobile devices called Apple Pay. In operation, Apple Pay is similar to Google Wallet; however, the infrastructure and revenue model is different. Apple Pay charges the issuing banks a fee of 0.05 percent of the transaction amount and guarantees each transaction; that is, if the transaction is fraudulent, Apple will cover the loss. Credit card companies normally charge merchants a fee ranging between 2 and 3 percent of the transaction amount, so the additional Apple Pay fee serves as a low-priced insurance plan for them. Consumers will not be charged at all for using Apple Pay and will not be given advertising messages. Further, Apple has stated that it does not collect information about consumer buying habits from Apple Pay data. Apple arranged for American Express, Discover, MasterCard, and Visa credit cards to be included in their system, along with a group of large card-issuing banks. They also included major retailers such as Bloomingdales, Disney, Staples, Walgreens and Whole Foods. These participants will be able to collect data on consumer buying habits, but only on those consumers that use their card or shop at their stores. Apple reported that more than a million credit cards were registered with Apple Pay in the first three days it was available. After Apple Pay's introduction, an increase in the number of retailers that accept NFC payments (as you learned in this chapter, NFC technology is used by both Google Wallet and Apple Pay) caused an increase in the use of Google Wallet.

REQUIRED:

1. In about 300 words, compare the benefits and drawbacks of Google Wallet and Apple Pay from a consumer's standpoint, a retailer's standpoint, and a bank's standpoint.

2. In 2015, Google announced the introduction of a new service called Android Pay. Using your favorite search engine or the resources of your library, learn more about Android Pay and, in about 200 words, explain why you think Google decided to develop this new product. In your answer, be sure to consider why Google also decided to continue offering its Google Wallet product.

3. A product named CurrentC that combines mobile payments and loyalty benefits was announced in 2015 by the Merchant Content Exchange, a company owned by a consortium of large U.S. retailers. CurrentC avoids the charges imposed by credit card issuers by using debit cards, but debit cards do not provide the same level of fraud protection as credit cards. Using your favorite search engine or the resources of your library, learn more about CurrentC and, in about 200 words, outline this product's chances for success. Be sure to include a discussion of the benefits and drawbacks of CurrentC in your answer.

4. Some banks are considering creating and offering a digital wallet product. Using your favorite search engine or the resources of your library, learn more about these banks and their plans and, in about 200 words, evaluate the likelihood of a bank's success in introducing its own digital wallet.

Note: Your instructor might assign you to a group to complete this case, and might ask you to prepare a formal presentation of your results to your class.

C2. The Moose Hut

Rod and Martha Nelson started The Moose Hut (TMH), a gift shop in Calgary, Alberta, more than 15 years ago. The Nelsons have capitalized on the tourist trade drawn by the Calgary Stampede, which is one of the largest rodeos in the world. The shop sells a wide range of Canadian-themed items to rodeo fans and other tourists who visit central Alberta throughout the year. TMH's offerings range from inexpensive food items, such as pure Canadian maple syrup and smoked salmon, to much more expensive handcrafted gifts, including Inuit and First Nations artwork. The company's trademark product, the Moose Mug, is one of its biggest-selling items.

Many of TMH's customers return to the store whenever they visit Calgary. TMH's line of Canada Day Party Favours is especially popular with homesick Canadians who have moved to other countries, and TMH has been selling those products by mail order for the past several years. After reviewing the sales numbers for these mail order items, Martha has decided that it might be a good idea to expand the mail order operation and begin accepting orders through a Web site. Many of the store's items have a high value-to-weight ratio and would be easy to ship to customers around the world.

TMH currently accepts only checks denominated in Canadian or U.S. currency in its mail order operation; however, taking orders on a Web site will probably require the company to be more flexible in accepting multiple payment methods. Rod and Martha asked you to help them examine payment processing alternatives for TMH's new Web business.

To be acceptable, a payment processing method needs to handle all major credit cards, perform currency conversions, and be available to a Canadian merchant. Most important is that the payment processing method must be reasonably priced. The margins on most gift items at TMH are between 10 percent and 30 percent of the selling price, but the extra costs of shipping and handling items sold through the Web site reduce those margins by another 5–10 percent of the selling price. TMH would like to keep overall payment processing costs below 4 percent of the selling price, if possible.

REQUIRED:

1. Using the Web Links for this case, identify at least three payment processing options that might be suitable for TMH. Write a report of about 400 words in which you describe each of the three payment processing options. Include specific advantages and disadvantages for each option. Prepare a one-page memorandum in which you make a specific recommendation to Rod and Martha. Include an explanation of the reasons for your recommendation.

2. Rod and Martha have heard about digital cash products such as Bitcoin and are thinking about accepting Bitcoins or some other digital cash from customers in person and online. Using your favorite search engine or the resources of your library, research this possibility and summarize your findings in a report of about 100 words addressed to Rod and Martha. In your report, outline the advantages and disadvantages to TMH of accepting one or more digital cash products as payments. Conclude your report with a recommendation based on your analysis.

3. During the Calgary Stampede, Rod and Martha rent booth space near the event and sell their products to event attendees. In the past, they have only made cash sales, because the electricity supply is not reliable in the booth area and their credit card reader needs electric power to operate. They believe they might be losing sales because customers cannot use their credit cards. Using your favorite search engine or the resources of your library, investigate portable credit card reader products, such as Square, that Rod and Martha might use to increase their sales at the booth. In about 100 words, summarize your findings and make a recommendation to Rod and Martha.

Note: Your instructor might assign you to a group to complete this case and might ask you to prepare a formal presentation of your results to your class.

For Further Study and Research

American Banker. 2009. "Online Merchants Cut Fraud Losses," December 1, 11.

Ammons, J., G. Schneider, and A. Sheikh. 2012. "Accounting for Retailer-Issued Gift Cards: Revenue Recognition and Financial Statement Disclosures," *Journal of the International Academy for Case Studies*, 18(1), 1–8.

Bigdoli, H. and R. Phillips. 2012. *Online Banking*. Hoboken, NJ: Wiley.

Berthiaume, D. 2015. "Amazon Shuts Digital Wallet," *Chain Store Age*, January 21. http://www.chainstoreage.com/article/amazon-shuts-digital-wallet

Carter, M. 2015. "Mobile Wallets Are Not Convenient Enough for Consumers," *PaymentsSource*, August 27. http://www.paymentssource.com/news/paythink/mobile-wallets-are-not-convenient-enough-for-consumers-3022186-1.html

Clark, M. 2012. "Visa US Offers Mobile Services," *Near Field Communications World*, February 10. http://www.nfcworld.com/2012/02/10/313104/visa-us-offers-mobile-services/

CyberSource. 2015. *15th Annual Online Fraud Report: Online Payment Fraud Trends, Merchant Practices and Benchmarks*. San Francisco, CA: Visa-CyberSource.

Daly, J. 2014. "Report Documents the March of Online Alternatives to the Payments Mainstream," *Digital Transactions*, March 9. http://digitaltransactions.net/news/story/Report-Documents-the-March-of-Online-Alternatives-to-the-Payments-Mainstream

The Economist. 2015. "The Fintech Revolution: A Wave of Startups Is Changing Finance; for the Better," May 9, 13–14.

EMC Corporation. 2013. *The Year in Phishing*. Bedford, MA: RSA, The Security Division of EMC.

Galbraith, J. 1995. *Money: Whence it Came, Where it Went*. London: Penguin Books.

Grant, D. 2001. "Internet Banking Nightmare: Couple Sue after Access to Their Funds Was Cut Off for 10 Crucial Days," *EastSideJournal.com*, June 10.

Henning, P. 2014. "More Bitcoin Regulation Is Inevitable," *The New York Times*, February 3. http://dealbook.nytimes.com/2014/02/03/more-bitcoin-regulation-is-inevitable/

Hill, K. 2014. "Bitcoin's Legality Around the World," *Forbes*, January 31. http://www.forbes.com/sites/kashmirhill/2014/01/31/bitcoins-legality-around-the-world/

Hof, R. 2015. "Most Stores Still Aren't Ready for Apple Pay or Android Pay," *Forbes*, September 17. http://www.forbes.com/sites/roberthof/2015/09/17/most-stores-still-arent-ready-for-apple-pay-or-android-pay/

Hoffman, C. 2015. "Explaining the Implications for Merchants of EMV and the Liability Shift," *Data Privacy Monitor*, May 18. http://www.dataprivacymonitor.com/data-breaches/explaining-the-implications-for-merchants-of-emv-and-the-liability-shift/

Javelin Strategy & Research. 2013. *Fifth Annual Online Retail Payments Forecast 2012–2017*. Pleasanton, CA: Javelin Strategy & Research.

Javelin Strategy & Research. 2015. *Mobile Online Retail Payments Forecast 2015*. Pleasanton, CA: Javelin Strategy & Research.

Lee, N. 2015. "With Android Pay, Google Gets Mobile Payments Right," *Engadget*, May 29. http://www.engadget.com/2015/05/29/android-pay-google-io/

Lewis, H. 2001. "NetBank, CompuBank Merge, Customers Get Squashed," *Bankrate.com*, May 22. http://www.bankrate.com/bzrt/news/ob/20010521a.asp

Livingstone, R. 2012. "Chasing the Digital Wallet," *Technology Spectator*, January 31. http://technologyspectator.com.au/industry/financial-services/chasing-digital-wallet

Magder, J. 2015. "Now Is the Time for Banks to Determine Mobile Pay Strategy," *PaymentsSource*, September 9. http://www.paymentssource.com/news/paythink/now-is-the-time-for-banks-to-determine-mobile-pay-strategy-3022268-1.html

Martin, J. 2015. "The State of Mobile Payments in 2015," *CIO Magazine*, April 22. http://www.cio.com/article/2912896/mobile/the-state-of-mobile-payments-in-2015.html

Millward, S. 2014. "China's Banks Give Deadline for Bitcoin Exchanges to Close Their Trading Accounts," *Tech in Asia*, April 10. https://www.techinasia.com/china-banks-must-close-bitcoin-trading-bank-accounts/

Montgomery, M. 2015. "Bitcoin Is Only the Beginning for Blockchain Technology," *Forbes*, September 15. http://www.forbes.com/sites/mikemontgomery/2015/09/15/bitcoin-is-only-the-beginning-for-blockchain-technology/

Nash, K. 2014. "Disruption Déjà Vu," *CIO Magazine*, February 1, 18–24.

Nevius, A. 2009. "IRS Expands Electronic Payment Options," *Journal of Accountancy*, 208(6), 78.

Peck, M. 2012. "Bitcoin: The Cryptoanarchist's Answer to Cash," *IEEE Spectrum*, May 30. http://spectrum.ieee.org/computing/software/bitcoin-the-cryptoanarchists-answer-to-cash

Perez, S. 2014. "Apple Announces Mobile Payment Solution Called Apple Pay," *TechCrunch*, September 9. http://techcrunch.com/2014/09/09/announces-mobile-payments-solution-called-apple-pay/

Ptacek, M. 2001. "CompuBank's Demise May Signal a New Era," *American Banker*, 166(63), April 2, 16.

Ramstad, E. 2004. "Hong Kong's Money Card Is a Hit," *The Wall Street Journal*, February 19, B3.

Ray, B. 2012. "Google Wallet PIN Security Cracked in Seconds," *The Register*, February 9. http://www.theregister.co.uk/2012/02/09/google_wallet_pin/

Rob, M. and E. Opara. 2003. "Online Credit Card Processing Models: Critical Issues to Consider by Small Merchants," *Human Systems Management*, 22(3), 133–142.

Roth, A. 2001. "CompuBank Merge Nettles NetBank," *American Banker*, 166(119), June 21, 1–2.

Say, M. 2014. "Why We Accept Bitcoin," *Forbes*, February 13. http://www.forbes.com/sites/groupthink/2014/02/13/why-we-accept-bitcoin/

Stoneman, B. 2003. "FAQs Lighten Service Load at First Internet Bank of Indiana," *American Banker*, 168(2), January 13, 12.

Torian, R., R. Schrader, O. Ireland, and R. Stinneford. 2008. "Current Developments in Electronic Banking and Payment Systems," *The Business Lawyer*, February, 63(2), 689–702.

Wingfield, N. and J. Sapsford. 2002. "eBay to Buy PayPal for $1.4 Billion," *The Wall Street Journal*, July 9, A6.

Yurcan, B. 2012. "Visa Rolls Out New Suite of Mobile Products for U.S. Financial Institutions," *Bank Systems & Technology*, February 9. http://www.banktech.com/payments-cards/232600563

Zhou, T. 2015. "An Empirical Examination of Users' Switch from Online Payment to Mobile Payment," *Technology and Human Interaction*, 11(1), 55–66.

PART 4

Integration

Blend Images Photography/Neer

Managing Electronic Commerce Implementations

LEARNING OBJECTIVES

In this chapter, you will learn:

- How to identify benefits and estimate costs of online business initiatives
- How online business startups are evaluated and financed
- When and how to outsource online business initiative development
- How to manage and staff electronic commerce implementations

INTRODUCTION

When she was three years old, Michelle Crosby's parents began a bitter and protracted divorce that exposed her to lawyers and the legal system. She grew up to become a successful business lawyer in Boise, Idaho, but her unpleasant childhood memories stayed with her. After completing mediation training at Harvard University, she returned to Boise and started a divorce mediation service. Crosby wanted to expand her business using online advertising to drive the creation of a national network of offices, but local bankers balked at funding the enterprise.

In 2013, Crosby left her home in Boise to spend three months at a startup coaching enterprise called **Y Combinator**. She had been selected for the program by Y Combinator after completing an application and a grueling 10-minute interview that Crosby described as harder than either of the two bar exams she had taken. Y Combinator accepts a small number of applicants for its programs twice each year. After supplying a small amount of money (generally under $100,000), Y Combinator works closely with startups to develop their businesses and, at the end of the three-month coaching period, arranges "Demo Day" presentations to investors.

Crosby is now back in Boise, operating her business, Wevorce. In the year following her presentation at Y Combinator, she obtained more than a million dollars from investors and was operating divorce mediation centers in five states. Her online service, Wevorce Anywhere, offers the services of "divorce architects" that can guide couples through a mediated settlement that can save them thousands of dollars in legal fees.

In this chapter, you will learn how online business startups plan, manage, and find investors for their ideas, including how they use companies such as Y Combinator to help them do so. You will also learn how larger businesses manage their internal online business implementations.

Identifying Benefits and Estimating Costs of Online Business Initiatives

The ability of companies to plan, design, and implement cohesive online business strategies can make the difference between success and failure. The tremendous leverage that firms can gain by being the first to do business a new way on the Web has caught the attention of top executives and investors in many industries. The keys to successful implementation of any information technology project are planning and execution. This chapter provides some guidelines to help those readers who will manage the planning, implementation, and continuing operations of electronic commerce initiatives. A successful business plan for an online business initiative should include activities that identify the initiative's specific objectives and link those objectives to business strategies (strategies that you learned about in Chapters 3, 4, 5, and 6).

In setting the objectives for an online business initiative, managers should consider the strategic role of the project, its intended scope, and the resources available for executing it. In this section, you will learn how to identify objectives and link those business objectives to business strategies. In later sections of this chapter, you will learn about Web site development strategies and how to manage the implementation of an electronic commerce initiative.

Identifying Objectives

Businesses undertake electronic commerce initiatives for a wide variety of reasons. Objectives that businesses typically strive to accomplish through electronic commerce include: increasing sales in existing markets, opening new markets, serving existing customers better, identifying new vendors, coordinating more efficiently with existing vendors, or recruiting employees more effectively.

Organizations of different sizes will have different objectives for their electronic commerce initiatives. Decisions regarding resource allocations for electronic commerce initiatives should consider the expected benefits and costs of meeting the objectives. These decisions should also consider the risks inherent in the electronic commerce initiative and compare them to the risks of inaction—a failure to act could concede a strategic advantage to competitors.

Linking Objectives to Business Strategies

Businesses use tactics called **downstream strategies** to improve the value that the business provides to its customers. Alternatively, businesses can pursue **upstream strategies** that focus on reducing costs or generating value by working with suppliers or inbound shipping and freight service providers.

In earlier chapters of this book, you learned about many of the things that companies are doing on the Web. The Web is an attractive sales channel for many firms; however, companies use electronic commerce to do much more than sell. They can use the Web to complement their business strategies and improve their competitive positions. Online business opportunities include activities such as:

- Building brands
- Enhancing existing marketing programs
- Selling products and services
- Selling advertising
- Developing a better understanding of customer needs
- Improving after-sale service and support
- Purchasing products and services
- Managing supply chains
- Operating auctions
- Building or using virtual communities to maintain relationships with customers and suppliers

The success of these activities can be difficult to measure. In the first wave of electronic commerce, many companies engaged in these activities on the Web without setting specific, measurable goals. In the late 1990s, companies that had good ideas could find plenty of investors and start a business activity on the Web. These early activities were often highly speculative. Successes and failures were measured in broad strokes. A company would either become a leader in its industry (perhaps after being acquired by a larger company) or would disappear into bankruptcy—all within a few short years.

In the second wave of electronic commerce, companies started taking a closer look at the benefits and costs of their electronic commerce initiatives before committing resources to them. It became necessary for online business ideas to have specific objectives for benefits to be achieved and costs to be incurred. Companies began creating pilot Web sites to test their online business ideas and then released production Web sites to handle full implementations. Companies started specifying clear goals that their pilot tests had to meet before they would launch new Web sites in their full production versions.

In the third wave, companies are moving beyond a conceptualization of online business as a Web site that communicates to individual users running Web browser software on their computers. The pervasiveness of smartphones and tablet devices puts the power of a Web browser into many more hands in many more locations. It also changes the nature of online communication. Messaging between a Web client running on a fixed location computer and a Web browser is a communication from one point to another, much like a landline telephone. Web clients running on multiple devices (some of which might be used simultaneously by a single user) make the types of communication and interaction richer and able to accomplish a wider array of tasks. The ease of acquiring the benefits of a technology is also increasing. For example, a company might never need to develop its own microblogging-based social media tool (such as Twitter), because it can use the functionality Twitter provides to participate in a virtual community in ways that cement its relationships with customers, suppliers, and even its own employees. The most profound change in the third wave, however, is likely to be the increase in online activities by smaller businesses. These firms can use the existing communication infrastructure of the world's Facebooks, Twitters, and similar social media tools to get information out to potential customers very effectively without investing large amounts of money in their own Web infrastructures. Some experts even suggest that small businesses might be better off investing their promotional resources in social media than in traditional Web sites.

Identifying and Measuring Benefits

Some benefits of electronic commerce initiatives are obvious, tangible, and easy to measure. These include such things as increased sales or reduced costs. Other benefits are intangible and can be much more difficult to identify and measure, such as increased customer satisfaction. When identifying benefits, managers should try to set objectives that are measurable, even when those objectives are for intangible benefits. For example, success in achieving a goal of increased customer satisfaction might be measured by counting the number of first-time customers who return to the site and buy.

Companies that create Web sites to build brands or enhance their existing marketing programs can set goals in terms of increased brand awareness, which they can measure with market research surveys and opinion polls. Companies that sell goods or services online can measure increases in sales volume. One complication that can occur when measuring either brand awareness or sales is that the increases can be caused by other things that the company is doing at the same time or by a general improvement in the economy. A good marketing research staff or outside consulting firm can help a company identify the specific effects of their online marketing or sales initiatives. Marketing research staff or outside consultants can also help a firm set and evaluate its specific goals for online business initiatives.

Companies that want to use Web sites to improve customer service or after-sale support might set goals of increased customer satisfaction or reduced costs of providing customer service or support. For example, Philips Lighting wanted to use the Web to provide an ordering system for its smaller customers. The primary goal for this initiative was to reduce the cost of processing smaller orders. Philips had identified that responding to inventory availability and order status inquiries accounted for over half the cost of processing smaller orders. Customers that placed small orders often called or sent faxes asking for this information. Philips built a pilot Web site and invited a number of its smaller customers to try it. The company found that customer service phone calls from the test group of customers dropped by 80 percent. Based on that measurable increase in efficiency, Philips decided to invest in additional hardware and personnel to staff a version of the Web site that could handle virtually all of its smaller customers. The reduction in the cost of handling small orders justified the additional investment.

Companies can use a variety of similar measurements to assess the benefits of other electronic commerce initiatives. Supply chain managers can measure supply cost reductions, quality improvements, or faster deliveries of ordered goods. Auction sites can set goals for the number of auctions, the number of bidders and sellers, the dollar volume of items sold, the number of items sold, or the number of registered participants. The ability to track such numbers is usually built into auction site software. Virtual communities and Web portals measure the number of visitors and try to measure the quality of their visitors' experiences.

Some sites use online surveys to gather this data; however, most settle for estimates based on the length of time each visitor remains on the site and how often visitors return. A summary of benefits and measurements that companies can make to assess the value of those benefits (these measurements are often called **metrics**) appears in Figure 12-1.

No matter how a company measures the benefits provided by an online business implementation, it usually tries to convert the raw activity measurements to monetary units. Having the benefits expressed in monetary units lets the company compare benefits

Electronic Commerce Initiatives	Common Measurements of Benefits Provided
Build brands	Surveys or opinion polls that measure brand awareness, changes in market share
Enhance existing marketing programs and create new marketing programs	Change in per-unit sales volume, frequency of customer contact, conversion (to buyers) rate
Improve customer service	Customer satisfaction surveys, quantity of customer complaints, customer loyalty
Reduce cost of after-sale support	Quantity and type (telephone, fax, e-mail) of support activities, change in net support cost per customer
Improve supply chain operation	Cost, quality, and on-time delivery of materials or services purchased; overall reduction in cost of goods sold
Hold auctions	Quantity of auctions, bidders, sellers, items sold, registered participants; dollar volume of items sold; participation rate
Provide portals, social networks, and virtual communities	Number of visitors, number of return visits per visitor, duration of average visit, participation in online discussions

© 2015 Cengage Learning

FIGURE 12-1   Measuring the benefits of electronic commerce initiatives

to costs and compare the net benefit (benefits minus costs) of a particular initiative to the net benefits provided by other projects. Although each activity provides some value to the company, it can be difficult to measure the value in monetary units precisely. Usually, even the best attempts at these measurement conversions yield only rough approximations.

Identifying and Estimating Costs

At first glance, the task of identifying and estimating costs may seem much easier than the task of setting benefits objectives. However, many managers have found that information technology project costs can be just as difficult to estimate and control as the benefits of those projects. Because Web development uses hardware and software technologies that change even more rapidly than those used in other information technology projects, managers often find that their experience does not help much when they are making estimates. Most changes in the cost of hardware are downward, but the increasing sophistication of software often requires more of the newer, less-expensive hardware. This often yields a net increase in overall hardware costs. The more sophisticated software often costs more than the amount originally budgeted, too. Even though electronic commerce initiatives are often completed within a shorter time frame than many other information technology projects, the rapid changes in Web technology can quickly destroy a manager's best-laid plans.

TOTAL COST OF OWNERSHIP

In addition to hardware and software costs, the project budget must include the costs of hiring, training, and paying the personnel who will design the Web site, write or customize the software, create the content, and operate and maintain the site. Many organizations now track costs by activity and calculate a total cost for each activity. These cost numbers, called **total cost of ownership (TCO)**, include all costs related to the activity. Increasing some costs can reduce other costs, so most managers find the TCO of a project to be a more appropriate focus for their cost control efforts than the individual elements of the project's cost.

The TCO of an electronic commerce implementation includes the costs of hardware (server computers, routers, firewalls, and load-balancing devices), software (licenses for operating systems, Web server software, database software, and application software), Internet connections, design work outsourced, salaries and benefits for employees involved in the project, and the costs of maintaining the site once it is operational. A good TCO calculation would, for example, include assumptions about how often the site would need to be redesigned in the future.

OPPORTUNITY COSTS

For many companies, one of the largest and most significant costs associated with electronic commerce initiatives is the opportunity lost by not undertaking such an initiative. The foregone benefits that a company could have obtained from an electronic commerce initiative that they chose not to pursue are costs. Managers and accountants use the term **opportunity cost** to describe such lost benefits from an action not taken.

Opportunity costs of not undertaking an online business initiative could include the value of customers never obtained, sales not made, suppliers not identified, or cost reductions not achieved in the company's supply chain. Although opportunity costs never show up in the accounting records, they are real and avoidable losses. Good managers try to think of opportunity costs whenever they make business decisions of any kind.

WEB SITE COSTS

Since companies began setting up Web sites, information technology research firms (such as International Data Corporation and Gartner) and management consulting firms (such as PwC's strategy& and McKinsey & Company) have regularly estimated the costs of implementing various types of online business operations. Although the total dollar amounts required to create and operate a Web site have varied over the years (and across specific types of businesses), the relative proportion of startup costs has remained surprisingly stable. About 10 percent of the cost is for computer hardware, another 10 percent is for software, and about 80 percent of the cost is for labor (including both internal labor and the cost of outside consultants). The annual cost of operating an online business Web site generally ranges between 50 and 200 percent of the initial cost of the site.

As you learned in Chapter 9, a small online store can be placed in operation for under $1000, but most small to midsize online business operations with full transaction and payment processing capabilities cost between $10,000 and $1 million to launch. Current estimates of the cost to launch electronic commerce sites for larger companies, especially those that must be integrated with existing business operations, are substantially higher. Figure 12-2 summarizes recent industry estimates for the cost of creating and operating online Web sites for various sizes of businesses.

	Small Online Store	Midsize Online Business	Large Online Business	Large Company's Online Business Integrated with Other Business Operations
Initial costs	$400–$7,000	$10,000–$1 million	$1 million–$5 million	$5 million–$100 million
Ongoing annual costs	$400–$14,000	$25,000–$2 million	$500,000–$10 million	$2.5 million–$200 million

FIGURE 12-2 Estimated costs for business Web sites

Many industry observers have noted that costs are generally heading downward. Startup firms increasingly find they can get their operations launched for dollar amounts that are in the low end of the range in each category. Lower costs for broadband access and computer hardware play a major role, but the most significant trend is that the cost of developing and maintaining software to run an online business (a cost that includes a substantial labor component) is decreasing.

Sarah Lacy, a journalist who writes about high-tech companies, compared one of the Internet's first successful startups, Netscape, with more recent startup companies. She noted that Netscape needed more than $40 million to buy equipment, bandwidth, and to pay people to build the software it needed just to get started in the early 1990s.

Kevin Rose started his online business, Digg, with an investment of under \$500,000 in 2004. Today, a programmer could develop a smartphone app and submit the idea to the Apple App Store and Google Play for less than \$1000.

When considering hosting options for a Web site, a business must consider the functions it needs now and in the future, the reliability of the hosting provider, the volume of customers and transactions it needs to handle, security, provisions for backup, and the cost. A summary of these factors appears in Figure 12-3.

Feature	Typical Measures
Functionality	Bandwidth, number of different operating systems and databases supported, disk space, number of e-mail accounts allowed, number and type of software provided (for Web site construction, traffic analysis, and so on)
Reliability	Guaranteed uptime percentage, guaranteed speed of service reinstatement when it does fail
Scalability	Ease of expansion of bandwidth, disk space, additional software (database, traffic analysis, and so on) that can be added to an account as it grows
Security	Employee background checks, features that provide physical protection of the facilities (fences, alarms, guards, security cameras, and so on) and protection against online intrusions (firewalls, network security software, and devices)
Backup and recovery	Frequency of backups, automation of backups, off-site storage of backup media
Cost	Initial and ongoing charges for setup and operation, additional charges for specific software and other features

FIGURE 12-3   Important Web hosting service features

Funding Online Business Startups

In the early days of the Web, many businesses were started by individuals who knew something about computers and technology and who had an idea for a business. For example, both eBay and Yahoo! were started by computer enthusiasts who decided they might be able to make a little money with their hobbies.

Online businesses that are startup companies (rather than ideas launched by existing businesses) cannot, in general, borrow from a bank or offer bonds or stock to investors. Banks are reluctant to lend money on the strength of a good idea alone, and access to stock and bond markets is limited to companies with long track records of profitability. Most startup businesses of any kind are funded out of the founders' savings, along with investments or loans from friends and relatives.

As business interest in the Web grew in the late 1990s, many online startups became attractive to investors who wanted a chance to make some fast money in what had become the Internet boom. A person would pitch an idea for an online business to a group of businesspersons who had money and enough business knowledge to evaluate the idea's potential. These investors, often called **angel investors**, would fund the initial startup. This remains a good option for online business ideas that need more money than they can raise from relatives and friends. In return for their capital, angel investors become stockholders in the business. In many cases, the angel investors end up owning more of the business than the founder. Typical funding by angel investors ranges between a few hundred thousand dollars and a few million dollars. Angel investors, in general, hope that the business will grow rapidly so that in a short time they can sell their interest in the company at a profit to the next round of investors, called venture capitalists.

Venture capitalists are very wealthy individuals, groups of wealthy individuals, or investment firms that look for small companies that are about to grow rapidly. They invest large amounts of money (between a million and a few hundred million dollars) hoping that in a few years the company will be large enough to sell stock to the public in an event called an **initial public offering (IPO)**. In the IPO, the venture capitalists take their profits and once again search for a new small company in which to invest.

The supply of angel investors and venture capitalists (and their willingness to invest in new startups) has waxed and waned with the booms and busts of online business activity. It has always been easier to find money for electronic commerce initiatives when business is good than when it is declining.

This system of financing startup and initial growth of online businesses has both benefits (it provides access to large amounts of capital early in the life of the business) and costs (angel investors and venture capitalists can end up with most of the profits and can put great pressure on the business to grow rapidly) for the founders of those businesses. With the high costs of launching online business Web sites in the first wave of electronic commerce, business founders had few alternatives. Now that the costs of creating an online business have gone down, the number of founders who can avoid venture capitalists and even angel investors is increasing. By relieving the pressure to grow rapidly, online entrepreneurs can be more creative and have a chance to learn from their mistakes. Industry observers expect this trend toward more and smaller online ventures to continue as the cost of creating an online business continues to fall.

Comparing Benefits to Costs

Most companies have procedures that call for an evaluation of any major expenditure of funds. These major investments in equipment, personnel, and other assets are called **capital projects** or **capital investments**. The techniques that companies use to evaluate proposed capital projects range from very simple calculations to complex computer simulation models. However, no matter how complex the technique, it always reduces to a comparison of benefits and costs. If the benefits exceed the costs of a project by a comfortable margin, the company invests in the project.

A key part of creating a business plan for electronic commerce initiatives is the process of identifying potential benefits (including intangibles such as employee satisfaction and company reputation), identifying the total costs required to generate those benefits, and evaluating whether the value of the benefits exceeds the total of the costs. Companies should evaluate each element of their electronic commerce strategies using this cost/benefit approach. A representation of the cost/benefit approach appears in Figure 12-4.

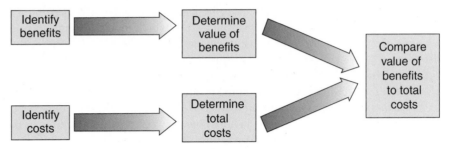

FIGURE 12-4   Cost/benefit evaluation of electronic commerce strategy elements

Return on Investment (ROI)

You might have learned techniques for capital project evaluation, such as the payback method, the net present value method, or the internal rate of return method, in your accounting or finance courses. These evaluation approaches are called **return on investment (ROI)** techniques because they measure the amount of income (return) that will be provided by a specific current expenditure (investment). ROI techniques provide a quantitative expression of whether the benefits of a particular investment exceed their costs (including opportunity costs). They can also mathematically adjust for the reduced value of benefits that the investment will return in future years (benefits received in future years are worth less than those received in the current year).

Although most companies evaluate the anticipated value of electronic commerce initiatives in some way before approving them, some companies see these projects as absolutely necessary investments. Thus, businesses might not subject these initiatives to the same close examination and rigid requirements as other capital projects because they fear being left behind as competitors move into online business activities.

Newspaper Web sites are one example of an industry's willingness to incur losses to establish an online presence. In the first wave of electronic commerce, only a few newspaper sites (such as Gannet's USA Today and *The Wall Street Journal's* WSJ.com sites) were profitable. Most newspaper sites took many years to become profitable, and a significant number remain unprofitable today. As you learned earlier in this book, newspaper sites have experimented with various ways to generate revenue, such as charging for subscriptions, charging for access to certain content, or charging for access to archived articles. Despite their continuing losses, most newspaper companies believe that they cannot afford to ignore the long-term potential of the Web. These companies estimate that the opportunity costs of not being present on the Web (for example, the loss of future profits to be earned from the Web site or the risk of losing market share to competitors) are greater than the losses they are experiencing in their online operations.

In the second wave of electronic commerce, more companies began taking a harder look at Web-related expenditures. Many companies have turned to ROI as the measurement tool for evaluating new electronic commerce projects because that is what they used for other IT projects in the past. ROI is a simple-to-understand tool that is easily applied; however, managers should be careful when using it to evaluate online business initiatives. ROI has some built-in biases that can lead managers to make poor decisions.

First, ROI requires that all costs and benefits be stated in monetary units. Because it is usually easier to quantify costs than benefits, ROI measurements can be biased in a way that gives undue weight to costs. Second, ROI focuses on benefits that can be predicted. Many electronic commerce initiatives have returned benefits that were not foreseen by their planners. The benefits developed after the initiatives were in place. For example, Cisco Systems created online customer forums to allow customers to discuss product issues with each other. The main benefits from this initiative were to reduce customer service costs and increase customer satisfaction regarding the availability of product information; however, the forums turned out to be a great way for Cisco engineers to get feedback from customers on new products that they were developing. This second use was not foreseen by the project's planners and has become the most important and beneficial outcome of the customer forums. An ROI analysis would have missed this benefit completely.

Yet another weakness of ROI is that it tends to emphasize short-run benefits over long-run benefits. The mathematics of ROI calculations do account for both correctly, but short-term benefits are easier to foresee, so they tend to get included in the ROI calculations. Long-term benefits are harder to imagine and harder to quantify, so they tend to be included less often and less accurately in the ROI calculation. This biases ROI calculations to weigh short-term costs and benefits more heavily than long-term costs and benefits, which can lead managers who rely on ROI measures to make incorrect decisions. You can learn more about this topic at the CIO Budgets Web page.

In the third wave, companies undertake highly sophisticated analyses of any planned online business activity. For example, a bank that is planning to launch mobile banking services would develop ROI estimates for each element of the implementation, including the Web site for mobile users, any apps that would be offered for various smartphone operating systems, and social media promotions that would entice users to switch their accounts to the bank or use more bank services (and thus generate more fee revenue for the bank).

Strategies for Developing Electronic Commerce Web Sites

When companies first established presences on the Web, the typical Web site was a static brochure that was not updated frequently and seldom included any transaction-processing capabilities. The next generation of Web sites included transaction processing and a variety of other automated business processing capabilities. Web sites became important parts of companies' information systems infrastructures. These transaction-processing capabilities were eventually enhanced with personalization (in which sites customized the Web site's presentation to each specific user) and the customer relationship management features you learned about in earlier chapters. More recently, Web sites became integrated with social media networks such as Facebook and Twitter. Companies also added separate Web sites with formatting that provides specific functionality for the smaller screens of smartphones and tablet devices. This evolution of Web site functions is shown in Figure 12-5.

These transformations have required organizations to review, update, and sometimes completely rebuild their Web sites and related computing infrastructure. Many large companies have developed tools for managing their software development projects. As more companies begin to see their Web sites as collections of software applications,

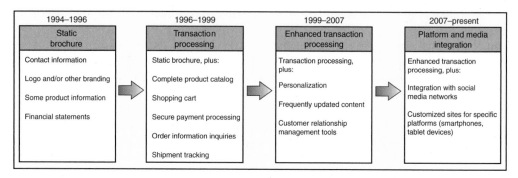

FIGURE 12-5   Evolution of Web site functions

they are starting to use these software development tools to manage the updating and rebuilding of their Web sites. A number of companies have been able to respond to these changes rapidly by using alternatives to traditional systems development methods, including the incubator approach that you will learn about later in this chapter.

Internal Development versus Outsourcing

Some companies try to avoid online business site development problems by finding a contractor who can handle the entire project for them. This practice is called **outsourcing**. Most leading companies understand that these sites can be too important to the future success of the company to risk outsourcing. An online business initiative's success depends on it being integrated into the activities in which the business is already engaged. Using internal people to lead all projects helps to ensure that the company's specific needs are addressed and that the initiative is congruent with the goals and the culture of the organization. Outside consultants or outsourcing companies are seldom able to learn enough about an organization's culture to accomplish these objectives. However, few companies are large enough or have sufficient in-house expertise to launch an electronic commerce project without some external help. The key to success is finding the right balance between outside and inside support for the project.

THE INTERNAL TEAM

The first step in determining which parts of an electronic commerce project to outsource is to create an internal team that is responsible for the project. This team should include people with enough knowledge about the Internet and its technologies to know what kinds of things are possible. Team members should be creative thinkers who are interested in taking the company beyond its current boundaries, and they should be people who have distinguished themselves in some way by doing something very well for the company. If they are not already recognized by their peers as successful individuals, the project may suffer from lack of credibility.

Some companies make the mistake of appointing as electronic commerce project leader a technical wizard who does not know much about the business and is not well-known throughout the company. Such a choice can greatly increase the likelihood of failure. Business knowledge, creativity, and the respect of the firm's operating function managers are all much more important than technical expertise in establishing successful electronic commerce. Project leaders need a good sense of the company's goals and culture to manage an implementation effectively.

Measuring the achievements of this internal team is very important. The measurements do not have to be monetary. Achievement can be expressed in whatever terms are appropriate to the objectives of the initiative. Customer satisfaction, number of sales leads generated, and reductions in order-processing time are examples of metrics that can provide a sense of the team's level of accomplishment. The measurements should show how the project is affecting the company's ability to provide value to the consumer. Many consultants advise companies to set aside between 5 percent and 10 percent of a project's budget for quantifying the project's value and measuring the achievement of that value.

Companies today recognize the value of the accumulated mass of employees' knowledge about the business and its processes. The value of an organization's pool of this type of knowledge is called **intellectual capital**. Although the value of intellectual capital is hard to measure and does not appear in the accounting records or financial statements, most companies today develop estimates of it and try to manage its growth.

The internal team should hold ultimate and complete responsibility for the electronic commerce initiative, from the setting of objectives to the final implementation and operation of the site. The internal team decides which parts of the project to outsource, to whom those parts are outsourced, and what consultants or partners the company needs to hire for the project. Consultants, outsourcing providers, and partners can be extremely important early in the project because they often develop skills and expertise in new technologies before most information systems professionals.

EARLY OUTSOURCING

In many online business projects, the company outsources the initial site design and development to launch the project quickly. The outsourcing team then trains the company's information systems professionals in the new technology before handing the operation of the site over to them. This approach is called **early outsourcing**. Because operating an online business site can rapidly become a source of competitive advantage for a company, it is best to have the company's own information systems people working closely with the outsourcing team and developing ideas for improvements as early as possible in the life of the project.

LATE OUTSOURCING

In the more traditional approach to information systems outsourcing, the company's information systems professionals do the initial design and development work, implement the system, and operate the system until it becomes a stable part of the business operation. Once the company has gained all the competitive advantage provided by the system, the maintenance of the online business system can be outsourced so that the company's information systems professionals can turn their attention and talents to developing new technologies that will provide further competitive advantage. This approach is called **late outsourcing**. Although for years late outsourcing has been the standard for allocating scarce information systems talent to projects, most managers find that early outsourcing works better for online business initiatives.

PARTIAL OUTSOURCING

In both the early outsourcing and late outsourcing approaches, a single group is responsible for the entire design, development, and operation of a project—either inside or outside the company. This typical outsourcing pattern works well for many information systems projects. However, electronic commerce initiatives can benefit from a partial outsourcing approach, too. In **partial outsourcing**, which is also called **component outsourcing**, the company identifies specific portions of the project that can be completely designed, developed, implemented, and operated by another firm that specializes in a particular function.

For example, many smaller Web sites outsource their e-mail handling and response functions. Customers expect rapid and accurate responses to any e-mail inquiry they make of a Web site with which they are doing business. Many companies send the customer an automatic order confirmation by e-mail as soon as the order or credit card payment is accepted. A number of companies act as outsourcers by providing these e-mail auto response functions to other companies. Another common example of partial outsourcing is outsourced payment processing. Many vendors are willing to provide complete customer payment handling. These companies provide a site that takes over when customers are ready to pay, processes the payment transaction, then returns the customers to the original site.

One of the most common elements of electronic commerce initiatives that companies outsource using this approach is Web hosting activity. Web hosting service providers are usually willing to accommodate requests for a variety of service levels. Small businesses can rent space on an existing server at the ISP's location. Larger companies can purchase the server hardware and have the service provider install and maintain it at the service provider's location. The service provider has the continuous staffing and expertise needed to keep an electronic commerce site up and running 24 hours a day, seven days a week (this kind of service is often called **24/7 operation**).

A number of service providers offer services beyond basic Internet connectivity to companies that want to do business on the Web. Many of these services were described earlier as candidates for partial outsourcing strategies and include automated e-mail response, transaction processing, payment processing, security, customer service and support, order fulfillment, and product distribution.

Incubators

An **incubator** is a company that offers startup companies a physical location with offices, accounting and legal assistance, computers, and Internet connections at a very low monthly cost. Sometimes, the incubator offers seed money, management advice, and marketing assistance as well. In exchange, the incubator receives an ownership interest in the company, typically between 10 percent and 50 percent.

When the company grows to the point that it can obtain venture capital financing or launch a public offering of its stock, the incubator sells all or part of its interest and

LEARNING FROM FAILURES

Nordisk Aviation

Nordisk Aviation is a subsidiary of the Norwegian Norsk Hydro Group. It designs, manufactures, and repairs air cargo containers for both freight and passenger baggage for major airlines throughout the world and for freight carriers such as FedEx and UPS. It also designs and sells handling systems and pallets that work with the containers. The company has annual sales of more than $100 million and employs more than 150 people at its locations around the world.

Nordisk was a strong believer in using the outsourcing approach for its IT projects—its IT Department included only two people. These two IT staff members worked as the overseers of every IT design and implementation project for the company. They also managed the ongoing IT services provided to Nordisk by other companies.

In late 2000, Manfred Gollent, the president of Nordisk, decided it was time to upgrade the company's Web site—which had been operating as an information site for several years—to include portal features that would allow Nordisk customers to check order status and learn about current developments in container and container-handling systems design. The logical approach for Nordisk was to find a company to which it could outsource the project.

The two members of Nordisk's IT staff went to work finding suitable Web developers. The previous Web developer had disappeared; they were unable to find any trace of the person who had created the existing Web site. The developer had created the Web site so that it used a number of programs to deliver dynamic pages. Unfortunately, the developer had given Nordisk only the executable code and not the actual programs. He also did not provide Nordisk with any documentation of the programs.

When the Web site was initially created, it was not an important strategic project for Nordisk. The IT staff members, who were busy with other important projects, did not ensure that the application code and documentation were received. Nordisk had to hire a company to rebuild the site completely to obtain the additional portal functions it wanted to add to the site. The lesson from the Nordisk case is that even when a company is outsourcing virtually all of its Web development, it must have procedures in place to ensure that the project is internally managed and documented.

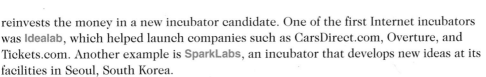

reinvests the money in a new incubator candidate. One of the first Internet incubators was Idealab, which helped launch companies such as CarsDirect.com, Overture, and Tickets.com. Another example is SparkLabs, an incubator that develops new ideas at its facilities in Seoul, South Korea.

Some companies have created internal incubators. A number of companies used internal incubators in the past to develop technologies that the companies planned to use in their main business operations. Most of these were unsuccessful and, ultimately, were shut down. Employees in internal incubators found it difficult to maintain an entrepreneurial spirit when they knew that the technology they were developing would ultimately be taken away and controlled by the parent company.

More recently, companies such as Matsushita Electric's U.S. Panasonic division started internal incubators to help launch new companies that will grow to become important strategic partners. The business ideas developed in the incubator are eventually launched as separate companies that assume ownership of the assets used to create the ideas or products. The incubator development team also stays on as the managers of the new company. These strategic partner incubators have yielded much better results than old-style technology development incubators.

Accelerators

An **accelerator** is a company that performs a function similar to that of an incubator; however, accelerators structure their activities differently. Also, accelerators tend to work with entrepreneurs who have already developed their idea into a business as opposed to incubators, which often work with entrepreneurs who are still at the "I have a great idea" stage.

Accelerators generally have a formal application process that often involves a competitive series of proposals and presentations. In that process, the entrepreneurs have their businesses examined by the accelerator's staff, who take a very close look at both the current operations and future plans of the business. Most of the proposals are rejected. Those that survive are entered into a formal program in which the entrepreneurs spend a set period of time (ranging from a few weeks to a few months) working closely with a group of mentors (called a **mentor network**) assembled by the accelerator to convert the idea into a viable business.

When a proposal is accepted, the accelerator makes a monetary investment in the startup in exchange for a small equity interest. In an accelerator, the real value to the entrepreneurs is not the monetary investment, but access to the mentor network. These mentor networks can include more than 100 people for some startups. The idea is to gather together the expertise needed to develop the startup and take it to the next level.

At the end of the development period, in which a number of startups are run through the accelerator process together in a cohort, the entrepreneurs make presentations to the media and potential investors at a demonstration day event. These pitches are designed to gain publicity and the interest of investors for each startup in the cohort. Y Combinator, the company mentioned in the chapter introduction, is a highly successful accelerator. Other companies that operate accelerators include TechStars and the Brandery.

Managing Electronic Commerce Implementations

The best way to manage any complex electronic commerce implementation is to use formal management techniques. Project management, project portfolio management, specific staffing, and postimplementation audits are methods businesses use to efficiently administer their electronic commerce projects.

Project Management

Project management is a collection of formal techniques for planning and controlling the activities undertaken to achieve a specific goal. Project management was developed by the U.S. military and the defense contractors that worked with the military in the 1950s and the 1960s to develop weapons and other large systems. Not only was defense spending increasing in those years, but individual projects also were becoming so large that it became impossible for managers to maintain control over them without some kind of assistance.

The project plan includes criteria for cost, schedule, and performance—it helps project managers make intelligent trade-off decisions regarding these three criteria. For example, if it becomes necessary for a project to be completed early, the project manager can compress the schedule by either increasing the project's cost or decreasing its performance.

Today, project managers use specific application software called **project management software** to help them oversee projects. Commercial project management software products, such as Oracle Primavera and Microsoft Project, give managers an array of built-in tools for managing resources and schedules. The software can generate charts and tables that show, for example, which parts of the project are critical to its timely completion, which parts can be rescheduled or delayed without changing the project finish date, and where additional resources might be most effective in speeding up the project. Open Workbench, OpenProj, and Redmine are open-source project management software packages that offer many of the same features as the leading commercial products.

In addition to managing the people and tasks of the internal team, project management software can help the team manage the tasks assigned to consultants, technology partners, and outsourced service providers. By examining the costs and completion times of tasks as they are completed, project managers can learn how the project is progressing and continually revise the estimated costs and completion times of future tasks.

Information systems development projects have a well-deserved reputation for running out of control and ultimately failing. They are much more likely to fail than other types of projects, such as building construction projects. The main causes for information systems project failures are rapidly changing technologies, long development times, and changing customer expectations. Because of this vulnerability, many teams rely on project management software to help them achieve project goals.

Although electronic commerce certainly uses rapidly changing technologies, the development times for most electronic commerce projects are relatively short—often they are accomplished in under six months. This gives both the technologies and the expectations of users less time to change. Thus, electronic commerce initiatives are, in general, more successful than other types of information systems implementations.

You can learn more about project management by reading the references listed in the For Further Study and Research section at the end of this chapter, or by clicking the Web Link for the Project Management Institute, a not-for-profit organization devoted to the promotion of professional project management practices.

Project Portfolio Management

Larger organizations often have many IT implementation projects going on simultaneously—a number of which could be electronic commerce implementations or updates. A company's top technology manager is its **chief information officer (CIO)**. CIOs of some larger companies now use a portfolio approach to managing these multiple projects. **Project portfolio management** is a technique in which each project is monitored as if it were an investment in a financial portfolio. The CIO records the projects in a list (usually using spreadsheet or database management software) and updates the list regularly with current information about each project's status. By managing each project as a portfolio element, project portfolio managers can make trade-offs between cost, schedule, and quality across projects as well as within individual projects. This gives the organization more flexibility in allocating resources to achieve the best set of benefits from all of the projects in the timeliest manner.

Project management software performs a function similar to this for the tasks within a project, but most project management software packages are designed to handle individual projects and do not do a very good job of consolidating activities across multiple projects. Also, the information used in project portfolio management differs somewhat from the information used to manage specific projects. Project management software tracks the details of how each project is accomplishing its specific goals. In project portfolio management, the CIO assigns a ranking for each project based on its importance to the strategic goals of the business and its level of risk (probability of failure).

To develop these rankings, managers can use any of the methods that are commonly used to evaluate the risk of making investments in business assets. Indeed, using these tools helps the IT function explain electronic commerce projects as investments in assets, which makes it easier for other top managers in the company to understand the business characteristics of these projects.

Staffing for Electronic Commerce

Regardless of whether the internal team decides to outsource parts of the design and implementation activity, it must determine the staffing needs of the electronic commerce initiative. The general areas of staffing that are most important to the success of an electronic commerce initiative include:

- Chief information officer (CIO)
- Business managers
- Project managers
- Project portfolio managers
- Account managers
- Applications specialists
- Web programmers
- Web graphics designers
- Content creators
- Content managers or editors
- Social networking administrators

- Online marketing managers
- Customer service reps
- Systems administrators
- Network operators
- Database administrators

In addition to implementing IT projects, the CIO is responsible for overseeing all of the information systems and related technological elements required to undertake and operate online business activities. The CIO's perspective is strategic and the person holding this position often serves as an important advocate for online business initiatives. CIOs frequently have an undergraduate degree in computer information systems (or a similar field) and a graduate degree in business or information technology management. They must have many years of experience in increasingly responsible management positions.

The business management function should include internal staff. The **business manager** should be a member of the internal team that sets the objectives for the project. The business manager is responsible for implementing the elements of the business plan and reaching the objectives set by the internal team. If revisions to the plan are necessary as the project proceeds, the business manager develops specific proposals for plan modifications and additional funding and presents them to the internal team and top management for approval.

The business manager should have experience and knowledge related to the business activity that is being implemented on the electronic commerce site. For example, if business managers are assigned to a retail consumer site, they should have experience managing a retail sales operation.

In addition to including the business manager, the business management function in large electronic commerce initiatives may include other individuals who carry out specialized functions, such as project management or account management, that the business manager does not have time to handle personally. A **project manager** is a person with specific training or skills in tracking costs and the accomplishment of specific objectives in a project. Many project managers are certified by organizations such as the Project Management Institute (which you learned about earlier in this chapter) and have skills in the use of project management software.

The **project portfolio manager** is usually promoted from the ranks of the project managers and has the responsibility for tracking all ongoing projects and managing them as a portfolio. This is the person who makes the trade-offs in cost, schedule, and quality across projects and balances the needs of the organization with the resources devoted to all projects.

An **account manager** keeps track of multiple Web sites in use by a project or keeps track of the projects that will combine to create a larger Web site. Most larger projects will have a test version, a demonstration version, and a production version of the Web site located on different servers. The test version is the "under construction" version of a Web site. Because most sites are frequently updated with new features and content, the test version gives the company a place to make sure that each new feature works before exposing it to customers. The demonstration version has features that have passed testing and must be demonstrated to an internal audience (for example, the Marketing

Department) for approval. The production version is the full operating version of the site that is available to customers and other visitors. The account manager supervises the location of specific Web pages and related software installations as they are moved from test to demonstration to production. In smaller projects, the business manager handles the project and account management functions.

As more vendors provide packaged software solutions for electronic commerce, such as those you learned about in Chapter 9, companies need information systems staff that can install and maintain the software. Most large businesses have **applications specialists** who maintain accounting, human resources, and logistics software. Similarly, electronic commerce sites that buy software to handle catalogs, payment processing, and other features need applications specialists to maintain the software. Although the installation of these software packages can be outsourced, most companies prefer to train internal staff to install the software so they can be better prepared to manage the software when the site becomes operational.

Web sites have evolved from static HTML to more complex designs built with dynamic Web page generation technologies and XML data integration. As Web sites have become more complicated, the need for **Web programmers**, who design and write the underlying code for dynamic database-driven Web pages, has increased. Good Web programmers are familiar with several different dynamic Web page generation technologies and are highly skilled in at least one of them. Many Web programmers also have database manipulation and query skills, such as the ability to write SQL or PHP code.

Because the Web is a visual medium, the role of graphic elements on individual Web pages is important. A company must either retain the services of a graphics design firm, a Web design firm that includes graphics designers, or must hire employees with graphics design skills. A **Web graphics designer** is a person trained in art, layout, and composition and who also understands how Web pages are constructed. The Web graphics designer, or design team for larger sites, must ensure that the Web pages on the site are visually appealing, easy to use, and make consistent use of graphics elements from page to page.

Most larger sites and many smaller sites include content created specifically for the Web site. Other sites adapt content from existing sources within the company for use on the Web site, or purchase content to use on the site. These activities require that the company hire **content creators** to write original content and **content managers** or **content editors** to purchase existing material and adapt it for use on the site.

Many online business teams include a **social networking administrator**, who is responsible for managing the virtual community elements of the Web operation. These administrators might have backgrounds in technology, sales, customer service, or in widely diverse fields such as sociology or anthropology. They must coordinate all of the technologies that make the site work as a social network in ways that create value for the organization.

Although many organizations operate their online marketing function out of their traditional marketing departments, employees with the position of **online marketing manager** specialize in the specific techniques used to build brands and increase market share using the Web site and other online tools, such as e-mail marketing. These managers often have an extensive background in marketing and combine that with knowledge of technologies that allow them to manage the organization's online marketing function.

The Web offers businesses a unique opportunity to reach out to their customers. Thus, business-to-consumer and business-to-business sites that want to capitalize on that opportunity must include a customer relationship management function. **Customer service** personnel help design and implement customer relationship management activities in the electronic commerce operation. They can, for example, issue and administer passwords, design customer interface features, handle customer e-mail and telephone requests for service or follow-up action, and conduct telemarketing for the site. Companies strive to provide the best possible service to satisfy the demands of their customers. The increasing power of customers to organize and express their expectations on the Web is a natural extension of the increase in consumerism that has occurred over the past two decades.

Some companies outsource parts of their customer relationship management operation to independent call centers. A **call center** is a company that handles incoming customer telephone calls and e-mails for other companies. Using a call center often makes sense for smaller companies that do not have the volume of customer inquiries to justify creating an internal call center operation. Some call centers work with a variety of businesses; others focus on one specialty area. For example, a specialized call center might contract with software manufacturers to provide installation help for their software products. Call center employees who are skilled in helping customers install one software package are often able to learn how to support other software packages very quickly.

A systems administrator who understands the server hardware and operating system is an essential part of a successful electronic commerce implementation. The **systems administrator** is responsible for the system's reliable and secure operation. If the site operation is outsourced to a service provider, the service provider supplies this function. If the site is hosted by the company, it needs to devote at least one person to this job. In addition, the internal system administrator needs sufficient staff to maintain full 24/7 operation and site security. These **network operations** staff functions include load estimation and load monitoring, resolving network problems as they arise, designing and implementing fault-resistant technologies, and managing any network operations that are outsourced to service providers or telephone companies.

Most electronic commerce sites require a **database administration** function to support activities such as transaction processing, order entry, inquiry management, or shipment logistics. These activities require either an existing database into which the site is being integrated, or a separate database established for the electronic commerce initiative. It is important to have a database administrator who can effectively manage the design and implementation of this function.

Postimplementation Audits

After an electronic commerce site is successfully launched, most of the project's resources are devoted to maintaining and improving the site's operations. However, an increasing number of businesses are realizing the value of a postimplementation audit. A **postimplementation audit** (also called a **postaudit review**) is a formal review of a project after it is up and running.

The postimplementation audit gives managers a chance to examine the objectives, performance specifications, cost estimates, and scheduled delivery dates that were established for the project in its planning stage and compare them to what actually happened. In the past, most project reviews focused on identifying individuals to blame for cost overruns or missed delivery dates. Because many external forces in technology projects can overwhelm the best efforts of managers, this blame identification approach was generally unproductive, as well as uncomfortable, for the managers on the project. Today, the postimplementation audit is used by most organizations to gather lessons learned from both successful and unsuccessful projects. These lessons can be accumulated and, over time, used to create and update a set of standard best practices for the organization.

A postimplementation audit allows the internal team, the business manager, and the project manager to raise questions about the project's objectives and provide their "in-the-trenches" feedback on strategies that were set in the project's initial design. By agreeing beforehand not to lay blame, the company obtains valuable information that it can use in planning future projects and gives the participants a meaningful learning experience.

The audit should result in a comprehensive report that analyzes the project's overall performance, how well the project was administered, whether the organizational structure was appropriate for the project, and the specific performance of the project team(s). Each section of the report should compare actual results to the project's objectives. Many companies modify their project management organization structure after completing each project based on the contents of postaudit review reports. Many companies also include a confidential section in the report that evaluates each team member's performance on the project. Summaries of member performance can help managers decide which employees should be included in future team projects.

Change Management

Any information system project involves change, and change can be upsetting to people. As employees of an organization become accustomed to their specific duties, many of them draw comfort from their knowledge and develop a sense of security because they know their jobs well and are good at doing them. When changes are introduced into a workplace, employees become concerned about their abilities to cope with the changes and with their ability to continue to do good work. They often become worried that they might lose their jobs. These concerns can lead to increased stress that can be damaging to morale and work performance.

Management researchers have developed strategies for **change management**, which is the process of helping employees cope with these changes. Change management techniques include communicating the need for change to employees, including employees in the decision processes leading up to the change, allowing employees to participate in the planning for the change, and other tactics designed to help employees feel that they are a part of the change. This helps employees overcome the feelings of powerlessness that can lead to stress and reduced work performance.

Summary

This chapter provides an overview of managing the implementation of online business initiatives for both startups and existing companies. After overall goals are set, specific objectives are derived from them and include planned benefits and costs. The benefit and cost objectives should be stated in measurable terms, such as dollars or quantities, and they should be linked to the organization's business strategies. Before undertaking the initiative, the company should evaluate the initiative's estimated costs and benefits. Some costs, such as opportunity costs, can be difficult to identify and estimate.

Funding for online business implementations can come from internal sources in midsize or large firms. Small new businesses can be funded from personal savings or loans and investments made by family and friends. As the startup increases in size, it can turn to angel investors and, eventually, venture capitalists before turning to a public offering of its stock.

The most common evaluation technique for online business initiatives is ROI. The benefits of electronic commerce projects can be harder to define and quantify in monetary units than the benefits expected from most other IT projects, so managers should be careful when using quantitative measures such as ROI to evaluate electronic commerce projects.

Online business initiatives undertaken by established companies can be internally developed, outsourced in full or in part, or can use an internal business incubator. These companies should form an internal team that includes knowledgeable individuals to develop the specific project objectives and is responsible for meeting those objectives. The internal team can select from specific strategies, such as using incubators or outsourcing various parts of the project, and should supervise the staffing of any part of the project that is to be developed internally. Smaller companies or startups can develop their own online business initiatives, but some use an incubator or accelerator operated by another firm to facilitate the process. Using either approach will generally require the owners to give up some equity interest in the new initiative.

Project management is a formal way to plan and control specific tasks and resources used in a project. It provides project managers with a tool they can use to make informed trade-offs among the project elements of schedule, cost, and performance. Large organizations are beginning to use project portfolio management techniques to track and make trade-offs among multiple ongoing projects. Electronic commerce initiatives are usually completed within a short time frame and thus are less likely to run out of control than other information systems development projects.

The company must staff the online business implementation regardless of whether portions of the project are outsourced. Critical staffing areas include business management, application specialists, customer service staff, systems administration, network operations staff, social network marketing staff, and database administration.

A good way for all participants to learn from project experiences is to conduct a postimplementation audit that compares project objectives to the actual results. This comparison can provide lessons learned from the experience that will improve future projects.

Online business implementations always require change, and change can be upsetting to people. Change management techniques can help employees adjust to the changes and be more cooperative in helping implement them.

Key Terms

24/7 operation

accelerator

account manager

angel investors

applications specialists

business manager

call center

capital investments

capital projects

change management

chief information officer (CIO)

component outsourcing

content creators

content editors

content managers

customer service

database administration

downstream strategies

early outsourcing

incubator

initial public offering (IPO)

intellectual capital

late outsourcing

mentor network

metrics

network operations

online marketing manager

opportunity cost

outsourcing

partial outsourcing

postaudit review

postimplementation audit

project management

project management software

project manager

project portfolio management

project portfolio manager

return on investment (ROI)

social networking administrator

systems administrator

total cost of ownership (TCO)

upstream strategies

venture capitalists

Web graphics designer

Web programmers

Review Questions

1. What are the two keys to successful implementation of an information technology project?
2. Provide two brief examples of business strategies that might be included in the plan for an online business initiative.
3. What is the goal of a downstream strategy?
4. What is the goal of an upstream strategy?
5. How might an online retailer measure increased customer satisfaction?
6. What is total cost of ownership?
7. Provide one brief example of an opportunity cost.
8. What is an angel investor?
9. What is a venture capitalist?
10. What is an initial public offering (IPO)?

11. What is a capital project?
12. What specific information is provided by a return-on-investment (ROI) calculation?
13. What is late outsourcing?
14. What is component outsourcing?
15. What is project management?
16. What is the function of a database administrator in an online business operation?
17. What is a postimplementation audit?
18. .What is change management?

Exercises

1. Midtown Bistro, a local restaurant, has hired you to help them develop a new online business initiative. The company wants to use social networking actively in its marketing plan and integrate it into its Web site. In one or two paragraphs, identify three benefits that Midtown Bistro might hope to obtain from this initiative and then write one additional paragraph about how it might measure its achievement of each benefit objective.

2. In about 100 words, name four activities that a business might want to accomplish online and for each activity, briefly explain why its success might be difficult to measure.

3. In about 100 words, explain why companies began creating pilot Web sites during the second wave of electronic commerce.

4. In a paragraph or two, outline two online activities that businesses can use to improve the value they provide to customers.

5. In about 100 words, list and briefly describe four specific activities that a company might undertake in the formation of an online business initiative.

6. In the third wave of electronic commerce, businesses no longer limit their vision of online activity to Web sites. In two or three paragraphs, outline at least two online business implementations that would not be accomplished by building or improving a Web site.

7. No matter how a company measures the benefits provided by an online business implementation, it usually tries to measure those benefits in monetary units. In a paragraph or two, explain why this is a good practice.

8. In one paragraph, name and briefly describe two specific costs that might be included in the total cost of ownership of an online business initiative.

9. The cost of launching an online business has increased steadily since the early years of electronic commerce. In about 100 words, explain why this change has occurred

10. In about 100 words, explain the advantages and disadvantages of using ROI to evaluate online business proposals.

11. In two or three paragraphs, explain why early outsourcing is often used for some parts of online business initiatives.

12. In about 300 words, explain how incubators and accelerators work. In your answer, compare these two approaches and provide at least one example of each.

13. In about 100 words, outline the functions of project management software. In your answer, explain what problems this type of software is designed to prevent.

Cases

C1. IdeaMarket

Bill Gross started his first company (a solar-powered device manufacturer) when he was 15 years old. After graduating from Caltech, he started an audio equipment manufacturer that was sold to Lotus and an educational software company that was sold to Cendant. With the proceeds of those sales, he decided to act on his fascination with the idea of converting ideas into profitable businesses and the business potential of the Web and, in 1996, joined with several partners to create Idealab.

Idealab was one of the first companies to provide an incubator that was open to individual entrepreneurs. Idealab provided venture capital and gave entrepreneurs a place to work and develop their business ideas alongside other entrepreneurs. In the first wave of electronic commerce, Idealab was very successful. Although many of its incubated companies eventually failed, enough of them succeeded that Idealab was able to fund several generations of new businesses through its operations. In its first year, it supported 10 new businesses, including the very successful CitySearch Web site. In its second year, Idealab helped create another 10 businesses, including the successful sites Shopping.com, Tickets.com, and WeddingChannel .com. In subsequent years, Idealab incubated companies such as NetZero, Cooking.com, CarsDirect.com, Picasa, and GoTo.com (which later became Overture and was eventually acquired by Yahoo!). Not all of Idealab's companies were successful, however. One of the most dramatic failures of the first wave of electronic commerce, eToys, had been an Idealab company. Idealab had more winners than losers, though; by early 2000, the company had more than $4 billion in assets.

In 2000, Gross decided to go beyond Idealab's original purpose as an incubator and developed a plan to compete with Amazon using existing Idealab companies. His plan was to combine about 10 of the companies in the incubator (including specialty retailer Eve.com and online jewelry store Ice.com) and promote them (using large amounts of money that would be raised from outside investors) as a single marketplace under the name Big.com. However, just as Gross began raising money to support the launch of this new marketplace, the pool of dot-com investment funds dried up. The new combined company failed. Eve.com and Big.com no longer exist. The founders of Ice.com bought their company back from Idealab and moved it to their home in Montreal (where the company is now operating profitably).

Within a few months, the failure of Big.com and a decline in the market value of Idealab's other holdings cut the company's asset value from $4 billion to $200 million. In January 2002, 44 Idealab investors sued Gross and other Idealab managers for $750 million, alleging mismanagement of funds. Eighteen months later, the suit was dismissed and Gross was once again able to devote his time to operating Idealab as an incubator; however, Idealab laid off more than two-thirds of its employees and stopped accepting outside venture capital. Idealab stopped providing incubator space for entrepreneurs who had developed ideas on their own and started funding only ideas generated by the Idealab management team. In 2012, Idealab returned once again to funding outside entrepreneurs and has returned to incubating successful ideas, such as New Matter, a company that makes low-cost 3D printers.

In 2014, Gross launched IdeaMarket, a crowdsourced marketplace that matches ideas with entrepreneurs who might be able to turn them into businesses and investors who can finance the startup. Anyone with an idea for which they have neither the skills nor the resources to develop themselves can post it on IdeaMarket. The people proposing the idea can invest some of their own money in the project if they wish, but most of the funding is provided by other investors who have been approved by IdeaMarket. Entrepreneurs who are interested in developing the idea into a business can submit a plan for doing so. Visitors to the Web site can suggest improvements to the business plan and can vote for or against it. The plans are eventually reviewed by the investors or IdeaMarket to reach a decision on whether to move forward or not. The person with the idea gets a 5 to 20 percent interest in the new venture (depending on how much money they invest, if any), site visitors who contribute to the plan share in a pooled interest of 5 percent, IdeaMarket gets 5 percent, and the rest is given to the team of entrepreneurs and the main investors.

REQUIRED:

1. Bill Gross, in a widely viewed TED Talk, made the point that the most important key to success when introducing a new product or service is timing. In about 200 words, analyze Idealab's 2000 decision to change its focus from being an incubator to merging its companies in an attempt to compete with Amazon.com. In your analysis, discuss whether the decision was a strategic error or just a case of bad timing.

2. In about 200 words, explain why you think Gross decided to reverse his decision to develop only internally generated ideas. Be sure to consider whether this change will help Idealab succeed in the third wave of electronic commerce.

3. In 2009, a company, Quirky, was launched that used crowdsourcing to evaluate ideas submitted by inventors. Quirky would fund the development of the most popular product ideas that it decided were feasible to create and sell profitably and shared the profits with the inventors. Despite some successful products, the company closed in 2015. Using your favorite search engine or the resources of your library to learn more about Quirky, write a report of about 500 words in which you compare Quirky to IdeaMarket. In your report, evaluate the revenue models of the two companies, identify reasons for Quirky's failures, and comment on the likelihood that IdeaMarket will be able to avoid a similar fate based on your comparison and analysis.

Note: Your instructor might assign you to a group to complete this case and might ask you to prepare a formal presentation of your results to your class.

C2. Davis Humanics

Davis Humanics (DH) is a company founded in 1982 that provides human resources services to about 7000 companies with a total of nearly 100,000 employees. These services include payroll processing, tax filing, health insurance and claims management, and retirement plan management. DH has annual sales of $2 billion and about 1000 employees. In 1997, DH launched a Web site that has since grown to include a variety of tools for connecting with customers. DH has expanded rapidly and has clients of all sizes, ranging from smaller companies with fewer than 50 employees to Fortune 500 companies.

As DH grows, it is having trouble maintaining a consistent quality of service. Account managers each must handle more clients, making it more difficult for them to maintain personal contact with the human resources executives who control DH's contracts. In the past, account managers worked with a small set of client contact people, but now account managers must work with more people, many of whom they have never met. Further, a number of different client employees have regular contacts with DH operations staff (who handle input tasks), DH systems staff (who help customize the interfaces between DH systems and client systems), and DH professional staff (lawyers, actuaries, and human resources professionals who consult with DH clients and their legal counsel regarding the operation of their retirement and benefits plans).

Because DH's clients vary so much in size and how they operate, DH has to be flexible in handling input data. For example, DH's payroll-processing service allows clients many different ways to send in time card data. The largest clients arrange for customized computer-to-computer transfer of information. Some large clients use EDI transfers. Most medium and smaller-sized clients e-mail the time card information, but some mail paper lists that DH must scan into its systems. The health insurance claims-handling operation is even more troublesome. In addition to having clients submit information in various formats, the insurance companies demand that DH submit information in specific formats that are different for each insurance company.

The complexity of DH's operations is growing as rapidly as the company adds new clients. Sandi Higbee, DH's Director of Operations, asks for your help in outlining a Web-based customer relationship management (CRM) system that will help manage the account managers' ever-increasing levels of customer contact (recall that you learned about CRM systems in Chapter 9). Sandi reviewed the products offered by several leading CRM vendors and believes that one might work as a base product, but no matter which product is chosen, she believes that substantial customization will be necessary because DH's operations are so complex and different from most companies that sell products or simple services to customers. A good CRM system for DH would need to monitor all types of customer interactions with DH account managers, operations staff, systems staff, and professional staff. In addition, the system's Web interface should allow DH clients to access parts of the CRM system so they can track DH's follow-up on their work requests and pending inquiries.

DH evaluates all capital projects, including IT projects, using ROI. Sandi is worried about this because she believes that many of the benefits of this CRM project will be hard to quantify. On the other hand, the costs of the CRM project (software and hardware purchase and cost of consultants who will customize the CRM software to meet DH's specific needs) will be very easy to quantify and will be large. Sandi expects the vendor-consultant teams to submit bids of between $1 million and $2 million for this project.

REQUIRED:

1. Prepare an outline of the benefits that DH might expect to obtain from this CRM project. Use categories to organize your list of benefits; for example, you might identify benefits that will accrue to DH's account managers, operations staff, IT staff, and professional staff. Because DH's clients will also benefit, you might be able to identify benefits that will accrue to DH's Marketing and Sales departments or to DH's New Product Development department. Be sure to include any long-term benefits that you think might occur after the CRM system has been in place for several years.

2. Prepare a one-page memorandum to the DH board of directors in which you argue against using ROI as the primary method for evaluating this project. Keep in mind that these directors have little time to review your arguments and are very much inclined to use ROI for all project evaluations.

Note: Your instructor might assign you to a group to complete this case and might ask you to prepare a formal presentation of your results to your class.

For Further Study and Research

Alton, L. 2015. "Five Reasons Why a Good Business Idea Is Never Enough to Succeed," *Entrepreneur*, September 2. http://www.entrepreneur.com/article/249886

Anthes, G. 2008. "What's Your Project Worth?" *Computerworld*, 42(11), March 10, 29–31.

Aragon, L. 2004. "Idealab: Bubble Fund Finds Itself Back at Square One," *Venture Capital Journal*, 44(6), June, 20.

Armour, P. 2010. "Return at Risk: Calculating the True Likely Cost of Projects," *Communications of the ACM*, 53(9), September, 23–25.

Blazier, A. 2003. "Far from Dead, Idealab Continues to Build for Future," *San Gabriel Valley Tribune*, July 12, C1.

Boyer, A. 2012. "Social Media for Small Businesses with 'No Time,' " *BlogWorld*, February 25. http://www.blogworld.com/2012/02/25/social-media-for-small-businesses-with-no-time/

Brandel, M. 2008. "Xtreme ROI," *Computerworld*, 42(7), February 11, 30–33.

Casserly, M. 2013. "Can This Y-Combinator Startup's Technology Keep Couples Out of Divorce Court?" *Forbes*, April 10. http://www.forbes.com/sites/meghancasserly/2013/04/10/wevorce-y-combinator-technology-divorce-court/

Cendrowski, S. 2012. "Nike's New Marketing Mojo," *Fortune*, February 27, 81–88.

Cerpa, N. and J. Verner. 2009. "Why Did Your Project Fail?" *Communications of the ACM*, 52(12), December, 130–134.

The Economist. 2014. "Special Report: Tech Startups, a Cambrian Moment," January 14, 1–14.

Fisher, T. 2009. "ROI in Social Media: A Look at the Arguments," *Journal of Database Marketing & Customer Strategy Management*, 16(3), September, 189–195.

Fleming, Q. and J. Koppelman. 2003. "What's Your Project's Real Price Tag?" *Harvard Business Review*, 81(9), September, 20–21.

Forrest, C. 2014. "Accelerators vs. Incubators: What Startups Need to Know," *TechRepublic*, November 17. http://www.techrepublic.com/article/accelerators-vs-incubators-what-startups-need-to-know/

Gerber, S. 2015. "Thirteen Things Tech Founders Should Look for in an Incubator or Accelerator," *Mashable*, June 4. http://mashable.com/2015/06/04/tech-incubator-accelerator/#Rigzv47apqkN

Grimes, A. 2004. "Court Deals Blow to Investors' Suit against Idealab," *The Wall Street Journal*, June 30, B6.

Gross, B. 2015. "The Single Biggest Reason Why Startups Succeed," *TED2015*, March. http://www.ted.com/talks/bill_gross_the_single_biggest_reason_why_startups_succeed

Haeussler, C., H. Patzelt, and S. Zahra. 2012. "Strategic Alliances and Product Development in High Technology New Firms: The Moderating Effect of Technological Capabilities," *Journal of Business Venturing*, 27(2), March, 217–233.

Hof, R. 2014. "With IdeaMarket, Idealab's Bill Gross Wants to Create One Million Startups," *Forbes*, September 8. http://www.forbes.com/sites/roberthof/2014/09/08/with-ideamarket-idealabs-bill-gross-wants-to-create-1-million-startups/

Jepson, K. 2009. "How Two Credit Unions Are Achieving Banner ROI on Their Web Sites," *Credit Union Journal*, September 21, 1–15.

Keefe, P. 2003. "Backing Up ROI," *Computerworld*, 37(12), March 24, 22.

Keen, J. and R. Joshi. 2011. *Making Technology Investments Profitable: ROI Roadmap from Business Case to Value Realization*. Second edition. Hoboken, NJ: Wiley.

Keil, M. and D. Robey, 1999. "Turning Around Troubled Software Projects: An Exploratory Study of the De-Escalation of Commitment to Failing Courses of Action," *Journal of Management Information Systems*, 15(4), 63–87.

Kerzner, H. 2013. *Project Management: A Systems Approach to Planning, Scheduling, and Controlling*. Eleventh edition. New York: John Wiley & Sons.

Kirsner, S. 2015. "Incubator and Accelerator Update: Mobile, Financial Services, Healthcare," *beta Boston*, February 17. http://www.betaboston.com/news/2015/02/17/incubator-accelerator-update-mobile-financial-services-healthcare/

Lacity, M. and L. Wilcocks. 2013. "Outsourcing Business Processes for Innovation," *MIT Sloan Management Review*, 54(3), 63–69.

Lagorio-Chafkin, C. 2015. "What Happened to Quirky?" *Inc. Magazine*, September 15. http://www.inc.com/christine-lagorio/what-happened-to-quirky.html

Levy, S. 2013. "Y Combinator Is Boot Camp for Startups," *Wired*, May 17. http://www.wired.com/magazine/2011/05/ff_ycombinator/all/

Mathiassen, L. and T. Tuunanen. 2011. "Managing Requirements Risks in IT Projects," *IT Professional*, 13(6), November–December, 40–47.

McConnell, S. 1996. *Rapid Development: Taming Wild Software Schedules*. Redmond, WA: Microsoft Press.

Metz, R. 2012. "The Startup Whisperer," *Business Impact*, February, 16.

Nocera, J. and E. Florian. 2001. "Bill Gross Blew Through $800 Million in Eight Months (and He's Got Nothing to Show for It): Why Is He Still Smiling?" *Fortune*, 143(5), March 5, 70–77.

Phillips, J., W. Brantley, and P. Phillips. 2012. *Project Management ROI*. Hoboken, NJ: Wiley.

Reitzig, M. 2011. "Is Your Company Choosing the Best Innovation Ideas?" *MIT Sloan Management Review*, 52(4), 47–52.

Rich, N. 2013. "Pitch. Eat. Sleep. Pitch. Eat. Sleep. Pitch. Eat. Sleep. Pitch. Eat. Sleep. Pitch. Eat… Silicon Valley's Startup Machine," *The New York Times*, May 5, MM36–MM48.

Sawhney, M. 2002. "Damn the ROI, Full Speed Ahead: 'Show Me the Money' May Not Be the Right Demand for E-Business Projects," *CIO*, 15(19), July 15, 36–38.

Schonfeld, E. 2007. "The Startup King's New Gig," *Business 2.0*, 8(9), October, 68.

Schwalbe, K. 2013. *Information Technology Project Management*. Seventh edition. Boston, MA: Course Technology.

Schwalbe, K. 2015. *Introduction to Project Management*. Fifth edition. Minneapolis, MN: Schwalbe Publishing.

Shu, C. 2013. "Seoul-based Accelerator SparkLabs' Latest Class Includes Wearable Tech and Mobile Game Makers," *TechCrunch*, December 4. http://techcrunch.com/2013/12/04/seoul-based-accelerator-sparklabs-latest-class-includes-wearable-tech-and-mobile-game-makers/

Silverster, J. 2015. "The Rise and Fall of Quirky: The Start-Up That Bet Big on the Genius of Regular Folks," *New York Magazine*, September 13, 2015. http://nymag.com/daily/intelligencer/2015/09/they-were-quirky.html

Taylor, H., E. Artman, and J. Woelfer. 2012. "Information Technology Project Risk Management: Bridging the Gap Between Research and Practice." *Journal of Information Technology*, 27, 17–34.

Wortham, J. 2013. "A Missing Revenue Stream from Mobile Apps," *The New York Times*, December 14, BU3.

Yourdon, E. and P. Becker. 1997. *Death March: The Complete Software Developer's Guide to Surviving "Mission Impossible" Projects*. Upper Saddle River, NJ: Prentice Hall.

Glossary

24/7 operation The operation of a site or service 24 hours a day, seven days a week.

Abandoned cart management A software that enables the shopping cart to retain a record of what customers have added to their shopping carts when their session is terminated for some reason.

Accelerator A company that performs a function similar to that of an incubator; however, accelerators structure their activities differently.

Acceptance An expression of willingness to take an offer, including all of its stated terms.

Access control list (ACL) A list of resources and the usernames of people who are permitted access to those resources within a computer system.

Account aggregation A feature of online banks that allows a customer to obtain bank, investment, loan, and other financial account information from multiple Web sites and to display it all in one location at the bank's Web site.

Account manager A person who keeps track of multiple Web sites in use by a project or keeps track of the projects that combine to create a larger Web site.

Accredited Standards Committee X12 (ASC X12) A committee that develops and maintains uniform EDI standards in the United States.

Acquirer fees Fees charged by an acquiring bank for providing payment card processing services.

Acquiring bank Synonymous with merchant bank, which is a bank that does business with merchants who want to accept credit cards.

Acquisition cost The total amount of money that a site spends, on average, to draw one visitor to the site.

Active content Programs that are embedded transparently in Web pages that cause action to occur.

active RFIDs RFIDs that have their own power supply.

Active wiretapping An integrity threat that exists when an unauthorized party can alter a message.

ActiveX An object, or control, that contains programs and properties that are put in Web pages to perform particular tasks.

ad exchange network A network that coordinates ad sharing so that other sites run one company's ad while that company's site runs other exchange members' ads.

Ad view A Web site visitor page request that contains an advertisement.

adaptive supply chain A condition that leads to higher efficiency, lower costs, and greater profits.

Ad-blocking software A program that prevents banner ads and pop-up ads from loading.

Addressable media Advertising efforts sent to a known addressee; these include direct mail, telephone calls, and e-mail.

Advance fee fraud A scam in which the perpetrator offers to share the proceeds of some large payoff with the victim if the victim will make a "good faith" deposit or provide some partial funding first. The perpetrator then disappears with the deposit.

Advanced Encryption Standard (AES) The encryption standard designed to keep government information secure using the Rijndael algorithm. It was introduced in February 2001 by the National Institute of Standards and Technology (NIST).

Advertising-subscription mixed revenue model A revenue model in which subscribers pay a fee and accept some level of advertising.

Advertising-supported revenue model A revenue model in which Web sites provide free content along with advertising or messages provided by other companies that pay the Web site operator for delivering the advertising or messages.

Affiliate marketing An advertising technique in which one Web site (called an "affiliate") includes descriptions, reviews, ratings, or other information about products that are sold on another Web site. The affiliate site includes links to the selling site, which pays the affiliate site a commission on sales made to visitors who arrived from a link on the affiliate site.

Affiliate program broker A company that serves as a clearinghouse or marketplace for sites that run affiliate programs and sites that want to become affiliates.

Amazon law State laws that require online retailers to collect and remit sales taxes on sales they make in their states, even though the online retailers do not have nexus with the state.

American National Standards Institute (ANSI) The coordinating body for electrical, mechanical, and other technical standards in the United States.

Analytical processing A technique that examines stored information and looks for patterns in the data that are not yet known or suspected; also called data mining.

Anchor tag The HTML tag used to specify hyperlinks.

Angel investors Investors who fund the initial startup of an online business. In return for their capital, angel investors become stockholders in the business and often own more of the business than the founder. Typical funding by angel investors is between a few hundred thousand dollars and a few million dollars.

Animated GIF Animated Web ad graphics intended to grab a visitor's attention.

Anonymous digital cash The digital cash like bills and coins cannot be traced back to the person who spent it.

Anonymous Web service A service that provides a measure of secrecy to Web surfers who use them by replacing the user's IP address with the IP address of the anonymous Web service on the front end of any URLs that the user visits.

Antivirus software Software that detects viruses and worms and either deletes them or isolates them on the client computer so they cannot run.

Applet A program that executes within another program; it cannot execute directly on a computer.

Application program (application, application software) A program that performs a specific function, such as creating invoices, calculating payroll, or processing payments received from customers.

Application program interface (API) A general name for the ways programs interconnect with each other.

Application server A middle-tier software and hardware combination that lies between the Internet and a corporate back-end server.

Application service provider (ASP) A Web based site that provides management of applications such as spreadsheets, human resources management, or e-mail to companies for a fee.

Application software Synonymous with application, which is a program that performs a specific function.

Applications specialist The member of an electronic commerce team who is responsible for maintenance of software that performs a specific function, such as catalog, payment processing, accounting, human resources, and logistics software.

Apps Application software that is sold for use on mobile phones.

AS2 (Applicability Statement 2) A specification based on the HTTP rules for Web page transfers.

AS3 (Applicability Statement 3) A more secure version of AS2.

Ascending-price auction A type of auction in which bidders publicly announce their successively higher bids until no higher bid is forthcoming; also called an English auction.

Asymmetric connection An Internet connection that provides different bandwidths for each direction.

Asymmetric digital subscriber line (ADSL) Internet connections using the DSL protocol with bandwidths from 16 to 640 Kbps upstream and 1.5 to 9 Mbps downstream.

Asymmetric encryption Synonymous with public-key encryption, which is the encoding of messages using two mathematically related but distinct numeric keys.

Asynchronous transfer mode (ATM) Internet connections with bandwidths of up to 622 Gbps.

Attachment A data file (document, spreadsheet, or other) that is appended to an e-mail message.

Auction consignment services Companies that take an item and create an online auction for that item, handle the transaction, and remit the balance of the proceeds after deducting a fee. These services are performed on behalf of people and small businesses who want to use an online auction but do not have the skills or the time to become a seller.

Auctioneer The person who manages an auction.

Authority to bind The ability of an individual to commit his or her company to a contract.

Automated clearing house (ACH) One of several systems set up by banks or government agencies, such as the U.S. Federal Reserve Board, that process high volumes of low dollar amount electronic fund transfers.

Backbone routers Computers that handle packet traffic along the Internet's main connecting points; they can each handle more than 50 million packets per second.

Backdoor An way of accessing software left open, accidentally or intentionally, that allows users to run the program without going through the normal authentication procedure for access to the program.

Back-end processor A banking service provider that handles charge backs and any other reconciliation items through the interchange network and the acquiring and issuing banks, including the ACH transfers.

Bandwidth The amount of data that can be transmitted in a fixed amount of time. Also, the number of simultaneous site visitors that a Web site can accommodate without degrading service.

Base 2 (binary) A number system in which each digit is either a 0 or a 1, corresponding to a condition of either "off" or "on." Also known as a binary system.

Bayesian revision A statistical technique in which additional knowledge is used to revise earlier estimates of probabilities.

Behavioral segmentation The creation of a separate experience for customers based on their behavior.

Benchmarking Testing that compares hardware and software performances.

Bid An offer of a certain price made on an item that is up for auction.

Bidder A potential buyer at an auction; one who places bids.

Big data Very large stores of information such as that collected by online sellers about their customers.

Bill presentment A Web site feature that allows customers to view and pay bills online.

biller-direct EBPP systems The systems used by large companies who want to manage and maintain their own systems.

Biometric security device A security device that uses an element of a person's biological makeup to confirm identification. These devices include writing pads that detect the form and pressure of a person writing a signature, eye scanners that read the pattern of blood vessels in a person's retina, and palm scanners that read the palm of a person's hand (rather than just one fingerprint).

Black hat hackers Hackers who use their skills for harmful purposes.

Black list spam filter Software that looks for From addresses in incoming messages that are known to be spammers. The software can delete the message or put it into a separate mailbox for review.

Blade server A server configuration in which small server computers are each installed on a single computer board and then many of those boards are installed into a rackmounted frame.

Blog Synonymous with Web log, which is a Web site on which people post their thoughts and invite others to add commentary.

Bluetooth A wireless standard that is used for short distances and lower bandwidth connections.

Bonded warehouse A secure location where incoming international shipments can be held until customs requirements are satisfied or until payment arrangements are completed.

Border router The computers located at an organizations point of connection to the Internet that decide the best path on which to forward each packet of information as it travels on the Internet to its destination. Synonymous with gateway computer and gateway router.

Bot (robot) A program that automatically searches the Web to find Web pages that might be interesting to people.

Botnet A robotic network that can act as an attacking unit, sending spam or launching denial-of-service attacks against specific Web sites. Synonymous with zombie farm.

Brand Customers' perceptions of the attributes of a product or service, including name, history, and reputation.

Breach of contract The failure of one party to comply with the terms of a contract.

Broadband Connections that operate at speeds of greater than about 200 Kbps.

Browser-wrap acceptance Synonymous with Web-wrap acceptance, which is the compliance with EULA conditions with which a user agrees through the act of using a Web site.

Buffer An area of a computer's memory that is set aside to hold data read from a file or database.

Buffer overrun, buffer overflow An error that occurs when programs filling buffers malfunction and overfill the buffer, spilling the excess data outside the designated buffer memory area. Also called buffer overflow.

Bulk mail Electronic junk mail that can include solicitations, advertisements, or e-mail chain letters. Also called spam or unsolicited commercial e-mail.

Bulletin board system (BBS) Computers that allow users to connect through modems (using dial-up connections through telephone lines) to read and post messages in a common area.

Business activity A task performed by a worker in the course of doing his or her job.

Business logic Rules of a particular business.

Business manager The member of an electronic commerce team who is responsible for implementing the elements of the business plan and reaching the objectives set by the internal team. The business manager should have experience in and knowledge of the business activity being implemented in the site.

Business model A set of processes that combine to yield a profit.

Business process offshoring The distribution of nonmanufacturing business activities to international suppliers.

Business process patent A patent that protects a specific set of procedures for conducting a particular business activity.

Business processes The activities in which businesses engage as they conduct commerce.

Business rules The way a company runs its business.

Business unit A unit within a company that is organized around a specific combination of product, distribution channel, and customer type. Synonymous with strategic business unit.

Business-to-business (B2B) Transactions conducted between businesses on the Web.

Business-to-consumer (B2C) Transactions conducted between shoppers and businesses on the Web.

Business-to-government (B2G) Business transactions conducted with government agencies, such as paying taxes and filing required reports.

Call center A company that handles telephone calls and e-mails for other companies.

Cannibalization The loss of traditional sales of a product to its electronic counterpart.

Capital investment A major outlay of funds made by a company to purchase fixed assets such as property, a factory, or equipment.

Capital project Synonymous with capital investment.

Card not present transaction A credit card transaction in which the card holder is not at the merchant's location and the merchant does not see the card. Includes mail order, online, and telephone sales.

Card verification number (CVN), card code verification (CCV), card verification data (CVD), card verification value (CVV or CV2), card verification code (CVC), card verification value code (CVVC), card security code (CSC), verification code (V-Code or V Code) A three- or four-digit number that is printed on the credit card, but is not encoded in the card's magnetic strip, which establishes that the purchaser has the card (or has seen the card) and is likely not using a stolen card number.

Cascading Style Sheets (CSS) An HTML feature that allows designers to apply multiple predefined page display styles to Web pages.

Casher The participant in a phishing scam who uses the acquired information.

Catalog On electronic commerce sites, a listing of goods or services that may include photographs and descriptions, often stored in a database.

Catalog model A revenue model in which the seller mails printed catalogs mailed to prospective buyers who can place orders by mail or by calling the seller's toll-free telephone number.

Cause marketing An affiliate marketing program that benefits a charitable organization.

Centralized architecture A server structure that uses a few very large and fast computers.

Certification authority (CA) A company that issues digital certificates to organizations or individuals.

Challenge-response A content-filtering security technique that requires an unknown sender to reply to a challenge presented in an e-mail. These challenges are designed so that a human can respond easily, but a computer would have difficulty formulating the response.

Change management The process of helping employees cope with changes in the workplace.

Channel conflict The problem that arises when a company's sales in one sales outlet interfere with its sales in another sales outlet; for example, when sales through the company's Web site interfere with sales in that company's retail store.

Channel cooperation A strategy that coordinates sales and credit among various sales outlets, including online, catalog, and brick and-mortar sales.

Chargeback The process in which a merchant bank retrieves the money it placed in a merchant account as a result of a cardholder successfully contesting a charge.

Charge card A payment card with no preset spending limit. The entire amount charged to the card must be paid in full each month.

Check 21 A U.S. law that permits banks to replace the physical movement of checks with transmission of scanned images.

Chief information officer (CIO) An organization's top technology manager; responsible for overseeing all of the business's information systems and related technological elements.

Cipher text Text that is composed of a seemingly random assemblage of bits. Cipher text is what messages become after they are encrypted.

Circuit A specific route between source and destination along which data travels.

Circuit switching A way of connecting computers or other devices that uses a centrally controlled single connection. In this method, which is used by telephone companies to provide voice telephone service, the connection is made, data is transferred, and the connection is terminated.

Click Synonymous with click-through.

Clickstream Data about site visitors.

Click-through The loading of an advertiser's Web page that results from a visitor clicking an advertisement on another Web page.

Click-wrap acceptance A user's compliance with a site's EULA or its terms and conditions through clicking a button on the Web site.

Client-level filtering An e-mail content filtering technique in which the filtering software is placed on the individual user's computer.

Client/server architecture A combination of client computers running Web client software and server computers running Web server software.

Client-side digital wallet An electronic or digital wallet that stores a consumer's information on the consumer's own computer.

Client-side scripting The generation of active content through software on the browser.

Closed architecture The use of proprietary communication protocols by computer manufacturers in the early days of computing, preventing computers made by different manufacturers from being connected to each other. Also called proprietary architecture.

Closed loop system A payment card arrangement involving a consumer, a merchant, and a payment card company (such as American Express or Discover) that processes transactions between the consumer and merchant without involving banks.

Closing tag The second half of a two-sided HTML tag; it is identified by a slash (/) that precedes the tag's name.

Cloud computing The practice of replacing a company's investment in computing equipment by selling Internet-based access to its own computing hardware and software.

collaborative commerce Using Internet technologies to integrate the design, development, construction, testing, and refinement of products.

Collector In a phishing attack, the computer that collects data from the potential victim.

Co-location (collocation, colocation) An Internet service arrangement in which the service provider rents a physical space to the client to install its own server hardware.

Commerce service provider (CSP) A Web host service that also provides commerce hosting services on its computer.

Commodity item A product or service that has become so standardized and well-known that buyers cannot detect a difference in the offerings of various sellers; buyers usually base their purchase decisions for such products and services solely on price.

Common law The part of English and U.S. law that is established by the history of law.

Communication modes Ways of identifying and reaching customers.

Companies The business activity occurring within large hierarchical business organizations.

Component outsourcing Synonymous with partial outsourcing; the outsourcing of the design, development, implementation, or operation of specific portions of an electronic commerce system.

Component-based application system A business logic approach that separates presentation logic from business logic.

Computer forensics The field responsible for the collection, preservation, and analysis of computer-related evidence to be used in legal proceedings.

Computer forensics expert An individual hired to access client computers to locate information that can be used in legal proceedings.

Computer network Any technology that allows people to connect computers to each other.

Computer security The protection of computer resources from various types of threats.

Computer virus Synonymous with virus, which is software that attaches itself to another program and can cause damage when the host program is activated.

Configuration table Information about connections that lead to particular groups of routers, specifications on which connections to use first, and rules for handling instances of heavy packet traffic and network congestion.

Conflict of laws A situation in which federal, state, and local laws address the same issues in different ways.

Consideration The bargained-for exchange of something valuable, such as money, property, or future services.

consolidator EBPP system An electronic bill payment and presentment system in which separate company (the consolidator) aggregates all of a customer's bills on its system.

Constructive notice The idea that citizens should know that when they leave one area and enter another, they become subject to the laws of the new area.

Consumer-to-business An industry term for electronic commerce that occurs in general consumer auctions; bidders at a general consumer auction might be businesses.

Consumer-to-consumer (C2C) A category of electronic commerce that includes individuals who buy and sell items among themselves.

Content creator A person who writes original content for a Web site.

content delivery networks (CDNs) A service in which the companies store large file contents on multiple servers located throughout the Internet.

Content editor A person who purchases and adapts existing material for use on a Web site.

Content management software Software used by companies to control the large amounts of text, graphics, and media files used in business.

Content manager Synonymous with content editor.

Contextual advertising An advertising technique in which ads are placed in proximity to related content.

Contract An agreement between two or more legal entities that provides for an exchange of value between or among them.

Contract purchasing Direct materials purchasing in which the company negotiates long-term contracts for most of the materials that it will need. Also called replenishment purchasing.

Conversion The transition of a first-time visitor to a customer.

Conversion cost The total amount of money that a site spends, on average, to induce one visitor to make a purchase, sign up for a subscription, or (on an advertising-supported site) register.

Conversion rate Used in advertising to calculate the percentage of recipients that respond to an ad or promotion.

Cookies Bits of information about Web site visitors created by Web sites and stored on client computers.

Copy control An electronic mechanism for providing a fixed upper limit to the number of copies that one can make of a digital work.

Copyright A legal protection of intellectual property.

Cost per click (CPC) A pricing metric in which a site monitors the number of visitors who click an ad and charges for each click rather than for each time the ad is shown on a Web page.

Cost per thousand (CPM) An advertising pricing metric that equals the dollar amount paid to reach 1000 people in an estimated audience.

Countermeasure A physical or logical procedure that recognizes, reduces, or eliminates a threat.

Cracker A technologically skilled person who uses his or her skills to obtain unauthorized entry into computers or network systems, usually with the intent of stealing information or damaging the information, the system's software, or the system's hardware.

Crawler Synonymous with spider, which is the first part of a search engine, which automatically and frequently searches the Web to find pages and updates its database of information about old Web sites.

Credit card A payment card that has a spending limit based on the cardholder's credit limit. A minimum monthly payment must be made against the balance on the card, and interest is charged on the unpaid balance.

Credit card associations Member-run organizations that issue credit cards to individual consumers. Also called customer issuing banks.

Crowdfunding site Also called a crowdsourcing site, a social networking site that allows users to solicit investments or contributions from other users.

Crowdsourcing site Also called a crowdfunding site, a social networking site that allows users to solicit investments or contributions from other users.

Cryptocurrency An encrypted form of currency.

Cryptography The science that studies encryption, which is the hiding of messages so that only the sender and receiver can read them.

Culture The combination of language and customs that are unique to a particular population.

Customer issuing banks (issuing banks) Member-run organizations that issue credit cards to individual consumers. Also called credit card associations.

Customer life cycle The five stages of customer loyalty.

Customer portal A corporate Web site designed to meet the needs of customers by offering additional services such as private stores, part number cross-referencing, product-use guidelines, and safety information.

Customer relationship management (CRM) Synonymous with technology-enabled relationship management, it is the obtaining and use of detailed customer information.

Customer relationship management (CRM) software Software that collects data on customer activities; this data is then used by managers to conduct analytical activities.

Customer service The people within an electronic commerce team who are responsible for managing customer relationships in the electronic commerce operation.

Customer value The cost that a customer pays for a product, minus the benefits the customer gains from the product.

Customer-based marketing strategy An approach to Web site design that accommodates the differing needs of various types of customers.

Customer-centric The Web site development approach of putting the customer at the center of all site designs.

Customs broker A company that arranges the payment of tariffs and compliance with customs laws for international shipments.

Customs duty (duty) A tax levied on a product as it enters a country.

Cyberbullying Threats, sexual remarks, or pejorative comments transmitted on the Internet or posted on Web sites.

Cybersquatting The practice of registering a domain name that is the trademark of another person or company with the hope that the trademark owner will pay huge amounts of money for the domain rights.

Cybervandalism The electronic defacing of an existing Web site page.

Data analytics Sophisticated statistical tools for investigating patterns and knowledge contained in big data.

Data Encryption Standard (DES) An encryption standard adopted by the U.S. government for encrypting sensitive information.

Data Interchange Standards Association (DISA) A not-for-profit organization devoted to the development of cross-industry electronic business information interchange standards such as EDI and XML.

Data mining A technique that examines stored information and looks for patterns in the data that are not yet known or suspected. Also called analytical processing.

Data warehouse In a CRM system, the database containing information about customers, their preferences, and their behavior.

Database The storage element of a search engine.

Database administration The person or team that is responsible for defining the data elements in an organization's database design and the operation of its database management software.

Database manager (database management software) Software that stores information in a highly structured way.

Database server The server computer on which database management software runs.

data-type definitions (DTDs) Many companies follow the common standards for XML tags such as data-type definition or XML schemas.

Dead link A Web link that when clicked displays an error message instead of a Web page.

Debit card A payment card that removes the amount of the charge from the cardholder's bank account and transfers it to the seller's bank account.

Decentralized architecture A server structure that uses a large number of less-powerful computers and divides the workload among them.

Decrypted Information that has been decoded. The opposite of encrypted.

Decryption program A procedure to reverse the encryption process, resulting in the decoding of an encrypted message.

Dedicated hosting A Web hosting option in which the hosting company provides exclusive use of a specific server computer that is owned and administered by the hosting company.

Deep Web Information that is stored in databases and is accessible to users through Web interfaces.

Defamatory A statement that is false and injures the reputation of a person or company.

Delay attack A computer attack that disrupts normal computer processing.

Demographic A group of customers who share common characteristics.

demographic information Customer or site visitor characteristics such as age, gender, family size, income, education, religion, or ethnicity.

Demographic segmentation The grouping of customers by characteristics such as age, gender, family size, income, education, religion, or ethnicity.

Denial-of-service (DoS) attack (denial attack) A computer attack that disrupts normal computer processing or denies processing entirely.

Descending-price auction Synonymous with Dutch auction, which is an open auction in which bidding starts at a high price and drops until a bidder accepts the price.

Dictionary attack program A program that cycles through an electronic dictionary, trying every word in the book as a password.

Digital cash A general term that describes any value storage and exchange system created by a private (nongovernmental) entity that does not use paper documents or coins and that can serve as a substitute for government-issued physical currency.

Digital certificate (digital ID) An attachment to an e-mail message or data embedded in a Web page that verifies the identity of a sender or Web site.

Digital content revenue model A revenue model in which a business sells subscriptions for access to the information it owns.

Digital rights management (DRM) Software that limits the number of copies that can be made of an audio file.

Digital signature An encryption message digest.

Digital Subscriber Line (DSL) Telephone line ISP connectivity that is a higher grade than standard 56K connectivity.

Digital wallet (electronic wallet, e-wallet) A software utility that holds credit card information, owner identification and address information, and provides this data automatically at electronic commerce sites; electronic wallets can also store electronic cash.

Digital watermark A digital code or stream embedded undetectably in a digital image or audio file.

Direct connection EDI The form of EDI in which EDI translator computers at each company are linked directly to each other through modems and dial-up telephone lines or leased lines.

Direct materials Materials that become part of the finished product in a manufacturing process.

Disintermediation The removal of an intermediary from a value chain.

display ad Banner ad A small rectangular object on a Web page that displays a stationary or moving graphic and includes a hyperlink to the advertiser's Web site.

display advertising network A broker between advertisers and Web sites that carry ads.

Distributed architecture Synonymous with decentralized architecture, which is a server structure that uses a large number of less powerful computers and divides the workload among them.

Distributed database system A database within a large information system that stores the same data in many different physical locations.

Distributed denial-of-service (DDoS) attack A simultaneous attack on a Web site (or a number of Web sites) from all of the computers in a botnet.

Distributed information system A large information system that stores the same data in many different physical locations.

Distribution (place) The need to have products or services available in many different locations.

Domain name The address of a Web page, it can contain two or more word groups separated by periods. Components of domain names become more specific from right to left.

Domain name hosting A service that permits the purchaser of a domain name to maintain a simple Web site so that the domain name remains in use.

Domain name ownership change The changing of owner information maintained by a public domain registrar in the registrar's database to reflect the new owner's name and business address.

Domain name parking Synonymous with domain name hosting, which is a service that permits the purchaser of a domain name to maintain a simple Web site so that the domain name remains in use.

Domain name servers (DNSs) The computers on the internet that maintain directories that link domain names to IP addresses.

Dot-com A company that operates only online.

Dotted decimal The IP address notation in which addresses appear as four separate numbers separated by periods.

Double auction A type of auction in which buyers and sellers each submit combined price-quantity bids to an auctioneer. The auctioneer matches the sellers' offers (starting with the lowest price, then going up) to the buyers' offers (starting with the highest price, then going down) until all of the quantities are sold.

Double-spending The spending of the same unit of electronic cash twice by submitting the same electronic currency to two different vendors.

Download bandwidth Also called downstream bandwidth or downlink bandwidth, a measure of the amount of information that can travel from the Internet to a user in a given amount of time.

Downstream bandwidth (downlink bandwidth) The connection that occurs when information travels to your computer from your ISP.

Downstream strategies Tactics that improve the value that a business provides to its customers.

Due diligence Background research procedures.

Dutch auction A form of open auction in which bidding starts at a high price and drops until a bidder accepts the price.

Dynamic catalog An area of a Web site that stores information about products in a database.

Dynamic content Nonstatic information constructed in response to a Web client's request.

Dynamic page A Web page whose content is shaped by a program in response to a user request.

dynamic pricing management A software that adjusts pricing in real time based on customer category, past purchase volume (in units or dollars). Order size, or any other variable the seller chooses.

Early outsourcing The hiring of an external company to do initial electronic commerce site design and development. The external team then trains the original company's information systems professionals in the new technology, eventually handing over complete responsibility of the site to the internal team.

Eavesdropper A person or device who is able to listen in on and copy Internet transmissions.

Edge router A routing computer or other networking device that is located at the border between the organization and the Internet or at the edge of the organization.

EDI compatible Firms that are able to exchange data in specific standard electronic formats with other firms.

EDI for Administration, Commerce, and Transport (EDIFACT) The 1987 publication that summarizes the United Nations' standard transaction sets for international EDI.

EDIINT (Electronic Data Interchange-Internet Integration or EDI-INT) A set of protocols for the exchange of data (EDI, XML, and other formats) over the Internet.

E-government The use of electronic commerce by governments and government agencies to perform business-like activities.

Electronic bill presentment and payment (EBPP) systems A system that delivers bills and accepts payment for them online.

Electronic business (e-business) Another term for electronic commerce; sometimes used as a broader term for electronic commerce that includes all business processes, as distinguished from a narrow definition of electronic commerce that includes sales and purchase transactions only.

Electronic commerce (e-commerce) Business activities conducted using electronic data transmission over the Internet and the World Wide Web.

Electronic customer relationship management (eCRM) Synonymous with technology enabled relationship management, it is the obtaining and use of detailed customer information.

Electronic data interchange (EDI) Exchange between businesses of computer-readable data in a standard format.

Electronic funds transfer (EFT) Electronic transfer of account exchange information over secure private communications networks.

Electronic funds transfer at point of sale (EFTPOS) cards Another term for debit cards, usually used outside the United States.

Electronic mail (e-mail) Messages that are exchanged among users using particular mail programs and protocols.

E-mail client software Programs used to read and send e-mail.

E-mail server A computer that is devoted to handling e-mail.

Encapsulation The process that occurs when VPN software encrypts packet contents and then places the encrypted packets inside an IP wrapper in another packet.

Encryption The coding of information using a mathematical-based program and secret key; it makes a message illegible to casual observers or those without the decoding key.

Encryption algorithm The logic that implements an encryption program.

Encryption program A program that transforms plain text into cipher text.

End-user license agreement (EULAs) A contract that the user must accept before installing software.

English auction A type of auction in which bidders publicly announce their successively higher bids until no higher bid is forthcoming.

Enterprise application integration The coordination of all of a company's existing systems to each other and to the company's Web site.

Enterprise-class software Commerce software used by large-scale electronic commerce businesses.

Enterprise resource planning (ERP) Business software that integrates all facets of a business, including planning, manufacturing, sales, and marketing.

Entity body The part of a message from a client that contains the HTML page requested by the client and passes bulk information to the server.

E-procurement The use of Internet technologies in a company's purchasing and supply management functions.

E-procurement software Software that allows a company to manage its purchasing function through a Web interface.

Escrow service An independent third party who holds an auction buyer's payment until the buyer receives the purchased item and is satisfied that it is what the seller represented it to be.

E-sourcing The use of Internet technologies in the activities a company undertakes to identify vendors that offer materials, supplies, and services that the company needs.

Ethical hacker A computer security specialist hired to probe computers and computer networks to assess their security; can also be hired to locate information that can be used in legal proceedings.

Extensible Business Reporting Language (XBRL) The standards that help in accounting and financial information standards.

Extensible Hypertext Markup Language (XHTML) A new markup language proposed by the WC3 that is a reformulation of HTML version 4.0 as an XML application.

Extensible Markup Language (XML) A language that describes the semantics of a page's contents and defines data records on a page.

Extensible Stylesheet Language (XSL) A language that formats XML code for viewing in a Web browser.

Extranet A network system that extends a company's intranet and allows it to connect with the networks of business partners or other designated associates.

Fair use A doctrine in U.S. law that permits limited use of copyrighted material under certain circumstances without obtaining permission from the copyright holder.

False positive An e-mail message that is incorrectly rejected by an e-mail filter as being spam when it is actually valid e-mail.

Fan Someone who follows a company's discussion activity on a social media site.

Fan base A collection of fans.

Fee-for-service revenue model A revenue model in which payment is based on the value of the service provided.

Fee-for-transaction revenue model A revenue model in which businesses charge a fee for services based on the number or size of the transactions they process.

File Transfer Protocol (FTP) A protocol that enables users to transfer files over the Internet.

Firewall A computer that provides a defense between one network (inside the firewall) and another network (outside the firewall, such as the Internet) that could pose a threat to the inside network. All traffic to and from the network must pass through the firewall. Only authorized traffic, as defined by the local security policy, is allowed to pass through the firewall. Also used to describe the software that performs these functions on the firewall computer.

Firms The business activity that occurs within large hierarchical business organizations.

First-mover advantage The benefit a company can gain by introducing a product or service before its competitors.

First-party cookie A cookie that is placed on the client computer by the Web server site.

First-price sealed-bid auction A type of auction in which bidders submit their bids independently and privately, with the highest bidder winning the auction.

Fixed-point wireless A data transmittal service that uses a system of repeaters to forward a radio signal from an ISP to customers.

Float The delay that occurs between the time that a person writes a check and the time that check the person's bank.

Forum selection clause A statement within a contract that dictates that the contract will be enforced according to the laws of a particular state; signing a contract with a forum selection clause constitutes voluntary submission to the jurisdiction named in the forum selection clause.

Four Ps of marketing The essential issues of marketing: product, price, promotion, and place.

Fourth-generation (4G) wireless technology Wireless technology that offers download speeds up to 12 Mbps and upload speeds up to 5 Mbps.

Frame relay A routing technology.

Freight forwarder A company that arranges shipping and insurance for international transactions.

Front-end processor A banking service provider that obtains authorization for a transaction by sending the transaction's details to the interchange network and storing a record of the approval or denial.

Fulfillment integration A software that connects a seller's shopping directly to the fulfillment service provider's computers so that shipping can be triggered by the shopping cart software automatically when the sale transaction is completed.

Funnel model of customer acquisition, conversion, and retention A method of evaluating specific marketing strategy elements.

Gateway computers Synonymous with routers, which are computers that determine the best way for data packets to move forward.

Gateway server A firewall that filters traffic based on applications requested by clients on the trusted network.

Generic top-level domain (gTLD) The main top-level domain names, including .com, .net, .edu, .gov, .mil, .us, and .org.

Geographic segmentation The grouping of customers by location of home or workplace.

Gift card A prepaid card sold to be given as a gift.

Graphical user interface (GUI) Computer program control functions that are displayed using pictures, icons, and other easy-to-use graphical elements.

Green computing The reduction of the environmental impact of large computing installations.

Group purchasing site (group shopping site) A type of auction Web site that negotiates with a seller to obtain lower prices on an item as individual buyers enter bids on that item.

Groupon The site that offered one coupon offer per day in Chicago.

Hacker A dedicated programmer who writes complex code that tests the limits of technology; usually meant in a positive way.

Hardware-based digital wallets Smartphones and tablets that can store a variety of identity credentials.

Hash algorithm A security utility that mathematically combines every character in a message to create a fixed-length number (usually 128 bits in length) that is a condensation, or fingerprint, of the original message.

Hash coding The process used to calculate a number from a message.

Hash value The number that results when a message is hash coded.

Hexadecimal (base 16) A number system that uses 16 digits.

Hierarchical business organization Firms that include a number of levels with cumulative responsibility. These organizations are typically headed by a top-level president or officer. A number of vice presidents report to the president. A larger number of middle managers report to the vice presidents.

Hierarchical hyperlink structure A hyperlink structure in which the user starts from a home page and follows links to other pages in whatever order they wish.

Home page In a hierarchical Web page structure, the introductory page of a Web site. Synonymous with start page.

Hot spot A wireless access point (WAP) that is open to the public.

hybrid cloud computing The companies move their large-volume and routine work to a cloud provider, but retain their more sensitive data and process on internal servers.

Hyperlink A type of tag that points to another location within the same or another HTML document. Also called a hypertext link.

Hypertext A system of navigating between HTML pages using links.

Hypertext elements HTML text elements that are related to each other within one document or among several documents.

Hypertext link (hyperlink) A type of tag that points to another location within the same or another HTML document.

Hypertext Markup Language (HTML) The language of the Internet; it contains codes attached to text that describe text elements and their relation to one another.

Hypertext Preprocessor (PHP) A Web programming language that can be used to write server-side scripts that generate dynamic Web pages.

Hypertext server Synonymous with Web server, which is a computer that is connected to the Internet and that stores files written in HTML that are publicly available through an Internet connection.

Hypertext Transfer Protocol (HTTP) The Internet protocol responsible for transferring and displaying Web pages.

Idea-based networking The act of participating in Web communities that are based on the connections between ideas.

Idea-based social media A Web site that creates communities based on the connections between ideas.

Identity theft A criminal act in which the perpetrator gathers personal information about a victim and then uses that information to obtain credit in the victim's name. After establishing credit accounts, the perpetrator runs up charges on the accounts and then disappears.

Impact sourcing Offshoring that is done to benefit training or charitable activities in less developed parts of the world. Also called smart sourcing.

Implied contract An agreement between two or more parties to act as if a contract exists, even if no contract has been written and signed.

Implied warranty A promise to which the seller can be held even though the seller did not make an explicit statement of that promise.

Impression The loading of a banner ad on a Web page.

Income tax Taxes that are levied by national, state, and local governments on the net income generated by business activities.

Incubator A company that offers start-up businesses a physical location with offices, accounting and legal assistance, computers, and Internet connections at a very low monthly cost.

Independent exchange A vertical portal that is not controlled by a company that was an established buyer or seller in the industry.

Independent industry marketplace A vertical portal that is focused on a specific industry.

Index A list containing every Web page found by a spider, crawler, or bot.

Indirect connection EDI The form of EDI in which each company transmits and receives EDI messages through a value-added network.

Indirect materials Materials and supplies that are purchased by a company in support of the manufacturing of an item, but not directly used in the production of the item.

Industry Multiple firms selling similar products to similar customers.

Industry consortia-sponsored marketplace A marketplace formed by several large buyers in a particular industry.

Industry marketplace A vertical portal that is focused on a single industry.

Industry value chain The larger stream of activities in which a particular business unit's value chain is embedded.

infrastructure as a service (IaaS) Cloud computing

Initial public offering (IPO) The original sale of a company's stock to the public.

Inline text ad A text ad consisting of text in an article or story that is displayed as a hyperlink and that leads to an advertiser's Web site.

Integrity The category of computer security that addresses the validity of data; confirmation that data has not been modified.

Integrity violation A security violation that occurs when a message is altered while in transit between sender and receiver.

Intellectual capital The value of the accumulated mass of employees' knowledge about a business and its processes.

Intellectual property A general term that includes all products of the human mind, including tangible and intangible products.

Intentional tort A tortious act in which the seller knowingly or recklessly causes injury to the buyer.

Interactive Mail Access Protocol (IMAP) A newer e-mail protocol with improvements over POP.

Interactive marketing unit (IMU) ad format The standard banner sizes that most Web sites have voluntarily agreed to use.

Interchange fees Fees charged by a card association to an acquiring bank that are usually passed to the merchant.

Interchange network A set of connections between banks that issue credit cards, the associations that own the credit cards (such as MasterCard or Visa), and merchants' banks.

internal search engine A software that allows customers to enter descriptive search terms, such as "men's shirts," so they can quickly find the Web page containing what they want to purchase.

Internet access provider (IAP) Synonymous with Internet service provider.

Internet backbone Routers that handle packet traffic along the Internet's main connecting points.

Internet EDI EDI on the Internet.

Internet of Things The subset of the Internet that connects computers and sensors to each other for communication, data exchange, and automatic transaction processing.

Internet Protocol (IP) Within TCP/IP, the protocol that determines the routing of data packets. See TCP/IP.

Internet Protocol version 4 (IPv4) The version of IP that has been in use for the past 20 years on the Internet; it uses a 32-bit number to identify the computers connected to the Internet.

Internet Protocol version 6 (IPv6) The protocol that will replace IPv4.

Internet service provider (ISP) A company that sells Internet access rights directly to Internet users.

Internet, internet A global system of interconnected computer networks. An internet (small "i") is a group of computer networks that have been interconnected.

Internet2 A successor to the Internet used for conducting research; it offers bandwidths in excess of 1 Gbps.

Interoperability The coordination of a company's information systems so that they all work together.

Interstitial ad An intrusive Web ad that opens in its own browser window, instead of the page that the user intended to load.

Intranet An interconnected network of computers operated within a single company or organization.

Intrusion detection system A part of a firewall that monitors attempts to log in to servers and analyzes those attempts for patterns that might indicate a cracker's attack is under way.

IP address The 32-bit number that represents the address of a particular location (computer) on the Internet.

IP tunneling The creation of a private passageway through the public Internet that provides secure transmission from one extranet partner to another.

IP wrapper The outer packet in the encapsulation process.

Jailbreaking Modifying an Apple iPhone's operating system.

JavaScript A scripting language developed by Netscape to enable Web page designers to build active content.

Judicial comity An accommodation by a court in one country in which it voluntarily enforces another country's laws or court judgments when no strict requirement to do so exists.

Jurisdiction A government's ability to exert control over a person or corporation.

justin-time inventory management Companies use justin-time inventory management to reduce inventory stocks of component parts purchased by arranging for delivery of those parts to occur very close to the time at which they are used in the manufacturing process.

Key A number used to encode or decode messages.

Knowledge management The intentional collection, classification, and dissemination of information about a company, its products, and its processes.

Knowledge management (KM) software Software that helps companies collect and organize information, share the information among users, enhance the ability of users to collaborate, and preserve the knowledge gained for future use.

Late outsourcing The hiring of an external company to maintain an electronic commerce site that has been designed and developed by an internal information systems team.

Latency The delay in transmission caused by the inability of the network to handle the full traffic load momentarily.

Law of diminishing returns The characteristic of most activities to yield less value as the amount of consumption increases.

Leaderboard ad Web site banner ad that is designed to span the top or bottom of a Web page.

Lean production The process of eliminating waste and unnecessary processes throughout the manufacturing process.

Leased line A permanent telephone connection between two points; it is always active.

LegalXML The information in the legal profession.

Legitimacy The idea that those subject to laws should have some role in formulating them.

Life-cycle segmentation The use of customer life cycle stages to identify groups of customers that are in each stage.

Linear hyperlink structure A hyperlink structure that resembles conventional paper documents in which the user reads pages in serial order.

Link checker A site management tool that examines each page on the site and reports any URLs that are broken, that seem to be broken, or that are in some way incorrect.

Link rot The undesirable situation of a site that contains a number of links that no longer work.

Liquidation broker An agent that finds buyers for unusable and excess inventory.

Load-balancing switch A piece of network hardware that monitors the workloads of servers attached to it and assigns incoming Web traffic to the server that has the most available capacity at that instant in time.

Local area network (LAN) A network that connects workstations and PCs within a single physical location.

Localization A type of language translation that considers multiple elements of the local environment, such as business and cultural practices, in addition to local dialect variations in the language.

Localized advertising Online advertising in which ads are generated in response to a search for products or services in a specific geographic area.

Location-aware services Customized services or advertising that are based on the location information transmitted by a user's mobile device.

Lock-in effect The inherent greater value to customers of existing companies than new sites.

Logical security The protection of assets using nonphysical means.

Long Term Evolution (LTE) A 4G wireless technology that offers download speeds up to 12 Mbps and upload speeds up to 5 Mbps.

Long-arm statute A state law that creates personal jurisdiction for courts.

Machine translation Language translation that is done by software; such translation can reach speeds of 400,000 words per hour.

Macro virus A virus that is transmitted or contained inside a downloaded file attachment; it can cause damage to a computer and reveal otherwise confidential information.

Mail bomb A security attack in which many computers (hundreds or thousands) each send a message to a particular address, exceeding the recipient's allowable mail limit and causing mail systems to malfunction; the computers are often under the surreptitious control of a third party.

Mailing list An e-mail address that forwards messages to certain users who are subscribers.

Mail-order model Synonymous with catalog model.

Maintenance, repair, and operating (MRO) Commodity supplies, including general industrial merchandise and standard machine tools, that are used in a variety of industries.

Mall-style commerce service provider A CSP that provides small businesses with an Internet connection, Web site creation tools, and little or no banner advertising clutter.

Managed service provider (MSP) A Web site hosting service firm; synonymous with ASP and CSP.

Man-in-the-middle exploit A message integrity violation in which the contents of the e-mail are changed in a way that negates the message's original meaning.

Many-to-many communications A model of communications in which a number of entities communicate with a number of other entities.

Many-to-one communications model A model of communications in which a number of entities communicate with a single other entity.

Market A real or virtual space in which potential buyers and sellers come into contact with each other and agree on a medium of exchange (such as currency or barter).

Market segmentation The identification by advertisers of specific subsets of their markets that have common characteristics.

Marketing channel Each different pathway that a business uses to reach its customers.

Marketing mix The combination of elements that companies use to achieve their goals for selling and promoting their products and services.

Marketing strategy A particular marketing mix that is used to promote a company or product.

Marketspace A market that occurs in the virtual world instead of in the physical world.

Markup tags (tags) Web page code that provides formatting instructions that Web client software can understand.

Masquerading Pretending to be someone you are not (for example, by sending an e-mail that shows someone else as the sender) or representing one Web site as another. Synonymous with spoofing.

Mass media The method of contacting potential customers through the distribution of broadcast, printed, billboard, or mailed advertising materials.

Massive open online course (MOOC) An online course often offered at no or very low cost and can attract hundreds of thousands of students.

MathML The information for mathematical and scientific information.

Meetup An in-person meeting between people who are acquainted through a blog.

mentor network A group of mentors.

Merchandising The combination of store design, layout, and product display intended to create an environment that encourages customers to buy.

Merchant account An account that a merchant must hold with a bank that allows the merchant to process payment card transactions.

Mesh routing A version of fixed-point wireless that directly transmits Wi-Fi packets through hundreds of short-range transceivers that are located close to each other.

Message digest The number that results from the application of an encryption algorithm to plain text information.

Metalanguage A language used to make statements about statements in another language or to define other languages.

Metrics Measurements that companies use to assess the value of site visitor activity.

Microblog A Web site such as Twitter that functions as a very informal blog site with entries (messages, or tweets) that are limited to 140 characters in length.

Microlending The practice of lending very small amounts of money to people who are starting or operating small businesses, especially in developing countries.

Micromarketing The practice of targeting very small and well-defined market segments.

Micropayments Internet payments for items costing very little—usually $1 or less.

Middleware Software that handles connections between electronic commerce software and accounting systems.

Minimum bid In an English auction, the price for an item at which the auctioning begins.

Minimum bid increment The amount by which one bid must exceed the previous bid.

Mobile ads Advertising messages that appear as part of mobile apps.

Mobile apps Programs that run on wireless devices such as smart phones and tablets.

Mobile commerce (m-commerce) Resources accessed using devices that have wireless connections, such as stock quotes, directions, weather forecasts, and airline flight schedules.

Mobile wallet A mobile phone that operates as a credit card.

Monetizing The conversion of existing regular site visitors seeking free information or services into fee-paying subscribers or purchasers of services.

Money laundering A technique used by criminals to convert money that they have obtained illegally into cash that they can spend without having it identified as the proceeds of an illegal activity.

Multipurpose Internet Mail Extension (MIME) An e-mail protocol that allows users to attach binary files to e-mail messages.

Multivector virus A virus that can enter a computer system in several different ways.

Näive Bayesian filter E-mail filtering software that classifies messages based on learned patterns indicated by the e-mail user's categorization of incoming mail. The filter eventually learns to recognize spam and filter it out.

Name changing (typosquatting) A problem that occurs when someone registers purposely misspelled variations of well-known domain names. These variants sometimes lure consumers who make typographical errors when entering a URL.

Name stealing Theft of a Web site's name that occurs when someone, posing as a site's administrator, changes the ownership of the domain name assigned to the site to another site and owner.

Near field communication (NFC) Contactless wireless transmission of data over short distances.

Necessity The category of computer security that addresses data delay or data denial threats.

Necessity threat The disruption of normal computer processing or denial of processing. Also called delay, denial, or denial-of-service threat (DoS).

Negligent tort A tortious act in which the seller unintentionally provides a harmful product.

Net bandwidth The actual speed information travels, taking into account traffic on the communication channel at any given time.

NetSuite It offers subscriptions to ERP software for all sizes of businesses.

Network access points (NAPs) The four primary connection points for access to the Internet backbone in the United States.

Network access providers The few large companies that are the primary providers of Internet access; they, in turn, sell Internet access to smaller Internet service providers.

Network Address Translation (NAT) device A computer that converts private IP addresses into normal IP addresses when they forward packets to the Internet.

Network Control Protocol (NCP) Used by ARPANET in the early 1970s to route messages in its experimental wide area network.

Network economic structure A business structure wherein firms coordinate their strategies, resources, and skill sets by forming a long-term, stable relationship based on a shared purpose.

Network effect An increase in the value of a network to its participants, which occurs as more people or organizations participate in the network.

Network operations Web site staff whose responsibilities include load estimation and monitoring, resolving network problems as they arise, designing and implementing fault resistance technologies, and managing any network operations that are outsourced to ISPs, CSPs, or telephone companies.

Newsgroup A topic area in Usenet where people read and post articles.

Nexus The association between a tax-paying entity and a governmental taxing authority.

Nonrepudiation Verification that a particular transaction actually occurred; this prevents parties from denying a transaction's validity or its existence.

Notice The expression of a change in rules (usually, legal or cultural rules) typically represented by a physical boundary.

N-tier architecture Higher-order client-server architectures that have more than three tiers.

Occasion segmentation Behavioral segmentation that is based on things that happen at a specific time or occasion.

Offer A declaration of willingness to buy or sell a product or service; it includes sufficient details to be firm, precise, and unambiguous.

Offshoring Outsourcing that is done by organizations outside the country.

One-to-many communication model A model of communications in which one entity communicates with a number of other entities.

One-to-one communication model A model of communications in which one entity communicates with one other entity.

One-to-one marketing A highly customized approach to offering products and services that match the needs of a particular customer.

Online marketing manager An employee who specializes in the specific techniques used to build brands and increase market share using the Web site and other online tools, such as e-mail marketing.

Ontology A set of standards that defines, in detail, the structure of a particular knowledge domain; in the Semantic Web, it defines the relationships among RDF standards and specific XML tags.

Open architecture of the Internet The philosophy behind the Internet that dictates that independent networks should not require any internal changes to be connected to the network, packets that do not arrive at their destinations must be retransmitted from their source network, routers do not retain information about the packets they handle, and no global control exists over the network.

Open auction (open-outcry auction) An auction in which bids are publicly announced (such as an English auction).

Open EDI EDI conducted on the Internet instead of over private leased lines.

Open loop system A payment card arrangement involving a consumer and his or her bank, a merchant and its bank, and a third party (such as Visa or MasterCard) that processes transactions between the consumer and merchant.

Open session A continuous connection that is maintained between a client and server on the Internet.

Opening tag An HTML tag that precedes the text that a tag affects.

Open-outcry double auction A double auction in which buy and sell offers are announced publicly. Typically conducted in exchange floor or trading pit environments for items of known quality, such as securities or graded agricultural products, that are regularly traded in large quantities.

Open-source software Software that is developed by a community of programmers who make the software available for download and use at no cost.

Opportunity cost Lost benefits from an action not taken.

Optical fiber A data transmission cable that uses glass fibers to achieve bandwidths up to 10 Gbps.

Opt-in A personal information collection policy in which the company collecting the information does not use the information for any other purpose (or sell or rent the information) unless the customer specifically chooses to allow that use.

Opt-in e-mail The practice of sending e-mail messages to people who have requested information on a particular topic or about a specific product.

Opt-out A personal information collection policy in which the company collecting the information assumes that the customer does not object to the company's use of the information unless the customer specifically chooses to deny permission.

Organized crime Unlawful activities conducted by a highly organized, disciplined association for profit. Also called racketeering.

Orphan file A file on a Web site that is not linked to any page.

Outsourcing The hiring of another company to perform design, implementation, or operational tasks for an information systems project.

Packet-filter firewall A firewall that examines all data flowing back and forth between a trusted network and the Internet.

Packets The small pieces of files and e-mail messages that travel over the Internet.

Packet-switched A network in which packets are labeled electronically with their origin, sequence, and destination addresses. Packets travel from computer to computer along the interconnected networks until they reach their destination. Each packet can take a different path through the interconnected networks, and the packets may arrive out of order. The destination computer collects the packets and reassembles the original file or e-mail message from the pieces in each packet.

Page view A page request made by a Web site visitor.

Page-based application system Application server software that returns pages generated by scripts that include the rules for presenting data on the Web page with the business logic.

Paid placement (sponsorship) The purchasing of a top listing in results listings for a particular set of search terms.

Partial outsourcing The outsourcing of the design, development, implementation, or operation of specific portions of an electronic commerce system.

Participatory journalism The practice of inviting readers to help write an online newspaper.

passive RFID tag A small device that receives a radio signal from a nearby

transmitter and extracts a tiny amount of power from that signal. It uses the power it extracts to send a signal back to the transmitter. That signal includes information about the item to which the RFID has been affixed.

Passphrase A sequence of words or text that is easy to remember, but is complex enough to serve as either a good password itself or as a prompt to remember a good password.

password manager A software that stores securely all of a person's passwords.

Patent An exclusive right to make, use, and sell an invention granted by a government to the inventor.

Patent assertion entity Also called patent troll, person or company can buy patents from the original inventors and then enforces the rights granted by the patents by suing others who use the patents without permission.

Patent troll Also called patent assertion entity, a person or company that buys patents from the original inventors and then enforces the rights granted by the patents by suing others who use the patents without permission.

Pay wall A digital control mechanism that limits the number of times a visitor may visit a site to a specific number of visits before the user must pay for continued access.

Payment card A general term for plastic cards used instead of cash to make purchases, including credit cards, debit cards, and charge cards.

Payment gateway Front-end processors or the hardware and software that are used to obtain transaction approvals.

Payment processing service provider, payment processor A third-party company that handles payment card processing for online businesses.

Pay-per-click model A revenue model in which an affiliate earns payment each time a site visitor clicks a link to load the seller's page.

Pay-per-conversion model A revenue model in which an affiliate earns payment each time a site visitor is converted from a visitor into either a qualified prospect or a customer.

pCell The approach operates at about 35 times the speed of current telephone wireless network technologies.

Per se defamation A legal cause of action in which a court deems some types of statements to be so negative that injury is assumed.

Perimeter expansion The increase in firewall limits beyond traditional borders caused by telecommuting.

Permission marketing A marketing strategy that only sends specific information to people who have indicated an interest in receiving information about the product or service being promoted.

Persistent cookie A cookie that exists indefinitely.

Personal area network (PAN) A small, low bandwidth Bluetooth network of up to 10 networks of eight devices each. It is used for tasks such as wireless synchronization of laptop computers with desktop computers and wireless printing from laptops, PDAs, or mobile phones. Synonymous with piconet.

Personal contact A method of identifying and reaching customers that involves searching for, qualifying, and contacting potential customers.

Personal firewall A software-only firewall that is installed on an individual client computer.

Personal jurisdiction A court's authority to hear a case based on the residency of the defendant; a court has personal jurisdiction over a case if the defendant is a resident of the state in which the court is located.

Personal shopper An intelligent agent program that learns a customer's preferences and makes suggestions.

Phablet A very large smartphone with a highresolution screen.

Pharming attack The use of a zombie farm, often by an organized crime association, to launch a massive phishing attack.

Phishing expedition A masquerading attack that combines spam with spoofing. The perpetrator sends millions of spam e-mails that appear to be from a respectable company. The e-mails contain a link to a Web page that is designed to look exactly like the company's site. The victim is encouraged to enter his or her username, password, and sometimes credit card information.

Physical security Tangible protection devices such as alarms, guards, fireproof doors, fences, and vaults.

Piconet A small, low-bandwidth Bluetooth network of up to 10 networks of eight devices each. It is used for tasks such as wireless synchronization of laptop computers with desktop computers and wireless printing from laptops, PDAs, or mobile phones. Synonymous with personal area network.

Place (distribution) The need to have products or services available in many different locations.

Plain old telephone service (POTS) The network that connects telephones; it provides a reliable data transmission bandwidth of about 56 Kbps.

Plain text Normal, unencrypted text.

platform as a service (PaaS) Cloud computing

Platform neutrality The ability of a network to connect devices that use different operating systems.

Plug-in An application that helps a browser to display information (such as video or animation) but is not part of the browser.

Pop-up ad An ad that appears in its own window when the user opens or closes a Web page.

Portal A Web site that serves as a customizable home base from which users do their searching, navigating, and other Web-based activity. Synonymous with Web portal.

Post Office Protocol (POP) The protocol responsible for retrieving e-mail from a mail server.

Postimplementation audit (postaudit review) A formal review of a project after it is up and running.

Power A form of control over physical space (such as a state) and the people and objects that reside in that space.

Prepaid card A purchased card that contains a limited value and that can be used for making purchases from retailers.

pre-roll video ad A form of rich media ads is used on Web sites that deliver video.

Presence The public image conveyed by an organization to its stakeholders.

Pretty Good Privacy (PGP) A popular technology used to implement public-key encryption to protect the privacy of e-mail messages.

Price The amount a customer pays for a product.

Primary activities Activities that are required to do business: design, production, promotion, marketing, delivery, and support of products or services.

Privacy The protection of individual rights to nondisclosure of information.

Private company marketplace A marketplace that provides auctions, requests for quotes postings, and other features to companies that want to operate their own marketplace.

private industrial networks The expanded arrangements of many private company marketplaces to include functions to allow supply chain participants to manage multiple functions including manufacturing, tier-one and tier-two suppliers, distribution centers, transportation, orders, invoicing, and payments.

Private IP addresses A series of IP numbers that have been set aside for subnet use and are not permitted on packets that travel on the Internet.

Private key A single key that is used to encrypt and decrypt messages. Synonymous with symmetric key.

Private network A private, leased-line connection between two companies that physically links their individual computers or intranets.

Private store A password-protected area of a Web site that offers individual customers negotiated price reductions on a limited selection of products and other customized features.

private trading exchanges The expanded arrangements of many private company marketplaces to include functions to allow supply chain participants to manage multiple functions including manufacturing, tier-one and tier-two suppliers, distribution centers, transportation, orders, invoicing, and payments.

Private valuation The amount a bidder is willing to pay for an item that is up for auction.

Private-key encryption The encoding of a message using a single numeric key to encode and decode data; it requires both the sender and receiver of the message to know the key, which must be guarded from public disclosure.

Procurement The business activity that includes all purchasing activities plus the monitoring of all elements of purchase transactions.

Product The physical item or service that a company is selling.

Product-based marketing strategy A logical way to think of a business because companies spend a great deal of effort, time, and money to design and create those products and services.

Product disparagement A statement that is false and injures the reputation of a product or service.

Product recommendation triggers The software tools that respond to a customer's product selections with suggestions for related products or refills for products that have consumable elements (such as blades for a razor).

Product review management The software that allows customers to post reviews to products.

Production strategy The way a company achieves competitive advantage in its product creation activities.

Project management Formal techniques for planning and controlling activities undertaken to achieve a specific goal.

Project management software Application software that provides built-in tools for managing people, resources, and schedules.

Project manager A person with specific training or skills in tracking costs and the accomplishment of specific objectives in a project.

Project portfolio management A technique in which each project is monitored as if it were an investment in a financial portfolio.

Project portfolio manager An employee who is responsible for tracking all ongoing projects and managing them as a portfolio.

Promotion Any means of spreading the word about a product.

Promotion management The software that allows sellers to create special offers (promotions) on specific products in response to variations in customer demand, seasonal preference, introduction of new product verities or package sizes, and any other variables chosen.

Property tax Taxes levied by states and local governments on the personal property and real estate used in a business.

Proprietary architecture The use of vendor specific communication protocols by computer manufacturers in the early days of computing, preventing computers made by different manufacturers from being connected to each other. Also called closed architecture.

Prospecting The part of personal contact selling in which the salesperson identifies potential customers.

Protocol A collection of rules for formatting, ordering, and error-checking data sent across a network.

Proxy bid In an electronic auction, a predetermined maximum bid submitted by a bidder.

Proxy server firewall A firewall that communicates with the Internet on behalf of the trusted network.

Psychographic segmentation The grouping of customers by variables such as social class, personality, or their approach to life.

Public key One of a pair of mathematically related numeric keys, it is used to encrypt messages and is freely distributed to the public.

Public marketplace A vertical portal that is open to new buyers and sellers just entering an industry.

Public network An extranet that allows the public to access its intranet or when two or more companies link their intranets.

Public-key encryption The encoding of messages using two mathematically related but distinct numeric keys.

Purchasing card (p-card) Payment cards that give individual managers the ability to make multiple small purchases at their discretion while providing cost-tracking information to the procurement office.

Pure dot-com A company that operates only online; also called dot-com.

Racketeering Unlawful activities conducted by a highly organized, disciplined association for profit. Also called organized crime.

Radio frequency identification device (RFID) Small chips that include radio transponders; they can be used to track inventory as it moves through an industry value chain.

Ransomware A Trojan that encrypts files on a victim computer and demands a payment for the key to unlock them.

Rational branding An advertising strategy that substitutes an offer to help Web users in some way in exchange for their viewing an ad.

Real-time location systems (RTLS) Tracking systems that use bar codes to monitor inventory movements and ensure that goods are shipped as quickly as possible.

rectangle ad A banner ad rectangle in shape.

Reintermediation The introduction of a new intermediary into a value chain.

Remote server administration Control of a Web site by an administrator from any Internet-connected computer.

Remote wipe Removing personal information from a lost or stolen mobile device by clearing all of the data stored on the device, including e-mails, text messages, contact lists, photos, videos, and any type of document file.

Repeat visits Subsequent visits a Web site visitor makes to a particular page.

Repeater A transmitter-receiver device used in a fixed-point wireless network to forward a radio signal from the ISP to customers. Synonymous with transceiver.

Replenishment purchasing Direct materials purchasing in which the company negotiates long-term contracts for most of the materials that it will need. Also called contract purchasing.

Representational State Transfer (REST) A principle that describes the way the Web uses networking architecture to identify and locate Web pages and the elements (graphics) that make up those Web pages.

Request header The part of an HTTP message from a client to a server that contains additional information about the client and more information about the request.

Request line The part of an HTTP message from a client to a server that contains a command, the name of the target resource (without the protocol or domain name), and the protocol name and version.

Request message The HTTP message that a Web client sends to request a file or files from a Web server.

Reserve price (reserve) The minimum price a seller will accept for an item sold at auction.

Resource description framework (RDF) A set of standards for XML syntax.

Response header field In a client/server transmission, the field that follows the response header line and returns information describing the server's attributes.

Response header line The part of a message from a server to a client that indicates the HTTP version used by the server, status of the response, and an explanation of the status information.

Response message The reply that a Web server sends in response to a client request.

Response time The amount of time a server requires to process one request.

RESTful applications (REST) Web services that are built on the REST model.

RESTful design The use of the REST model in building Web services.

Retained customer A customer who returns to a site one or more times after making his or her first purchase.

Retention costs The costs of inducing customers to return to a Web site and buy again.

Return on investment (ROI) A method for evaluating the potential costs and benefits of a proposed capital investment.

Revenue model The combination of strategies and techniques that a company uses to generate cash flow into the business from customers.

Reverse auction (seller-bid auction) A type of auction in which sellers bid prices for which they are willing to sell items or services.

Reverse bid The process in which an auction customer seeks products by describing an item or service in which he or she is interested, and then entertains responses from merchants who offer to supply the item at a particular price.

Reward-based crowdfunding A type of crowdfunding in which the investors pay in advance for products (or services) to be delivered when the company makes them using the invested funds.

rich media ads The ads that generate graphical activity that "floats" over the Web page itself instead of opening in a separate window.

Right of publicity A limited right to control others' commercial use of an individual's name, image, likeness, or identifying aspect of identity.

Roaming The shifting of Wi-Fi devices from one WAP to another without requiring intervention by the user.

Robot (bot) A program that automatically searches the Web to find Web pages that might be interesting to people.

Robotic network A network that can act as an attacking unit, sending spam or launching denial-of-service attacks against specific Web sites. Synonymous with botnet or zombie farm.

Rogue apps Apps that contain malware or that collect information from mobile devices and forward it to perpetrators.

Rooting Modifying an Android smartphone's operating system.

Router A computer that determines the best way for data packets to move forward to their destination.

Router computers (routing computers) The computers that decide how best to forward each packet of information as it travels on the Internet to its destination. Synonymous with gateway computers and routers.

Routing algorithm The program used by a router to determine the best path for data packets to travel.

Routing table Synonymous with configuration table, which is information about connections that lead to particular groups of routers, specifications on which connections to use first, and rules for handling instances of heavy packet traffic and network congestion.

Sandbox A functional subset of the full browser in which applets or scripts can run without affecting other operations on the client computer.

Scalable A system's ability to be adapted to meet changing requirements.

Scripting language A programming language that provides scripts, or commands, that are executed.

Sealed-bid auction An auction in which bidders submit their bids independently and are usually prohibited from sharing information with each other.

Search engine Web software that finds other pages based on key word matching.

Search engine optimization (search engine positioning, search engine placement) The combined art and science of having a particular URL listed near the top of search engine results.

Search engine placement broker A company that aggregates inclusion and placement rights on multiple search engines and then sells those combination packages to advertisers.

Search engine ranking The weighting of the factors that search engines use to decide which URLs appear first on searches for a particular search term.

Search term sponsorship The option of purchasing a top listing on results pages for a particular set of search terms. Also called paid placement or sponsorship.

Search utility The part of a search engine that finds matching Web pages for search terms.

Second-price sealed-bid auction A type of auction in which bidders submit their bids independently and privately; the highest bidder wins the auction but pays only the amount bid by the second-highest bidder.

Secrecy The category of computer security that addresses the protection of data from unauthorized disclosure and confirmation of data source authenticity.

Secure envelope A security utility that encapsulates a message and provides secrecy, integrity, and client/server authentication.

Secure Hypertext Transfer Protocol (S-HTTP) An encryption approach that is used to establish secure connections between Web servers and clients.

Secure Sockets Layer (SSL) A protocol for transmitting private information securely over the Internet.

Secure Sockets Layer-Extended Validation (SSL-EV) digital certificate A more secure certificate for which a certification authority must confirm the legal existence of the organization by verifying the organization's registered legal name and other facts.

Security policy A written statement describing assets to be protected, the reasons for protecting the assets, the parties responsible for protection, and acceptable and unacceptable behaviors.

Segment Also called a market segment; a subset of a company's potential customer pool that has common demographic characteristics.

Self-hosting A system of Web hosting in which the online business owns and maintains the server and all its software.

Semantic Web A project initiated by Tim Berners-Lee intended to blend technologies and information to create a next-generation Web in which words on Web pages are tagged (using XML) with their meanings.

Server A powerful computer dedicated to managing disk drives, printers, or network traffic.

Server architecture The different ways that servers can be connected to each other and to related hardware such as routers and switches.

Server farm A large collection of electronic commerce Web site servers.

Server software The software that a server computer uses to make files and programs available to other computers on the same network.

Server-level filtering An e-mail content filtering technique in which the filtering software resides on the mail server.

Server-side digital wallet An electronic or digital wallet that stores a customer's information on a remote server that belongs to a particular merchant or to the wallet's publisher.

Server-side scripting A Web page response approach in which programs running on the Web server create Web pages before sending them back to the requesting Web clients as parts of response messages.

Service mark A distinctive mark, device, motto, or implement used to identify services provided by a company.

Session cookie A cookie that exists only until you shut down your browser.

Session key A key used by an encryption algorithm to create cipher text from plain text during a single secure session.

Session negotiation When establishing S-HTTP security, the process of proposing and accepting (or rejecting) various transmission conditions.

Sexting The illegal practice of sending sexually explicit messages or photos using a mobile phone.

Shared hosting A Web hosting arrangement in which the hosting company provides Web space on a server computer that also hosts other Web sites.

Shill bidder An individual employed by a seller or auctioneer who makes bids on behalf of the seller, sometimes artificially inflating an item's price. Shill bidders may be prohibited by the rules of a particular auction.

Shipping profile The collection of attributes, including weight and size, that affect how easily a product can be packaged and delivered.

Shopping cart An electronic commerce utility that keeps track of items selected for purchase and automates the purchasing process.

Short message service (SMS) A protocol used to transmit short text messages to cell phones and other wireless devices.

Shrink-wrap acceptance A buyer's acceptance of the conditions of the EULA, demonstrated by removing the shrink wrap from the product box.

Signature Any symbol executed or adopted for the purpose of authenticating a writing.

Signed (message or code) The status of a message or Web page when it contains an attached digital certificate.

Simple Mail Transfer Protocol (SMTP) A standardized protocol used by a mail server to format and administer e-mail.

Simple Object Access Protocol (SOAP) A message-passing protocol that defines how to send marked-up data from one software application to another across a network.

Single-use card A payment card with disposable numbers, which gives consumers a unique card number that is valid for one transaction only.

Site sponsorship The opportunity for an advertiser to sponsor part or all of a Web site to promote its products, services, or brands. Site sponsorships are more subtle than banner or pop-up ads.

Skyscraper ad A large banner ad on the side of a Web page that remains visible as the user scrolls down through the page.

Small payment Any payment of less than $10.

Smart sourcing Offshoring that is done to benefit training or charitable activities in less developed parts of the world. Also called impact sourcing.

smart-follower strategy An approach in which a business observes first-mover failures and enters a business later, when large investments are no longer required and business processes have been tested.

Smartphone A mobile phone that includes a functional Web browser and a full keyboard.

Sniffer program A program that taps into the Internet and records information that passes through a router from the data's source to its destination.

Snipe The act of placing a winning bid in an online auction at the last possible moment.

Sniping software Auction software that observes auction progress until the last second or two of the auction clock, and then places a bid high enough to win the auction.

Social commerce The use of interpersonal connections online to promote or sell goods and services.

Social media Web sites that allow participants to exchange ideas and report news and information updates to each other.

Social networking A Web site designed to facilitate interaction among a community of users.

Social networking administrator An employee who is responsible for managing the virtual community elements of the Web operation.

Social networking site A Web site that individuals and businesses can use to conduct social interactions online.

Social shopping The practice of bringing buyers and sellers together in a social network to facilitate retail sales.

Software agent A program that performs information gathering, information filtering, and/ormediation on behalf of a person or entity. Synonymous with intelligent software agent.

software as a service (SaaS) The practice of offering software use online.

Sourcing The part of procurement devoted to identifying suppliers and determining the qualifications of those suppliers.

Spam (unsolicited commercial e-mail or bulk mail) Electronic junk mail.

Spear phishing A phishing expedition in which the e-mails are carefully designed to target a particular person or organization.

Spend The total dollar amount of the goods and services that a company buys during a year.

Spider The first part of a search engine, it automatically and frequently searches the Web to find pages and updates its database of information about old Web sites.

Sponsored top-level domain (sTLD) A toplevel domain for which an organization other than ICANN is responsible.

Spoofing Synonymous with masquerading, which is pretending to be someone you are not (for example, by sending an e-mail that shows someone else as the sender) or representing one Web site as another.

Spot market A loosely organized market within a specific industry.

Spot purchasing Direct materials purchasing that occurs within a spot market.

Stakeholders The various entities involved in a business; these include customers, suppliers, employees, stockholders, neighbors, and the general public.

Standard Generalized Markup Language (SGML) An old, complex textmarkup language used to create frequently revised documents that need to be printed in various formats.

Start page In a hierarchical Web page structure, the introductory page of a Web site. Synonymous with home page.

Stateless system A system, such as the Web's hypertext transfer protocol (HTTP), that does not retain information from one session to the next.

Static catalog A simple list of products written in HTML and displayed on a Web page or a series of Web pages.

Static page A Web page that displays unchanging information retrieved from a disk.

Statistical modeling A technique that tests theories that CRM analysts have about relationships among elements of customer and sales data.

Statute of Frauds State law that specifies that contracts for the sale of goods worth more than $500 and contracts that require actions that cannot be completed within one year must be created by a signed writing.

Statutory law That part of British and U.S. law that comprises laws passed by elected legislative bodies.

Steganography The hiding of information (such as commands or identification) within another piece of information.

Stickiness The ability of a Web site to keep visitors at its site and to attract repeat visitors.

Sticky The condition of having stickiness.

Stockout A loss of sales suffered by a retailer when it does not have specific goods on its shelves that customers want to buy.

Store charge card (store-branded card) A charge card issued by a specific retailer.

Stored-value card Either an elaborate smart card or a simple plastic card with a magnetic strip that records currency balance, such as a prepaid phone, copy, subway, or bus card.

Strategic alliance The coordination of strategies, resources, and skill sets by companies into long-term, stable relationships with other companies and individuals based on shared purposes.

Strategic business unit (SBU) A unit within a company that is organized around a specific combination of product, distribution channel, and customer type.

Strategic partners The entities taking part in a strategic alliance.

Strategic partnership Synonymous with strategic alliance.

Streamlined Sales and Use Tax Agreement (SSUTA) An agreement between U.S. states that would simplify state sales taxes by making the various state tax codes more congruent with each other while allowing each state to set its own rates.

Style sheet A set of instructions used for Web page formatting. It is stored in a separate file and lets designers apply specific formatting styles to a page.

Subject-matter jurisdiction A court's authority to decide a dispute between entities based on the issue of dispute.

Subnetting The use of reserved private IP addresses within LANs and WANs to provide additional address space.

Sufficient jurisdiction A court's ability to hear a matter if it has both subject-matter jurisdiction and personal jurisdiction.

Supply alliances Long-term relationships among participants in the supply chain.

Supply chain The part of an industry value chain that precedes a particular strategic business unit. It includes the network of suppliers, transportation firms, and brokers that combine to provide a material or service to the strategic business unit.

supply chain competition The use of technologies to improve the efficiency of a company's operations

Supply chain management The job of managing the integration when companies integrate their supply management and logistics activities across multiple participants in a particular product's supply chain.

Supply chain management (SCM) software Software used by companies to coordinate planning and operations with their partners in the industry supply chains of which they are members.

Supply management Synonymous with procurement, which is the business activity that includes all purchasing activities plus the monitoring of all elements of purchase transactions.

Supply web An industry value chain that includes many participants that are interconnected in a web or network configuration.

Supporting activities Secondary activities that back up primary business activities. These include human resource management, purchasing, and technology development.

SWOT analysis Evaluation of the strengths and weaknesses of a business unit, and identification of the opportunities presented by the markets of the business unit and threats posed by competitors of the business unit.

Symmetric connection An Internet connection that provides the same bandwidth in both directions.

Symmetric encryption The encryption of a message using a single numeric key to encode and decode data. Synonymous with private key encryption.

Systems administrator A member of an electronic commerce team who understands the server hardware and software and is responsible for the system's reliable and secure operation.

Tablet device A small computing device with wireless connectivity that is larger than a mobile phone but smaller than most laptop and notebook computers.

Tags (markup tags) Web page code that provides formatting instructions that Web client software can understand.

Tariff A tax levied on products as they enter the country; also called duty or customs duty.

TCP/IP The set of protocols that provide the basis for the operation of the Internet. The TCP protocol includes rules that computers on a network use to establish and break connections. The IP protocol determines routing of data packets.

Technology-enabled customer relationship management Synonymous with technology enabled relationship management.

Technology-enabled relationship management The business practice of obtaining detailed information about a customer's behavior, preferences, needs, and buying patterns and using that information to set prices, negotiate terms, tailor promotions, add product features, and provide other customized interactions.

Teergrubing A antispamming approach in which the receiving computer launches a return attack against the spammer, sending e-mail messages back to the computer that originated the suspected spam.

Telecommuting An employment arrangement in which the employee logs in to the company computer from an off-site location through the Internet instead of traveling to an office.

Telework Synonymous with telecommuting.

Terms of service (ToS) Rules and regulations intended to limit the Web site owner's liability for what a visitor might do with information obtained from the site.

Text ad A short promotional message that does not use any graphic elements.

Text markup language A language that specifies a set of tags that are inserted into the text.

Texting The practice of users sending short text messages to one another via a mobile phone network or the Internet.

Third-generation (3G) wireless technology Wireless mobile phone technology that offers download speeds up to 2 Mbps and upload speeds up to 800 Kbps and also uses the SMS protocol to send and receive text messages.

Third-party cookie A cookie that originates on a Web site other than the site being visited.

Third-party logistics (3PL) provider A transportation or freight company that operates all or most of a customer's material movement activities.

Threat An act or object that poses a danger to assets.

Three-tier architecture A client/server architecture that builds on the two-tier architecture by adding applications and their associated databases that supply non-HTML information to the Web server on request.

Throughput The number of HTTP requests that a particular hardware and software combination can process in a unit of time.

Tier-one suppliers The capable suppliers that work directly with and have long-term relationships with businesses.

Tier-three suppliers Suppliers that provide components and raw materials to tier-two suppliers.

Tier-two suppliers Suppliers that provide components and raw materials to tier-one suppliers.

Top-level domain (TLD) The last part of a domain name; the most general identifier in the name.

Tort An action taken by a legal entity that causes harm to another legal entity.

Total cost of ownership (TCO) Business activity costs including the costs of hiring, training, and paying the personnel who will design the Web site, write or customize the software, create the content, and operate and maintain the site. TCO also includes hardware and software costs.

Touchpoint Online and offline customer contact points.

Touchpoint consistency The provision of similar levels and quality of service in all of a company's interactions with its customers, whether those interactions occur in person, on the telephone, or online.

Tracert A route-tracing program that sends data packets to every computer on the path (Internet) between one computer and another computer and measures the packets' round-trip times, providing an indication of the time it takes a message to travel from one computer to another and back, pinpointing any data traffic congestion, and ensuring that the remote computer is online.

Trade name The name (or a part of that name) that a business uses to identify itself.

Trademark A distinctive mark, device, motto, or implement that a company affixes to the goods it produces for identification purposes.

Trademark dilution The reduction of the distinctive quality of a trademark by alternative uses.

Trading partners Businesses that engage in EDI with one another.

Transaction An exchange of value.

Transaction costs The total of all costs incurred by a buyer and seller as they gather information and negotiate a transaction.

Transaction processing Processes that occur as part of completing a sale; these include calculation of any discounts, taxes, or shipping costs and transmission of payment data (such as a credit card number).

Transaction server The computer on which a company runs its accounting and inventory management software.

Transaction sets Formats for specific business data interchanges using EDI.

Transaction taxes Sales taxes, use taxes, excise taxes, and customs duties that are levied on the products or services that a company sells or uses.

Transceiver A transmitter-receiver device used in a fixed-point wireless network to forward a radio signal from the ISP to customers. Synonymous with repeater.

Transfer taxes Taxes that are levied on transactions between companies or companies and consumers.

Transmission Control Protocol The protocol that includes rules that computers on a network use to establish and break connections. See TCP/IP.

Trial visit The first visit a Web site visitor makes to a particular page.

Trigger word A key word used to jog the memory of visitors and remind them of something they want to buy on the site.

Triple Data Encryption Standard (Triple DES or 3DES) A robust version of the Data Encryption Standard used by the U.S. government that cannot be cracked even with today's supercomputers.

Trojan horse A program hidden inside another program or Web page that masks its true purpose (usually destructive).

Trusted (network) A network that is within a firewall.

Tweet A short message sent from one Twitter user to another.

Two-tier client/server architecture A client/server architecture in which only a client and server are involved in the requests and responses that flow between them over the Internet.

Ultimate consumer orientation A focus on the needs of the consumer who is at the end of an industry value chain.

Ultra Wideband (UWB) A wireless communication technology that provides wide bandwidth (up to about 480 Mbps in current versions) connections over short distances (30 to 100 feet).

Uniform Resource Locator (URL) Names and abbreviations representing the IP address of a particular Web page. Contains the protocol used to access the page and the page's location. Used in place of dotted quad notations.

Universal ad package The four most common standard Web ad formats.

Universal Description, Discovery and Integration (UDDI) specification The set of protocols that identify locations of Web services and their associated WSDL descriptions.

Unsolicited commercial e-mail (UCE) Electronic junk mail that can include solicitations, advertisements, or e-mail chain letters. Also called spam or bulk mail.

Untrusted (network) A network that is outside a firewall.

Upload bandwidth Synonymous with upstream bandwidth.

Upstream bandwidth The connection that occurs when you send information from your connection to your ISP.

Upstream strategies Tactics that focus on reducing costs or generating value by working with suppliers or inbound logistics.

URL broker A business that sells or auctions domain names that it believes others will find valuable.

Usability testing The testing and evaluation of a company's Web site for ease of use by visitors.

Usage-based market segmentation Customizing visitor experiences to match the site usage behavior patterns of each visitor or type of visitor.

Use tax A tax levied by a state on property used in that state.

Usenet (User's News Network) One of the first mailing lists; it allows subscribers to read and post articles within topic areas.

Usenet newsgroup Message posting areas on Usenet computers in which interested persons (primarily from the education and research communities) can discuss those topic areas.

Value chain A way of organizing the activities that each strategic business unit undertakes to design, produce, promote, market, deliver, and support the products or services it sells.

Value system Synonymous with industry value chain.

Value-added network (VAN) An independent company that provides connection and EDI transaction forwarding services to businesses engaged in EDI.

Venture capitalist A very wealthy individual or investment firm that invests in small companies that are about to grow rapidly. By investing large amounts of money (between a million and a few hundred million dollars), venture capitalists attempt to help these growing companies become large enough to sell stock to the public.

Vertical integration The practice of an existing firm replacing one of its suppliers with its own strategic business unit that creates the supplied product.

Vertical portal (vortal) A vertically integrated Web information hub focusing on an individual industry.

Vicarious copyright infringement The violation of an organization's rights that occurs when a company capable of supervising the infringing activity fails to do so and obtains a financial benefit from the infringing activity.

Vickrey auction Synonymous with second-price sealed-bid auction. Named for William Vickrey, who won the 1996 Nobel Prize in Economics for his studies of the properties of this auction type.

video ad The video ads that can be either free standing or integrated into videos that the site visitor selects to watch.

Viral marketing Tactics that rely on existing customers to tell other persons—the company's prospective customers—about the products or services they have enjoyed using.

Virtual community An electronic gathering place for people with common interests.

Virtual company A strategic alliance occurring among companies that operate on the Internet.

Virtual fitting room An online equivalent of an in-store fitting room.

Virtual learning network A virtual community used for distance learning.

Virtual model A graphic image built from customer measurements and physical traits on which customers can try clothes. Typically found on sites selling clothing and accessories.

Virtual private network (VPN) A network that uses public networks and their protocols to transmit sensitive data using a system called "tunneling" or "encapsulation."

Virus Software that attaches itself to another program and can cause damage when the host program is activated.

Visit The request of a Web site visitor for a page from a Web site.

The Wall Street Journal A daily newspaper.

Warchalking The practice of placing a chalk mark on a building that has an easily entered wireless network.

Wardrivers Network attackers who drive around in cars using their wireless-equipped laptop computers to search for unprotected wireless network access points.

Warranty disclaimer A statement indicating that the seller will not honor some or all implied warranties.

Web See World Wide Web.

Web 2.0 Technologies that include software that allows users of Web sites to participate in the creation, editing, and distribution of content on a Web site owned and operated by a third party.

Web APIs Techniques for interconnection of programs with each other over the Web.

Web beacon A tiny graphic that a third-party Web site places on another site's Web page.

Web browser (Web browser software) Software that lets users read HTML documents and move from one HTML document to another using hyperlinks.

Web bug A tiny, invisible Web page graphic that provides a way for a Web site to place cookies.

Web catalog revenue model A revenue model of selling goods and services on the Web wherein the seller mails catalogs to prospective buyers who can place orders online.

Web client computer A computer that is connected to the Internet and is used to download Web pages.

Web client software Software that sends requests for Web page files to other computers.

Web directory A listing of hyperlinks to Web pages that is organized into hierarchical categories.

Web EDI EDI on the Internet.

Web graphics designer A person trained in art, layout, and composition who also understands how Web pages are constructed and who ensures that the Web pages are visually appealing, are easy to use, and make consistent use of graphics elements from page to page.

Web log A Web site on which people post their thoughts and invite others to add commentary. Synonymous with blog.

Web portal Synonymous with portal, which is a Web site that serves as a customizable home base from which users do their searching, navigating, and other Web-based activity.

Web programmer A programmer who designs and writes the underlying code for dynamic database-driven Web pages.

Web server A computer that receives requests from many different Web clients and responds by sending HTML files back to those Web client computers.

Web server software Software that makes files available to other computers on the Internet.

Web services A combination of software tools that let application software in one organization communicate with other applications over a network using the SOAP, UDDI, and WSDL protocols.

Web Services Description Language (WSDL) A language that describes the characteristics of the logic units that make up specific Web services.

Web-wrap acceptance The compliance with EULA conditions with which a user agrees through the act of using a Web site.

White hat hackers Hackers who use their skills for positive purposes.

White list spam filter Software that looks for From addresses in incoming messages that are known to be good addresses.

Wide area network (WAN) A network of computers that are connected over large distances.

Wi-Fi (wireless Ethernet, 802.11b, 802.11a, 802.11g, 802.11n) The most common wireless connection technology for use on LANs; it can communicate through a wireless access point connected to a LAN to become a part of that LAN.

Winner's curse A psychological phenomenon that causes bidders to become caught up in the excitement of competitive bidding and bid more than their private valuation.

Wire transfer Synonymous with electronic funds transfer, which is the electronic transfer of account exchange information over secure private communications networks.

Wireless access point (WAP) A device that transmits network packets between Wi-Fi-equipped computers and other devices that are within its range.

Wireless Application Protocol (WAP) A protocol that allows Web pages formatted in HTML to be displayed on devices with small screens, such as PDAs and mobile phones.

Wireless Encryption Protocol (WEP) A set of rules for encrypting transmissions from wireless devices.

Wireless Ethernet The most common wireless connection technology for use on LANs.

Worldwide Interoperability for Microwave Access (WiMAX) A 4G wireless technology that offers download speeds up to 12 Mbps and upload speeds up to 5 Mbps.

World Wide Web (Web) The subset of Internet computers that connects computers and their contents in a specific way, and that allows for easy sharing of data using a standard interface.

World Wide Web Consortium (W3C) A notfor-profit group that maintains standards for the Web.

Worm A virus that replicates itself on other machines.

Writing A tangible representation of the terms of a contract.

XML parser A program that can format an XML file so it can appear on the screen of a computer, a wireless PDA, a mobile phone, or other device.

XML schemas Many companies follow the common standards for XML tags such as data-type definition or XML schemas.

XML vocabulary A set of XML tag definitions.

Yankee auction A type of English auction that offers multiple units of an item for sale and allows bidders to specify the quantity of items they want to buy.

ZigBee A short-range wireless technology that was developed to be low cost and run on very little power.

Zombie A program that secretly takes over another computer for the purpose of launching attacks on other computers. Zombie attacks can be difficult to trace to their perpetrators.

Zombie farm A group of computers on which a hacker has planted zombie programs.

Index

Note: **Bold** page numbers indicate where a key term is defined in the text.

A

C

Q

R

X